CW01424841

Routledge International Handbook of Contemporary Social and Political Theory

The triangular relationship between the social, the political, and the cultural has opened up social and political theory to new challenges. The social can no longer be reduced to the category of society, and the political extends beyond the traditional concerns of the nature of the state and political authority.

This *Handbook* will address a range of issues that have recently emerged from the disciplines of social and political theory, focusing on key themes as opposed to schools of thought or major theorists. It is divided into three parts which address:

- The most influential theoretical traditions that have emerged from the legacy of the twentieth century
- The most important new and emerging frameworks of analysis today
- The major theoretical problems in recent social and political theory.

The *Routledge International Handbook of Contemporary Social and Political Theory* encompasses the most up-to-date developments in contemporary social and political theory, and as such is an essential research tool for both undergraduate and postgraduate students, as well as researchers, working in the fields of political theory, social and political philosophy, contemporary social theory, and cultural theory.

Gerard Delanty is Professor of Sociology and Social & Political Thought at the University of Sussex. He has edited several volumes, including (with Krishan Kumar) the *Handbook of Nations and Nationalism* (Sage, 2006), and the *Handbook of Contemporary European Social Theory* (Routledge, 2006). His most recent book is *The Cosmopolitan Imagination* (Cambridge University Press, 2009).

Stephen P. Turner is Graduate Research Professor of Philosophy at the University of South Florida. He is the author or editor of a number of books on Max Weber, including the *Cambridge Companion* (Cambridge University Press, 2000), and other books including *The Social Theory of Practices* (Polity Press, 1994), *Liberal Democracy 3.0* (Sage, 2003), and *Explaining the Normative* (Polity Press, 2010).

Routledge International Handbook of Contemporary Social and Political Theory

Edited by Gerard Delanty and Stephen P. Turner

Routledge
Taylor & Francis Group

LONDON AND NEW YORK

First published in paperback 2014
First published 2011
by Routledge
2 Park Square, Milton Park, Abingdon, Oxon OX14 4RN

Published in the USA and Canada
by Routledge
711 Third Avenue, New York, NY 10017

Routledge is an imprint of the Taylor & Francis Group, an informa business

© 2014 selection and editorial material Gerard Delanty and Stephen P. Turner; individual chapters, the contributors

The right of the editors to be identified as the authors of the editorial material, and of the authors for their individual chapters, has been asserted in accordance with sections 77 and 78 of the Copyright, Designs and Patents Act 1988.

All rights reserved. No part of this book may be reprinted or reproduced or utilised in any form or by any electronic, mechanical, or other means, now known or hereafter invented, including photocopying and recording, or in any information storage or retrieval system, without permission in writing from the publishers.

Trademark notice: Product or corporate names may be trademarks or registered trademarks, and are used only for identification and explanation without intent to infringe.

British Library Cataloguing in Publication Data
A catalogue record for this book is available from the British Library

Library of Congress Cataloging-in-Publication Data
A catalog record has been requested for this book

ISBN: 978-0-415-54825-0 (hbk)
ISBN: 978-0-415-71446-4 (pbk)
ISBN: 978-0-203-87557-5 (ebk)

Typeset in Bembo
by Integra Software Services Pvt. Ltd, Pondicherry, India

Printed and bound by CPI Group (UK) Ltd, Croydon, CR0 4YY

Contents

Contents

Contents

Notes on Contributors

Adam Arvidsson is Associate Professor of Sociology at the University of Milano, Italy. He also works with a research project on reputation economy at the Copenhagen Business School. His main research interests concern new forms of value and labor in the information economy. His latest book, *Brands, Meaning and Value in media Culture* (London, Routledge 2006) investigated the brand as a key institution in the information economy). His forthcoming book, *The Ethical Economy. Business and Society in the 21st Century* (New York Columbia University Press, 2010, with Nicolai Peitersen), elaborates on a vision for the 'new economy' that is emerging out of today's open and socialized productive practices.

Amelia Arsenault serves as the George Gerbner Post-Doctoral Fellow and a research fellow at the Center for Global Communication Studies at the University of Pennsylvania, Annenberg School for Communication. Her research interests include: communication and power; media and ICT ownership; media and ICT for development; and public diplomacy. Her recent publications on the subject of networks include: 'The Power of Multi-Media Global Networks: An Analysis of the Media, Telecom, Gaming and Computing Industries' in Winseck & Jin (Eds.) *Media Political Economies: Hierarchies, Markets and Finance in the Global Media Industries.* (London: Bloomsbury Academic, forthcoming); 'The Structure and Dynamics of Global Multi-Media Business Networks', *International Journal of Communication* (with Manuel Castells, 2008); and 'Switching Power: Rupert Murdoch and The Global Business Of Media Politics. A Sociological Analysis', *International Sociology* (with Manuel Castells, 2008).

Mauro Basaure Ph.D. (University of Frankfurt), Assistant Professor at the Instituto de Humanidades of the Universidad Diego Portales, Santiago de Chile, and member of the *Groupe de Sociologie Politique et Morale* (EHESS/CNRS), Paris-France. Research fellow at the *Institute of Social Research,* Frankfurt/M. (2004–9), where he was the initiator of the *International Study Group for Critical Theory.* Research Fellow at the Lateinamerika Institut of the Freie Universität Berlin (2003). He attended the University of Chile, where he studied sociology (1993–99) and received his M.A. in political philosophy (2000–2002). His areas of research and teaching include social theory, critical theory, new french sociology and political philosophy. Recent publications: *Erneuerung der Kritik. Axel Honneth im Gespräch* (New York, Frankfurt/M.: Campus, 2009) (with Jan Philipp Reemtsma and Rasmus Willig, eds.); Foucault et la Psychanalyse. (Paris: Éditions Le félin, 2009) (with Emmanuel Gripay and Ferhat Taylan, eds.).

Patrick Baert is Reader in Social Theory at the University of Cambridge where he is also a Fellow of Selwyn College. Amongst his recent books are *Social Theory in the Twentieth Century* *and Beyond* (with Carreira da Silva, 2010), *Philosophy of the Social Sciences: Towards Pragmatism* (2005) and the co-edited volume *Conflict, Citizenship and Civil Society* (2010).

Peter Beilharz is Professor of Sociology and Director of the Thesis Eleven Centre for Cultural Sociology at La Trobe University in Australia. He is author or editor of 23 books, beginning with *Trotsky, Trotskyism and the Transition to Socialism* (1987), ending, most recently, with *Socialism and Modernity* (2009). He is a founding editor of *Thesis Eleven*. He is author of many works on the history of socialism, on Zygmunt Bauman and Bernard Smith. He was Professor of Australian Studies at Harvard, and is a Fellow of the Centre for Cultural Sociology at Yale.

Richard Bellamy is Professor of Political Science and Director of the School of Public Policy, University College London (UCL), University of London. Recent publications include *Liberalism and Pluralism: Towards a Politics of Compromise* (Routledge, 1999), *Rethinking Liberalism* (Continuum, 2000, 2005) and (as co-editor) *The Cambridge History of Twentieth Century Political Thought* (CUP, 2003), *Lineages of European Citizenship* (Palgrave, 2004) and *Making European Citizens* (Palgrave, 2006). His *Political Constitutionalism: A Republican Defence of the Constitutionality of Democracy* was published by Cambridge University Press in 2007 and his *Citizenship: A Very Short Introduction* by OUP in 2008.

Charles Blattberg is Professor of Political Philosophy at the Université de Montréal. Educated at Toronto, McGill, the Sorbonne (Université de Paris I), and Oxford, his publications include *From Pluralist to Patriotic Politics* (Oxford University Press, 2000); *Shall We Dance? A Patriotic Politics for Canada* (McGill-Queen's University Press, 2003); and *Patriotic Elaborations: Essays in Practical Philosophy* (McGill-Queen's University Press, 2009).

Paul Blokker is a Postdoctoral Fellow at the department of Sociology, University of Trento, Italy. In 2007–8, he was a Marie Curie Postdoctoral Fellow at the School of Social and Cultural Studies, University of Sussex. His current research is on constitutionalisms, constitutional rationalities, plurality, and (local) democratic participation in the new member states of the EU. Recent publications include: *Multiple Democracies in Europe. Political Culture in New Member States,* Routledge, 2009.

James Bohman is Danforth Professor of Philosophy at Saint Louis University. He is the author of *Democracy Across Borders* (MIT Press, 2007), *Public Deliberation* (MIT Press, 1996), and *New Philosophy of Social Science* (MIT Press, 1991). He is currently working on a book on difficulties with current conception of citizenship.

Stewart Clegg is Research Professor and Director of the Centre for Management and Organization Studies Research at the University of Technology, Sydney. A prolific publisher in leading academic journals in social science, management and organization theory, he is also the author and editor of many books, including the *Handbook of Power* (with Mark Haugaard 2009).

Patricia Hill Collins is Distinguished University Professor of Sociology at the University of Maryland, College Park. Her books include *Black Feminist Thought: Knowledge, Consciousness, and the Politics of Empowerment* (1990, 2000), winner of the American Sociological Association's (ASA) Jessie Bernard Award, and the C. Wright Mills Award of the Society for the Study of Social Problems; *Race, Class, and Gender: An Anthology, 7th ed.* (2010), edited with Margaret Andersen, a widely-used reader in colleges and universities; and *Black Sexual Politics: African*

Americans, Gender, and the New Racism (2004), recipient of ASA's 2007 Distinguished Publication Award. In 2008–9 she served as the 100th President of ASA, the first African American woman to hold this position in the organization's 104-year history.

Clare Colebrook is Edwin Erle Sparks Professor of English at Penn State University. She has written on Gilles Deleuze, contemporary philosophy, feminist theory, literary theory and poetry. Her latest book is *Deleuze and the Meaning of Life* (2010).

Brian D. Cook is a PhD candidate in the Department of Sociology at Stanford University. He received his M.Phil. in Development Studies at the University of Oxford. His current work focuses on the role of social movements in the transition to democracy. He has conducted research in South Africa and is currently engaged in a long-term project on post-apartheid social movements. He has also examined the impact of conflict on cross-national patterns of migration and is interested more broadly in civil society and economic development.

Karen S. Cook is the Ray Lyman Wilbur Professor and Chair of Sociology at Stanford University. She is also Director of the Institute for Research in the Social Sciences (IRiSS). She is one of the co-editors of the Russell Sage Foundation Series on Trust and the editor, co-editor, or co-author of *Trust in Society, Trust and Distrust in Organizations, Cooperation without Trust?, eTrust: Forming Relationships in the Online World*, and *Whom Can You Trust? How Groups, Networks and Institutions Make Trust Possible*. She has published on social exchange, social justice, social networks and trust.

Gerard Delanty is Professor of Sociology and Social & Political Thought, University of Sussex. In 2006 he was a visiting professor at Deakin University Melbourne and has previously held visiting professorships in Kyoto and Toronto. He has written on various issues in social and political theory, European identity and the cultural and historical sociology of modernity. He is editor of the *European Journal of Social Theory* and author of several books including *Inventing Europe: Idea, Identity, Reality* (Macmillan, 1995), *Social Theory in a Changing World* (Polity Press, 1999), *Modernity and Postmodernity: Knowledge, Power, the Self* (Sage, 2000), *Citizenship in the Global Age* (Open University Press, 2000), *Community* (Routledge, 2003) and (with C. Rumford) *Rethinking Europe: Social Theory and the Implications of Europeanization* (Routledge, 2005) He has edited many volumes, including the *Handbook of Contemporary European Social Theory* (Routledge 2005), *Europe and Asia Beyond East and West* (Routledge, 2006) and (with Krishan Kumar) *The Handbook of Nations and Nationalism* (Sage 2006). His most recent publication is *The Cosmopolitan Imagination: The Renewal of Critical Social Theory,* Cambridge University Press, 2009.

Thomas Docherty is Professor of English and Comparative Literature at the University of Warwick, having previously held Chairs of English at Trinity College Dublin and at the University of Kent. He is the author of many books, including *Postmodernism* (Columbia University Press), *After Theory* (Edinburgh University Press), *Criticism and Modernity* (Oxford University Press), *Alterities* (Oxford University Press), *Aesthetic Democracy* (Stanford University Press), and *The English Question; or, Academic Freedoms* (Sussex Academic Press). He is currently completing a book about confession and writing, provisionally entitled *I Confess,* and is writing another about the state of the University as an institution, provisionally called *The University of the Idea*.

José Maurício Domingues holds a PhD from the London School of Economics and Political Science and is Professor at Rio de Janeiro University Research Institute (IUPERJ). His main books are *Sociological Theory and Collective Subjectivity* (Macmillan and Saint Martin's Press, 1995), *Social Creativity, Collective Subjectivity and Contemporary Modernity* (Macmillan and Saint Martin's Press, 2000), *Modernity Reconstructed* (University of Wales Press, 2006), and *Latin America and Contemporary Modernity* (Routledge, 2008).

Natalie J. Doyle is Senior Lecturer in French and European Studies at Monash University, Melbourne, and Deputy Director of the Monash European and EU Centre. Her research and publications have mainly dealt with French social and political thought, classical and contemporary, with particular reference to interpretations of modernity. She is also interested in the question of the place of religion in modern European culture and issues of European identity with special respect to the history and future of the European Union. Recent publications include Doyle, N.J., Martinez Arranz, A., and Winand, P. (Eds.). *New Europe, New Governance, New Worlds?* Brussels: Presses Interuniversitaires Européennes/Peter Lang, 2009; and Arnason, J. P. and Doyle, N.J. (Eds). *Domains and Divisions of European History,* Liverpool: Liverpool University Press, 2010.

Erik O. Eriksen is Professor and Director of ARENA – Centre for European Studies at the University of Oslo. His main research fields are political theory, democratic governance, public policy and European integration. The interest in conditions for legitimate governance has led to publications on democracy in the EU, functions and limits of the state, deliberative democracy, communicative leadership, regional politics, and the welfare state. He has directed several big research projects including: CIDEL – Citizenship and democractic legitimacy in the EU. 2003–5; and RECON – Reconstituting Democracy in Europe. 2007–11. His main books in English include: *Democracy in the European Union – Integration through deliberation?* (co-ed. J.E. Fossum), London: Routledge, 2000. *Understanding Habermas. Communicative action and deliberative democracy,* (J. Weigård co-author), London: Continuum Press, 2003; *Developing a Constitution for Europe,* (J. E. Fossum and A. J. Menéndez co-editors), London: Routledge, 2004; *Making the European Polity. Reflexive integration in the EU,* London: Routledge, 2005; *The Unfinished Democratization of Europe.* Oxford: Oxford University Press 2009.

Thomas Faist is Professor of Transnational and Development Studies at the Department of Sociology, Bielefeld University. He directs the Center on Migration, Citizenship and Development (COMCAD). His research interests focus on international migration, immigrant integration, citizenship, and social policy. Thomas Faist held visiting appointments at Malmö University and the University of Toronto. He serves on the editorial board of Ethnic and Racial Studies, Migration Letters, and South Asian Diaspora. Thomas Faist recently published *Beyond a Border: The Causes and Consequences of Contemporary Immigration,* with Peter Kivisto (SAGE Pine Forge Press 2010).

Marcel Fournier is Professor of Sociology, Université de Montréal. His main interests are in the history of sociology social theory, sociology of science and higher education, sociology of culture. His publications include: (edited with Michèle Lamont) *Cultivating Differences, Symbolic Boundaries and the making of Inequalities,* University of Chicago Press, Chicago, 1992; *Marcel Mauss,* Paris, Fayard, 1994 (translated in English by Princeton University Press); (edited with Arnaud Sales) *Knowledge Society, Creativity and Communication,* Sage, 2007; and *I, Emile Durkheim,* Paris, Le Seuil, 2008 (translated in English by Polity Press).

Steven Grosby, Professor, Clemson University, is the author of *Nationalism: A Very Short Introduction* (2005), *Biblical Ideas of Nationality: Ancient and Modern* (2002); and co-editor of

Nationalism and Ethno-Symbolism: History, Culture and Ethnicity in the Formation of Nations (2007) and the four volume *Nationality and Nationalism* (2004). In addition to other books and numerous articles, he translated and edited *Hans Freyer, Theory of Objective Mind: An Introduction to the Philosophy of Culture* (1999).

John G. Gunnell is Distinguished Professor, Emeritus, in the Department of Political Science at the State University of New York at Albany, and he is currently affiliated with the Department of Political Science at the University of California, Davis. His main research is in political theory and the history and philosophy of social science. Recent publications include *Imagining the American Political: Political Science and the Discourse of Democracy* (Pennsylvania State University Press, 2004); "Can Social Science be just?" *The Philosophy of Social Science* (forthcoming); "Political Inquiry and the Metapractical Voice: Weber and Oakeshott," *Political Research Quarterly.* Fall, 2008; "Are We Losing Our Minds? Cognitive Science and the Study of Politics," *Political Theory.* December, 2007.

Austin Harrington is Reader in Sociology at the University of Leeds, UK, and Research Associate at the Max Weber Kolleg für kultur-und sozialwissenschaftliche Studien at the University of Erfurt, Germany. His publications include *Art and Social Theory: Sociological Arguments in Aesthetics* (Polity Press, 2004) and *Modern Social Theory: An Introduction* (Oxford University Press, 2005, editor). He is currently completing a monograph on ideas of Europe and Europeanism in the thought of German liberal cosmopolitan intellectuals from the years of the Weimar Republic.

Joel Isaac is Lecturer in American History at Queen Mary, University of London, and holds the Balzan-Skinner Lectureship in Modern Intellectual History at the University of Cambridge, 2010–11. His work has appeared in the *European Journal of Social Theory, Modern Intellectual History,* the *Historical Journal,* and the *Journal of the History of Ideas.*

Byron Kaldis is Associate Professor of Philosophy and Academic Course Coordinator at the Hellenic Open University and has previously taught at Universities in the UK and USA. He works and publishes in the areas of metaphysics, the philosophy of the social sciences and their relation to natural sciences, the ethics of technoscience, as well as on the relationship between ethics and political philosophy. He is on the Editorial Board of the new Springer Academic Book *Series Studies in the Philosophy of Sociality,* the General Editor of the forthcoming multi-volume SAGE Encyclopedia of *Philosophy and the Social Sciences* and Editor of the *Mind and Society: Cognitive Science meets the Social Sciences* Synthese Library Series, Springer (2012).

Krishan Kumar is University Professor, William R. Kenan, Jr., Professor and Chair, Department of Sociology, University of Virginia, USA. He was previously Professor of Social and Political Thought at the University of Kent, UK. He has been a Visiting Scholar at Harvard, a Member of the Institute for Advanced Study, Princeton, and a Visiting Professor at the Ecole des Hautes Études en Sciences Sociales, Paris, as well as at the universities of Bergen, Bristol, Colorado (Boulder) and Kent (Canterbury). Among his publications are *Utopia and Anti-Utopia in Modern Times* (1987), *1989: Revolutionary Ideas and Ideals* (2001), *The Making of English National Identity* (2003), and *From Post-Industrial to Post-Modern Society,* second edition (2005). He is currently working on empires.

Fuyuki Kurasawa is Associate Professor in the Department of Sociology at York University in Toronto, Canada, Faculty Fellow of the Center for Cultural Sociology at Yale University, and

Co-President of the International Sociological Association's Research Committee on Socio-logical Theory. Kurasawa has been a Visiting Scholar at Cornell, Harvard, New York and Yale universities, as well as at the Ecole des Hautes Etudes en Sciences Sociales. He is the author of *The Ethnological Imagination: A Cross-Cultural Critique of Modernity* (2004) and *The Work of Global Justice: Human Rights as Practices* (2007). His current research focuses on humanitarianism and the historical constitution of a visual economy of distant suffering.

Daniel Levy is Associate Professor in the Department of Sociology at Stony Brook University in New York. As a political sociologist he is interested in issues of globalization, collective memory studies and comparative-historical sociology. Among his books are: *The Holocaust and Memory in the Global Age* (Temple University Press 2005) and *Memory and Human Rights* (Penn State University Press 2010), both with Natan Sznaider. Forthcoming is *The Collective Memory Reader* (Oxford University Press – with Jeffrey Olick and Vered Vinitzky-Seroussi). For more information on his work please visit http://www.sunysb.edu/sociol/?faculty/Levy/levy.

Moya Lloyd is Professor of Political Theory at Loughborough University. She has published widely in the areas of contemporary political theory and gender theory. Her most recent books include *Beyond Identity Politics: Feminism, Power, Politics* (Sage 2005), *Judith Butler: From Norms to Politics* (Polity 2007), and with Adrian Little (eds) *The Politics of Radical Democracy* (Edinburgh University Press, 2009). She is currently at work on two projects: a book on *Sex, Gender and Sexuality* for Acumen Press and a project examining the relation between social orders, norms, and 'who counts'.

Timothy W. Luke is University Distinguished Professor of Political Science at Virginia Poly-technic Institute and State University in Blacksburg, Virginia. He also serves as the Program Chair for Government and International Affairs in the School of Public and International Affairs, and as the Director of the Center for Digital Discourse and Culture (CDDC) in the College of Liberal Arts and Human Sciences at Virginia Tech. His main research interests are directed at applying political and social theory to understand contemporary processes of governance and globalization in cultural economics, environmental conflicts, and world politics.

Raffaele Marchetti is Lecturer on International Relations at LUISS University, Rome, and the University of Naples L'Orientale. He holds a Laurea in Philosophy from the University of Rome La Sapienza, and a Ph.D. in Political Theory from the London School of Economics and Political Science. He coordinated the FP6 Strep project *SHUR. Human Rights in Conflicts: The Role of Civil Society,* was Jean Monnet Fellow at the European University Institute, and research fellow in the FP6 research project *DEMOS. Democracy in Europe and the Mobilisa-tion of Society*. He received the 2005 ISA-Lawrence S. Finkelstein Award on International Organisation. His research interests concern International Political Theory and Global politics, especially the role of civil society actors both at the local and transnational level and global democracy.

Aurea Mota is a PhD student at IESP (formerly VERJ), Rio de Janeiro, Brazil. Her research is an attempt to apply approaches in modern social theory and political philosophy to explain the process of attenuation of the liberal framework in Latin America. She has a particular interest in the incorporation of collective rights in the late twentieth century in Latin American countries. She is the recipient of a research prize for the Latin America Social Science Council for her work and she is a member of the council's Political Philosophy Research Group.

Donatella della Porta is Professor of sociology in the Department of Political and Social Sciences at the European University Institute. She is on leave of absence from the University of Florence, where she was full professor of Political Science, president of the corso di laurea in Administrative Sciences, and Director of the Department of Political Science and Sociology at the University of Florence. Professor Della Porta received a Diplôme d'Etudes Approfondies at the Ecole des Hautes Etudes en Sciences Sociales of Paris and a Ph.D in political and social sciences at the European University Institute in Florence. She directs the DEMOS project (Democracy in Europe and the Mobilisation of the Society), financed under the VI FP by the EC. She coordinated the Gruppo di Ricerca sull'azione collettiva in Europa (GRACE), and has conducted research also at Cornell University, Ithaca N.Y, and at the Wissenschaftszentrum Berlin für Sozialforschung. In 1990 she received a Career Development Award of the H.F. Guggenheim Foundation; in 1997 a Stipendium of the Alexander von Humboldt Stiftung. Her main research interests concern social movements, political violence, terrorism, corruption, police and policies of public order. On these issues she has conducted investigations in Italy, France, Germany and Spain. She has directed a project of comparative research on control of public mass demonstrations in Europe and one on the police in Italy. Currently she is involved in several comparative projects on citizenship and social movements. She is co-editor of the *Europeoan Political Science Review* (ECPR and Cambridge University Press; journals.cambridge.org/epsr).

Sheila Nair is Professor of Political Science at Northern Arizona University, USA. Her research and teaching interests include migration, human rights, security, political economy, postcolonial and international relations theory, and Southeast Asian politics. She is the author of several articles and chapters. She is editor (with Shampa Biswas) of *International Relations, and States of Exception: Margins, Peripheries and Excluded Bodies* (Routledge 2010).

Elena Ruiz–Aho is Assistant Professor of Philosophy at Florida Gulf Coast University in Fort Myers, Fl, where she teaches in the areas of Latin American philosophy, feminist ethics, and 19th and 20th century continental philosophy. Her research interests include Latin American social theory and postcolonial theory, especially as they intersect with feminism. Her current projects focus on the impact of European colonialism on Amerindian discursive practices, as well as on developing feminist models of discourse ethics specific to Latin America.

Saskia Sassen is the Robert S. Lynd Professor of Sociology and Member, The Committee on Global Thought, Columbia University (www.saskiasassen.com). Her new books are *Territory, Authority, Rights: From Medieval to Global Assemblages* (Princeton University Press 2008), *A Sociology of Globalization* (W.W.Norton 2007), the forthcoming 4th fully updated *Cities in a World Economy* (Sage 2010). She also recently edited *Deciphering the Global* (Routledge 2007), and co-edited *Digital Formations: New Architectures for Global Order* (Princeton University Press 2005).

Jeremy Shearmur was educated at the L.S.E., where he also worked for eight years as assistant to Karl Popper. He subsequently taught philosophy at Edinburgh, political theory at Manchester, was Director of Studies at the Centre for Policy Studies, and was a Research Associate Professor at the Institute for Humane Studies, George Mason University – prior to teaching political theory and then philosophy at the Australian National University. His publications include *The Political Thought of Karl Popper,* and *Hayek and After,* and he and Piers Turner were recently the editors of Karl Popper's *After the Open Society,* which comprises previously unpublished or uncollected writings by Popper on social and political themes.

Yannis Stavrakakis studied political science at Panteion University (Athens) and Essex, where he completed his doctoral thesis on the 'Ideology and Discourse Analysis' PhD Programme. He has worked at the Universities of Essex and Nottingham and is currently Associate Professor at the School of Political Sciences, Aristotle University of Thessaloniki. He is the author of *Lacan and the Political* (London and New York: Routledge, 1999) and *The Lacanian Left* (Edinburgh: Edinburgh University Press/Albany: SUNY Press, 2007) and co-editor of *Discourse Theory and Political Analysis* (Manchester: Manchester University Press, 2000) and *Lacan & Science* (London: Karnac, 2002).

Robert B. Talisse is Professor of Philosophy at Vanderbilt University. He works primarily on political philosophy, but also pursues research in American pragmatism, especially the epistemology of Charles Peirce. His articles have appeared in leading journals such as *Transactions of the C. S. Peirce Society, Journal of Social Philosophy, Journal of Moral Philosophy, Res Publica, Argumentation,* and *Episteme.* He has four authored books, including *A Pragmatist Philosophy of Democracy* (Routledge 2007) and *Democracy and Moral Conflict* (Cambridge, 2009).

Meyda Yeğenoğlu is a professor of Sociology at Middle East Technical University, Ankara, Turkey. She has held visiting appointments at Columbia University, Oberlin College, Rutgers University, New York University, University of Vienna and Oxford University. She has published in the fields of orientalism, globalization, postcolonial theory, cultural studies, and migrancy. She is currently working on a book entitled *Secular Apprehensions: Islam, Migrancy and Hospitality in Europe.* She is the author of internationally well-cited *Colonial Fantasies; Towards a Feminist Reading of Orientalism* (Cambridge University Press, 1998). She has published numerous essays in various journals and edited volumes such as *Feminist Postcolonial Theory, Postcolonialism, Feminism and Religious Discourse, Nineteenth Century Literature Criticism, Postmodern Culture, Race and Ethnic Relations, Culture and Religion, Radical Philosophy, Inscriptions, Toplum ve Bilim, Defter, and Doğu-Bat.* She has extensively contributed to the literature on post-colonial theory and orientalism. She teaches in the fields of cultural studies, postcolonial theory, contemporary critical theory, orientalism and feminist theory.

Georg Sørensen is Professor of Political Science at Aarhus University, Denmark. Recent books include *The Transformation of the State. Beyond the Myth of Retreat* (2004), *Democracy and Democratization* (3rd ed. 2008) and *Introduction to International Relations. Theories and approaches* (4th ed. 2010, with R. Jackson). Recent articles in: *European Journal of International Relations, Security Dialogue, International Relations, Cooperation and Conflict.*

Piet Strydom, an Apartheid émigré, is Statutory Lecturer in Sociology at University College Cork, Ireland. Since the 1980s, the cognitive approach has been central to his research on social theory, the history and philosophy of the social science, and substantive areas such as rights, ecology, risk, South African land reform, and cosmopolitanism. His publications include *Discourse and Knowledge* (Liverpool University Press, 2000); *Risk, Environment and Society* (Open University Press, 2002); *New Horizons of Critical Theory: Collective Learning and Triple Contingency* (Shipra Publications, 2009); 'Philosophies of the Social Sciences', UNESCO *Encyclopaedia of Life Support Systems* (EOLSS Publishers, 2009); and *Contemporary Critical Theory and Methodology* (Routledge, 2011). He edited and introduced *Philosophies of Social Science* (Open University Press, 2003) with Gerard Delanty; and edited a special issue of the *European Journal of Social Theory* on the theme of 'Social Theory after the Cognitive Revolution: Varieties of Contemporary Cognitive Sociology' (Vol 10/3, Aug 2007). Cognitive sociology and the philosophy of social science served as focus of his visiting professorship at the Université de Provence, Aix-en-Provence, France, in 2009. Recently, a book of essays in his honour edited by Séamus ÓTuama appeared under the title *Critical Turns in Critical Theory: New Directions in Social and Political Thought* (Tauris Academic Studies, 2009).

Stephen P. Turner is Graduate Research Professor in Philosophy at the University of South Florida. His writings on social theory include books on explanation, such as *Sociological Explanation as Translation* (1980), Weber and Durkheim, and on such topics as practice (*The Social Theory of Practices,* 1994), and politics (*Liberal Democracy 3.0: Civil Society in an Age of Experts,* 2003), as well as articles and chapters on charisma, rationality, agency theory, fascism, organizational culture, constitutions, and the Frankfurt School. His most recent book was *Explaining the Normative* (2010). He is currently working on Kelsen, Weber, and the relation of liberalism to law.

Gary Wickham is Professor of Sociology at Murdoch University in Perth, Western Australia, where he has worked for 25 years. He has published five books (three of them on Foucault) and over 50 articles (more than 10 of which are on Foucault or on Foucault-related themes). His current work focuses mostly on the project of civil-peace rule, a distinctive mode of ruling a bounded territory and its peoples which was developed in sixteenth- and seventeenth-century Europe, eventually bringing to an end a protracted period (nearly one hundred and fifty years) of religion-driven civil war. In particular it focuses on the way this type of rule fostered a separate domain of safe interaction in which individual freedom may be responsibly pursued (a domain known as 'the social') and a separate domain in which individual and collective wealth may be responsibly pursued ('the economy'), which operate alongside the five 'primary' elements of this type of rule: politics, law, sovereignty, state, and a tradition which combines, in varying ways, a commitment to life over death and a commitment to the goals of individual freedom and individual responsibility.

Peter Wagner is ICREA Research Professor at the University of Barcelona. His research aims to connect social and political theory to comparative-historical sociology focusing on the transformations and re-interpretations of modernity, democracy and capitalism. His recent publications include *Modernity as experience and interpretation* (Polity Press, 2008) and *Varieties of world-making: beyond globalization* (ed. with Nathalie Karagiannis, Liverpool University Press, 2007).

Iain Wilkinson is a Senior Lecturer in Sociology at the School of Social Policy, Sociology and Social Research at the University of Kent, UK. He also directs a researcher centre dedicated to the study of charity, philanthropy, humanitarianism and social justice (CPHSJ). His publications include *Anxiety in a Risk Society* (2001 Routledge), *Suffering: a Sociological Introduction* (2005 Polity) and *Risk, Vulnerability and Everyday Life* (2009 Routledge).

Guanjun Wu is Lecturer and Research Fellow at Fudan institute for Advanced Study in Social Sciences in Shanghai. He also serves as deputy editor of *Fudan Political Philosophy Review*. His books include *Multiple Modernities* (2002), *The Perverse Core of Everyday Reality* (2006), and *The Spectral Analysis of Love and Death* (2008), all in Chinese.

Introduction: Social, Political, and Cultural Theory since the Sixties

The Demise of Classical Marxism and Liberalism, the New Reality of the Welfare State, and the Loss of Epistemic Innocence

Stephen P. Turner and Gerard Delanty

The publication of John Rawls' *A Theory of Justice* in 1971 coincided with a complex set of changes in the political situation of the west, the role of intellectuals, the state of the social sciences and humanities, and in the development of the welfare state itself. These changes provided the conditions for the creation of a body of thought quite different from the one the sixties had produced, and a significant change from the discipline-dominated thinking of the period after the Second World War. The immediately relevant events included the effective demise of Parsons' systems theory, the waning of the passions of 1968, and an enrollment crisis in universities' humanities and social science departments as economic fear drove students into professional programs, creating a sharp downturn in demand for faculty. The optimism that had characterized disciplines in these fields during the 1960s quickly faded. The idea that sociology was soon to become a "science," the source of the positivism dispute of the sixties, faded along with it. Logical Positivism as a coherent movement collapsed under the weight of the problems of the theory-observation distinction (Suppe 1977 [1974]: 45–50). At the same time Political Theory, which had been taught largely as an historical study – a history of error, as Leo Strauss described the standard textbook of the time, George Sabine's *A History of Political Theory* (1961), or as a continuation of the mood of *Kulturpessimismus*, as in the writings of Sabine's critic, Leo Strauss – revived, partly in response to the stimulus from the success of Rawls, partly in response to new ideas about participatory democracy rooted in the experience of the sixties. Social theory also changed: the role that Parsons had played as a focus of theoretical discussion was replaced; the work of Jürgen Habermas, particularly his *Theory of Communicative Action* (1984–87 [1981]), reassessed and re-appropriated the classical theoretical tradition in social theory to replace Parsons' synthetic account, and this work coincided with a systematic reconsideration of the classic social theorists, especially Weber. An additional source of new thinking came from the "dependent" periphery, as thinkers such as Ernesto Laclau and Chantal Mouffe (Laclau 1997; LaClau and Mouffe 1985), which emancipated Socialist theory from received dogmas about class struggle and recognized the centrality of other antagonisms and the need for open democracy.

This comprehensive rethinking of the areas of social and political theory had many startling results, especially when it combined with new social movements, and the seventies produced a series of them. The student movement of the sixties was followed by one even more powerful, the Women's Movement, which asserted its issues within each of the relevant fields and created a new field of Women's Studies, with a new model of activist scholarship and identity politics. Marxism took a cultural turn. New thinkers who were unclassifiable in disciplinary terms, such as Michel Foucault and Stuart Hall, emerged as fashionable. "Cultural studies" became a rubric under which humanistic Marxists could gather. Ironically, it also became a rubric under which followers of Parsons, such as Clifford Geertz, could replace the Parsonian conception of society dominated by a central value system with an equally "cultural" image of "the mind full of presuppositions" provided by cultural codes (Geertz 1973: 89, 112–13). The content and subject matter of these theories also changed. The sociology of the mid-twentieth century was concerned to a significant extent with "professionalization" as a major social transformation replacing class and class antagonism. Foucault produced a startling inversion of this paradigm. The practicing theories which governed and justified the work of the "professionals" who had taken over such things as the care of the mad and criminal, usually under the flag of progress and humanitarian reform, were treated by Foucault as ideological constructions which represented their own form of rule. The paradigms of incarceration and punishment established in the nineteenth century were the prime example of this (Foucault 1977). Foucault broadened this treatment into a more encompassing critique of governmentality (Foucault 1991 [1978]) as the underside of liberalism – the enabling practices of dominance and exclusion from power that liberal political theory had largely ignored in favor of abstract theories of representation, but which was undeniably a large part of the way liberal democratic regimes actually governed.

The generation of these new perspectives and radical variations on old perspectives was accompanied and justified by a new set of meta-theoretical ideas. "Structuralism," an idea associated with disciplines, especially anthropology, was followed by post-structuralism, which soon morphed into deconstruction, and postmodernism – an even more encompassing idea which spread throughout the humanities and social sciences. The same emphasis on discourse, and the idea that the institutions of society and politics rested on ideological constructions, appeared in such forms as the idea that history should be understood as a system of rhetorical structures rather than as a science-like study of the facts, the recognition that different disciplines constructed the world in incommensurable ways, and deconstruction, the recognition that construction was an active process of discursive activity which could itself be reconstructed. Identities, which were contested by the social movements that flourished in the seventies and after, were themselves understood in these terms: the social construction and contestation of identities became the subject of the politics of the street. The world appeared as a set of interpretations, or "texts," which could only be interpreted rather than treated as facts. These ideas came to be called "postmodernism," and, by the eighties, this name came to be applied to the period itself.

Disciplinary Projects and the New Form of Theoretical Discussion

Postmodernism reaction produced its own reaction. The relativism of postmodernism became old news. But the period left behind a strong sense that the ideas that had been contested so strongly in the 1960s – positivism, Marxism, and the various disciplinary projects that had been defined in retrospect as "modernist" were impossible to return to or take seriously in the form that they had presented themselves – namely as projects grounded in a uniquely valid methodology, a uniquely true grand narrative, or a unique connection to reality. The idea that one could play a philosophical trump card in favor of one set of descriptions of the social world – a characteristic feature of the lengthy and inconclusive methodological debates of the 1950s and 60s – was seen as a product of a kind of intellectual innocence that was now lost.

The loss of innocence had consequences for what followed. New projects emerged, and flourished, but these projects derived their legitimacy from their relation to problems that had emerged from the inadequacies of past projects: the failure, for example, of traditional organic and juridical conceptions of state and society to account for such central facts of their own domain as citizenship or sovereignty in the face of the phenomenon of globalization. The new projects understood themselves to be trafficking in the domain of constructions. These new projects were intrinsically concerned with connections between domains that had traditionally been divided into the categories of social, political, and cultural. Cosmopolitanism, to take an example from the globalization literature, was simultaneously a cultural and social as well as a political phenomenon at the level of interstate legal relations, just as the national identities with which it competed were cultural constructions (Delanty 2009; Zolo 1997). The properties of cosmopolitanism could not be confined to a single discipline. Mass entertainment was consumed across the world and constructed for world markets. The agents of globalization included a highly internationalized elite that exercised influence in national politics. States were often juridically irrelevant to the settlement of issues of international business, which took place by arbitration in lawyers' offices, with the effect of creating new forms of global law.

These phenomena and many more depended on the theoretical structures of the past – notions of sovereignty as part of international law, for example – in order to be formulated, but the loss of innocence meant that the validity of these theories as a source of the language of description could no longer be taken for granted. The prior ideological formulations of the nature of the state and of law were built into the conduct and practice of the state: to account for conduct and practice there is no alternative to accounting for this ideology and placing it in a larger and different perspective from the one which originally produced it and validated it. The new theories and theoretical approaches were thus not new grand narratives, but rather meta-narratives. As part of their own project of analyzing new forms of sociality, politics, and cultural life they incorporated, and at the same time accounted for, the limitations of past conceptualizations.

This new form of theory – interdisciplinary, meta-theoretically aware, skeptical of grand narratives, recognizing the role of social and ideological construction in the creation of its subject matter – has not been without its opponents. The reactions have taken various forms, but the central element of each is the reassertion of disciplinary boundaries. In the case of philosophy, we now have "philosophical social theory," which is concerned largely with the affirmation of the doctrine of collective intentionality. This concept, which has been taken up in ethics and in some contexts of metaphysics, and had been used by John Searle as a means of accounting for the ontological status of social institutions and making the social world (Searle 1995, 2010), is a self-conscious rejection of explanations from other disciplines which undermine conventional philosophical claims. Philosophical arguments deriving concepts (such as "collective intentions") from other concepts, such as the use of "we" and "together" in ordinary language (Gilbert 1989, 1990, 1996), can be performed apart from empirical issues, such as the question of whether anything explanatory about the real social world is added by reference to collective intentions (cf. Turner 2010). The goal is to get an ontology of the social that avoids skeptical conclusions of the kind associated with postmodernism. The result is a form of intellectual conservatism that makes some preferred set of terms immune from "external" criticism.

The "philosophical" version of social theory also wants it both ways: to claim a specialized knowledge of ontology, but also to have these results accepted as true in a sense relevant to other concerns. But the "authority" of philosophy in the case of collective intentionality rests on nothing more than the bankrupt project of analytic philosophy based on the idea that linguistic usage tells us what the contents of the world are. The "meaning" that matters is the meaning in common life: the political meaning. Similarly, in sociology, one finds the rejection of interdisciplinary social theory, theory which is not wedded to the relatively narrow range of "facts" of concern to empirical sociology, on the grounds that social theory ought to preserve a close relation to empirical sociology (Joas and Knöbl 2009: xi). Implicitly, this simply means that "sociological" social theory may reject or ignore "philosophical" theories, political theories, and the like, and refer only to disciplinary concerns, while at the same time asserting intellectual authority over "the social" and speaking to the common life. But the authority derives from nothing more than the equally bankrupt project of extracting a science of social life from the kind of data that sociologists traditionally have preferred. Neither claim to authority is credible: these concepts belong to no fields, but to the common life itself.

Apart from these defensive disciplinary reactions, however, contemporary social and political thought is largely free from the kind of compartmentalization that marked the era of disciplinarization in the early and mid-twentieth century. The kinds of new approaches and new problematics discussed in this volume depend neither on disciplinary identities, and therefore authority, nor on the aspiration to be the scientific last word. They typically depend on and incorporate, but critically or at a meta-level, the ideological constructions of the past: one cannot understand issues of citizenship, marginality, and the like without references to the historical concept of citizenship as it is built into the institutions and laws of the nation state and international law. Any meaningful alternative understanding must also be an understanding of these institutions and facts. To go beyond Freud in a Lacanian way is to incorporate Freud. To focus on the underside of the liberal order as in Foucault is also to recognize and reinterpret the liberal order.

The New Problem of the Welfare State

The sixties left a rich but ambiguous legacy. Some of the changes that occurred early in the period after the sixties were rooted in the sixties or earlier; some of them were reactions to the events of the sixties and the successes and failures of the Old and New Left during that period. But the publication of Rawls' *Theory of Justice*, and its astonishing impact, reflected an important shift in the political concerns of academic social and political thinkers. The publication of this book coincided with struggles over the welfare state, which was consolidated throughout the west in the 1960s. By the 1970s, it was evident that the changes produced by the welfare state were irreversible − that opposition to the welfare state in the future would concern marginal issues of policy and philosophy and questions about the extent of its reach and its goals. But the basic fact of a larger, more intrusive, and more powerful state had become a taken for granted premise, still poorly understood and undertheorized, across the political spectrum.

The welfare state in Europe was rooted in a political lesson. The lesson that had been learned in the 1930s was that the price, and risks, of open class conflict were impossible for modern societies to bear, that the working class needed to be taken care of in the framework of a caring state, and that the traditional, and traditionally hazy, idea of socialism as the property-free brotherhood of man was neither achievable nor, perhaps, desirable. In Europe, the threat of Soviet Communism and fear of the defection of the working class drove the right to accept the compromises that led to the welfare state. The Left, for its part, accepted (often tacitly) that without the recovery of industry and business there would be nothing to redistribute.

The effect of the welfare state, ironically, was to eliminate the traditional working class as a meaningful political category and force. In the 1930s, and even into the 1950s, the working class was a distinct group, with its own culture and amusements: class difference was pervasive, especially in Europe. By the 1980s, and in most societies earlier, these distinctions– which were originally highly visible, for example in modes of dress – were largely submerged, or had vanished. New media and public education produced a common culture. New wealth produced common patterns of consumption.

The 1970s saw threats to, and a building reaction against, the welfare state. Not everyone shared fully in the benefits of the new order. The remnants of the older Left that had not been raised up in the economic expansion of the 1950s and 60s – miners, in Britain, for example – faced off against the government, producing scenes of violence, and disrupting the economy. The least attractive forms of labor were taken up by immigrants and minority members. The means open to the state to include the least advantaged were often unpopular. Affirmative action programs for minorities, for example, threatened the traditional working-class supporters of the Left. And Left governments came to represent austerity and economic malaise. At the same time, and not unconnected with this, the core loyalists of the Left became public employees – teachers, for example – rather than industrial workers.

The Left of the past is now seen through the powerful distorting lens of these changes. The figures we now celebrate from this period, the Frankfurt School and the critical social theory tradition generally, including cultural critics such as Walter Benjamin and Alexandre Kojève and the *Collège de Sociologie*, Antonio Gramsci, and George Lukaćs, were minor players at the time. The dominant Left of the 1930s was very different: concerned with such ideas as comprehensive "planning": of the economy, and life generally – even the planning of values, in the writings of Karl Mannheim (1940). The language of rights, prior to 1945, was largely disdained as bourgeois ideology. The state was a subject of no interest: in theory, it was to wither away once socialist revolution swept away class antagonism and property. Relations between states were to become pacific once class vanished, so international relations were of no interest. Neither were the traditional ideas of political theory: sovereignty, the idea of the state as resting on the exchange of protection for obedience, legality, legitimacy, and so forth.

The face of the old Left was firmly fixed on the socialist future and its benefits: the present was interregnum or purgatory; the practical realities of socialist governance as seen in Stalin's Soviet Union were misrepresented, as they were in the writings of the Webbs (1936, 1942) and John Desmond Bernal (1939), or ignored – a pattern which continued long after the war, especially in the writings of French intellectuals such as Jean Paul Sartre (Judt 1992). The Hungarian revolt of 1956 put an end to this for many intellectuals on the Left, but not all of them, and not the Communist parties of Europe: as a result, the issue of defending the Soviet Union continued to paralyze them old Left well into the 1960s.

Yet this period also saw an evolution on the Left. The language of human rights, extended to social rights, was embraced, however cynically, by the Soviet Union in the context of such documents as the United Nations Charter. And the Left in the west loudly asserted its liberal rights to speak freely in support of illiberal regimes in which these rights did not exist. The fifties saw the spectacle of McCarthyite persecution of former Communists who asserted their rights under law, and their innocence under law, to admiring audiences, despite being, in several important cases, compromised by the fact of their participation in espionage. Similarly, in Eastern Europe, prominent intellectuals on the Left who proclaimed their intellectual independence were sometimes involved with the security apparatus itself.

Freedom: The New Solution

The New Left of the sixties freed itself from these contradictions, but at a cost to intellectual and political coherence. It was a short step from the assertion of liberal rights against McCarthyism to the unqualified affirmation of these rights, and to freedom – the Free Speech movement in Berkeley is an example – against the security regime of the state generally. But freedom in the here and now was not part of the Old Left's program. The language of freedom itself both relied on the cold war dichotomy of communism and freedom and radicalized it. And in doing so it made freedom into a value as powerful and important as equality itself.

Rawls represented a powerful intellectual response to this conflict: freedom was reconcilable with equality and there was a rational means, something approaching a metric, for balancing the two. The basic idea was that once the rules of the game in society were fair, meaning that they led to egalitarian outcomes, people should be free to act within these rules. His conception of "the basic structure of society" was sociological, rather than legal or ethical: "the way in which the major social institutions fit together into one system, and how they assign fundamental rights and duties and shape the division of advantages that arises through social cooperation" (Rawls 1993: 258). These were open to manipulation to shape the division of advantages to produce the greatest well-being consistent with fairness of distribution. The principle of fairness was that the arrangements should benefit the worst off in society first.

This was a justification of the welfare state not merely as a problematic compromise, short of true socialism and scarcely better than capitalism, but as a positive order based directly on fundamental considerations of justice itself, considerations grounded directly in moral reason. Whatever reservations they had about the details of Rawls' highly technical argument, among academics in the social sciences and humanities at least, with the exception of economists, the general thrust of these arguments was accepted. The goal of equality was grounded in justice; justice was grounded in reason. Moreover, these were ideals that did not imply the use of revolutionary violence, outright expropriation, or terror. The means available were means familiar to modern states. Moreover, the ideal of justice was understood to be implicit in common morality. Thus it could function as a critical standard that was implied by the basic moral commitments underlying the society and the state itself: still critical, because the state and society characteristically fail to live up to their own implicit aspirations, but, nevertheless, grounded in the morality of the citizens rather than an imposition from outside or on high.

This form of argument put Marxism in a peculiar position. Rawls did not need to appeal to the historical mission of the working class to bring about Communism through revolution, a dead letter by this time, nor indeed any need to appeal to history at all. The goal of equality, something that was a powerful motivator for socialism but not the whole of it (brotherhood, the abolition of the exploitation of man by man, human dignity, and the end of property were more traditional goals), was now ordained by reason directly. Freedom as a normal part of a fair social arrangement was a useful ideal. Concerns about "more" freedom could be dismissed as, by definition, attempts to preserve unfair advantages, and an obsession of right-wing cranks. Whatever reservations one might have about the details of Rawls' arguments paled: it showed that there could be a powerful defense of the present state that pointed in a "progressive" direction of improvement that preserved the values of liberalism that deserved preservation.

It is important to understand the peculiar double-edged character of this argument. On the one hand, it was a defense of the existing order. On the other, it was the source of a form of critique that had no natural limits and could be varied extensively. No actually existing welfare state lived up to the idea of justice in Rawls. This was the simple form of the critique, and it was the source of much of the attraction of Rawls: as Richard Rorty often said, it represented the best extant account of what a good society should aspire to be, which happens also to have fit the prejudices of the faculty at Harvard. But the nature of the critique had much more radical implications. The fact that existing social arrangements were not "just" in Rawls' sense raised questions about the political forms, including the form of liberal democracy itself. If they failed to produce justice, there was something wrong with them, or with the citizens who voted in them. And these flaws might be rooted more deeply, in, for example, a flawed culture, a flawed social order that produced false consciousness, or something else.

The project of the defense of the welfare state thus shaded into the critique of liberal democracy as such, and then into anti-liberalism. Both the extension of the idea of equality and the issue of the failure of liberal democracy to bring about genuine equality could tap into a vast well of non-standard Left criticism, including the critiques developed by the Frankfurt School. The welfare state as it actually existed of course had its own problematic history – the paternalistic mental health and prison institutions created in the early period of liberalism were integral to the actual welfare state. And its subjects could be understood also as its victims. Similarly, forms of inequality not countenanced by Rawls, especially forms of inequality that excluded people, degraded them, stigmatized them, or otherwise defined them in institutional ways which conflicted with their own identities, could be made the basis for new forms of critique. Racism, sexism, and other symbolic and tangible forms of harm were themselves sources of inequality, and therefore of the liberal democratic order that produced them and by extension the welfare state in its present form.

The project of constructing a defense of the welfare state has continued unabated in various forms other than Rawls' own. These approaches constitute a major part of the contemporary literature in social and political thought, and are well represented in this volume. Critical Theory as presently practiced represents a development of the same project of reconciling egalitarianism to liberal ideas, notably the idea of civil society. Republicanism is an attempt to give an account of freedom other than the liberal account and at the same time justifies the welfare activities of the state, including its assertion of paternalistic powers. Communitarianism is another. The return of interest in such traditions as pragmatism, which was on the Left, in Dewey's hands, but opposed to the dominant Left of Bernal, is in part an attempt to find a philosophical account of the social sciences and the modern welfare state order that is consistent with the lessons of the postmodern revolt against modernism, but which is nevertheless positive and not merely relativistic. The discussions of racism, of the Foucaultian state, "recognition" in the thought of the Frankfurt School, as well as the revival of the discussion of notions of sovereignty, reflect the use or plundering of the received conceptual tradition in order to make sense of the new reality of the modern state.

Social Democracy vs. Liberalism

One important issue that underlies this discussion could be put as follows: despite serving as an ideal that much of academic thinking accepts without reservation, "social democracy" has been opposed, or rejected in its details, by electorate after electorate. People have not, it appears, acted in accordance with the demands of reason. But at the same time, the welfare state, or at least many of its institutions, is popular. People fiercely defend the benefits of the welfare state when they are threatened by austerity programs. But they do not want to pay for them. Moreover, they have acted against their own interests by rejecting forms of redistribution that would benefit them and which "reason" justifies. This problem – which is a problem only under the assumption that reason in fact justifies the order in question – runs through the literature. Is there something intrinsic to the nature of public discussion, the psychological formation of people, or culture, or in the hidden or overt power of the opponents of redistribution, that gets in the way of reason and prevents the realization of the kind of social order that reason demands? There is, in short, an analogue to the Marxian problem of false consciousness produced by the failure of the ideal of social democracy to be realized.

False consciousness is not the only model for this question. One of the great puzzles of twentieth-century politics is the fact that liberalism, which in its political as well as economic forms, brought enormous benefits, both economically and in terms of rights, also produced an extraordinarily fierce opposition. Fascism, Nazism, and the Left generally rejected liberalism as an ideology and a practice, and in the most vitriolic terms. The history of liberalism in the twentieth century is largely a history of struggles against liberalism, and the affirmation of anti-liberal ideas against the hidden ideological grounds of liberalism. The terms sovereignty, recognition, and the like are each terms that liberalism either rejects or ignores, or redefines.

The case of "social democracy" is similar: it produced its own reaction, or more accurately its own discontents, though some of these discontents were very powerful. On the Left, these discontents involved the excluded and the issues of equality that the simple economic model of the distribution of wealth left unaddressed – issues arising from ingrained race and gender biases in the law, in policy, and the like, as well as issues involving the status of previously despised groups, such as gays, the disabled, and ethnic minorities. Here the opposition is less fierce, but the reasoning is nevertheless fundamental: the very existence of these claims on the state calls into question the idea of blind justice derived from reason alone.

Liberalism itself fought back, both at the level of electoral resistance to the welfare state, and intellectually. For liberals, the problem of freedom was no more resolved by Rawls than the problem of the nature of equality itself. Robert Nozick, in a famous text of the 1970s, *Anarchy, State, and Utopia* (1974), made the point that Rawls had conveniently omitted consideration of the ways in which the distribution of wealth was the product of the free choices of individuals, and ignored the rights they had to the disposition of the wealth that they had acquired through their own effort. Even Marx accepted the idea that there was some deep connection between work and the control of the products of work. He merely rejected the institution of alienable private property as the proper form of this relation.

The problem of liberalism is rooted in the political compromises that produced the welfare state itself. Writers like Carl Schmitt (1988 [1923]), Albert Venn Dicey (1962 [1914]), and Joseph Schumpeter (1950 [1942]) had questioned whether democracy and liberalism were themselves compatible: in the end, they thought, the temptation of the working class to overturn property arrangements and impose not only direct egalitarian socialism but an authoritarian regime to enact it would be too great. The restraints on political action implied by the idea of the self-limited state, and the rule of open discussion of the use of the limited powers of the state, would soon fall under the pressure of the misguided desire to kill the golden goose of capitalism and expropriate the wealth of those who ran it. Along with it, the liberal idea of government by discussion would also vanish.

The philosophical form of these ideas produced a similar conflict with liberalism. If it was indeed the case that reason demanded an egalitarian regime, what was the point of liberal discussion or representative institutions other than to provide legitimacy or symbolic acquiescence to the dictates of reason? Kant's followers, and Hegel, had already faced this implication of the idea that politics was justice grounded in reason: they concluded that the role of the representative was to act in accordance with reason on behalf of those who were represented (Bluntschli 2002 [1869]). It followed that "consent" was genuine only when it was in accordance with the dictates of reason. Liberal discussion was tolerable if it led to the acceptance of reason. Michael Beresford Foster, in his classic discussion of Hegel and Plato, characterized this as "the pitiless domination of reason" (1965 [1935]: 85).

And if one believes that reason does not dictate the solution to political questions, "reason" is being used by these thinkers as a warrant for the exercise of authoritarian power – a means of usurping power in the name of reason and of controlling and eliminating politics and contestation in the name of the end of justice grounded in reason. This is a conflict that is present today in the writings of Chantal Mouffe in response to the Habermasian idea of political reason in a fully realized civil society (Mouffe 1999). And it is posed, in a practical way, by the question of the role of intellectuals in society: if they are the representatives of reason, and have the role of bringing about the public acceptance of reason, they are either – depending on one's choices in the face of this conflict, merely instruments of public enlightenment and servants of reason or active political agents promoting ideological solutions to the problems of the present.

The Present and the Past

These issues underlie much of the discussion in Part 1 of this volume. In one way or another, the chapters deal with issues with liberal democracy and the welfare state, and with the need to replace, supplant, analyze, or extend and transform the images of man and politics inherited from liberal political thought, and with the responses to these attempts. The responses take two basic forms: a "French" critique, which understands liberalism as a form which organizes hidden means of distinction, suppression, and harm in the name of universalism and equity. The other, the "German" critique, is an attempt to consider the conditions for the full realization of the liberatory aspirations contained in the original liberal impulse. There is also a kind of American variation on these in the form of pragmatism, and a critique originated from liberalism itself, as well as still living traditions of European liberalism transplanted into the Anglo-American universe, and a resurgence of interest in Republicanism as an alternative to liberalism that allows in an unproblematic way for an extensive welfare state.

The "French" critique follows Foucault's basic thought that we are complicit in our own oppression as a result of accepting forms of thought and practice that serve to oppress us. These forms acquire a kind of autonomy. They are controlled by no one, but enacted by everyone. "Liberal democracy" is made up of these bodies of practice – they are the underside of the liberal democratic state, and the true significance of the seemingly neutral practices of the liberal state is in these practices, which are the means by which citizens are disciplined, punished, labeled, excluded and included, and the like. Concentrating the project of reform on the refinement of these practices and modes of thought, their equal application, or the production of fair outcomes, as in Rawls' procedural liberalism, misses the point fundamentally: the procedures themselves are the source of the oppressive power by which people are excluded, suppressed, labeled, and controlled.

This was a powerful idea. It avoided the problem of identifying power with a ruling class or elite – a project which in the 1950s and 60s had produced numerous efforts, which tended to discover beneficiaries of the system and people who maintained it, but few examples of classes which could "rule." We ourselves, with our complicity in the basic arrangements of such things as the liberal penal and justice system, were the source of its power. Moreover, our complicity was unconscious: part of the fact of an order of practices of this kind is the fact that they supply our own mental apparatus for thinking about these things: conceptual practices.

As Gary Wickham points out, this idea, along with Foucault's array of technical terms, was eagerly absorbed, especially in the Anglo-Saxon world, where it represented a way of continuing critique despite the disappearance of the most overt forms of the traditional Marxist form of class conflict. It fit nicely with anti-totalitarianism, and indeed had the effect of converting liberal democratic regimes, including the welfare state itself, into totalizing institutions embodying ideologies of control. Power is about repression in both totalitarian and liberal regimes. But liberal regimes repress in covert ways, ways that are covert even to the repressors, who simply see themselves as dealing with the damaged or deranged and defending society, rather than as taking sides in a conflict. The task of the analyst is to identify and make visible these practices of power.

This was a mode of reasoning that applied widely, and applied at the point that procedural liberalism was especially vulnerable: the problem of minorities and those who are excluded or harmed by the procedural order of liberalism, and the hidden injuries which the welfare state produced when it managed these populations. Indeed, the history of feminist thought in this period as well as thinking about race, reproduces the transition from a kind of procedural liberalism, or a faith in the use of ordinary political and legal processes to attain justice and equality, to a recognition that the issues of racism and sexism, and the kinds of repression and inequality that they generate, are intrinsic to the order of practices themselves and require new forms of theorizing.

Foucault's topics ranged from madness to sexuality, and typically were concerned with the grand historical sweep – the turning points in which new orders of repression were created, usually in the distant past, and the long process of their playing out and development by largely unwitting administrators and minor thinkers. His focus, typically, was on the organizing ideas behind these systems, the ideas which provided their practitioners with ways of thinking about their subject. Pierre Bourdieu, who derived his own thought from the same general French tradition, but was more deeply rooted in the social sciences, carried out an analogous project, but concentrated on the more immediate range: systems of education which conferred and decided academic distinction, the organization of the relation between inside the house, the domain of women, and the outside, the domain of men, in the Algerian household, and so forth.

As Marcel Fournier notes, these studies had their own dramatic effects. In the case of schooling, the perception of schools as relatively autonomous "Republican" institutions was changed: Bourdieu exhibited them as systems for the reproduction of hierarchy, which operated in subtle ways to exclude the poor and advantage the beneficiaries of current hierarchies. And they did so precisely by the adherence to practices, which Bourdieu labeled with the distinctive term "habitus," that had unconscious distinction-producing effects which the analyst could reveal. Bourdieu, as Fournier shows, was able to do something that Foucault did not: to create an academic corps of followers and collaborators.

Bourdieu is in some ways the symptomatic figure of the transformation of discussion. He recognized that the old questions of class were no longer determinative and that the possibility of struggle now resided in the realm of the symbolic or cultural, against symbolic power and distinction based on symbolic power, and also recognized that the new class to which an appeal needed to be made was the class of government workers created by the expanded welfare state. His main audience and following was among teachers, who were frequently members of the French Communist party. Bourdieu's intellectual and ideological problem was to think through the problem of culture and cultural practices – the locus of hierarchy in the new society produced by the welfare state. This required the development of such notions as symbolic violence, which, as Fournier notes, he used to analyze male domination.

But the thinker with the most distinctive approach to these issues is Jacques Lacan. As Stavrakakis shows in his chapter on Lacan and his influence, his radicalization of Freudian analysis and his terminology of the real, the imaginary, and the symbolic run through thinkers like Cornelius Castoriadis (1998), Bourdieu, and Slavoj Žižek (1989) and represent a particularly powerful kind of means of deconstruction and critique of ideology. For Lacan, as Stavrakakis notes, the realm of the symbolic is, as it is for Bourdieu and Foucault, the precondition for interaction, including the interaction out of which collectives and individuals are formed – thus this realm is the starting point and subject of analysis.

For Lacan, this was not merely a talking point: it was the basis for a replacement of the notion of the autonomous desiring individual of liberalism with a conception of subjectivity that makes desire into the attempt to overcome a lack, and doing this through such means as consuming or identifying with a political ideology. The lack, however, is never possible to overcome – the autonomous individual never happens, and the solutions to the lack are themselves in the realm of the imaginary. It is this lack that powers capitalism, which provides consumption products that address this lack, including such things as prestige goods that confer identity. But the process never ends. And this endlessness generates its own response in the form of ascetic rationalism, as in Weber, in which pleasure is deferred. Present consumerism is a response to, and of course a rejection of, deferred pleasure in favor of consumption. But it is intrinsically doomed to fail to produce the fulfillment it promises, and constrains us to seek our pleasure in the channels provided by a consumer economy.

These thinkers were each influenced by, or identified with, Marxism. But at the end, appeals to Marx in France came to have little meaning beyond the ceremonial. The larger fate of Marxism, however, is more complex. Peter Beilharz examines the complex fate of Marx and Marxism. Marx, he notes, can be read in many ways, but at the core of his thought was the critique of political economy, especially its disembodied notions of labor. The early Marx had a romantic image of work as a freely given contribution to a collective whole. This image, which made sense only in characteristically rural settings, was set aside when he recognized that the industrial order was here to stay. He expected capitalism to collapse of its own accord. When Marxism became an official ideology of the Social Democratic Party it came to be accepted that socialism could be produced through voting. But the rhetoric of revolution was still employed, both as a motivator for the working classes, and as a promise of a radically changed future. The far Left rejected this cynical strategy, which in any case ended in grief – the revolutionary rhetoric and the far Left itself so terrified the voters that only the least threatening socialist parties attained power. Those that were wedded to this rhetoric were suppressed by force when the opportunity arose – as it did in Austria, for example.

The great exception to this was Russia. Lenin developed an unMarxian doctrine of the vanguard party that justified party rule in the name of the proletariat. The Russian revolution succeeded: it became a model for intellectuals in developing countries and was imposed on Eastern Europe. It retains its power in the poorest parts of the world as a solution to backwardness. In Europe it was recognized more or less explicitly by the Left to be deeply flawed, but the principle of refusing to denounce socialist regimes prevented these flaws from being discussed except in the form of a complex theoretical code. In France, because of the influence and omnipresence of the Communist party, this necessity vanished: one could either operate within the limits of the official party, which many intellectuals were willing to do, or one was free to invoke Marx in a wide variety of ways. The same could not be said for Germany or German Left socialist thought, where an unwillingness to explicitly reject the Soviet Union went hand-in-hand with a willingness to criticize with respect to such matters as aesthetic theory, and the development of a code which allowed for an alternative Left critique.

The Frankfurt School was the master of this kind of encoded discussion, and used it to develop a form of Marxism that had its roots not only in Marx and Hegel but also in Max Weber, the theorist of western rationalization and bureaucratization. As Beilharz puts it, they combined a Marxist critique of commodification with Weber's dystopian critique of rationalization. The product of this marriage was a socialist humanism concerned not so much with capitalism as with the characteristic forms and products of modernity itself, including the Soviet state. Louis

Althusser and Étienne Balibar (1970) and Nicos Poulantzas (1987 [1975], 2001 [1978]) provided a strongly "for Marx" critique of this body of thought, exposing the distance it had come from Marx himself. The collapse of the Soviet sphere in 1989 and the death of both leading figures put an effective end to this line of thought.

The Marxian impulse lives on in various forms. The model pioneered by the Frankfurt School when it added Weber to Marx (and Freud to Marx) continues to be a method of prolonging the life of Marxian ideas: Lacan, Schmitt, deconstruction, and other ideas can be combined with Marx to generate a "position." And the basic anti-capitalist animus of Marx also takes ever new forms: as a source for the critique of globalization, the current financial crisis of the west, and so forth. But these Marxisms are all post-Marxisms: the proletariat as a revolutionary force exists only in the romantic rhetoric of far Left politics, and not in the realm of social and political theory.

The problem of race is a central example of a source of pluralism. On the one hand, race exemplifies the kinds of inequality rooted in the realm of ideas and the symbolic. As Patricia Hill Collins shows, race theory both has a scientific lineage and serves as a kind of working theory that serves to harm the subjects of its theorizing. It is thus a natural target for critical theory – for a critique that not only rejects it, which she calls traditional theory with a critical intent, but shows the hidden racial assumptions of universalistic accounts, and goes beyond this to identify what she calls "contemporary racial formations of social injustice," meaning the racially unjust meaning of social formations which appear to have nothing to do with race. Justice, in the case of race, requires not just equality, or the elimination of a harmful form of thought, but the recognition and elimination of these hidden, harmful, racial significances. The nature of the harms, however, is not obvious, so one task of critical race theory is precisely that of theorizing these harms. In this form, critical race theory takes every institution as its subject, because every institution is inveigled in the racial ordering of society.

The same kind of case can be made for gender. As Claire Mary Colebrook points out, one form of feminism would be an extension of the basic language of liberalism, the language of rights and free choice, as well as the language of equality, to domains that were of special concern to women: reproductive rights and sexual rights. And the same "feminization" could be performed on other theories and approaches, so that one could construct a feminist variant of Marxism or post-modernism. But this would keep the forms of theory intact. The larger claim and promise of feminism is that the form of theorizing can and should itself change: that the present form of theory is itself masculine in character, and could be replaced by something with a preference for inclusion and empathy and a rejection of the notion of individual autonomy as a part of masculine ideology. As she notes, the notion of inclusion, both in theory and political practice, opens up realms of experience to theoretical discussion that not only undermine the liberal model of the individual, but raise questions about the notions of sexual difference that the feminist critique of liberalism assumes, and thus about the sexual binary, and ultimately about the notion of difference itself.

If we question, or deconstruct, the very basis of our distinctive form of critique, is this deconstruction tantamount to a kind of political quietism? This is a question that is raised by Judith Butler's rhetorical analyses of gender difference talk discussed by Colebrook, and Butler's famous slogan "everyone is in drag." Thomas Docherty discusses this problem in terms of the infusion of ideas from literary criticism into social theory, especially in the form of Jacques Derrida's philosophy of decentering and his critique of the philosophy of presence. As Docherty notes, the kinds of analysis of difference promoted by thinkers like Derrida does indeed dissolve the naïve binaries that "political" critiques by academics often depend on. Nevertheless, he points out, this has led, in the thought of such philosophers as Deleuze, to a quest for a stopping point beyond these distinctions and binaries, such as "the event" and the idea of "becoming" as a way of getting beyond the fixity of difference thinking. In this respect this new turn of thought resembles the response of *Lebensphilosophie* to the rigid categories of neo-Kantianism. But in the hands of thinkers like Alain Badiou this critique becomes a form of the critique of ideology and false consciousness which opposes forms of consciousness to an engagement which cannot be reduced to forms.

Habermas, the embodiment of the second generation of the Frankfurt School, began his career close to Marxism, but like the first generation his thought was motivated in large part by the question of false consciousness, the question which originally was "why did the proletariat fail to fulfill its historical mission." But Habermas pursued it in the updated form of the question of why people did not vote for Social Democracy, and specifically for the Social Democratic Party in Germany, which in the early years of the German Federal Republic was unable to achieve a parliamentary majority. Habermas, in his classic work on the *Structural Transformation of the Public Sphere* (1992 [1962]), inverted the analysis of the Weimar republic and its "sham parliamentarism" produced by Carl Schmitt. Schmitt argued that the possibility of genuine rational discussion and persuasion – the precondition of liberal democracy – had been made impossible by the emergence of anti-liberal "totalizing parties," such as the Communists and Nazis, and by extension also the largely ideological SPD, which aimed to absorb the state into its own encompassing ideology and viewed parliamentary action as only a means to advance this ultimate objective: the absorption of the state by the party and the subordination of the state to the exclusive ideology of the party. Habermas argued that the public sphere itself was a sham in the conditions of modern liberal democracy, because the kind of rational discussion that should motivate political choice was undermined fatally by the false "news" and sham discussion among peers that actually decided elections. Eventually this argument turned, as suggested above, in the direction of a positive argument for a particular as yet unachieved public sphere in which uncoerced rational consensus would prevail.

James Bohman explains the meaning of the notion of "critical" in the "Critical Theory" that is the enduring contribution of this school to present discussion, and indeed which makes it a paradigm of the kind of social theory and philosophy that became central after the de-disciplinarization of this discussion after the seventies. Bohman notes that these theories have a special explanatory structure that makes them both explanatory and normative. They are liberatory theories – designed to account for the obstacles to liberation and to have practical implications for the practice of liberatory politics itself.

In some of its earlier incarnations, this goal seemed to involve a comprehensive social and historical account which would provide its possessors with the means of identifying, from an epistemically privileged and theoretically grounded vantage point, instances of false consciousness in terms of an account of the stages of historical development of capitalism. Bohman argues for a more modest notion of "critical" which is nevertheless consistent with the project of a liberatory politics: critical theory as a form of inquiry consistent with a democratic politics in which a plurality of voices are not only heard but incorporated into critical inquiry itself. As he describes the lessons of pragmatism for critical theory, the kind of inquiry that is envisioned by pragmatism is a form of experimentalism in which there is democratic participation, especially in the judging of consequences. This kind of inquiry contrasts to technocratic, expert-driven inquiry of the kind criticized by Habermas.

Yet, as Bohman notes, there is an unresolved tension in Habermas himself with respect to the issue of theoretical unification. He is open to methodological pluralism, but not quite ready to abandon the idea that at the highest level of thought a unifying philosophy of history is required. Bohman argues that we lose nothing by abandoning this idea, and that we gain by access to the variety of explanatory strategies found in the pluralistic world of perspectives. But we also gain something in the way of means of verification – something that Critical Theory wedded to a philosophy of history had to give up – in the form of the public verification of the success of particular liberatory measures and policies. This kind of verification can rely, democratically, on the reflexive ability of individuals in the public itself, rather than on technocratic methods.

Pragmatism, however, as Robert Talisse explains, does not speak in a univocal way about the correct methods: he identifies four distinct "pragmatist" approaches to the social and political, including Dewey's perfectionism, Rorty's ironism, Richard Posner's realism, and Cheryl Misak's deliberativism, which, perhaps combined with Dewey's slogan that democracy is a way of life, comes closest to Bohman's development of Habermas. For Dewey as for Habermas, discussion led to solidarity and a recognition of common values. The role of the state is to facilitate moral grown in this direction, a direction whose destination is not fixed in advance, as socialist thinking ordinarily assumed. But as Talisse notes, this is one conception of human flourishing among others.

Richard Rorty, in contrast, faces up to the relativism of conceptions of the human good, and sees the message of pragmatism in its openness to improvement and willingness to experiment with new forms of flourishing. He accepts the need to stand unflinchingly for our values in the face of the reality that there is and can be no grounding for them in philosophy, reason, nature, and the like – echoing in this respect Isaiah Berlin, Schumpeter, and Weber. Posner goes on to describe the democratic mindset that he identifies with pragmatism, which is anti-philosophical and disdains appeals to transcendental reason and transcendental values. He rejects democracy as deliberation, questioning whether this is anything more than utopianism, and suggests that democracy be understood as a competition for votes and nothing more – by reference to Schumpeter as well, who gets this conception from Weber.

As these references make clear, there is a conception of democracy that does not rely on classical liberal philosophy, but which is nevertheless liberal. Weber is one crucial representative of this kind of liberalism, and Schumpeter is another. In each case these liberals operate with minimal assumptions about human nature, and are reluctant to appeal to any kinds of transcendental assertions, whether they are about "rights" or "democracy." But they are particularly immune to appeals to collective entities – society, race, and the like – and to assertions about the rationality of political values. Jeremy Shearmur discusses two thinkers in this category, Karl Popper and Friedrich Hayek: each of them anti-utopians who applied their arguments to the Marxism of their time, but whose arguments remain relevant. For them, the attempt to assert values as truths leads more or less directly to tyranny: either the market, in Hayek's case, should decide, or, for Popper, a politics of piecemeal reform which concentrated not on the good life, about which we can never be expected to agree, but on the elimination of bad things about which we can agree.

The Frankfurt School is now in its third "generation." With the work of Axel Honneth, it has returned to a deeply anti-liberal concept: recognition. The key to the concept is that recognition, unlike, for example the distribution of goods in Rawlsian distributive justice, cannot be generated by ordinary procedures of liberal democracy, by universal law, by government mandates, and the like. It is something that is achieved in history by struggle, by demands. It is a pre-political concept, in the family of the concept of honor, which is a condition for a certain kind of politics, rather than its product. As Mauro Basaure shows, for Honneth this level is fundamental to social life. For Honneth the concept of recognition is a return to the true social order – an order of reciprocal claims and demands whose mutual acceptance does such things as allow the individual to appear in public without shame, without hiding aspects of their identity. It arises in the sphere of community life and in such forms as maternal love. A positive form of this mutual recognition affirms ones identity and makes possible successful self-realization in general. Honneth takes reciprocal recognition and affirmation to be a condition for the kind of subjectivity that allows genuine democratic political participation. In its critical form, as an account of failure of recognition and the processes that prevent recognition, this account is a novel form of the false consciousness problem itself, though for Honneth the problem now takes the form of asking what failures of recognition now stand in the way of is genuine "social democracy" with genuine democratic participation.

It is easy enough to dismiss the emphasis on recognition as a form of political romanticism, in Schmitt's sense, and to point to the affinities of the idea of recognition with the totalitarianism of the Soviet Union, the totalizing parties of the European Left in the interwar years, and to fascist and Nazi doctrine: the fascist idea of the idea of duty, and therefore of the soldier as its exemplary instance, as a model for the new order and the Nazi concern with the dignity of the working man in the face of his capitalist bosses and with considerations of honor more generally. The association of these ideas and identity politics in general with the notion of race – with the Mexican immigrant *party La Raza* as the exemplary party of identity politics – is also difficult to avoid. Nevertheless, it is clear that there are elements of the notions of human belongingness and attachment that lie beyond the spare and formal liberal legal forms of citizenship, legal rights to due process, the vote, and the relations of the market.

The question is what role these elements should play. Are they "private" and politically irrelevant? Or are they the secret essence of all politics and of realized human life? There is a sharp division over this. Liberalism has an affinity with the Protestant idea that human dignity and the like are ultimately irrelevant and a distraction: the true test for salvation is the individual's relation with God, a god who is "no respecter of persons," as the market and the liberal legal state are. For liberalism, they are private. Against liberalism, both on the Right and the Left, is the idea that true human life is possible only in the context of the rooted, the participatory, and the ecstatic communal: without this humans are atomized Hobbesian individuals incapable of genuine human relations. Liberalism, from this point of view, imposes atomization in the name of freedom and procedural justice, and employs the public private distinction to suppress and reject the desire for recognition that those whose being is rooted in ethnic, class, gender, and communal identities wish to see acknowledged in order for them to participate as bearers of these identities.

Communitarianism brings these issues into the open. Is there a fundamental conflict between liberalism, including liberal justice in the rather abstract form originally advocated by Rawls, and the kinds of human relations that make up actual communities? Does well-being and social solidarity require more than a neutral framework in which we each pursue our individual ideas of the good? Is liberalism itself not so much neutral as an ideology of its own that contains a conception of the good that is itself problematic? Charles Blattberg points out that these issues are difficult for liberals to answer – if they reduce liberalism to a very spare notion of the good, such as autonomy – and define liberalism in terms of people's freedom to pursue their autonomously chosen ends, and add to this the idea of value-pluralism, that there is no rational ground for choice between these ends, we implicitly exclude the possibility of various forms of human relation – such as those captured by the notion of recognition – and replace these possibilities with the possibility of a society based on the much different notion of toleration.

Republicanism has emerged as an alternative to liberalism that preserves freedom, but does so by redefining it, and allows the state to act in a non-neutral manner in terms of values – a key condition for the defense of the modern, intrusive, welfare state as it actually operates. Richard Bellamy shows how republican arguments serve to avoid the kinds of problems detailed by

Blattberg's chapter, replacing liberalism with a notion of political community in which interventions that liberalism would treat as violations of freedom can be justified in terms of the values of the community itself. This kind of interference – such as interfering in ways that protect a person from self-harm – is neither arbitrary nor an expression of domination.

Moreover, the republican political community can, and to have a genuine community must, intervene to protect its members from the domination of others. Liberalism, in contrast, permits certain forms of domination by shielding it under the heading of rights – the right, for example, of a druggist to arbitrarily deny a drug to a purchaser on the basis of their personal beliefs, or for no reason at all. Political discourse which protects the right to be heard is the key to the prevention of domination: even a minority whose views might otherwise be ignored by the political process can have their voices heard and enter into political coalitions to secure their wishes.

Non-domination, like recognition, is a fact in the social realm. Liberalism secures rights against the state; non-domination is a social condition assured by the state as a means of securing the conditions for genuine democratic participation. What counts as domination, and what kinds of interventions by the state are warranted, are determined by the democratic process itself. But it is a democratic process undistorted by the relations of domination that liberalism allows. Thus republicanism incorporates the idea of assuring recognition and protecting community as these pre-political conditions relate to the integrity of the political process of discussion and exchange itself – and this can allow for very extensive interventions, which produce a *de facto* egalitarianism.

Natalie Doyle describes developments in French political thought that go in what is in some respects the opposite direction. She notes that thinkers like Aron and Francois Furet uncovered a French liberal tradition prior to French republicanism, with a prepolitical notion of freedom – a notion of human sovereignty. Where this notion is similar to the "Republicanism" discussed above is in the idea that this kind of freedom requires the protection of the state, and is fragile. Where it differs is in the way the problem of the state is itself understood: the state is not, so to speak, a natural product of collective willing which legitimates its intrusions on us, but is rather an invention, a mythologized or imagined thing, with no grounding in a legitimacy other than its own constructed imaginary being – no external legitimating fact such as God or the sacred. This reasoning reflected a suspicion of the totalitarian implications of Rousseau's general will. But it also reflected the idea of the state as a human project, an ideological construction, consisting of representations, to use the language of Durkheim as well as these thinkers.

The outcome of this reasoning is that that state, society, and the like – including of course the Foucauldian order of governmentality – are not treated as objects or forces outside of human control, but that the history of the state becomes a history of the humanization of state power, and the exclusion of religious grounding – a kind of disalienation and de-sacralization of the state. The implications of this reasoning for liberal democracy are in a sense the obverse of the lesson one finds in Foucault: that we are the creators, rather than the passive victims, of the state. But we are also engaged in a continuous process of emancipating ourselves from the monarchical, religiously grounded state of the European past, and of creating the subjectivity that makes democratic politics and collective action possible without the sacralized forms of monarch and nation. Individualizaton is not so much a theoretical error or theoretical premise, or a sign of failure to achieve collective unity, as a product of this process, and of the creative making of states and imaginaries of the state which drives this process.

This kind of more fundamental rethinking of the nature of liberal democracy as an achievement is relevant to the understanding of the political development of Latin America. The early leaders of Latin American republics were also characteristic modernizing intellectuals of the kind that in the twentieth century, in the decolonizing world, looked to Marxism as an alternative path to development. As José Maurício Domingues and Aurea Mota point out, they reasoned that liberal democracy was not possible with the populations of their country and the Spanish legal and social inheritance, so they opted for more of a Napoleonic model, which gradually settled, in the nineteenth century, into a practice of state centralism. But these nations were also, for the most part, artificial, sometimes highly heterogeneous constructions which concealed a vast collection of minorities. These were for the most part politically excluded and regarded as a nuisance, as the chapter points out.

In the twentieth century, the ideas of the Left had a special influence: the compromises that made for the Welfare state in Europe did not take place in Latin America, and the poor remained, a decisive political reality – appealed to both by Left and in the case of Perón in Argentina, a kind of populist Right. Theorizing about the problem of the poor developed in contact with political movements of various kinds which sought to assert minority rights and regional demands. The possibility of a stable liberal constitutional order was always under threat by these movements. Yet a gradual development of a kind of liberal constitutionalism nevertheless took place, and the preponderance of military dictatorship diminished.

The Latin American experience is a mirror of western European modernity – both a challenge to the standard model of development, which raises questions about its universality, and a reminder of the conditions of its achievement – conditions such as relative ethnic and linguistic homogeneity. It is also a challenge to the notion of democratic participation, which takes on different and problematic meanings when the participation occurs under the flag of collective identities. Liberalism depended on effacing these identities: the price of recapturing them is to render ordinary liberal politics of discussion more difficult.

Deliberation, reason, and critique, to the extent that they become the basic content of politics, place intellectuals in a special position. Although there is a long tradition of discussing intellectuals as a social category in social theory, little of the earlier discussion reflected on the phenomenon of the public intellectual itself. From the time of Zola to the present, however, the forms of public intellectual assertion and presence have evolved, and a more serious discussion of the bearers of public reason, if that is what they are, is needed. Patrick Baert and Joel Isaac point to Bourdieu as an example of a thinker who was a public political intellectual who also theorized about public intellectuals and to some extent thought reflexively about the role of the public intellectual. Behind him was always the example of Sartre, the consummate public intellectual, who had discredited himself as a public thinker by his devotion to the Communist line. Much recent writing on intellectuals in sociology has been concerned with careerism – how an intellectual makes it. But there are other strands: the philosophy of expertise, the contextualist approach in the history of ideas, and an ongoing literature on the conflict between devotion to intellectual goals and political commitment. This is clearly a topic that requires more effort, but which is ready to emerge from its somnolence.

New and Emerging Frameworks: Plurality, Contingency, Relationalism, and Transformation

Part 1 covers a range of theories that in very different ways have emerged out of the crisis and transformation of liberal political thought over the past three decades or so. As we have seen, developments within the French and German traditions opened up entirely new perspectives on the fate of the political in a period of major social and political change. The topics under discussion in Part 2 of this volume are less defined in terms of major schools of thought than by frameworks that have emerged around specific themes. The chapters concern topics that in part represent continuity with the older traditions of social and political analysis, but mostly they deal with topics reflecting new and emerging frameworks of analysis. Many of the topics covered here are not easily positioned within what have now become established theoretical traditions, though they have been clearly influenced by post-Foucauldian theory, constructivism and interpretivism. The topics under discussion in Part 2 of the volume are largely concerned with challenges to social and political theory that have arisen from the crisis of the very understanding of the social that has come as a result of issues that are often summed under the heading of globalization or, in other words, the crisis of late modern or global society. Some of the more specific problems that this concerns are discussed in the next section of the volume.

A striking feature of current theorizing is the persistence of some of the central questions of social and political theory but which escape normative closure. Indeed the very possibility of a normative critique of society, which was taken for granted in the classical traditions of modern social and political thought, is increasingly questioned – though rarely rejected – in these new approaches. The older assumptions about the objectivity of society, or the reality of the social, and the possibility of an alternative politics has been supplanted by approaches that appear to foreground plurality, contingency, relationalism, and transformation. Until recently cultural theory, under the more general rubric of postmodernism, provided a framework of analysis that challenged the core of classical or modern social theory. As the approaches discussed in this part illustrate, culture is now no longer a domain outside the social and the political, but is constitutive of the social world. But we need to go beyond a notion of culture as such to a understanding of the different processes that it entails. In many ways the postmodern challenge has been normalized around a view of the social world as a site of conflicting interpretations. With this comes a return to some of the older questions and themes, but in new theoretical guises. These chapters cannot be located in a disciplinary field of social science. Most, if all, the chapters are also good illustrations of the merging of the concerns of social and political theory around conceptions of social life that stress plurality, contingency, relationalism, and transformation. In different ways these four conceptions of social life are emphasized in the chapters in Part 2.

The theory of power and the legitimation of authority, the subject of Stuart Clegg's chapter, has been a theme in sociological theory since Weber. Since Lukes' introduction of the third dimension of power in his seminal 1974 publication, which high-lighted a conception of power as the systematic delusion about interests. However Lukes' analysis was beset by the problem of objective interests and the assumption that the theorist might know what these are. Clegg's chapter shows how current theorizing on power goes beyond Lukes' own radical theory of the third dimension of power with greater emphasis on transformative processes at work in situations of power. Noteworthy in this regard is consciousness-raising through the conversion of practical consciousness knowledge into discursive consciousness knowledge. Practical consciousness is a tacit knowledge used in everyday life while discursive consciousness is knowledge that is more reflexive, critical and is potentially transformative. These two forms of knowledge are not entirely separate, but social order – and that is to say the legitimacy of social institutions – often depends on its separation. In other words, people have experiences of power but also have the capacity to understand these in ways that might cast light on their situation in a way that will allow them to challenge power. Alternative discursive consciousness is possible but this will depend on alternative definitions of what had been taken for granted and the capacity to make claims on the basis of such new understandings of the world. Real interests can only be discursively articulated in the generation of new ways of seeing the world. They do not reside in objective truths.

The radical contingency of the social world and the plurality of interpretations are the themes of Peter Wagner's chapter on theories of modernity. The term "modernity" expresses the need for a new language for interpreting the contemporary socio-political condition in light of a situation that cannot be fully explained in terms of postmodernity. A range of new theories of modernity aimed at re-assessing that the older sociological concept of modern society in view of experiences that were increasingly seen in terms of major societal transformation. But modernity, which cannot be theorized today as a universal or unlinear condition, should also not be pluralized to a point that is ceases to refer to anything common. His argument, which is developed around a critique of the varieties of modernity literature, is that the main features of modernity consist of a "limited set of basic problématiques" that all human societies need to address. These are the questions as to what certain knowledge a societal self-understanding is seen to rest upon; how to determine and organize the rules for the life in common; and to how to satisfy the basic material needs for societal reproduction. Modernity is not a universal condition; against what recent approaches might suggest, it is a condition in which certain questions are posed while the answers to them are not externally given but need to be always open. As with the previous chapter on power, contestation of the validity of existing answers and arrangements is always possible. But here greater emphasis is given to plurality. Thus the plurality of modernity consists of a plurality of possible answers to the problems that all modern societies are faced with.

The legacy of the Enlightenment and modernity is everywhere present. The vision of a social order based on legitimate authority as opposed to violence constituted the basis of the very possibility of society in classical social theory. In this vision, human beings armed with reason, which comes with the advancement of knowledge, could create a political order that makes possible the progress of freedom. To do this they had to conquer both the social world and the natural world. The fact that they were unable to do so fully gave rise to the problem of modernity. As Wagner argues, modernist social and political thought problematized in different ways the tension between the pursuit of freedom and rational mastery, on the one hand, and on the other side the often unintended, collective outcome in the form of major societal institutions. This tension resides in the heart of the very conception of power, as domination and as legitimate authority, as Clegg shows. The fragile condition of modernity and the kinds of power that it creates is in many ways encapsulated as a problem of trust.

Karen Cook and Brian Cook explore the problem of trust in an analysis that distinguishes between social and political trust. Political trust is about the belief in the reliability of the legitimacy of government. Social thrust refers to more practical concerns, which are often discussed in terms of the capacity for social capital to be mobilized; it concerns not only confidence in the institutions and organizations but also trust in other individuals. The problem of trust becomes acute in modernity due to the world-wide growth of democracy and increase in human agency and interconnectedness leading to the need for new bonds but ones that cannot be reduced to either force or domination. Complex societies need to find ways to make cooperation possible. The existence of uncertainty and risk is what makes the act of trusting another significant. Trust and risk are inextricably connected. If there is no risk of something going wrong, then there is no real need for trust to be an issue. The act of trusting another party, person, or institution places one at risk. This is the condition of radical contingency that defines the predicament of modernity. Trust is not a psychological state, but it is relational and contingent on the terms of the relation. So trust, like much of the condition of modernity, is not underpinned by an objective reality. Much of the interest in trust is about exploring what factors facilitate cooperation under varying conditions. But, and it is the key point, modernity may not simply give rise to more trust – in so far as this is a general condition – than a desire for trustworthiness. If we want anything, it is likely more trustworthiness since we cannot always trust that our interests will be severed by societal norms. Thus, trust networks, especially in high risk contexts in which distrust rather than trust may best characterize the social situations often lead to a more limited application of trustworthiness. So trust is highly fragile and contingent; it is inextricably bound up with risk.

The analysis of society in terms of risk has been at the forefront of social theory since Beck's theory of the risk society. Risks are assessments – and thus they are interpretations – of problems in the objective order of the social world, and they are the site of new political controversies. The risks may be entirely products of the risk discourse, which itself has the capacity to shape much of contemporary social life and public policy. Tim Luke's chapter explores the important linkages between risk and the environment as contested topics in social and political theory in the more advanced industrial societies of the world. His chapter reflects a certain distance towards social constructionist accounts of risk while at the same time not following a simplistic view of risk as reducible objectively measurable dangers. Risks are real but real in different ways. The embedded necessities of living with risky technologies have become so routinized by expert managers and economic conditions that few question this inescapable fact of life. Much of government is about the reduction of potential risks in conditions of contingent complexity. Nonetheless, the very same energy-intensive systems of mass consumption, which make a high standard of living possible, also arguably are responsible for the increasing endangerment of even living at all well amidst today's environmental crises. As the noxious greenhouse gases generated by fossil fuel use have been identified by the scientific community as the most likely cause of global warming, the many important linkages between risk and the environment clearly need to be more fully explored, particularly with regard to the inequalities behind their initial creation as well as their ultimate impact. This chapter explores how risk becomes widespread as both naturalized abnormality within a society as well as routinized irrationality in the economy. When ordinary unintended irrationalities are recast as the achievements of late modernity, the truly accidental normality of coexisting with systems of complex systems make the environment and risk crucial concerns for social and political thinkers.

The transformation of the social is the topic of several other chapters which all in different ways explore the theme of the plurality, relationalism, contingency, and transformation of social. One of the most influential developments in recent interpretations of the social is network theory. This is not a single field, but includes the diverse fields of Network-Theory, first developed by Bruno Latour and Michael Callon, and generally referred to as Actor Network Theory or ANT, Manuel Castells' conception of the Network Society as the social structure characteristic of the information age, and the expanding field of network analysis, as in the work of Wellman, Fisher, and Granovetter. The notion of the social as a network is of course not new and was an important aspect of the sociology of Simmel who stressed a conception of the social in terms of relationships and, too, was a feature of the sociology of Bourdieu. What is new is the emphasis on the materiality of networks in terms of communication technologies and the current context of globalization. The significance of network theory lies in a relational conception of the social. Society is not an objective reality in itself, as Durkehim claimed. Networks are sets of relationships between nodes and are heterogeneous in terms of their composition, which can include humans, machines and organizations. As Amelia Arsenault says, "the study of networks is, in essence, the study of relationship," and as such suggests a relational conception of society. The social is constructed out of associations and relations rather than out of agents and structures.

This approach blurs the distinction between society and nature since in networks elements of both are present and what is important is the combination. There is no determining structure and no reliance on agency as the prime mechanism in the generation of social configurations. But networks are constitutive; they are, as Arsenault says, "building blocks," but in the sense not of specific networks but the network as a societal form in itself. Thus for Castells, we can speak of the "network society" as a contrast to, for example, the class society. Network theorists might be agreed on the importance of networks as the sociological unit of analysis, but there are huge differences in how networks are theorized. ANT theory sees the key aspect the connections and especially between different kinds of connectors (humans and non-humans, for instance), while Castells stresses the network itself, not the associations. In any case networks are not outside the social, but constitutive of the social. Such a view would lead to a different conceptualization of mobile phones, for instance: they could be seen as technologies human beings use to communicate or they could be seen as part of a new kind of society, which might be termed the network society. The object of study is the relational field, not the objects in it.

As in other chapters in this volume, the question of power is ever-present. Arsenault considers the subject of network effects. That is, what are the major social and political implications of the rise of networks as a mode of social organization? For Castells, the sphere of power resides in communication. The new privileged sites of power lies in the media. The general point that emerges from this is that "switchers" – or a connection point between different networks, such as those of media, the political and the economic – are increasingly important. While power relations figure less in ANT, the key point here is that the difference between social actors operating between or within networks resides in their successes or failures in constructing associations. Nevertheless, network theory undermines the centrality of the social actor as it does of objective structures.

Performativity, like network theory, has emerged as one of the most important theoretical approaches of recent times, with an extraordinarily varied take-up. The starting point for many contemporary discussions of performativity in social and political thought is J. L. Austin's *How To Do Things With Words* (Austin 1962). The key idea in this work that was later taken up by social and political theorists is that language is action upon, rather than a description of, the world. The implication of this is that language is potentially transformative. The idea that words could do things – that communication is a mode of action – was to prove hugely influential. It gave rise to one of the main fault-lines within contemporary theories of performativity: between those treating performativity as a formal property of language, as Habermas, and those, such as Butler and Alexander, treating it as a social or cultural practice. As Moya Lloyd shows, a division began to emerge in theories of performativity with the ideas of Derrida and Bourdieu, who took up different notions of performativity, marked between those conceptualizing it as a linguistic phenomenon and those defining it as a social practice. The formal pragmatics of Jürgen Habermas, who brought performativity into his theory of communicative action, marked a further level of complexity in the concept. But the most influential approach is Judith Butler's argument that gender is performative. The controversial account of symbolic action as social performance developed by Jeffery Alexander *et al.* is yet another illustration of the diversity of appropriations of this notion. For Moya, if it is to operate as an effective social and political theory, a theory of performativity has to be capable of explaining both the reproduction and perpetuation of relations of power (gendered, capitalist, racial, and so on) and how those relations can be contested. The nature of performance is that it may be a failure or a success. Performative success is thus reconceptualized by Bourdieu as a function of social power, dependent upon the "symbolic capital" of a particular actor, and performative failure of their lack. This reasoning, Moya argues, allows the concept of performativity to be transformed from a purely linguistic phenomenon into one concerned with the social conditions, including gender and class, that impact on language use.

The question of networks, discussed earlier, and the relational conception of the social that it implies raises many questions for the meaning of social institutions and related notions of structure and agency. For institutions, the implication is that they are now in an era of change and not necessarily place specific. The advent of the network society undermines the importance of spatial proximity. Of the many implications that this raises, one concerns the fate of the nation-state and the kinds of belonging that it entails. The chapters on nationalism and empire in different ways attest to the continued relevance of these geopolitical forms. Instead of withering away, much of recent social and political theory has engaged extensively with the legacy of the modern nation-state. Steve Grosby argues that nationality poses a number of significant problems for social and political theory; and, in turn, the insights of social and political theory can importantly contribute to clarifying the character of nationality. However, in order to make that contribution, social and political philosophy will have to put aside the antiquated schema of the historical disjunction between *Gemeinschaft* and *Gesellschaft* – a contrast that still largely dominates many of the theoretical investigations into nationality.

The question of empire is rather more complicated. As Krishan Kumar shows in his chapter, empires have existed throughout much of recorded history but imperialism, as an ideology and practice, is relatively recent. This chapter looks at the interaction of empire and imperialism. It analyzes the concept of empire, distinguishing between land and overseas empires, and examines the relation between empires and nation-states. It traces the rise of imperialism, as a European phenomenon, and its reflection in largely critical accounts of empire, in the works of Hobson, Lenin, and others. Kumar shows the persistence of empire in the twentieth century, despite increasing resistance, and argues that nation-states have lived for much of their time in the shadow of empire. He also considers the condition of empire after the great decolonizations of the second half of the twentieth century, including the fall of the Soviet Union. Is empire now dead? This seems a premature judgement, in the light of the persistence of the "American empire" and the widely-held view that the nation-state is in crisis. Empires not only have an after-life in the cultures of colonizers and colonized alike, but may also be instructive for thinking about possible forms beyond the nation-state.

Whatever forms political community might take beyond the nation-state, the imperial form is unlikely to be Alexandrian, that is embracing cosmopolitan cultures covering the entire earth in a single ecumene. Contemporary cosmopolitan theory is largely post-imperial and, too, post-universalistic. Fuyuki Kurasawa's chapter on cosmopolitanism discusses the multi-faceted dimensions of this concept in recent social and political thought. Cosmopolitanism refers to a perspective on the world that stresses openness to others. This can be reflected in political, economic and cultural forms depending on the claims being made. The prevalence of cosmopolitanism in recent times has much to do with globalization and the rise in transnationalization more generally. However, it is not directly a product of globalization and in many ways it expresses a normative critique of globalization. In this respect, cosmopolitanism reflects the themes of pluralisation and transformation that mark much of recent theorizing on the social. Cosmopolitanism is a concept that refers both to normative criteria – one's world as a dwelling-pace or the belief in the moral primacy of human unity and love of humankind – and to empirical phenomena that reflect normative principles. The latter is increasingly associated with notions of vernacular cosmopolitanism or rooted cosmopolitanism, grounded in the realities of everyday life where an ethos of multiperspectivism has become embedded in peoples's lives. For this reason cosmopolitanism is often taken to be an analytical approach in recent social science. Kurasawa identifies three analytical paradigms within cosmopolitan theory: formalism (focussed on intersubjective procedures of public deliberation to develop norms of universal moral equality), ethicism (focussed on the ethics of engagement with alterity), and materialism (focussed on the link between cosmopolitanism and global capitalism).

The next three chapters deal with emerging frameworks of analysis relating to issues that go beyond the traditional scope of social and political theory. These concern cognitive theory, neuroscience, and socio-biology all of which point towards the naturalisation of the social. Byron Kaldis addresses developments of the relation between the natural and the social by charting the epistemological and social-theoretic standing of human sociobiology. The general idea of the relationship between nature and society is delineated in a discussion that shows what is involved when social theory is attempted to be derived from natural–scientific discourse. The most celebrated and most vilified such attempt, sociobiology, has, along with evolutionary psychology, advanced theses about the nature of society and the evolutionary origin of ethics. Much of this amounts to a strong naturalism, a scientist reduction of the study of human thought and action and economic behavior, to its biological basis. This has all led to the return in a new guise of determinism and reduction, with the twist that human freedom is now only a matter of enhancing evolution by the most suitable forms of technology. The result is that social theory is forced into a normative critique against claims made in the name of science, which have taken on a counter-normative force in the alleged capacity of evolutionary biology to explain social life in all its facets.

Piet Strydom's chapter opens with an argument in favor of a weak naturalistic rather than either a strong naturalistic or a strong idealistic conception of the cognitive approach. Against this background, it seeks to clarify this approach by identifying the principal mechanisms operative in the process of constitution and organization of society: generative (new ideas and claims-making), relational (association), transformative (collective learning), and context-setting mechanisms (state, economy, civil society). The mechanisms are illustrated by way of a cognitive reconstruction of social and political theory as it reflexively ran parallel to the unfolding of modernity through its three major historical phases: from the early modern, through the modern, up to the currently emerging transnational constellation. Central to the account is the dialectical conception of the cognitive immanent in social life and the metacognitive reflexively available in context-transcendent cultural models. It allows a critical analysis of the way in which context-transcendent normative guidelines – e.g. the idea of a democratically self-governing society – can and do play a positive role in structuring immanent social orientations and relations, but are often deformed or even blocked by the interference of context-setting political, economic and cultural factors which themselves have a significant cognitive component. Deformations and/or blockages of this kind blighted modern society by way of such pathologies as authoritarianism, ideologisation, marketisation, instrumentalism, repression and obfuscation, and some of these are in danger of being reproduced in a new form and on a new scale under transnational conditions. A vital aspect of the constitution and organization of the emerging world society in an adequate form is to be found in subject formation, the formation of a subject appropriate to the emerging constellation. On the basis of this analysis the task of a cognitively inspired contemporary social and political theory is restated. This task, Strydom argues, is the practically meaningful one of studying and critically analysing the constitution and organization of the emerging world society so as to contribute to the mitigation, if not avoidance, of unjustifiable interferences in the process and their undesirable pathogenic and pathological consequences.

Strydom's rejection of both strong naturalism – for instance some notion of biological determinism – and of social constructionism with its relativistic implications, is also reflected in the chapter by John Gunnell on neuroscience. A difficulty with cognitive theory is the diversity of approaches and what often enters into social science is in fact philosophical speculation by neuroscientists. Nevertheless it is now widely recognized that it is has important implications for social and political theory. Gunnell makes the point that one impetus behind the contemporary interest in cognitive science has been declining interest in rational choice theory. One of the implications of cognitive neuroscience is a new significance for the role of the emotions and social interaction. This relates very much to the relational conception of the social discussed earlier, but in a much more extensive manner. The key concept is connectionism, which, as

Gunnell explains, seeks to explain a wide range of human capacities by reference to neural processes. Neuroscience attests to "social areas" in the brain, but which cannot be reduced to determinism: it is rather a weaker form of naturalism and cannot also be explained in the universalistic terms of Chomsky. However, it does show that consciousness is not something entirely subjective and thus purely relativistic conclusions are not valid. Emotions have a neural basis. Thinking and feeling is multilayered with biology mixed into the social. In this context he refers to William Connolly's (2002) notion of a "deep pluralism" as an outcome of neuroscience. The resulting neuropolitics draws attention to how political choice and action may be in part shaped by neural processes.

The final two chapters in Part 2 deal with relatively new perspectives in contemporary social and political theory beyond the horizons of the established approaches in western thought. Elena Ruiz-Aho's chapter introduces the main themes and ideas in feminist border thought, broadly construed as an emerging paradigm for theorizing the lived experience of political borderlands, especially along the U.S.–Mexico border. Specifically, it offers a framework through which the complex experiences of multicultural subjects, and women of color in particular, who are situated at the crossroads of two or more cultures can be articulated. As a leading example in the field, Gloria Anzaldúa's seminal descriptions of postcolonial life (as they appear in her landmark *Borderlands/La Frontera*, 1987) are presented in the context of recent Latin American social and cultural theory, including Walter Mignolo's notion of "border thought". As a political theory that articulates the barriers towards inclusiveness and recognition of cultural differences in multiethnic societies with attention to race and gender, feminist border thought is also presented as a powerful ally in addressing post-9/11 rhetorical constructions of national identity based on assimilation rather than plurality and difference.

Guanjun Wu's chapter is addressed to new Chinese political thought since the break with the Maoist period (1949–78). The post-Maoist Chinese period saw the rise of intellectuals as a leading group in Chinese society. Whereas it was the Party leadership that had previously set the tone of cultural and intellectual life, academics and independent scholars have increasingly become involved in Chinese social and political thought as this develops in the public sphere. His topic concerns the rise of public intellectuals in contemporary China and "May Fourth Enlightenment" which emerged in the 1980s but which consolidated in the wake of the Tiananmen student protest after 1989 and gained further momentum after 1992 the easing of censorship on intellectuals. This movement invoked an earlier opposition to Confucianism, going back to the early twentieth century, but today it is defined against Maoism and one of the new ideas that has emerged is a new thinking around Confucianism. However, as Wu argues, these ideas were largely confined to cultural critiques as opposed to political ones. As an example of more political orientations within recent Chinese thought, Wu refers to the movement known as "critical intellectuals," including the prominent thinker Wang Hui, as this took shape in the late 1990s. A key idea is that it is not modernity but China's premodern past that may offer a resource for new ideas today. His work can be seen as an attempt to find a new intellectual framework for social and political critique on China's path to modernity and its place and role in the global context. Such attempts to reconstruct Chinese modernity are frequently linked with the revival of classical Confucian thought and serve as a reminder to alternative conceptions of modernity beyond the western experience.

Emerging Problems

The chapters collected in Part 3 of this volume concern emerging problems and are closely related to the new frameworks of analysis discussed in Part 2. These reflect a sense of crisis, in particular the fragmentation of the social and the political order of modernity. Much of this is related to the consequences of globalization, which has forced a re-assessment of many of the presuppositions of modern social and political thought. But we also find in these chapters the exploration of alternative scenarios to the discourse of the end of modernity that pervaded some of the earlier theories of postmodernity. As discussed also above, the chapters collected here cannot be so easily located within the context of the cultural turn in the social and human sciences. Many of the topics can be seen as revitalized classical themes addressing major social and political transformations relating to economy and state. These are topics that have been relatively marginalized by the cultural turn, which saw a general turning away from the analysis of large-scale processes such as capitalism and the state. These chapters can be summed up under three broad thematic fields: the crisis of sovereignty and new conceptions of the political, the consequences of transnationalism for political community and social justice, and changes in the constitution of subjectivity and social values.

Sheila Nair discusses how sovereignty, sovereign power, *homo sacer*, and the ban coincide in the making of "the state of exception" and the camp as developed in Giorgio Agamben's work. She explores how Agamben exposes the ways in which sovereign power depends upon and is sustained by the exception, and how bare life – suspended in a zone of indistinction – is exemplified in the modern camp. While disrupting established notions of sovereignty and security in international relations, and drawing attention to their exclusions, these characterizations of the exception, are nevertheless, seen by some critics as limiting. The chapter then turns to a discussion of the postcolonial exception, governmentality, and sovereignty in the context of critics' claims that Agamben does not properly account for imperial and colonial narratives in his arguments. Her conclusion is that a postcolonial counter-narrative should matter in the framing of arguments round the exception.

The next chapter offers a case for the continued relevance of the state despite some of the claims made about its demise as a result of globalization. For Georg Sørensen, there are three major modalities of state in the present international system; they are the postmodern states in the OECD-world, the weak postcolonial states mostly in Sub-Saharan Africa, and the modernizing states, mainly in Asia, Latin America, and parts of Eastern Europe. They display new patterns of violence and conflict: large-scale violent conflict is now within weak states while advanced states face an increasing number of transnational bads. In the political sphere, democracy is challenged; modernizing states are not on any secure path towards stable democracy, weak states lack the preconditions for democratic rule, and advanced states face a number of new challenges emerging from cross-border integration. In the economic realm, global capitalism is not in existential crisis, but a stable liberal economic order with benefits for all is not in the cards. As regards common values and identities, there is no strong trend towards the emergence of common liberal values on a global scale. Processes of modernization and processes of decay both help produce more nationalistic or fragmented and divisive responses in terms of identity. Finally, the institution of sovereignty remains in place, but it is being transformed in ways that exposes it to significant challenges. The conclusion is that the sovereign state is alive and well. By no means has it been obliterated by the forces of globalization. But it has been transformed in significant ways and it will continue to change. These changes may not always be for the better. The major types of state discussed here all face considerable challenges to which they have so far not found very good answers. Many observers are too optimistic when they consider processes of political and societal change; the outcome of such processes may not always be development; it might as well be decay.

The following chapter by Paul Blokker addresses a key feature of the modern polity: the constitution. The abstract idea of a written constitution as the foundational basis of modern democratic societies is a largely undisputed element in much of social, political, and legal theory. At the same time, the nature, form, and distinct functions of the constitution in, and increasingly also beyond, modern democratic societies is an evermore frequent object of dispute. Notwithstanding the identification of a global trend, of the last half century or so, of convergence to an "amplified" form of modern constitutionalism around a form of "new constitutionalism," more recent trends of pluralization seem to provoke profound changes in the nature of modern constitutionalism and its theorization. While the trends in some ways seem to amplify legalistic and monistic tendencies, they also indicate strong corrosive and diversifying implications for the modern constitutional template. The trends discussed are the fragmentation of sovereignty, cultural pluralism, and substantive or interpretative pluralism. Blokker's argument is that the challenges of complex pluralism undermine many of the constraining features of modern constitutionalism, but, while in some cases forms of autonomy and democratic participation are strengthened, in many others, constitutional pluralism tends to further compromise the democratic dimension of constitutionalism. In a normative sense, the chapter critically discusses a number of theoretical reflections on these challenges, and in particular emphasizes those approaches that search for the potential reinforcement of participatory, open-ended, and inclusive dimensions in the current constitutional predicament.

The EU is clearly a major example of state formation and of constitutional experimentation. As Erik Eriksen demonstrates, Europe has been transformed from an order of largely independent nation-states to an integrated order with some capacity to rule in the name of all. The European integration process has resulted in a set of institutions premised on a complex mixture of supranational, transnational and intergovernmental principles. It is difficult to understand how this could have happened voluntarily when the Union lacks important enabling conditions, such as a collective European identity based on a common language and culture. The pragmatist approach depicts cooperation as a response to problematic situations, and institution formation as a response to the indirect consequences of such, which increasingly catches on and has polity consequences. The effect is more legal regulation, which triggers claims to democracy. The integration process is to a large degree driven by contestation and opposition. The chapter also addresses "the nature of the beast." What could the EU possibly amount to? A *regional subset* of an emerging larger cosmopolitan order or a specfically European route? It is however difficult to draw the conclusion that the EU is itself cosmopolitanism, though it could be seen as creating certain conditions for the emergence of cosmopolitics.

The next four chapters are more explicitly addressed to the consequences of transnationlism. Saskia Sassen's chapter is concerned with the micro shifts that are amounting to a new immigration reality. Central to this is are changes in the position of the state in a world that is not only increasingly interdependent but also one where the national is itself being partly denationalized. States create distinction between nationals and non-nationals, members and non-members. But the de-nationalization of the state means the erasure of this distinction of inside and outside, by developments such as the institutionalizing of the human rights regime and claims for rights made by unauthorized immigrants in all major immigration countries. According to Sassen, the significance of immigration goes beyond immigration policy narrowly defined. The theme of power returns in this chapter which demonstrates that the powerless can challenge the state. Even the most powerful states can reach limits in getting their way in the world and as a consequence they have to negotiate with the powerless who become enpowered as a result. The reality she describes does not quite fit into either postnationalism or transnationalism. It assumes neither the end of the state nor does it extend beyond the territory of the state. For this reason the notion of the de-nationalization of the state may be more relevant as a characterization of the phenomena she discusses.

The theme of contestation is the focus of the next chapter but the concern here is rather with transnationalist activism and the emergence of a global justice movement. Donatella della Porta and Raffaele Marchetti examine the conceptual innovations for social and political theory that have been inspired by transnational activism. These constitute significant bridges between empirical and normative research on civil society and social movement and concerns mobilization around collective claims that pertain to global issues. They argue the global justice movement has redefined major political issues around global justice. Unlike the new social movements of the 1980s, which were largely products of societal change in western countries, the global justice movement incorporates elements of diverse movements – gender, class, race, religion, environment – and is not therefore a single issue movement. Under the heading of global justice diverse elements of various cultures are combined in a movement based on transnational activism. Della Porta and Marchetti see the global justice movement as an expression of subaltern and rooted cosmopolitanism and characterize it around the following principles: it is placed based as opposed to be located in global space, it affirms autonomy, diversity and solidarity. The following chapter by Thomas Faist takes up the theme of transnationalism in a discussion of social question. In his view the point of departure for a discussion of the new transnational social question is a growing awareness of cross-border interdependence along crucial issues of social inequalities and the implications not only for so-called developing countries. The contention around inequalities takes recourse to international conventions declaring social rights, moral convictions and actually existing social standards. To survey the theories able to capture the new transnational question yields insights into the framing of social inequalities. Current theory raises the question whether concepts such as social rights and citizenship are adequate to describe contemporary social inequalities. While such concepts arose in the context of the geopolitical framework of modernity, we do not have adequate terms to capture the current situation. It would appear that cosmopolitan currents are largely oppositional and transnational social rights.

As indicated in the chapter discussed earlier by Sassen, the most pervasive implications of transnationalism for political community lie within the nation-state and concern immigrants. While her account emphasizes the capacity of immigrants to challenge the state, other perspectives stress the condition of exclusion and the need for a politics of hospitality. Meyda Yeğenoğlu, in her chapter on hospitality, rights and migration, discusses the concept of hospitality in an attempt to understand the relation between immigrants, exiles, foreigners, refugees, and other displaced populations who are in transit and/or without a home and their hosts or the "new" socio-cultural and political "homes" they are situated in. A series of concepts and issues such as the host, what does to welcome and receive mean, subjectivity, *ipseity*, and interruption of the self, conditional and unconditional hospitality, hospitality as right versus ethics of hospitality, hostility, home, ownership, and expropriation (or dispossession) are explicated. The chapter highlights the problematic and complex nature of the relation between the ethics and politics of hospitality by focussing on three figures: Immanuel Kant, Emmanuel Levinas, and especially Jacques Derrida and his recasting of our understanding of the nature of the relation between the ethics and politics of hospitality that this relation entails.

A theme running throughout all these chapters concerns changes in the constitution of subjectivity and the generation of new social values. This is present in the cosmopolitan current in the previous chapters on social justice and the transformation of political community. It is particularly present in the final four chapters. Adam Arvidsson investigates important new forms of value production that are emerging within the information economy. He argues that the information economy is marked by a radical socialization of processes of wealth production. Empowered by networked digital media the production of immaterial, but increasingly also material wealth is located to networks of productive collaboration that unfold beyond established forms of corporate control, and that sometimes coincide with the ordinary life process. He also suggests that such forms of "social production" are endowed with a particular logic of value, where value is less related to inputs of labor time or other scarce resources and more to the ability to construct the kinds of virtuous social relations that give purpose and coherence to diffuse forms of cooperation. In other words, social production is part of an emerging ethical economy.

Iain Wilkinson offers an overview of "social suffering" both as a term of analysis and as an inter-disciplinary field of study that has been widely adopted in social science to refer to lived experiences of pain, damage, injury, deprivation and loss. He offers some explanations for the gathering of interest around the topic of "social suffering" in contemporary social science and outlines the contribution of figures such as Pierre Bourdieu and Arthur Kleinman to this development. The critical praxis of "social suffering" is explored in terms of its contribution to contemporary discourse on human rights and the politics of humanitarianism. In this setting, "social suffering" is identified as a critical concern wedded to a new politics of sensibility. This revisits some longstanding ethical debates over the virtue "fellow-feeling" and its bearing upon the establishment of social ties and social commitments to care for others. These are set within a new analytical frame that aims to pay heed to intensifying forces of "mediatization," "commercialization," and "rationalization" within late modern society.

The experience of suffering is mirrored in another major theme in recent social and political theory: namely temporalities, especially those that are connected with trauma and collective memory. Both memory and suffering and other related concepts are not static concepts that can be easily defined. Their meaning is rather defined in its historical and social contextualization. Daniel Levy explores the significance of memory for political, social and cultural theory. Rather than viewing memory as epiphenomenal, he argues that memory is an integral and constitutive part of theory. The contemporary preoccupation with memory is reflected in terms of a com-memorative boom and the concomitant emergence of memory studies. Memory is omnipresent as it is situated in social frameworks (i.e. family, nation, and personal experiences anchored by symbolic markings), manifested in cultural practices (i.e. externalized into archival repositories such as memorials and museums), and shaped by political circumstances (i.e. wars, catastrophes, and debates generating lasting meanings of these events). Social frameworks and historical cir-cumstances change over time and with them the aforementioned alignments of temporalities (e.g. the discourse of progress in modernity). Studying (and theorizing) memory allows us to shift our focus from time to temporalities, and thus to understand what categories people, groups, and cultures employ to make sense of their lives, their social, cultural and political attachments and the ideals that are validated – in short, the political, cultural and social theories which command normative attention. Levy's chapter connects memory with the theme of cosmopolitanism reflected in other chapters in this volume. He makes the point that particular orientations towards the past need now to be reevaluated against the background of "global memory scapes." The upshot of this is not the decline of national collective memories but the pluralization of memory and the cosmopolitan impulse towards the critical engagement with past injustices.

In the final chapter in this volume, Austin Harrington explores recent ideas about the emergence of a consciousness of "post-secular society" in contemporary western democracies. "Post-secular society" may be seen as pinpointing some significantly new dimensions of reflexivity at play in the conduct of states and civil-society actors toward religious as well as non-religious value-orientations in contemporary public spheres. Harrington surveys four bodies of literature: challenges to "classical secularization theory"; debates about religion in public spheres; work on religion in comparative historical-sociological studies of civilizations; and recent engagements with religion from the side of left-wing traditions of social and political theory. What this chapter highlights is how the logic of pluralization is present within nationality. Nations today can, to varying degrees, accommodate a pluralistic vision of political community in which religion can have a place. The implication is that religious life is not only compatible with modernity but is itself one manifestation of modernity's reflexive self-renewal.

Conclusion

Liberalism and the socialist Left, as well as European Conservatism and Fascism, presented simplified but compelling images of society which were integrated into the subjectivity and self-reflective activity of the people whose activity created their politics and society. The modern welfare state struck a balance between the claims produced under these images, to justice, freedom, and stability. Contemporary social, political, and cultural theory is not so much a continuation of this project as the continuation of the reflective activity of the people who experience modern society. As with past social theory, this reflection is aided and stimulated by social movements and counter-movements. But for the most part it is not concerned with inventing new simplifications or claiming external authority – from God, Science, or Reason itself – for new simplifications. Instead, it is focused on the problem of understanding what is, and what is not comprehensible in terms of these past images.

Critics on the Left sometimes complain nostalgically about the loss of utopia in modern social theory, and the complaint is well-founded. The thinkers and problems discussed in this volume, and the new approaches that have been made to these problems, are for the most part dealing with obdurate facts that the old utopian self-images of society no longer can be claimed to fit. Globalization, cosmopolitanism, the problems of statelessness, border existences between cultures and identities, suffering beyond the reach of the bureaucratic practices of the welfare state, all anomalous from the point of view of traditional images of societies as contracts, as inclusive hierarchic orders, as caring bureaucracies, and so forth. Even the most ingrained legal and political ideas, such as modern constitutionalism, are problematic in the face of these new facts and the forms they have produced.

Understanding these phenomena needs new approaches: to the memories that constitute new identities, to the generation of new values such as global justice in these new or previously ignored situations, to the networks, new transnational formations and what connects them, to the extension of such things as hospitality and trust, to the mediatized environments in which subjectivities arise and are sustained, and so forth. At the same time, social and political theory cannot rely on the older kinds of philosophical anthropologies, invented images of humanity, that traditional liberalism and collectivism invented. The image of humanity is itself challenged by biology and neuroscience, as well as by the de-stabilizing approach to subjectivity found in Lacan and in theories of the performative.

Finally, contemporary social and political thought has come to recognize that modernity itself is not one thing, produced in one process. The modernities being produced in China, the alternative forms generated in Latin America, and the weak-state chaos of much of the post-Colonial "developing world" remind us that the western welfare state is itself increasingly operating by making "exceptions" to the practices of governance that originally defined it. Today the "normal" of the welfare state itself is not normal. The challenge of contemporary social and political thought is to understand what has changed, and to address the question of whether the modern inheritance of democratic forms of deliberation and decision can be extended to deal with these changes.

References

Althusser, L. and E. Balibar (1970) *Reading Capital*, trans. Ben Brewster, London: NLB.

Austin, J. (1962) *How to Do Things with Words*, Oxford: Oxford University Press.

Bernal, J. D. (1939) *The Social Function of Science*, Cambridge, MA: MIT Press.

Bluntschli, J. C. (2002 [1869]) "What Is a Political Party?", in S. E. Scarrow (ed.) *Perspectives on Political Parties: Classic Readings*, New York: Palgrave Macmillan, 75–81.

Castoriadis, C. (1998) *The Imaginary Institution of Society*, trans. Kathleen Blamey, Cambridge: MIT Press.

Connolly, W. (2002) *Neuropolitics*, Minneapolis: University of Minnesota Press.

Delanty, G. (2009) *The Cosmopolitan Imagination: The Renewal of Critical Social Theory*, Cambridge: Cambridge University Press.

Dicey, A. V. (1962 [1914]) *Law and Public Opinion in England during the Nineteenth Century* 2nd edn, London: Macmillan & Company.

Foster, M. B. (1968 [1935]) *The Political Philosophies of Plato and Hegel*, Oxford: Clarendon Press.

Foucault, M. (1977) *Discipline and Punish: The Birth of the Prison*, trans. Alan Sheridan, New York: Pantheon Books.

——(1991 [1978]) "Governmentality", trans. Rosi Braidotti and revised by Colin Gordon, in Graham Burchell, Colin Gordon and Peter Miller (eds) *The Foucault Effect: Studies in Governmentality*, Chicago, IL: University of Chicago Press, 87–104.

Geertz, C. (1973) *The Interpretation of Cultures: Selected Essays*, New York: Basic Books.

Gilbert, M. (1989) *On Social Facts*, London: Routledge.

——(1990) "Walking Together: A Paradigmatic Social Phenomenon", *Midwest Studies in Philosophy*, VI, 1–14.

——(1996) *Living Together: Rationality, Sociality, and Obligation*, Lanham, MD: Rowman & Littlefield.

Habermas, J. (1984–87 [1981]) *The Theory of Communicative Action*, trans. Thomas McCarthy, vols 1 & 2, Boston, MA: Beacon Press.

——(1992 [1962]) *The Structural Transformation of the Public Sphere*, Cambridge: Polity.

Joas, H. and W. Knöbl (2009) *Social Theory: Twenty Introductory Lectures*, Cambridge: Cambridge University Press.

Judt, T. (1992) *Past Imperfect: French Intellectuals 1944–1956*, Berkeley: University of California Press.

Laclau, E. (1977) *Politics and Ideology in Marxist Theory: Capitalism, Fascism, Populism*, London: NLB.

Laclau, E. and C. Mouffe (1985) *Hegemony and Socialist Strategy: Towards a Radical Democratic Politics*, trans. Winston Moore and Paul Cammack, London: Verso.

Mannheim, K. (1940) *Man and Society in an Age of Reconstruction: Studies in Modern Social Structure*, New York: Harcourt, Brace & World.

Mouffe, C. (1999) *The Challenge of Carl Schmitt*, London: Verso.

Nozick, R. (1974) *Anarchy, State, and Utopia*, New York: Basic Books.

Poulantzas, N. (1987 [1975]) *Political Power and Social Classes*, trans. Timothy O'Hagan, London: Verso.

——(2001 [1978]) *State, Power, Socialism*, London: Verso.

Rawls, J. (1971) *A Theory of Justice*, Cambridge, MA: Harvard University Press.

——(1993) *Political Liberalism: The John Dewey Essays in Philosophy*, 4, New York: Columbia University Press.

Sabine, G. (1961) *A History of Political Theory*, New York: Holt, Rhinehart & Winston.

Schmitt, C. (1988 [1923]) *The Crisis of Parliamentary Democracy*, trans. Ellen Kennedy, Cambridge, MA: MIT Press.

Schumpeter, J. (1950 [1942]) *Capitalism, Socialism and Democracy*, New York: Harper & Row.

Searle, J. (1995) *The Construction of Social Reality*, New York: Free Press.

——(2010) *Making the Social World: The Structure of Human Civilization*, Oxford: Oxford University Press.

Suppe, F. (1977 [1974]) "The Search for Philosophic Understanding of Scientific Theories", in *The Structure of Scientific Theories*, Urbana: University of Illinois Press, 3–241.

Turner, S. (2010) *Explaining the Normative*, Cambridge: Polity Press.

Webb, S. and B. Webb (1936) *Soviet Communism: A New Civilization?* New York: C. Scribner's Sons.

——(1942) *The Truth about Soviet Russia. With an essay on the Webbs by Bernard Shaw*, New York: Longmans, Green.

Žižek, S. (1989) *The Sublime Object of Ideology*, London: Verso.

Zolo, D. (1997) *Cosmopolis: Prospects for World Government*, Cambridge: Polity Press.

Part 1
Living Traditions

The Marxist Legacy

Peter Beilharz

What is the fate of marxism, a hundred and fifty years after its original inception at the hands of Marx and Engels? The results of this story are mixed, and contradictory. On the one hand, marxism seems completely exhausted, expired, perhaps returned to the mainstream as the renewed common sense that capitalism is the central world power and protean agent of creative destruction. We are all Marxists now, perhaps again especially after the Global Meltdown. On the other hand, the status of marxism is newly marginal, at least in the hands of transatlantic university radicals, for whom marxism remains the truth. For marxism became the *de facto* consciousness of a good part of the global radical or university left into the 1960s, and its residual influence is still apparent but often unworldly.

At the beginning of the twentieth century, it was apparent that marxism had some significant influence in civil society, at least in countries such as Germany, where the Social Democratic Party claimed to enshrine Marxist values. But the SPD was, infamously, a society within a society, and socialism has long acted historically as the counterculture of modernity. At the end of the twentieth century the picture was unrecognizably different. After the Russian Revolution, which no one had expected in 1900, marxism became the ideology of Soviet state power. After 1989, the world power that was Soviet communism had disintegrated, and marxism was presented in the media a museum piece. But then there was globalization, and marxism again became a presence, as the mistranslated image of *The Communist Manifesto*, 'all that is solid melts into air' was rediscovered as the *urtext* of the creative destruction process itself. For the other side, meantime, for the opponents of marxism, Marx could be portrayed as the evil genius who somehow was vitally responsible for the Soviet disaster itself.

How do we find a way through all these trails and clues, to begin to make sense of the Marxist legacy today? This chapter makes five moves in this direction. The first, on Marx, addresses the moment of theoretical establishment. All discussion here must still begin from the question of the nature of Marx's project. The second section addresses the theoretical main-streaming of marxism after Marx. Often referred to as the period of classical marxism, this centres on the experience of the German Social Democrats and the challenges they faced in seeking to reconcile reformist practice with (often) revolutionary rhetoric. But this moment was lost to vision, in effect, when the Bolsheviks seized Russian state power in the name of Marx, and marxism henceforth was identified with Soviet state power, a political and historic elision from which the emancipatory project of Marx would never recover. The third phrase discussed here involves the revival of the marxian legacy, often via the heritage of critical theory, into the 1960s. Humanist marxism reemerged in this period, only to be suppressed again in a fourth phase, here referred to as the Return of the Hard Left. Under the influence of Louis Althusser and his followers, marxism took a scientific and renewed Bolshevik, first pro-Soviet, then pro-Chinese turn. Fifth, and finally for our purposes there, there is the intriguing and divided phenomenon of postmarxism, itself formed in the wake of the postmodern. The postmarxist moment bifurcates into two streams, one of which is fundamentalist and revivalist, the other of which wears its marxism as a light cloak.

Marx's Project

Did Marx have a project, or is this a category we impose on his work, like that of others, after the fact? There are many ways to read Marx, or various Marxes available to us. If we begin from the necessary sense that Marx is the starting point, then we also need to accept that we are all after Marx, and in this sense we are all postmarxists, literally after Marx and after marxism, the latter understood as the world-historic project of transforming the world announced by Marx in his Theses on Feuerbach.

Marx can be read as poet, follower of world literature, journalist, revolutionary, historian, or philosophical anthropologist. These days we often classify him as a sociologist, though that thought would never have occurred to him. One way to identify the unity of his thought is to read it as the critique of political economy. This is one arc that holds together the major instalments of his work, from the *Economic and Philosophical Manuscripts* (1844) to the *Grundrisse* (1857–8), *Contribution to the Critique of Political Economy* (1859) through to its culmination in *Capital* (1867).

If economics was to become the dominant discipline into the twentieth century, political economy was already making this claim to hegemony a century earlier. Of course its ambit was broader than that of economics. Political economy was a moral philosophy, that discourse which enquired into the origin of new wealth and its social consequences. Marx's original critique of political economy was based on its failure to historicize. Rather than explaining capital as private property, political economy universalized it. Rather than viewing capital as a process, it viewed capital as the effective cause of labour, whereas in fact, Marx claimed, it was the other way around: labour produced capital, capital was only dead or stored-up labour. As he was later to suggest, capital was like the vampire or the werewolf that consumed labour up without mercy. And this was to become a significant part of Marx's style, or dramaturgy, where images of magic, enchantment, and the supernatural all jostled together, where capitalism was a phenomenon like the world of the sorcerer's apprentice. The spells that had let loose these demonic forces could no longer easily be controlled or reversed. This, in turn, becomes a significant tension throughout Marx's work, where humans both have agency to change the world, and are simultaneously entrapped within processes beyond their ken and influence. But can we be both, at the same time, or only one or other?

Marx's early critique of political economy asserted the centrality of alienated labour to capitalism. The object of socialism, then, would be the pursuit of the autonomous or creative capacity to labour, to make the world through expression. This is what pitted Marx against 'primitive communism'. Socialism, for Marx, could only be imagined as the freely achieved results of the collective labourer. In this, while Marx is often pictured as the man of Enlightenment, he is also the best son of Romanticism (Beilharz 1994). For like Schiller, and differently, Rousseau, Marx dreams of a human wholeness, of a world before the division of labour and its cult of fragmentation. Marx's original utopia, concealed behind his and Engels' public disdain for writing recipes for the cook shops of the future, is plainly rural and romantic (Beilharz 1992). Marx's utopia only becomes grey, rather than green, as he himself adjusts to the sense of industrialism's permanency, its non-reversibility. While the younger Marx identifies freedom or autonomy with this sense of return to control over the labour process, the later Marx concedes that perhaps freedom may be found only outside labour, in the creative space mode available by the free time afforded by automation. This is part of the fascination of Marx's work, that it changes colour irreversibly across the opening phase of the cultural revolution of modernity.

Marx and Engels confuse this situation by insisting that their position is that of communism, not socialism (Beilharz 1992). This is proleptic, for as Durkheim showed in his Bordeaux lectures on socialism, the commune is passed; socialism, understood rather as the response to scale, complexity, and the need for regulation is modern, whereas the idea of communism historically rendered is indeed premodern. Marx and Engels sought what we would now call product differentiation, or at least distinction for their views. They wanted to insist not only that their view was distinct from that of the crackpot dreamers (seas of lemonade, etc.) of utopia, but also that their socialism was in some sense or other necessary or scientific, evolutionary, the necessary consequence of feudal and capitalist development and its crowning glory. Marx thus built his project on an unresolved tension between the need for action, revolutionary or other, and the dull compulsions of material life, where the working class had no alternative but to sell their labour in order to survive. His hopes for revolution were pinned on various possibilities, some voluntary, some structural. He believed that the association of labourers on the factory floor itself would encourage socialism; that it was necessary actively to change the world, not just to interpret it; that capitalism would collapse under the weight of its own contradictions, such as the tendency of the profit rate to fall; and that socialism would be the next, best evolutionary form for capitalist dynamism to take. He believed all these things at once, or at different moments of his life, or more precisely he left a series of hints as to possible sources of change without ever developing a coherent theory of revolution (Draper 1977).

Marx projected revolutionary capacity onto the proletariat itself. Socialism became the world-historic vocation of the proletariat. But the wage-slaves remained tied to the wheel, and then later, after the postwar boom, their political and labour representatives became the best lieutenants of capitalist expansion (Bauman 1972). One thing, however, that Marx did not do, in all this, was develop a theory of the vanguard party. The essential revolutionary sympathy of Marx is with the idea of working-class self activity or capitalist collapse leading to socialism. Very few Marxists, Russians included, believed in the combat communist party, the object of which was to seize state power, before 1917. Even Trotsky was still sympathetic to menshevism, or the reforming stream in Russian marxism. The idea of the combat or conspirational party, 'one wise man worth a hundred fools', arrived only with Lenin in *What Is To Be Done?* (1902). And even Lenin adhered to the principles of classical marxism in his greater achievement, *The Development of Capitalism in Russia* (1899).

Marxism after Marx

Marx died in 1883. It was only after his death that marxism became identified with a party, or movement: the German Social Democratic Party. Karl Marx called himself a communist, but he was no Bolshevik. He would have called himself a revolutionary, but he was no putschist.

Engels died in 1895. By that stage, Engels had conceded the possibility of an electoral or parliamentary road to socialism. Indeed, if the proletariat made up the vast majority of the population, why should they not simply vote socialism in, once the popular franchise had been sufficiently expanded? This was the context for the formation of classical marxism.

The SPD combined any number of political tendencies, but it is conventional to differentiate between three (Beilharz 1992). One was represented by Rosa Luxemburg, a spontaneist revolutionary in the spirit of Marx, an opponent of what she called 'barracks socialism' but a revolutionary all the same. By the dawn of the new century, the status quo in the SPD was predictable but embarrassing. It was a party of reform, but with revolutionary credentials. It worked through the networks of civil society, generating a thick, alternative culture of clubs, societies, mutual aid facilities, and so on. But it never put away the Sunday china which called for Revolution. This is where the standard jokes about pragmatic socialists come from: parlour pinks, or else like radishes, red on the outside, white on the inside. Luxemburg's revolutionary response was to demand that the SPD's politics be brought into line with its rhetoric. If it claimed to be revolutionary, then the SPD should be prepared to behave in a revolutionary way. The best representative of the second view, the reformist, or right-wing alternative, was Eduard Bernstein. Bernstein called not only for reform, for the adjustment of rhetoric towards the reformist practice of the SPD, but also for revision, for the rejection of Marx's axioms about class bipolarization and the alleged decline of the middle class. As far as Bernstein could see, the middle class was expanding. And marxism, or social democracy, would need to factor this vital change into its worldview and practice if it was to have a significant effect on the world locally, in Germany.

The third dominant position in the SPD, which in a sense was hegemonic, was associated with the views of the 'Pope of Marxism', Karl Kautsky. Kautsky was happy to sit on the contradiction, to argue for the necessity of maintaining revolutionary rhetoric and reformist practice. Comrades could live with contradiction. 'We are a revolutionary, but not a revolution-making party.' Kautsky held onto the automatic theme in Marx, where in the fullness of time socialism would emerge, later. Always later. As August Bebel, another Social Democratic father put it, socialism would drop into our laps like a ripe fruit. And this, indeed, was widespread Marxist commonsense until the political arrival, later in Italy, of Antonio Gramsci. Gramsci's great realization was that, left to itself, the way the world worked was that the other guys won; or to put it more precisely, whoever mobilized hegemony successfully would win. Gramsci returned marxism, in a sense, to its 1840s inflexion in Marx's project. Here, will was everything; necessity was a theological category, and the idea that socialism would necessarily arrive by itself was a political disaster, an invitation to reaction or at least to the reactionaries at the door.

The achievement of German Social Democracy was thus an extraordinary combination of institution- and culture-building in this world, held together with the redemptive or religious belief in the coming of the new world. This German culture in turn dominated that of the Second International. The Second International collapsed in August 1914, after German SPD parliamentary representatives voted for war credits, and the hope of internationalism foundered on that great emergent reality of the twentieth century, nationalism. But the dominance of the SPD in the world socialist movement was really punctured only in October 1917, when the Russian Bolsheviks took state power.

Enthusiasm for the Russian Revolution was initially widespread. After all, the Bolsheviks had done something, whereas the grand old men of social democracy only ever talked about it. While Gramsci was not a hard Leninist, he too enthused for the radical and voluntarist nature of the breach they had entered into. Gramsci indicated this in an essay entitled 'The Revolution Against Capital' (1918). His argument was twofold. The Russian Revolution was a revolution against capital, but it was also a revolution against the complacency that had followed *Das Kapital*. Waiting for the revolution had finally been shown as the sham it was; the Bolsheviks had shown the will to act, to lead.

Gramsci's own enthusiasm got the better of him. The Russian Revolution was not a Revolution Against Capital, but a revolution against a decadent feudalism which held some major nodes of capitalist development developing within it. This was precisely Gramsci's later insight, that while it was courageous the Bolshevik Revolution really just pushed over a rotting Tsarist edifice. This meant that the enormity and ultimate impossibility of the task that the Bolsheviks had set themselves only slowly became apparent. After Lenin's death in 1924 and Trotsky's exile in 1927, Stalin set out to build the primary accumulation of capital in the Soviet Union by coercion and terror of a kind that made the Enclosure Acts pale into insignificance in their own levels of violence and destruction. Gramsci's insight shifted into the sense that, again contra Marx, the presenting issue for Marxists now was not the anatomy of political economy but the power and persuasion of civil society.

The banner and beacon of revolutionary marxism, meanwhile, was taken on by the lonely figure of Leon Trotsky. Originally in sympathy with the spontaneism and anti-Jacobinism of Rosa Luxemburg, Trotsky in power became the best of Bolsheviks (Beilharz 1982). Marginalized, expelled, and finally murdered by Stalin in Mexico City in 1940, Trotsky became the leader of the loyal opposition, and a major intellectual influence on the postwar left (Beilharz 1987). Always full of revolutionary optimism, Trotsky remained convinced that the conditions for world revolution were ripe, that all that was lacking was the appropriate kind of Trotskyist leadership. His advocacy of the idea and slogan of Permanent Revolution also indicated a doubling. One aspect of Permanent Revolution was the claimed inevitability of socialist revolution; whatever form a revolution initially now took, it would consequently grow over into socialist revolution. But second, all revolutions would spread globally; revolution could no longer be contained at national borders, except by the treachery of Stalin's 'socialism in one country'. Many of the finest left wing minds came to follow this position of Trotsky's, from Isaac Deutscher to Ernest Mandel, C. L. R. James, Raya Dunayevskaya, Perry Anderson, and *New Left Review* more generally. The sticking point, for this tradition, was to be found in the question of the nature of the Soviet Union, and whether the traditional categories of Marxist thinking could explain it. Was the Soviet Union, by the 1930s, still recognizably socialist? Should it rather be called capitalist, or state capitalist? Only the more innovative of thinkers, from Bruno Rizzi and James Burnham to Heller, Fehér, and Markus could step outside of the conventional Marxist categories in order to argue that Soviet societies were a new kind of modernity *sui generis* (Fehér, Heller, and Markus, 1982). Whether analytically or politically, the Soviet Union had become a kind of fatal attraction for Marxists the world about. Yet some, from Kautsky on, had always refused the possibility that socialism could be built in the USSR. They were right, and Marx would have agreed with them. Socialism would come after capitalism, or it would not come at all.

The Marxian Legacy

If we understand Marx's project as the critique of political economy, a social-philosophical critical theory with an emancipatory intention, then its ethical distance from Bolshevism, let alone Stalinism, will be apparent. Yet the elision of these differences, and the careless identification of Marx and Bolshevism, remains. Marx is widely, and quite mistakenly viewed as a totalitarian. But even viewed simply as an historical trend, totalitarianism is twentieth century, Marx nineteenth, and while culture is fundamental, ideas do not themselves have this kind of causal effect. Marx wanted to change the world, or that we should ourselves change it, but what he bequeathed us intellectually was a critical theory with an emancipatory intent.

The idea of critical theory, in the context of the history of marxism, is usually associated with the Frankfurt School for Social Research. In terms of its reception, critical theory is often reduced to the cultural pessimism associated with works such as Horkheimer's and Adorno's

Dialectic of Enlightenment (1944) and Marcuse's *One-dimensional Man* (1964). The Frankfurt School achieved much else beside (Wiggershaus 1994), but its main theses did indeed include this idea of modernity as entrapment, Marx plus Weber, as it were in the early period spirit of Kafka's *Metamorphosis*. Critical theory can indeed be viewed as Marx plus Weber, commodification plus rationalization. Two earlier intellectual links helped to make this bond, well before *Dialectic of Enlightenment*, and long before critical theory became a kind of household word for radicals.

The first significant link in this process was provided by Georg Lukács, in his 1923 essay 'Reification and the Consciousness of the Proletariat' (Lukács 1971). Lukács was a Hungarian marxist taken in by Weber to his Sunday circle. His essay was a brilliant synthesis of Marx's and Weber's themes of commodification and rationalization, the more remarkable as it anticipated the motifs of Marx's Paris writings, unavailable in any language until 1932. Lukács' work anticipated the work of Karl Löwith, who in that year (1932) pinned Weber and Marx together in his brilliant essay *Max Weber and Karl Marx*. Löwith viewed Marx and Weber not as combatants, as in the infamous image of Weber as 'the bourgeois Marx', but as social philosophers with a primary interest in the human condition in modernity. The difference between them, according to Löwith, was that they characterized this condition differently – Marx through the image of alienation (the Paris writings now having become available), Weber through the master-image of rationalization (Löwith 1932). Obviously there remained significant differences between Marx and Weber, not least those of disposition, over the ethics of responsibility versus the ethics of ultimate ends, the respective weight given to material and ideal factors in history and so on. Yet Marx's revolutionary rhetoric became hollow when read against the fatalistic logic of the argument concerning commodity fetishism. The problem, for Marxists, seemed now to be that we were stuck with capitalism, and that things only got worse when hothead Bolsheviks tried to shortcircuit history by barging into 'socialism' now.

For the critical theorists the scenario was different. The German working-class movement had failed to rise to the moment into the later 1920s. Even without the disastrous experience of fascism, capitalism had shown enormous resilience and integrative capacity. This argument was revived into the 1960s, when Marx's early work became available in English, and student radicalism peaked. Its best exemplification was in Marcuse's *One-dimensional Man* (1964). By this stage, the idea of totalitarianism, further popularized by Orwell's *1984* (1948), had spread to the west. The inmates of modernity, or at least their radical representatives, began to fear that totalitarianism was not specific to Stalinism or Nazism, but was endemic to capitalism, even to modernity itself. The iron cage was everywhere; conformism was abundant. The United States was bombing the daylights out of Vietnam, and governments such as that in Australia had reintroduced military conscription. It may not have been totalitarian, but on some days it seemed hard to tell.

Critical theory was sometimes teased for its aristocratic components, its disinclination to praise popular culture, jazz or Americanism, its sometimes overwhelming sense of cultural pessimism, and all these sentiments echo the larger and older traditions of aristocratic radicalism, for which the old world, in general, was better than the brashness and shock of the new. The European critique of modernity was born as a critique of the mass, mass society, mass production, mass migration, the mass man, the image of life based on the factory, on its regimentation and yes-men, the conformism of following orders. This was also Marcuse's anxiety into the 1960s – that the lucid or erotic components of being had been submerged into dull regimes of compliance, consumption, and getting on. Perhaps this was the moment when sociology began to shifts its focus from the realm of production to that of consumption. Gramsci had already anticipated the cultural turn in marxian thirty years earlier.

Marcuse was not the only high-profile critical theorist, though the fact that he remained in the USA after Horkheimer and Adorno returned to Germany placed him strategically to be more significantly influential into the 1960s. More, he wrote in jeremiad form, unlike the laconic and dense Adorno, anticipating, in this sense, the later popularity of Zygmunt Bauman, another critical Cassandra figure. The second generation of critical theory became associated especially with the work and figure of Jürgen Habermas, who turned back to the inspiration of Kantian universalism. Where Marcuse saw systemic closure and frustration, Habermas saw possibilities for change, reform, and democratization. His early work drew together marxian and weberian themes and filaments, again seeking a critical theory with a practical or emancipatory intention in the manner of Marx.

Critical theory simultaneously began to pluralize in the East European regimes which had been established as extensions of the Soviet empire after World War Two. Into the 1960s dissident forms of humanist marxism were emerging in Yugoslavia, Czechoslovakia, Hungary, and Poland. In Hungary the students of Lukács formed the Budapest School, who like others held the radical principles of Marx against the state which claimed to rule in the name of Marx. Its leading figures – Agnes Heller, Ferenc Fehér, Ivan Szelenyi, George and Maria Markus – left to seek exile in Australia, where they made significant contributions to the critique of Soviet-type societies, among other things. Leading dissidents in Poland, including Zygmunt Bauman, Leszek Kolakowski and Wlodzinierz Brus, were 'allowed to leave' in 1969. The Yugoslav movement gave birth to *Praxis* and then to *Praxis International*. Of all these, Bauman perhaps became the most significant follower of the critical theory of modernity. His most influential mid-career book, *Modernity and the Holocaust*, both builds on and extends the classical Frankfurt tradition of *Dialectic of Enlightenment* (Bauman 1989). Here modernity also turns back and feeds upon itself (Beilharz 2000).

These kinds of developments were more influential in the United States than in Britain. British marxism, powerfully influenced by *New Left Review*, began with some sympathy for radical humanism but soon cashed this in for the harder edge and stiffer scientific claims of Althusserian marxism. Journals like *Telos*, whose earlier sympathies were for phenomenological marxism, gave critical theory a better reception across the Atlantic, while purpose-built or dedicated journals like *New German Critique* also promoted critical theory and its co-currents and trends. *Telos* also further promoted the work of Gramsci, which was kick-started in Australia by Alastair Davidson in 1968, three years before *Selections from the Prison Notebooks* became available (Davidson 1968; Gramsci 1971). Finally, *Telos* and then *Thesis Eleven* helped to profile the work of Cornelius Castoriadis, where the marxian project was reformed as the project of autonomy. As Dick Howard showed in his *Marxian Legacy* (1977), there was a libertarian line that ran from the young Marx through to Rosa Luxemburg, then later to Castoriadis. Raya Dunayevskaya had anticipated this lineage earlier, in significant period works such as *Marxism and Freedom* (1958). For these thinkers, socialism would be democratic or it would not be at all. Only this urging failed sufficiently to contemplate its own outcome: that it would not be at all.

The Hard Left

Humanism was a sitting duck for those with harder heads. What did it mean, to say that because we (or our forebears) had made this world, we could remake it, make it anew? Were there not harder structures or systems which would bounce back, fail to respond to hippie enthusiasms and the wash of good intentions? The hard left was not given to endorsing Marcuse, but they often seemed to share his sense that the beast of modernity (or rather, capitalism) would not respond to suggestion, or to the ballot box. Something more forceful, more revolutionary, would be required. The work of Louis Althusser offered the necessary toolkit. Althusser wanted marxism to be a science, and its politics to be revolutionary, the latter at least until the French events of May 1968, when revolution was made by Althusser to look more like a good idea than a practical project. Althusser intervened powerfully into a dispute which now likely looks arcane, but kept marxologists in work for a long time. This was the dispute over the Young versus the Mature Marx.

Into the 1960s the new Marx, the newly discovered Marx, was the Marx of the Paris Manuscripts. These are, as Marx once wrote to Engels in their later years, green, in contrast to the later grey of theory and the dull industrial culture of factory civilization which it sought to explain. Reading the young Marx was fun, more or less; reading *Capital*, in contrast, was hard work. Althusser sternly took on the duty of reading *Capital*, writing a very serious book called *Reading Capital*, and insisting that we should all read *Capital* seriously, in its multiple volumes, preferably in the original (Althusser and Balibar 1970). The early Marx was Marx before he was Marx, foreplay rather than the real action. *Capital* was taken to represent a new form of knowledge, building upon a significant epistemological break or rupture. We all became epistemologists. Nobody seemed to notice that this was a step away from practice, rather than towards it. But these were times of great seriosity, and high illusions, as well as very serious scholarship.

Yet there was something important in this mission. Marx's early writings give us the perspective of his laboratory. We can watch him thinking, and it can be an exhilarating experience. But his life's work was *Capital*, and the architectonic of that work repays serious close reading. Rightly or wrongly, Marx had become convinced that the mode of presentation of this work was crucial; that there was a best way to explain capital, and that he had sorted it out. He was also convinced that capital was the privileged category, to be accessed via the logic of the commodity form. It did seem something of an irony that none, or few, of the Marxists had read Marx, because it was too hard. And this was part and parcel of the story of the fate of marxism. Engels, Kautsky (the pope of Marxism), then Lenin, and finally Stalin had reduced Marx's theory to a series of axioms or platitudes about surplus value, historical and finally dialectical materialism. Marxists got by reciting these axioms in their daily denunciations of capitalism. Marxism had become its own caricature.

Althusser blew the whistle on this state of affairs. After Althusser, it was inadmissible for Marxists to cut corners. They were now compelled to deal with their own theoretical heritage. A few clichés concerning the ubiquity of alienation and the need for revolution would no longer do.

Some followed Althusser slavishly, replacing old clichés with new. Others such as Nicos Poulantzas took more interesting paths. Poulantzas picked upon some of the staples of Marxist sociology, such as class and the state, and history, with reference to the problems of fascism and dictatorship. But all of this ended badly. Poulantzas committed suicide, leaving a fine book, *State, Power, Socialism* (Poulantzas 1979) which also responded to the legacy of Rosa Luxemburg. Althusser murdered his wife, and himself died a sad and lonely death (Althusser 1993). Althusser flirted with Maoism; Poulantzas with the then significant European trend called Eurocommunism.

Across the Channel, Althusserianism had the peculiar echo-effect apparent in the work of Hindess and Hirst. They took on the period interest of Marxist historians and anthropologists in modes of production. Their initial purpose was to generate a non-historical theory of history. As their collaboration eased, Hindess turned via Foucault to matters of political philosophy, Hirst to broad problems of radical English ideas, Thatcherism, and the critique of globalization-talk.

One of the ironies of the Althusserian experiment was that while it was dismissive of history, in contrast to theory, historians drank here as well. Marxist history had been steered hitherto by humanists such as E. P. Thompson, who bombed Althusser in *The Poverty of Theory* (1978). Marxist historiography nevertheless became more sophisticated in dialogue with Althusser, as is evident in the work of the *Radical History Review* or *History Workshop Journal*. Stronger Marxist views like those of Immanuel Wallerstein, mediated by the work of the *Annales* School and Fernand Braudel, became highly influential as world-systems analysis via the Braudel Centre's *Review*. Althusserian marxism remains influential still today in journals such as *Rethinking Marxism*.

Alternative positions had been sketched out by culturally sensitive thinkers such as Henri Lefebvre in Paris and Stuart Hall in London. Marxism's influence spread out through the cultural turn, into cultural studies and later into geography and urban studies. The work of Castells helped to carry it through into work on networks, globalization and the information society. The stiff edge of structural marxism shifted into the school called analytical marxism, where analytical logic was taken to be the vital supplement which would fill Marx's deficit or add the newly necessary ingredient. This is indeed one way to view the history of academic marxism, especially with its institutionalization in western universities after World War Two. Marxists often respond to their predicament in an additive or supplementary manner. Some add phenomenology, some add structuralism. Some add epistemology, some add analytic logic or psychoanalysis or mathematics. Some seek to add culture, following Gramsci. The difference between this way of thinking, often fashion-prone and sometimes smelling of desperation, and the tradition of Critical Theory is that when Weber meets Marx the result is transformative, a synthesis of both theoretical perspectives. For critical theory, the contribution of Weber is not regional, but fundamental. It is not catalytic, but is itself transformed in the process. This might be one reason explaining its persistence.

Postmarxism

After Marx, there are the Marxists. Karl Marx famously denied that he was a Marxist. Then, after the Marxists, there are now the postmarxists. All this is historically necessary. We are all, now, after Marx, and in a different sense we are also after marxism, in its classical form. As a theoretical legacy, classical marxism in the manner of Kautsky persists. But in an historical sense, the classical marxism of the German Social Democrats is eclipsed by the victory of the Bolsheviks, who successfully appropriated the name of marxism for themselves. Into a bipolar, and then Cold War world, it suits both protagonists, American and Soviet alike, to identify marxism and Stalinism. Marxists, of course, persist, not least as the bearers of the Trotskyist illusion, that they are the true inheritors of Lenin and the loyal opposition. Castoriadis, himself momentarily a Trotskyist in the 1940s, later called Trotskyists 'the Stalinist bureaucracy in exile'. But while the remnants of marxism in this form still persist, there are also further developments, often characterized as postmarxism.

Postmarxism makes sense; if we are after Marx, we are also after marxism. The phenomenon bifurcates, however, and in this it follows the postmodern, whose semantics it extends from the realm of modernism and modernity into that of marxism.

Debates about the postmodern often split over the relative weight given to each term (Beilharz 1994, 2010). As Bernard Smith put it, postmodern enthusiasts often mistook the tail for the kite (1997: 159). The modern was the kite, the postmodern its tail, rather than the other way around. In some arguments, the post was valued above the modern, which was now presented as archaic. In others, the post was merely the appendage, representing cultural forms in aesthetics and architecture which emerged after the collapse of the Long Boom. Similar differences in possibility emerge with the idea of the postmarxist.

All this takes on a different light, in addition, after the fall of the Berlin Wall in 1989 and the subsequent collapse of communism. A post-Soviet world is also, in a particular sense, a postmarxist world, though the subsequent triumph of capitalism also called out the revival of a kind of generalized marxism in the anti-WTO movement. Globalization, ironically, revived the analytical fortunes of Marxists, as did the GFC and the return of the Spectre of Depression. In a perverse, historical sense Marx's triumph was best exemplified by the Chinese experience, where a residual kind of institutional marxism in the form of the Chinese Communist Party went together with the victory of Chinese quasi-capitalist productive forces.

To be postmarxist, then, is in a sense now unavoidable. Some of the best Marxists have been historians, such as Bernard Smith and Eric Hobsbawm, or sociologists such as Stuart Hall, differently geographers such as David Harvey or critical theorists such as Fred Jameson who have worn their categories lightly, combined interests in the critique of culture and power, taken technology as seriously as cultural development. Different radical journals, from *New Left Review* to *Thesis Eleven*, have worked the field after marxism in distinct ways. Other bodies of work, such as those associated with Laclau and Mouffe, have followed versions of the additive approach indicated above: add psychoanalysis, add Wittgenstein, add Schmitt. The exemplary, or foundational, text here was *Hegemony and Socialist Strategy* of Laclau and Mouffe (1985), where marxism and other intellectual currents are juxtaposed, perhaps, rather than integrated. But the predominant influence in postmarxism globally has been more stridently Marxist, less post- than Marxist.

The two most influential postmarxist contributions come from Zizek, and Negri and Hardt respectively. Both have developed cult-followings, and blockbuster sales, and in the case of Zizek, cults of personality (try Youtube). Zizek's approach has also been additive: add Lacan, in particular, but also comedic: add Hitchcock, and jokes about Lenin. Zizek's approach is also contrarian, essentially provocative. Sometimes this style is defended as a kind of agonism; often it is simply offensive, as in Zizek's claim that Lenin (now without humour) was basically a nice guy who strayed into politics (Zizek 2002). This is reminiscent of the Woody Allen joke in which Albert Speer is surprised to discover that Hitler was a Nazi.

Zizek's marxism is a kind of postbolshevism rather than postmarxism, where the semantic weight falls on the Bolshevik rather than the post. In some circles he has been called a Bolshevik clown, though here the weight is on the adjective more than the noun (Zizek 2002; Beilharz 2005). Where Lenin in 1917 calls for socialism as electrification plus Soviets, Zizek today calls for socialism free Internet access plus Soviets. Neither seems especially likely.

Negri and Hardt offer a different kind of postmarxism, which perhaps is really best defined as neomarxism, for its purpose is to renew and refresh the old, stale revolutionary project. Negri connects back to the Italian ultra-left tradition of the *autonomista*, where, in contrast to Castoriadis' more open and ontological use of the idea, it is workers' autonomy or *autogestion* that matters (Wright 2002). Negri also connects back to the notion of Engels, adopted by the Trotskyists C. L. R. James and Dunayevskaya into the 1950s of 'the invading socialist society', for which the most powerful trend towards socialism apart from autonomous proletarian struggle is the internal evolution towards socialism within the heart of capitalism itself. Where others, earlier, viewed capitalism as doing socialism's work via the internal socialization of capital, Negri and Hardt project this capacity onto globalization. In contrast to the dominant, reactive mood of most radical critique of globalization, their book *Empire* (2000) returns to the axioms of automatic marxism, only Empire now itself lays the ground for socialism. Socialism, once again, is imagined as the egg or embryo of socialism within late capitalist developments. Immaterial labour, exemplified in the new communications technology, represents the promise of socialism *in nuce*. Little wonder that *Empire*, with or without the later added enthusiasm for the idea of the Multitude, should have been such a hit with a needy residual left. For it works like a kind of mosaical or magical marxism, reinstalling both spontaneism and revolutionary guarantees at the same time, bringing the millennium closer in ways that echo Cecil B. DeMille more than Karl Marx. The problem with this kind of automatic marxism is precisely that it is too Marxist, too orthodox in its millennial hope and desire to inscribe the future of socialism within the path of capitalist development. Yet again, it results in a combination of public militancy with a long term strategy of waiting for the revolution.

Conclusion

What then, finally, was Marx's legacy? The specificity of the question is important. Marx's legacy: not Lenin's, or that of Bolshevism, or Marxism–Leninism. What is the marxian legacy?

Marx is the proverbial son of the Enlightenment, but also of romanticism. As Berman shows, his project is deeply imbued with the modernist spirit, of embracing the whirlwind of creative destruction (Berman 1984). Yet Marx also longs for a gentler, slower Renaissance world. The moment of his intellectual formation, in the Roman-French town of Trier, connected him to these European legacies and also meant that he could imagine modernity as reversible (a prospect we have now well and truly lost). Marx elaborates on Schiller's critique of fragmentation in developing his youthful theory of alienation. He develops a critical theory with an emancipatory intention. He learns to historicize, to think and explain the new world in terms of drama, dramaturgy, ghosts and spirits, fetishes, mythologies, masking, in images as powerful as that of the sorcerer's apprentice. He proceeds via the critique of political economy to theorize power and culture, to centre on technology as a culture.

The power of Marx's diagnosis of modern times is not equalled by his prognosis. Marx shows a fundamental weakness in his attraction to populism, the image of two fundamental working classes, especially early. He installs the proletariat as the motor of history, an imputation which the proletariat never quite understands correctly. His sense of the permanent revolution of capital spills over into the telos of guaranteed socialism, which it never is. He was a powerful critic of capitalism as modernity, who understood the centrality of capital as a relation and as a self-naturalizing illusion. He was a dreamer. His intellectual origins were before modernity, but the scope of his vision was beyond it. His legacy is best imagined as what Ernst Bloch called the warm stream of marxism.

Was he an original? Yes, and no. The power of Marx's work lies in the brilliant synthesis that he generated from the work of others, working within on the critical horizons of both the streams we conventionally separate as Enlightenment and Romanticism. Perhaps, in our own times, the fate of his thought is to return to the cultures from which it was initially created, as avant-garde returns, finally, to the mainstream.

References

Adorno, T. and M. Horkheimer (1944) *Dialectic of Enlightenment*, London: Allen Lane, 1973.
Althusser, L. (1993) *The Future Lasts a Long Time*, London: Chatto & Windus.
Althusser, L. and E. Balibar (1970) *Reading Capital*, London: New Left Books.
Bauman, Z. (1972) *Between Class and Elite*, Manchester: Manchester University Press.
——(1989) *Modernity and the Holocaust*, Oxford: Polity.
Beilharz, P. (1982) 'The Other Trotsky', *Thesis Eleven*, 2.
——(1987) *Trotsky, Trotskyism and the Transition to Socialism*, London: Croom Helm.
——(1992) *Labour's Utopias: Bolshevism, Fabianism, Social Democracy*, London: Routledge.
——(1994) *Postmodern Socialism: Romanticism, City and State*, Melbourne: Melbourne University Press.
——(2000) *Zygmunt Bauman – Dialectic of Modernity*, London: Sage.
——(2005) 'Postmarxism', in G. Ritzer (ed.), *Sage Encyclopedia of Social Theory*, London: Sage.
——(2010) 'Modern and Postmodern', in J. Hall, I. Grindstaff, Ming-Cheng Lo (eds), *Handbook of Cultural Sociology*, London: Routledge.

Berman, M. (1984) *All that is Solid Melts into Air*, New York: Knopf.

Davidson, A. (1968) *Antonio Gramsci – The Man, His Ideas*, Sydney: Australian Left Review.

Draper, H. (1977) *Karl Marx's Theory of Revolution*, New York: Monthly Review, 4 volumes.

Dunayevskaya, R. (1982 [1958]) *Marxism and Freedom*, Sussex: Harvester.

Fehér, F., A. Heller, and G. Markus (1982) *Dictatorship Over Needs*, Oxford: Blackwell.

Gramsci, A. (1971) *Selections from the Prison Notebooks*, London: Lawrence & Wishart.

——(1975 [1918]) 'The Revolution Against Capital', in Cavalcanti and Piccone (eds), *History, Philosophy and Culture in the Young Gramsci*, St Louis: Telos.

Howard, D. (1977) *The Marxian Legacy*, London: Macmillan.

Laclau, E. and C. Mouffe (1985) *Hegemony and Socialist Strategy*, London: Verso.

Lenin, V. I. (1899) *The Development of Capitalism in Russia*, Progress: Moscow.

——(1902) *What Is To Be Done?* Progress: Moscow.

Löwith, K. (1932) *Max Weber and Karl Marx*, London: Allen & Unwin, 1982.

Lukács, G. (1923) 'Reification and the Consciousness of the Proletariat', in *History and Class Consciousness*, London: Merlin, 1971.

Marcuse, H. (1964) *One-dimensional Man*, Boston, MA: Beacon.

Marx, K. (1975 [1844]) 'Economic and Philosophical Manuscripts', in L. Colletti (ed.), *Marx – Early Writings*, Harmondsworth: Penguin.

——(1973 [1858]) *Grundrisse*, Harmondsworth: Penguin.

——(1970 [1859]) *A Contribution to the Critique of Political Economy*, Moscow: Progress.

——(1867) *Capital Volume One*, Progress: Moscow, n.d.

Negri, A. and M. Hardt (2000) *Empire*, Cambridge, MA: Harvard University Press.

Poulantzas, N. (1979) *State, Power, Socialism*, London: New Left Books.

Smith, B. (1997) *Imagining the Antipodes: Theory, Cuture and the Visual in the Work of Bernard Smith*, Cambridge: Cambridge University Press.

Thompson, E. P. (1978) *The Poverty of Theory and Other Essays*, London: Merlin.

Wiggershaus, R. (1994) *The Frankfurt School: Its History, Theories and Political Significance*, Cambridge, MA: MIT Press.

Wright, S. (2002) *Storming Heaven: Class Composition and Struggle in Italian Autonomist Marxism*, London: Pluto.

Zizek, S. (2002) *Revolution at the Gates*, London: Verso.

Foucault and the Promise of Power without Dogma

Gary Wickham

Foucault's work on power, governance, and society holds out the promise of power without dogma. To help the reader to understand the allure of such a promise, I will begin with a sketch of Foucault's reception in the Anglophone academy (those wanting a sketch of Foucault as an especially French thinker, operating in a French and broader European context, would do well to consult Tribe 2009). My sketch, then, is from the perspective of someone who first encountered Foucault in the late 1970s, who has only ever dealt with him in translation, who is still a fan, but who now has serious doubts about many aspects of Foucault's legacy.

Like many other Anglophone academics who took up Foucault, I first came across him as a mysterious figure lurking on the fringe of what then seemed, for some reason, a vital debate. This debate sought to find a way to advance Marxist thinking in the light of the obvious fact (obvious to many, but not all) that the Marxism of Marx was not particularly relevant to people living in advanced Western democracies like Britain, the USA, Canada, and, in my case, Australia. I was, this is to say, spending a lot of time wondering whether thinkers like Althusser on the one hand and the British Cultural Marxists on the other (people like Raymond Williams and Stuart Hall, themselves working closely with translations of the work of Antonio Gramsci) offered a genuine alternative to the dogmatic Marxism that I, along with many others, had never been keen to take up.

The name 'Foucault' was first spoken to me in dark, conspiratorial tones, as if he were a threat to the then-alluring project of combining Althusser's ideology-centred thinking and the British culture-and-hegemony thinking. Foucault, along with Weber, Popper, Berlin, and many others (the list was a tiresomely long one) had to be rejected, or so I was told. My mind was soon changed on that score. The exciting work of Barry Hindess and Paul Hirst (see esp. Hindess and Hirst 1975, 1977), who had worked through the Althusser and British Cultural Marxist possibilities more thoroughly than anyone else I had then read (or have read since), indirectly opened up the idea that Foucault was not only *not* a threat to the best-alternative project I shared with hundreds of others, but was the key to that project's success.

At last, here was a thinker who could treat power seriously yet undogmatically, someone who could relate power to society without making it read like the script of a prison movie. I was hooked. I tried my best to understand (or to sound like I understood) all the methodological innovations that came with the Foucault package – 'archaeology', 'genealogy', 'discourse', 'episteme', and so on. My excitement reached its peak when, using these tools, Foucault appeared to have succeeded in crafting an entirely new approach to the study of government, under a term of his own invention, 'governmentality'. But, as so often happens in life, the peak of excitement turned out to be the moment when doubts emerged. These doubts became stronger, eventually leading me to think that Foucault's works from this period too often pronounce and too rarely argue from the historical evidence.

I will return to this point in the conclusion. I wish to spend most of my chapter in positive voice (remember, I am still a fan), trying to capture what was and still is so attractive about Foucault's work on power–governance–society. To put this in another way, while I am nowadays often irritated by the vast fields of governmentality investigations being grown around the world, many of which give the impression that projects of governing one's self or one's tennis club or one's university are equivalent to the government of nation states, I am nonetheless still attracted to the project Foucault launched. I am especially attracted by work – whether by promising young scholars or by one or another of the 'old hands' – which uses Foucault's thinking on power in novel and productive ways. An example of such work by a young scholar is Ryan Walter's determination to treat Foucault as an historian of the formation of the modern state, alongside but different from Quentin Skinner (see esp. Walter 2008b). In this quest, Walter is respectful of Foucault but by no means slavish, arguing, for instance, that he and his govern-mentality followers are weak on 'the constitution of an economic terrain', because they mistakenly focus on 'the general use of liberal understandings of agency' (Walter 2008a: 95).[1] An example of such work by an old hand is Keith Tribe's sympathetic yet incisive reading of two of the recent books in the series of Foucault's lectures at the Collège de France (Tribe 2009), a piece in which Tribe provides some wonderful detail about what Foucault was reading in the 1970s and, more importantly, what he was not reading. Speaking of these lectures, I am also impressed by the unflagging energy of Foucault scholars in bringing all of Foucault's lectures at the Collège (right up to those given in 1984, the year in which he died) to the attention of both the Francophone and Anglophone reading publics. The dedication and scholarship involved in finding taped versions of the lectures and in so diligently transcribing, editing, and, in the Anglophone case, translating them are highly laudable (details of this project, and many other things Foucault, can be found on the website founded by Clare O'Farrell: Michel-Foucault.com).

Foucault's Power–Governance–Society Work as a Positive Contribution to Social and Political Theory

Three of the four main things about Foucault's power–governance–society body of work that made it (and still make it) so appealing are: its marked differences from Marxism;[2] the tools Foucault fashioned to help make it so; and the way in which he made the transition from power analysis *per se* to a study of governmentality. I will deal with these first three strengths one at a time. The fourth strength runs through all of these and cannot be separated from them. It is the dramatic and exciting way in which Foucault put so many of his points, not just in his books but especially in his many interviews. Not since Marx, paradoxically, has a major theorist written so well that one might want to read the work for the writing alone, even if one had no interest in the ideas.

A Feasible Alternative to Marxism

Here, for example, is Foucault summarising his account of power, and in doing so encapsulating the differences between him and the Marxists:

Power is not something that is acquired, seized, or shared, something that one holds on to or allows slip away; power is exercised from innumerable points, in the interplay of nonegalitarian and mobile relations ... Power comes from below; that is, there is no binary and all encompassing opposition between ruler and ruled at the root of power relations ... One must suppose rather that the manifold relations of force that take shape and come into play in the machinery of production, in families, limited groups, and institutions, are the basis for wide-ranging effects of cleavage that run through the social body as a whole.

(Foucault 1998: 94)

Power is within society, Foucault is telling us, working as a part of its fabric, not imposed upon it from the outside. It can be repressive, but this is not its main face. It is productive more than it is destructive, positive more than it is negative:

If power were never anything but repressive, if it never did anything but to say no, do you really think one would be brought to obey it? What makes power hold good, what makes it accepted, is simply the fact that is doesn't only weigh on us as a force that says no; it also traverses and produces things, it induces pleasure, forms knowledge, produces discourse. It needs to be considered as a productive network that runs through the whole social body, much more than as a negative instance whose function is repression.

(Foucault 2001b: 120)

Foucault's achievement in so quickly building such an enthralling account of the operation of power in society is all the more remarkable when one remembers the dominant hold that Marxist and neo-Marxist accounts had in the Anglophone academy in the 1970s and even into the 1980s. The key to his success probably lies in the fact that he did not initially present his insights in abstract terms but instead allowed them to emerge from his painstaking histories of various knowledge endeavours, or sciences, particularly psychiatry, psychology, penology, and sexology. Without bludgeoning his readers, Foucault allowed them to see mostly power where others would see mostly science. For example:

Tuke and Pinel opened the asylum to medical knowledge. They did not introduce science, but a personality, whose powers borrowed from science only their disguise, or at most their justification. These powers, by their nature, were of a moral and social order; they took root in the madman's minority status, in the insanity of his person, not of his mind.

(Foucault 1971: 271–2)

This is a wonderful feeling for the reader, as anyone who has taught Foucault to undergraduate or graduate students will attest, giving her or him a sense of discovering power, as if for the first time. And the magic is multiplied by the fact that Foucault insists that he himself did not at first see power where he later came to see it, that he too was initially blinded by the claims of knowledge and science:

When I think back now, I ask myself what else it was that I was talking about in *Madness and Civilization* and *The Birth of the Clinic*, but power? Yet I'm perfectly aware that I scarcely ever used the word and never had such a field of analyses at my disposal. I can say that this was an incapacity linked undoubtedly with the political situation in which we found ourselves. It is hard to see where, either on the Right or the Left, this problem of power could then have been posed. On the Right it was posed only in terms of constitution, sovereignty, and so on, that is, in juridical terms; on the Marxist side, it was posed only in terms of the state apparatus. The way power was exercised – concretely, and in detail – with its specificity, its techniques and tactics, was something that no one attempted to ascertain … This task could only begin after 1968, that is to say, on the basis of daily struggles at grass-roots level, among those whose fight was located in the fine meshes of the web of power. This was where the concrete nature of power became visible, along with the prospect that these analyses of power would prove fruitful in accounting for all that had hitherto remained outside the field of political analysis. To put it very simply, psychiatric internment, the mental normalization of individuals, and penal institutions have no doubt a fairly limited importance if one is only looking for their economic significance. On the other hand, they are undoubtedly essential to the general functioning of the wheels of power.

(Foucault 2001b: 117)

It might be, of course, that the dazzling prose prevented most readers (including me) from noticing that sometimes Foucault was saying things that were in fact not all that far from what the Marxists of the time were saying, as can be glimpsed in the above quote when he uses the phrase 'daily struggles' and when he dismisses 'the Right's' obsession with sovereignty and state, but I will leave that matter for now and move on to the second thing that made (and still makes) this body of Foucault's work so appealing, its use of very particular and seemingly quite exotic tools of analysis.

Foucault's exotic tools for power analysis

I have room only for a brief discussion of archaeology, genealogy, and discourse (this section is based on my treatment of these methodological devices in Wickham 2002, which itself owes a debt to Kendall and Wickham 1999). This means that I am leaving out things like *dispositif*, event, and a host of others, though I will touch on *episteme* in dealing with discourse. In developing these tools Foucault did not, of course, start from scratch, nor did he claim to; the tools may be exotic but they are not totally new. He readily acknowledged the influence on his thinking of a number of others, most especially Canguilhem, the historian of science, Nietzsche, the philosopher/historian, and Blanchot and Bataille, who resist easy classification (Gane 1986).

Archaeology's main task is to describe statements in the archive (Foucault 1972: 131), statements covering the sayable and the visible (as, for example, in the invention and maintenance of the asylum or the prison). Foucault thinks of the archive as 'the general system of the formation and transformation of statements' (Foucault 1972: 130). His main concern in using this tool was to develop a 'general' history (Foucault 1972: 164), by which he meant a history that captures a broad range of features of power without being overwhelmingly 'total' or 'essentialist', that is, without having to insist that every historical tidbit be viewed in the terms of the battle between capital and labour or some other such 'grand' battle. In particular, he wanted archaeology to describe: regularities of statements in a non-interpretive manner (content to remain at the level of appearances, eschewing any quest to go 'beyond' this level in search of 'deeper meanings'); statements in a non-anthropological manner, as a means to avoid the habit of seeking meaning in human beings themselves; the relation between one statement and other statements; 'surfaces of emergence' or places within which objects are made objects of discourse; the institutions that acquire authority and provide limits within which discursive objects may act; and the 'forms of specification' in which discursive objects are targeted (for more on the complexities of Foucault's use of archaeology, see esp. Bevis, Cohen, and Kendall 1989; Brown and Cousins 1986).

There has been some dispute within the secondary literature as to whether Foucault's use of genealogy marks a complete break with his use of archaeology, with some claiming that genealogy was the tool Foucault invented to explicitly explore power because he felt that archaeology was not up to the job. In this way, it is said that archaeology is a pale academic tool whereas genealogy, with more blood in its veins, is archaeology plus power, a sort of archaeology on speed. I do not intend to go into the details of that dispute because for me there is no dispute. When Foucault says, alluringly, 'what else it was that I was talking about in *Madness and Civilization* and *The Birth of the Clinic*, but power?', I take him to mean that he thinks he was doing power analysis all along, he just didn't realise it. As such, I think of genealogy as a slightly adjusted form of archaeology – adjusted to acknowledge power's importance – not a break from it. The main difference involved is that in using genealogy Foucault makes more effort to link his careful histories to the present, but this is not really all that much of a change. In truth any assiduous reader would all along have been doing this with the analyses marked 'archaeology'. Stressing that genealogy is a route to a 'history of the present' certainly helped Foucault to get across his point that the knowledge endeavours (or sciences) he was investigating, especially psychiatry, had 'disreputable origins and unpalatable functions' (Rose 1984), which is no bad thing, but it is not really saying anything new. After all, which history is not, at least in some sense, a history of the present? Let me just say that genealogy entails a more overt attempt to answer problems about the present than does archaeology, and leave it at that.

Discourse is an altogether more difficult tool for Anglophone readers to come to grips with, mainly because Foucault did not use the term in the same way in which it is normally used in English – to describe formal speech. However, inasmuch as the standard English meaning does allow the term to be extended to formal writing, Foucault's usage should not be entirely foreign to an Anglophone audience. Perhaps herein lies the source of the difficulty – that Anglophone readers respond to Foucault's usage of the term as if it is a simple extension of the English usage, when, I suggest, he meant it to be doing much more work than that.

For Foucault, language is only one component of a discourse. To think of English words like 'institution', 'procedure', and 'practice' might help the novice to come to grips with what Foucault was trying to do when he used this tool, but to gain a stronger command of it, it is necessary to grapple with his proposition that a discourse has no 'inside' and no 'outside'.[3] The first step on the road to doing so is to understand that in Foucault's hands a discourse is primarily about production. In this way, discourses about sex, for example, produce the very category 'sexuality' and in doing so produce particular 'types of person', such as 'homosexual', 'heterosexual', 'deviant', etc. This does not mean, of course, that Foucault is proposing that before the existence of these discourses, none of these things existed. As he makes clear in the first volume of his *History of Sexuality* project (1998), discourses on 'sexuality' emerged in the eighteenth and nineteenth centuries, not out of thin air but as more and less dramatic refinements of certain kinship ties, certain Christian 'sins of the flesh', certain ancient but long-lasting techniques of 'self-mastery', etc. Foucault is not is suggesting, this is to say, that sex 'itself' exists in a 'pure' non-discursive place and time. While we can reasonably think of the 'raw materials' of Foucault's discourses – in this case bodies, sex, death, etc. – as non-discursive, we cannot gain access to this realm without discourse. The relation of the discursive to the non-discursive is therefore always fraught and complex.

By insisting that discourses have 'no inside', Foucault is insisting that there is no hidden mechanism that makes discourses work, nothing we should be digging for beyond or behind the use of words and symbols that make their use possible. All we need for discourse analysis, by Foucault's way of thinking, is what is right there in front of us. If we remember that when Foucault was invited to name his Chair at the Collège de France he chose 'Professor of the History of Systems of Thought' it should help us to understand discourses in terms of visible 'systems of thought'. This will help, for it makes clear that 'thought' is not a special domain, the product of a higher order of existence called 'thinking', it is simply the name given to the 'surfaces of appearance' involved in the operation of various institutions, procedures, apparatuses, etc., all of them quite public and visible.

By saying that discourses have no 'outside', Foucault is, in an important sense, simply expanding his argument that discourses have no 'inside'. If we accept that Foucault is right that discursive surfaces are all that we have to work with and right that we need no more than this, then we are accepting that there is nothing 'outside' them, nothing that somehow guarantees their existence and operation. This is to say, we need not trouble ourselves by trying to anchor discourses in 'the world', or in some other such supposedly fixed point of reference.

Finally, the best way to understand Foucault's notion of *episteme* is to think of an episteme as a large, loose collection of discourses built up over time and space. Epistemes are not in any way determinate of discourses, rather the term is used by Foucault to allow us to occasionally consider the vaguely co-ordinated operation of discourses over certain time periods and in certain places: 'Sometimes he treats the discourses separately; at other times, he looks at their contribution to the possibility of each period having an overall view of the world (which he calls "the Western episteme")' (McHoul and Grace 1992: 32).

Power analysis becomes governmentality analysis

It would be reasonable to say that Foucault's late-1970s turn from power, as it exists in the 'smallest elements of society' and as it operates through various knowledge endeavours, to power as it operates specifically as a form of governing was simply another stage in his long-term quest to capture the complexities of the relations between power and knowledge. Indeed, in making this turn Foucault was so concerned to emphasise the links between his long-term stress on power's intimate connections with knowledge and his later governing-focused body of work that he coined the term 'governmentality', to stress the 'knowing' aspects of governing.

It would be reasonable to say this but to do so would be to risk missing the crucial fact that what is now called governmentality analysis was forged as much by Foucault's followers – initially in Britain and Australia but soon spreading to New Zealand, Canada, and the United States – as much as it was forged by Foucault himself. Foucault provided the raw materials, particularly in his seminal essay 'Governmentality' (1979), and then both he and his followers made it into a new way of dealing with questions concerned with the way societies and individuals are governed, including the way individuals govern themselves.

The raw materials were a set of connected propositions, focusing first on the emergence, in the sixteenth century or before (Foucault's periodisations are rarely exact), of a distinctive way of thinking about the state, which allowed the state to be treated as an entity *sui generis*, as opposed to an entity entirely under the control of God. Once that development had occurred, Foucault argues, 'reason of state' thinking then produced a special object of governing, 'the population', which in turn spawned special sciences, such as political economy and statistics. These sciences allowed governments to govern in terms that dealt with both whole populations and, increasingly, with the different individual members of the populations, leading to various 'liberal' technologies of rule, whereby individuals achieve 'more' freedom by governing themselves.

As with his earlier work, these propositions – all of them interesting in themselves – were made compelling by the way in which Foucault put them. Here, as a first example, is Foucault explaining the emergence of reason of state:

> To put it very schematically: the art of government finds at the end of the 16th century and the beginning of the 17th its first form of crystallisation: it organises itself around the

theme of the reason of State, understood not in the negative and pejorative sense we attribute to it today (namely as that which infringes on the principles of law, of equality and humanity in the sole interests of the State), but in a full and positive sense: the State is governed according to rational principles which are intrinsic to it and which cannot be derived solely from natural or divine laws or the principles of wisdom and prudence; the State, like Nature, has its own proper rationality, even if this is of a different sort. Conversely, the art of government instead of seeking its foundation in transcendental rules, cosmological models or philosophical-moral ideals, must find the principles of its rationality in that which constitutes the specific reality of the State.

(Foucault 1979: 14)

And here, as a second example, is Foucault explaining the crucial role played by the notion of population:

[I]t was thanks to the perception of the specific problems of the population, related to the isolation of that area we call the economy, that the problem of government finally came to be thought, reflected and calculated outside of the juridical framework of sovereignty ... prior to the emergence of population, the art of government was impossible to conceive except on the model of the family and in terms of economy conceived as the management of a family; from the moment when, on the contrary, population appears as absolutely irreducible to the family, the latter becomes secondary with respect to the population, comes to appear as an element internal to population, no longer that is to say as a model, but as a segment ... [T]he family becomes an instrument rather than a model: the privileged instrument for the government of the population ... [P]opulation comes to appear above all else as the ultimate end of government, that is the welfare of the population since this end consists not in the act of governing as such but in the improvement of the condition of the population.

(Foucault 1979: 16–17)

While I am not convinced, as I said in the introduction and will say in more detail in the conclusion, that Foucault achieved with this body of work anything like what he seemed to be claiming for it, or anything like what his followers have claimed for it, I can see why it was attractive at the time and why it remains attractive. The followers were given a wonderful opportunity to insist on the differences between Foucault's approach to questions of government and those traditional approaches that worked with traditional understandings of state and sovereignty. The followers took this opportunity with both hands and have built an impressive framework for future studies (if not, I would add, a convincing one). Two examples of what this group of Foucault's followers achieved will have to suffice, one from Mitchell Dean and one from Pat O'Malley. Dean (1999: 10–16) argues that the key to understanding Foucault's governmentality analysis is to understand Foucault's break with 'the characteristic assumptions of theories of the state', a break, Dean says, which freed him to think about government in a new way, as 'the conduct of conduct', yet without severing all links with some familiar figures from the canon of social theory:

It deals with how we think about governing, with the different mentalities of government ... The notions of collective mentalities and the idea of a history of mentalities have long been used by sociologists (such as Emile Durkheim and Marcel Mauss) and by the *Annales* school of history in France ... For such thinkers, a mentality is a collective, relatively bounded unity, and is not readily examined by those who inhabit it … The idea of mentalities of government, then, emphasizes the way in which the thought involved in practices of government is collective and relatively taken for granted … the way we think about exercising authority draws upon the theories, ideas, philosophies and forms of knowledge that are part of our social and cultural products.

(Dean 1999: 16)

O'Malley, writing for a legal audience in the late 1990s, provides some useful background to the way in which governmentality analysis developed as a separate approach as well as attempting to define the term itself still further:

There is a considerable literature exploring and developing this approach … advanced primarily in recent years by British and Australian scholars. The journal *Economy and Society* has been a principal site for the development of this approach, which is frequently referred to as the "governmentality" literature. While "governmentality" refers to a particular technology of government that emerges in the eighteenth century, the term is more generally used to refer to the approach adopted in its study. The approach is characterized by two primary characteristics. The first is a stress on the dispersal of "government," that is, on the idea that government is not a preserve of "the state" but is carried out at all level and sites in societies – including the self government of individuals … The second is the deployment of an analytic stance that favors "how" questions over "why" questions. In other words it favors accounts in terms of how government of a certain kind becomes possible: in what manner it is thought up by planners, using what concepts; how it is intended to be translated into practice, using what combination of means? Only secondarily is it concerned with accounts that seek to *explain* government – in the sense of understanding the nature of government as the effect of other events.

(O'Malley 1998–9: 679, n7)

Conclusion

My focus in this chapter has been on the attractiveness of Foucault's work on power–government–society as a contribution to social and political theory, broadly understood. As well as offering a basic summary of the direction of this body of work, I have tried to make plain why it became such a force within the domain of social and political theory. In doing these two things, however, I have not attempted to hide the fact that I share with a number of other scholars considerable disquiet about the trajectory of some of the arguments Foucault put so well and helped to make so influential. In this conclusion I wish to summarise the arguments behind my doubts (for fuller versions of these arguments, see esp. Wickham 2006, 2008), though I will not let these harsher words be my final words.

I can begin my critical commentary with a point introduced earlier: that in formulating his insights on the operation of power Foucault's propositions often differed little from standard Marxist pronouncements of the day. To give just two examples, both of which fly in the face of his aforementioned caution against over-emphasing the repressive nature of power:

[I]t is in the nature of power – particularly the kind of power that operates in our society – to be repressive, and to be especially careful in repressing useless energies, the intensity of pleasures, and irregular modes of behavior.

(Foucault 1998: 9)

Panopticism is … a type of power that is applied to individuals in the form of continuous individual supervision, in the form of control, punishment, and compensation, and in the form of correction, that is, the moulding and transformation of individuals in terms of certain norms.

(Foucault 2001a: 70)

As well as being a clue to Foucault's residual Marxism, I suggest that these two snippets also provide an indication that while Foucault explicitly said that he was keen not to be seen to be a theory-for-its-own-sake type of theorist, in the sense of a priest-like figure making pronouncements from on high about the operation of power in society – 'The aim of the inquiries that will follow is to move less toward a "theory" of power than toward an "analytics" of power: that is, toward a definition of the specific domain formed by relations of power, and toward a determination of the instruments that will make possible its analysis' (Foucault 1998: 82) – he sometimes was precisely such a theorist. This tendency is most marked in his theory-driven distinction (as opposed to a distinction driven by historical evidence) between governmentality power and an older style of power built around sovereignty and law, and in his theory-driven insistence that governmentality power replaced 'outmoded' sovereignty-law power:

[A]s long as sovereignty remained the central question, as the institutions of sovereignty remained fundamental and as the exercise of power was conceived as the exercise of sovereignty, the art of government could not develop in a specific and autonomous manner.

(Foucault 1979: 15)

As David Saunders (1997: 103) puts it, in this particular essay Foucault imposes on history 'perfectly antithetical ways of exercising power' and in doing so ignores 'inconvenient' historical specificities, most notably the fact that religion had inspired over a hundred and fifty years of civil war in Europe, a bloody period which was only brought to an end by a certain combination of forces featuring sovereignty and law, a combination that was no less important in the late twentieth century, when Foucault was writing, than it was in the eighteenth century (the supposed birthing period of governmentality) or than it is in the twenty-first century (though it has to be admitted those of us writing in the early twenty-first century have the 'advantage' of working in the wake of 9/11, which made it easier to see the importance of this combination of forces, an advantage Foucault did not have).

This theory-as-pronouncements-from-on-high problem, in leading him to underestimate the importance of sovereignty and law, also led him to underestimate the on-going importance of the state. For example:

[T]he State is no more than a composite reality and a mythical abstraction whose importance is a lot more limited than any of us think. Maybe what is really important for our modern times, that is, for our actuality, is not so much the State-domination of society, but the "governmentalisation" of the State.

(Foucault 1979: 20)

Ian Hunter goes so far as to suggest that Foucault's governmentality 'theory' is a type of Kantian philosophical theory. The 'governmentality schema', Hunter argues, 'seems to have much in common with post-Kantian philosophical history in that it portrays an inappropriately objectifying reason being replaced by one less inclined to impose its cognitive will on the immanent order of things' (Hunter 1998: 246).

In making these various critical points, I am not proposing that Foucault should lose his place in the social and political theory hall of fame. He undoubtedly deserves his berth (as well as deserving what all the other inductees have won as a right: the right to be constructively criticised). I am not even suggesting that Foucault's writings on power are totally tainted by the problems I have highlighted. Certainly, many of his pronouncements about surveillance, for instance, along with the examples offered above look overblown now. The fact that the panopticon was never actually built should have alerted more readers (including me) to this at the time his main power pieces were being published, as should have the fact that the 'eye of power' arrangements of hospitals, schools, factories, and so forth (see esp. Foucault 1980: 146–65) were more a matter of architectural fashion, among other things, than they were an attempt to enhance the surveillance of subjects. But making claims that now look overblown is not much of a charge; it was the 1970s after all. I think that in this context I should dismiss that charge as trivial and concentrate instead on the fact that the second and third volumes of the History of Sexuality project (both published posthumously: Foucault 1986a, 1986b) – books in which the problem of 'theorising' stressed above is totally absent – were inspirational to Peter Brown in producing some of the most exciting and convincing work on power produced in the last thirty years (see esp. Brown 1988). This is both Foucault on power *and* Foucault at his very best: 'the author of descriptive genealogies – "grey, meticulous and patiently documentary"' (Saunders, quoting Foucault, 1997: 105–6).

Notes

1 Walter's work reminds me of the early work of Gavin Kendall, who used his training as a classicist to respectfully correct some errors in Foucault's historical treatment of the ancient world while simultaneously promoting the value of Foucault's approach to the study of power and society (see esp. Bevis, Cohen, and Kendall 1989).

2 Foucault of course was fond of saying that he was moving away from phenomenology as much as he was moving away from Marxism. I suggest that for those interested in his power–governance–society work the main break was with Marxism.

3 The following discussion of a discourse's lack of an 'inside' and lack of an 'outside' owes a considerable debt to Hunter 1984.

References

Bevis, P., M. Cohen and G. Kendall (1989) 'Archaeologizing Genealogy: Michel Foucault and the Economy of Austerity', *Economy and Society* 18:3, pp. 323–45.

Brown, P. (1988) *Power and Persuasion in Late Antiquity: Towards a Christian Empire*, Madison, WI: University of Wisconsin Press.

Brown, B. and M. Cousins (1986) 'The Linguistic Fault: The Case of Foucault's Archaeology', in M. Gane (ed.) *Towards a Critique of Foucault*, London: Routledge & Kegan Paul, pp. 33–60.

Dean, M. (1999) *Governmentality*, London: Sage.

Foucault, M. (1971) *Madness and Civilization: A History of Insanity in the Age of Reason*, trans. R. Howard, London: Tavistock/Routledge.

——(1972) *The Archaeology of Knowledge*, London: Tavistock

——(1979) 'Governmentality', *I & C*, 6, pp. 5–21.

——(1980) *Power–Knowledge*, ed. C. Gordon, New York: Pantheon.

——(1986a) *The Care of the Self*, trans. R. Hurley, New York: Pantheon.

——(1986b) *The Use of Pleasure*, trans. R. Hurley, New York: Pantheon.

——(1998) *The Will to Knowledge: The History of Sexuality*, Volume 1, trans. R. Hurley, Harmondsworth: Penguin.

——(2001a) 'Truth and Juridical Forms', in *Power*, ed. J. Faubion, trans. R. Hurley, Harmondsworth: Penguin, pp. 1–89.

——(2001b) 'Truth and Power', in *Power*, ed. J. Faubion, trans. R. Hurley, Harmondsworth: Penguin, pp. 111–33.

Gane, M. (1986) 'Introduction: Michel Foucault', in M. Gane (ed.) *Towards a Critique of Foucault*, London: Routledge & Kegan Paul.

Hindess, B. and P. Q. Hirst (1975) *Pre-capitalist Modes of Production*, London: Routledge & Kegan Paul.

——(1977) *Mode of Production and Social Formation: An Auto-critique of Pre-capitalist Modes of Production*, London: Macmillan.

Hunter, I. (1984) 'Michel Foucault: Discourse versus Language', unpublished MS, Griffith University, Brisbane.

——(1998) 'Uncivil Society: Liberal Government and the Deconfessionalisation of Politics', in M. Dean and B. Hindess (eds) *Governing Australia: Studies in Contemporary Rationalities of Government*, Cambridge: Cambridge University Press, pp. 242–64.

Kendall, G. and G. Wickham (1999) *Using Foucault's Methods*, London: Sage.

McHoul, A. and W. Grace (1992) *A Foucault Primer: Discourse, Power and the Subject*, Melbourne: Melbourne University Press.

Michel-Foucault.com website: www.michel-foucault.com/.

O'Malley, P. (1998–9) 'Imagining Insurance: Risk, Thrift and Industrial Life Insurance in Britain', *Connecticut Insurance Law Journal*, 5:2, pp. 676–705.

Rose, N. (1984) 'The Formation of the Psychology of the Individual in England 1870–1939', unpublished PhD thesis, University of London.

Saunders, D. (1997) *Anti-lawyers: Religion and the Critics of Law and State*, London: Routledge.

Tribe, K. (2009) 'The Political Economy of Modernity: Foucault's Collège de France Lectures of 1978 and 1979', *Economy & Society*, 38:4, pp. 679–98.

Walter, R. (2008a) 'Governmentality Accounts of the Economy: A Liberal Bias?', *Economy & Society*, 37:1, pp. 94–114.

——(2008b) 'Reconciling Foucault and Skinner on the State: The Primacy of Politics?', *History of the Human Sciences*, 21:3, pp. 94–114.

Wickham, G. (2002) 'Foucault and Law', in M. Travers. and R. Banakar (eds) *Introduction to Law and Social Theory*, Oxford: Hart, pp. 249–65.

——(2006) 'Foucault, Law and Power: A Reassessment', *Journal of Law and Society*, 23:4, pp. 596–614.

——(2008) 'The Social Must Be Limited: Some Problems With Foucault's Approach to Modern Positive Power', *Journal of Sociology*, 44:1, pp. 29–44.

Accidental Conditions

The Social Consequences of Poststructuralist Philosophy

Thomas Docherty

Much of the most invigorating social theory in recent times has its origins in the ostensibly unpromising field of literary criticism. The advent of structuralist and then poststructuralist work in literary theory provoked what became known as the 'theory wars' in university literature departments. Among literary theorists, one of the most abiding arguments in recent decades was that described by Paul de Man in his 'The Resistance to Theory' paper, originally written in 1982. Surprisingly, that paper argues that the greatest resistance to theory comes not from the avowed opponents of theoretical criticism (usually caricatured as 'common-sense empiricists'), but rather from within theory itself. Key to the logic of the piece is a consideration of the vexing question of linguistic reference: that is, the question of how it is that linguistic *signs* map on to the non-linguistic *material* of history and reality. That question, at first glance one that is of purely literary interest, actually contains a major theoretical problem for social and political theory. Here is what de Man writes:

> It would be unfortunate, for example, to confuse the materiality of the signifier with the materiality of what it signifies. This may seem obvious enough on the level of light and sound, but it is less so with regard to the general phenomenality of space, time or especially the self; no one in his right mind will try to grow grapes by the luminosity of the word 'day,' but it is very difficult not to conceive the pattern of one's past and future existence as in accordance with temporal and spatial schemes that belong to fictional narratives and not to the world. This does not mean that fictional narratives are not part of the world and of reality; their impact upon the world may be all too strong for comfort. What we call ideology is precisely the confusion of linguistic with natural reality, of reference with phenomenalism.
> *(de Man 1986: 11)*

This – a problem of linguistic reference that becomes the problem of ideology – is a major issue for poststructuralist philosophy. In what follows, I shall show how it also informs social theory.

For many on the political left, poststructuralism has little to offer social theory, and it has much less to yield that will be of use for socio-cultural practice. In one fairly prevalent view, poststructuralist thought, specifically in the form of its deconstructive turn, leads to a crippling political indecisiveness and consequent quietist inaction. The logic here is straightforward, if based on a slight caricature of Derrida's practices of deconstruction. At the core of deconstruction is a realization that all our thinking is organized around conceptual oppositions: to make meaning at all, we need a structural opposition between (for examples) up and down, left and right, inside and outside, male and female, work and leisure, and so on. The logic of deconstruction is that the hierarchy that governs the opposition (and that would propose one polarity of the opposition as normative, against a deviant or abnormal secondary term) becomes, in Derrida's preferred term, 'undecidable'. This may be best explained by an example, one that is by now well-rehearsed in the literature.

Consider how we make sense of our society in terms of gender. For the most part, we operate as we do and live as we do thanks to (among many other structural and conceptual oppositions) a meaningful opposition between male and female. There is nothing 'essential' about this opposition: rather, it is simply one way that we have of making sense of our world as we do. It is useful in that it helps us to organize whatever socio-sexual arrangements we find congenial, for example; and, in this way, sexual activity can become meaningfully regulated for us. Now, for whatever reason (and, as far as deconstruction is concerned, the reason need not be clarified), the society that we currently live in and through proposes a hierarchical organization of that opposition, such that the male pole is often or usually proposed as normative, and the female is seen as derivative or secondary, as if 'female' meant 'not quite fully male'. We usually call this organization either 'sexism' or 'masculinism'. Deconstruction argues that the opposition, its intrinsic alleged hierarchy, and (perhaps most significantly) its consequential value-system (in this case, a system based on masculinism) is not stable, but rather 'undecidable'.

In the sexist logic and value-system described above, we ask how we would define 'male'; and, typically, the answer comes back along the lines of 'in possession of a phallus'. In this, 'female' is defined by absence or lack, specifically the lack of a phallus 'possessed' by the male. Deconstruction argues, however, that, in order to define the male in the first place, we have clearly had to have recourse, for comparison and contrast, to some entity that *lacks* the phallus: the *presence* of the phallus in the male is only meaningful – indeed only conceptually perceptible – once we are aware of its *absence* elsewhere. If no creature was marked by the absence of the phallus, then we could not use the phallus as a marker of gender, and we would thus still not be able to identify one entity as 'male'. Thus, says deconstruction, it turns out that if woman is defined by her *lack* (the alleged absence of the phallus), then man, paradoxically, is defined by *lack to the second degree*, because in order to define itself, the male turns out to be lacking its opposite (woman), which is itself defined by lack (the absence of the phallus). Far from the female being an incomplete male, the male, it turns out, is but a special case of the female – provided we are defining these in terms of lack, in terms of the presence or absence of the phallus.

The alleged hierarchy, therefore, in which male is a central norm and woman but a special case of maleness (the male who supposedly lacks the phallus), is reversed. We might be inclined to call this answer to sexism something like 'feminism'. *However* – and here is the problem with deconstruction and, indeed, all poststructuralist thought, for those on the political left – we still have a structural opposition (this time between, say, 'new man' and 'emancipated woman' or some such); and that opposition, as an opposition that governs our concept of gender, is available for further deconstruction and indeed *must* in turn be deconstructed. In this sense, with an analysis that is potentially interminable, we reach a position where the hierarchical organization between male and female remains, in the end, *radically undecidable*. This is not much use for those who would wish to change actual gender relations, say, or the property relations on which capitalism is built (worker against owner of the means of production, say); nor does it help those who would wish to legitimize the revolutionary potential of the claim that the proletariat should overthrow the ruling class.

It is unsurprising, then, that many on the political left have construed poststructuralism as being, at best, a mode of thought that is in conformity with liberal bourgeois idealism or, at worst, a practice that is complicit with, even encouraging of, a quietist nihilism that has given the field of practice over to dangerous right-wing tendencies. The argument would be that poststructuralist logic takes us ever further away from material reality or history and into the realm of signs; and, indeed, this was explicitly Edward Said's argument when he favoured the work of Foucault over that of Derrida, seeing deconstruction as something that took us deep into the text, certainly, but preferring Foucauldian analysis as something that took us deep into textuality but also brought us back to the realm of reference again (Said 1984: 183). In what follows here, I shall attempt to nuance this concern about poststructuralism's legacy for social theory more fully, and to re-assert the power of poststructuralist thinking for a progressive and emancipatory social theory.

First, I shall explore the issue of the relation between, on one hand, linguistic and conceptual *form* (the ways in which we literally formulate thought), and, on the other hand, the brutal historical realities of *force* (as something that is not amenable to straightforward formalization). Second, I shall consider the relations of force to matters of desire, including the desire for social change; and here, the work of Deleuze will be of importance. Finally, I will examine how a very specific *play of forces* can shape history. The play of forces I have in mind here is that which we usually associate with love, itself an abiding issue in social theory and philosophy at least since Plato's *Symposium* and *Republic*, and one that has been revived as a major concern in the thought of Badiou.

The Origins of the Problem: Force

In what we should regard as a key founding document of poststructuralism, the review essay 'Force and Signification', Derrida realizes that the great strength – and also the great limitation – of the prevailing structuralist thought that emerged in the late 1950s is its ability to deal with matters of *form*. Structuralism, with its ability to consider all things under the terms of *sign* and *signification*, is able to give a full understanding of what de Man, in the passage I quoted at the start of this piece, would come to call 'linguistic reality'. Yet, Derrida already finds, in this 1963 piece, that structuralism *as such* is complicit with ideology; and this is all the more true precisely at those moments when it believes it is actually unmasking ideology in the name of critique, because it confounds the understanding of form or of linguistic reality with the understanding of phenomena themselves. As he puts it in his review-essay, '*Form* fascinates when one no longer has the force to understand force from within itself. That is, to create. This is why literary criticism is structuralist in every age, in its essence and destiny' (Derrida 1978: 4–5). In short, structuralism triumphs when one cannot deal with *force*, or when one reduces force to signification. 'Force' here is, as it were, Derrida's term for phenomenalism or for the material reality of history; and the key theoretical issue that is relevant to our present concern is the issue of *representation*.

The problem with structuralism, in these terms, is that it reduces the fact of history to the merest 'signs of history', shifting attention from ontology to epistemology as it were (McHale 1987: 10–11); and thereby, it evacuates history of its material content. The argument becomes focused on re-presentations of history, and not on the factual presence of historical events in their specificity. This, with its attention to the relation between presence and representation, is akin to the kind of argument advanced much earlier in the last century by Walter Benjamin in his much-cited 'Work of Art in the Age of Mechanical Reproduction' essay. There, Benjamin indicates that, prior to the age of mechanical reproduction, the work of art is characterized by an aura, the 'unique phenomenon of a distance' (Benjamin 1973: 224) given to it by its absolute singularity (its absolute 'otherness' from us), its location at the nexus of a specific play of forces that made the production of the artifact not only possible but also somehow necessary. When we consider such a work of art, what we become aware of is the struggle – the tensed play of forces, if you will – that inhabits and informs or shapes the work, the play of tensions that concretize or realize themselves in the work. The work of art is, as it were, the momentary arrest of those forces, their arrangement into a form, or their illusory 'freezing' into a material reality a 'now-time' or *Jetztzeit*, as Benjamin has it (Benjamin 1973: 263, 265; Agamben 2005: 2 and *passim*).

By contrast, in the age of mechanical reproduction, where we have multiple copies of the work, we lose the specificity of that uniqueness, the specificity occasioned by our realization of the work's absolute alterity or the fact that it does not care about our conscious perception of it; and instead we have what can be described as the purely *aesthetic* form of the work, a *form* devoid of the *content* that is historical struggle, or force. When the work is not designed primarily to be *available* to our consciousness, then, paradoxically, its value becomes *determined* by our consciousness; and we call this 'aesthetics'. Attention is diverted away from the forces that shape material history, and instead directed inwards to the 'linguistic' or signifying shaping of the work 'in itself', as it were. For Benjamin – as later for Derrida – the real task of the critic is to find a way to re-awaken the force of that singularity in all its telling force, to 'understand force from within itself'.

This, though it may sound abstruse, has a profound contemporary relevance. Recent years have witnessed the rise of a managerialist class in most of the advanced economies, which now organize themselves according to the logic of what Adorno and Horkheimer called a culture 'brought within the sphere of administration' (Adorno and Horkheimer 1974: 131), or, as it is more commonly known, the 'administered society'. Less philosophically, it is now a commonplace that the political class no longer *represent* people, but rather *manage* them; and, as for politics, so also for all aspects of social life. We are all managers now, either managing other people or managing ourselves according to bureaucratically established norms and expectations, sometimes called 'projects', 'targets', 'personal goals', or 'outcomes'. For the ascendant managerialist class, historical specifics matter little: instead of an attention to the specific details or content of any problem or issue, they inspect instead the form of dealing with it, or matters of process. In project management, it matters little what the project actually is ('running the economy', as a project, becomes functionally equivalent to 'organizing the school-run'): all that matters is the process by which we arrive at the conclusion whereby we show that we have, in the cliché, planned the work and worked the plan (we have 'run the economy', say – well or badly, it matters not).

In this state of affairs, we essentially establish two orders of being. The first of these is that which we might call material historical reality (running the economy well or badly), while the second is the level at which we *represent* that reality (the bald fact of running the economy, tables and spreadsheet figures to hand). Increasingly, the representation has supplanted the original, such that material historical realities now lead a rather clandestine existence, sometimes even becoming invisible, as if wished or magicked away. This is easily exemplified by the recent world financial crisis, in which the representation of wealth and profit in spreadsheets supplanted the actual debt and poverty that the representation had occluded. Or, in an equally chilling example, we can have inquiry after inquiry into the Iraq War, all of which turn out to be inquiries into the procedures that are followed to arrive at and manage decisions – and thus we evacuate our inquiry of any matters pertaining to the actual *content* of those decisions, instead merely confirming that the *forms* by which decisions were made were adhered to. This is what we can call fantasy politics: the politics of 'I wish it so, therefore it is so.' In crude terms, it is what journalists refer to as the triumph of spin over substance; but, as fantasy politics, it is much more dangerous than just 'spinning' the news, for, as in other fantasies, real hurts – real forces – can be ignored.

It is worth remembering what is at stake in this: for Benjamin, such a thinking is complicit with an ideology of fascism. As he put it, 'The masses have a right to change property relations', but 'Fascism sees its salvation in giving these masses not their right, but instead a chance to express themselves' (Benjamin 1973: 243). For Benjamin, writing in the shadow of the 1929 Crash and the rise of a European right-wing scenting power, this aestheticisation of the political leads inexorably to war and to fascism; and his response is that we must politicize aesthetics. For poststructuralist thinking, the tendency is much the same: the ignoring of content under the signs of form leads to a situation where we have two separate realms, the world of material force, where people suffer pain; and the world of the forms of these things – which we usually call 'government'.

Of Desire, Accident, and Death

Seeing representation as an issue, some philosophers and commentators look for a way of addressing, as directly as possible and without the fall into mere signification, something that is profoundly historical; and they find it in death. For Baudrillard, for example, death was a kind of liminal point that calls into question the very possibility of 'symbolic exchange' (Baudrillard 1976: *passim*). For many, it is in a profound sense 'unthinkable' in that it is structurally impossible to re-present one's own death, if we construe representation as something that is dependent upon the priority of something really occurring, something 'present': one would need to survive one's own death in order to represent it, and, by definition, that is impossible. There are large consequences of this fact.

The first of these is that death becomes linked to a kind of radical and absolute 'singularity', to something that is unamenable to representation and that therefore falls outwith the structural impasse given to us by the 'ideological' thinking that I outlined above. As Derrida has it:

> Death is very much that which nobody else can undergo or confront in my place. My irreplaceability is therefore conferred, delivered, "given," one can say, by death … It is from the site of death as the place of my irreplaceability, that is, of my singularity, that I feel called to responsibility. In this sense only a mortal can be responsible.
>
> *(Derrida 1995: 41)*

Death, thus, becomes a theoretical test-case for our attempt to come to grips with the absolute singularity of the historical event. If history can be defined as that which eschews repetition (Blumenberg 1983: 596), then death becomes its central element. Yet, as Derrida has indicated, with this singularity comes the call for an ethical responsibility. Thus, in the first place, death as that which is inevitable becomes aligned with a force of history that can be described, as in ancient classical tragedy, as conditioned by *Ananke*, necessity. Yet also, in the second place, death calls us forth to answer the fundamental question governing all social theory and social practice, 'What shall I do?' or 'How shall I live?' The logic of poststructuralism, remember, has made this a major problem, given that it has rendered us into the realm of the undecidable.

In the face of this, Deleuze offer us a series of major possible moves. The subscription to history-as-necessity is complicit with the prioritization of the formal structures of history over the specifics of the material content: events. For Deleuze, the event is absolutely central. In brief, the major turn that he gives to poststructuralist thinking is one that re-establishes the centrality of the event, in all its evanescence, to any radical thinking. Yet this is not the material event as we usually think it; that is, it is not a definite something that is occasioned or brought about in a world of supposed 'exteriority' by an 'interiority' of consciousness that allegedly determines material conditions in the world. The world 'as such' does not exist, in fact: rather, there are only *arrangements of forces* that are episodic, radically singular, and productive of desire.

History as it is lived does not feel like the living out of a formal story, the fulfilling of a pattern. For Deleuze, this fact is important: although he is very aware of Derrida and other philosophers who find their sources in Hegel, Husserl and Heidegger, Deleuze works instead through an ontology derived largely from Bergson and Spinoza. From Bergson, what he takes as central to his thought is the importance of *time* and of *movement*. Considering Bergson's notion of duration, however, he already gives it his own inflection, arguing that duration 'is a becoming that endures, a change that is substance itself' (Deleuze 1988a: 37) In Spinoza, he finds a very specific sense of *difference* and of *singularity*. In this, Deleuze indicates the 'scandal' of Spinoza as the scandal that essentially dismisses any notion of a world of duality: 'According to the *Ethics* … what is an action in the mind is necessarily an action in the body as well, and what is a passion in the body is necessarily a passion in the mind. There is no primacy of one series over the other' (Deleuze 1988b: 18). Deleuze's ontology is not a philosophy of being but rather a philosophy of becoming and, indeed, a philosophy of *accidental becoming*. This, and specifically the role of the accidental, is of lasting importance in social theory.

There are overlaps with deconstruction. Deconstruction and associated forms of poststructuralist thought base themselves on a notion of *difference*, deriving largely from the linguistics of Saussure. Saussure famously argued that language is a system of differences without positive terms: meaning is produced through differential structures. Thus, we see a structuralist world based on binary oppositions; and, in Derrida, we move from the restricted economy of this simple opposition to a generalized economy of difference as such. However, in all these cases, there remains a notion of difference *as opposed to* identity: in short, within difference, there lurks a remnant of *substantive identity* as such. Deleuze takes this in another and contrary direction.

In Spinoza, he finds a notion of what we might call absolute or primary difference: not difference that defines itself in opposition to something else, something 'self-same' or self-identical; but difference, rather, as an absolute condition of the very possibility of identity, so to speak. Spinoza begins his *Ethics* with a meditation on the substantiality of God; and his case is that God is at once infinite (and thus containing an infinity of possible attributes) while at the same time unique (and thus not amenable to re-presentation): 'God is both unique and absolute' (Hardt 1993: 61). For Deleuze, this offers a consistency with his reading of time and movement in Bergson, for it offers a version of substance that is *intrinsically different*: not 'different from' something else, for there is no something else (God is infinite), and not differing from itself in time (God is one thing). Rather, this is pure difference as constitutive of the substance of being.

The result, for Deleuze, once the theological issue is removed from the equation, is that one is never in a state of being (a being that would allow me to give an account of 'my identity'), but only becoming (in which 'I' never quite coincide with myself, since my temporal condition precludes any such possibility, and since the 'I' is a product of the movement or arrangement of forces). Being would equate with death, and is negative; becoming is equivalent to living and is affirmative, joyful.

This means, though, that all things are necessarily always in flux. In fact, it is even more radical than that: anything that we might want to identify as a specific 'somewhat' (or some 'thing') is nothing more than a pure instantiation of a play of forces that makes the somewhat as it 'is', an interruption in the otherwise continuous flow of becomings; yet more, the perceiver of this 'somewhat' is herself or himself but an accident of the play of forces that phenomenologically brings the perceiver into line, however momentarily, with the perceived. To perceive is momentarily to arrest the flow of becomings, the play of forces that constitutes history, as it were. Within this, therefore, any 'event' – such as the event of perception – is itself an 'accidental condition' of history.

There is, thus, no 'I' other than the play of forces that allows me, at whatever moment, to pretend to arrest the flow of becoming. This has a massive effect on the notion of agency, and beyond that, of freedom. This is a way of describing how Deleuze thinks of 'events'. At one level, events are what constitute history; but, according to Deleuze, we must be careful to distinguish events from spectacle. The event takes place in what he thinks of as '*le temps mort*':

> ... the event is inseparable from dead time. It's not even that there is dead time before and after the event, rather that dead time is in the event, for example the instant of the most brutal accident confounds itself with the immensity of empty time in which you see it arriving, as a spectator of that which has not yet happened, in a long suspense. ... Groethuysen said that every event was, as it were, in the time when nothing happens.
>
> *(Deleuze 1990: 218; my translation)*

Now, the event, therefore, is not something that is determined or even predetermined by a consciousness; rather, the emergence of the consciousness is that which comes about precisely as a result of the encounter that *is* the event itself, the play of forces that constitutes this 'dead time', a time that is taken out of formal narrative but that allows for the constitution of a subject.

In many other philosophies or social theories, especially those based either upon forms of psychoanalysis or upon forms of 'identity-politics', the subject is often typically characterized and described by her or his desire. For Deleuze, such desire is not a matter of exerting a will upon exteriority, much less a matter of 'choice', either consumerist or existentialist – in short, the desire does not 'bring something about'. Again, the desire is that which is produced through the encounter that, in the first place, is constitutive of both subject and object, and constitutive of them *as* subject and object. What Deleuze is trying to do is to find a way of addressing movement as the fundamental form of ontology, but ontology considered as the conditions of our becoming rather than as being.

The result is the production of what we can call the accidental conditions of consciousness or of desire. It is important to note that we are not here talking of desire as a set of 'wants' or 'choices' based on lack or need or wish. Rather, this desire is a way of describing the product of force. The play of forces or the arrangement of forces that constitutes becomings-in-time is something that is itself in constant flux; and it thus produces desire simply as the condition of producing yet more arrangements, more becoming. In this way, desire can be thought of as a pure 'affirmation', the affirming of positive becoming; and the significance of this is that it flies directly in the face of most radical 'critical' thinking that derives from Hegel or from any notion of criticism as negation. Desire, here, is what philosophy – and, by extension, radical social theory – should be about: it is about the production of more becoming, more *concepts*. This – the 'production of concepts' – is indeed, Deleuze's answer to the great question, 'What is philosophy?' (Deleuze and Guattari 1991: 8)

It will be seen, though, that the affirmation that is desire nonetheless leaves us with some practical difficulties. If there is no I determining of exteriority, then it follows that we have a difficulty with the very idea of conventional historical agency. Further, if we have such a difficulty, then we have a corollary problem concerning freedom. Deleuze and Badiou (most especially this latter) have some ways of considering this that are helpful; and, interestingly, some of these answers return us to some foundations of poststructuralist philosophy.

Accident and the Encounter that is Love

The question of agency, and with it the attendant issue of human freedom, is an abiding concern for all social theory. If we put together poststructuralism's legacy, in which we can think of ideology as a problem concerning the confounding of linguistic with phenomenal orders of being (what I called 'fantasy politics' above) with the emergence of a desire that is not based in the negating power of an individuated human consciousness (Deleuze's implicit critique of individualism), then we reach, in a very different inflection, a concern expressed by Marx. In his eleventh thesis on Feuerbach, Marx famously argued that 'Until now, the philosophers have only interpreted the world. The point, however, is to change it' (Marx 1976: 65). Yet he also knew that such change was not a matter easily brought about, for in *The Eighteenth Brumaire*, just five years later, he points out:

> Men make their own history, but they do not make it just as they please; they do not make it under circumstances chosen by themselves, but under circumstances directly encountered and inherited from the past. The tradition of all the generations of the dead weighs like a nightmare on the brain of the living.
>
> *(Marx 1978: 9)*

In this, he is actually rather close to Deleuze, except that Marx, working still within Hegelian dialectic and valuing therein the power of critical negation, believes that change can be 'chosen', as it were. For Deleuze, taking seriously the realization that history, material history, is 'event', we cannot stand aside from the flow of history and make such choices: 'we' – the very idea that there is a communal 'we' in the first place – is but an accident of flows and arrangements of forces.

History becomes what it really is: encounter, encounters that produce subjects, however fleeting, and that enable further encounters through the fact of desire, now better construed simply as ongoing Bergsonian motion. In this final section, we should consider what is at stake in the issue of the encounter, and try to discover what remains of agency or freedom after these recent philosophical turns.

In recent times, Badiou has placed considerable emphasis on the question of the encounter. Indeed, he places the *amorous* encounter, along with a philosophy of number, at the centre of his philosophy. Deriving from set theory, Badiou's mathematics argues that there is no grounding or foundational 'one' from which we can establish ordinal or cardinal amplitude or difference; rather, difference is again basic, for set theory shows that 'There is no "one"'; rather, there are multiples 'and every multiple is itself a "multiple of multiples"' (Badiou 1988: 37). In Badiou, any 'singularity' approximates to Deleuzian 'substance', and specifically the substance of an encounter. Where, for Derrida, the question of singularity emerges with a contemplation of death, for Badiou (and for Deleuze) singularity emerges from the encounter we call love.

To explore this, let us return to the problem given to us by poststructuralism: the problem of reference. This is also a problem regarding truth, it should now be clear. In many cases, we test the truth-claim of a linguistic proposition by measuring it against some non-linguistic reality: if I say 'it is raining', then I can test the truth of my statement by feeling the rain on my skin when I step outdoors. What happens if you do not believe me? In this case, truth is conditioned by an ethical demand: while avoiding coercion and while remaining purely disinterested (i.e. wanting only to test the claim), I must try to persuade you. In most existing philosophies or social practices, what this amounts to is the erection of a philosophy of identity, of identity-politics: 'you' must be 'I', in that you must see things as I see them. You must identify your own statement with mine (we call it agreement); and thus you and I are the same, identical, equal.

Behind this, there lurks a fallacious notion of an intrinsic or possible 'equality' among the participants in a dialogue. It is fallacious because it presupposes the division of the world into interiority (my feeling or opinion) and exteriority (the rain). It is misleading also because it is based upon the idea that difference can be resolved into sameness or identity, that difference is not 'really' difference but simply two variant representations of an underlying sameness. It is false because it believes that two different views can be one; false in terms of equality because it believes that it can occlude differences of power in the arrangement of forces between you and me through something called agreement or consensus.

Against this, let us simply consider the encounter in a more neutral fashion. Let us tie it certainly to truth; but, now, following Deleuze, we can have truth not as something epistemological to be tested by what will turn out inevitably to be an ideological claim for verification by assenting to an alleged real. Rather, let us present truth as the eruption of an event. Further, let us consider the event that is the encounter; and let us characterize that encounter with desire's ethical variant, love.

Badiou rejects the notion that love is a fusion of different entities. Against the kind of claim that suggests that love is a coupling (a two-becomes-one) that can form the basis of the social, Badiou writes instead that 'Love is not that which, from a Two supposedly given structurally, makes the One of an ecstasy ... Love is not the deposition of the Same on the altar of the Other ... love is not even the experience of the other' (Badiou 1992: 255–6; my translation). Instead, Badiou sees love as an experiencing of the world, by the world: it is not simply the experiencing by a pre-existing 'One', distinguished from other 'one's, of some equally pre-existing 'Other'. Love, in this encounter, becomes the production of truth; but truth as an event, as a something-that-happens, and thus as historical fact.

For Badiou, truth is intimately tied to events. A truth is not a validated knowledge-claim, as it were, for 'knowledge-claims' presuppose the divisibility of events into consciousness and exteriority. A truth, for Badiou, is something that happens, an irruption into the existing order of things. In Marxist terms, Badiou's truth is a changing of the world instead of a mere knowing or interpreting it.

He turns to the amorous encounter, that shocking changing of the world that we can experience and that shocks us into truth. The argument goes as follows:

1. Assume two positions of experience (Badiou calls them 'male' and 'female', but stresses that this has no biological or essentialist overtones);
2. Recognize that these two positions, insofar as they cannot be identical with each other, are in fact radically disjunctive with respect to each other (they are what Lyotard might have called incommensurables);
3. Now realize that this disjunction cannot be the object of a knowledge for either of the two positions, for, to assume such a knowledge is to assume a third position outside of the encounter itself. It is also to assume an identity between that third position and either the male or the female and, by definition, that would be a modification of the male or female position in the first place. In any case, finally
4. There is no third position in the encounter. This final point is crucial for Badiou's purpose, for, given the lack of such a 'transcendent' or third position, it is impossible to *know* that there are two positions in the first place; rather, the encounter in question is not at all the object of a *knowledge* at all. Instead, it is an *event*. We move from love as epistemology (and all that it entails: the whole idea of criticism as taste, or as preference for this over that), to criticism as ontology.

Now, Badiou also claims that truth must be 'transpositional'; that is, not simply dependent upon point-of-view. How can truth – the truth of this love, say – be transpositional, given the absolute and radical disjunction of man/woman? The usual answer is to claim that there is a masculine science (or knowledge) and a feminine one; or, more fundamentally for social theory, that there is a bourgeois science and a revolutionary science. Such a view will always resolve itself into the dialectic whereby difference is reduced to identity, for we will have to adjudicate between competing truth-claims; and, in this, we will always have a situation whereby one consciousness (or individual) exerts its authority over another, claiming not only truth but also a greater legitimacy than the individual who 'loses the argument'. Instead of such a neo-Hegelian master/slave scenario, Badiou begins from his paradox: truth is transpositional, and yet there remains a radical disjunction between positions *within* this truth. Love, he claims, is the arrangement in which this paradox is treated: love does not rid us of the paradox, but gives it to us as an event that must be engaged with.

Conclusion

The legacy of poststructuralist thought, especially in the hands of late Derrida, Deleuze, and Badiou, is one where we must review our relation to knowledge, to ideology and, perhaps above all, to democracy. Democracy as we usually consider it is based on a struggle, between competing 'opinions'; but that struggle occludes the deeper struggle between an alleged world of exteriority and that of a supposed interiority. Any such arrangement is condemned to live in the fantasy of ideology. Against this, say these thinkers, we have a duty to explore multiplicity, radical becoming, and the accidental conditions or truths of love.

References

Adorno, Theodor, and Horkheimer, Max, 1974: *Dialectic of Enlightenment* (trans. John Cumming; London: Verso).

Agamben, Giorgio, 2005: *The Time that Remains* (trans Patricia Dailey; Stanford, CA: Stanford University Press).

Badiou, Alain, 1988: *L'Etre et l'événement* (Paris: Seuil).

——, 1992: *Conditions* (Paris: Seuil).

Baudrillard, Jean, 1976: *L'Echange symbolique et la mort* (Paris: Gallimard).

Benjamin, Walter, 1973: *Illuminations* (London: Fontana).

Blumenberg, Hans, 1983: *The Legitimacy of the Modern Age* (trans. Robert M. Wallace; Cambridge, MA: MIT Press).

Deleuze, Gilles, 1988a: *Bergsonism* (trans. Hugh Tomlinson and Barbara Habberjam; New York: Zone Books).

——, 1988b: *Spinoza: Practical Philosophy* (trans. Robert Hurley; San Francisco, CA: City Lights Books).

——, 1990: *Pourparlers* (Paris: Editions de minuit).

Deleuze, Gilles and Guattari, Félix, 1991: *Qu'est-ce que la philosophie?* (Paris: Editions de minuit).

Derrida, Jacques, 1978: *Writing and Difference* (trans. Alan Bass; London: Routledge).

——, 1995: *The Gift of Death* (trans. David Wills; Chicago, IL, and London: University of Chicago Press).

Hardt, Michael, 1993: *Gilles Deleuze: An Apprenticeship in Philosophy* (London: UCL Press).

McHale, Brian, 1987: *Postmodernist Fiction* (London: Methuen).

de Man, Paul, 1986: *The Resistance to Theory* (Manchester: Manchester University Press).

Marx, Karl, 1976: 'Theses on Feuerbach', in Frederick Engels, *Ludwig Feuerbach and the End of Classical German Philosophy* (Peking: Foreign Languages Press).

——, 1978: *The Eighteenth Brumaire of Louis Bonaparte* (Peking: Foreign Languages Press).

Said, Edward, 1984: *The World, the Text, and the Critic* (London: Faber & Faber).

Lacanian Theory

Ideology, Enjoyment, and the Spirits of Capitalism

Yannis Stavrakakis

Every attempt to use psychoanalytic categories and logics in social and political theorization and analysis inevitably raises the spectre of psychological reductionism. Yet, already from the early days of the psychoanalytic movement, every new realization of the limits of mainstream socio-political explanations – especially of the rationalistic and deterministic tendecies implicit in them – shifted attention to the insights psychoanalysis could offer. It was to psychoanalysis the Frankfurt School turned in order to account for the unexpected lure of Nazi ideology and the 'failure' of the Enlightenment project it signalled. Likewise, in the 1960s, it was to psychoanalysis that Louis Althusser turned in order to grasp the role of ideology in producing docile social subjects and in limiting the scope of resistance. The Lacanian Left, an expanding group of critical theorists and philosophers appreciative of the work of the French psychoanalyst Jacques Lacan and determined to explore its numerous socio-political implications, is today shaping this orientation with a dynamism similar to that of the Freudian Left,[1] but with very different preoccupations and priorities.

At the forefront of this new trend in social and political theory, Slavoj Žižek has put forward what he often describes as an *explosive combination of Lacanian psychoanalysis and Marxist tradition* in order to question the very presuppositions of the circuit of capital. For his part, Alain Badiou has re-appropriated Lacan in his radical *ethics of the event*. Pointing out that 'Lacanian theory contributes decisive tools to the formulation of a theory of hegemony', Ernesto Laclau and Chantal Mouffe have included Lacanian psychoanalysis in the list of contemporary theoretical currents necessary 'for understanding the widening of social struggles characteristic of the present stage of democratic politics, and for formulating a new vision for the Left in terms of radical and plural democracy' (Laclau and Mouffe 2001 [1985]: xi). Obviously, Lacanian theory is not used in the same way by all these theorists and philosophers. Nor is politics and the Left understood by all of them in an identical fashion. Yet the mere possibility of formulating these different positions clearly presupposes the slow emergence of a new theoretico-political horizon: this broad horizon is what I have called the 'Lacanian Left'.[2]

This category is proposed not as an exclusive or restrictive categorization, but as a signifier capable of drawing our attention to the emergence of a distinct field of theoretical and political interventions seriously exploring the relevance of Lacan's work for the critique of sedimented social processes and contemporary hegemonic orders. At the epicentre of this emerging field one would locate the enthusiastic, if increasingly idiosyncratic, endorsement of Lacan by Žižek; next to him, one finds the Lacan-inspired insights of Laclau and Mouffe; at the periphery – negotiating a delicate balancing act between the outside and the inside of the field, often functioning as its intimate 'others' or adversaries – one would have to locate the critical engagement of thinkers like Cornelius Castoriadis and Judith Butler. Drawing on the work of such theorists – especially Žižek and Laclau – I will try, in this short text, to familarize the reader with the most basic Lacanian logics and conceptual innovations and to briefly sketch some of their implications for social and political theory and the analysis of culture, as well as for reflecting on the cultural, political, and ethical dimensions of the current economic crisis.

Lacan emerges, for the first time, as a distinct post-Freudian theorist, in the 1930s and 1940s, with his work on the image and the 'mirror stage' as foundational aspects of both subjective self-recognition and alienation: identifying with an external image introduces the prospect of a stable identity for the newborn, but the irreducible externality of this image entails the cost of an unavoidable alienation. Registering the linguistic and cultural turns in the social sciences, Lacanian theory will become, in the 1950s and 1960s, an integral part of the structuralist revolution, formulating a new, anti-humanist understanding of subjectivity, now focusing on language and culture as the terrains in which identity is simultaneously constructed and negated, formulated and alienated. Yet, Lacan's theoretical boldness will allow him to successively question, throughout his teaching but especially in its final part, the all-encompassing role of both *Imaginary* and *Symbolic* representation; hence his insistence on the importance of what he calls *the Real*, of a radically alienating and inaccessible fullness beyond-representation, in accounting for the complex dialectic between symbolic and affect, language and enjoyment, that sustains and/or dislocates social and political identifications, cultural dynamics, ethical and economic orders. It is precisely these aspects of Lacan's work that are today highlighted and further developed by the Lacanian Left. Not least because they allow a non-reductionist and thoroughly illuminating confluence between psychoanalysis and socio-political theory.

From Individual to Subject, from Subject to Other, from Wholeness to Lack

The very different but equally fascinating journeys of the Freudian and the Lacanian Left would not make sense and would never have happened if the individual and the social were autonomous, self-sufficient realms. Indeed, the fact that they actually took place seems to corroborate the observation of a great sociologist, Norbert Elias, that categories like 'individual' and 'society' do not refer to *a priori* different objects 'existing separately', but rather to 'different yet inseparable' sides of the same object, 'of the same human beings' (Elias 1983 [1968]: 228–9); their 'autonomization' can only be the result of a contingent process of historical – and/or intellectual – construction and sedimentation and not of any kind of analytical or empirical necessity. In a similar vein, in his famous *Rome Discourse* (1952), referring to the relation between psychoanalysis and history and to his use of historical concepts and examples in the illumination of clinical problems and challenges, Lacan denies the need for the slightest conceptual displacement, 'translation', or adaptation: there is no need to carry these remarks into the analytic domain 'since they are there already' (Lacan 1977 [1966]: 52). It is, thus, far from surprising that as we enter his highly sophisticated work of the 1960s and 1970s, the distinction between individual and collective itself becomes the object of a relentless deconstruction. From a Lacanian point of view, such a distinction *does not exist*; it cannot claim any validity beyond its artificial elevation within Enlightenment's self-understanding in scientific and political discourse. It is not a coincidence, then, that Lacan's major conceptual innovations are always articulated at the threshold between individual and collective, subjective and objective. Categories such as the *real*, the *symbolic* and the *imaginary* are neither individual nor collective. They are both or, rather, they are located beyond such conventional distinctions.

This is, after all, the paradox revealed in the psychoanalytic clinic, the major source of inspiration for psychoanalytic theory. The clinic is not about an extra-social encounter, that between analyst and analysand conceived as pre-constituted individual, if not solipsistic, entities or personalities. On the contrary, the analytic relationship itself is made possible through the mediating role of social institutions such as discourse and language, without which no social bond can be established. The symbolic universe of civilization and culture provides the terrain within which the analytic relation – the so-called 'talking cure' – acquires its (inter-subjective) meaning and from which it draws its material. No wonder, then, that an 'individual' symptom – if the formulation of such an abstraction is momentarily allowed – is never alien to what Freud calls *discontents in civilization*. Indeed, what initially appears as purely individual is always implicated within a social dynamic. And *vice versa*: every social regulation and political command calls for its subjective inscription, its embodiment. Without them it remains powerless, impotent. For example, isn't it the case that, in modernity, individuation and individualism have progressed hand in hand with state sanctioned disciplinary and biopolitical techniques and the massification of culture? Isn't it the case that, already from the historical beginnings of capitalism, the idea of individual interest as the central axis of human behavior was posited as a social duty?[3] And isn't today the drive to individual consumption functioning as a social force *par excellence*, which sustains the whole economic, social, and political edifice of late capitalist societies?[4]

This constitutive and continuous dialectic between individual and collective/social is, of course, not entirely new. If one goes back to Hegel and Kojève, for example, (s)he will encounter the classical Hegelian intuition that human desire is never purely individual. According to Kojève, 'Human Desire must be directed toward another Desire':

> [A]nthropogenetic Desire is different from animal Desire … in that it is directed, not toward a real, 'positive', given object, but toward another Desire … it is human to desire what others desire, because they desire it. Thus, an object perfectly useless from the biological point of view (such as a medal or the enemy's flag) can be desired because it is the object of other desires. Such a Desire can only be a human Desire, and human reality, as distinguished from animal reality, is created only by action that satisfies such Desires; human history is the history of desired Desires.
>
> *(Kojève 1980 [1947]: 5, 6)*

We can see now how private acts of consumption are inextricably linked to an inter-subjective conditioning that sustains particular types of economic, social and political ordering. It is here that the full socio-political potential of Lacan's famous dictum is revealed, anticipating the emphasis on *homo symbolicus* and the plasticity of desire in sociological analyses of late capitalist consumer society: 'man's desire is the desire of the Other' (Lacan 1977 [1966]: 78).

Simply put, even when psychoanalysis insists that the role of the subject needs to be taken seriously into account in social and political analysis – or, rather, precisely then – this call does not imply a return to an individual level marked by some intrinsic essentialist features of humanity. Subjectivity marks, above all else, the site where all such features evaporate, where they fail and falter. It marks an ontological gap, always implicated in a dialectic of civilizational, social and political dynamics. Moving beyond banal individualism – which, today, is more likely to be found in mainstream social science currents like the rational choice paradigm, rather than in psychoanalytically inspired social and political theory – Lacan stresses the importance of the subject as *lacking*. Now, we can locate the origins of this understanding in the Freudian notion of *Spaltung* (splitting). This notion is important because it shapes Lacan's conception of the subject, in which this split appears as an ontological condition of subjectivity as such. According to Lacan, ignoring the implications of this constitutive split would amount to a betrayal of psychoanalysis: '[I]f we ignore the self's radical ex-centricity to itself with which man is confronted, in other words, the truth discovered by Freud, we shall falsify both the order and methods of psychoanalytic mediation' (Lacan 1977 [1966]: 171). The subject of psychoanalysis is thus the ex-centric subject, a subject structured around a radical split, a radical lack. It is this specific understanding of subjectivity that creates the conditions necessary for a productive confluence of psychoanalytic theory and socio-political inquiry.

Indeed, there are several benefits that accrue to such a conceptualization. If objectivist versions of (social) science foreclose the subject, psychoanalysis is determined to pursue a different path. However, such a path does not legitimate simplistic or reductionist accounts of subjectivity because it avoids attributing to subjectivity a positively defined essence (such as a privileged notion of true interests/needs, a certain type of inherent rationality or a humanist foundation). Most crucially, by moving beyond individualism, by conceptualizing subjectivity in terms of lack, we can also achieve a thorough grasping of the socio-symbolic dependence of the subject: owing to the centrality of lack in the Lacanian conception of the subject, subjectivity becomes the space where a whole 'politics' of *identification* takes place. Simply put, the idea of the split subject cannot be separated from the recognition that the subject is always attempting to cover over its constitutive lack, to achieve some integration, a semblance of wholeness, through continuous identification acts. Lack stimulates *desire* and thus necessitates the constitution of every identity through processes of identification with socially available objects of identification such as political ideologies, patterns of consumption, and social roles. And this is what creates a truly *symbiotic* relation between subjectivity and the social world.

Such a radical questioning of individualism is also consistent with developments in social and political theory. We have already alluded to the work of Norbert Elias, but this is also the case in the study of ideology, discourse, and the social imaginary. In fact, Marxism had already emphasized the limits of the traditional 'atomised, contained subject which ignores the latter's socio-economic formation and, for some, its determination by external forces' (Williams 2002: 24). Marxism, however, has often relied on reductionist models of identity incapable of grasping a more complex dialectic of social institution and reproduction. Althusser, Foucault, and Castoriadis try to offer more sophisticated critiques of individualism. Althusser pictures the human subject as an ideological effect rather than a self-constituting agent (Althusser 1984; Howarth 2000: 94), whereas in Foucauldian discourse analysis the individual is likewise seen not as the source, the producer of discourse, but as a 'function and effect of discourse' (Howarth 2000: 53). As Cornelius Castoriadis has formulated it, the social-historical is what 'shapes' individuals (Castoriadis 1991: 84). A variety of (anti-humanist) traditions in social and psychoanalytic theory seem to converge on that: the individual cannot be constituted outside 'society'; he or she should, rather, be seen as a product, an ideological effect of the social conditioning of human existence. And this social conditioning is revealed not as something that simply erodes individuality and individual freedom but as what has historically constructed it, not as an obstacle to individual desire but as its (intersubjective) condition of possibility.

Yet, for Lacan, this is not the end of the story. Obviously this construction is never complete; this social conditioning is never total, and social and political structures are ultimately unable to fully determine identity and fix desire. This is where, from a psychoanalytic point of view, a moment of subjective freedom emerges, precisely because, as Lacan has repeatedly highlighted, it is not only the subject that is lacking: the socio-symbolic framework of reality is also incomplete, marked by a somewhat symmetrical 'lack in the Other'. As a result, the relationship between subjectivity, society, and politics can be theorized only as a function of political identification within a horizon of ontological impossibility, leading to a picture characterized by a complex play of (ultimately failed) identifications, dis-identifications and renewed identifications.

Ideological Domestications of Lack: Between Language and Enjoyment

As we have seen, the inability of identification acts to produce a full identity by subsuming subjective division (re)produces the radical ex-centricity of the subject and, along with it, a whole (negative) dialectics of partial fixation. At the same time, this radical alienation constitutes the condition of possibility of our (partial) freedom. Subjectivity, then, in Lacan's work, is linked not only to lack but also to our attempts to eliminate, domesticate or, at any rate, negotiate a relation with this lack that, for better or worse, does not stop re-imposing itself. One question that emerges here concerns the precise grasping of the level at which identification and identity (and its failure) matters, under what conditions and in what contexts. For instance, can socio-political analysis remain at the level of meaning or signification? If not, how should one theorize the 'material' irreducible to signification? Here, one needs to stress the productivity of the Lacanian distinction between the 'subject of the signifier' and the 'subject of enjoyment (*jouissance*)', marking Lacan's trajectory from structuralism to post-structuralism and beyond: beyond imaginary and symbolic representation.

Let us discuss these issues with reference to a crucial debate in social and political theory, the one surrounding the category of 'ideology'. From a Lacanian point of view, 'ideology' would connote all our attempts to manage subjective lack and the 'lack in the Other' through discursive articulations of reality promising to restore wholeness, to guarantee integration and harmony. The critique of such ideological fantasies would then be recast as an effort to deconstruct ideological discourse, traverse its impossible promise of utopian wholeness and fullness, and ethically register ontological lack. Lacanian theory has a lot to offer on all these fronts.

First of all, it can help us develop the tools necessary to analyse this reality as a symbolic construction. Lacanian semiology, for example, and especially such concepts as the *point de caption*,[5] have influenced immensely the way discourse analysis deconstructs ideological signification – providing the impetus behind the conceptualization of the *nodal point* as the point of reference necessary in every articulation of meaning (Laclau and Mouffe 1985: 112): 'At first sight it could seem that what is pertinent in an analysis of ideology is only the way it functions as a discourse, the way the series of floating signifiers is totalized, transformed into a unified field through the intervention of certain "nodal points"' (Žižek 1989: 124). Indeed, this approach has been employed extensively in the analysis of a variety of contemporary ideologies. Thus, to refer to a concrete empirical example, Green ideology can be seen to comprise an articulation of differential positions, of distinct ideological moments with no *a priori* Green meaning (direct democracy, decentralization, non-violence, post-patriarchal principles, etc.). What retroactively transforms this aggregate of largely pre-existing principles into a coherent ideological chain, what stops their ideological sliding, limits re-signification, and (partially) fixes their meaning, is the intervention of the nodal point 'Green', of 'Nature' as a discursive principle of organization. Following this intervention – and the ideological process of re-naming it initiates – direct democracy becomes 'Green democracy', the subordination of women is linked to the exploitation and destruction of nature, and so on.[6]

As Slavoj Žižek has cogently pointed out, this is a crucial first step in the analysis of ideological constructions. Yet, the appeal of ideological discourse and the depth of ideological identification cannot be explained solely on ideational or semiotic grounds (Žižek 1989: 125). Ideological investment and hegemony seem to presuppose a particular relation to ideas that cannot be adequately explained with reference to ideas themselves and their rhetorical manipulation. Due to Freud's and Lacan's determination to conceptually encircle the beyond-representation, psychoanalytic theory is eminently qualified to illuminate this non-ideational aspect of ideological identification. A conceptual apparatus drawing on theorizations of libido, affect, fantasy, and enjoyment (*jouissance*) can provide valuable insights in analyzing this dimension. In the words of Slavoj Žižek:

> the last support of the ideological effect (of the way an ideological network of signifiers 'holds' us) is the non-sensical, pre-ideological kernel of enjoyment. In ideology 'all is not ideology (that is, ideological meaning)', but it is this very surplus which is the last support of ideology. That is why we could say that there are also two complementary procedures of the 'criticism of ideology':
>
> one is *discursive*, the 'symptomal reading' of the ideological text bringing about the 'deconstruction' of the spontaneous experience of its meaning – that is, demonstrating how a given ideological field is a result of a montage of heterogeneous 'floating signifiers', of their totalization through the intervention of certain 'nodal points';
>
> the other aims at extracting the kernel of *enjoyment*, at articulating the way in which – beyond the field of meaning but at the same time internal to it – an ideology implies, manipulates, produces a pre-ideological enjoyment structured in fantasy.
>
> (*Žižek 1989: 124–5*)

Hegemony and ideological attachment cannot be fully explained at a formal level, the level of discursive articulation and signification. The *force* of a discourse, its hegemonic appeal, cannot be reduced to its *form*. Form and force need to be conceptually distinguished, and this is something Ernesto Laclau forcefully registers in his recent work:

> For what rhetoric can explain is the *form* that an overdetermining investment takes, but not the *force* that explains the investment as such and its perdurability. Here something else has to be brought into the picture. Any overdetermination requires not only metaphorical condensations but also cathectic investments. That is, something belonging to the order of *affect* has a primary role in discursively constructing the social. Freud already knew it: the social link is a libidinal link. And affect … is not something *added* to signification, but something consubstantial with it. So if I see rhetoric as ontologically primary in explaining the operations inhering in and the forms taken by the hegemonic construction of society, I see psychoanalysis as the only valid road to explain the drives behind such construction – I see it, indeed, as the only fruitful approach to the understanding of human reality.
>
> (*Laclau 2004: 326*)

Enjoyment: A Political Category

It is necessary, at this point, to say a few words about the concept of enjoyment (*jouissance*) Lacan uses, which differs markedly from notions of pleasure or satisfaction currently used in socio-political reflection, ranging from the banal (Breslin 2002) to the more sophisticated (Foucault 1998). Indeed, Lacan posits *jouissance* as always-already lost, as the part of ourselves that is sacrificed, castrated, upon entering the world of language and social norms. The prohibition of *jouissance* – the nodal point of the Oedipal drama – is exactly what permits the emergence of desire, a desire structured around the unending quest for the lost, impossible *jouissance*. When subjectivity is conceived in terms of lack, then, this lack can be understood as a lack of *jouissance*. The fact that this *jouissance* is always-already lost, however, does not mean that it does not influence the fate and structure of identification processes. On the contrary, it may even be possible, starting from this ontological premise, to introduce a complex typology of the modes of interaction between enjoyment and the dialectics of socio-political identification.

For a start, it is the imaginary promise of recapturing our lost/impossible enjoyment that provides the fantasy support for many of our political projects, social roles, and consumer choices. For example, a good portion of political discourse focuses on the delivery of the 'good life' or a 'just society', both fictions (imaginarizations) of a future state in which the current limitations thwarting our enjoyment will be overcome. The politics of utopia provides the exemplary case of the structure described here.[7] In Green discourse, to return to our previous example, this role is played by the utopian vision of a 'sustainable society' in which the harmonious balance between humanity and nature will be fully restored, simultaneously resolving all other socio-political imbalances.[8]

But this is not the full story. What sustains desire and motivates our acts of identification at an affective level is not merely reducible to some abstract fantasmatic promise of fullness. This desire and motivation is sustained also by the subject's limit-experiences linked to a *jouissance* of the body. Without such experiences, our faith in fantasmatically inflected political projects – projects which, after all, never really manage to deliver the fullness they promise – would gradually vanish. Celebratory practices associated with the defeat of a national enemy, even the success of a national football team, are examples of such experiences of enjoyment sustaining national(ist) identifications.

Yet, all these experiences remain partial, to the extent that the enjoyment experienced never equals the enjoyment promised and anticipated: '"That's not it" is the very cry by which the jouissance obtained is distinguished from the jouissance expected' (Lacan 1998 [1972–3]: 111). Its momentary character, unable to fully satisfy desire, fuels dissatisfaction. It reinscribes aliena-tion and lack in the subjective economy, the lack of another *jouissance*, thereby reproducing the fantasmatic promise of – and desire for – its recapture. Nevertheless, this persisting deficit has to be persuasively explained if an ideology is to retain its hegemonic appeal. Thus, very often, ideologies attribute this failure to encounter the promised harmony and enjoyment to the action of a localized enemy (the Jews, who always plot to rule the world; the immigrants, who steal our jobs; the national enemy, etc.).

Indeed, oftentimes the cause of the lack of enjoyment is attributed to someone who has 'stolen it'. Romantic national(ist) histories, for example, are frequently based on the supposition of a golden era (Ancient Greece and/or Byzantium for modern Greek nationalism, the Jewish kingdom of David and Solomon in many versions of Jewish nationalism, etc.). During this imagined golden age, the nation was prosperous and happy, only to be later destroyed by an evil 'Other', someone who deprived the nation of its enjoyment. Typically, national(ist) narratives are rooted in the desire of each generation to try to heal this (metaphoric) castration, and give back to the nation its lost full enjoyment. The identity of the evil agent who prevents the nation from recouping the enjoyment it has lost shifts as a function of historical context. In this view, the obstacle to full enjoyment shifts depending on the specificity of the fantasmatic narrative at stake, but the formal logic remains the same. The important point is that *fantasy* fosters the solidarity of the national community, consolidates national identity, and animates national desire. It does this by structuring the social subject's partial enjoyment through a series of collective practices (celebrations, festi-vals, consumption rituals, etc.) and by reproducing itself at the level of representation in official and unofficial public discourse (both as a beatific narrative of future harmony and as a traumatic scenario of 'theft of enjoyment') (Žižek 1993; Stavrakakis and Chrysoloras 2006).

Facing such ideological mechanisms and utopian desires, a democratic political ethics can only point to the traversing of fantasy and the need to institutionalize social lack. Inscribing again and again the unbridgeable distance between our ideological/utopian reality and an always escaping *real*, which is impossible to control fully and represent, it challenges us to embrace the partiality of enjoyment, moving in a post-fantasmatic direction.

The Crisis and Its Spirit

From a Lacanian point of view, the *symbolic* of discursive articulation (simultaneously enabling and alienating), the *imaginary* of fantasies (both harmonious and castrating), and the *real* of enjoyment (fantasmatic and partial) are always dialectically implicated in producing and sustaining ideological identifications and socio-political orders. But what about the economy? For example, what can the Lacanian framework offer to an attempt to grasp the implications of the global crisis rocking the international system, state structures and subjective trajectories, at least since 2008? Up to now, the majority of analyses circulating in the public sphere have remained on a largely technical level, as if the economy was a technical problem for economists and technocrats, independent of any social, political and cultural context; as if economic behaviour was taking place in a vacuum. Yet, this crisis is not merely a financial crisis; it is also a social, a political, and an ethical crisis, above all else a *spiritual* crisis – provided, of course, that 'spirit' is used here in its Weberian sense, where it implies a particular form of obligation, a distinct ethical mode, a type of categorical imperative (Weber 2006 [1905]: 45, 267). Indeed, one cannot understand economic behaviour without mapping its spiritual, ethical and cultural framing; without exploring the multiple ways in which the symbolic attempts to regulate affect, libido, enjoyment. This leads us directly to the debate around the 'spirit of capitalism' initiated by Max Weber and revisited by Boltanski and Chiapello (2006) and others. It also demands that we understand the economy, first of all, as 'symbolic economy' (Goux 1990), 'affective economy' (Elias 1983), and 'libidinal economy' (Lyotard 1993). And here Lacanian theory has a lot to offer.

From such a viewpoint, the current crisis should be discussed against the background of a broad cultural and ethical transformation, which took place after the Second World War. In a nutshell, what I have in mind is the gradual dislocation of the so-called *society of prohibition*. What emerges in its place is a *society of commanded enjoyment*, as Lacanian social theorist Todd McGowan has put it (McGowan 2004: 2). While more traditional forms of social organization 'required subjects to renounce their private enjoyment in the name of social duty, today the only duty seems to consist in enjoying oneself as much as possible' (McGowan 2004: 2). This is the call that is addressed to us from all sides: the media, advertisements, even our very own friends and family.

Societies of prohibition – including early capitalist society – were founded on an idealization of sacrifice, of sacrificing enjoyment for the sake of social duty. In its initial phases, with its reliance on 'work ethic' and delayed gratification, 'capitalism sustained and necessitated its own form of prohibition' (McGowan 2004: 31). According to this perspective, the classical bourgeois attitude – and bourgeois political economy – was initially based on 'postponment, the deferral of jouissances, patient retention with a view to the supplementary jouissance that is calculated. Accumulate in order to accumulate, produce in order to produce' (Goux 1990: 203–4). This is the *first spirit of capitalism*, associated with a sense of professional duty based on 'rational asceticism' – a gradually secularized version of protestant asceticism – and the concomitant tabooing of enjoyment, conspicuous consumption (in Thorstein Veblen's sense) and luxury (Weber 2006 [1905]: 149). One of the nodal points of this framework of sacrifice is 'saving':

> In the form of the first spirit of capitalism that dominated the nineteenth century and the first third of the twentieth, saving constituted the main means of access to the world of capital and the instrument of social advancement. It was, in large part, by means of

inculcating an ethic of saving that the values of self-control, moderation, restraint, hard work, regularity, perseverance, and stability prized by firms was transmitted.

(Boltanski and Chiapello 2006: 152)

In our societies of commanded enjoyment, with the increasing hegemony of a *second spirit of capitalism*, 'the private enjoyment that threatened the stability of the society of prohibition becomes a stabilizing force and even acquires the status of a duty' (McGowan 2004: 3). Hence the domination of consumerist hedonism, of the endless pursuit of 'individual' enjoyment at any cost (financial, social, ecological, etc.). Isn't today's crisis a crisis of this model and of its 'spirit'? Doesn't it bring us face to face with limitations, paradoxes and contradictions deeply inscribed in the fabric of the ethical and cultural constitution of late capitalist societies? Even though the 'society of commanded enjoyment' describes itself ideologically as a *liberating* society, elevating the consumerist quest for enjoyment into the central regulative principle of the social bond does not mean that we actually enjoy more, that we can experience the fullness and wholeness promised by advertising discourse. The fantasy of a perfect, final enjoyment may stimulate our desire for consumption, but as soon as the desired product, our *object-cause of desire*, comes into our posession a first momentary experience of partial enjoyment is followed by discontent and a second moment of alienation. Once more, it seems, that the *jouissance* obtained is no match for the *jouissance* expected.

In societies of commanded enjoyment, enjoyment makes sense predominantly as a duty: 'duty is transformed into a duty to enjoy, which is precisely the commandment of the superego' (McGowan 2004: 34). The seemingly innocent and benevolent call to 'enjoy!' – as in 'Enjoy Coca-Cola!' – embodies the violent dimension of an irresistible commandment. Lacan was perhaps the first to elaborate on the importance of this paradoxical hybrid when he linked the command 'enjoy!' with the superego: 'The superego is the imperative of *jouissance* – Enjoy!' (Lacan 1998 [1972–3]: 3). He was, indeed, one of the first to detect in this innocent call the unmistakable mark of power and authority. Thus Lacan is offering a revealing insight on what has been described as the 'consuming paradox': while consumerism seems to broaden our opportunities, choices and experiences as individuals, it also directs us towards predetermined channels of behaviour and thus it 'is ultimately as constraining as it is enabling' (Miles 1998: 147).

The command to enjoy is nothing but an advanced, much more nuanced – and much more difficult to resist – form of power. It is more effective than the traditional model not because it is less constraining or less binding but because its violent exclusionary aspect is masked by its fantasmatic vow to enhance enjoyment, by its productive, enabling *facade*: it does not oppose and prohibit but openly attempts to embrace and appropriate *the subject of enjoyment*. Not only is this novel articulation of power and enjoyment hard to recognize and to thematize; it is even harder to de-legitimize in practice, to dis-invest consumption acts and dis-identify with consumerist fantasies. However, without such a dis-investment and the ethical cultivation of alternative (post-fantasmatic) administrations of *jouissance* no real change can be effected. And this is the challenge, both political and subjective, that the current crisis addresses to each and every one of us.

Conclusion

If it is today possible to speak about a Lacanian Left, if Lacanian theory constitutes one of the most dynamic resources in the ongoing reorientation of social and political theory, it is because Lacan's re-elaboration of Freudian psychoanalysis has allowed a non-reductionist formulation of subjectivity. The subject, marked by a constitutive lack, becomes the locus of a complex politics of identification. Lack stimulates *desire* and thus necessitates the constitution of every identity through processes of identification with socially available objects. Ideology constitutes precisely such an object of identification. Incorporating but, simultaneously, moving beyond the effects of the 'linguistic turn' on social and political theory, a Lacan-inspired approach to ideology and discourse highlights the two axes on which every identification operates: semiotic and affective/libidinal, discursive articulation and administration of enjoyment, form and force.

Indeed enjoyment, Lacan's *jouissance*, emerges here as a central political category. It refers to what is sacrificed through the socialization process, to the castrated part of ourselves that, as lacking, does not stop conditioning our desire. It is the imaginary promise of recapturing this lost/impossible enjoyment that provides the fantasy support for many of our political projects, the most obvious case being utopian constructions. Such fantasmatic promises, however, cannot sustain their hegemonic appeal without partial experiences of enjoyment and, most crucially, without blaming someone else for their ultimate inability to restore subjective wholeness and social fullness, for the 'theft of enjoyment'. It is here that the other side of the pursuit of harmony is revealed: hatred, demonization, persecution.

Far from being a technocratic issue beyond social and political control, the economy is also conditioned by the dynamic dialectic between the *symbolic* level of ethical command, the *imaginary* of fantasy and the *real* of (partial) enjoyment. In late capitalist *societies of commanded enjoyment* this dialectic leads to the hegemony of a duty to enjoy that conceals its violent constraining aspect behind its fantasmatic vow to enhance enjoyment, behind a liberating promise securing our 'voluntary servitude'. The current crisis may offer an opportunity to bring this into consciousness and to explore alternative post-fantasmatic forms of ethical, socio-political and economic ordering.

Notes

1 An earlier 'movement' that included Marcuse, Reich, and Roheim; see Robinson 1969.
2 For a detailed account of the Lacanian Left and a critical presentation of the most prominent figures associated with this orientation, see Stavrakakis 2007.
3 See, for a paradigmatic articulation of this argument, Hirschman 1977.
4 We shall return to this question in the final section of this text.
5 A concept originating from the Lacanian theorization of psychosis; see Lacan 1993 [1955–6]: 267–8.
6 This analysis of Green ideology is elaborated in detail in Stavrakakis 1997a.
7 For an analysis of utopian discourse along these lines, see Stavrakakis 1999, especially ch. 4.
8 This argument is developed in more detail in Stavrakakis 1997b.

References

Althusser, L. (1984) *Essays on Ideology*, London: Verso.
Boltanski, L. and Chiapello, E. (2006) *The New Spirit of Capitalism*, London: Verso.
Breslin, Th. (2002) *Beyond Pain: The Role of Pleasure and Culture in the Making of Foreign Affairs*, Westport, CT: Praeger Publishers.
Castoriadis, C. (1991) *Philosophy, Politics, Autonomy*, New York: Oxford University Press.
Elias, N. (1983 [1968]) 'Appendix I: Introduction to the 1968 Edition', in *The Civilizing Process*, vol 1: *The History of Manners*, Oxford: Blackwell.
Foucault, M. (1998) *The History of Sexuality*, vol. 1: *The Will to Knowledge*, London: Penguin.
Goux, J.-J. (1990) *Symbolic Economies*, Ithaca, NY: Cornell University Press.
Hirschman, A. (1977) *The Passions and the Interests*, Princeton, NJ: Princeton University Press.
Howarth, D. (2000) *Discourse*, Buckingham: Open University Press.
Kojève, A. (1980 [1947]) *Introduction to the Reading of Hegel*, Ithaca: Cornell University Press.
Lacan, J.(1977 [1966]) *Écrits: A Selection*, London: Tavistock/Routledge.
——(1993 [1955–6]) *The Seminar of Jacques Lacan*, Book III: *The Psychoses, 1955–56*, London: Routledge.

——(1998 [1972–3]) *The Seminar of Jacques Lacan*. Book XX: *Encore, On Feminine Sexuality, The Limits of Love and Knowledge, 1972–3*, New York: Norton.

Laclau, E. (2004) 'Glimpsing the Future: A Reply', in S. Critchley and O. Marchart (eds) *Laclau: A Critical Reader*, London: Routledge.

Laclau, E. and Ch. Mouffe (2001 [1985]) *Hegemony and Socialist Strategy*, London: Verso.

Lyotard, J.-F. (1993 [1974]) *Libidinal Economy*, London: Athlone Press.

McGowan, T. (2004) *The End of Dissatisfaction? Jacques Lacan and the Emerging Society of Enjoyment*, Albany: SUNY.

Miles, S. (1998) *Consumerism – As a Way of Life*, London: Sage.

Robinson, P. (1969) *The Freudian Left*, New York: Harper & Row.

Stavrakakis, Y. (1997a) 'Green Ideology: A Discursive Reading', *Journal of Political Ideologies*, 2(3), 259–79.

——(1997b) 'Green Fantasy and the Real of Nature: Elements of a Lacanian Critique of Green Ideological Discourse', *Journal for the Psychoanalysis of Culture and Society*, 2(1), 123–32.

——(1999) *Lacan and the Political*, London and New York: Routledge.

——(2007) *The Lacanian Left*, Albany, NY: SUNY Press.

Stavrakakis, Y. with N. Chrysoloras (2006) '(I can't get no) Enjoyment: Lacanian Theory and the Analysis of Nationalism', *Psychoanalysis, Culture and Society*, 11, 144–63.

Weber, M. (2006 [1905]) *The Protestant Ethic and the Spirit of Capitalism*, Athens: Gutenberg (in Greek).

Williams, C. (2002) 'The Subject and Subjectivity', in A. Finlayson and J. Valentine (eds) *Politics and Poststructuralism: An Introduction*, Edinburgh: Edinburgh University Press.

Žižek , S. (1989) *The Sublime Object of Ideology*, London: Verso.

——(1993) *Tarrrying with the Negative*, Durham, NC: Duke University Press.

Pierre Bourdieu and His Legacy

Marcel Fournier

Pierre Bourdieu (1930–2002) was a distinguished and prolific researcher and the author of some of the most seminal works of the twentieth century. His influence in France and elsewhere in the world is almost beyond measure: if the number of times he has been cited by other academics is any indication, he is probably the best-known sociologist in the world. Pierre Bourdieu always recognized his indebtedness to other thinkers, yet it is true to say that his own theoretical stance was both original and ambitious. His goal was to combine a theory of action (with notions of practice, habitus, capital, and strategies), a theory of society (with the concepts of field, domination, reproduction, and symbolic violence), and a theory of sociological knowledge (that included a theory of the role of intellectuals in the public place). Bourdieu's status as a sociologist therefore puts him on the level of Durkheim, Marx, Weber, or Parsons.

Durkheim and Bourdieu shared several similarities in their professional and intellectual lives: they both studied philosophy and were awarded the *agrégation*; they became professors and worked with a group of collaborators and disciples; they published a form of manifesto (*Les Règles de la méthode sociologique* and *Le Métier de sociologue*), they became publishers (Bibliothèque de l'Année sociologique, Alcan, and "Le Sens commun", Éditions de Minuit) and both founded an interdisciplinary journal (*L'Année sociologique* and *Les Actes de la recherche en sciences sociales*). They were, however, dissimilar in two important aspects of their careers. Durkheim taught at the University of Bordeaux and then at the University of Paris (Sorbonne), while Bourdieu taught first at the University of Lille and then mainly at the École Pratique des Hautes Études (later to became the École des Hautes Études en Sciences Sociales) and at the Collège de France where he held the Chair of Sociology, as had Marcel Mauss in the 1930s. Pierre Bourdieu recognized his debt not only to the uncle (Durkheim) but also to the nephew (Mauss) in a conference paper he gave in 1997 entitled, "Marcel Mauss Aujourd'hui" (Bourdieu 2004b) in which he wrote short commentaries on such quotations from Mauss as: "Everything in society is nothing but relations"; "In point of fact, everything social is both simple and complex"; "People talk first and foremost to act and not only to communicate"; "Sociology is simply the principal means of educating society, not the way to make people happy."

Pierre Bourdieu was not *stricto sensu* a Durkheimian. As is clear from *The Craft of Sociology* (1968), a work that included a wide selection of short texts ranging from Bachelard to Wittgenstein, his theoretical perspective was eclectic enough to accommodate Durkheim, Marx, and Weber.

When he defended sociology as a science, he meant science that dealt with an object that could speak and had an observer who was part of that object (society). His approach was both epistemological and sociological, with a strong defence of the sociology of sociology. Later, Bourdieu developed the idea of "participative objectivation" and in place of a radical relativism he proposed a more nuanced position inviting every scholar to produce his own auto or reflexive sociology. The theme of his final lecture at the Collège de France was "Science de la science et réflexivité" (Bourdieu 2001).

Bourdieu's work can be divided into three great areas of investigation: 1) the progression from an epistemological reflection to a sociology of science (and of sociology); 2) the development of an ethnology of Kabyle society to a theory of practice; 3) the evolution from a sociology of education and cultural practices to a sociology of the fields of symbolic production. His two most ambitious scientific projects defended a new conception of sociology (with Jean-Claude Chamboredon and Jean-Claude Passeron)[1] and developed a theory of practice around the famous notion of habitus (as a set of cultural dispositions).[2]

Pierre Bourdieu enjoyed polemical debate (as illustrated by his opposition to Levi-Strauss, structural Marxism, symbolic interactionism, and, later, postmodernism), defended eclecticism (in Marx, Durkheim and Weber, for instance), and supported interdisciplinarity (in disciplines such as anthropology, linguistics, economics, history, and political science). He also rejected canonical dichotomies (such as determinism/liberty, subjectivism/objectivism, and structure/history). In order to identify his own theoretical perspective, Bourdieu used the term "structural analysis" (different from structuralism), with the central notion of field. As we can see in *La Reproduction* which offered a systematization of his theoretical perspective with the notions of symbolic violence, cultural capital, cultural arbitrary, and habitus, the perspective is structural in the sense that it gives primacy to the structure of social positions between social groups and classes. Bourdieu also liked to define his approach as a kind of constructivism or structuralist constructivism, the method he used in his analysis of the relationship between fields, which was based on the principle of "structural homology" first introduced by E. Panofky in *Architecture et pensée scholastique*.

A Research Group, a Journal

While he certainly had philosophical leanings (as had Merleau-Ponty and Wittgenstein) and epistemological concerns – as his work shows – Pierre Bourdieu never disconnected his theoretical reflections from the study of concrete problems or objects (as seen in his examination of matrimonial strategies in the Béarn, workers in Algeria, European museums, photography, and the French school system).

His first "laboratory" was his weekly session with his PhD students at the École Pratique des Hautes Études in the rue Varennes in Paris. It was the pedagogical formula he preferred most of all: a seminar where he would present new ideas to a relatively small group of students and young researchers and test new hypotheses. Always careful to have a page of written notes in front of him, he nevertheless liked to improvise, introducing questions and injecting comments into his own work. Reflexivity was very much a part of his work. His objective was to transmit to his students the habitus of the researcher: intellectual rigour, seriousness, and teamwork, moving back and forth from theory to empirical investigation. He liked to say that the sociologist walks shod in a pair of sabots and that most of his own experiences dealt with things that appeared visible and obvious. Many of his first collaborators were his own students such as Luc Boltanski whose doctoral thesis was published as *The Making of a Class: Cadres in French Society* and Monique de Saint-Martin whose doctoral work was entitled 'Les fonctions sociales de l'enseignement scientifique supérieur'. Bourdieu co-authored many articles with them and other close collaborators.

For Pierre Bourdieu, research was a collective enterprise that needed an institutional basis (seminars, research centres, grants).[3] He was director of the Centre de sociologie européenne, founded by Raymond Aron, and founder of his own Centre de sociologie de la culture et de l'éducation. Many of his first books were the result of inquiries carried out with the help of assistants and colleagues, first in Algeria[4] and later in France. One of his main collaborators was Jean-Claude Passeron. Together they published *Les Étudiants et leurs études* (1964, with the collaboration of Michel Éliard), *Rapport pédagogique et communication* (1965, with Monique de Saint-Martin,[5] *Academic Discourse. Linguistic Misunderstanding and Professorial Power*) and two other important books, *Les Héritiers* (1964, *The Inheritors*) and *La Reproduction* (1970, *Reproduction in Education, Society and Culture*), which changed the perception contemporary Western societies had of schools: schools that enjoy relative autonomy or independence are not mainly a means of social mobility but a mechanism of reproduction for social classes.

As his title indicated, *The Inheritors: French Students and Their Relation to Culture*, Bourdieu had a strong interest in the cultural tastes and practices of students (reading matter, music, movies, etc.). During those same years he carried out two extensive pieces of empirical research, one into the uses of photography, *Un art moyen: essais sur les usages sociaux de la photographie* (1964, with Luc Boltanski, Robert Castel, Jean-Claude Chamboredon, Gérard Lagneau, and Dominique Schnapper), and the other into the type of people who visit museums, *L'amour de l'art: les musées d'art européens et leur public* (1966, with Alain Darbel and Dominique Schnapper). The central question concerned the democratization not only of schools but also of culture, a question that received considerable attention in France at the end of the 1960s at the time of the May 1968 social movement. Bourdieu proposed a sociology of symbolic power that addressed the important topic of the relationship between culture, social structure, and action and analysed the logic of distinction that for him was the fundamental dimension of social life.[6]

In almost all of his books, Bourdieu used empirical data that had been collected by his collaborators and students and had benefited from the technical assistance of a documentalist (Rosine Christin) and of a computer specialist (Salek Bouhedja): *La Distinction*, *Homo Academicus*, *La Noblesse d'État*, *Les Règles de l'art*, etc. The methodological approach he preferred was the most qualitative among quantitative methods: data analysis, a kind of factorial analysis devised by J.-P. Benzécri.

The first issue of the *Actes de la recherche en sciences sociales* was published in January 1975. It had a director, Pierre Bourdieu, but no editorial board. The journal was innovative in its objective (to present research in action with working papers, different kinds of documents, data, and archives) and its graphic design: large format, photographs, and the use of comic strips (Boltanski 2008). The stated theme of the issue was the social hierarchy of objects and the main articles were written by Bourdieu and his close collaborators: i.e. Pierre Bourdieu and Yvette Delsault ("Le couturier et sa griffe: contribution à une théorie de la magie"), Luc Boltanski ("La constitution du champ de la bande dessinée"), Francine Muel, ("L'école obligatoire et l'invention de l'enfance anormale"), and Claude Grignon ("L'enseignement agricole et la domination symbolique de la paysannerie"). This was more than just the formation of a new research group – it was the birth of a new school of thought.

It is possible to identify different circles, sub-groups and generations among his collaborators. The first group comprised A. Sayad, Jean-Claude Passeron, and Jean-Claude Chamboredon (who, as *caïman*, or teacher, at the École normale supérieure, would "lure" into sociology a group of young philosophy students, Jean-Louis Fabiani, François Héran, and Pierre-Michel Menger, all of whom were fascinated by the strength of Bourdieu's intellect). The second group came together when Bourdieu was made Director of Studies at the EPHE: Luc Boltanski, Monique de Saint-Martin, Francine Muel-Dreyfus, Jean-Claude Combessie, Patrick Champagne, Christophe Charle, and others. The third one formed after he had been elected to the Collège de France: Gisèle Sapiro, Frank Poupeau, Frédéric Lebaron, and others. Bourdieu agreed to hand over the direction of the Centre de sociologie européenne to some of these collaborators: Monique de Saint-Martin, Jean-Claude Combessie, and Rémi Lenoir. The Bourdieu School quickly acquired an international influence, in the first instance thanks to some of his former students: Sergio Miceli in Brazil, Marcel Fournier in Canada, Yves Winkin in Belgium, and Loïc Wacquant in the USA.[7] The journal *Actes de la recherche en sciences sociales* now has an editor (Maurice Aymard), an editorial board (including Pierre Bourdieu's son, Jérôme), a scientific committee (with many American scholars including Rogers Brubaker, Craig Calhoun, Aaron Cicourel, Robert Darnton, William Julius Wilson, etc.) and more than fifty associated members (*rédacteurs associés*).

The Collection "Le Sens commun" to Liber-Raisons d'agir

Bourdieu's influence extended to the choice of sociological texts published by the publisher Éditions de Minuit where he was given charge of the series "Le Sens commun". One of his most important and original contributions to his field of research was the publication in this collection of many American, English, and German authors: Panofsky, Cassirer, Bateson, Goffman, Labov, Bernstein, Richard Hoggart, Marcuse, Ralph Linton, Edward Sapir, Joseph Schumpeter, and Radcliffe-Brown.

Further books appeared with the creation of a new publishing venture, Liber-Raisons d'agir. Bourdieu's last great collective enterprise was his *La Misère du monde*, an impressive work of monumental size (1993): more than twenty collaborators[8] conducted a series of interviews with people about "their lives and the difficulties they had encountered". The aim was "to understand the conditions of production of the contemporary forms of social suffering (*misère sociale*)". It was a huge success and was adapted several times for the theatre.

Debates

Each one of Bourdieu's individual and collective works gave rise to considerable controversy inside and outside academic circles in France and around the world. Leaving aside the epistemological debate about *The Craft of Sociologist* and the later question of relativism in science, we can identify one major theoretical debate on the theory of practice (the notion of habitus, etc.), two more specific debates on education and culture, and a final and more general one at the end of his life concerning his political "interventions".

All these debates have structured the French sociological field setting up oppositions between schools of thought and scholars: the opposition between Bourdieu and Baudrillard was the opposition between scientific research/essay; between Bourdieu and Boudon it was holism/individualism; between Bourdieu and L. Althusser or N. Poutantzas it was structural-Marxism/critical sociology; between Bourdieu and Touraine it was order/change and agents/actors; between Bruno Latour and Bourdieu it was the opposition between two conceptions of science, one more relativist and the other more objectivist, etc. We can see the result of some of this opposition in the reactions that Bourdieu's publications on education provoked. There was the Marxist perspective (Christian Baudelot and Roger Establet, *L'École capitaliste en France*, 1971), and there was the Rational Choice Theory (Raymond Boudon, *L'Inégalité des chances*, 1973). Boudon's theory of action, methodological individualism, clearly placed him at odds with

Bourdieu's theory of practice. Alain Touraine, the expert on collective movements whose theoretical perspective had been set out in his *Sociologie de l'action* (1965),[9] reacted to *La Reproduction* by publishing *The Self Production of Society*. The opposition between Bourdieu and Touraine was further exacerbated when they both competed in 1981 for the Chair of Sociology at the Collège de France.

In the 1960s, Bourdieu and Passeron were among the first sociologists to take a critical look at public policy and its implications for the democratization of education and culture. Their sociological analysis showed that, in spite of adopting formal meritocratic practices, schools enhanced rather than attenuated social inequalities. Their attack was against what Bourdieu called the "ideology of gift", by which he meant the ideology of the institution and of its members who understandably were reluctant to accept a theory that appeared to them to offer no chance of change. The Left accused them of not being sufficiently Marxist while the Right accused them of criticizing the meritocratic system. Bourdieu was also accused of attacking elitism when he published his *Homo academicus*, a strong structural analysis of the French academic system characterized by the dichotomy between the universities and the Grandes Écoles (institutions that cater to the power structure of the state and recruit their students in large measure from the upper classes of society).

There was a similar reaction when Bourdieu published *Distinction: A Social Critique of the Judgement of Taste* (1979). This book earned him a huge audience outside the academic world in France. Defining social class position in terms of the volume and structure of various forms of capital (economic, cultural), he marked his proximity to (notion of domination) and his distance from Marxist class analysis that explains everything by means of the social relations of production and class struggle. Class struggle is not just economic; it also has a cultural and symbolic dimension. On the other side, some sociologists criticized the thesis of the homologous relations between social milieu and cultural consumption. In France, where every four years the government conducts a survey of the cultural practices of the total population, Olivier Donnat (2004) used the data to distinguish different systems of practice and taste or "cultural worlds" that are not directly dependent on social backgrounds: from exclusion to eclecticism.[10]

Philosophers and art specialists were irritated by the "bourdieusian" sociological approach deeming it to be "reductionist" in the sense that it reduces taste to a question of social status: tell me what your social background is and I will tell you what you read and what kind of theatre you like. Where is the freedom for each of us to acquire the information and skills we are looking for to build our own system of taste? In general, in philosophical circles and the world of art, there was strong resistance against Bourdieu's sociology of art for presenting the field and not the individual artist as the "creator": "In France I have lots of enemies but no opponents, a term I use for people who carry out the necessary research to propose a refutation of my own position" (Bourdieu and Chartier 2010: 16)

Bourdieu provoked a similar reaction (as did Durkheim more than a century earlier) when he proposed a sociological theory of (scientific) knowledge. He summarized his analysis in a few provocative sentences: "The subject, the agent of science, is not the individual but the field"; "Reflexivity is not the cogito, it is the field. So it is collective." It is understandable why philosophers were angry with him and often remain so. His objective was to reconcile two opposing theoretical positions: historicism and rationalism. The title of one of his last books read *Méditations pascaliennes, Éléments pour une philosophie negative* (1997).

Masculine Domination, which was developed from an article of the same name published in *Actes de la recherche en sciences sociales* in 1990 is one of Bourdieu's shortest and one of his most controversial books (Bourdieu 1998a). The power of masculine domination is analysed as a symbolic violence: in the way it is imposed, this domination is "the prime example of this paradoxical submission" through which "the most intolerable conditions of existence can so often be perceived as acceptable and even natural". Some scholars regretted that the only "data" that inform this study come from anthropological information about the Kabyle that Bourdieu gathered in the 1960s. Others criticized his decision to ignore almost all of the work of the French feminist theorists. The counter-attack has been instant and two questions have been central to this debate. One, more personal: is this analysis a "masculinist" point of view? The other, more theoretical: is the masculine domination only a symbolic violence?

Divergences[11]

Both inside and outside Bourdieu's research group, as is normal in all dynamic research groups, discussions continued unabated. It was a "collective enterprise" (de Singly 1998) with a great deal of collaboration and exchange. Bourdieu would often rewrite his collaborators' articles or reanalyse the data they had collected. These debates led to differences of opinion and divergences that eventually spilled over into the public space. The first example was the debate about the notion of popular culture when Bourdieu published *Distinction*. Is it a dominant culture? Do people have the resources to resist it (the dominant culture)? Jean-Claude Passeron and Claude Grignon strongly denounced the "misérabilisme" and the populism in sociology and literature in their *Le Savant et le populaire* (1989). Passeron distanced himself geographically (he moved from Paris to Marseilles) and intellectually from his friend Bourdieu and worked with other sociologists, Jean-Claude Chamboredon, Robert Castel, Claude Grignon, and Raymonde Moulin, who were also close to Bourdieu. His main interest then became the sociology of culture and the arts which led to the publication of an important book entitled *Le Raisonnement sociologique* (1991). This epistemological reflection on the social sciences re-evaluated the position he had defended with Bourdieu in *The Craft of Sociology* by returning to Max Weber's epistemological dualism (historical sciences/natural sciences): sociology adopts a scientific approach but is not a science in the sense of a "science réfutable" (*dixit* Karl Popper). Admiration and criticism were the two attitudes that linked Passeron to Bourdieu: "With Bourdieu but against Pierre Bourdieu" summarizes his position.[12]

Another Example: The Theory of Practice

The notion of habitus gave rise to feelings both of fascination and rejection and set many sociologists against him: they considered his theory to be too deterministic, allowing little place for freedom of choice or the capacity for action and lacking a fully comprehensive dimension. How can one demonstrate that habitus is class habitus? How can one explain why two people with the same habitus do not think or act alike?

The 1980s were characterized by two things: first, the *retour du sujet* ("the subject is back", as Touraine's book, Le retour de l'acteur announced), and a subject who, by definition, had the skill to account for his actions; second, the (re)discovery of pragmatism. The title of a new journal launched in the 1990s was *Raison pratique*, and the theme of the first issue was "Les formes de l'action: sémantique et sociologie" (editor: Patrick Pharo). The central idea was that the social actor is plural. The title of a François Dosse work (1995) on the new spirit of the human sciences was *L'Empire du sens*.[13]

Luc Boltanski, who had been seen as Bourdieu's *dauphin*, shifted position, his so-called "pragmatist turn", and placed himself at some considerable critical distance from his *maître à penser*, abandoning the notions of habitus and field and developing a totally new theoretical perspective with new objects (forms of injustice, controversies) and new concepts (*cités*, or regimes of argumentation; *épreuves*, or trials). He established a close collaborative relationship with an economist, Laurent Thévenot, published a "programmatic" book, *The Justification* (1991), and set up a research group, the Groupe de sociologie politique et morale, where he worked with students and collaborators (Élizabeth Claverie, Bernard Conein, Nicolas Dodier, and Cyril Lemieux). His most ambitious work was his *Le Nouvel esprit du capitalisme* (1999) with Eva Chiapillo. One of his objectives was to develop not a critical sociology but a sociology of criticism.

In a move to distance himself from Bourdieu's research group, Boltanski agreed to link up with Bruno Latour's group, the Centre de sociologie de l'innovation, that was strongly opposed to Bourdieu's social theory. His research group welcomed researchers who kept themselves at arm's length from Bourdieu – people such as Nathalie Heinich, an active sociologist of art at the Centre National de Recherches Scientifiques (CNRS); this former Bourdieu disciple became, as she said so herself, "a renegade" (Heinich 2007). Sometimes, the distancing of oneself turned into an excessively aggressive rebellion against Bourdieu, as happened in the intellectual trajectory of Jeannine Verdès-Leroux (1998) who described Bourdieu as a "terrorist" in sociology.

"What use can we make of great men?" asked Robert Castel, a former collaborator of Bourdieu. His answer was "Keep them at a safe distance", by which he meant that it was possible to work with Bourdieu but it was advisable not to become his disciple. Bernard Lahire has adopted a similar position though his critical opposition to Bourdieu's theory of cultural legitimacy is less clear-cut: there is, he claims, a plurality of legitimate cultural orders and considerable variations between individuals. The title of one of his books, *La Culture des individus:* dissonances culturelles et distinction de soi (Lahire 2004) gives a clear idea of his distance from Bourdieu.

Another work, *Le travail sociologique de Pierre Bourdieu: dettes et critiques* (Lahire 1999), a collaborative affair edited by Lahire, brought together a number of researchers prepared to engage in critical dialogue with Bourdieu's work. Among them were Philippe Corcuff, Jean-Louis Fabiani, Cyril Lemieux, Emmanuel Ethis, and Alain Viala. Fabiani, a former Bourdieu student and author of *Les philosophes de la République* (1988), edited *Le goût de l'enquête* (2001) as a tribute to Passeron who had been his colleague at the École des Hautes Études en Sciences Sociales in Marseille. In *Le Monde* he wrote a hard-hitting review (entitled "Sociologie et télévision, arrêt sur le mage") of Bourdieu's book *Sur la television*, a small red book which has been a bestseller. Fabiani slated it for being poorly documented and resembling a pamphlet in that it insulted journalists among others and relied on quick generalization rather than on rigorous research (Fabiani 1997).

The intellectual

There are two public images of Bourdieu. The first is that of the rigorous and sophisticated sociologist who defended the "craft of sociology", a profession requiring a long and difficult training, as demanding as a high-level sport. The second is that of the public sociologist or committed intellectual who presented sociology as a martial sport: Pierre Carles' 2001 film *La sociologie est un sport de combat: Pierre Bourdieu* showed Bourdieu mobilizing workers at the Gare de Lyon in Paris and discussing issues with young Arabs in a Paris suburb.

Were there two Bourdieus, the one before and the one after 1990? From the outset of his career, Bourdieu was preoccupied by political questions (the independence of Algeria, etc.) but in the 1970s and 1980s he strongly advised his students not to enter politics (Fournier 2003). Those who worked or studied with him all agreed on two things: first, the most important thing was to defend academic freedom from all outside intrusion; and, second, the best way to change the world was to understand it, and the only way to achieve more freedom was to discover the constraints limiting that freedom.

After publishing his best-selling *La Misère du monde* (1993), Bourdieu became even more active in politics, criticizing the media (in particular television) and politicians. He founded his own series of books, the Liber-Raisons d'agir, helped create a Parliament for writers, supported the anti-globalization movement ATTAC, and published many short political essays (Bourdieu 1998b) that attacked neoliberalism and globalization and defended the necessity of criticizing contemporary societies (Bourdieu 2002). Pierre Bourdieu was an intellectual, not an ideologue. While striving to achieve the status of Jean-Paul Sartre, he was markedly different from him in two ways. His political interventions as an intellectual (his model was Michel Foucault) came in areas where he had a specific competence (in the field of education, for example), when he spoke out on behalf of science, or when acting as part of what he termed as the "intellectual collective".

His activism on the left of the Left irritated many colleagues and some former students who, for one reason or another, disapproved of his public stance or took exception to some of the positions he adopted on political matters. But he attracted a wide audience beyond the narrow confines of the academic world and came to be recognized as a critical sociologist, opening up his work to new interpretations and appealing to a younger generation of social scientists. It is interesting to observe that Luc Boltanski who has published a joint paper with Bourdieu, entitled "La production de l'idéologie dominante", in *Les Actes de la recherche en sciences sociales*, the title of *De la critique: précis de sociologie de l'émancipation*. Was this a comeback? His new move was to rehabilitate the notion of domination and to defend a more pragmatic and critical approach to sociology (Boltanski 2009).

Conclusion

What has happened in the few years since Bourdieu's death? The sociology of the intellectual and scientific fields can teach us something about the way a research group reorganizes and a field restructures after the death of a *maître à penser*, a predominantly inspirational figure. First, there was a period of collective celebration – the creation of the Fondation Pierre Bourdieu (*Pour un espace des sciences sociales européen*/For a European Research Space in the Social Sciences) with more than 125 members, collective books (Pinto, Sapiro, and Champagne 2004), a biography (Lescourret 2008), and publication of posthumous papers and books (Bourdieu 2004a); second, there was a quarrel among the members of the group over the inheritance – who were the real heirs apparent? – with the group dividing into different sub-groups, some orthodox, others less so. The orthodox group was then viewed as a sect composed of epigones rigidly defending the original theory.

If further innovation is to come, will it be from the "centre" or from the edge, and who are likely to be the innovators? To answer this question and to explain why since Bourdieu's death there has been no sociologist (*stricto sensu*) in the Collège de France, an empirical study of the French sociological field (and of other academic fields, linguistic, political, etc.) over the past decade is needed. There will always be strong opposition between the "old" schools of thought or research groups: Bourdieu's school, Boudon's research group, and the Touraine–Wievorka's research groups. But there are new research groups and new schools of thought (Boltanski–Latour, MAUSS. or the Antiutilitariian Movement in Social Sciences, etc.). And, what is more important, the structure of the sociological field is changing with the reorganization of research: the creation of large research centres that are federations of research groups (e.g. the new Centre européen de sociologie et de science politique which is the merger of the Centre de sociologie européenne and of the Centre de recherches politiques de la Sorbonne), and the beginning of the Agence nationale de recherche and of the European system of grants. Research activities are more specialized and also more interdisciplinary, and the centres of scientific research are not so much "laboratories" as networks, both national and international. Each network has its intellectual leaders and organizers and a group of autonomous researchers, as for example in the sociology of art with Raymonde Moulin, Jean-Claude Passeron, Jean-Louis Fabiani, Alain Quemin, and Pierre-Michel Menger or in the sociology of family with François de Singly, Jean-Claude Kaufmann, Agnès Pitrou, and Irène Théry. All these changes have had an impact on the organization of teaching (professional specialization or masters) and also of the profession (the new Association française de sociologie with its networks and thematic groups).

In this new context, there is no doubt that Bourdieu's work remains vibrant and may even be more relevant than ever since the results of his research are used or discussed in many different fields of teaching and research (health, sport, art, literature, and education). Pierre Bourdieu was an innovative thinker and an avant-garde intellectual. As such he deserves to be considered as one of the great sociologists of all time, and our last classical sociologist.

Notes

1 *Le Métier de sociologue*, 1968 (*The Craft of Sociology: Epistemological Preliminaires*).
2 *Esquisse d'une théorie de la pratique*, 1972 (*Outline of a Theory of Practice*), *Le Sens pratique*, 1980 (*The Logic of Practice*).
3 See Pierre Encrevé and Rose-Marie Lagrave 2003.
4 *Travail et travailleurs en Algérie* (1963, with Alain Darbel, Jean-Paul Rivet, and Claude Seibel) and *Le Déracinement : la crise de l'agriculture traditionnelle en Algérie* (1964, with Abdelmalek Sayad). Bourdieu also published a short work, *Sociologie de l'Algérie,* in the "Que sais-je?" collection (1958, Presses Universitaires de France).
5 In the appendix, there is a study by Christian Baudelot of a library in Lille.
6 See David Swartz 1997.
7 For the international diffusion of Bourdieu's works, see the series of papers in the italian electronic journal *Sociologica*.
8 F. Bonvin, É. Bourdieu, P. Champagne, R. Christin, J.-P. Faguer, R. Lenoir, F. Muel-Dreyfus, M. Pialoux, L. Pinto, A. Sayad, L. Wacquant, etc.
9 Touraine founded two research centres, the Centre d'études des mouvements sociaux and the Centre d'analyse et d'intervention sociale, and carried out research and published books with his students and collaborators: F. Dubet, Z. Hedegus, and M. Wieviorka.
10 Richard A. Petterson and R. Kern (1996) in the USA introduced the notion of "omnivorous cultural consumption" by which they meant that people can like things or activities that can extend from the fine arts to popular and folk expressions. For an evaluation of *The Distinction*, thirty years on, see Viviana Fridman and Michèle Ollivier (2004).
11 It would be interesting to analyse the reception of Bourdieu's thought in the USA. Paul DiMaggio, professor at Princeton University, published Bourdieu-inspired articles (1977, 1982). Loïc Wacquant, professor at the University of California, Berkeley, played an active role in translating Bourdieu's papers and co-authoring with Bourdieu, *An Invitation to Reflexive Sociology* (1992). Michèle Lamont's position has been more ambiguous, at the same time using and criticizing Bourdieu's theoretical perspective. Now a professor at Harvard University, she has progressively moved away from Bourdieu to become closer to the Boltanski-Thevenot group (Lamont forthcoming). One of the harder-hitting American critics to have published an attack on Bourdieu's work is the sociologist Jeff Alexander who was close to the Touraine research group (see Alexander 1995).
12 See Encrevé and Lagrave 2003. Shortly before Bourdieu died, it seems that the two friends who had closely worked together were reconciled.
13 On the "new spirit", see Corcuff 1995.

References

Alexander, Jeffrey (1995), "The Reality of Reduction: the Failed Synthesis of Pierre Bourdieu", in *Fin de Siècle Social Theory: Relativism, Reduction, and the Problem of Reason*, London: Verso, pp. 128–217.
Boltanski, Luc (2008), *Rendre la réalité inacceptable*, Paris: Éditions Demopolis.

——(2009), *De la critique: précis de sociologie de l'émancipation*, Paris: Gallimard.

Bourdieu, Pierre (1998a), *La Domination masculine*, Paris: Seuil, coll. Liber.

——(1998b), *Contre-feux: propos pour servir à la résistance contre l'invasion néo-libérale*, Paris: Seuil, coll. Liber.

——(2001), *Science de la science et réflexivité*, Paris: Raisons d'agir.

——(2002), *Interventions 1961–2001, Science sociale et action politique*, Texts edited by Franck Poupeau and Thierry Discepolo, Marseilles: Agone and Comeau & Nadeau, Montréal.

——, (2004a), *Esquisse pour une socio-analyse*, Paris: Raisons d'agir.

——(2004b), "Marcel Mauss, aujourd'hui", in Marcel Fournier (ed.), "Présences de Marcel Mauss", *Sociologie et Sociétés*, 36 (2), Fall, 15–23.

Bourdieu, Pierre and Loïc Wacquant (1992), *An Invitation to a Reflexive Sociology*, Chicago, IL: University of Chicago Press.

Bourdieu, Pierre and Roger Chartier (2010), *Le sociologue et l'historien*, Paris: Agone & Raisons d'agir.

Corcuff, Philippe (1995), *Les nouvelles sociologies: constructions de la réalité sociale*, Paris: Nathan.

DiMaggio, Paul (1977), "Social Capital and Art Consumption: Origins and Consequences of Class Differences in Exposure to the Arts in America", *Theory and Society*, 5, 109–32.

——(1982), "Cultural Capital and Schoool Success: The Impact of Status Culture Participation on the Grades of U.S. High School Students", *American Soicological Review*, 47, 189–201.

Donnat, Olivier (2004), "Les univers culturels des Français", *Sociologie et Sociétés*, 36 (1), Spring, 87–103.

Dosse, François (1995*), L'Empire du sens: l'humanisation des sciences humaines*, Paris: La Découverte.

Encrevé, Pierre and Rose-Marie Lagrave (eds) (2003), *Travailler avec Bourdieu*, Paris: Flammarion.

Fabiani, Jean-Louis (1997), "Sociologie et télévision, arrêt sur le mage", *Le Monde*, 12 February.

Fournier, Marcel (2003), "Pierre Bourdieu: la sociologie est un sport de haut niveau", *Awal, Cahiers d'études berbères*, 27–8, 55–69.

Fridman, Viviana and Michèle Ollivier (eds) (2004), "Tastes, Cultural Practices and Social Inequalities: In Fashion and Out", *Sociologie et Sociétés*, 36 (1), Spring.

Heinich, Nathalie (2007) *Pourquoi Bourdieu*, Paris: Gallimard-Le Débat.

Lahire, Bernard (ed.) (1999), *Le travail sociologique de Pierre Bourdieu*, Paris: Éditions la Dévouverte.

Lahire, Bernard (2004), *La Culture des individus: dissonances culturelles et distinction de soi*, Paris: Éditions la Découverte.

Lamont, Michèle (forthcoming), "Looking Back at Bourdieu", in Elizabeth Silva and Alan Warde (eds), *Cultural Analysis and Bourdieu's Legacy: Settling Accounts and Developing Alternatives*, London: Routledge.

Lescourret, Marie-Anne (2008), *Bourdieu, vers une économie du bonheur*, Paris: Flammarion.

Passeron, Jean-Claude (1991*), Le Raisonnement sociologique: l'espace non-poppérien du raisonnement naturel*, Paris: Nathan.

Passeron, Jean-Claude and Claude Grignon (1989), *Le Savant et le populaire, misérabilisme et populisme en sociologie et en littérature*, Paris: Seuil.

Petterson, R. A. and R. Kern (1996), "Changing Highbrow Taste: From Snob to Omnivore", *American Sociological Review*, 61, 900–7.

Pinto, Louis, Gisèle Sapiro, and Patrick Champagne (eds) (2004), with the collaboration of Marie-Christine Rivière, *Pierre Bourdieu, sociologue*, Paris: Fayard.

de Singly, François (1998), "Bourdieu: nom propre d'une entreprise collective", *Le Magazine littéraire*, 369, october, 39–44.

Swartz, David (1997), *Culture and Power: The Sociology of Pierre Bourdieu*, Chicago, IL: University of Chicago Press.

Verdès-Leroux, Jeannine (1998), *Le Savant et la politique: essai sur le terrorisme sociologique de Pierre Bourdieu*, Paris: Éditions Grasset.

Rediscovering Political Sovereignty

The Rebirth of French Political Philosophy

Natalie J. Doyle

1975 was a significant year for French political thought. Two books signalled its rebirth after its domination by Marxism: Michel Foucault's *Discipline and Punish* and Cornélius Castoriadis's *The Imaginary Institution of Society* (Foucault 1977; Castoriadis 1987). Both constructed theoretical accounts of modern power. The former attracted a following in the English-speaking world. The latter, on the other hand, inspired a reflection on democracy still informing the French contemporary debates on democracy explored in this chapter. I will show how their definition of modernity goes against some of the central assumptions of Foucault's work by situating them in a conceptual framework that highlights their limitations, how the forms of submission Foucault analysed are the perverse by-products of a wider project of liberation, that of human sovereignty. This discussion of sovereignty is distinguished by its historical perspective, specifically by its engagement with the revolutions of the eighteenth century outside Foucault's concerns. I must point out, in this respect, that all the authors discussed were at some point associated with the centre for political research created by the historian François Furet at the *École des Hautes Études en Sciences Sociales* (EHESS, Paris), in honour of the sociologist and liberal thinker, Raymond Aron, who died in 1983: a historian of the French Revolution, Furet gave the Centre de Recherches Politiques Raymond Aron a cross-disciplinary character by bringing together historians, philosophers, sociologists, and economists to reflect on the principles that inform contemporary liberal democracy through the prism of a re-interpretation of eighteenth-century history, especially of the contrast between the genesis of French and American democracy. The centre pioneered the rediscovery of a French tradition of liberalism obscured by Republicanism.

French liberal thought originated in the encounter of Enlightenment thinking with the Revolution of 1789. From the Enlightenment, it retained a universalistic conception of freedom and an attachment to the pursuit of peace through moderate government. To these, it added one of the key principles of the Revolution of 1789: the separation of the political sphere from the religious one as guarantee of human rights. A paradox characterizes it: its conception of freedom as absolute, first political principle outside religion or philosophy but as fragile and dependent on political institutions, just as much as on the virtue of individual citizens. This conception stresses the absolute autonomy of political action from technological and economic progress. It relies on the morality of universal reason. Its attitude to history is suspicious of its presumed transcendent meaning. It is committed to representative politics, the best form of government to safeguard freedom against all those other currents of political thought that exercised their attraction over European political life over the course of two centuries. French political liberalism entertains an ambivalent relationship to its Anglo-American counterpart: it defines citizenship as incompatible with religion, the outcome of a process whereby individuals shed their family, ethnic, or religious ties to become sovereign over their destinies. In this respect, French liberalism intersects with British individualism but it does not put any faith in the market as principle of social organization and invests the state with the task of protecting social harmony (Baverez 1999).

The revolutions of 1989 that brought the Cold War to an end should have given the rediscovery of French liberalism a wider audience but the concern with the need to fight totalitarianism that constituted one of its major themes after the Second World War appeared as obsolete. Its cautious historicism was defeated by the theories of American thinkers such as Fukuyma and Huntington that reinvested history with a deterministic logic. Instead, Foucault's brand of radical suspicion towards liberal democracy emerged triumphant. The victory of democracy over totalitarianism, of nation-states over empires changed the framework within which freedom grew: the nation-state, in its universal suffrage and legal architecture, its increasing economic interventionism leading to the provision of welfare, and its insertion in a system of international relations grounded in the principle of state sovereignty. The nation-state is now challenged in its monopoly: forces empowered by technology operating across national borders; new regional groupings, and supra-national law are fostering ways of being no longer confined within national identity. Civic participation, individual freedom, and the role of the state can no longer be explored in the same way. The old tensions (those between autonomy and alienation, individualism and universal values, local and global identities, economic development and economic crisis, inclusion and exclusion) remain, however, as pertinent as ever. Contemporary French political thought deals with these by highlighting the complex and somewhat contradictory character of modern freedom.

Democracy and Autonomy: Cornelius Castoriadis and Claude Lefort

Castoriadis's *The Imaginary Institution of Society* opened up a new way to approach democracy by contextualizing its discussion within a theory of modern power that stresses its emancipating dimension predicated on the liberation of individual and societal creativity from its submission to the authority of the past. It opposed Foucault's and Lyotard's unequivocal indictment of modernity as the imposition on individuals of a restrictive social discipline of exclusion and control, legitimized by recourse to "grand narratives" of ultimate progress and liberation. For Castoriadis, democracy is inseparable from the discovery of political society. It is the creation of an autonomous realm of rational debate on the normative framework of social life (Castoriadis 1997 [1983]). Pioneered in Athens, democracy departed from an anthropological norm: it abandoned the traditional heteronomous framework of social life with its reference to an external authority (the ancestors, the Gods, etc.) and made society institute itself *autonomously*. This definition of democracy is grounded in a reflection on the question of historical innovation that develops three key ideas: the notion of social imaginary, the distinction between instituted and instituting society, and the distinction between "infra" and "explicit" power.

Societies, Castoriadis stresses, are endeavours of *self-creation* and this creative process is irreducible to rational cognitive thought, for what is involved with each type of society or culture is a coherent pattern of symbolical interpretation of the world. Societies in fact create their own worlds, through a complex but unified web of meanings that permeate not only their institutions but the very psyche of the individuals who constitute society. The origin of such a system of meaning cannot be found in any given subject, in physical reality or in the realm of concepts, for the creation of society is the work of what Castoriadis calls the *radical social imaginary* or the *instituting* society, a realm of absolute freedom and creativity, in opposition to the *instituted* society (Castoriadis 1997). The *instituted* society or the realm of social, imaginary significations – in shorthand, the *social imaginary* – is only the end-product of the process of creation performed by the instituting society (Castoriadis 1987 [1975]). In this respect, it must be stressed that Castoriadis offers a much more nuanced conception of modern power than Foucault who apprehends the political exclusively through the notion of the "will to power".[1] Foucault blurs the distinction made by Castoriadis between "infra-power", the power through which human societies institute themselves and in the process produce and reproduce the individuals that define them, and "explicit power", that of the state which the invention of democratic politics opened up to collective debate allowing the "infra-power" of society itself to be contested (Castoriadis 1991 [1988]).

Castoriadis's cultural definition of democracy also responds to the attempts made by such thinkers as Rawls and Habermas to move away from the classical definitions of democracy as a *regime* involving the formulation of substantive ends to be pursued collectively in favour of a procedural understanding that sees in democracy a mode of conflict resolution arrived at through inter-subjective negotiation. By contrast, Castoriadis stresses the social project of autonomy that underpins it. His understanding of traditional heteronomy is crucial to his belief in the emancipating force of democratic autonomy but, throughout his writings, remains largely synonymous with religion. It is in the work of his main intellectual interlocutor, Claude Lefort, that the contrast between autonomy and heteronomy becomes the basis for a full political philosophy that goes beyond Castoriadis's denunciation of procedural liberalism and offers a theory of the specificity of *modern* autonomy as opposed to the Greek "breakthrough".

Lefort's political philosophy deepens Castoriadis's notion of democratic autonomy by establishing a connection between autonomy and historicity. To control division, heteronomous societies establish social relationships predicated on the assertion of humanity's difference from the natural world. A supernatural order justifies tradition and forbids transformative action upon the natural world. By contrast, historical societies open themselves up to the new. However, societies cannot function without possessing a symbolic representation of their unity. Collective life involves the institution of a closed discourse maintaining the illusion of a superior identity. In non-historical societies, this closed discourse is provided by religion; in historical societies by ideology (Lefort 1986a [1978]). Modern ideology calls into question religious transcendence but does so by erecting another kind of transcendence, the rationalist transcendence of ideas such as Humanity, Progress, Science, Property or Family …

However, at the same time as it reproduces humanity's alienation from its own creative power, ideology crucially opens up the space for a symbolic representation of humanity's sovereignty, that performed by the law (Lefort 1988 [1981]). In modern liberal societies, the law acquires an autonomous presence outside political power. Its foundation is fundamentally external to political power and those who occupy the place of authority do not possess it. Modernity thus possesses a locus of ideological sovereignty external to political power. Modern, *liberal* democracy maintains an essential distance between the symbolical realm and empirical reality because it does not rely on any substantive notion of community derived from an authority external to the social space. It resists all attempts to enclose the symbolic in specific institutions. Lefort's analysis thus leads to a different assessment of liberal democracy from that of Castoriadis. Liberal democracy defines power as an *empty* locus, devoid of any empirical embodiment, which is far more radical than the Greek idea that power cannot be appropriated. The Greek idea of power remained indeed tied to a closed, heteronomous definition of the social community: the insertion of individuals in that community is what prevents them from exercising despotic power over one another. The Greek idea that "power belongs to no one" really means that power belongs to "none of *us*" because it only belongs to the *us*. On the other hand, the liberal definition of power does not rely on any positive, unitary conception of community which power would incarnate. Modern democratic power thus remains a purely symbolic notion, the ideal of popular sovereignty. Popular sovereignty is exercised by people who do not possess it but merely *represent* it, for a limited time. Modern sovereignty is *de jure* an indeterminate space: all are equal in the face of this fundamental indeterminacy.

Power is always the power of *representation*, the power to give a human community a symbolical representation of itself – that is, an identity which subsumes its inner divisions.[2] The radical, historical novelty of European modernity resides in the way the political came to replace religion in this cultural function, a phenomenon which was most evident in the French Revolution. Lefort's work thus involves the reappraisal of French revolutionary history, in which, as Tocqueville before him, he sees a *social* revolution, the democratic revolution establishing an ontological equality of status between individuals and with it a new type of social regime, which he argues culminated in the establishment of liberal democracy. Both Lefort and Castoriadis saw this democratic revolution as still unfolding, in constant contest with attempts to re-establish the reassuring, closed meanings that characterise heteronomous cultures. For their younger collaborator, Marcel Gauchet, this contest reveals the original reliance of human communities on traditional religion or its modern, ideological equivalent, civil religion, for the formulation of a unitary, collective identity that transcends their inner divisions. In this respect, the "Democratic Revolution" constitutes a kind of anthropological mutation, the moving away from religion as cultural framework of social life, with or without the belief in God.

Democracy and Historicity: Marcel Gauchet

Gauchet's political history of religion sees in the advent of liberal democracy the outcome of a process of religious "disenchantment": the disengagement of European societies from a religion conception of human power (Gauchet 1997 [1985]). Gauchet's definition of "disenchantment" extends Émile Durkheim's sociological insight into the political function of religion for all human societies prior to modernity (Durkheim 1995 [1917]). Human imaginary creativity, Castoriadis's central theme, was indeed first explored by Durkheim: his sociology shows that before the advent of the state, humanity's capacity to institute its social world expressed itself through its apparent *denial* in religion.[3] Gauchet explores this paradox: he analyses modernity as the process whereby social life emancipates itself from its grounding in the sacred defined by religion, in which the state played a leading role. Gauchet's account of this long-term transformation reveals its civilizational import extending the French sociological tradition founded by Durkheim.

The civilizing influence of modern democracy involves the acceptance of pluralism based on the discovery of human power. This discovery removed humanity from its state of religious unreflexivity and dictated its entry into a *historical condition*. From the nineteenth century, historicity as new consciousness of human power has primarily been channelled into economic activity and technological change (Gauchet 2003). With the development of economic modernity into capitalism, it took the form of ideologies that sought to transcend the *political condition* of human life and to do away with the state's authority over collective life. The problems Western societies have experienced since the 1970s can only be understood through a re-assessment of their eighteenth-century political foundations (Gauchet 2005a). This re-assessment concerns the intellectual representations of society encouraged by modern historicity and examines the question formulated in the early nineteenth century by Benjamin Constant, that of defining the crucial difference between the collective liberty of ancient democracy and modern freedom Constant sought to explain how the French Revolution's principle of popular sovereignty could have justified oppression (Gauchet 2005b). He reached the conclusion that the fault lay in Jean-Jacques Rousseau's concept of democratic sovereignty: Rousseau's doctrine was correct in stressing the people's general will as the only legitimate form of authority but radically wrong in its definition of popular sovereignty's unlimited scope. Modern democracy, however, is based on the split between liberty as exercise of collective power and liberty as the pursuit of private independence from this very power.

Gauchet invokes history to question the validity of this assessment: the democratic state's evolution has seen it considerably expand its sphere of action but in keeping with the respect for freedoms protected though the liberal principles stressed by Constant: the separation of powers, the autonomy of individuals. On an ideological level also, Constant's critique of Rousseau's political philosophy is problematic. Is the idea that the people are sovereign compatible with the rejection of the principle that popular sovereignty cannot be alienated, nor divided? Constant betrays Rousseau's thinking when he believes that it is possible to retain the notion of popular sovereignty, yet limit its sphere of exercise. Despite this, Constant's critique reveals that Rousseau's definition of democratic sovereignty was predicated on a conception of social cohesion at odds with the culture of liberalism allowing individuals to express their autonomy in civil society.

Rousseau's thinking developed against the representation of power underpinning monarchical absolutism, yet retained its emphasis on the state's exclusive responsibility for society's very existence. His democratic reformulation of the contract-notion historically linked to the promotion of state sovereignty – allowed British liberalism to produce an *economic* representation of society questioning the state's monopoly over the representation of social life: the market. (Gauchet 2005c).[4] In this respect, Gauchet's work counters the "economism" underpinning the rise of the "social sciences" in the twentieth century, which viewed "society" as totally autonomous from any political value. The evolution of democratic societies in the last three decades reveals how the notion of society encouraged the social sciences to reify their object by ignoring its cultural, normative dimension.

In the late 1970s, Western societies entered a new stage of individualism, making the law mediate between individuals and groups: on the practical level, as mode of regulation of social relationships and, on an ideological level, through the notion of individual right as the primary principle of social life. Modern "disenchantment" involved three crucial political innovations (Gauchet 2005f). In the sixteenth century the *theologico-political revolution* of political realism created the modern state, followed in the seventeenth by the *juridical revolution* establishing the foundations of the new political order in law and reformulating the meaning of juridical legitimacy through the idea of natural right. "Disenchantment" was made complete by the emergence in the eighteenth and nineteenth centuries of the historical perspective: historicity addressed the political question of what constitutes the ends of social life through the suggestion that it was *progress*. The state's assertion of human *collective sovereignty* was obscured by the concept of society.[5]

Economic modernity, predicated on the liberal upheaval or inversion of values *(l'inversion libérale)* involved the de-hierarchization of society. It was produced through a new future-oriented relationship to history seeing in historical change the expression of human creativity and involves a transformative conception of human power. This notion emancipated "civil society" from political will and was originally associated with an individualistic and primarily materialistic interpretation of human creativity. This influential interpretation of human power was revived in the 1970s in the form of "neo-liberalism" and awareness of the collective, political dimension of social life was further reduced. The economic crisis of the early 1980s promoted the view that this return of liberalism was in essence an economic, and not *political* phenomenon. The end of Fordism and the difficult transition to a "post-industrial" economy were in fact mere symptoms of a new societal transformation: "intensified liberal individualization", affecting all sectors of social life, from education to family relationships (Gauchet 2000 [1998]).

"Intensified liberal individualization" was encouraged by the decline of the modernist ideology of progress and its faith in a better future, bringing back to the fore the *political problem*: the question of understanding what in modern societies maintains collective existence (Gauchet 2005f). Having lost tradition's all-encompassing normative order, modern societies first held together through the promise of *progress*, be it that of democracy or that of its communist rival. Looking for an answer to the political problem and no longer able to locate it in a golden future, Western intellectuals turned to the past, instead, through a philosophical reflection on the notion of political right. Western societies re-activated their juridical foundations – established in the seventeenth century by natural law philosophy – that had been thought obsolete in the first half of the twentieth century when the "social question" revealed the need for representative politics. This revival of juridical thinking highlights the significance of the French Revolution as the "Revolution of the Rights of Man": its debates *anticipated* the concerns of contemporary democracy and the fact that human rights constitute its sole regulative ideal or critical utopia (Gauchet 1989). The Revolution's ideals failed to find an empirical realization as they remained predicated on the belief in the transcendent authority of the state. Their quest for political sovereignty is however still crucial for an understanding of modern democracy, even if it acquired a different form through liberalism (Gauchet 1995). Gauchet's writings have made a strong contribution to the rebirth of political philosophy but remain insufficiently acknowledged next to the authors thought in the English-speaking world to have best defined the problems of contemporary democracy such as Rawls or Habermas.

Democracy and the Nation-state: Pierre Manent vs Marcel Gauchet

In France, the rediscovery of liberalism was fostered by intellectual collaboration within the Centre de Recherches Politiques Raymond Aron. The tensions of contemporary liberal democracy discussed by Gauchet are thus, unsurprisingly, also explored in the work of other centre members, such as Pierre Manent and Pierre Rosanvallon, who share the concern with the contemporary fate of political sovereignty. In what follows, I discuss Manent's influential critique of the ideology underpinning European integration *Democracy Without Nations: The Fate of Self-government in Europe* (Manent 2007 [2006]).[6]

Democracy Without Nations analyses a problem also explored by Gauchet: the decline in Europe of the political form of the nation-state (Gauchet 2005e) and presents a similar diagnosis. There are, however, substantial differences between the two authors to do with their treatment of the question of the place of the sacred in democratic societies, originating in their different understanding of Tocqueville's contribution. Manent sees in the rise of democracy the progress of ontological equality as first described by Tocqueville. This progress was facilitated by the nation-state as the framework within which both difference and similarity could be expressed, in the international arena, and within the national sphere itself. His interpretation of liberal democracy's history accords with Gauchet's. It stresses the existence of three periods in the humanization of state power. The oldest, identified with its symbolic apex, the 1651 publication of Hobbes's *Leviathan*, established the nation-state's prerogatives, today under question but without an alternative having yet been designed. The second one started with the American Revolution and saw the principle of popular sovereignty define the legitimacy of state power. From 1848 to 1968, the third one established as the object of political representation *society* and its divisions.

Manent, like Gauchet, sees in the contemporary crisis of political representation a problem attributable to the paradoxical tendency of liberal democracy to make the state's role increasingly invisible and more broadly, to obscure the project of sovereignty (Gauchet 2004b). In Europe, the "social" state was so successful in eliminating the markers of class identity that it weakened the sense of difference that underpinned political representation and narrowed down the state's mission to that of guaranteeing the equal rights of individual citizens. This crisis – evident in other forms in other Western liberal democracies – is not primarily motivated by economic insecurity: whilst a new form of inequality tied to the risk of unemployment contributes to the fear that the state no longer adequately represents the interests of its citizens impartially, Western societies have overall become more prosperous, enjoying unprecedented health and longevity. Here Manent accords with Gauchet's judgement that the crisis of political representation has a deeper cause: the perception of individuals that they no longer form a cohesive body for the state to represent, either in social or national form. Representative government has been replaced by a purely administrative state exclusively concerned with the need to balance individual rights: representative *government* had given way to *governance*, a purely managerial role.

The same logic motivates the discourse of globalization promoted by the United States but in a less radical form that does not proclaim the nation-state's obsolescence in the same way as the European Union. The American version holds that a leading nation, model and champion of democracy, can encourage all peoples to embrace democratic mores in accord with human nature itself, irrespective of history or geography and join a new, interconnected world unified by the rules of trade and respect for the law.[7] In contrast with European countries, the United States reserves the right to use military force to punish those "rogue states" that threaten the advent of this natural harmony. American "hard power" and European "soft power", however, both perpetuate the illusion of classical liberalism: cultural conflict can be eliminated through commerce and humanity be united by rational communication. It is an illusion because communication relies upon the existence of a political community and does not create it. The European nation-states formed over time and came to play the same role as the city in Ancient Greece: to create social unity, through the provision of a neutral public space. Manent, like Castoriadis, stresses the lessons that can still be found in the comparison between contemporary democracy and its distant precursor. Both the Greek *polis* and the nation-state allowed the fusion of *civilization* and *liberty*.

The link between the nation-state and civilization is also the main focus of Gauchet's discussion of European transnational cooperation. His analysis similarly challenges the tendency to conflate the nation-state with nationalism – tendency apparent in the discourse of "integration" that accompanied the creation of the European Union – but presents a different assessment of the cosmopolitan understanding of international relations that permeates the European Union. Gauchet's use of the notion of cosmopolitanism refers back to its appearance in the late Enlightenment period and the evolution of the notion of nation as political and historical society. The notion of civilization in the singular, it is clear, has never recovered from its association with colonial imperialism and has more or less disappeared from contemporary intellectual debates. Gauchet, however, resurrects the notion to suggest that Europe is now confronted with the need to resolve the tension between the existence of a plurality of

European nations and a common ideal of civilization. The product of the European notion of nation, this idea is predicated on the belief in the historical movement of nations towards a form of union, which transcends them but to which they each contribute their particularities.

The nineteenth-century notion of nation drew on very old material: on a pre-modern understanding of community that promoted a sense of cultural superiority. This narrow understanding of nation gave European countries their ambition to be the exclusive embodiment of a universal civilization, thereby fuelling nationalism and colonial imperialism. By definition, however, the notion of nation was plural: European nations defined themselves in contest with one another. Whilst they accepted one another's legitimacy, they competed for the leadership of Europe and, through it, for that of the world. The European notion of nation-state was both belligerent and peaceful and drew on the cosmopolitan spirit of the second half of the eighteenth century that gave birth to an ideal of universal community. With scientific rationality becoming the new model of universality, this ideal of international community fused with that of scientific progress and matured with the development of historicity: it converged with the acceptance of the plural contribution to history made by nations. In the second half of the nineteenth century, the rise of nationalisms undermined the belief in a natural harmony of nation-states and the compatibility of their objectives no longer appeared compatible. A new era of competition opened up in the name of civilization seeing leading European countries staking their claims to being the embodiment of civilization, with disastrous consequences for Europe and the world in the first half of the twentieth century. The end of the Second World War resurrected the ideal of civilization but in opposition to the idea of patriotism and renamed *integration*. Like the eighteenth-century ideal of civilization, "integration" assumed a materialistic expression: cooperation in science, industry, technology, and trade. The old project's new incarnation brought European countries closer to one another. It did not, however, create the *political* community envisaged by theories of functionalism. European "integration" or cosmopolitanism was an *ethical project*, uncontainable within geographical or cultural boundaries, the natural extension of the pluralism gaining ground in national societies.

This assessment of "Europeanization" overlaps with Manent's analysis which additionally provides a detailed account of the shift symbolized by the Treaty of Maastricht: the European Union as administrative creation of some nation-states led by France and Germany acquired a legitimacy of its own. European integration ceased to be the tool of some nation-states to become an a-political project of expansion. European countries in the name of "European democratic values" undermined the political action that gave its legitimacy to the political form of the nation-state already shaken by the crisis of traditional political representation.

Democracy and Liberalism: Marcel Gauchet

Despite their similar critique of the European Union, Manent and Gauchet reach different conclusions regarding the significance of the civil religion of patriotism. Manent considers that the transfer of sacredness from the Church to the State was a *logical* necessity: for him, the modern state's legitimacy, its neutrality, can be derived only from a different kind of sacred transcendence, that of the nation (Manent 2007). For Gauchet, civil religions were only a *historical* necessity: transitional phenomena in de-sacralization (Gauchet 2004a). This is linked to his different interpretation of liberalism which I will contrast with that of Manent in what follows.

As mentioned in the introduction, a re-assessment of French revolutionary history was central to the rediscovery of the tradition of French liberalism, which drew on Tocqueville's interpretation. There is, however, a significant difference in its understanding that demarcates different conceptions of liberalism: Lefort and Gauchet acknowledge the value of its definition of democratic equality but fundamentally question the belief that it leads to a moral and intellectual consensus. For them, democracy is the principled acceptance of society's *division*. In this respect, totalitarianism always shadowed it, at least in its European version still permeated by the memory of hierarchy and its organic definition of society (Lefort 1986b; Gauchet 2005d). Tocqueville's failure to recognize that in democracy everything is put into question is due to the fact that his theory is based on the United States, a country without a pre-democratic history which made its allegiance to the principle of popular sovereignty appear much more clearly but concealed its pre-history in monarchical state absolutism: absolutism's elevation of the state above society, its centralization of political power paradoxically created the conditions in which hierarchy could later be contested. Hierarchy, however, remained an obstacle to the assertion of the principle of popular sovereignty. Democracy could triumph only when individualism had given state action a radically new objective: the creation of a new type of society, *a society of individuals*. The advent of democracy, in other words, was dependent on the liberal inversion of values analysed above.

Tocqueville's discussion of democracy still remains most perceptive: it reveals its logic, the deconstruction of hierarchy, and its principle of ontological difference. It points to the existence of what Castoriadis called "a central imaginary signification". The equality he discusses is far more than juridical. Nor is it economic. By equality, he referred to the possibility of *individual mobility* created by the disappearance of the group identities of hierarchical societies. In aristocratic societies, equal wealth did not in any way abolish the ontological inequality of classes whilst economic inequality in modern societies is not synonymous with radical difference: individuals are "equals" because for one another, they are *semblables* (alike). Modern societies reject the principle of "Otherness" underpinning traditional societies because of the role of the state. The invention of the state made this Otherness *immanent*, rather than transcendent, triggering the discovery of human subjectivity. The state induced a transformation of the sacred manifest in the birth of new systems of religious beliefs that establish a radical divide between two orders: that of the mundane and that of the divine, invisible Other.

Gauchet's treatment of Christianity offers an insightful account of the radical novelty associated with the evolution of the state in Western Europe that ultimately led to its complete desacralization. Unlike Manent, Gauchet does not attribute this novelty exclusively to the internal logic of Christianity's evolution but rather to its interaction with *state reconstruction* following the failure to re-establish an effective imperial framework after the demise of Rome. The discovery of political subjectivity was the outcome of the encounter of pre-Christian tribal visions of sacred power with an imperial vision affected by the specific evolution of Western Christianity. This encounter gave birth to a radically new conception of political sovereignty, no longer based on mediation with the sacred sphere but on the *representation* of the earthly one. The monarchical, territorial state signalled the birth of an original symbolic matrix of social organization based on new sacred entities: the state and the nation. This new form of sacredness, however, ultimately served to *desacralize* the political by conferring on the state a radically new, *transformative* power: reshaping the world, both natural and human.

Desacralization gave birth to *modern subjectivity* which did not only take the form of collective sovereignty as discussed above but also that of individualism. From Hobbes to Rousseau, the first conceptualizations of this ideal of subjectivity relied on a conception of citizenship in which the individual was reduced to his social identity. Sovereignty, in other words, was purely collective. It only became individual also, in the course of the nineteenth century through a myth of natural autonomy defining the individual as self-created that gradually pushed off the stage the aspiration to collective, political sovereignty. This foundational myth has weighed negatively on all the discussions of modern political philosophy of modernity, on its definitions of freedom, autonomy, and democracy. The modern notion of subjectivity is indeed essentially ambiguous because it encompasses the two meanings of autonomy, epistemological and ethical. As Castoriadis pointed out, autonomy defines *being*, whose archetypal primary reflexivity is teleological in the sense that existence is its own end. Self-awareness as self-care or self-preservation must thus be distinguished from the ethical, Kantian notion of subjectivity: to be an autonomous individual is to choose *for oneself*, by individualizing the ends of one's actions (Descombes 2004).

Despite appearing as derived from the individual's presumably natural autonomy, these ends, however, remain essentially social in character: autonomy is *an end-point*, not a starting point as defined by liberalism. It is the outcome of a process of social education that educates the individual psyche by teaching it to see the other in itself and itself in the other, that is, to acquire the capacity for self-limitation. It has been associated with the state not, as Foucault argued primarily, through the discipline it imposed on individuals but, far more importantly, through its capacity to emancipate individuals from personalized relationships of dependency. It replaced these with the respect for *democratic generality* that emerges from equality, the rejection of radical otherness. Gauchet's writings on the development of psychiatry co-authored with Gladys Swain counter Foucault's assertion that early modernity was synonymous with exclusion (Foucault 1965 [1961]; Gauchet and Swain 1999 [1980]). The mad in traditional societies may have rubbed shoulders with all the other members of the community but only because they were thought to be radically *other*, and as a result appeared non-threatening. The exclusion was mental. In contrast, modern societies excluded them *physically*: their difference had ceased to be alien and had to be understood. Foucault's mistake was to take the immediate, discriminatory expression of modernity at face-value.

Conclusion

Post-structuralism's success in the 1980s and 1990s contributed to obfuscating another French school of thought, which rejected all radical attacks on liberalism and affirmed the empowering dimension of modern culture through its discussion of political sovereignty. Marcel Gauchet and Pierre Manent have done much to re-assert the traditional French concern for the political dimension of social life. Against the form of political thinking known as *neo*-liberalism, they have stressed the historical significance of nineteenth- and twentieth-century *democratic* liberalism: it created a system of government capable of recognizing the two imperatives of individual rights and collective responsibility (Gauchet, 2001). Liberal democracy was established in the form of the nation-state whose sovereignty is questioned by a new form of capitalism. Globalization in fact challenges *popular*, rather than *national* sovereignty: it relies on national states far more than commonly acknowledged (Lefort 2000). The nation-state merged the two notions of nation and people but the notion of nation lacks democratic grounding as a result of its pre-modern history. From this stems the ambivalence of the principle of national sovereignty explored by Gauchet in contrast with Manent.

Despite this, the principle of national sovereignty was invoked to counter neo-liberalism's economism in a way that was detrimental to efforts to construct the new form of sovereignty needed to re-invigorate the political. The crisis of 2008 brought into great relief the need to formulate a common, political purpose on a bigger stage than the nation or, as Pierre Rosanvallon calls it, a *démocratie-monde* that not only requires the re-activation of the democracy of state action at the national level but also that of public opinion (Rosanvallon 2009). The active participation of citizens, indeed, constitutes the *counter-democracy* that addresses the shortcoming of electoral-representative government (Rosanvallon 2008). Rosanvallon's discussion of these shortcomings accords with Gauchet's definition of liberal democracy as a political regime of compromise between democratic power and liberalism (Gauchet 2007) whose legitimacy was secured after 1945 through reforms that, amongst other things, constructed a public apparatus capable of steering the historical change produced by market autonomy. The current economic crisis reminds us that democratic societies should direct their history, rather than suffer it. They will only do so if they rediscover their *political sovereignty*.

Notes

1 As Vincent Descombes argues (1977: 998–1027), Foucault's political philosophy reduces social life to conventionality. It discusses the political significance of social life but at the same reduces it to the notion of power relations, to the strategies these engender. Power becomes *potentia* but power as *potentia* depends on *potestas*, the cultural authority conferred upon it by social opinion or, to use Castoriadis's terminology, by the social imaginary. This reduction engenders a tautological form of reasoning that plays on the dual grammatical function of the French word for power, *pouvoir*, both noun and verb. Power becomes will to, which paradoxically erases the distinction between power and its abuse. By definition, power goes as far as it can go; by definition all power is abuse: " ... it is in the nature of power – particularly the kind of power that operates in our society – to be repressive ... " (Foucault 1984: 9).

2 Lefort expresses this idea through a play on words when he says that a society's *mise en sens* (structuring of meaning, in others words the creation of its identity) is both a *mise en forme* (the creation of a specific form given to human coexistence, the creation of a *regime*) and a *mise en scene* (staging, in the sense of theatrical representation).

3 I have explored the affinity between Durkeim's work and that of Castoriadis, Lefort, and Gauchet in "The Sacred, Social Creativity, and the State" (Doyle 2007).

4 I have developed the question of British economic liberalism's debt to French political modernity in "Alternatives within the West: French and British Roads to Modernity" (Doyle 2010).

5 Gauchet's engagement with the history of psychiatry cannot be dissociated from his longstanding interest in psychoanalysis, an interest shared with Castoriadis, who practised psychoanalysis. Gauchet incorporates the Freudian notion of unconscious in his account of the birth of modern individual subjectivity. See his *L'Inconscient cérébral* (1992) and *Le Vrai Charcot. Les chemins imprévus de l'inconscient*, co-authored with Gladys Swain (1997).

6 Rosanvallon's books on democratic political representation are part of the intellectual paradigm discussed in this chapter. They have been extensively translated and discussed in English and thus do not need any additional commentary. I therefore refer to this author only in the conclusion.

7 Gauchet's different interpretation of liberalism leads him to formulate a different assessment of the apparent divergence of European and American contemporary interpretations of the West as leader of the democratic world. In a postscript to an article on Tocqueville entitled "La Dérive des continents" (see Gauchet 2005c), he argues that the American interpretation can be explained by the specificity of American history but that the differences are less significant than they appear.

References

Baverez, N. (1999) "De L'Esprit du libéralisme français ", in *Le Magazine littéraire*, 380, 63–6.

Castoriadis, C. (1987 [1975]) *The Imaginary Institution of society*, trans. Kathleen Blamey, Cambridge: Polity Press.

——(1991 [1988]), "Power, Politics, Autonomy", in *Philosophy, Politics, Autonomy*, ed. and trans. David Ames Curtis, Oxford: Oxford University Press.

——(1997 [1993]) "The Greek Polis and the Creation of Democracy", in *Philosophy, Politics, Autonomy*, ed. and trans. David Ames Curtis, Oxford: Oxford University Press.

Descombes, Vincent (1977), "Pour elle un Français doit mourir", *Critique*, 366.

——(2004) *Le Complément de sujet: enquête sur le fait d'agir soi-même*, Paris: Gallimard.

Doyle, N. J. (2007) "The Sacred, Social Creativity and the State", in Jean-Phillipe Deranty, Danielle Pentheridge, John Rundell, and Robert Sinnerbrink (eds), *Recognition, Work, Politics: New Directions in French Critical Thought*, Leiden: Brill.

——(2010) "Alternatives within the West: French and British Roads to Modernity", in J. P. Arnason and N. J. Doyle (eds) *Domains and Divisions of European History*, Liverpool: Liverpool University Press.

Durkheim, E. (1995 [1917]) *The Elementary Forms of Religious Life*, trans. Karen E. Fields, New York: Free Press.

Foucault. M. (1965 [1961]) *Madness and Civilization: A History of Insanity in the Age of Reason*, trans. R. Howard, London: Tavistock.

——(1977) *Discipline and Punish*, New York: Random House.

——(1984) *The History of Sexuality*, London: Penguin.

Gauchet, M. (1992) *L'Inconscient cérébral*, Paris : Éditions du Seuil.

——(1997) *The Disenchantment of the World*, trans. Steve Rothnie, Princeton, NJ: Princeton University Press.

——(1989) *La Révolution des droits de l'homme*, Paris: Gallimard.

——(1995) *La Révolution des pouvoirs*, Paris: Gallimard.

——(2000 [1998]) "A New Age of Personality: On the Psychology of Our Times", *Thesis Eleven*, 60 (1), 23–41.

——(2001) "Le Socialisme en redéfinition", *Le Débat*, 151, 87–109.

——(2003) *La Condition Historique*, Paris: Stock.

——(2004a) *Un Monde désenchanté*, Paris: L'Atelier/Éditions ouvrières.

——(2004b) *La Démocratie contre elle-même*, Paris: Gallimard.

——(2005a) "Introduction: les figures du politique", in *La Condition Politique*, Paris: Gallimard.

——(2005b) "Constant: le libéralisme entre le droit et l'histoire", in *La Condition Politique*, Paris: Gallimard.

——(2005c) "De L'avènement de l'individu à la découverte de la société" in *La Condition Politique*, Paris: Gallimard.

——(2005d) "L'Expérience totalitaire et la pensée de la politique", in *La Condition Politique*, Paris: Gallimard.

——(2005e) "Le Problème européen", in *La Condition Politique*, Paris: Gallimard.

——(2005f) "Les tâches de la philosophie politique", in *La Condition Politique*, Paris: Gallimard.

——(2007) *L'Avènement de la démocratie I – La Révolution moderne*, Paris: Gallimard.

Gauchet, M. and G. Swain (1997) *Le Vrai Charcot: Les chemins imprévus de l'inconscient*, Paris: Calmann-Lévy.

——(1999 [1980]) *Madness and Democracy: The Modern Psychiatric Universe*, Princeton, NJ: Princeton University Press.

Lefort, C., (1986a [1978]) "Outline of the Genesis of Ideology in Modern societies", in John B. Thompson (ed.), *The Political Forms of Modern Society*, Cambridge: Polity Press.

——, (1986b) "The Logic of Totalitarianism", in John B. Thompson (ed.), *The Political Forms of Modern Society*, Cambridge: Polity Press.

——(1988 [1981]) "The Permanence of the Theologico-political?", in *Democracy and Political Theory*, trans. David Macey, Oxford/Cambridge: Polity Press with Basil Blackwell.

——(2000) "Nation et souveraineté", *Les Temps Modernes*, 610, 25–46.

Manent. P. (2007 [2006]) *Democracy Without Nations? The Fate of Self-government in Europe*, trans. Paul Seaton, Wilimington, DE: ISI Books.

Rosanvallon, P. (2008) *Counter-democracy: Politics in an Age of Distrust*, trans. Arthur Goldhammer, Cambridge: Cambridge University Press.

——(2009) " Réinventer la démocratie", *Le Monde*, 29 April.

Continuity through Rupture with the Frankfurt School

Axel Honneth's Theory of Recognition*

Mauro Basaure

The vitality of a school of thought is based more on its capacity for self-criticism, change and continuous development through waves of rediscovery than on devotedly clinging to "the classics." This dynamic of *continuity through rupture* explains the power of the Frankfurt School's (*FS*) tradition of critical theory. Just as Jürgen Habermas, the most renowned representative of that tradition's second generation, both continues and breaks with the work of Max Horkheimer, Theodor Adorno and Herbert Marcuse (to name only the most central authors of the founding generation of the *FS*), Axel Honneth – as both a disciple of Habermas and the most prominent member of a third generation of that tradition – forges his own path in regard to the work of both those founding authors and with respect to Habermas. The *FS* tradition's survival is now to a large extent dependent on Honneth's theoretical effort to achieve continuity through rupture with Habermas' work. The purpose of this chapter is to provide readers who are interested in the current state of the *FS* tradition with a guide to the main aspects of Honneth's work and, based on this description, in the second section, to explore certain key ruptures with his predecessors, particularly Habermas.

Axel Honneth's Theoretical Project: A Brief Reconstruction

Honneth's social theory (1995a) is based on the thesis of a formal-anthropological order – one that is shared by authors such as Tzvetan Todorov (2001), Avishai Margalit (1996) and Charles Taylor (1992) – namely, that recognition is a fundamental mechanism of our social existence. This concept implies, on the one hand, that the development of subjectivity depends on recognition and that we can only conceive of ourselves as members of society to the extent that we are, and feel we are, recognized in certain essential aspects of our personality. It also means, on the other hand, that the social structures by which the forms of reciprocal recognition are established are fundamental to the very existence (or integration) of society.

Honneth's thesis is strengthened by his use of aspects of both *developmental psychology* and *moral sociology*. On the one hand, with the aid of Winnicott's object relations theory and certain aspects of Freudian psychoanalysis, Honneth (1995a, 2009) shows that people depend on an environment that is characterized by affirmative treatment from the earliest moments of their lives and that there is a direct connection between their personal identity and the intact nature of relationships of recognition, as they acquire a free relationship with themselves and individual autonomy only to the extent that they enjoy the affirmation of the social environment. Thus Honneth asserts that there is a strong link between the psychological dimension of subjectivity and social transformations – as a source of changes in the experiences of subjects in society –: that is, between personal identity and social structures. On the other hand, he also analyzes these social structures in terms of a moral-sociological theory of "spheres of recognition" (Honneth 1995a; Fraser and Honneth 2003). Honneth's basic question is the following. What social practices are institutionalized in our society to the extent that they imply forms of reciprocal recognition and are based on normative principles that can be reconstructed as a moral grammar of social life? With Hegel's help, Honneth (1995a, 2000b) notes that modern societies are stabilized by a moral infrastructure that can be reconstructed in terms of three forms of interaction or "spheres" governed respectively by three normative principles: *love*, *rights* and *social esteem*. *Love* is the general name for a form of reciprocal recognition and emotional attention that subjects grant one another and also expect or even demand in the context of their primary relationships (with romantic partners, family members and friends). According to the principle of modern *rights*, all members of society should recognize each other and respect each other as equals in their rights and obligations, in particular, as legal persons. Finally, modern societies also are characterized by the principle of *achievement*, by which subjects mutually grant one another social esteem on the basis of contributions they make to the realization of shared social values while making use of their specific capacities and qualities.

Coinciding to a certain extent with pluralist theories of justice such as that of Michael Walzer (1983; see Miller 1999), Honneth (Fraser and Honneth 2003) asserts that the modern idea of justice as equal treatment has been institutionalized in three different ways. Love, equality of rights and the principle of achievement represent normative principles in relation to which individuals may legitimately assert the different demands of equal treatment. These spheres have a historic nature and, as such, express a certain degree of maturity in social relationships. A single anthropological need for recognition was diversified to the extent that spheres of recognition have been differentiated historically: the need for recognition is expressed through emotional support, cognitive respect and social esteem depending on whether one refers to primary relationships, legal relationships of rights or relationships of solidarity in light of shared values, respectively (Honneth 1995a, 2007b; Fraser and Honneth 2003).

Based on the assertion of this intimate link between the comprehensive development of subjectivity and affirmative experiences of recognition, Honneth identifies three positive modes of practical relationship-to-self that correspond to the above-mentioned spheres: basic self-confidence, self-respect and self-esteem (Honneth 1995a, 1995b; Fraser and Honneth 2003). Accordingly, there are three characteristic types of experiences of disrespect or social injury that would harm the integrity of said relationships. Experiences of physical abuse and rape threaten that aspect of the personality which is rooted in the physical integrity. Experiences of the dispossession of rights and exclusion and underprivileging do the same with regard to one's social integrity. Finally, experiences of humiliation, denigration and degradation negatively affect one's sense of honor and personal dignity (Honneth 1995a, 1995b).

Honneth uses the above to develop a theory of struggles for recognition and to endow the demands expressed therein with normative support, seeing them as the fundamental factor in a dynamic that broadens society's normative structure (a) and to justify the normative perspective of his own critical theory (b).

a. Honneth's theory of social struggles has two key argumentative axes (L. C. Basaure 2011). The first is the *moral-sociological explanatory* axis that rotates around the motivational sources of social struggles. The second is a *philosophical-historical reconstructive* axis that rotates around the historical meaning of those struggles. In a way, Honneth rehabilitates the strong positive reference of critical theory to specific social struggles that, from the perspective of its Marxist program of the 1930s, constituted a central aspect of the *FS*. While during that period and in classic Marxism in general that reference was thought of mainly in terms of an explanatory model based on the notion of interest, Honneth proposes an alternative model of a *moral-sociological* order based on the notion of recognition. Honneth does not ignore the explanatory potential of the concept of interest, but rejects its inscription in a utilitarian paradigm, especially one with a totalizing intent according to which all motivations of action are traced back to the maximization or increase of utility. In contrast, the model of recognition starts from the idea that subjects are *constitutively* oriented to mutually shared expectations of recognition that are reflected in moral norms, and that, when they perceive or feel a threat to their personal identity, which is rooted in these expectations, they react with moral feelings of resentment, disrespect, outrage, etc., which could potentially incite the beginning of a social struggle (Honneth 1995a, 2007b; Fraser and Honneth 2003).

The reconstruction of the principles of recognition also informs the diversity of normative references with respect to which actors can raise justified demands for equal treatment, thus allowing for the analytical differentiation of social conflict. Based on this differentiation, for example, in response to Nancy Fraser, Honneth (Fraser and Honneth 2003) can not only assert that problems of redistribution are better understood if they are treated as problems of recognition, but also that, depending on the type of demand in question, they can be understood as conflicts related to the privation of social *rights* or an *unjust valorization* of the contribution that social groups make to society through their work.

In contrast to classical Marxism with its one-dimensional concept of social struggle, Honneth (Fraser and Honneth 2003; Jay 2008) does not have a specific social movement in mind, but rather an area of experiences, feelings and ordinary moral judgments that are potentially – in other words, not necessarily – political in the sense that they can be the basis for generating a collective struggle that achieves public visibility (Fraser and Honneth 2003). Honneth is interested in describing the broad spectrum of feelings and moral experiences that can provide motivation for and sustain social struggles. In contrast to the theory of social movements and the political-theoretical thesis of civil society (Cohen and Arato 1994), the Honnethian concept of struggle intends to be sensitive to forms of social suffering and moral reactions to negative experiences or conflicts that have not necessarily reached high levels of collective organization and thus have not managed to cross the threshold of public visibility in the political realm (Fraser and Honneth 2003).

Honneth (1995a, 2007b) takes up the practical-philosophical thesis that the basic source of the social dynamic and moral development of society is social conflict and struggles for recognition. In this way, the *philosophical-historical reconstructive axis* of Honneth's work suggests that such struggles are not only guided by the principles of recognition – which lend normative direction and validity to the struggles – but that the struggles themselves gradually contribute to the further entrenchment and broadening of the moral structures of reciprocal recognition. As such, specific and concrete struggles for recognition can be inscribed in a larger process of societal development and moral learning.

b. The set of elements presented thus far constitute the basis upon which Honneth constructs his critical theory of society. Accordingly, the normative point of view of that theory may be justified in universalist terms. An anthropological thesis translated into a psychology of development embodies a universalist intention given its non-relative nature. This intention also can be extended to the normative principles of recognition. To the extent that these norms or principles are implicitly accepted by the actors themselves – as having a validity that transcends specific social historical contexts, like in Honneth's approach – the critical theorist can assert them vis-à-vis those actors assuming that his own position is not idiosyncratic or specific but universally valid (Honneth 2007b, 2009). The combination of anthropological elements, the psychology of development and social theory that Honneth takes up allows him to justify and practice different forms of social critique. Depending on how these elements are emphasized, the critique may address injustices or social pathologies that can be said to refer to the notion of personal self-realization or a theory of rationality.

Primarily emphasizing his pluralist social-theoretical perspective, Honneth proposes to broaden the liberal concept of justice in two intimately related senses (Fraser and Honneth 2003). On the one hand, the concept includes forms of equal treatment that go beyond the universalist sphere of law (Honneth 2007b). On the other, it seems to Honneth that the notion of justice should incorporate a reference to the pre-political conditions that allow subjects to participate in public life, that is, the realization of the principle of democratic participation (Fraser and Honneth 2003). Once again, these pre-political conditions are not reduced to a matter of law but are broadened to include affirmative experiences mainly in the sphere of social solidarity. Honneth defends a concept of social democracy based on a notion of justice that, echoing a thesis of Adam Smith (1977 [1776]), may be defined in terms of a type of social relationship in which all members of society can appear in public without shame, and where this does not require anyone to hide any crucial aspects of their own identity (in contrast to the exclusions which typically occur at present regarding people of various social groups or classes). For Honneth, this can only take place to the extent that one enjoys a positive relation-to-self achieved in the context of intact relationships of recognition (Honneth 1995a). The critique of injustice thus involves the critic drawing out and asserting – in concert with the perspective of the actors involved or not – the implicit normativity of the social world, i.e. the principles of recognition as plural principles of just treatment. Based on them, one cannot only denounce the injustices to which certain social groups are subjected but also demonstrate how such injustices represent an attack on the basic conditions for the realization of the universal principle of democratic participation (Honneth 2007b; Fraser and Honneth 2003).

Secondly, stressing the anthropological and social-ontological aspects of his perspective, Honneth also develops a critical theory of social pathologies (Honneth 2003). He considers pathological those global social developments – that is, those that do not only affect certain groups, but all of society – that can be said to systematically damage the conditions necessary for successful self-realization in each person, i.e. the conditions required for a good and successful life. The normative criterion of this assessment is clearly the idea of an undistorted form of social relationship that would guarantee all members of society the opportunity to achieve self-realization (Honneth 1995b, 2000b, 2009). While this idea is intimately related to the institutional historical condition of the different spheres of recognition, the analytical emphasis here is not so much placed directly on the normativity that the different moral principles of recognition impose as principles of justice, as it is on the description of the rational foundations of human social existence and various threats to them which occur in the course of the social practices themselves. Echoing Hegel and Durkheim, Honneth highlights the pathological consequences of processes of individualization that cause social disintegration and lead to forms of suffering arising from an increase in the indeterminacy, insecurity and uncertainty experienced by members of society in their lives (Honneth 2010).

Thirdly, the concept of social pathologies referred to above should be differentiated from a second, more recent concept that Honneth (2008) has tried to develop, this time along the lines of a theory of rationality. The critique of social pathologies is based once again on an accentuation of anthropological or social–ontological dimensions that are no longer immediately related to the prerequisites of personal self-realization. More than the socio-historical configuration of relationships of *reciprocal recognition*, what is now in question is the *original mode* in which each individual comes to perceive him- or herself, others and the surrounding world. Honneth shifts the analytical perspective away from the critical evaluation of the quality of social relationships towards that of the most primordial forms of perception of the interior and exterior world. In this context, Honneth's (2008) thesis is that our original form of understanding the world – both in a *genetic* sense, regarding psychological development from birth onwards, and a *categorical* one, regarding conceptual relationships of priority among the cognitive capacities of mature adults – is not a cognitive–rational one but rather a pre-cognitive one of affective involvement or participation. In order to designate this primordial form, Honneth introduces the concept of *existential recognition*, which should not be confused with the concept of *reciprocal recognition* that refers to the affirmation of the person's specific characteristic by the social medium. Honneth (2003) states that existential recognition (*Anerkennung*) is prior to knowledge (*Erkennen*) and a constitutive aspect of it. If the notion of *disrespect* is opposed to that of *reciprocal recognition* (Honneth 1995a, 2007b), the concept of *existential recognition* has as its counterpart *reification* (Honneth 2008), a Lukácsian concept that Honneth takes up for the purpose of a critique of social pathologies that is consciously conceived as an attempt to renew the critique of instrumental rationality of the first- and second-generation of the *FS* (Basaure, Reemtsma and Willig 2009).

The concept of reification refers to a situation in which a *forgetting of existential recognition* has taken place, that is a consubstantial aspect of our human existence that cannot be renounced is suspended or repressed. This forgetting cannot be more than a fiction. It is a fiction that, therefore, has the performative capacity to transform practices. Reification originates where the rational cognitive aspect of perception appears to be radically independent from the pre-cognitive and affective aspect of said perception, that is of existential recognition. Reification refers to a process – and its results – in which the reigning forms of *knowledge* embody a purely objectifying and instrumentalist cognitive relationship to oneself, others and nature to such an extent that one can no longer recognize the traces of existential recognition upon which human cognition is necessarily founded. In short, it is a matter of strong and systematic disequilibrium between existential recognition and knowledge in favor of the latter. Honneth is therefore not critiquing objectification itself but rather pathological situations in which one can identify an excessive form of instrumentalist objectification that implies a repression or forgetting of existential recognition. One concrete example of what Honneth (2008) has in mind here is the increasing prevalence in contemporary society of forms of self-reification by way of self-presentation such as that which is exhibited by subjects on the modern job market or in organized dating services, etc.

Continuity through Rupture with the Tradition of the Frankfurt School

This final concept of pathology developed by Honneth may serve as a point of departure for exploring certain ruptures that he makes regarding his predecessors, particularly Habermas. By using this notion, Honneth attempts to maintain continuity with one of the key efforts of the *FS* authors (Basaure, Reemtsma and Willig 2009). In contrast to what Adorno (1986, 1990) had done with the concept of mimetic behavior and what Habermas (1987, 1992, 1994) does with that of communicative rationality, until his recent writings on existential recognition Honneth (2008) had not managed to link his theory of recognition to a critical theory of instrumental rationality and concomitant social pathologies, that is to a critique based on the notion of an asymmetrical development or a disequilibrium among forms of rationality that are constitutive of the human species. If Habermas (1987) continued the Lukácsian program of a critique of reification by reformulating it in terms of a critique of the threat that expanding spheres of instrumental (or functional) rationality represent regarding those necessarily governed by communicative rationality, Honneth (2008), for his part, reconceptualizes this program in terms of the threat of *a 'forgetfulness' of existential recognition*. Habermas (1987, 1996) could speak of pathologies of the modern world to the extent that the dimensions of social life which are threatened are a constitutive aspect of our sociocultural form of human life, i.e. intersubjective communication. For Honneth, however, the most primordial, and hence constitutive, realm of human life would no longer be that of communicative rational understanding, but one of affective participation (Honneth 2008): existential, pre-cognitive and pre-linguistic recognition. On this point, Honneth draws closer to Adorno's concept of mimetic behavior than to Habermas' concept of communicative rationality given that the former, like the notion of existential recognition, involves a non-conceptual or pre-conceptual way of understanding the world.

In this attempt to overcome a lack in his own program – namely, not having a key concept for developing a critique of instrumental rationality – and with a notion of existential recognition, Honneth limits himself to proposing a nucleus of non-cognitivist rationality that is useful for the critical assessment of social pathologies (Honneth 2008, 2009; Basaure, Reemtsma and Willig 2009). He does not develop that critique itself because it does not translate the distinction between existential recognition and knowledge into a useful social-theoretical analysis of the process of reification as Habermas (1987) does when he translates the concepts of instrumental and communicative rationality into two dimensions of society, namely functional systems and the lifeworld. Based on this conceptualization, Habermas (1987, 1996) can understand the pathologies of the modern world as being caused by a colonization of the lifeworld by systemic logics of the bureaucratic state and the market economy. By not making a translation of this type, Honneth offers only the basic conceptual infrastructure upon which a critical social theory of pathologies might be based. Rather than offering a social theory that translates a conceptual distinction at the level of the theory of rationality, Honneth (2008) limits himself to indicating the empirical incidence of a set of convictions whose performative capacity would systematically force the adoption of an objectifying attitude towards oneself and others. This issue, which can be seen as a shortcoming, is linked at the social–theoretical level in Honneth's work to a central aspect of his attempt to achieve a break with Habermas.

On the one hand, like others authors (McCarthy 1991; Joas 1991) Honneth (1993; Basaure, Reemtsma and Willig 2009) gives a series of reasons for rejecting the Habermasian distinction between systems and lifeworld. In part, Honneth claims that this distinction encourages the fiction that, in contrast to the lifeworld, bureaucratic and economic orders constitute completely denormativized social spheres that operate under relatively autonomous logics which are detached from the intentional practices of the actors. Honneth rejects the introduction of systems theory in the conceptual context of critical theory and holds to the conceptual framework of a strictly action-theoretical and practical-philosophical perspective. In fact, in the line of the *FS* authors, Franz Neumann (1972 [1944]) and Otto Kirchheimer (1969) – and, if one wishes, in another tradition, that of Karl Polanyi (1957) or, more recently, Luc Boltanski and Ève Chiapello (2005) – Honneth assumes that such orders, and capitalism in general, cannot be truly understood if one distances them from the structuring normativity of social life and conflicts concerning it. This remains true even under the assumption that those orders are nothing more than the imposition of one symbolic power over another, as in the case of Bourdieu (Bourdieu and Passeron 1990; Wacquant and Bourdieu 2005). On the other hand, however, it is clear that

Honneth lacks a social-theoretical account of the phenomena addressed by institutional and systemic theories which, if not a direct competitor to, at least provides a workable substitute for, the explanatory work done by those sociological approaches. Honneth (Basaure, Reemtsma and Willig 2009) has said that he is aware that it does not seem possible to explain the dynamics of social structures solely on the basis of the normative and conflictive practices of actors and that there are highly robust forms of institutional sedimentation whose dynamics cannot be addressed properly from a purely practical-philosophical perspective. Whether he is conscious of it or not, up to this point Honneth has not offered a satisfactory response to this key aspect of modern social theory.

Above and beyond this problematic, the concept of existential recognition reveals another dimension of Honneth's effort to establish a rupture-in-continuity with the work of Habermas. This concept is constructed on the intuitive understanding that the critique of the pathologies of rationality should overcome a certain cognitivist prejudice (Honneth 2008). It is thus anchored to a pre-linguistic, pre-cognitive and qualitative experience of a "caring" engagement with the world. The intuition that – now moving beyond the issue of rationality – marks the theory of recognition is of the same variety. Honneth links the intersubjective paradigm to a concept of intersubjective communication that is broader than that of linguistic communication. The linguistic turn effected by Habermas – with the help of which he managed to overcome the "production paradigm" that had trapped the work of the first generation of *FS* authors – is a fundamental step forward for Honneth (1993, 1995b, 2007b, 2009), though it does not quite go all the way, or at least goes a bit astray. In this context, Honneth's critique of Habermas involves a charge of a reductionism: by exclusively highlighting linguistic communication (Honneth and Joas 1988), Habermas loses sight of non-linguistic forms of intersubjective communication that are equally important for both the construction of subjectivity and social reproduction (Honneth 2000a). This broadened concept of communication is most clearly evidenced in the importance that Honneth gives to pre-linguistic communication in the sphere of love – mainly in the mother–child relationship – from the point of view of the development of subjectivity (Honneth 1995a). In general, Honneth is careful not to lose sight of the importance of the *materiality* of recognition: corporeal, gestural or mimetic communication and the symbolic aspects of the world of things, that is how, for example, rooms, streets, urban spaces, educational organizations, etc., indirectly express a certain level of development or a state of relationships of reciprocal recognition (Basaure, Reemtsma and Willig 2009), which, incidentally, elucidates the difference between this approach and Foucauldian critical theory (Basaure 2009).

This broadening of the concept of communication has its origin in the manner in which Honneth assumes or specifies the intersubjective turn, that is the legacy of the young Hegel (Honneth 1995a, 1995b, 2007b). Habermas' (1970, 2003) return to the Hegelian intersubjective turn is a decisive conceptual move that led Honneth to search through Hegel's earlier work for the deep social and normative meaning of reciprocal recognition. In Honneth, however, the intersubjective medium in which the development of subjectivity takes place is strictly related to the normative infrastructure of social relationships and their link to people's need for recognition. The anthropology taken up by Honneth does not refer so much to communication and linguistic capacities as to the needs and demands of recognition. These demands, which people constantly make, would be governed by principles anchored in the intersubjective structures of social action according to their level of development in a specific, historical moment of social reproduction (Honneth 1995a). The conceptual expression of this is the paradigm of recognition, where recognition is understood more broadly than in the context of Habermas' discourse ethics (Honneth 2000a). There the concept remains fundamentally linked to the normative principles involved in non-distorted practices of *linguistic* communication.

A different nature is revealed in the description of experiences in which deep-seated behavioral expectations are disappointed (Honneth 2000a). It is no longer a matter of distortions of intersubjective communication but rather of feelings of injustice or disrespect in social subjects. For Honneth, the ethics of discourse does not provide an adequate description of typical negative moral feelings because the normative criteria or principles of justice are not directly linked to those feelings but to the achievement of discursive agreement or the undistorted course of linguistic communication. From the point of view of a moral phenomenology, Honneth (2000a) argues that the primary feelings of injustice do not occur when certain rules of argumentation are not respected; rather, those moral feelings appear when our legitimate expectations of recognition from others or society at large are not fulfilled. Another of Honneth's most significant criticisms of Habermas is based on this fundamental disagreement.

With his differentiation of the concept of rationality and spheres of rationalization, Habermas managed to open a socially immanent practical, moral space in which processes of moral learning, social emancipation and democratization could be anchored. For Honneth, this opening – which constitutes a fundamental advance within the *FS* tradition that cannot be renounced (Honneth 1993, 2007b) – was achieved by paying a very high price: namely, the loss of the possibility of *theoretically* conceiving processes of societal rationalization as inherently bound up with social struggles and conflicts (Honneth 1993; Basaure, Reemtsma and Willig 2009). According to Honneth, in Habermas' work an unbridgeable gap is produced between these processes and the dynamics of social conflicts based on the concrete modes in which relations of social power are expressed. Seeing this as a fundamental shortcoming, Honneth (2000a) seeks to describe the internal, constantly conflictive nature of the lifeworld starting from his construal of the specifically moral feelings, a conceptual moment in which anthropological and social-theoretical theses are unified on the basis of the notion of recognition.

Drawing on an important stream of social philosophy and sociological theory, Honneth holds that society's processes of integration – in addition to being necessarily based on the mechanism of recognition – are also accompanied by continuously emerging conflict. He understands moral consensus and social struggle as two inseparable aspects, two phases, of the process of social reproduction (Basaure, Reemtsma and Willig 2009). This neo-Hegelian proposal can be understood as a perspective that integrates *normativity and conflict* (Honneth 1995a, 1995b, 2007b): members of society are integrated through mechanisms of reciprocal recognition that, nonetheless, by their own logic, are controversial and, as a result, the object of struggles for recognition. In this way, the Honnethian notion of moral-historical learning is not based on the idea of a rationalization of the lifeworld oriented by the *telos* of communication. This learning is instead the historical result of social conflicts and struggles for recognition (Honneth 1995a, 2007b).

With the notion of a *sociological deficit*, Honneth has asserted that the entire *FS* tradition has displayed a tendency to ignore the true nucleus of the social, which, for him, is the fact of a *permanent conflict within and about orders of reciprocal recognition*. As such, this nucleus can be ignored in two different ways from which two different types of sociological deficit are derived. One refers to the *normativity* and the other to the *conflictuality* of social life. On the one hand, the early *FS* authors ignored the normative aspect of this nucleus, i.e. in Honneth's theory, the moral infrastructure of society in the form of spheres and principles of recognition. According to Honneth (1993), here more or less agreeing with Habermas' own diagnosis, a productivist notion of rationality and society and a reductionistic functionalism prevented these authors from being able to describe the normative logic that animates social life and social conflicts. When Habermas (1987) then replaced the production paradigm with one of communicative understanding and with differentiated concepts of rationality and society, he managed to overcome, in his own way, this *first sociological deficit* since he recognized the normative mechanism of social integration in communicative action. But, according to Honneth, Habermas' one-sided reconceptualization produced what can be called a *second sociological deficit* referring to the aspect linked to the conflictive nature of society (Honneth 2007b). That is, there is a strong tendency built into the conceptual scheme of Habermas' work to undervalue the meaning of conflicts and social struggles in the reproduction of the social order. This idea was clearly present in the early stages of the *FS* tradition in the form of a Marxist theory of history.

For this reason, Honneth's proposal can be understood as a sort of synthesis of elements derived from the first phase of the tradition of critical theory and the one that begins with Habermas' work. To put it briefly, while he obtains, though in a very transformed and selective manner, a normative and moral view of society from Habermas, he takes from the founders of the *FS* tradition the idea that social struggles have a constitutive significance for social reproduction. This integrating perspective guides Honneth (1995b, 2009) in his efforts to take up the work of certain authors of the *FS* tradition who, unlike Adorno, Horkheimer and Marcuse, were not part of the *inner circle* of the first generation of that tradition and did not determine the general trend of the work done in the Institute for Social Research. In what in this sense are the peripheral works of Franz Neumann, Otto Kirchheimer in political economy, Erich Fromm in social psychology, and Walter Benjamin in the theory of culture, Honneth identifies a concept of social integration which is determined by the results of fragmentary daily struggles among social groups and by the communicative and aesthetic-interpretive capacities of the actors themselves. It is not subject to anonymous processes that impose themselves stealthily, as in the image of a society integrated in a purely functional manner or a managed world like the one found in the works of Adorno, Horkheimer or Marcuse (Honneth 1993, 1995b).

There is another area in which Honneth's work marks a rupture with Habermas' perspective on politics and social struggles. In order to describe the internal and continual conflicts inherent to the lifeworld, Honneth starts from a broad concept of social struggle – one that in principle can be private and individual as well – which is more or less identified with a set of reactions to negative moral experiences (Honneth 1995a). This wider perspective stands in contrast to that of Habermas (1987), who understood the contemporary presence of certain social movements in civil society – acting directly and visibly in the public political sphere – as cultural struggles in defense of the autonomy of the lifeworld from colonization by the systemic logics of the bureaucratic state and the market economy. These social movements, which were associated with the moral and critical conscience of progressive bourgeois sectors, would embody a legitimate critique of the uncontrolled installation of relationships oriented by instrumental and strategic rationality, either in the sense of an excess of bureaucratization or an undue expansion of economic relationships in areas of action that in principle cannot be coordinated by means of power and money (Honneth 2007b).

Honneth holds that perspectives like that of Habermas lose sight of two fundamental issues. The first is a concern for the prerequisites for political participation in the public life of a community (Honneth 2007a). According to his concept of justice, Honneth finds it necessary to give importance to those non-universalist spheres of action that in fact help enable the realization of universal values such as that of equal participation in the public sphere. It is in particular a question of spheres of action that are not subject to universalist principles of action such as that of private relationships and that of recognition in the context of work relationships (Honneth 1995a; Fraser and Honneth 2003). On the other hand, Honneth argues that Habermas also tends to ignore the fact that the public sphere involves mechanisms of exclusion and thematic selection such that if critical theory refers only to social conflicts involving groups that are already organized and participate in the public sphere, then it will suffer a certain blindness regarding other latent struggles that do not (yet) do so. They remain beneath a threshold of relevance and public thematization as hidden forms of social suffering, and moral experiences of humiliation and injustice. These daily struggles can (and often should) lead to a fight to make publicly visible demands for change or restitution and the collectives behind them. For Honneth, these conflicts over visibility are not an external matter but rather constitutive of the democratic public sphere. Drawing on the work of Bourdieu (Basaure 2011), he refers to the issue of representation below the threshold of the public perspective and criticizes the exclusively theoretical focus on the presence of social movements (Honneth 2007b; Fraser and Honneth 2003). Taken together, these two doubts about Habermas' theoretical perspective amount to a critique of any conceptual and political program that centers exclusively on the category of civil society. For Honneth, that category brings with it a certain idealization because the privileged place acquired by the representation of organized bodies of subjects in political society tends to be too far removed from the conditions for participation in that society as well as from the complex ideological-political dynamic that allows for cognitive and public representation of certain forms of social suffering in the first place and the struggles for recognition aimed at making that possible (Basaure, Reemtsma and Willig 2009).

Debates about the complex continuity through rupture discussed here with regard to Honneth and Habermas certainly will play an important role in determining the future of the *FS* tradition.

Note

* For valuable help in the preparation of this text, I thank Nora Sieverding, Jonathan Trejo-Mathys, Simon Susen, and Jaeho Kang. I also would like to thank Katherine Goldman for her support in the development of this text.

References

Adorno, T. W. (1986) *Aesthetic Theory*, London: Routledge & Kegan Paul.
——(1990) *Negative Dialectics*, London: Routledge.
Basaure, M. (2009) "Foucault and the 'Anti-Oedipus Movement': Psychoanalysis as Disciplinary Power", *History of Psychiatry*, 20 (3), 340–59.
——(2011) "The Grammar of an Ambivalence: On the Legacy of Pierre Bourdieu in the Critical Theory of Axel Honneth," in B. Turner and S. Sassen (eds) *Pierre Bourdieu and Classical Sociology*, London: Anthem Press.
Basaure, M., J. P. Reemtsma and R. Willig (2009) *Erneuerung der Kritik: Axel Honneth im Gespräch*, Frankfurt, New York: Campus.
Boltanski, L. and È. Chiapello (2005) *The Spirit of Capitalism*, New York: Verso.
Bourdieu, P. and J. C. Passeron (1990) *Reproduction in Education, Society, and Culture*, London: SAGE.
Cohen, J. L. and A. Arato (1994) *Civil Society and Political Theory*, Cambridge, MA: MIT Press.
Fraser, N. and A. Honneth (2003) *Redistribution or Recognition? A Political-Philosophical Exchange*, New York: Verso.
Habermas, J. (1970) *Technology and Science as "Ideology"*, Boston, MA: Beacon Press.
——(1987) *The Theory of Communicative Action*, vol. 2: *Lifeworld and System: A Critique of Functionalist Reason*, Boston, MA: Beacon Press.
——(1992) *Moral Consciousness and Communicative Action*, Cambridge, MA: MIT Press.
——(1994) *Postmetaphysical Thinking: Philosophical Essays*, Cambridge, MA: MIT Press.
——(1996) *The Philosophical Discourse of Modernity*, Cambridge, MA: MIT Press.
——(2003) *Truth and Justification*, Cambridge, MA: MIT Press.
Honneth, A. (1993) *The Critique of Power: Reflective Stages in a Critical Social Theory*, Cambridge, MA: MIT Press.
——(1995a) *The Struggle for Recognition: The Moral Grammar of Social Conflicts*, Cambridge: Polity Press.
——(1995b) *The Fragmented World of the Social: Essays in Social and Political Philosophy*, Washington: SUNY Press.
——(2000a) "Anerkennungsbeziehungen und Moral: Eine Diskussionsbemerkung zur anthropologischen Erweiterung der Diskursethik", in R. Brunner and P. Kelbel (eds) *Anthropologie, Ethik und Gesellschaft. Für Helmut Fahrenbach*, Frankfurt, New York: Campus, 101–11.

——(2000b) *Suffering from Indeterminacy: An Attempt at a Reactualization of Hegel's Philosophy of Right*, Assen: Uitgeverij Van Gorcum.

——(2003) *Unsichtbarkeit: Stationen einer Theorie der Intersubjektivität*, Frankfurt: Suhrkamp.

——(2007a) "Democracy as Reflexive Cooperation: John Dewey and the Theory of Democracy Today", in *Disrespect: The Normative Foundations of Critical Theory*, Cambridge: Polity Press, 218–39.

——(2007b) *Disrespect: The Normative Foundations of Critical Theory*, Cambridge: Polity Press.

——(2008) *Reification: A New Look at an Old Idea*, Oxford: Oxford University Press.

——(2009) *Pathologies of Reason: On the Legacy of Critical Theory*, New York: Columbia University Press.

——(2010) *The Pathologies of Individual Freedom: Hegel's Social Theory*, Princeton, NJ: Princeton University Press.

Honneth, A. and H. Joas (1988) *Social Action and Human Nature*, Cambridge: Cambridge University Press.

Jay, M. (2008) "Introduction", in A. Honneth, *Reification: A New Look at an Old Idea*, Oxford: Oxford University Press, 3–13.

Joas, H. (1991) "The Unhappy Marriage of Hermeneutics and Functionalism", in A. Honneth and H. Joas (eds) *Communicative Action*, Cambridge: Polity Press, 97–118.

Kirchheimer, Otto (1969) *Politics, Law and Social Change*, New York: Columbia University Press.

Margalit, A. (1996) *The Decent Society*, Cambridge, MA: Harvard University Press.

McCarthy, T. (1991) "Complexity and Democracy: Or the Seducements of Systems", in A. Honneth and H. Joas (eds) *Communicative Action*, Cambridge: Polity Press, 119–39.

Miller, D. (1999) *The Principles of Social Justice*, Cambridge, MA: Harvard University Press.

Neumann, F. L. (1972 [1944]) *Behemoth: The Structure and Practice of National Socialism, 1933–1944*, New York: Octagon Books.

Polanyi, K. (1957) *The Great Transformation: The Political and Economic Origins of Our Time*, Boston, MA: Beacon Press.

Smith, Adam (1977 [1776]) *An Inquiry into the Nature and Causes of the Wealth of Nations*, Chicago, IL: University of Chicago Press.

Taylor, C. (1992) *Multiculturalism and "The Politics of Recognition": An Essay*, Princeton, NJ: Princeton University Press.

Todorov, T. (2001) *Life in Common: An Essay in General Anthropology*, Nebraska: University of Nebraska Press.

Wacquant, L. and P. Bourdieu (2005) *Pierre Bourdieu and Democratic Politics: The Mystery of Ministry*, Cambridge: Polity Press.

Walzer, M. (1983) *Spheres of Justice: A Defense of Pluralism and Equality*, New York: Basic Books.

Lessons from Twentieth-century Political Philosophy before Rawls

Jeremy Shearmur

It has sometimes been suggested that political philosophy was dormant – if not dead – before Rawls brought it back to life, if not with a kiss, then with work which was both impressive and has given rise to a daunting quantity of secondary literature.

A few minutes reflection, however, would make clear to the enquirer that this was far from the case. While what was going on before Rawls wrote was diverse, and while those who have contributed to the Rawls industry may well not have liked what was going on, there is no question but that a lot was taking place. In addition to work in the 'ordinary language' tradition, there was, after all, R. G. Collingwood and Michael Oakeshott, and also Leo Strauss. There was also work in the orthodox Marxian tradition, to say nothing of the Frankfurt School. In the present chapter, however, I am going to concentrate on two rather different figures – Popper and Hayek. My concern will be to try to spell out the kind of work in which they were involved, how it differs from more recent work, and to argue that a lot has been lost by virtue of its having been given insufficient attention.

First, however, something must be said. For, in retrospect, there is something rather odd about the work of both Hayek and Popper if looked at from a contemporary perspective. It might be summed up by saying that, while neither of them were crusading non-cognitivists in respect of moral and political values, the general temper of the times at which they wrote had in many respects cowed them. This is most obvious in the case of Popper – for he has addressed, explicitly, the way in which in his early work he was restricted in what he said as a consequence of not having to hand a theory in terms of which he could defend the rationality of ideas like truth and of metaphysical theories (such as realism). This led to his writing *The Logic of Scientific Discovery* in such a way that all that was appealed to were notions of rationality in respect of logical and mathematical issues, empirical ideas, and methodology. While it is perfectly true – as Popper was himself to stress – that by the time he wrote his *Open Society and Its Enemies* he placed emphasis on the significance of a rational attitude (of the idea that we can't be sure that our ideas are correct, and that we might have something to learn from one another), there is a sense in which, at key points, his approach comes over as decisionistic. (Indeed, in some earlier writing – of which there are still traces in *The Open Society* – there seems to be an appeal just to the individual's conscience as a moral authority, in a manner which contrasts sharply with his anti-subjectivism and stress on inter-subjective appraisal, in *The Logic of Scientific Discovery*.)

Hayek, too, is – to say the least – rather muted about values, and rather than arguing about them, tends to simply assume certain minimal values, the thrust of his work lying elsewhere.

The task that I will address here is as follows. I will concentrate on the very different approaches to political philosophy of Friedrich Hayek and Karl Popper. I will not be concerned to address their work in its own terms, but will, rather, consider the following question. What might contemporary political theorists miss, if they do not pay attention to their work but, instead, write as if twentieth-century political philosophy had been asleep until the advent of John Rawls? Clearly, there are many other figures whose work one might equally consider from such a perspective, but I have chosen Hayek and Popper because these are people about whom I can write most easily, and also because I think that their work has interesting (if rather different) things to say to us today.

First, some commonalities. As I have mentioned, given the time at which Hayek and Popper were writing, they did not have much confidence in strongly cognitive approaches to moral and political theory. Popper, in much of his work, was faced with the problem of responding to the challenge of people whom he knew from Vienna, who had questioned the cogency of anything that went beyond the empirical and the formal. Through all of his work, Popper disagreed with the approach from the early Wittgenstein, and the Vienna Circle, that it was cogent to debar various kinds of discourse as 'meaningless'.[1] But he nonetheless struggled with the problem of how to explain that metaphysical claims were open to critical assessment, and was somewhat ambivalent about the status of ethical claims.[2] Hayek was, by training, an economist, and also had reservations about ethical cognitivism. In certain respects, this leads to problems about their work – e.g. that anyone who wishes to explore what their responses should have been to certain questions in this area, would be faced with a task involving a lot of reconstruction, often speculative. However, there are certain advantages to their approach. For they tended to minimize the degree to which they were involved in founding their approaches upon substantive ethical claims, and also to be well aware of the fact that there would be likely to be continuing disagreements about ethical issues, to which it could not be assumed that there was a rational resolution.

This, I think, is important in two respects. First, what they have to say is, it seems to me, highly pertinent to the situation in which we find ourselves. For while those writing today would probably wish to claim that more could be done by way of cognitive argument about social and ethical issues than Hayek and Popper would have allowed for, we are apt to over-rate what can be achieved, and to proceed as if everybody in fact found our own approach rationally telling. This, in a situation in which people's views on ethical (to say nothing of religious) matters are diverse, and in which the practical impact that rational argument about such matters can make is somewhat limited,[3] can pose real problems, as we are apt to treat the world as if everyone would agree that our ideas are compelling. Second, a consequence of all this, is that what Hayek and Popper did concentrate upon – issues which can be addressed with relatively minimal ethical assumptions – is I believe of real interest and importance.

Two points, however, must at once be made. The first is that they both worked with what might be called minimal, but recognisably liberal, assumptions – in the sense that they respected the preferences of individuals, and were concerned about both their liberty and their well-being, and took themselves to be addressing others who shared these concerns. Clearly, given the time at which they were writing, they hardly needed to be reminded that the world contained Hitler and Stalin – and also people who supported them. Their concern in the bulk of their writings was not to address those who were genuinely anti-humanitarian in their views; but they did wish to engage with people who were humanitarian, but who they thought were misled into the support of such people, because they held mistaken social, political, and methodological theories. Happily, this is not a major problem today – although certainly there are difficult issues posed by those who hold certain religious views[4] – and by those who embrace certain kinds of fashionable relativism. (My concern here is not that people are led to deny what is obviously true, but, rather, that relativism may make it difficult for them to admit that they and others hold views which are mistaken or in other ways problematic.)[5]

Second, Hayek's and Popper's views should not be identified with what one might call the non-moralistic contractarian tradition in political thought; i.e. with those who wish to restart what they see as a Hobbesian project, but couched in terms of rational choice theory. Such work is often intellectually interesting, and I think that we may have a lot to learn from it with regard to issues of institutional design.[6] But it seems to me problematic because in actual social and political circumstances, people may well be motivated by specific religious or moral commitments and they may simply not be interested in what those in this tradition tell them would be in their interest if they were, instead, more narrowly and rationally self-interested.

Rather, both Hayek and Popper address the world as it is, and they do not suppose that we can be expected to agree with our fellow-citizens on high-level priorities and on the plans for their implementation. There are, in the work of each of them, arguments – which are rather different in their character[7] – directed against the idealistic would-be planners of their own day. And while the targets of their criticism are no longer with us, there is I believe a lot in their arguments which needs to be taken on board. Instead of talking in abstract terms, however, it would I think be most useful if I were turn to consider Hayek and Popper separately, before – in the conclusion to this chapter – returning to more general matters.

Hayek

In approaching political theorists, one might usefully make a distinction between those who start with moral issues, and those who start with a picture of society as they believe that it currently stands and what the realistic prospects for changing it might be. It is not that the latter group do not have moral concerns, so much as that, for them, what we should do once it has been determined what our society is like, is pretty much a 'no-brainer'. *Our* customary way of addressing issues in political philosophy is typically of the first kind (such that, say, where we find elements of the latter approach within what we take to be 'our' kind of political theory, as with the elements of social relativity and the reference to Akbar in Mill's *On Liberty*, we tend to treat it as if it was an unfortunate lapse).[8] But clearly, we cannot, say, make much sense of Marxism other than in terms of the second approach. My suggestion is that Hayek is usefully considered to be a theorist of the second kind, and that we have a lot to learn from him and from that second tradition.

As looking at things in such a way may be unfamiliar, let me start with a few words about Marx, when seen from this perspective. For him, our key starting-point, if we were to do political philosophy, would be to appreciate what our society is like. Here, Marx would offer us his well-known analysis. Given this, what needs to be done is, in a sense, obvious.[9] For given basic good-will – or, indeed, pretty much any ordinary moral motivation – the key issue would be to see what could be done to work with those in a position to transform our society into one in which people could live genuinely human lives. Clearly, there were other facets to Marx's work – from the way in which he transformed his understanding of the Hegelian tradition, to more scientistic and 'historicist' readings of these matters which one got later in the Marxian tradition. But at a certain level, *given* his social analysis, what needs to be done would be fairly obvious from most ordinary ethical perspectives.

Now it seems to me that, while lots of other things are also going on in Hayek's work, an important insight into his ideas is offered by a parallel with Marx. For a key aspect of Hayek's work was provided by the impact made on him personally by, and then by his reworking of, Ludwig von Mises' arguments about the problems facing socialism.[10] Of special importance here, is the idea that there was a fatal flaw to the socialist tradition; namely, that it had assumed that the practical benefits of capitalist society would still be available to us, even if we moved away from a market-based society. Socialism in anything like Marx's sense was, Mises argued, simply not possible, for within such societies we would not have access to the information, and be able to undertake the kinds of economic calculations, upon which such societies vitally depend.

It is here that a glance back at Marx becomes again important. For he argued that, within capitalism, there were various structural limitations on what could be accomplished politically. For capitalism to work, certain mechanisms played a key role, and power was also distributed in various distinctive ways. Within such a system, it literally made no sense to ask the main players to behave differently: to do so was to ask them to behave in ways that were at odds with how the system both did and had to operate, and also, given that the system was in place, to operate in ways which might be drastically against their interests. Clearly, most people would, today, have considerable reservations about the explanatory theories that Marx offered, and even those sympathetic towards Marxism as a programmatic approach, would agree that there seems to be much more leeway to make changes, and for working people to make improvements within the system, than Marx had suggested.[11] However, if one puts to one side the Marxian hope of a dramatic resolution of our key social problems,[12] a lot of *critical* work written about Western politics within the Marxist tradition has much force. Not only does it throw light upon features of 'liberal' political systems that liberals often do not talk about. But it also raises important problems about left-liberal hopes that the state can be expected to work to the advantage of the poor and downtrodden.

Now Hayek isn't Marx. But there is a sense in which his work shares some features of a structural approach to politics, like Marx's. At one level, he argued that Marx was wrong in thinking that a transformation of our society to socialism is possible. There is, for Hayek, nowhere else to go – not least because of the vast numbers of people whose continuing existence, he came to argue, depends on something like the market-based forms of social organization that we have at present remaining in place. At the same time, for Hayek societies of this kind have structures which limit what actions we can take if our society is still to thrive, and if people are to be able to continue to enjoy individual freedom. In his view, however, we may be attracted to doing things which will lead us from this path, and one of his continuing concerns was to try to warn us that various things which might well seem appealing in themselves, are problematic in terms of their likely systematic consequences for the functioning of our society.

Hayek's worry is that it is all too tempting to do things which seem attractive – but which are likely to have dire consequences for the structural characteristics of societies like ours, and the benefits that they can bring us.

In this respect, Hayek's work has an aspect which is like that of eighteenth-century social theorists: that while there is a concern for values – and with different people's aspirations – there is also a concern for the operations of society as a system, and with the fact that if it is going to work in certain ways, then this may depend on people's having certain particular characteristics, and values. Such concerns – which are obvious enough in Montesquieu, in Rousseau, in the American Founding Fathers, and also in Adam Smith, and which also spill over into the nineteenth century – tend not now to play a significant role in political theory.[13] Yet in Hayek, they play a key role. For what he offers us is a picture of a society that functions in powerfully productive ways, and which at a certain level furnishes the individual citizen with an important kind of liberty. Yet, on his account, how this society does or might best work is horribly vulnerable, often to the likely consequences of actions which we will be inclined to take on the basis of some of our best impulses. Some of these, Hayek believes, are in fact misplaced – i.e. they are ideals, like that of a society in which people merit what they receive, which he thinks cannot be realized in a society like ours. Others like the wish for a welfare state of a certain kind, are fine, provided that they are pursued in the right way – which, here, means that they are pursued in such a way that they do not damage those institutions which are responsible for key functional roles being performed, and for the safeguarding of people's freedom.

Hayek has specific ideas about how our institutions do – and can – work; he also has ideas (sometimes highly speculative) about how such institutions may have developed, and about the characteristics of them that need to be preserved. These are certainly worthy of examination; but I would have thought that the value of his work is rather more general.

For what Hayek does is to offer us a picture in which we have inherited social mechanisms which perform various functions for us, which typically were not designed (or, if they were, were often not planned to operate as they currently do). What these are, and how they operate, may not be evident to us. And it may – e.g. if Mises and Hayek were right about the economic calculation argument – be the case that we cannot achieve things that we wish to have, without specific such mechanisms being in place. The most obvious example, in Hayek's work, is the price system. But he went on to generalize his argument, and to suggest that we have inherited social institutions, habits, traditions, and so on, of many different kinds, which may have this broad character. It is clear that many of these are likely not to have the same 'There is no alternative' character, that he argued was the case for the price system in a society like ours. But at the same time, we need, I think, to take seriously his point that we typically make use of specific mechanisms which may well rule out the achievement, while we use them, of other things that we think to be valuable. To this one might add a Burkean perspective; that is to say, that *we* have been formed by particular traditions, values, and ways of behaving, which may have the consequence that some institutions and ways of doing things which are possible for *other* people, may not be possible for us, either as we are currently, or for how we might feasibly become.

At the same time, it must be stressed that, in Hayek's work, there is also emphasis upon the idea that institutions which we have inherited may not work particularly well, and that we may need to change and reform them. This seems to me a key part of his approach (even if how exactly this fits with some of what he says when pursuing other aspects of his views, is not altogether clear: it seems to me that there is much in Hayek's work which is unresolved).[14]

What, then, is the contemporary significance of Hayek's approach? I think that his work stresses to us the importance of understanding that we operate under all kinds of institutional and traditional constraints; ones which we may tentatively set out to improve upon, but which will typically limit our ability to accomplish all that we might like to. In this sense, Hayek's approach is strongly anti-utopian; but from a Hayekian perspective, the charge of utopianism could be made not just at the Marxists and would-be large-scale social planners of his own day, but also at people inspired by visions of 'social justice', domestically or internationally, in our own. While his approach does have a significant value basis to it – valuing people's freedom, and their well-being – what he has to say can and should speak to people with a variety of values and concerns. In his own day, he dedicated his *Road to Serfdom* (Hayek 1944) to 'socialists of all parties', and he had a strong concern to speak to people on both the left and the right of politics. In my view, a key corrective which emerges from his work, is the idea that we should pursue our normative concerns with as much knowledge as we can obtain about how our institutions and traditions operate, how they constrain us, and about what choices are feasibly open to us. It would, I think, lead us back to an approach to political theory in some ways closer to that which was taken in the eighteenth century, and to working against a backdrop of a big-picture view of these issues, than that which tends to be found in our work on political theory today.

Popper

Karl Popper is best known in political philosophy for his *Open Society*, and for a number of essays which appeared in his *Conjectures and Refutations* (Popper 1963) and in subsequent collections (including various rather general addresses which appeared in essay collections in his old age). More recently, a lot of hitherto scattered or unpublished material on social and political themes has appeared in his *After the Open Society*. I have addressed his views in my *Political Thought of Karl Popper*, while Malachi Hacohen has provided a brilliant and detailed account of his earlier work, in his *Karl Popper: The Formative Years* (see Hachohen 2000). Here, as in the previous section on Hayek, I will concern myself not with Popper's views in their own right, but with what they may have to say to us today.

While there were certain commonalities between Popper and Hayek – a background in early twentieth-century Austria; emigration to England; an attachment to certain themes which would today be recognized as 'republican' in character[15] – and while they were friends, there were also deep differences between them. Their social backgrounds were different, and they first met in London in the 1930s. Hayek was an economist, with a family background in biology. Popper's interests were in psychology and subsequently the physical sciences. In addition, Popper's background was much more strongly socialist, and while he became critical of socialism (see particularly his letter to Rudolf Carnap on this subject, now included in his *After the Open Society*), he never shared the systematic liberal economic perspective which pervaded Hayek's work. It was all this that made it somewhat strange that he and Hayek came to in some ways similar perspectives in *The Open Society* and *The Road to Serfdom*. What they shared, particularly, was an ethical individualism which contrasted with various collectivist ideas which were then popular, a disagreement with 'historicism' in social theory, and misgivings about then-popular ideas about social planning. However, it seems to me that their criticism of planning, while it came to similar (negative) conclusions, was developed in rather different ways. For Hayek, ideas from the debate about socialist economic calculation played an important role, as did issues about the social distribution of information, the importance of the rule of law to the operations of a market-based society, and the degree to which people within such a society are likely to be able to agree, rationally, only to a limited extent about collective projects and their priority.[16]

Popper's perspective was very different. He was struck, particularly, by the diversity of our ideals,[17] and by the fallibility of our knowledge. In a paper written in 1946, Popper considered the diversity in terms of their ideals between, say, Christians, utilitarians, liberals, and socialists[18] – and the fact that it is not likely that they will convince one another that they are in error.[19] He argues that while in our private relations we may pursue our ideals (e.g. by way of pushing our tastes in music upon our friends), such conduct is not appropriate for the public realm. There, rather, he argues that we should concentrate upon those things which we can agree as being problematic, and develop a political agenda in which they are addressed. Thus, the agenda for politics – beyond a basic agenda for the protection of individuals from aggression and exploitation (including, in his view, economic exploitation), which is to be secured by the laws and the power of the state – is the pursuit of an agreed agenda of social ills which should be remedied. Here, however, the issue of our fallibility comes into play. In Popper's view, any action which the government takes in the pursuit of such concerns is likely to have unintended consequences – and these may be adverse in their character. What then becomes important is that each and every citizen be recognised as a source of potential criticism – they may be the people who know that there are unanticipated problems with these policies, not least because they affect them or the people or situations that they know all about. Popper here discusses the Kantian idea of the 'rational unity of mankind', but he re-interprets it in terms of his own fallibilistic epistemology. The ability to offer such feedback – and to have governments which respond to it – is, for Popper, a key characteristic of a good political order.

All this, clearly, would require that we have institutions in place which are not ordinary features of modern Western democracies. Neither presidential-style nor parliamentary-style systems work effectively for such purposes. In particular, the public services – which in many countries play a key role not just in the formulation of policy, but whose conceptions about what is and what is not politically possible or even advisable constitute a framework for all policy which is given serious consideration – seldom have *their* ideas opened to critical scrutiny. And, in general terms, for any senior politician to admit that their ideas were flawed, typically ensures that they lose (and perhaps also their party loses) the next election. What would seem to be needed are bodies concerned with the scrutiny of what is taking place in our society, to which those with political power are accountable. However, there is more. For suppose that someone does report that there are unintended, problematic consequences from some measure. Such claims need to be checked out and their significance evaluated. In addition, only certain such things will receive protection – we typically, say, don't protect a small store from competition from a larger store that opens up near it; while in other cases, it might be thought most appropriate to assist people to adapt to problematic and disruptive change, rather than to try to prevent it.

Indeed, this serves to highlight an issue in respect of which Popper's work is, I think, vulnerable to a Hayekian critique.[20] Popper was critical of what he called the 'essentialism' of the Marxian tradition, by which he meant the picture of structural constraints under which Marxists saw what could be achieved, politically, as severely limited. Popper's critique was in part political – he was concerned with what he thought to be some disasters which a historicist version of these ideas had led to in Europe between the wars. It was also in part methodological. It seems to me, however, that both points are open to correction. As I have argued elsewhere, Popper's methodological criticism seems to stand in need of correction in the light of the fallibilistic realism about science which he was himself to adopt. There seems every reason to believe that our actions may have consequences which constrain us politically, in ways that may not be obvious, as may our traditions and choices of systems of social institutions. Further, if we consider these constraints as being of the kind that Hayek described – i.e. less as telling us that there are things that are impossible, so much as telling us about things that it would be problematic to try to realise, given our existing institutions and ways of doing things – the case seems to me pressing.

If there is anything in this, however, it points to a major difficulty. For what we would seem to need, from the perspective of either of these theorists (Hayek, directly; Popper, if he can be pushed in the direction that I have indicated), is a reflective body of people, who can advise, in a fallible but reasonably authoritative way, about these institutional issues. That is to say, while we do not need the Guardians of Plato's *Republic*, we do seem to need an informed body playing a more negative but theoretically informed role. Hayek was led, in his old age, to make some suggestions about the possible role of a senate-like body, to be elected on a cohort-basis by people over a certain age, to constrain the government on the basis of their ideas about what would make for just laws. But clearly, *these* people would not have the kind of theoretical knowledge that would be needed to play the task that, it seems to me, Hayek himself has indicated that we need. What, I think, is patently clear, is that no institutions currently play this role, and that tendencies in the development of the media are, if anything, leading us away from a situation in which a knowledge of these matters can be presumed to be something like a common possession of those in leading positions in our society.[21] In making this point, however, I am not suggesting that such an institution could currently be set up – only that, for reasons that I think become clear in rather different ways in the work of Hayek and of Popper, we are likely to face some real difficulties without there being such institutions in place.

Conclusion

My aim in this piece was to suggest that important points would be lost if we were to treat political philosophy as something that was asleep until it was awoken by Rawls. In what I have written, my concern has implicitly been with the Rawlsian tradition, and the kind of work which has been developed in response to it. To these people, my message is that our starting-point should be with a historical and theoretical understanding of our institutions, traditions, and customs, and the way in which they both enable and constrain us. It may or may not be the case that, in the end, the specific concerns and claims of Hayek will prove to be correct; but – or so it seems to me – he was at least asking the right *kinds* of questions. Further, while one can go a lot further towards cognitivism in respect of ethical and political issues than did Hayek or Popper, what we can achieve there should not mislead us. For among people of good will there are likely to be value-based disagreements which go all the way down – and in the face of which, Popper's concerns about what we can agree needs basic protection, and what we can agree we should try to remedy, look important.[22] Such concerns would, I think, lead us towards a bringing together of the normative and the positive in a manner that was last found in eighteenth-century social theory. At the same time, while I would endorse Hayek's and Popper's criticisms of Marxism's ability to resolve our problems, I think that there is a lot of value in the *critical* aspects of the Marxist tradition, because of its concern for the interplay between our systematic social institutions and what happens in society.

It could, however, be said that the work of Rawls, and analytical work of a similar kind, while important, is by no means all there is. Let me conclude, by indicating briefly how my suggestions could be extended elsewhere.

As I argued in some detail in my *Political Thought of Karl Popper*, there are considerable commonalities between the later Habermas and Popper. At the same time, Habermas' expectations about dialogue and consensus seem to me hopelessly over-optimistic. Clearly, we may be able to operate in something like this fashion in certain areas of science.[23] But, if this is the case, it depends upon those involved sharing an intellectual background, having a shared, and detailed, knowledge of their subject-matter, and upon their concentrating on a restricted range of problems. Popper suggested that we might be able to aim for consensual judgements about those things which we may need to remedy, politically. But his argument for this required that we put our ideological commitments to one side (as relating to the private sphere).[24] Further, I have suggested that issues become more complex once one brings in theoretical knowledge – just because, when looked at from a Hayekian perspective, some of the things that citizens agree are regrettable and in need of remedy, may well be things that the theoretically informed would tell us can't be addressed, without giving rise to much greater problems. From such a perspective, ideas in the Habermasian tradition, and in the work of those concerned with 'deliberative democracy', look hopelessly – and dangerously[25] – over-optimistic.

In this respect, there is a degree of commonality between the writers with whom I have been concerned, and those who stress the 'agonistic' character of politics. But, it seems to me, there are two problems about the latters' work. First, while Hayek and Popper urge us to restrict the scope of politics to that about which we can reasonably expect to get agreement, those who favour an agonistic approach seem expansive in their views about the political, but not to tell us how we can hope to resolve our disagreements without them leading to our taking up arms against one another. For if someone else comes after us, our friends and family, or our possessions, on a basis which from our perspective is unreasonable, we are not likely to take to it kindly, and may well find ways of resisting. It is, after all, worth bearing in mind the degree to which the kind of peace and security that many of us can take for granted is a social and historical artefact rather than being something like a default condition for human life. We should not take risks with it lightly. Second, those who favour such perspectives often take a viewpoint which might be referred to as 'postmodern'. But in the light of the issues with which this chapter deals, this is a disaster. For it calls into question – often, it seems to me, without fully understanding the implications of what it is doing – the very notion of our acting under constraints, the character of which we may be able to come to understand theoretically.[26] In this respect, the Marxist tradition – shorn of its optimistic teleology – seems to me infinitely to be preferred, and also to speak much more truly to the concerns of the disadvantaged.[27]

One final comment. Should – against, it should be said, my expectations, there be a shift towards the concern for an interplay between large-scale (and also pertinent empirical) social theory and normative theory, of the kind that attention to these ideas would again lead us, we would have a lot on our hands. It is not, however, typically work that could easily be undertaken within the relatively short, and tightly analytical, papers which we are currently expected to write. Much would need reform, in terms of our academic institutions and the bureaucracies who currently seek to control the research that takes place within them.

We would, nonetheless, return to something that could hope to make a real contribution towards the societies in which we are living, and to the difficult problems that confront us. There is also much that is intellectually challenging. To conclude with one brief example, in Hayek's work, a great deal of weight is placed upon tradition, and upon the dangers of destroying valuable things that it accomplishes, by way of certain kinds of rationalistic planning. In Popper's later work, emphasis is placed on tradition, too. But each of them faces a problem here. Hayek wishes to be a traditionalist, but also to embrace market institutions, and the kinds of radical change for which they allow. Popper favours piecemeal social engineering, controlled by feedback from citizens, about how things had not turned out as we have hoped. But if our earlier practices involved traditional practices, we may well not be able to return to where we were before – and to such traditions – after we have gone through some period of experimentation. To address such issues seems to me a pressing, and interesting, task.[28]

Notes

1 See, for discussion of this, Popper 1959, first published in German in 1934.
2 See, for discussion, Shearmur 1986a and 2009.
3 As a recent period of sabbatical leave in the United States brought home to me all too clearly.
4 My argument here is not that religious theories are distinctively problematic, so much as that, in difficult situations or times of rapid social change, people may embrace certain religious views which can pose problems for everyone else.
5 A concern about relativism may, thus, be grounded not in a belief that we are correct, but in a fallibilist concern that we may well *not* be correct, even about those things about which we seem most sure.
6 There is, though, the risk that institutions designed to work in the public interest even if people are narrowly self-interested, may well lead people who were initially altruistic to react negatively and to start to behave in a narrowly self-interested way, in the face of the kinds of incentives and systems of accountability introduced by the new systems.
7 Popper's arguments are concerned, particularly, with our fallibility and with the problems posed by the unintended consequences of governmental action; Hayek's, with issues about the social division of information.

8 That is, there is a degree of relativity to what kind of society we are living in, to Mill's *On Liberty*, with which his modern readers often feel unhappy.

9 I am not wishing to denigrate issues like those raised by Alan Buchanan, as to the situation of a potential labour leader, whose material interests might well be to allow himself to be bought out by the bosses; rather just to say that for anyone who had a strong moral motivation (be it a concern for human happiness, or individual flourishing), what was to be done was obvious.

10 Seen, here, as a theory addressing the situation of people living in large, populous, industrial societies: neither Mises nor Hayek doubted that some form of socialism might be possible for those living in small face-to-face societies.

11 Popper was explicitly critical of the idea that there were such limitations; e.g. in what he wrote against 'essentialism'. But this is a respect in which, or so it seems to me, his work is open to criticism from a Hayekian direction.

12 And also does not restrict the basis on which constraints on politics are understood to Marxian political economy.

13 Or if they do – as in certain of the discussions round Putman's worries about changes in the character of Western societies and their consequences – tend to be relegated to a sort of lower league of political theory, or to be treated in terms of over-optimistic and patently unrealistic ideas about the remedial power of civic education.

14 See, for some discussion, Shearmur 2007.

15 In the sense of Philip Pettit and Quentin Skinner. They can be seen in the Rechtsstaat character of Hayek's legal theory, and at various points in Popper's work – e.g. in what he referred to as 'protectionism'.

16 In this respect it is odd that Alex Nove, who had little time for Hayek, in many respects re-invented Hayek's arguments from *The Road to Serfdom*, in his *Economics of Feasible Socialism* (Nove 1983), and, indeed, put them in a particularly effective way.

17 I am here drawing, particularly, on his 'Public and Private Values', written, it would seem, in 1946 (see, now, Popper 2008), which I think throws a lot of light on some of the concerns underlying Popper 1945.

18 His concern – both in 'Public and Private Values' and in Popper 1945 – is with people who are humanitarian and democratic in their orientation. His concern for people who don't share such views is, typically, with those who are led to oppose their own underlying proclivity towards such ideas, by what Popper takes to be the appeal of mistaken intellectual ideas.

19 Popper did not have to hand, at the time, a theory of the rational discussability of such matters, although he welcomed what he called a 'rational attitude' the possessors of which might learn from one another.

20 I might mention that to a degree Shearmur 1986a brought, *inter alia*, Hayekian issues into the critical appraisal of his work, while I was explicit about the fact that in Shearmur 1986b, I drew upon material from Popper and Lakatos's ideas about 'research programmes' in providing a framework for the assessment of the development of Hayek's views over time.

21 I address this issue, among other things, in my *Living with Markets* (see Shearmur forthcoming).

22 It is tempting to see Popper's approach, here, as involving the emancipation of the 'political' from the wider Rawlsian structure.

23 But note, in this context, the reservations that have been expressed by people in the discipline of science studies. My suspicion is that much of what they say may be correct – but that what it points to is the need to improve on our institutions, so that they operate so as better to further the development of knowledge.

24 It is interesting to note the way in which issues of this kind have once again become a focus of attention, as Rawls and Habermas turned to consider the role of religion in the public sphere.

25 Precisely because, as Hayek stressed in *The Road to Serfdom*, one of the real risks to liberty is a government that *claims* that it is acting on the basis of a rational consensus – which it then empowers itself to press upon everyone, in the name of reason.

26 There is a striking parallel, here, with the ideas which Hayek addressed in his Inaugural Address at the LSE, 'The Trend of Economic Thinking'. See now on this, Hayek 1991.

27 It is striking that Rorty, for example, left with no account of the possibilities of social change illuminated by theory, is left appealing, with Charles Dickens, for a change of heart. Cf. on this in Dickens, George Orwell's brilliant essay, available at <http://www.orwell.ru/library/reviews/dickens/english/e_chd>, accessed 1 November 2010.

28 This is one issue with which I am concerned in my *Living with Markets* (Shearmur forthcoming).

References

Hacohen, M. (2000) *Karl Popper: The Formative Years*, Cambridge: Cambridge University Press.

Hayek, F. (1944) *The Road to Serfdom*, London: Routledge.

——(1991) *The Trend of Economic Thinking*, ed. W. W. Bartley and S. Kresge, Chicago, IL: University of Chicago Press.

Nove, A. (1983) *The Economics of Feasible Socialism*, London: Allen & Unwin.

Popper, K. (1945) *The Open Society and Its Enemies*, London: Routledge.

——(1959 [1934]) *The Logic of Scientific Discovery*, London: Hutchinson.

——(1963) *Conjectures and Refutations*, London: Routledge.

——(2008) *After the Open Society*, ed. J. Shearmur and P. Turner, London: Routledge.

Shearmur, J. (1986a) *The Political Thought of Karl Popper*, London: Routledge.

——(1986b) *Hayek and After*, London: Routledge.

——(2007) 'Hayek's Politics', in E. Feser (ed.) *The Cambridge Companion to Popper*, Cambridge: Cambridge University Press.

——(2009) 'Critical Rationalism and Ethics', in Z. Parusnikova and R. Cohen (eds) *Rethinking Popper*, Dordrecht: Springer.

——(forthcoming) *Living with Markets*, London: Routledge.

Liberalism after Communitarianism

Charles Blattberg

The 'liberal–communitarian debate' arose within Anglo-American political philosophy during the 1980s. The liberals were led by John Rawls along with Ronald Dworkin, Thomas Nagel and T.M. Scanlon while the communitarian critique was mainly advanced by Alasdair MacIntyre, Michael Sandel, Charles Taylor and Michael Walzer. The critique can be said to have focused on one of two (perhaps incompatible) approaches found, for example, within Rawls' *A Theory of Justice* (1971). In order to arrive at what he believes is the best possible theory, Rawls calls on us to take both a universalist route, that which is associated with his idea of 'the original position', and a more contextual one, according to which we should aim to achieve 'reflective equilibrium' in our thinking about political justice. The original position is a hypothetical perspective that we attain by stepping behind a 'veil of ignorance' in order to disregard knowledge of our personal capacities or place in society. By so doing we are said to be able to deliberate in a truly representative manner since we can 'regard the human situation not only from all social but also from all temporal points of view' (Rawls 1971: 587) and so formulate principles of justice that could serve as the basis of a social contract affirmed by everyone. Reflective equilibrium, by contrast, requires us to start from – and so remain relative to – a given society: beginning with the considered judgments contained within the society's practices, judgments should serve as no more than provisional fixed points, we are to tack back and forth from practice to theory until we achieve a state of balance over a set of systematic principles. According Rawls, both the original position and reflective equilibrium approaches culminate in the same theory of justice, though the scope of its applicability would, one would think, be different for each.

Communitarians tended to focus their critique on liberals who were attracted to one form or other of the universalist approach. Two basic claims were advanced. First, it was argued that reasoning from such a perspective is not only undesirable but also impossible. It is undesirable because it both undermines those aspects of our way of life that must by their very nature be practised in common with others, from friendship and family to the various forms of community, and because it is too abstract to be compelling to ordinary citizens. And it is impossible because people just cannot make moral decisions from such a detached perspective. Second, universalism was said to assume a misguided conception of the self, one that Taylor has labelled 'atomist' (1985 [1979]) and Sandel 'unencumbered' (1982, 1992 [1984]). This self is both misconceived, since it assumes that all of our ends can be matters of choice for us, and unsuitable, since psychologically, socially and politically speaking it once again undermines those ends that underlie common practices and so is only compatible with individualistic ones.

Rawls responded with 'Justice as Fairness: Political not Metaphysical' (1985), a paper that was largely included in the first chapter of his *Political Liberalism* (1993). In it he emphasises the reflective equilibrium (now also called 'Kantian constructivist') approach and downplays that of the original position, the latter being characterised as no more than a device of representation. Rawls also points out that reflective equilibrium never assumes that we can or should choose our life plans *ex nihilo*, only that we can evaluate some of our ends on the basis of a background of others – none of which, again, are to be treated as anything more than provisional fixed points. And Rawls claims that he is not taking a position on any particular conception of the self since such ontological as well as metaphysical questions are outside the purview of his approach's 'political' perspective, one that ought to be distinguished from those based upon 'comprehensive' worldviews. To Rawls, it is possible to achieve reflective equilibrium on what is simply a more systematic formulation of the principles that underly the public political culture to be found within liberal democratic regimes, one that is shared by all of the reasonable ways of life within those regimes. Such principles may thus be said to represent an 'overlapping consensus' between these ways of life, albeit one that can be detached from their other, non-political aspects.

In consequence, Rawls and other 'political liberals' (e.g. Larmore 1996 [1990]) are sometimes said to have taken a 'hermeneutical' turn (e.g. Richardson 1990: 22). But while the systematic reformulating they favour is indeed a form of interpretation, it is too 'theoretical' to be associated with the approaches of those such as Hans-Georg Gadamer (1989) which tend to come to mind when one thinks of contemporary hermeneutics. Because Rawls' aim is, after all, to reach a settled resting point in equilibrium, the theory of justice whose application is to guide political practice. Hermeneutical interpretation, by contrast, is something always ongoing, always 'on the way', to borrow an expression from Gadamer's teacher Martin Heidegger (1971 [1959]; see also Gadamer 1981 [1972]: 105). This means that while the hermeneutical social critic also aims for a better interpretation of political justice, it is not one that could be represented by a set of fixed and systematic principles. Indeed we might even say that, since hermeneutics entails a thoroughly contextual, 'practical' rather than 'theoretical' form of holism (Dreyfus 1980), its practitioners should avoid any talk of principles.[1]

In time, the debate between liberals and communitarians both dissolved and ramified. It dissolved because it came to be recognised that most of the communitarians reject the label (except, notably, Daniel Bell 1993) and that many of them, including Taylor and Walzer, even consider themselves liberals of a sort. Moreover, the liberals they had been criticising declared that they, too, affirmed a conception of community (e.g. Dworkin 1992 [1989]), something that Sandel (1982: 149) and Taylor (1995a [1989]: 195), among others, have acknowledged. Out of this dissolution, however, and alongside other subjects that have become the foci of contemporary Anglo-American political philosophy (including deliberative democracy, human rights and global justice), emerged three distinct but related developments, each of which may be described as pertaining to 'liberalism after communitarianism'.

Liberalism as an Ideology

Whether they view their theories as universally applicable or not, liberals such as Rawls see them as providing a neutral framework: a conception of right within which citizens may pursue their different conceptions of the good. This is in keeping with popular expressions such as 'liberal democracy' with their implication that liberalism is something more than 'but another sectarian doctrine' (Rawls 1985: 246), which is to say more than a mere ideology on par with others such conservatism, socialism, feminism, green ideology and so on. That is why Dworkin, for example, may propose, without acknowledging the contradiction that an explicitly liberal common ground can serve as the fair playing field upon which both liberals and conservatives should confront each other within American politics (Dworkin 2006: 7). However those, liberal and otherwise, who conceive of liberalism as an ideological 'fighting creed' (Taylor 1995b [1992]: 249) do so because they reject the separation of right from the good and so favour what has been called a 'perfectionist' as distinct from neutral state. In consequence, they also reject the thoroughly pejorative, Marxist-inspired conception of ideology according to which ideologies are no more than masks for material or other interests. To Michael Freeden, for example, an ideology is simply a way of 'political thinking, loose or rigid, deliberate or unintended, through which individuals and groups construct an understanding of the political world they, or those who preoccupy their thoughts, inhabit, and then act on that understanding' (Freeden 1996: 3).

Freeden is the leading student of liberalism as an ideology today. His morphological approach, which focuses on the evolving meanings and configurations of the political concepts that make ideologies up, allows him to be sensitive to the variety of forms that liberalism has taken. For given the various ways that its core, adjacent and peripheral concepts have been identified, related and decontested, liberalism has indeed meant different things not only in different countries but also throughout history (Freeden 1996, 2005, 2008). It is because he recognises this that Freeden has been able to point out how inward-looking, narrow and impoverished the leading American variant – the one that was the target of communitarian criticisms – has been. Freeden can thus be said to have helped make way for liberalisms that avoid the American variant's ahistoricism, depoliticisation and over-emphasis on individual rights to the expense of a concern for well-being and social solidarity.

One problem with Freeden's approach, however, is that it is overly analytical, by which I mean that it is not holistic enough. A central feature of his studies of ideologies in general and of liberalism in particular consists of 'assembling', of moving 'from concepts to ideologies' as one of his chapter titles puts it (Freeden 1996: ch. 2). But hermeneutics teaches that we should always begin the other way around, which is to say with the whole instead of with its parts. This is not only because all parts, and so all concepts, always remain more or less connected to that whole, but also because a continual grasp, however limited, of it is necessary if the parts are to be properly conceptualised. Now while Freeden does occasionally begin his study of a given ideologist with a general characterisation, he more often than not opens with an account of their ideology's core concepts taken one at a time. And even when he does begin with the ideology as a whole he often fails to return to it when examining its individual concepts. As a result, while his studies are very sensitive to how adjacent concepts can shape each others' meanings both logically and culturally, they fail to capture how much the ideology as a whole can also do so. For example, while he does refer to the way L.T. Hobhouse sums-up his liberalism[2] as well as to how that summation 'informs' Hobhouse's particular understanding of 'the core liberal concepts of liberty, rationality, progress, individuality, sociability, a common good, limited and responsible power' (Freeden 2005: 25–6), Freeden nevertheless does not have very much to say about *how* it does so. Yet it is surely important to Hobhouse that this whole is always to some degree present in each and every part.

In addition, while decrying the ostensive neutrality of the American variant, Freeden nevertheless assumes that ideologies should be studied in a strictly impartial manner, by which he appears to mean without judging them as better or worse in the sense of more or less true. But can we really fully understand a given ideology without asking about the degree to which it succeeds in accurately expressing the values of the political community in which it is set?

Freeden's impartiality can also be said to take him to the opposite extreme of the Marxists in that he does not have very much to say about the limitations of ideological thinking (though see Freeden 2009). Indeed he is far from impressed by the well-known criticism that ideologies tend to encourage dogmatic attitudes (e.g. Namier 1955: 5–7), a critique that we might supplement here by pointing out how ideological inflexibility goes hand in hand with overly adversarial responses to political conflict. This applies not only to those responses which consist of force rather than dialogue but also to those of the latter that are limited to negotiation. Because while ideologies can certainly provide helpful guidance when it comes to negotiating, they only get in the way when one hopes to respond to a conflict with an open mind instead – which is to say with conversation instead of negotiation (Blattberg 2009).

Liberalism in the Face of Diversity: Autonomy

Another major development emerging from the liberal–communitarian debate has seen liberals strive to be more sensitive to questions arising from the significant levels of diversity to be found in Western societies, in particular, questions associated with identity politics and the place of minorities. This development has taken two major forms.

One is the defence of a perfectionist liberalism – a liberalism, again, of the good and not merely the right – that is centred around a particular conception of the core liberal value of the liberty of the individual. Of course this value has been interpreted differently, the rival inter-pretations going by such names as 'bourgeois', 'negative', 'self-ownership', 'authenticity' and 'non-domination'. The perfectionist liberalism that is our focus here favours 'autonomy', how-ever. While this term is also central to Immanuel Kant's account, according to which individual liberty should be equated with morality as a whole, understood as consisting of self-determined principles, in this case autonomy is meant to refer to the freedom of individuals *to choose* their own lives. As so understood, the idea plays a minor if significant role in Walzer's liberalism, according to which the 'autonomous person', who Walzer conceives, as an individual capable of choosing to participate in the various realms, associations, or spheres of modern society, is 'the ideal subject of the theory of justice' (Walzer 1983: 279; Walzer 2007 [1984]). Autonomy is, however, front and centre in the liberalisms of Joseph Raz and Will Kymlicka. (Though it should be noted that the latter is not as comfortable with the idea of perfectionism as the former – and this despite his willingness to countenance 'short-term state intervention designed to introduce people to valuable ways of life' (Kymlicka 2002: 277n6), i.e. to conceptions of the good.)

Raz and Kymlicka see their approaches as especially appropriate for multicultural societies. For though the liberalism that was the target of the communitarian critique purports to be neutral among different cultural groups, it is 'in fact implicitly tilted towards the needs, interests, and identities of the majority group; and this creates a range of burdens, barriers, stigmatizations, and exclusions for members of minority groups' (Kymlicka and Norman 2000: 4). Raz's and Kymlicka's liberalisms, by contrast, are much more sensitive to the issues arising from diversity, this being because, as Raz has put it, 'the conditions of autonomy require an environment rich in possibilities' (Raz 1994: 107; see also Raz 1986: chs 14–15; Kymlicka 1995: chs 5, 8; and Kymlicka 2002: ch. 6). Only a substantially diverse society can meet the needs of autonomy since, if freedom is indeed a matter of choosing, then there must, of course, be an adequate range of options to choose from. Instead of viewing ethnic or national minorities as potential threats to the unity of a liberal polity, then, Raz and Kymlicka argue that they can contribute to it by providing cultural options for citizens – as long, that is, as they do so within a framework that respects autonomy.

But is autonomy really the best way to conceive of the liberty of the individual? Raz recommends it to us as an ideal particularly suited to the often changing conditions of contemporary society (Raz 1986: 370), while Kymlicka views it as simply entailed by modernisation and globalisation (Kymlicka 2002: 369). Yet the notion of choice also points us towards one of modern society's least-attractive features, namely consumerism, and when we think of individual liberty in this way then it is hard not to wonder about Raz's claim that it is through our choices that we best define our morality. To Raz, autonomy requires 'morally acceptable options' (Raz 1986: 378) but one could argue that we often rightly conceive of a moral decision as something that was never really optional since there was no way to do otherwise and remain true to ourselves. (Note that this way of speaking betrays a sympathy for the authenticity conception of individual liberty.) The danger of conceiving of individual liberty as a matter of choosing, then, is that it can trivialise. As Taylor has written regarding the word 'choice', it 'occludes almost everything important: the sacrificed alternatives in a dilemmatic situation, and the real moral weight of the situation' (Taylor 2007: 479). The term 'options' is equally problematic since it suggests a number of independently distinct items to choose from whereas the moral reality, at least according to hermeneutical accounts of perception (e.g. Merleau-Ponty 1962), is once again usually much more holistic. This is so both because it tends to be a matter of shades and degrees and because the different interpretations of what to do remain connected to us even when they are the objects of criticism since they are, after all, possible expressions of the values that constitute who we are. To Kymlicka however, we can criticise certain values given the options they represent only because 'we can "stand apart" or "step back" from our current ends, and question their value to us' (Kymlicka 2002: 215, though see 278n2). Yet is this not distorting, and is such disengagement really necessary for criticism?

Liberalism in the Face of Diversity: Value Pluralism

Value pluralists would answer 'yes' and 'no' to these questions, for they affirm a conception of practical reason and so criticism that rejects disengagement. To Isaiah Berlin, Stuart Hampshire, and Bernard Williams, among others, we ought to recognise that there exists a plurality of often conflicting and incommensurable values and that we cannot properly respond to their conflicts by turning to an abstract, systematic theory of justice – whether neutralist or perfectionist – for guidance. Because such theories assume that the values have been commensurated, in the sense of interlocked within a unified system, and this is impossible without seriously distorting them. Instead of applying a theory, then, those involved in a political conflict should aim to negotiate with each other in good faith. They should be willing to make concessions, to compromise as part of a struggle to reach a balanced accommodation.

Why should they be so willing? The recognition of the plurality of values as well as of the plurality of ways of life that are made up of them leads value pluralists to assert that, even though we may not share the values of people we are in conflict with, we should still see those values as genuine and so accept that those affirming them are moral agents deserving of a certain minimum of respect. This means that we ought to *tolerate* them to a degree, hence make at least some concessions for reasons other than that we feel forced to do so.

But what concessions, exactly, and how much should we be conceding? It is here that value pluralists can be said to turn to ideologies for guidance since, among other things, ideologies tell us to give different values different weights. They diverge over this, of course, which is why, crudely put, socialists such as Hampshire tend to favour equality, conservatives such as John Kekes protecting tradition, and liberals such as Berlin and Williams individual liberty. But even one's most cherished value is never to be awarded an overriding status since all value pluralists agree that no value should be uncompromisable. This is so even – or perhaps especially – when a favoured value comes into conflict with others that one's ideology emphasises. That is why Berlin and Williams, at least, can be said to agree with William Galston for whom 'liberalism is a basket of ideals that inevitably come into conflict with one another if a serious effort is made to realize any one of them fully, let alone all of them simultaneously' (Galston 1991: 195).

Evidently, this liberalism is quite different from that of Raz or Kymlicka, its fulcrum being toleration rather than autonomy. Raz claims to subscribe to value pluralism but he endorses the plurality of values not because he recognizes a certain moral reality but because he sees pluralism as serving autonomy. This is why he believes that toleration should be subservient to autonomy (Raz 1986: 407). As for Kymlicka, he views toleration and autonomy as but 'two sides of the same coin' (Kymlicka 2002: 231), which is why it comes as no surprise that he, too, is unwilling to countenance autonomy's compromise (Kymlicka 2002: 245).

Liberals who affirm value pluralism cannot agree with this, and not only because of the centrality that they give to toleration. For there is also a deeper, philosophical reason. We have already noted how the recognition of a plurality of conflicting and incommensurable values leads value pluralists to reject systematic theories of justice in favour of negotiation. Here we can add that it also ensures (or at least should ensure) that value pluralists identify the ground of their liberalism with an untheorizable political culture instead of with a political philosophy. Otherwise put, liberalism is, once again, to be considered a fighting creed, an ideology rather than as a doctrine that could be in some sense logically derived from a systematic political philosophy. Only such a philosophy would be capable of 'sheltering' certain values from the vicissitudes of everyday politics, thus putting them beyond compromise. Yet to value pluralists politics – and, one would think, the philosophy of it – exist in an inherently disunified world, one, that is, 'where ends collide' (Berlin 1978 [1961]: 149). Theories of justice, then, are not only Procrustean but, because they are not really systematic, no specific ideology can ever be derived directly from them. And that is why we cannot go straight from pluralism in itself to liberalism. Hence Berlin: 'Pluralism and liberalism are not the same or even overlapping concepts. There are liberal theories which are not pluralistic. I believe in both liberalism and pluralism, but they are not logically connected' (Berlin and Jahanbegloo 1991: 44; see also Berlin and Williams 1994: 308–9). It should be noted that Berlin is often read as supporting the opposite position (e.g. Gray 1997: ch. 6) but for this to be true we would have to interpret his claim on behalf of an unbreachable minimal private sphere of individual liberty (as made, for example, in his famous 'Two Concepts of Liberty' essay) as being enough to support a full-blown liberalism. But Berlin's reply to what we might refer to as the question of 'how much' is: 'that which a man cannot give up without offending against the essence of his human nature' (Berlin 1969a [1958]: 126; see also 161, 164–6) and this suggests that value pluralism and liberalism can be logically linked only if one makes the implausible claim that the latter is somehow inherent to that nature.

If there is a problem with the liberalism of value pluralism, or indeed with any and all forms of value pluralist politics, it is that, by favouring negotiation, it virtually rules out that non-adversarial form of dialogue which is conversation. In a conversation interlocutors aim to integrate the conflicting values, to realise the whole of which they are assumed to be a part, by achieving a reconciliation as distinct from an accommodation. Instead of zero-sum compromising, then, the balancing of the values against each other, those who would converse must strive to learn from each other in order to develop synergistic solutions to their conflict. This is especially necessary when it comes to what has been called 'the politics of recognition', which arises when there are conflicts over a group's desire to have its uniqueness or distinctiveness within the polity recognised, usually by the state. Because recognition (as the German and French words for it, *Anerkennung* and *reconnaissance*, make especially clear) is about truth, and one either learns that something is true or one does not; the only form of dialogue that has the potential to bring the desired recognition, then, is conversation. Yet there is not only no place for it within the neutralist, anti-perfectionist liberalism that Walzer has dubbed 'Liberalism 1', that whose 'politics' consist mainly of adversarial 'pleading' before whatever authority is charged with applying the theory of justice, but it is also incompatible with the more value pluralist-friendly model that he calls 'Liberalism 2' (Walzer 1994). For the latter is still the home of strictly adversarial responses to conflict, of 'struggles' over recognition that begin when the need for it is advanced as a 'demand'. Now though the politics of recognition has often been portrayed in this way (e.g. Taylor 1995b: 225; Honneth 1995), one that is certainly compatible with the value pluralist's world of 'colliding ends' and so with negotiation, conversation can only be effective in response to a conflict that is considered 'oppositional' but not 'adversarial'. For values that collide (or 'clash', which is another adversarial metaphor popular in the literature) are not parts of a whole but (at least initially) separate, independently distinct things, since otherwise they could not have come into conflict in that particular way. Moreover, if one wishes to converse while others are willing only to negotiate then conversation, which is an extremely fragile mode of dialogue, will just not be viable. No surprise, then, that value pluralist writings are replete with references to the inescapability of tragedy and dirty hands in politics (e.g. Berlin 1969b: 11; Williams 1978; Hampshire 1989: 170–7). Because when politics at its best is about no more than compromise, then everyone must expect to lose something of value. Lacking a conception of the whole, of 'the common good' to strive to fulfil, value pluralists thus leave us with a politics from which there is nothing to gain, much less to learn (Blattberg 2000).

Conclusion

Like most ideologies, liberalism will continue to evolve. And identifying the best ways that it should to do so will, of course, remain a central topic for discussion among those of us who subscribe to it. But as the account above suggests, before confronting other ideologists we should try to engage with *all* of our fellow citizens, and in a way that encourages conversation and not merely negotiation. This means listening to them instead of to some preconceived doctrine, for only that way can we hope to fulfill not only the values that liberalism favours, but all values.

Notes

1 On why it makes sense to do so, see Dancy 2004.
2 'The heart of liberalism is the understanding that progress is not a matter of mechanical contrivance, but of the liberation of living spiritual energy. Good mechanism is that which provides the channels wherein such energy can flow unimpeded, unobstructed by its own exuberance of output, vivifying the social structure, expanding and ennobling the life of mind' (Hobhouse 1964 [1911]: 73; quoted in Freeden 2005: 25).

References

Bell, D. (1993) *Communitarianism and Its Critics*, Oxford: Clarendon Press.
Berlin, I. (1969a) 'Two Concepts of Liberty', in *Four Essays on Liberty*, Oxford: Oxford University Press.
——(1969b [1958]) 'Political Ideas in the Twentieth Century', in *Four Essays on Liberty*, Oxford: Oxford University Press.

——(1978 [1961]) 'Does Political Theory Still Exist?', in Henry Hardy (ed.), *Concepts and Categories: Philosophical Essays*, Princeton, NJ: Princeton University Press.

Berlin, I. and R. Jahanbegloo (1991) *Conversations with Isaiah Berlin*, London: Peter Halban.

Berlin, I. and B. Williams (1994) 'Pluralism and Liberalism: A Reply', *Political Studies*, 62 (2), 306–9.

Blattberg, C. (2000) *From Pluralist to Patriotic Politics: Putting Practice First*, Oxford: Oxford University Press.

——(2009) 'Political Philosophies and Political Ideologies', in *Patriotic Elaborations: Essays in Practical Philosophy*, Montreal and Kingston: McGill-Queen's University Press.

Dancy, J. (2004) *Ethics without Principles*, Oxford: Oxford University Press.

Dreyfus, H.L. (1980) 'Holism and Hermeneutics', *Review of Metaphysics*, 34 (1), 3–23.

Dworkin, R. (1992 [1989]) 'Liberal Community', in S. Avineri and A. de-Shalit (eds.) *Communitarianism and Individualism*, Oxford: Oxford University Press.

——(2006) *Is Democracy Possible Here?* Princeton, NJ: Princeton University Press.

Freeden, M. (1996) *Ideologies and Political Theory: A Conceptual Approach*, Oxford: Clarendon Press.

——(2005) *Liberal Languages: Ideological Imaginations and Twentieth-century Progressive Thought*, Princeton, NJ: Princeton University Press.

——(2008) 'European Liberalisms: An Essay in Comparative Political Thought', *European Journal of Political Theory*, 7 (1), 9–30.

——(2009) 'Editorial: What Fails in Ideologies?', *Journal of Political Ideologies*, 14 (1), 1–9.

Gadamer, H.-G. (1981 [1972]) 'Hermeneutics as Practical Philosophy', in *Reason in the Age of Science*, F.G. Lawrence (trans.), Cambridge, MA: MIT Press.

——(1989) *Truth and Method*, J. Weinsheimer and D.G. Marshall (trans.), New York: Crossroad, 2nd edn.

Galston, W.A. (1991) *Liberal Purposes: Goods, Virtues, and Diversity in the Liberal State*, New York: Cambridge University Press.

Gray, J. (1997) *Isaiah Berlin*, Princeton, NJ: Princeton University Press, 2nd edn.

Hampshire, S. (1989) *Innocence and Experience*, London: Allen Lane, Penguin Press.

Heidegger, M. (1971 [1959]) *On the Way to Language*, P.D. Hertz (trans.), New York: Harper & Row.

Hobhouse, L.T. (1964 [1911]) *Liberalism*, New York: Oxford University Press.

Honneth, A. (1995) *The Struggle for Recognition: The Moral Grammar of Social Conflicts*, Joel Anderson (trans.) Cambridge, MA: MIT Press.

Kymlicka, W. (1995) *Multicultural Citizenship: A Liberal Theory of Minority Rights*, Oxford: Clarendon Press.

——(2002) *Contemporary Political Philosophy: An Introduction*, Oxford: Oxford University Press, 2nd edn.

Kymlicka, W. and W. Norman (2000) 'Citizenship in Culturally Diverse Societies: Issues, Contexts, Concepts', in Kymlicka and Norman (eds) *Citizenship in Diverse Societies*, Oxford: Oxford University Press.

Larmore, C. (1996 [1990]) 'Political Liberalism', in *Morals and Modernity*, Cambridge: Cambridge University Press.

Merleau-Ponty, M. (1962) *The Phenomenology of Perception*, C. Smith (trans.) London: Routledge.

Namier, L. (1955) 'Human Nature in Politics', in *Personalities and Powers*, London: Hamish Hamilton.

Rawls, J. (1971) *A Theory of Justice*, London: Oxford University Press.

——(1985) 'Justice as Fairness: Political not Metaphysical', *Philosophy and Public Affairs*, 14 (3), 223–51.

——(1993) *Political Liberalism*, New York: Columbia University Press.

Raz, J. (1986) *The Morality of Freedom*, Oxford: Clarendon.

——(1994) 'Liberalism, Scepticism, and Democracy', in *Ethics in the Public Domain: Essays in the Morality of Law and Politics*, Oxford: Clarendon Press.

Richardson, H.S. (1990) 'The Problem of Liberalism and the Good', in R.B. Douglass, G.M. Mara and H.S. Richardson (eds) *Liberalism and the Good*, New York: Routledge.

Sandel, M. (1982) *Liberalism and the Limits of Justice*, Cambridge: Cambridge University Press.

——(1992 [1984]) 'The Procedural Republic and The Unencumbered Self', in S. Avineri and A. de-Shalit (eds) *Communitarianism and Individualism*, Oxford: Oxford University Press.

Taylor, C. (1985 [1979]) 'Atomism', in *Philosophy and the Human Sciences: Philosophical Papers 2*, Cambridge: Cambridge University Press.

——(1995a [1989]) 'Cross-purposes: The Liberal–Communitarian Debate', in *Philosophical Arguments*, Cambridge, MA: Harvard University Press.

——(1995b [1992]) 'The Politics of Recognition', in *Philosophical Arguments*, Cambridge, MA: Harvard University Press.

——(2007) *A Secular Age*, Cambridge, MA: Harvard University Press.

Walzer, M. (1983) *Spheres of Justice: A Defense of Pluralism and Equality*, New York: Basic Books.

——(1994) 'Comment', in A. Gutmann (ed.) *Multiculturalism: Examining the Politics of Recognition*, Princeton, NJ: Princeton University Press, 2nd edn.

——(2007 [1984]) 'Liberalism and the Art of Separation', in D. Miller (ed.) *Thinking Politically: Essays in Political Theory*, New Haven, CT: Yale University Press.

Williams, B. (1978) 'Politics and Moral Character', in S. Hampshire (ed.) *Public and Private Morality*, Cambridge: Cambridge University Press.

Republicanism

Non-domination and the Free State

Richard Bellamy

The recent resurgence of republican thinking has constituted one of the most notable and exciting developments within contemporary social and political thought (Laborde and Maynor 2008). Roughly speaking, there have been three strands within this republican revival. The first strand goes back to Aristotle and stresses the importance of civic participation for individual self-realisation. This view has been prominent within modern communitarianism, particularly the more left-leaning and democratic versions of this school of thought. It can be likened to Benjamin Constant's famous characterisation of 'ancient liberty' (Constant 1988 [1819]), in which political freedom is bound up with popular sovereignty and assumes a close identification between citizens and their political community, on the one hand, and among themselves, on the other (for an example, see Sandel 1996). The second strand, while retaining elements of this communitarian version of republicanism, draws more on the Enlightenment tradition of republican thought of Tom Paine and especially Kant. This view has figured within critical theory, particularly the writings of Jürgen Habermas (1996). It can be associated with Constant's characterisation of 'modern liberty' as combining liberal civil rights with a communitarian republican view of popular sovereignty to produce a system of constitutional democracy. The key difference with Constant's account is that these republican theorists have added social to the liberal civil rights of 'private autonomy' and connect them not to the market but to the political rights of 'public autonomy'. Rights on this account offer preconditions for citizens to deliberate on a free and equal basis with each other. The third strand looks to the neo-Roman tradition of republican thought of Cicero and Machiavelli (Pettit 1997; Skinner 1998). The distinctive feature of this view is a conception of freedom as non-domination. By contrast to the first two strands that conceive freedom in terms of collective self-mastery achieved through popular sovereignty, this view sees freedom in terms of freedom from mastery by another. On this account, political participation is valued more for its instrumental than its intrinsic virtues. Rather than being the expression of a sovereign popular will, democracy offers a system of government in which all are treated as equals and act as rulers and ruled in turn, so no one is regarded as the master of others or placed in a position to dominate them.

The three strands identified above are to some extent ideal types. Not only are there variations within each strand, but also many thinkers straddle more than one of them. For example, David Miller's liberal nationalism has elements of both the first strand, in its emphasis on

130

national community and the boundedness of citizenship, and of the second strand, in its commitment to certain international duties to meet basic human rights, while also criticising certain positions of thinkers in both these camps – such as Habermas's support for the EU (Miller 2000). There is also a common thread running through each of these strands in the emphasis placed on political citizenship, albeit for somewhat different reasons, as we have seen. For relatedly distinct reasons, all three also criticise what they regard as central features of contemporary liberalism – notably an abstract individualism that prioritises property and other market rights, and sees all laws and government regulation as *prima facie* inimical to freedom since they involve interference with an individual's supposed natural liberty.

In what follows I shall concentrate primarily on the third strand. As I noted, the first two strands have largely figured as aspects of other schools of thought: namely, communitariansm and critical theory respectively. Instead, the third strand forms a distinctive and to some degree self-contained republican school of thought, albeit with links to certain aspects of the other two from which some neo-Roman republican theorists have at various times drawn inspiration. In the rest of this chapter I will outline the concept of freedom as non-domination on which the distinctiveness of this strand rests, show how the resulting concept of the 'free person' is linked to an equally distinct account of the political and constitutional arrangements of a 'free state', and finally note the implications of this theory for distributive justice.

Freedom as Non-domination

In his famous essay 'Two Concepts of Liberty' Isaiah Berlin contrasted 'negative' with 'positive' liberty, characterising the first as 'freedom from interference' and the second as 'freedom to realise oneself' in some way (Berlin 1969). He argued that political participation was only contingently and instrumentally linked to negative liberty, offering one possible means to ensure the state interfered as little as possible with people's interests – something that might be even better achieved by a constitutional court or some other independent body such as an ombudsman. However, positive liberty allowed for an intrinsic link with participation in both democracy and the state as the means of realising oneself. Although such ethical naturalist reasoning has a distinguished pedigree going back, as I noted above, to Aristotle and, in a rather different form, to Kant, Berlin argued it was potentially 'totalitarian' in its implications even when espoused by avowedly liberal thinkers such as T. H. Green. Not only do such moralised accounts of freedom suggest that being free consists in pursuing certain possibly contentious ends that realise a person's 'true' self, but also they risk suggesting that 'real' freedom consists in obedience to a state that realises such ends. Within democratic theory, notions such as popular sovereignty suggest a similar conflation of individual with collective autonomy. As a result, Berlin's analysis has tended to discredit republicanism and the link it makes between freedom and politics. Instead, the view typical of freedom as non-interference has come to prevail, whereby intervention by the law or the state curtails freedom, albeit in many cases with justification. On this view, democratic participation necessarily sacrifices a degree of personal freedom that could be devoted to business or leisure to public service, something that may be far less rewarding for many (if not all) individuals and hence diminish their freedom over all. Democracy may also allow rent-seeking behaviour by particular individuals that unnecessarily expands the state beyond what is necessary to reduce interference with individual choice overall.

An important contribution of the rediscovery of the neo-Roman tradition has been to dispute Berlin's influential account by suggesting a 'third' concept of liberty, that while a 'negative' theory of freedom as 'freedom from domination' nevertheless regards the role of the law and state as furthering rather than constraining liberty (Pettit 1997; Skinner 1998). This account of freedom takes as its antonym the condition of a slave. According to what Berlin regarded as the standard view of negative liberty as 'freedom from interference', slaves remain free so long as their masters do not interfere with them. From this perspective, the slaves of benevolent and non-interfering masters are free in fact, even if they lack the status of free persons. Not being free persons may make their freedom less secure – if their master died they could be sold to a cruel owner, say, or he may undergo a personality change that turns him into a brute – but so long as their master remains alive and benevolent they may possess as wide a sphere of liberty as many a citizen, possibly even wider than some. Quentin Skinner has noted how this division between 'liberty' and 'security' was introduced by Hobbes and then re-proposed by Bentham in criticism of the Neo-Roman republican view that then prevailed and which made no such distinction. For the republican account holds a slave is dominated and his or her freedom curtailed not only by the interference of his or her master, but also by that master's ability to invigilate and inhibit the slave's actions in arbitrary ways – that is, in ways that reflect the master's not the slave's interests or preferences and that the master can impose on the slave wilfully and without consultation.

The neo-Roman concept of liberty highlights three dimensions missing from the standard account of liberty as non-interference. First, even when not actually interfered with, the fact that the slave is invigilated by someone who could interfere if they chose may be just as effective in leading him or her not to act in ways that he or she believes might lead to interference. Second, even with a good master, slaves may be inhibited from performing actions or expressing views they know their master would disapprove of. They might even choose to do or say things they know will please him or her despite these actions or opinions going against their own preferences, interests or beliefs. Third, a key feature of this condition of domination lies in being subject to the arbitrary rule of the master – that is, the master's capacity to determine at his or her own discretion how, when and for what purpose to interfere or not interfere with a slave. To the extent such a determination rests solely on the will of the master, then it will be dominating for the slave. The first two dimensions suggest we can have an absence of freedom without any actual interference, for both invigilation and inhibition place constraints on what agents do and lead them to actions that they would not otherwise choose to take. The third dimension goes further and indicates how interference may in some respects actually enhance freedom. For laws that oblige a system of rule to consult the interests of those it affects will liberate agents from the domination that attends arbitrary rule. When interference reduces arbitrariness, and hence domination, it promotes freedom and assists individuals to plan and act in autonomous ways. It may also facilitate collective choices and projects that are in the public interest and that would not be feasible without the coordination that common rules can bring.

The three dimensions of freedom highlighted by the non-domination view point to lacunas in the conception of freedom as non-interference that reveal it as doubly flawed: it overlooks those circumstances where freedom can be diminished without interference, and neglects the ways interference can promote freedom. These same points also build a quite different case for linking freedom to political participation to those offered by the two other strands of republican thinking outlined above. Freedom as non-interference regards liberty as a natural condition – individuals are freest when free from all constraints in a state of nature. The problem, graphically described by Hobbes (1996 [1651]) – the progenitor of this account of liberty – is that such natural freedom is thoroughly insecure, with the naturally free individual's life 'nasty, brutish and short'. Law and the state involve a rational sacrifice of a degree of natural liberty for greater security. Yet on this account an absolute monarch secures as good a quality and quantity of liberty for his subjects as any republic will for its citizens. Indeed, in Hobbes's view monarchies rate better than republics given that the latter generally place heavier demands on their members in terms of civic obligations and commitment to the public good. By contrast, the neo-Roman republican can respond by revealing monarchical rule as the epitome of unfreedom, for it institutionalises domination. Freedom and its absence on the non-domination account is a social condition. Domination results primarily from three circumstances: a power-imbalance, dependency and personal rule, all of which allow for a degree of arbitrariness on the part of rulers. All three are inherent features of monarchy, which involves hierarchy and ascribed status, with all members of the kingdom 'subjects' of the monarch to serve his pleasure rather than the other way round. The public welfare only emerges indirectly to the extent that that the personal wealth of the monarch depends on that of his or her kingdom. It is not just that these circumstances all make interference more likely and so freedom less secure. For interference *per se* is not what diminishes freedom on the republican account. Rather, they create domination and hence a loss of freedom in themselves by allowing the invigilation of the dominated by the monarch and inducing dominated behaviour, such as sycophancy, without the need for actual interference. Moreover, they do so because personal rule encapsulates arbitrary power by placing the lives and livelihood of all subjects of a monarchy at the pleasure of the King or Queen's majesty. To be 'free persons' individuals must be citizens of a 'free state', that is a polity that institutionalises a form of republican rule that unlike monarchy includes checks against domination. It is to the requirements of such a free political system that we now turn.

A 'Free State': How Republicanism Guards Against Domination

A 'free state' has both an internal and an external dimension. Domestically, it must put in place institutions that avoid and prevent the development of power imbalances, dependency and personal rule between citizens. Externally, it must protect against the domination of its citizens – either individually or collectively – by other states or agencies operating outside the state, such as multinational or transnational corporations or even international organisations. I shall explore each in turn.

Within the domestic sphere, Pettit (1997) has tended to emphasise the 'rule of law' and constitutional constraints as the most suitable mechanisms for meeting the criteria needed for non domination, rather than democracy *per se* – though he has advocated contestatory democracy as a means for allowing citizens to challenge rules and policies that do not track their interests. The slogan 'the rule of law, not men' makes such suggestions appear the natural means of overcoming 'personal' rule, given that even democracy could be regarded as allowing some persons – be it the political class within a representative system, or a tyrannical majority in a divided society, to consistently dominate others. Indeed, Pettit has seen 'counter-majoritarian' checks and balances, notably the separation of powers, as the natural complements to the 'rule of law' in securing a 'free state'. However, although the second strand of republicanism has adopted this tack, albeit not only as a constraint upon but also in more recent versions (such as Habermas 1996), as the basis for popular sovereignty, I believe it fails to capture the character of the third strand. For non-domination requires citizens enjoy an equal political status as the makers of laws and not just an equal legal status under the law. On its own, this latter condition is potentially itself one of subjecthood and, unless laws can truly rule without persons, potentially places citizens under the arbitrary rule of those few who administer and interpret the law. Indeed, to avoid just this possibility this strand has typically adopted a political rather than a legal form of constitutionalism, which equates a condition of non-domination with the status of citizenship and views the right to equal participation in ruling or selecting rulers as 'the right to have rights'.

Past republicans often expressed the link between non-domination and political equality using the language of consent (Skinner 2008). Only the need for all to be counted equally in consenting to government would ensure that everyone's interests were taken equally into account regardless of their wealth or social station. As Colonel Thomas Rainborough famously expressed it in the Leveller debates in Putney, the 'poorest he ... has a life to live as the greatest he; and therefore, ... it's clear that every man that is to live under a government ought first by his own consent to put himself under that government'. It is a requirement with revolutionary potential, implying 'that the poorest man ... is not at all bound in a strict sense to that government that he has not had a voice to put himself under'. However, if these conditions could only be met through unanimous consent to all policies, then – as R. P. Wolff (1970) demonstrated – it is unlikely that any workable system of democracy could satisfy these criteria. It is almost as implausible to assume that the basic structures of society could receive the actual consent of all those subject to them. Social contract theories have attempted to overcome these problems by modelling circumstances that might generate principles of political justice that all ought to consent to. Yet, such idealisations have a tendency to build their conclusions into their premises and be subject to numerous objections from those arguing from alternative premises of a similar plausibility and reasonableness. As such, there is a danger that a constitutional settlement that matches and is interpreted through the reasoning of a few – no matter how well-intentioned and knowledgeable they may be – will fail to treat all citizens as equal sources of reasoned argument and relevant information.

To overcome this difficulty suggests the need for a middle way – one that secures all involved with an equal weight in the process of decision-making, while allowing that not all may be equally happy with the result. Nevertheless, such equal weighting needs to be more than mere equality in the process and less than full substantive equality of outcome. As past republicans put it, procedures should aim 'to hear the other side'. In other words, the goal is decisions that are not only made impartially and fairly in a purely formal sense but also seek to consult the different interests of those concerned so that the resulting decisions do not oppress them. Historically republicans have advocated a number of devices to achieve this end. The choice of rulers by lot, for example, was hoped both to give all citizens an equal chance of power and an incentive to use it fairly and for the general interest rather than their own or that of their friends given that they could not know or influence who would rule after them. Likewise, the doctrine of mixed government sought to achieve a balance of power between the different classes within society. According to this doctrine, the monarch, aristocracy and people could only rule with the assent of the others – a view that continues to find a formal expression within the English constitutional formula of 'the queen in Parliament'. By contrast to the view of the first two strands of republicanism, the third strand does not propose these democratic mechanisms on the assumption that there is a single sovereign popular will. Rather, they assume the demos to be fragmented into multiple demoi with different and often conflicting ideals and interests. The aim is not achieve a consensus so much as an equitable accommodation between them. Nor do they see participation as a means to individual or collective self-realisation or even self-mastery. Instead, they are means to avoid mastery or domination by others.

The traditional republican devices also differ from the standard liberal view of constitutional government (Bellamy 1996, 2007). They regard constitutionalism not as the subjection of the normal process of legislation to a supposedly 'higher' law protected by a separate judicial body, immune to popular control, but as resulting from the involvement of the public in a set of political institutions that ensure the process of law-making and adjudication gives equal consideration to their views. This form of republican constitution rejects the view that a constitution can offer a resource of substantive political principles in the form of constitutional rights that might provide a set of public reasons to be applied by a court or the government to solve all questions touching issues of political justice. Law cannot rule in this way because within a pluralist society reasonable disagreements exist as to the nature of rights, how they relate to other values and considerations, and the ways they might be implemented in a given case. For example, it may be uncontentious that women have a right not to be raped but there are many contentious issues surrounding how best to secure this right so that an appropriate balance is met between protecting the interests of women wishing to bring accusations of rape forward and ensuring defendants get a fair hearing. So, rather than being a repository of acceptable public reasons, a republican constitution serves to ensure all the relevant reasons the public might wish to raise when deciding such questions get aired when framing legislation and policy.

The rules and procedures a republican constitution requires to pass a law or place a policy issue on the agenda attempt to promote conscientious, coherent and considered decision-making. They create feed-back mechanisms that render rulers responsive and accountable to the ruled, thereby giving governments incentives to treat citizens with equal concern and respect, pay attention to their interests and correct harmful mistakes and policy failures. On this model, public reasoning involves paying attention to the reasons of the public rather than being ruled by a set of supposedly authoritative public reasons. The republican constitutional constraint that prevents arbitrary rule comes from so balancing the input of citizens that they, and hence those who govern them, are obliged to consult each other's positions. Such a political constitutionalism has the removal of power imbalances, dependency and personal rule at its heart. By equalising power, each citizen is treated as an independent source of reasoning and information who must be consulted in the decision-making process, while none can rule without the active collaboration of others.

In contemporary democracies, a system of equal votes, majority rule and competing parties can be seen as offering an updated form of the republican system of mixed government (Bellamy 1996, 2007, 2008). One person, one vote and majority rule equalise power in decision-making and aggregate people's preferences in a fair way that is anonymous, neutral and positively responsive. That is, people's votes count equally whoever they are and whatever their views may be, and a change in balance of opinion is directly reflected in the outcome. Meanwhile, party competition plays a key role in the production of balanced decisions. To win elections, rival parties have to bring together broad coalitions of opinions and interests within a general programme of government. Even under PR systems, where incentives may exist for parties to appeal to fairly narrow constituencies, they need to render their programmes compatible with potential coalition partners to have a chance of entering government. In each of these cases, majorities are built through the search for mutually acceptable compromises that attempt to accommodate a number of different views within a single complex position.

Such compromises are sometimes criticised as unprincipled and incoherent, encouraging 'pork barrel politics' in which voters get bought off according to their ability to influence the outcome rather than the merits of their case. Despite a system of free and equal votes, some votes can count for more than others if they bring campaigning resources, are 'deciding' votes, or can ease the implementation of a given policy. However, within pluralist societies different political resources tend to be distributed around different sections of the community, while their relative importance and who holds them differs according to the policy. Democratic societies are also invariably characterised by at least some cross-cutting cleavages that bind different groups together on different issues. Of course, in ethnically, religiously or culturally divided societies the divisions on certain matters may be such as to make compromise agreements difficult to impossible, so that majority tyranny on the part of the largest group becomes a genuine worry. Yet in some cases at least it has been possible to use a mixture of executive power sharing, federalism and special rights to secure either a threshold or proportionate voice for all groups in decision-making that is sufficient to ensure their differences are respected.

In circumstances of reasonable disagreement, such compromises recognise the rights of others to have their views treated with equal concern as well as respect. They legitimately reflect the balance of opinion within society (Bellamy 1999). Naturally, some groups may still feel excluded or dissatisfied, while the balance between them can alter as interests and ideals evolve with social change. The counterbalances of party competition come in here. The presence of permanent opposition and regular electoral contests means that governments will need to respond to policy failures and alterations in the public mood brought about by new developments. Legislative programmes are remarkably close to the manifesto commitments that parties develop to win elections. Yet, in anticipating future elections and in tackling unforeseen issues – including certain unanticipated perverse consequences of their own policies – party programmes do evolve.

This willingness of parties to alter their policies is often seen as evidence of their unprincipled nature and the basically self-interested motives of politicians and citizens alike. However, this picture of parties cynically changing their spots to court short term popularity is belied by the reality. Leap-frogging is remarkably rare, not least because they and their core support retain certain key ideological commitments to which changes in policy have to be adapted. Nevertheless, that parties see themselves as holding distinctive rather than diametrically opposed views renders competition effective, producing convergence on the median voter, which is generally the Condorcet winner – that is, the proposal that best reflects the preference ordering of citizens overall. It also provides protection for minorities. Because an electoral majority is built from minorities and is prone to cycling coalitions, a ruling group will do well not to rely on a minimal winning coalition and to exclude other groups completely – thereby reducing the possibility of such cycles. In this respect, majority rule protects minorities. Either a currently excluded minority has a good chance of being part of a future winning coalition, or – for that very reason – is likely not be entirely excluded by any winning coalition keen to retain its long-term power.

Of course, one cannot deny either that all democratic systems often fail to be as responsive and as accountable as one might like, or that minorities or individuals sometimes are dominated by policies supported by the majority. However, all real systems are flawed. That does not mean we should accept these flaws and not seek to remedy them, merely that the failings of such systems should not lead to their being regarded as irremediable. In this respect, the third strand of republicanism offers a distinctive way for thinking about such institutional reforms – namely, that they should avoid domination by enhancing political equality in ways that lead citizens and their elected representatives to 'hear the other side'. Doing so not only serves political justice by guiding policy towards a conception of the public good that has equity at its core, but also has certain cognitive advantages of forcing policy-making to be more scrupulous and self-critical with regard to its likely costs and benefits over all.

The governance of relations between 'free states' follows the same rationale guiding the design of their domestic arrangements. Neo-Roman republicans have generally been wary of schemes for global or cosmopolitan democracy. The reasons are twofold. First, they worry that a concentration of power within a single institution would raise the risks of domination. Even with the best will in the world, it might be exceptionally difficult to frame collective policies that are responsive to the diversity of cultures and interests of the global population. Second, within states citizens lives are sufficiently interconnected for them to have a more or less equal stake in the decisions. Though globalisation has enhanced interconnectedness beyond the state, and many decisions within states affect the lives of citizens outside their borders, globalization has as yet to produce conditions whereby all are affected to any degree as equally by common decisions on a global scale as they are within states. As a result, there is a greater danger of majority tyranny and the oppression or neglect of minorities within a globalised democracy than within a national democracy.

To counter these two dangers, republicans have traditionally advocated a balance of power between states (Skinner 2010). The aim is to prevent any one state becoming hegemonic. By and large the most successful international organisations and agreements have been those that seek to guard against the negative externalities one state's domestic policies may have on other states and to help it recoup some of the costs of its providing positive externalities. They have also attempted to offer incentives for all states to become 'free states' on the grounds that such states are less likely to seek to dominate others. As with the domestic arrangements for avoiding non-domination, an advantage of the neo-republican programme is its political realism. The pursuit of political justice goes hand in hand with attentiveness to the need to equalise power and accommodate difference. The EU is probably the most successful set of arrangements in this regard (Bellamy and Castiglione 2000). On the one hand, free trade policies have been aimed at promoting the common prosperity of the member states, on the other hand the incentives to democratise have been focussed on securing peace and successfully helped sustain the transition from authoritarian rule that has characterised the majority of its current members. Its governance has been based on deep intergovernmental checks and balances that are designed to secure mutually advantageous agreements in areas where inter-state cooperation proves necessary.

Non-Domination and Social Justice

Republicanism is sometimes charged with having little to say about distributive justice, being exclusively concerned with political justice. However, the republican approach sees the two as intimately related. For grave social and economic disparities can be dominating and may require interventions to tackle them that a liberal approach would find illegitimate. In this respect, republicanism has a natural affinity to measures that promote social and economic as well as political equality.

From the point of view of the classical liberal, a free market will allow huge disparities in wealth and income that arise from the free choices of individuals. Any redistribution of wealth tends to be treated as an interference with these free choices and as such a constraint upon individual liberty. As a result, a presumption exists against redistribution (and, indeed, all regulation) so long as it cannot be shown that it effectively reduces interference overall – an extremely difficult point to illustrate. By contrast, the republican makes the opposite presumption that disparities of economic wealth tend to have a dominating effect. An employee with limited employment opportunities will be beholden to her employer in ways that inhibit her behaviour without there necessarily being any interference. So long as the regulations that constrain the possibility of dominating arbitrary behaviour by those possessing such power are not themselves the product of arbitrary power but result from a due process then they will be acceptable on the non domination account. There will be no comparable need to attempt to calculate whether the regulation enhances or diminishes domination over all if the rule is in and of itself non-dominating. So, whereas everything from health and safety measures to a minimum wage and unemployment benefit are *prima facie* interferences with liberty on the liberal negative liberty view, they can be regarded as *prima facie* enhancements of liberty on the non-domination, republican account because they remove arbitrariness and discretion on the part of those with power over others.

In a similar way, the republican will regard the poor and ill-educated as vulnerable to domination by others. Poverty, illiteracy and ignorance reduce people's ability to exercise their political rights on equal terms with the wealthy and better educated, to claim redress for any injustice through the courts and so on. Social and economic rights that are funded through regular laws by state authorities are not dominating in themselves and reduce the possibility of the weak being dominated by the strong. Moreover, as a number of theorists have recently noted (Bell 2010), similar considerations apply to considerations of global justice. Again, republicans will be sensitive to the ways wealthy states may dominate poorer ones, forcing them to enter inequitable trade agreements, for example. Likewise, as a matter of consistency they will seek to ensure the citizens of all states have the capacity to resist domination by others, with the meeting of basic levels of social and economic protection an important part of such resilience.

Conclusion

Republicanism offers a distinctive political and social programme deriving from the notion of freedom as non-domination. In particular, it offers a justification for a more participatory and egalitarian society – one that is democratic in the widest sense – that escapes the standard criticisms of such policies when they are tied to a theory of 'positive liberty'. It also offers a way of integrating social and political theory in that it emphasises how political and social relations interact, most particularly through its emphasis on power and status.

References

Bell, D. (ed) (2010) 'Global Justice and Republicanism', Special Issue *European Journal of Political Theory*, 9 (1).

Bellamy, R. (1996) 'The Political Form of the Constitution: The Separation of Powers, Rights and Representative Democracy', *Political Studies*, 44, 436–56.

——(1999) *Liberalism and Pluralism: Towards a Politics of Compromise*, London: Routledge.

——(2007) *Political Constitutionalism: A Republican Defence of the Constitutionality of Democracy*, Cambridge: Cambridge University Press.

——(2008) 'Republicanism, Democracy and Constitutionalism', in C. Laborde and J. Maynor (eds) *Republicanism and Political Theory*, Oxford: Blackwell, pp. 159–89.

Bellamy, R. and Castiglione, D. (2000) 'Democracy, Sovereignty and the Constitution of the European Union: The Republican Alternative to Liberalism', in Z. Bankowski and A. Scott (eds), *The European Union and its Order*, Oxford: Blackwell, pp. 170–90.

Berlin, I. (1969) *Two Concepts of Liberty*, Oxford: Oxford University Press.

Constant, B. (1988 [1819]) 'The Liberty of the Ancients Compared with that of the Moderns', in B. Constant, *Political Writings*, ed. B. Fontana, Cambridge: Cambridge University Press, 1988, pp. 307–28.

Habermas, J. (1996) *Between Facts and Norms: Contributions to a Discourse Theory of Law and Democracy*, Cambridge: Polity Press.

Hobbes, T. (1996 [1651]) *Leviathan*, ed. R. Tuck, Cambridge: Cambridge University Press.

Laborde, C. and Maynor, J. (eds) (2008) *Republicanism and Political Theory*, Oxford: Blackwell.

Miller, D. (2000) *Citizenship and National Identity*, Cambridge: Polity Press.

Pettit, P. (1997) *Republicanism: A Theory of Freedom and Government*, Oxford: Oxford University Press.

Sandel, M. (1996) *Democracy's Discontent: America In Search of a Public Philosophy*, Cambridge, MA: Harvard University Press.

Skinner, Q. (1998) *Liberty Before Liberalism*, Cambridge: Cambridge University Press.

——(2008) 'Freedom as the Absence of Arbitrary Power', in C. Laborde and J. Maynor (eds) *Republicanism and Political Theory*, Oxford: Blackwell, pp. 83–101.

——2010 'On the Slogans of Republican Political Theory', in D. Bell (ed) 'Global Justice and Republicanism', Special Issue *European Journal of Political Theory*, 9 (1), 95–102.

Wolff, R. P. (1970) *In Defence of Anarchism*, New York: Harper & Row.

Pragmatism and Political Theory

Robert B. Talisse

Pragmatism is the name of an unruly philosophical family. The first pragmatists – Charles Peirce, William James, and John Dewey – disagreed over fundamental philosophical issues; and when post-Deweyan pragmatists such as Sidney Hook, C.I. Lewis, Nelson Goodman, W.V.O. Quine, Hilary Putman, Richard Rorty, Robert Brandom, Richard Posner, and Susan Haack are included, the discord becomes more pronounced. Perhaps the most that can be said is that pragmatists hold that philosophical theories must not only be tethered to practice, but are to be evaluated according to their capacity to guide practice. Hence, throughout the pragmatist tradition, one finds as a common line of criticism the charge that certain long-standing philosophical problems should simply be abandoned because they have no practical relevance.

One should expect a philosophical program that demands practical relevance to be closely focused on political questions. Surprisingly, such matters were not among the central concerns of Peirce and James. It was Dewey who placed ethics and politics at the core of pragmatist philosophy, and much of the subsequent pragmatist theorizing follows from or is a reaction to Dewey's views. In what follows, I will explore four main trends within pragmatist political philosophy: John Dewey's perfectionism, Richard Rorty's ironism, Richard Posner's realism, and Cheryl Misak's deliberativism. After providing a brief description of each, I will sketch a few of the leading problems that each approach must face.

Dewey's Perfectionism

The core of Deweyan political philosophy can be stated in the slogan that is popular among contemporary Deweyans: *democracy is a way of life*. This slogan is intended to convey two main commitments. First, democracy is not merely a kind of state or a procedure for collective decision, but a *moral ideal* of human life. Second, the moral ideal that is democracy can be pursued and fulfilled only under certain kinds of social arrangements. In short, democracy is a way of life in which each individual exercises and cultivates his unique capacities in a way which contributes to the flourishing of the whole society.

In this way, Deweyans reject the common separation between ethics and politics. For them, the good life for humans can be achieved only within a certain kind of social order; democracy is the intrinsically social project of achieving a "truly human way of living" (Dewey 1969–91,

LW11: 218) for all individuals. According to Dewey, human flourishing necessarily involves participation in social life; and this involves *communication* among citizens with regard to matters of shared concern. Consequently, Dewey held that the "heart and guarantee of democracy is in free gatherings of neighbors on the street corner to discuss back and forth what is read in uncensored news of the day" (Dewey 1969–91, LW14: 227); by engaging in communication, citizens may "convince and be convinced by reason" (Dewey 1969–91, MW10: 404) and thus come to realize "values prized in common" (Dewey 1969–91, LW13: 71).

Dewey thought that such communicative processes were fit to govern the whole of social association. Thus, according to Dewey, democracy is a mode of social organization that "must affect all modes of human association, the family, the school, industry, religion" (Dewey 1969–91, LW2: 325). In this way, Deweyan democracy is a moral ideal that reaches into the whole of our lives, both individual and collective, aimed at human flourishing, what Dewey called "growth" (Dewey 1969–91, MW12: 181).

Employing some of the current verbiage, we can say that Deweyan democracy is a species of *perfectionism*. Perfectionists hold that it is the job of the state to promote or cultivate among citizens the dispositions, habits, and virtues requisite to human flourishing. The perfectionist is to be contrasted with the *neutralist*, who holds that, since people disagree about what human flourishing or the good life consists in, the state must be *impartial* with regard to such matters. According to the neutralist, politics is concerned strictly with the protecting rights of individuals to life, liberty, and property, not their moral development, happiness, or flourishing.

Unlike other forms of perfectionism, which hold that the project of forming citizens' dispositions is a task only for the state, Deweyan perfectionism holds that the perfectionist project is a task for *all* modes of human association (Dewey 1969–91, LW2: 325). Dewey held that "The struggle for democracy has to be maintained on as many fronts as culture has aspects: political, economic, international, educational, scientific and artistic, and religious" (Dewey 1969–91, LW13: 186). He saw the task of democracy to be that of "making our own politics, industry, education, our culture generally, a servant and an evolving manifestation of democratic ideals" (Dewey 1969–91, LW13: 197). For Dewey, then, *all* social associations should be aimed at the realization of his distinctive vision of human flourishing. And this aspiration is found throughout Dewey's corpus; in his writings on politics, education, psychology, religion, culture, and art, we are told that growth is the ultimate and proper end.

Perfectionist conceptions of politics face serious difficulties, and Deweyan perfectionism is no exception. Perfectionist views hold that the state (and, in the Deweyan case, all other forms of social association) must endeavor to promote some specified moral end, such as growth; consequently, perfectionism is rooted in the judgment that we *know* what it is for humans to flourish, and thus that further philosophical disputation over the question of human flourishing is superfluous. This is especially evident in the case of Deweyan democracy, for, as we've seen, the Deweyan wants to structure *all of society* around his own view of human flourishing. One must have a markedly high level of confidence in the correctness of one's conception of human flourishing if one is to prescribe it *for everyone*.

But it is hard to sustain the requisite level of confidence. When we survey the fields of philosophy, economics, theology, psychology, sociology, and biology, we find *several* competing conceptions of human flourishing. Similarly, when we canvass our fellow citizens, we discover a plurality of conceptions of what is best in life, what is most important, and what it means to live well. What's more, we find that, for the most part, each of these varied visions of human flourishing has its distinctive strengths and weaknesses; there are several competing conceptions of human flourishing that are philosophically viable and it is hard to declare any clear winner among them.

Hence the difficulty: Before we propose to organize society around any conception of human flourishing in particular, we had better be sure we have the right or best one, for it is clear that a state which imposes on its citizens a *false* or *defective* conception of human flourishing inflicts serious moral harms on them. The difficulty is especially pressing in the case of Deweyan democracy, which, as we have seen, envisions a society in which *all* modes of human association are aimed towards the promotion of Dewey's conception of flourishing.

Of course, the Deweyan contends that since he has the *correct* conception of human flourishing, he needn't worry about this difficulty. But how can he be so sure? Is his confidence warranted? How could he know? Deweyans like to reply that they embrace an *experimental* attitude towards these and every other question. They say that we should judge the appropriateness of the Deweyan conceptions of growth by the results which follow from implementing it.

But this response seems insufficient. For one thing, it is a stubborn fact that social and political institutions, once enacted, are difficult to dissolve and can be revised only very slowly. The Deweyan attitude of "try and see" seems fully appropriate for inquirers in a laboratory, or even for individuals pursuing their own life plans, but when it comes to designing institutions to govern the whole of social association, we must be cautious. Mistakes are morally costly to the lives of others. It is one thing to prescribe to individuals that they each should adopt an experimental attitude towards their own life, but it is quite another to say that we collectively should see each other's lives as things to be collectively experimented with. One might remind the Deweyan: My life is not *your* experiment!

Deweyans might reply that the democratic way of life is proposed as an *ideal* for human society, not as a requirement for individuals. They may say that in a democratic society, individuals are free to opt out of the Deweyan ideal. They may even say that there are distinctive goods that can be realized in non-Deweyan lives. The Deweyan hence comes to see Deweyan democracy as a "way of life" in a *personal* sense, and not something fit to be woven into the very fabric of our entire society.

But to personalize Deweyan perfection in this way would be to *abandon* Deweyan democracy to a very significant extent. A personalized Deweyan would have to reject the claim that all modes of human association should be organized around the aim of growth. But this commitment seemed to be the fulcrum of Deweyan democracy. The challenge facing Deweyan perfectionists, then, is to provide a conception of democracy robust enough to count as a "way of life" fit to govern all of society while also recognizing the fact that Dewey's conception of human flourishing is but one among several distinct but philosophically defensible conceptions about how human life – socially and individually – is best ordered.

Rorty's Ironism

At the center of Richard Rorty's view is a distinctive view of the task of political philosophy. According to Rorty, political philosophers ought to seek to inspire "social hope" (1999) and "national pride" (1998); that is, according to Rorty, political theorists should tell "inspiring stories" (1998: 3) which "[clear] philosophy out of the way" and "let the imagination play upon the possibilities of a utopian future" (1999: 239). Rorty holds that it is through inspiration, not argumentation – through appreciation of the lives of Walt Whitman and John Dewey (1998: 11) not through engagement with the arguments of philosophers – that citizens come to see themselves as "part of a great human adventure" (1999: 239).

Whereas thinkers such as Locke, Kant, Mill, and Rawls sought after philosophical principles which could provide the groundwork for a democratic order, Rorty insists that democracy "can get along without philosophical presuppositions" (1988: 178). In keeping with the general thrust of his pragmatism, Rorty holds that we should give up the idea that democracy is "subject to the jurisdiction of a philosophical tribunal" (1989: 196–7); he contends that the traditional hunt for a philosophical justification for democracy is merely a "distraction" (1996: 335).

Importantly, Rorty sees the traditional aspiration of political philosophy as a distraction because he believes that the very idea of a philosophical justification as nonsensical. He insists that the attempt to justify democracy is futile because it is couched in an obsolete philosophical paradigm. According to Rorty, "There is no way to beat totalitarians in argument" because there is no non-question-begging way to defend the premises about human nature and freedom from which democratic commitments follow (1987: 42). He continues that "attempts to ground a practice on something outside the practice will always be more or less disingenuous" (Rorty 1996: 333). The lesson we must learn is that "human beings are historical all the way through" (Rorty 1988: 176), that there are no facts about "human nature," "rationality," or "morality" which supply a case for democracy. Accordingly, he claims that any proposed argument for democracy will inevitably be "just a hypostatization of certain selected components" of existing democratic practice (Rorty 1996: 333–4).

Rorty offers a "circular justification" for his favored view of democracy; he "makes one feature of our culture look good by citing still another," and unabashedly compares our culture with others "by reference to our own standards" (1989: 57). By promoting a particular vision of his community, Rorty does not provide "philosophical backup" for those aspects of his community that he most admires. Rather, he is "putting politics first and tailoring a philosophy to suit" (Rorty 1988: 178). He insists that the purposes of democracy are *better served* by his strategy.

In Rorty's ideal "post philosophical" and "poeticized" (1989: 53) culture of "postmodernist bourgeois liberalism" (1983), citizens would openly acknowledge that their loyalties to democratic ideals are not based on philosophical arguments, but are the products of purely contingent facts about history, geography, and socialization. Yet they will not see this as a failure of any kind. They will nonetheless "stand unflinchingly" (Rorty 1989: 46) for their commitments *despite* the acknowledgement of their contingency. This "unflinching courage" (Rorty 1989: 47) in the face of radical contingency is the essence of what Rorty calls "ironism." His view, then, comes to this: there is no way to philosophically justify democracy, and those of us who favor democracy can offer only question-begging defenses of it; but in a properly pragmatic society, the absence of justification is no matter, because the very idea of justification is nonsense. The point of political philosophy in a democracy, then, is to encourage and inspire citizens to retain their devotion to democracy *despite* the fact that they recognize that there is no sense in which democracy is better than oligarchy or tyranny. We stand up for democracy despite having given up on thinking that democracy is best. That's Rortyan ironism.

There are many lines of criticism that could be pursued. But one of the interesting features of Rorty's view is that many of the obvious criticisms can be easily dismissed. For example, the charge of relativism is met by Rorty with the claim that "relativism" is a category that makes sense only against the backdrop of a philosophical model which admits of a distinction between the "relative" and the "objective"; these categories are rejected by Rorty. So let us consider Rorty's contention that democracy is better served by ironism. This, after all, seems like an empirical question.

Suppose that Rorty's ironic vision of democracy has been widely accepted. Imagine that the political theorists of the world no longer see their opponents as misguided and mistaken, but simply enchanted by different political visions. The contest between these different views is no longer understood as a search for the truth, but as something like a political campaign: each theorist *promotes* his vision and tries to inspire his fellow citizens. It seems that this would be in many respects undesirable. Most importantly, a Rortyized political culture would likely be unable to unable to inspire the kind of social hope he aims to invoke.

Consider, for example, Stalin's claim that his brutal regime is democratic "in a higher sense." Does it make sense to say that Stalinism is just another vision of democracy? The obvious response, one that Rorty endorses (1998: 57–8), is that Stalinist democracy is no democracy at all. However, it is unclear how Rorty can distinguish between *real* and *fake* democracy.

Rorty suggests that the way to treat Stalin is to simply dismiss him as *mad* (1988: 186). Of course, for Rorty, this is not a psychological diagnosis, but simply to say that "there is no way" to see Stalin as a fellow citizen; Rorty thinks Stalin is "crazy" because "the limits of sanity are set by what *we* can take seriously" (1988: 187). According to Rorty, these limits are, of course, "determined by our upbringing, our historical situation" (1988: 188). Rorty's "ethnocentric" (1988: 188) strategy founders once we consider the case of *fellow citizens* who promote visions of our democracy similar to those proffered by Stalin or any of Rorty's other paradigmatic madmen. Members of white-supremacist or other racist organizations certainly promote a certain vision of the "utopian future of our community" (Rorty 1996: 333), a particular image of what is best in our culture. We cannot treat racists as "mad" *and* maintain that "the limits of sanity" are set by the contingencies of community, for, in this case, the madmen are *members* of my community; for better or worse, the KKK is as much a part of our social inheritance as the ACLU. Rorty must either introduce some *ad hoc* qualifications such that the racist will necessarily not count as "one of us," or he will have to concede that the modern democratic state is home to persons who promote views that differ substantially from his own.

Although Rorty is surely aware of such threats, his view seems unable to produce an adequate response. He suggests that, when dealing with opponents of democracy, we "ask [them] to *privatize* their projects" (1989: 197). But what can we do when they refuse? We simply change the subject or end the conversation, we "refuse to argue" with them (Rorty 1988: 190). But this strategy of non-engagement seems like it could only be good news for the anti-democrats. Similarly, politically disengaged and apathetic citizens are not simply "uninspired," but often believe that they are *justified* in ignoring politics, they typically maintain that political action and engagement are futile.

Rorty sees these challenges as deriving not from failures of argument but from a breakdown of social hope. Again, the Rortyan response is to try to inspire in citizens a romantic affection for democracy. To be sure, this *is* important; however, an essential component of social hope is the confidence that what is hoped for is *worth* achieving and *better* than the alternatives. Yet Rorty does not allow one to maintain that democracy is in any relevant sense *better* than, say, tyranny or oligarchy. Hence Rorty's "social hope" must be "ironic" – we must hope to achieve that which we no longer can think is *worth* achieving, we must draw inspiration from that which we contend is essentially not inspiring. The idea of an "ironic" hope seems incoherent; Rorty's politics seems literally *hopeless*.

If there is anything inspiring in the works of Rorty's democratic heroes, it is precisely the sense that the visions of democracy they present are in a non-ironic sense *worth* trying for and *worth* hoping to achieve. This can be maintained only if one can point to some aspect of democracy which relevantly distinguishes it from tyranny. But to undertake the project of distinguishing tyranny from democracy is to engage in the kind of theorizing that Rorty has abandoned. It seems that we have hit upon an internal challenge to Rorty: ironic hope is uninspiring.

Posner's Realism

Richard Posner advocates "everyday pragmatism" (2003: ch. 1), "the mindset denoted by the popular usage of the word 'pragmatic', meaning practical and business-like, 'non-nonsense', disdainful of abstract theory and intellectual pretension, contemptuous of moralizers and utopian dreamers" (2003: 50). Posner continues that this mindset captures "the untheorized cultural outlook of most Americans" (2003: 50); it is the practice of prioritizing the "empirical over the theoretical" and the methodological directive to "start from what we have" (2003: 184). In Posner's view, then, pragmatism is a decidedly *anti-philosophical* stance which rejects the very idea of moral and political *theory*. According to the everyday pragmatist, moral and political questions fall within the purview of either the behavioral sciences, such as economics and psychology, or are simply matters to be settled by legislators and judges.

Posner develops his view of democracy in contrast with what he sees as a misguided alternative that he calls "deliberative democracy" and associates with Deweyan democracy. Much of recent theorizing about democracy has followed Dewey in holding that democracy requires communication and participation of citizens in the processes of self-government. In place of such views, Posner proposes that democracy is "a kind of market" (2003: 166), a "competitive power struggle among member of a political elite … for the electoral support of the masses" (2003: 130).

Posner's view is a standard form of *democratic realism*. Democratic realism has its source in the work of Joseph Schumpeter. Schumpeter famously defines democracy as "that institutional arrangement for arriving at political decision in which individuals acquire the power to decide by means of a competitive struggle for the people's vote" (1962: 269). Realists, then, hold that democracy *simply is* voting. In fact, Schumpeter claims that once a citizen casts his vote, his mission as citizen has been fulfilled: "once [citizens] have elected an individual, political action is his business and not theirs" (1962: 295). What may seem like ordinary democratic activities, such as standard forms of petition or contributing to grass-roots political organizations, are on Schumpeter's view "political back-seat driving" and are to be discouraged (1962: 295).

Posner professes to eschew the utopianism of deliberative theories (2003: 164) by sticking to what he sees as the humble facts about contemporary society: "Citizens do not care much about politics, they are not very intelligent, and they "have no interest in debate" (Posner 2004: 42). Posner reasons that democracy is therefore best conceived of as a market of "consumer sovereignty" (2004: 41) in which the "natural leaders" compete for the votes of the "sheep" (Posner 2003: 183). Contending that his view is "more respectful of people as they actually are," he characterizes his position as "unillusioned" (2003: 145).

A sustained evaluation of realism lies beyond the scope of the present essay. Let us raise the concern that everyday pragmatism and democratic realism are in fact not complementary views.

In order to build his everyday pragmatist case for democratic realism, Posner appeals to a formidable body of data that indicate sharp declines in voter participation and similarly sharp increases in voter ignorance. From the point of view of this data, the everyday pragmatist case for realism seems clear – citizens seem to care little for politics. However, that Posner should consider only the data collected by social scientists is puzzling. If we turn to other features of democratic politics, "the untheorized cultural outlook of most Americans" becomes more complicated.

One of the striking features of current modes of political discourse is that they are couched in a self-image that is deliberative. Television news channels profess to offer "no spin" zones and "fair and balanced" reporting that is "accurate" and "trusted." Popular books of political commentary, the publication of which is now a multi-million dollar industry, claim to expose "lying liars" and various other sources of "fraud" and "deception." On political talk radio programming across the nation, citizens participate daily in political discussion that at times involves significant degrees of complexity. Representatives and pundits are criticized for being "partisan," that is, blindly loyal to a party line and thus irresponsive to the arguments and reasons offered by the opposition.

To be sure, the incessant claims to fairness, reasonableness, trustworthiness, and honesty function mostly as slogans serving marketing objectives. However, in light of the market pressures operative in the modern media industry, we must conclude that such slogans are effective – they *sell*. And these slogans sell precisely because citizens tend to see themselves as well-informed and rational deliberators; they tend to see their political opinions as based on reasons and argument rather than expressions of raw preferences. At the very least, they hold that reasons, evidence, argument, and truth *matter* for political decision. As a characterization of our "untheorized cultural outlook," democratic realism seems inadequate.

Posner contends that "political rhetoric is deeply hypocritical" and that politicians must "flatter the people and exaggerate the degree to which the people actually rule" (2003: 153). He insists that no matter what we may *believe* about ourselves, the fact remains that people are disinterested in political participation of the sort that the deliberative democrat prescribes. But, if Posner is correct here, it is difficult to see why the hypocritical rhetoric is *necessary*. To repeat, the deliberative self-image may be merely a rhetorical device, but its effectiveness indicates that the deliberative image resonates positively with citizens. Were it true that citizens see their political activity as being no different from purchasing a toaster (Posner 2004: 41), the rhetoric of deliberation and participation would have no purchase. Yet it *does* have a purchase.

Of course, the realist cares not for what people *believe* of themselves or how they *understand* their political activity. However, if the everyday pragmatist's mission is to capture "the untheorized cultural outlook of most Americans" (Posner 2003: 50), then realism misses the mark.

Consequently, realism is not the view of democracy that the everyday pragmatist is looking for. We can push the criticism further to show that everyday pragmatism is not the philosophical framework most congenial to realism. Recall that Posner enlists democratic realism in his anti-theory campaign; he advocates realism as a hard-nosed alternative to abstract and aspirational political theories. However, no democratic realist can abide Posner's anti-theory stance. Standard versions of realism, such as Schumpeter's, are technically robust social scientific *theories* and so are highly academic – they are addressed mainly to social scientists for the purpose of explaining and predicting the political behavior of a given population. Accordingly, such views are decidedly *not* proposed as a description of "the untheorized cultural outlook of most Americans." In fact, realism is replete with ontological, methodological, and moral commitments that are "abstract" and "philosophical" in the senses Posner deplores. It is debatable whether democratic realism is a viable political theory, but it is in any case not an "everyday pragmatist" view.

Misak's Deliberativism

Cheryl Misak proposes a conception democracy based in Peircean pragmatism. She offers the following encapsulation of her view: "deliberative democracy in political philosophy is the right view, because deliberative democracy in epistemology is the right view" (2004: 15). In order to get a grip on Misak's politics, we need first to look to her epistemology.

Misak begins from Peirce's view about truth. Peirce held that "The opinion which is fated to be ultimately agreed to be all who investigate, is what we mean by truth" (Collected Papers: 5.407). Misak argues that Peirce did not think that truth was to be *defined* as the belief that would be adopted by inquirers at the ideal end of inquiry. She says that Peirce's characterization of truth is intended to help us to "get leverage on the concept, or a fix on it, by exploring its connections with practice" (Misak 2004: viii). That is, according to Misak, Peirce aims to *clarify* or *elucidate* the concept of truth, not *define* it.

The core of Peirce's elucidation is the intuitive thought that to take a proposition, *p*, to be true – that is, to believe that *p* or assert that *p* – is to hold that *p* would forever stand up to the test of experience and never be defeated (Misak 2000: 49, 2004: ix). Since believing that p is taking p to be true, and taking p to be true is to take p to be able to withstand the tests and travails of ongoing scrutiny, every believer is committed to being open to *inquiry*, the enterprise of squaring one's belief with reasons, arguments, and evidence by continually subjecting one's beliefs to objections and challenges. Indeed, Misak holds that the kind of responsiveness to reasons that inquiry is meant to secure is a *constitutive norm* of belief (2004: 12). To be sure, Misak's claim does *not* commit her to the view that no one ever holds beliefs for defective reasons or for no reason at all. To say that reason-responsiveness is a constitutive norm of belief is to say that when we believe *we take ourselves to be* reason-responsive.

From these considerations, we see that Misak's Peircean epistemology is inherently *social*. Again, to be a believer is to aim at truth. But truth-aiming is an ineliminably *diachronic* affair: we aim at truth by always standing ready to square our beliefs with new reasons, arguments, and evidence. Indeed, to believe that p is to be committed to the hypothesis that p will stand up under scrutiny and will square with all the evidence and argument that could be brought to bear on it. Consequently, believing "involves being prepared to try to justify one's views to others and being prepared to test one's beliefs against the experience of others" (Misak 2000: 94). For if we do not take seriously the arguments and criticisms of others, getting "the best or the true belief is not on the cards" (Misak 2000: 94). Accordingly, Misak holds, with Peirce, that in order to aim at truth, believers must have access to and participate in a *community* of inquirers. The very nature of belief commits us to processes of inquiry, which in turn commits us to participation in a certain kind of community, namely one in which inquiry can commence.

We can now see how Misak's conception of democracy emerges out of her epistemology. According to Misak, to hold beliefs at all is to be committed to inquiry, and thus to social processes of "debate and deliberation" (2000: 106) with others. These commitments entail a range of interpersonal norms that Misak sees as characteristically democratic. Specifically, Misak contends that the commitment to the enterprise of justification entails that one must subject one's beliefs to objections and challenges *from all quarters*, since anyone might have a relevant countervailing consideration or counter argument. Consequently, we must stand ready to "listen to others" (Misak 2000: 96) and take their arguments and experiences seriously. Perhaps more importantly, inquiry commits us to engaging with those whose experiences differ from our own; for if we are aiming at truth, we must seek out new and unfamiliar challenges. In this way, the norms of belief entail interpersonal norms of equality, participation, recognition, and inclusion.

From these interpersonal norms, a range of social norms emerges. In order for individuals to exchange reasons and collectively inquire, there must be norms of free speech, freedom of information, open debate, protected dissent, accountability, and so on. Additionally, if inquiry is to commence, the formal infrastructure of democracy must be in place, including a constitution, courts, accountable bodies of representation, regular elections, and a free press. Also, there must be a system of public schooling designed to equip students in the epistemic habits necessary for inquiry, and institutions of distributive justice to eliminate as far as justice allows the material obstructions to democratic citizenship. Further, democracy *might* also require more extensive provisions, such as special measures to preserve public spaces and to create forums for citizens to encounter new perspectives. In any case, Misak holds that the full range of democratic norms can be derived from her pragmatist epistemology.

The main worry is that Misak claims to have derived too much substance from the very meager insights from which she begins. Misak's holds that an entire conception of democracy can be derived from a few truisms of epistemology. Is this plausible? Here's one objection: Grant that the norms that govern belief commit us to inquiry, which in turn commits us to taking each other's reasons seriously. Grant further that taking each other's reasons seriously commits us to norms of inclusiveness, participation, and equality. But these are not sufficient for a democratic society, for seeing others as equal partners in inquiry is consistent with seeing those same others as *political* subordinates. That is, it seems consistent with Misak's epistemology for one to regard his fellow believers as *consultants*, whose arguments and objections have merely *recommendatory* force, rather than as *political equals* who are entitled to *equal* political power and *equal* influence over political decision.

Perhaps Misak would respond that in order for inquiry to truly commence, the upshot of inquiry must have political force. The way to ensure that inquiry has such force, Misak may argue, is to give to all believers an equal vote. Yet this kind of reply prompts another worry. If democracy is the political upshot of our epistemic commitment to aim at truth, and if we want our politics to reflect the outcomes of our inquiries, then what justification could there be for the *democratic nation state*? Why shouldn't persons who live in Italy be consulted on questions concerning policy in Canada? Surely people in Italy are inquirers and will have a distinctive view of Canadian politics. If the point of democracy is to have policy reflect our best reasons, then why should political power within a given state be restricted to those who happen to live within its borders? Does Misak's view entail a *global* democracy, a democracy without sovereign nations?

These institutional concerns may be met with practical considerations. Misak could say that a global democracy is impractical, and that we are stuck with the nation state. Perhaps she would be correct. But the thought of a world governed by global inquiry raises a different kind of worry. Misak thinks that believing commits us to norms of reason exchanging such that to believe that p is to stand ready to offer reasons for p and respond to arguments against p. The worry is that Misak has glossed over issues concerning what is to count as a reason for p. Disagreements over political matters often seem to be disagreements about the precise meaning of our epistemic commitments. In particular, many controversies involve disagreements about what should count as *evidence* for a given proposition. To take an easy example, some hold that the fact that the Bible condemns homosexuality constitutes *evidence*, and perhaps *conclusive evidence*, that homosexuality is immoral. Others hold that the Bible is morally irrelevant. Some take statistics concerning gun-related crime to provide evidence in favor of gun-control policies, whereas others think that even a very high incidence of gun-related crime is beside the point.

It would be easy to multiply examples. The point is that, even is we grant Misak's epistemic claims, we still may disagree in specific cases about whether some statement, s, counts as *evidence* for p. So, although we may all agree on the norms governing belief, we may yet be in conflict regarding the precise *content* of these norms. How are such conflicts to be resolved? To say that we should exchange our reasons is to make no progress, since we are divided over what should count as a reason. Some would say that we should look to the empirical sciences for guidance; others would say that we should follow our commonsense intuitions; some would recommend that we *pray* for the right answer; and still others would say that we should give up on the very idea of epistemic criteria. What could count as a reason to adopt one of these answers rather than another?

If the commitment to inquiry is going to form the core of our conception of democracy, we had better get specific about what we mean by *inquiry* and related notions. The trouble, however, is this: Once Misak provides the requisite details her description of the norms of belief will likely lose their intuitive resonance. But it is the intuitive character of her views about the tight connections between belief and evidence that accounts for much of the appeal of her epistemic deliberativism.

Conclusion

We have surveyed four prominent trajectories in contemporary pragmatist political philosophy, identifying the main difficulties confronting each view. That each pragmatist option occasions serious objections is no reason to regard pragmatism as an imperiled program. On the contrary, philosophical approaches thrive on the difficulties to which they give rise. The best current work in pragmatist political philosophy is addressed precisely to the task of working through the difficulties we have raised here.

References

Dewey, J. (1969–91) *The Collected Works of John Dewey: The Early Works, The Middle Works, The Later Works*. 37 vols. Jo Ann Boydston, ed. Illinois: Southern Illinois University Press.

Misak, C. (2000) *Truth, Politics, Morality*. New York: Routledge.

——. (2004) *Truth and the End of Inquiry*. New York: Oxford University Press.

Posner, R. (2003) *Law, Pragmatism, and Democracy*. Cambridge, MA: Harvard University Press.

——. (2004) "Smooth Sailing." *Legal Affairs*. January/February: 41–2.

Rorty, R. (1983) "Pragmatism without Method." In Rorty, *Objectivity, Relativism, and Truth*. Cambridge: Cambridge University Press.

——. (1987) "Science as Solidarity." In Rorty, *Objectivity, Relativism, and Truth*. Cambridge: Cambridge University Press.

——. (1988) "The Priority of Democracy to Philosophy." In Rorty *Objectivity, Relativism, and Truth*. Cambridge: Cambridge University Press.

——. (1989) *Contingency, Irony, Solidarity*. Cambridge: Cambridge University Press.

——. (1996) "Idealizations, Foundations, and Social Practices." In *Democracy and Difference*, Seyla Benhabib, ed. New Jersey: Princeton University Press.

——. (1998) "Pragmatism and Romantic Polytheism." In *the Resurgence of Pragmatism*, Morris Dickstein, ed. Durham: Duke University Press.

——. (1999) *Philosophy and Social Hope*. New York: Penguin.

Schumpeter, J. (1962) *Capitalism, Socialism, and Democracy*. New York: Harper Books.

Methodological and Political Pluralism

Democracy, Pragmatism, and Critical Theory

James Bohman

Although myriad in its forms, "critical theory" (or more generally critical social inquiry) has a distinctive purpose and overall structure. Critical social theorists generally aim at constructing social theories that link explanation and criticism and thus have both normative and explanatory features. Furthermore, such theories must also be "practical." "Practical" here does not simply mean useful; nor does it mean that critical theories are connected to practice generally, but rather to a particular purpose. As Horkheimer put it, such theories seek "to liberate human beings from the circumstances that enslave them" (Horkheimer 1982: 244). The philosophical problem of critical social inquiry is to identify precisely those features of its distinctive explanations that give them their distinctive normative character in underwriting social criticism. A closer examination of paradigmatic works of critical social science from Marx's *Capital* to the Frankfurt School's *Studies in Authority and the Family* and Habermas's *Theory of Communicative Action* does not reveal any distinctive form of explanation or special methodology that provide the necessary and sufficient conditions for such inquiry. Rather, the best such works employ a variety of methods and styles of explanation and are often cooperative and interdisciplinary in their mode of research (Horkheimer 1993). What then makes them works of critical social science?

There are two main answers to this question. The first is that they employ a distinctive theory which unifies such diverse approaches and explanations. This approach demands a comprehensive theory that will unify the social sciences and underwrite the superiority of the critic. The second is practical. According to this view, such theories are distinguished by the form of politics in which they are embedded and the method of verification that this politics entails. In this essay I want to defend a version of the second approach, grounded in the pragmatic conception of democracy as a mode of inquiry. Even if critical social science is best unified practically and politically rather than theoretically or epistemically, it is not thereby reducible to democratic politics. It is rather the moment of inquiry from the perspective of a participant within such practices.

As evidenced by the turn to historical materialism in Marx and its constant reconstruction thereafter, the practical solution has not been the favored one in the history of critical social science. The theoretical solution provides the critic with an epistemically superior status over

149

and above the limits of the participants' perspective; it underwrites the claims that such criticisms are "scientifically justified." It also provides the basis for going beyond a "mere" pluralism and for adjudicating among the often contradictory claims of theories and explanations in the social sciences; those explanations that cannot be organized into the unity of the comprehensive social theory are rejected. This theoretical conception is not devoid of politics. Rather, corresponding to this single comprehensive theoretical framework is the comprehensive political goal of human emancipation. If we reject such theoretical and political convergence, where does critical social science begin amidst such theoretical and political pluralism? Here pragmatism, especially as it has been developed in John Dewey's theory of democratic inquiry, provides the vocabulary for a more complex understanding of the goals and political contexts that make sense of what critical theorists can actually do. Pluralism requires that we abandon the criterion that Marx saw as the criterion of the theoretical approach and the superiority of historical materialism: a unique fit between critical explanation and the goals of a particular political practice. If empirical theories are indeterminate to the extent that they do not yield *unique* predictions, then critical theories are indeterminate if they do not establish a unique relation to human emancipation. I want to argue that we can accept such indeterminacy on the practical interpretation of critical social science and that it is the only possibility consistent with democratic politics.

Because Habermas was perhaps the first critical theorist to realize the full implications of methodological and theoretical pluralism in the social sciences, I shall focus on his account of critical theory to develop this practical account. He is a useful example precisely because there is an unresolved tension in his "reconstruction" of critical social science: the tension between retaining the Marxian theoretical project of a comprehensive social theory on the one hand and the pragmatic and Weberian insight into the benefits of irreducible pluralism on the other hand (Habermas 1979; Weber 1949). In pushing Habermas in the direction of pluralism, the practical argument needs to show that pluralism enhances rather than detracts from the public use of reason, just as it enhances rather than detracts from the value of social inquiry. Convergence on a "correct" theory, even as a regulative ideal governing inquiry, does by itself not give critical social science any special role in public self-reflection or in enriching democratic practice.

Pragmatism and Social Inquiry

Pragmatism owes its current appeal to two core ideas: its transformation of traditional epistemological, moral and metaphysical questions into practical problems and its emphasis on the relations between democracy and science. Dewey's pragmatism does both without being deflationary. His pragmatic rule, "judge any idea by its consequences" (Dewey 1948: 163), in no way suggests that ideas or norms should be reduced to their instrumental value. Rather, the pragmatic rule asks us to look at problems in a certain way. Take, for example, the problem of moral and epistemic disagreement. Pragmatism does not construe this as a metaphysical and epistemological problem to be solved once and for all by distinct criteria of judgment that apply in every case. Instead, it asks us to consider the role of disagreement in various practices. Rather than an epistemological problem to be solved by universal criteria of judgment, disagreement is better seen as a practical problem, indeed ultimately a political problem. When searching for a practical solution, we may not want to eliminate disagreement at all. Indeed, we may, for example, inquire about its practical role: How can disagreement become part of our practices so as to make them more fruitful and self-critical without making their continued existence impossible? Disagreement is an important part of inquiry, making the important question not how to get rid of it but how to make the diversity of opinions useful to the goals of our epistemic and political practices (Dewey 1988). Because it is related to problem solving in general, inquiry is part of all social practice.

The pragmatic conception of inquiry gives the old Enlightenment analogy between democracy and science a political twist. While it seems to suggest rule by experts, this objection does not apply to science as the pragmatists thought of it: for them, science itself is successful because it is organized democratically. Dewey, for example, saw the problem of inquiry as a political one. "Existing political practice, with its complete ignoring of occupational groups and the organized knowledge and purposes that are involved in the existence of such groups, manifests a dependence upon a summation of individuals quantitatively ... " (Dewey 1991: 50–1). In its proper form, analogy works both ways. Democracy, too, can be improved through directly incorporating epistemic features of the cooperative practices of socially organized knowledge upon which it is based in any complex society (Bohman 1995).

This distinctively political understanding of the relationship between theory and practice in social inquiry unites pragmatism and critical social science. But there are many political relationships and epistemic goals that are consistent with democracy. Dewey's insight is to define various modes of inquiry in terms of the different political relationships in which they can be carried out: those relations necessary for prediction and control, for strategic action, and finally for cooperation. While democracy does not exclude the possibility of any of these practical relationships, it makes cooperation fundamental. Indeed, any cooperative activity demands inquiry and critical social science is precisely the analysis of the basic terms and norms of cooperation. Once there is a fundamental agreement of these norms, then social inquiry more generally may also examine means and ends as well as the conditions for strategic action within a cooperative framework. As Putnam puts it, "all cooperative activity involves a moment of inquiry" (Putnam 1994: 174). Critical social science supplies methods for making explicit this moment of self-examination necessary for on-going democratic regulation of social life, including its own governing norms. Here the relation of theory to practice is a different one: more than simply clarifying the relation of means and ends for decisions on particular issues, these social sciences institutionalize reflection upon institutionalized practices and their norms of cooperation. Critical social science is also reflexive in the sense that among such practices is included the examination of practices and modes of inquiry itself, including underlying social norms and relationships. One such mode is critical social science, understood through democratic norms and goals.

As practices of inquiry embedded in other practices, all the social sciences establish specific relationships between inquirers and other social actors. Social inquiry that only develops optimal problem solving strategies in light of objective knowledge of the consequences of all available courses of action is rightly called "technocratic" by Habermas and other Critical Theorists and rejected by pragmatists from Mead to Dewey. It models the social scientist on the engineer, who masterfully chooses the optimal solution to a problem of design. For the social scientist as an ideally rational and informed actor, "the range of permissible solutions is clearly delimited, the relevant probabilities and utilities precisely specified, and even the criteria of rationality to be employed (e.g., maximization of expected utilities) is clearly stated" (Hempel 1965: 481). The pragmatic question here is *who* provides such solutions and *how* they were derived: the solutions are instrumental, derived without cooperative inquiry. Agency here belongs to the social scientist who, as an engineer, does not need a social relationship of cooperation, but only the ability to command acquiescence. Hempel certainly overestimated how well the social sciences can identify mechanisms that could contribute to instrumental success, particularly since even if an optimal solution emerges affected actors can make it suboptimal by raising its costs through noncompliance. Theories of strategic action go further, assuming that each actor has agency in so far as the analysis gets at the interdependent choices of each from the perspective of their particular beliefs and desires. As in instrumental action, the inquiry adopts a third-person perspective, judging actions according to criteria of success as set by independent standards of rationality. In both cases, inquiry is monological and thus need not be cooperative. Only the stance of the reflective participant is fully dialogical, giving inquirer and agent equal standing as agents in a shared practice (whatever the goals of that practice may be). It is this political relationship of equal agency that critical inquirers seek to establish, as they address their criticism to actors who will engage in public reflection on the nature and goals of the practices in which inquirer and actor both participate.

In this respect, critical social inquiry has a particularly important role. It examines the basis and terms of ongoing cooperation itself, particularly within the most basic social institutions. Besides social cooperation, such practices are also about developing policies for achieving socially valuable ends or for acquiring useful knowledge. Such policies must in turn be tested, and a variety social scientific theories and research programs have the epistemic resources for this task. Pragmatism suggests that the greater the variety of such theoretical perspectives, the better the public testing of such policies and problem solving strategies (Dewey 1986: 500). Given its relationships of inquiry among equals, critical social inquiry engages in a different second-order sort of testing. It asks: what are the consequences that social science should be looking for? How are the terms of cooperation determined and how are they influencing the ongoing practices in which they are embedded? What sort of blindspots have these terms of cooperation created, say in the distribution of benefits and burdens? How can these practices be organized and reorganized so as to make it possible to change those terms of cooperation that cannot pass the test of democratic self-reflection? If all cooperative practices have a moment of inquiry, then they also need a moment of self-reflection on such inquiry itself. Thus, critical social inquiry takes practical inquiry one reflective step further, a step that can only be carried out by a public. As in Kuhn's distinction between normal and revolutionary science, second-order critical reflection considers whether or not the framework for cooperation itself needs to be changed. Such criticism is directed at current institutions as well as towards formulating new terms of cooperation under which problems are solved. When participants hold norms constant, then instrumental and strategic modes of inquiry are useful in determining the objective and social consequences of policies and practices. Given that these consequences usually require at least the sort of behavioral expectations that legitimate social norms are an effective mechanism for bringing about, the examination of the normative expectations is often the best (and even least costly) way to solve problems when practices break down.

Consider the problem of the availability of experimental drugs for the treatment of AIDS as it developed in the United States over the last decade. It is clear to all that the development and testing of drugs is a matter for scientific experts who learn more and more about the virus and its development in the body. So long as experts unproblematically engaged in first-order problem solving, AIDS patients were willing to grant these experts certain authority in this domain. Nonetheless, the continued spread of the epidemic and lack of effective treatments brought about a crisis in expert authority, an "existential problematic situation" in Dewey's sense (Dewey 1986: 492). In response lay participants made the cooperative character of this division of labor problematic, pointing out the practical consequences and burdens of scientific activities. By defining expert activity through its social consequences and by making explicit the terms of social cooperation between researchers and patients, patients and other non-expert participants sought to reshape the practices of gaining medical knowledge and authority. Indeed, as Stephen Epstein points out, the effects of AIDS activists on medical research did not just concern extra-scientific problems such as research funding. Rather, they challenged the very standards of statistical validity employed in experimental trials (Epstein 1996: part 2). Such challenges required questioning central norms that organize and justify the authority of scientific enterprise itself, not just the dissemination of its results or its application outside the scientific domain. In this case, the social process of testing inquiry did not just change particular policies concerning experimentation, but transformed the structure and organization of medical research and public health and changed their underlying norms of cooperation. The very terms of cooperation and inquiry in this area were changed by the affected public in order that institutions could once again engage in acceptable first-order problem solving. Only by making scientific institutions more accountable to those who are affected by their research and on whose continued cooperation and consent such research depends could inquiry continue.

This public challenge to the norms on which expert authority is based may be generalized to all forms of research in cooperative activity. It suggests the transformation of some of the epistemological problems of the social sciences into the practical question of how to make their forms of inquiry and research open to public testing and public accountability. This demand also means that some sort of "practical verification" of critical social inquiry is necessary. What is its distinct practical problem for such testing and verification? How do we judge its practical consequences, especially if it is second-order rather than first-order problem solving? If such second-order reflection involves testing existing norms, then it also must test norms of social inquiry, including norms of public justification.

If we examine the writings of critical social theorists on their own activity, we find neither any clear answer to the problem of verification, nor any clear way to think about the social organization of critical inquiry itself. Two problems stand in the way, both having to do with the epistemic status of the social sciences. The first has to do with the way in which the epistemological problems of critical social inquiry have traditionally been dealt with. Instead of searching for practical transformations of epistemological problems, Critical Theorists have sought to ground their form of social inquiry in a comprehensive social theory. Failing that, many have considered it necessary to abandon appeals to social scientific explanations entirely (Adorno 1973; Wiggershaus 1994). This skepticism is, however, the result of a false conception of the verification of critical explanations.

The failure of this theoretical attempt leads to a second problem. The main reason to abandon the search for the best comprehensive social theory as providing the warrant for good social criticism is that there are many different theories and methods that provide critical insight into the normative organization of society. A non-skeptical response to methodological pluralism has become the centerpiece of the philosophy of social science in the work of Jürgen Habermas. However, Habermas has drawn back from the full implications of such pluralism, fearing that it will undermine the normative task of reflective social inquiry. It is here that pragmatism has something to offer critical social inquiry. Pragmatists have transformed the seemingly irresolvable epistemological and moral dilemmas of pluralism into tractable practical and political problems. Seen in this light, some of Habermas's own writings come remarkably close to the pragmatic solution to the problem of pluralism in inquiry, and the very problems he raises suggest that he ought to return to the pragmatism of his early writings in the philosophy of the social sciences. However, Habermas continues to seek theoretical rather than practical solutions in his recent writings, often leading to an unmotivated pessimism about the role of critical social inquiry in transforming cooperative practices and democratic institutions. Such a reliance on theory is undermined not only by Habermas's own insight that there is no one way to engage in social inquiry or in practical self-reflection, but also by his own critical practice. In what follows, I shall develop just such a pluralistic, practical and ultimately democratic conception of critical inquiry.

Methodological Pluralism and Theoretical Unification: An Unresolved Tension in Habermas

Before his more recent attempts at theoretical unification as a solution to the pluralism of the social sciences, Habermas's philosophy of social science and of critical social inquiry was initially both pragmatist and pluralist. He begins his first attempts to reconstruct the task of critical social science in a distinctly pragmatic way, emphasizing the purposes and goals constitutive of various forms of knowledge. In *Knowledge and Human Interests*, Habermas recognizes the inherent pluralism of the social sciences. He identifies three distinct and irreducible "knowledge constitutive interests," each with their own distinct presuppositions, modes of inquiry, and epistemic goals (Habermas 1971). Habermas also ties these interests to different "social media" of work, language, and power as distinct means of social organization. The technical cognitive interest aims at control and is connected with nomological sciences; the practical interest of the hermeneutic–historical sciences aim at increasing mutual understanding and unimpeded communication; and finally, the emancipatory interest of critically oriented science aims at liberating human beings from relations of force, unconscious constraints and dependence. While the first two interests can be developed through the "self-reflection of the existing sciences," the third, emancipatory interest has a unique status – at least insofar as it does not correspond to a single, well-developed form of inquiry. While Habermas thinks that there are exemplars for such activity in psycho-analysis and ideology critique, there is no determinate or well accepted form of inquiry that corresponds to "critical reflective knowledge."

Regardless of what we think of this analysis of cognitive interests as an epistemology of the social sciences, it is striking that the emancipatory interest has a particular status that already encompasses the two-sides of Habermas's conception of critical social theory. On the one hand, he recognizes a variety of epistemic goals or interests in social science and the role of critical self-reflection in achieving them; and yet, on the other hand, he argues that critical self-reflection (and with it critical social theory) has a special comprehensive status in that it unifies all forms of social inquiry as the inquiry into "the self-formation of all humanity." As I will argue later, we lose nothing of importance for the former by abandoning the unifying claims of a social theory that does the work of a philosophy of history.

The justification of this two-sided (pluralistic, yet comprehensive) approach is worked out in more detail in Habermas's writings on the philosophy of social science and is the common thread that connects *On the Logic of the Social Sciences* (originally 1967) to *The Theory of Communicative Action* (originally 1981). The problem of pluralism is not new in the philosophy of social science. As Habermas argues in *On the Logic of the Social Sciences*, Max Weber was among the first to recognize that the social sciences combine various cognitive operations: explanation and interpretation; historical comparison and transhistorical theoretical terms. This mixed status leads social scientists to combine seemingly contradictory and heterogeneous methods, aims and theories into more or less coherent wholes. Just as in the analysis of forms of inquiry tied to distinct knowledge-constitutive interests, Habermas accepts that various theories and methods each have "a relative legitimacy." Indeed, like Dewey he goes so far as to argue that it is "the apparatus of general theories" typical in the natural sciences, and not their causal or functional forms of inquiry, that cannot be applied to society. In the absence of any such general theories, the most fruitful approach to social scientific knowledge is to bring all the various methods and theories into relation to each other: "Whereas the natural and the cultural or hermeneutic sciences are capable of living in mutually indifferent, albeit more hostile than peaceful coexistence, the social sciences must bear the tension of divergent approaches under one roof ... " (Habermas 1988: 3). This indifference is a theoretical one. It is precisely when they are addressed to complex social situations that the sciences must find practical ways to resolve such methodological tensions.

Habermas's affirmation of pluralism in the social sciences always keeps the two sides in tension. Even while accepting pluralism, the social sciences cannot be satisfied with mere pluralism or indifference; they must also seek the relationships between the various fundamental approaches and modes of empirical research and explanation. It is establishing the connection among these various forms of research that is the hallmark of critical theory. To the extent that it is self-reflexive about the social scientific enterprise itself and the need to hold different approaches in tension, critical theory reveals how the social sciences as a whole can properly handle theoretical and methodological pluralism.

In *The Theory of Communicative Action*, Habermas casts critical social theory in a similar pluralistic, yet unifying way. In discussing various accounts of societal modernization, Habermas argues that the main existing theories have their own "particular legitimacy" as developed lines of empirical research, and that Critical Theory takes on the task of critically unifying the various theories and their heterogeneous methods and presuppositions. "Critical Theory does not relate to established lines of research as a competitor; starting from its concept of the rise of modern societies, it attempts to explain the specific limitations and relative rights of those approaches" (Habermas 1987: 375). Here Habermas adds a particular theoretical task that is not present in his previous recognition of methodological pluralism in the social sciences. However, recognizing the rights of diverse approaches implies also recognizing their limitations, and there must be some more comprehensive standpoint from which the Critical Theorist may do so: it is the comprehensive standpoint of a theory of modernization that incorporates what is right about each other approach while criticizing their weaknesses and limitations. From the point of view of the problem of inquiry with which Habermas began in *Knowledge and Human Interests*, Habermas sees critical theory as performing a self-reflective *Aufhebung* on other empirically valid approaches, eliminating none and locating them all in a more comprehensive framework (Habermas 1986).

This Hegelian response to the fact of pluralism in the social sciences contrasts sharply with the Kantian answer favored by Habermas in other philosophical domains, particularly in normative theory. The Kantian answer is given sharpest formulation by Weber in his philosophy of social science: Weber recognized the hybrid nature of social science, but saw different methods and theories as truly heterogeneous in their presuppositions. According to this contrasting approach, "the relative rights and specific limitations" of each theory and method are recognized by assigning them to their own particular (and hence limited) empirical domain (Habermas 1987: 375). Rather than establishing these judgments of scope and domain through a more comprehensive theory that encompasses all others and thereby shows their limitations, the Kantian approach proceeds case by case, seeing the way in which these theories run up against their limits in trying to extend beyond the core phenomena of their domain of validity (Bohman 1991). Such an approach need not deny the possibility of fruitful large-scale theories, so long as their success is established by a wide range of empirical evidence and by the diversity of sub-theories that they fruitfully integrate. It suggests a theoretically modest, but practically robust pragmatism about critical inquiry. Such a recognition brings the philosophy of critical social science closer to Dewey's pragmatism by transforming the irresolvable epistemological dilemmas of pluralism into practical problems for public reflection.

Before turning to such a practical interpretation of critical social inquiry, it may be appropriate to consider why the theoretical account of them has been favored for so long and by so many Critical Theorists. First, it has been long held that only a comprehensive social theory could unify critical social science and thus provide a "scientific" basis for criticism that goes beyond the limits of lay or participant knowledge. Second, not only must the epistemic basis of criticism be independent of agents' practical knowledge, the cogency of an explanation must be normatively distinct from its political effects on a specific audience. Rather than the inquiry that is part of a practice, social criticism ought to be a two-stage affair: first, inquirers independently discover the best explanation using the available comprehensive theory; then, second, they persuasively communicate its critical consequences to participants who may have false beliefs about their practices. Let me briefly consider why each of these interrelated claims is based on a false view of critical inquiry and upon anti-pluralist assumptions.

Such a form of inquiry does not to deny that there is an important role for general theories. They aim at possible explanations of large-scale social and historical processes and relate different phenomena together when they are successful and complete. As such they may also provide "general interpretive frameworks" on which it is possible to construct "critical histories of the present" (McCarthy in McCarthy and Hoy 1994: 229–30). But this more modest account of critical theories no longer sees general theories as comprehensive. Rather, they are interpretations that are validated by the extent to which they open up new possibilities of action which are themselves to be verified in democratic inquiry. General theories are then best seen as practical proposals whose critical purchase is not moral and epistemic independence but practical and public testing according to criteria of interpretive adequacy.

Pluralism and Agency: Pragmatism and the Adequacy of Criticism

Critical social theory has always sought to combine theoretical inquiry with intellectual and moral responsibility within a well-integrated interpretive and explanatory framework and a political practice aimed at human emancipation. More than any other social theorist, Habermas has advanced this endeavor. His actual critical practice, however, has more in common with Dewey's theoretical and methodological pluralism and with his realization that the goal of emancipation is not one but many different goals typical of full and rich human existence. Such a theory only serves the methodological purpose of correcting for the one-sidedness of existing theories and approaches while integrating them into adequate, critical and practical explanations. Historical materialism has long been tied to the project of a politically and scientifically determinate critical theory; abandoning this goal and accepting a weaker criterion of adequacy also entails that we accept a different picture of social scientific knowledge consistent with the irreducibility of heterogeneous methods and theories in the social sciences. A plurality of adequate theories and methods is not only required for good critical explanations with normative content; it is also more appropriate to the role that critics play in democratic political change.

Besides analyzing the "emancipatory interest" as the specific purpose of certain forms of social inquiry, Habermas's interpretation of the distinctive relationship of theory and practice in critical inquiry pushes him in yet another pragmatic direction. The problem is that his methodological writings have neglected this important relationship. Merely to identify a number of different methods and a number of different theories connected with a variety of different purposes and interests leaves the social scientist in a rather hopeless epistemological dilemma. *Either* the choice among theories, methods and interests seems utterly arbitrary, *or* the critical theorist has some special epistemic claim to survey the domain and make the proper choice for the right reason. While the former, more skeptical horn of the dilemma is one endorsed by "new pragmatists" like Richard Rorty (1991) who sees all knowledge as purpose-relative and by Weber in more decisionistic moments in his methodological writings, the latter demands objectivist claims for social science generally and for the epistemic superiority of the critical theorist in particular that Habermas and other Critical Theorists have been at pains to reject

(Habermas 1973: 38). Is there any way out of the epistemic dilemma of pluralism? The way out, it seems to me, has already been indicated by pragmatism's emphasis on the social context of inquiry and the practical character of social knowledge.

The problems of pluralism cannot be avoided simply by shifting the debate to practical criteria. Not only are there many distinct practical interests or purposes, the social sciences may also be practical in many different senses. To the extent that we can identify the epistemological basis of the social sciences in forms of practical knowledge, the dilemma of pluralism becomes more tractable as a problem: identifying the type of knowledge required by the specific social context of inquiry. The analysis of interests takes us some of the way toward a solution. Technical knowledge does not only represent a particular interest, say the interest in controlling outcomes; in the case of the social sciences, it also presupposes a particular practical relation between the social scientists and the subjects of their inquiry. In order to control certain social outcomes or processes, a particular context of inquiry must be created: the regulative control of institutions over certain kinds of practices or processes. As second-order reflection, critical social inquiry presupposes and sometimes attempts to create a different social context of inquiry. It addresses the subjects of inquiry as equal reflective participants, as knowledgeable social agents. In this way, the asymmetries of the context of technical control are suspended; this means that critical social inquiry must be judged by a different set of practical consequences, appealing to increasing the "reflective knowledge" that agents already possess to a greater or lesser degree. As themselves agents in the social world, social scientists participate in the creation of the sort of contexts in which their theories are publicly verified.

The goal of critical inquiry is not to control social processes or even to influence the sorts of decisions that agents might make in any determinate sort of way. Instead, its goal is to initiate public processes of self-reflection (Bohman 1996: ch. 5). Thus, critical social science can measure its success against the standard of attaining such a practical goal. In certain cases, the goal may be attained simply by addressing agents as members of a functioning public sphere; hence, the success of critical social inquiry may be measured by its practical consequences for the quality of discussion and debate in the public sphere. Such a standard is the same measure of success for the contributions of any reflective participant in the public sphere, particularly those who are concerned about its public character or the quality of public opinion formed within it (Bohman 1996: ch. 1). But it may not always be the case that a well-functioning public sphere exists; and even if one exists it may be difficult to initiate reflection on various social themes or self-reflection on aspects of the public sphere. Such cases are the subject matter of most critical theories, such as the theory of ideology, which seem to introduce certain asymmetric features into critical social knowledge, leaving the critic once again in a position of epistemic superiority. This problem, too, is less intractable from a pragmatic point of view: no such strong claims are required, since the critic's theory does not provide the practical warrant of critique. Indeed, Dewey's emphasis on the social organization and distribution of knowledge helps us to understand the role of the critical social scientist differently: as one among many reflective participants, engaging in an on-going process of deliberation and self-reflection.

Conclusion: Democracy as a Critical Practice of Social Inquiry

My argument here develops a contrast between two interpretations of critical social science: the one is theoretical and dependent on the heritage of German Idealism, and the other is practical and pluralistic in the spirit of pragmatism. The main epistemic weakness of the first interpretation is that it depends on the overly ambitious goal of a comprehensive social theory which can unify all the diverse methods and practical purposes of social inquiry. In the absence of such a theory, the choice between various approaches or methods seems fundamentally arbitrary. The practical alternative offers a solution to this problem by taking critical social theory in a pragmatic direction. In this respect, I have argued that a pragmatic reinterpretation of the verification of critical inquiry solves seemingly intractable epistemic problems for the social theorist. But it is also true that Critical Theory can help us in understanding pragmatism better, avoiding older pragmatism's often rather unanalyzed faith in the progressive power of knowledge and communication on the one hand and the relativistic pluralism of recent "new" pragmatism on the other. Critical Theory and pragmatism are therefore mutually informative, especially when united around a normative account of democratic practices of socially organized, critical judgment.

The relationship of critical social inquiry and democracy that I am developing here has more to do with Dewey's dynamic and transformative publics than with Habermas's conception of discursive practice. Suitably modified to deal with difficulties of communication and the potential for cooperative conflicts, an epistemic interpretation of democratic social inquiry properly combines the social role of inquiry in improving decision making with radical democracy's emphasis on egalitarianism and decentralization of power. It understands the excesses of the democratic will of the majority or the people, while avoiding excessive political rationalism typical of comprehensive theoretical approaches (Elster 1989). Social inquiry does not just economize on the costs of acquiring information; it is also a cooperative enterprise that democratizes the social distribution of knowledge. In this way, a politics of institutional reform inspired by pragmatism seeks to identify both institutional and non-institutional locations for democratization, especially as power in complex societies is organized around knowledge as a resource. When properly organized and defined, knowledge is a resource that may be democratically shared and publicly verified through first- and second-order reflection. Under these conditions critical social inquiry can have transformative consequences as the moment of inquiry in democratic practices. Clarifying the democratic context of practical verification goes a long way towards showing why critical social science provides the best model of inquiry in situations of theoretical and political pluralism.

References

Adorno, T. W. 1973. *Negative Dialectics*. New York: Seabury Press.
Bohman, James. 1991. *New Philosophy of Social Science: Problems of Indeterminacy*. Cambridge: MIT Press.
——1995. "Modernization and Impediments to Democracy: Hypercomplexity and Hyperrationality," *Theoria* 86: 1–20.
——1996. "Causal Pluralism Without Levels," *The Southern Journal of Philosophy* 34: 115–27.
Dewey, John. 1948. *Reconstruction of Philosophy*. Boston, MA: Beacon Press.
——1986. *Logic: The Theory of Inquiry* in *The Later Works*. Volume 12. Carbondale, IL: Southern Illinois University Press.
——1988. *The Public and Its Problems* in *The Later Works*. Volume 2. Carbondale, IL: Southern Illinois University Press.
——1991. *Liberalism and Social Action* in *The Later Works*. Volume 11. Carbondale, IL: Southern Illinois University Press.
Elster, Jon. 1989. *Solomonic Judgements*. Cambridge: Cambridge University Press.
Epstein, Stephen. 1996. *Impure Science: AIDS, Activism and the Politics of Knowledge*. Berkeley, CA: University of California Press.
Habermas, Jürgen. 1971. *Knowledge and Human Interests*. Boston, MA: Beacon Press.
——1973. *Theory and Practice*. Boston, MA: Beacon Press.
——1979. *Communication and the Evolution of Society*. Boston, MA: Beacon Press.
——1986. "Questions and Counterquestions," in *Habermas and Modernity*, ed. R. Bernstein. Cambridge, MA: MIT Press.
——1987. *The Theory of Communicative Action*. Volume 2. Boston, MA: Beacon Press.

——1988. *The Logic of the Social Sciences*. Cambridge, MA: MIT Press.

Hempel, Carl. 1965. *Aspects of Scientific Explanation*. New York: Free Press.

Horkheimer, Max. 1982. *Critical Theory*. New York: Seabury Press.

——1993. *Between Philosophy and Social Science*. Cambridge, MA: MIT Press.

McCarthy, Thomas and David Hoy. 1994. *Critical Theory*. London: Basil Blackwell.

Putnam, Hillary. 1994. *Words and Life*. Cambridge, MA: Harvard University Press.

Rorty, Richard. 1991. "Inquiry as Recontextualization," in *The Interpretive Turn*, ed. D. Hiley, J. Bohman, and R. Shusterman. Ithaca, NY: Cornell University Press.

Weber, Max. 1949. *The Methodology of the Social Sciences*. New York: Free Press.

Wiggershaus, Rolf. 1994. *The Frankfurt School*. Cambridge, MA: MIT Press.

What is "Critical" about Critical Racial Theory?

Patricia Hill Collins

Ideas about race as well as racial theory have long occupied a peculiar position in Western knowledge. For one, despite its ubiquitous nature in empirical work, race was not treated as centrally important to the *theoretical* concerns of Western social thought. Racial knowledge remained scattered across several academic disciplines, often as an unmarked signifier attached to some other concern. Biology, sociology, history, literature, political science, economics, medicine, and education have all had distinctive and often storied traditions of scholarship that produced knowledge about race, and that often used race as part of some other project. For example, sociology sought to understand class formations, it routinely subordinated race to class, arguing that race was a manifestation of class. Similarly, biology ostensibly sought to understand human intelligence and capacity for morality, yet scientific findings grounded in racial logic provided evidence for white superiority. These were not primarily theoretical discourses about race, even though ideas about race were central to their scholarly projects. Moreover, because racial scholarship focused on empirical questions and concerns, racial theory was an after-thought. In this collective disciplinary context, ideas about race permeated Western discourse, yet race was typically seen as derivative of some other seemingly more fundamental theoretical concerns associated with a particular discipline or school of thought.

A related issue concerns how Western conceptions of theory create special challenges for racial theory. One approach has been to categorize racial theory in relation to different conceptions of race, namely, race as designation, lineage, type, subspecies, status, class, and construct (Banton 1998). Yet because this thematic approach to racial theory traversed multiple disciplines in ways that signaled the (unrecognized) interpenetration of political, social, and cultural theories, racial theory's peripheral position within individual disciplines may have masked its centrality for intersecting political, social and cultural theories. Is racial theory primarily a political theory, a social theory, a cultural theory, all or is it none of the above? Moreover, this thematic approach suggests that, because conceptions of racism draw from these racial constructs, racial theory with anti-racist aspirations can be categorized using this same analytical framework. Yet can racial theory with critical, anti-racist aspirations be accommodated within this thematic frame?

The issue of the placement of intellectuals who do critical race theory constitutes yet another concern. For strategic reasons, racial theorists, especially those engaged in anti-racist projects, may have worked within the confines of Western knowledge, yet may have taken critical postures towards the corpus of what counts as racial knowledge (both empirical and theoretical) as well as the epistemological practices that produced such knowledge. Such thinkers were often clearly cognizant of how the interrelated political, social and cultural contexts of Western social thought affected their intellectual production as well as the bodies of knowledge that counted as theory. For example, late-nineteenth-, early-twentieth-century African-American intellectuals such as William E. B. Du Bois and Anna Julia Cooper recognized race was not simply an object of investigation but also a social force that shaped the knowledge production process itself (Cooper 1892; Du Bois 1979). In a similar fashion, subsequent generations of Black intellectuals have recognized that the outcomes of their research could have tangible effects on their everyday lived experiences.

These patterns suggest that, because neither critical racial theory nor the intellectuals who may be its practitioners fit comfortably within Western conventions of what counts as theory, and in fact, may have historically challenged these conventions, surveying critical race theory may require greater attention to the relationship between the epistemological criteria of theory and power relations that legitimate those definitions. Situating critical race theory within (1) the historical marginalization of race within numerous disciplinary fields where race often functioned as an unmarked signifier for disciplinary knowledge projects, (2) cross-disciplinary Western social theory where racial theory found varying thematic expressions that in turn contributed to an overarching Western racial project, and (3) how racial scholars within academic disciplines who took a critical posture toward race and racism responded to the challenges of their respective disciplines requires attending to the knowledge/power relations that frame critical racial theory.

Given this context, what makes critical racial theory *critical*? The term "critical race theory" that arose in the 1990s in U.S. legal circles certainly encapsulates these relations; yet the idea of racial theory that was critical of dominant theories of race contributed to various forms of racism has a much longer history. In the following sections, I draw upon Max Horkheimer's 1937 essay "Traditional and Critical Theory" to tease out the construct of "critical" within critical racial theory (Horkheimer 1982). Eschewing the tendency to define critical theory in opposition to traditional theory, Horkheimer examines points of convergence and divergence between traditional theories, primarily the positivism of Western science, and the critical theory of the Frankfurt School. A considerable corpus of work advances similar ideas, yet Horkheimer's essay provides a clear and comprehensive analysis of what makes theory "critical." Because Horkheimer's essay examines the epistemological underpinnings of Western social theory, it provides a useful framework for mapping the contours of *critical racial theory*.

Racial Theory: Traditional and Critical Distinctions

Within Western science, the definition of theory is straightforward. For most researchers, theory consists of the sum-total of propositions about a subject that are linked with each other such that a few remain basic and the rest derive from them. The fewer primary principles there are in any given theory, the better the theory. Containing conceptually formulated knowledge on the one hand and the facts to be subsumed under it on the other, traditional theory evolves by trying to ensure that the derived propositions remain consonant with the actual facts. If theory and the so-called facts contradict each other, one or both must be re-examined because either the scientist has failed to observe correctly or something is wrong with the principles of the theory (Horkheimer 1982: 188).

Horkheimer argues that traditional theory can exercise a positive social function in bringing informed scientific knowledge to bear on important social issues. Theory in its traditional form engages in the critical examination of data with the aid of an inherited apparatus of concepts and judgments. Western science makes substantial contributions to human well-being when its traditional theory concentrates on the problems raised within its own internal technical development and, addresses these problems by either changing its theoretical assumptions and/or by searching for new data (Horkheimer 1982: 205). In this sense, traditional theory can be profitably applied to social problems (for example, racism as a social problem). Yet Horkheimer also suggests that this form of traditional theory cannot address the political dimensions of society, primarily because its internal epistemology views such involvement by scientists as introducing bias into the theoretical enterprise.

Horkheimer offers critical theory as a complementary if not alternative form of social theory that draws from the strengths of traditional theory yet avoids its limitations. In contrast to the epistemological framework of traditional theory, which does not take a critical posture either toward its own scientific project or the processes that legitimate it, critical theory goes beyond the critical eye that a scientist might turn on the match between research findings, the data used to determine those findings, and the theoretical propositions that are upheld or challenged in the process. Instead, critical theory would be critical of the entire enterprise of constructing knowledge in the first place.[1]

Six elements of critical theory that distinguish it from its more traditional counterpart are of special significance for critical race theory. First, because actual social relations are inherently power relations, critical theory engages in a *dialectical analysis* that is cognizant of both structures of power as well as its own relationship to them. This attentiveness to social location mandates that critical theory should take into account its own participation in creating the society that it allegedly studies.[2] Racial theory engaged in a dialectical analysis would recognize that its own knowledge-claims and practices were not benign, but instead contributed to and reflected the systems of racial power in which it was situated. Second, and relatedly, critical theory expresses a *reflective accountability* concerning its own practice. Critical race theory would contain an inherent reflexivity about society as well as its own practices. Racial knowledge for knowledge's sake could not exist.

A third dimension of critical theory reflects its embeddedness in social relations, namely, how the social location of intellectuals shapes knowledge. Horkheimer offers a useful analysis of this dimension of critical theory: "critical thinking is the function/ neither of the isolated individual nor of a sum-total of individuals. Its subject is rather a definite individual in his real relation to other individuals and groups, in his conflict with a particular class, and, finally, in the resultant web of relationships with the social totality and with nature" (Horkheimer 1982: 210–11).[3] Depending on their placement in racial power relations, some intellectuals will garner more credibility than others for their knowledge.

Fourth, critical theory is not just part of a social world that lies outside intellectual production, but is also embedded within an *interdisciplinary* intellectual world characterized by power relations. Horkheimer and other Frankfurt School scholars brought different disciplines together; positing that working on social issues across disciplinary boundaries would yield insights that were unobtainable by working within narrow and increasingly specialized academic domains. Via this commitment to interdisciplinary work, they modeled an intellectual synergy across academic disciplines, but also potential synergies among theoretical approaches of traditional and critical theory that might be especially useful for critical race theory.

Fifth, critical theory aspires to better society by *both* understanding *and* transforming it. These ideas add an ethical component to critical theory that point to critical theory as a form of praxis necessary for social transformation. Here a framework that valorizes ethics replaces the value neutrality of traditional theory.[4] Because racial knowledge can be marshaled for oppressive or emancipatory purposes, questions of ethics explicitly or, more often, implicitly permeate all racial scholarship.

Finally, critical theory advances a distinctive theory of social change. Critical theory views change as inherent to society; it also posits that societies all contain certain core principles that remain the same even though they may change form and expression. As Horkheimer describes it, "theory has a historically changing object which, however, remains identical amid all the changes" (Horkheimer 1982: 239). Within this logic, racism constitutes a *changing same* social formation grounded not in linear, evolutionary processes, but rather in human agency. Racism exemplifies a changing-same racial formation, with varying expressions of racial theory operating to uphold or contest racist practices.

Table 1 summarizes these tenets of traditional and critical racial theory. Critical racial theory is more likely to reflect the following epistemological tenets: (1) a *dialectical analysis* that recognizes and takes into account its participation in the racial politics of its time and place; (2) *reflective accountability concerning its own practice* in producing racial knowledge; (3) an analysis of how the *social location of racial theorists* within societal power relations affect racial knowledge; (4) a recognition of an *interdisciplinary intellectual world* that encourages it to draw from many disciplines and approaches to theory (e.g., social, political, and/or cultural); (5) adherence to an *ethical, anti-racist framework* that aspires to better society by transforming it in the direction of social justice; and (6) a distinctive *theory of social change* concerning race within society and within its own knowledge base.

If a given racial theory reflects *none* of the above criteria, it clearly resembles the traditional racial theory developed to uphold dominant racial discourse. If, instead, *all* are present, racial theory can be comfortably classified as critical racial theory. Far more likely are expressions of racial theory that build upon the tenets of traditional theory and that also have varying combinations of criteria associated with critical theory. For example, in *Whitewashing Race*, a group of American social scientists surveyed contemporary social science literature on race and racism in order to use scientific evidence to refute growing references to the colorblindness of an ostensibly post-racial society (Brown *et al.* 2003). On the one hand, a project such as *Whitewashing Race* can be seen as traditional racial theory with critical intent. The scholars wish to counter a dominant racial discourse positing a post-racial society with scientific evidence claiming the opposite. On the other hand, the interdisciplinary range of scholars involved in the project coupled with the policy focus of the volume suggest that the impetus for the project did not come exclusively from *within* social science, but rather from events in society itself. The volume focused on the changing–same nature of racial inequality by marshalling evidence to prove

Table 1 Traditional and Critical Racial Theory

Traditional Racial Theory	Critical Racial Theory
Dominant Racial Discourse Uses tools of science to uphold dominant racial discourse	Uses tools of science Dialectical analysis Reflexive accountability
Traditional Racial Theory with Critical Intent Uses tools of science to challenge dominant racial discourse Implicit ethical, anti-racist goal	Attentive to social location of theorists Interdisciplinary Ethical, anti-racist goals and/or framework Theme of the changing-same

the persistence of racial disparities despite official policies of colorblindness. Thus, *Whitewashing Race* can be seen *both* as a work of traditional racial theory with critical intent *and* as critical racial theory.

Table 1 provides a roadmap for navigating the following arguments, and is not a rigid taxonomy for classifying theories in one box or the other. Yet as the case of *Whitewashing Race* suggests, the borders that distinguish one type of theory from another are typically blurred and porous. Critical racial theory is neither intrinsically opposed to all traditional racial theory and thus should not be defined as the antithesis of its traditional counterparts. Instead, some critical racial theory can easily be situated within the conventions of Western social theory whereas other versions mark its borders or stand outside it.

Keeping these caveats in mind, the distinctions between traditional and critical theory provide a useful starting point for categorizing racial theories, which can be situated as falling closer to the focal points of traditional or critical theory. Traditional racial theories may adhere more closely to the tenets of Western science in ways that uphold racism and thereby justify its practices; or have the opposite effect by using the very same tenets of Western science to challenge legitimated knowledge. Traditional racial theory may thus dispute dominant racial discourse from within the putative political safety provided by working within traditional norms. In this fashion, traditional racial theory can have critical effects without meeting the additional criteria associated with critical theory.

Challenging dominant racial discourse: traditional racial theory with critical intent

It is important to stress that dominant racial discourse emerged in conjunction with slavery, colonialism, imperialism, and apartheid, all major institutional expressions of racial oppression. The collective practices and resulting knowledges of scientific racism were dominant because they helped legitimate then dominant systems of racial power. The dominant racial discourse consisted of natural and social science as well as humanities disciplines that all constructed racial narratives that upheld white supremacy. Several well known monographs do an excellent job of analyzing the discourse of scientific racism (see, e.g., Gossett 1963; Stepan 1982; Gould 1981) as well as the content of explicitly racial theories (see, e.g., Bulmer and Solomos 1999; Back and Solomos 2000; Banton 1998). In essence, the bulk of racial theory has engaged in this version of being critical by using the tools of Western knowledge with the intent of refuting dominant knowledge claims. Here I survey selected examples drawn from social, political, and cultural theory respectively. Such theory need not affiliate with the more risky practices of an avowedly critical racial theory. Instead, such theory may work within the epistemological conventions of traditional theory; yet manage to advance a critique of some aspect of prevailing racial politics.

Traditional racial theory with critical intent is critical of the knowledges produced by conservative racial projects, such as those associated with scientific racism, yet is not necessarily critical of the processes of scientific knowledge-production. For example, throughout the first half of the twentieth century, eugenics was widely recognized as normal, legitimated science. Eugenics discourse appeared across a range of academic disciplines and within varying national traditions. Yet during this same period, and across these same disciplines, a different group of scholars aspired to correct the scientific record on race by using the same tools of positivist science to criticize the scientific merit of eugenics. Eugenics projects and anti-eugenics projects were both organized via appeals to traditional science, the traditional theory that shaped Western science, and subsequent ideas about race suggested by eugenics and anti-eugenics thinking (Duster 2003).

When it comes to social theory, the sociological career of William E. B. Du Bois provides an exemplar for this approach to traditional racial theory within the social sciences and the traditional racial theories most closely associated with them. In the early twentieth century, Du Bois could not help but develop a critical posture on prevailing knowledge that saw people of African descent as biologically inferior. Du Bois was certainly aware of the politics of knowledge production, but he also recognized that he was one of the first African-American intellectuals who possessed the educational credentials to launch a critique of the findings of Western science from within Western science. His ambitious program of empirical work on African-Americans questioned the naturalness, normality, and inevitability of early-twentieth-century racial theory. Du Bois's scholarly work, as did that of other African-American sociologists, used the tools of science and history to produce counter-discourses about African American life that contested prevailing discourses of scientific racism. For example, Du Bois's, masterful theoretical analysis *Black Reconstruction*, and Oliver Cox's important analysis of global racism *Caste, Class & Race* both illustrate efforts to re-theorize race within sociology using the tools of history, politics, and economics (Du Bois 1969; Cox 1948). Du Bois's sociological career also illustrates how critical projects on race within social science disciplines were ignored. Du Bois, for example, could not find steady work within sociology and eventually left the field altogether. Yet bringing Du Bois back into the sociological canon, and reading sociology in relation to how Du Bois's absence shaped the subsequent development of the field highlights the missed opportunities for a more robust critical racial theory within sociology.

Theoretical works can be overtly involved with theorizing race and racism, yet not be identified as works of racial theory. For example, Zygmunt Bauman's volume *Modernity and the Holocaust* can be read as a book about the internal contradictions of modernity, anti-Semitism, as well as the centrality of bureaucracy to the Holocaust, yet Bauman's book is less often analyzed as a book of racial theory. This is odd, especially since Bauman titles two of his chapters "Modernity, Racism, Extermination I and II" (Bauman 1989). Traditional race theory with critical intent may not be immediately recognizable as racial theory, and may routinely be classified as something else. Take, for example, Hannah Arendt's volume *The Origins of Totalitarianism* (Arendt 1968). Collectively, the three parts of this volume examine the workings of modern state power, a rendition that can be read as an important work within traditional race theory. Placing her analyses of anti-Semitism, imperialism, and totalitarianism in one volume enables Arendt to present an analysis of totalitarianism as total domination. Arendt is typically read as a political theorist, yet this volume can also be placed within the framework of traditional racial theory.

Neither Bauman nor Arendt would categorize their own work as racial theory, illustrating the need for a revised reading of all analyses of power where race seems to be absent or play a minor role. In this regard, the corpus of work by Michel Foucault provides a provocative case of traditional theory with critical intent that does not appear to be about race at all. Using texts and discourse analysis to examine social phenomena, Foucault's work on biopower created provocative new directions for the study of the body and of sexuality as a site of discipline. Foucault's work has implications for a racial theory within cultural theory, yet until the early twenty-first century, Foucault was not linked to racial theory. Yet the translation and publication of his 1975–6 lectures suggest substantial overlap between his discussions of biopower in the last chapter of volume one of *The History of Sexuality* and his newly-translated ideas in *Society Must Be Defended* (Foucault 1990, 2003). Despite the fact that Foucault died before he could develop these links, it seems clear that he either conceptualized or was coming to accept race as part of his analyses of biopower. Foucault used the epistemological framework of Western philosophy to critique Western analyses of numerous constructs, most prominently, sexuality. Foucault's scholarship was groundbreaking, but remained traditional in that he did not stray far from prevailing norms of Western philosophy. In this sense, the corpus of Foucault's work does fall within the framework of traditional theory with critical intent.

Challenging dominant racial discourse and practices: critical racial theory

Critical racial theory participates in a similar intellectual project as its traditional counterpart with critical intent; both are critical of dominant racial discourse and both draw upon the intellectual (scientific) traditions of Western social theory. At the same time, because there is no one firm definition of critical racial theory, merely expressions of varying combinations of its distinguishing features as summarized in Table 1, here I survey selected contemporary examples of critical racial theory that seem more closely aligned with the broad tenets of critical theory.

The field of Cultural Studies has stimulated some important developments within critical racial theory. Because cultural theorists have not been situated within the science paradigm of Western knowledge (the archetype for Horkheimer's understanding of traditional theory), the narrative, interpretive, and, most recently, poststructuralist orientations within cultural studies lend themselves to different analyses of race see, e.g. (Foucault 1980). Most significantly, cultural theorists have engaged in a project of reading race back into dominant narratives to reconceptualize formerly non-racial ideas and practices as raced. Recasting seemingly universalistic narratives as racial narratives challenges the assumed neutrality of Western social theory. For example, *Orientalism*, Edward Said's groundbreaking work of literary criticism within postcolonial studies, presents the provocative thesis that the West's understanding of Orient was in actuality a projection of the West's racialized (if not racist) fantasies about the racial Other (Said 1978). Following Said, postcolonial theory contests Western social theory's analyses of a host of themes, including race (Loomba 1998).

Unearthing the racial subtexts of Western social theory has been one of the more substantive contributions of critical racial theory. For example, Sander Gilman's groundbreaking book *Difference and Pathology: Stereotypes of Sexuality, Race, and Madness* draws on psychoanalytic traditions to examine how race functions within Western societies (Gilman 1985). Using the example of Africa, Anthony Appiah's volume *In My Father's House: Africa in the Philosophy of Culture* uses philosophical tools to examine the fiction of race (Appiah 1992). Cultural critics such as Anne McClintock and Ann Stoler have applied tools of critical analysis to racial, imperial, and colonial practices, revealing more explicitly how these practices were racial formations (McClintock 1995; Stoler 1995).

One of the most significant developments of the past several decades has been unmasking prevailing universalistic language of political discourse to reveal not only how ideas of freedom, democracy, and justice require a racial subtext but also how Western social institutions reflect these racialized meanings. The corpus of work by philosopher David Theo Goldberg, as illustrated in his volume *The Racial State* (Goldberg 2002), is exemplary in this regard. Goldberg traces how discourses of freedom advanced by liberal, democratic states only made sense in contrast to the non-freedom of people of color, both within such states and in the colonies. What made such states "racial states" was less their explicit racial policies (which were certainly present), but rather how issues of race made a broad range of policies comprehensible, many of which did not appear to be about race at all (Goldberg 2002).

The racial subtexts of constructs of nation, nationalism, and the nation-state have also been identified as central to the meaning of these specific ideas as well as power in general. Etienne Balibar's essay "Racism and Nationalism" presents a model of racism as having internal and external expressions that correlate with internal political mechanisms (the racism of anti-Semitism) and external political mechanisms (the racism of colonialism and imperialism) (Balibar 1991). Essays such as these lay the foundation for a theory of global racial formations that situates the nation-state as an important unit of racial analysis. Illustrating the interdisciplinary and increasingly transnational nature of critical racial theory, Wallerstein and Balibar engage in a similar project to examine the racialized nature of seemingly universalistic processes, not with the state as was the case with Goldberg's projects, but rather with world systems theory (Balibar and Wallerstein 1991).

This way of reading race back into dominant narratives to reconceptualize formerly non-racial ideas and practices as intelligible due to their racial meaning has been very useful in conceptualizing ideologies of colorblindness, a set of hegemonic beliefs arguing that race no longer has any meaning in producing racially disparate outcomes. Drawing upon post-structuralist frameworks and wedding them to material analyses, the field of Cultural Studies has spearheaded new avenues for analyzing the racial knowledges and practices that reproduce a seemingly colorblind society. British sociologist Stuart Hall, for example, discusses how useful he found the shift to the discursive framework of the metaphor of language to be in reconceptualizing ideology and its centrality to class politics and popular culture (Grossberg 1996). Texts as diverse as public policy documents (Van Dijk 1993), mass media representations of black popular culture (Collins 2009: 135–74), and racial statistics (Zuberi 2001) have been analyzed as sites that reproduce racism despite a commitment to universalistic criteria of colorblindness.

Unearthing the racial subtexts of actual social relations has proven to be invaluable in analyzing contemporary colorblind racism as a new racial formation, as well as colorblind ideologies that uphold it. Instead of assuming that nothing is raced – the stance of colorblindness – developing tools for reading colorblindness assumes that everything is raced. By assuming, for example, that all individuals have a "race" that can be performed and differentially deployed from one situation to the next, the burgeoning field of "whiteness studies" examines multiple forms of white identity, some conservative and others progressive (Andersen 2003; Lewis 2004). Similar efforts have been devoted to analyzing common social practices that reproduce colorblind racism, such as everyday strategies that whites use to avoid seeing race yet maintain racialized identities (Myers 2005; Bonilla-Silva 2003); and the methodological dilemmas in critical racial research (Twine and Warren 2000).

The field of Cultural Studies has greatly enhanced the traditions of traditional theory with critical intent as well as critical racial theories. Late-twentieth-century synergies among social, political, and cultural theory catalyzed a new theoretical language for critical racial theory itself. Racial formation theory provides a foundational vocabulary for examining race and racism in prior racial formations (slavery, colonialism, and apartheid, for example) as well as contemporary forms of racism (colorblind racism) (Omi and Winant 1994). In their groundbreaking work, *Racial Formation in the United States*, Michael Omi and Howard Winant describe racial formation theory:

> We define racial formation as the sociohistorical process by which racial categories are created, inhabited, transformed, and destroyed. Our attempt to elaborate a theory of racial formation will proceed in two steps. First, we argue that racial formation is a process of historically situated projects in which human bodies and social structures are represented and organized. Next we link racial formation to the evolution of hegemony, the way in which society is organized and ruled. Such an approach, we believe, can facilitate understanding of a whole range of contemporary controversies and dilemmas involving race,

including the nature of racism, the relationship of race to other forms of differences, inequalities, and oppression such as sexism and nationalism, and the dilemmas of racial identity today.

(Omi and Winant 1994: 55–6)

Several elements of this theory resonate with critical racial theory. For one, Omi and Winant's notion of racial formation is materially grounded – slavery, colonialism, colorblind racism and similar racial formations are sociohistorical processes, not just ideological constructs that can be accepted or rejected at will. Identifying their process as containing historically situated projects illustrates a dialectical sensibility of examining the connections of theory and society as well as a theory of change that sees racial categories as being "created, inhabited, transformed, and destroyed." They also see racial formation theory as facilitating understanding of a wide range of debates concerning race, in particular, how racism intersects with sexism, nationalism and similar projects. Rather than viewing race as a fixed entity, Omi and Winant's notion of racial projects presents an analytical infrastructure that can be used to assess critical racial theories as well as the practices that shape them.

Racial formation theory opens new door for crafting critical racial theory. Yet, as this survey suggests, the lion's share of critical racial theory occurs within the boundaries of Western social theory, here parsed out in more nuanced categories of traditional racial theory with a critical intent and critical racial theory that embraces more of the tenets of critical theory. What purports to be "critical" racial theory may in actuality be far more traditional than expected, albeit still critical when compared to dominant racial discourse. Conversely, what is traditional via choice of topic, research methodology, and interpretation may be far more critical than meets the eye. Keeping these blurred boundaries in mind, in the next section I sketch out a third approach to racial theory that also draws from prevailing concepts of the traditional and critical theory, but that further blurs these boundaries because it simultaneously draws from racial formation theory and adheres to more of the tenets of critical theory.

From Racial Theories to Critical Racial Projects

Distinguishing traditional and critical theory is helpful in shedding light on racial theory that is safely positioned within the contours of Western norms. Max Horkheimer's rendition of critical theory may have been a minority voice within the positivist Western canon, but Horkheimer's status as an intellectual and his framing of critical theory within the parameters of Western conventions assured that his ideas would be taken seriously. Yet focusing unduly on theoretical content while ignoring the people and practices that are associated with theoretical knowledge-production creates obstacles for critical racial theories that aim to develop comprehensive anti-racist theory and practices. Can a critical racial theory be fully "critical" if it remains solely in the terrain of the theoretical?

Because Western theory has been so central within prior forms of racism, broadening the parameters of Western theory to incorporate a more expansive array of intellectual practices under the umbrella of "theory" as well as including a broader range of social actors in the category of "theorist" might be especially crucial for racial theory. Stated differently, categorizing patterns of racial theory as traditional and/or critical solely within the framework of what counts as Western theory is a promising first step. Yet the greater challenge lies in identifying critical race projects that might intersect with and/or fall outside the parameters of Western social theory. One might then re-contextualize *both* traditional racial theory with critical intent *and* critical racial theory in relation to these projects.

Just as the notion of racial formation of Omi and Winant was useful in challenging the categories of political analysis, their notion of a *racial project* is useful here for projects that go beyond the goal of producing theory. As they define it, "A *racial project is simultaneously an interpretation, representation, or explanation of racial dynamics, and an effort to reorganize and redistribute resources along particular racial lines* [italics in original]. Racial projects connect what race *means* in a particular discursive practice and the ways in which both social structures and everyday experiences are racially *organized*, based upon that meaning" (Omi and Winant 1994: 56). In this sense, traditional racial theories, with or without critical intent, and critical racial theories are *all* racial projects, with the content and organization of any given theory functioning as the intellectual core of the more expansive and often unacknowledged social, cultural, and political dimensions of the racial project. Within the tenets of racial formation theory, Western theory has itself always been a racial project writ large, one that has often denied the terms of its participation in the racial formations that needed it.

A more expansive definition of *critical racial projects* refers to a broad constellation of contemporary and historical theories and practices that have actively engaged the prevailing racial theories and/or practices of particular times and/or social contexts. In essence, a critical racial project draws upon the distinguishing features of critical theory, and uses them to craft appropriate critical racial projects. For example, when it comes to contemporary racial formations such as colorblind racism, or the increasing recognition that racism is global, emphasizing racial projects creates space to develop critical racial projects that (1) draw upon both traditional racial theory as well as critical racial theory; (2) begin to reduce the artificial binary separating empirical and theoretical work on race; and, as a result, (3) are more explicitly targeted toward social transformation concerning contemporary racial formations of social injustice. Trying to excise the *critical* nature of racial theory from the overarching *critical* nature of the overall racial project thus runs the risk of misunderstanding both the theory and its set of related practices.

The corpus of Frantz Fanon's work illustrates this recursive relation between critical racial theory and a more expansive definition of a critical racial project. Frantz Fanon's *Wretched of the Earth*, for example, was widely read by intellectuals of color, not only for its critical and radical content, but also because Fanon wrote this volume in the context of the critical racial project of Algerian struggles for independence (Fanon 1963). This particular work of Fanon, whose intellectual core inspired a wide array of social theory that is not typically seen as critical racial theory, illustrates the significance of seeing how the overarching racial project shapes a particular expression of racial theory. Because white, Western social theorists were not Fanon's target audience, *The Wretched of the Earth* has been difficult to incorporate into the canon of traditional Western theory as a freestanding theory of violence, or of change, or of anything else. Fanon's work suggests that decolonization struggles and anti-racist social movements have been important catalysts for critical racial projects because theory has had close ties either to actual decolonization projects (emancipation in a colonial context) or to new political realities faced by migrants who were differently racialized in former colonial powers. Fanon's work raises questions about the status of postcolonial racial theory, requiring us to distinguish between academic theories of postcolonialism and knowledge projects that theorize and aim to change neocolonialism as a new form of racism.

The growth of centers within colleges and universities that bridge the gap between academia and the general public also demonstrate the difference between critical racial theories that are primarily academic and critical racial projects that require new institutional infrastructures. The constellation of scholars at the Center for Contemporary Cultural Studies in the 1980s illustrates the significance of diasporic intellectuals of color for critical racial projects and theories that might ensue. Stuart Hall served as the head of the Center, yet Hall's leadership involved collaborative work during a time when the term "black" was a political identity that housed migrants from the Caribbean, continental Africa, and Asia who became "ethnic" upon arrival in the U.K. Scholars at the Center not only worked collaboratively, they also aimed at praxis. Because the structural underpinnings of how they did racial theory differed so dramatically from their elite counterparts – the content of their theory was correspondingly distinct. Specifically, scholars identified culture as an important site of politics, thus rendering popular culture a worthwhile component of critical racial theory. Hall's articles "New Ethnicities" and "What Is This 'Black' in Black Popular Culture?" constitute core works for cultural studies and critical racial theory alike (Hall 1992, 1996). The significance of the intellectual production of CCCS was that the distinctiveness of the racial project catalyzed the significance of the ensuring critical racial theory.

To highlight the recursive nature of theory and social context within critical racial projects, I present two cases of critical racial projects that reflect the criteria of critical theory detailed in Table 1. These projects are not simply theoretical endeavors, although theory is central to each project, because the people and practices attached to these critical racial projects do not fit neatly within conventions of Western social theory. Both cases adhere to the criteria for critical racial theory but the identities and social locations of intellectuals who participate in these projects illustrate how these cases can also be seen as part of broader critical racial projects. I am suggesting a different way of reading these theories, not simply asking whether they meet the criteria of traditional racial theory with critical intent, or even of critical racial theory, but suggest that they are better understood as part of critical racial projects.

I have selected two contemporary examples of critical racial projects advanced primarily by people of color, in part because people of color have largely been treated as objects of study within traditional racial theory as well as within selected strands of critical racial theory; and in part because these examples provide a different social, political and cultural context for what counts as theory. Both examples illustrate how people of color as agents of knowledge produce critical racial theory within critical racial projects. The first case constitutes a critical racial project that that emerged within a social movement context and became institutionalized in an academic setting. The second case illustrates a critical racial project that emerged within an academic setting yet aimed to move beyond academic conventions to change society.

The first case concerns the development of intersectionality as the theoretical core of Black feminist thought, a critical racial theory, and its participation in the broader critical racial project of African American women. In the 1970s and 1980s, Black feminist thought reflected the heterogeneity of women who were involved in social movements. The goal of Black feminist thought was not a search for truth, for the latest theoretical innovation, or even to desegregate academic institutions, but rather aimed to foster Black women's empowerment through theoretical analysis of how race, class, gender, and sexuality as systems of power mutually constructed one another to shape oppression (Collins 2000). Initially, this intersectional framework suggested provocative links that might ground social justice projects, initially, of civil rights and feminism, the groups most directly affecting African-American women, but also of other groups with a shared goal of transforming society. This emphasis on intersections of race, class, gender and sexuality as they affected African-American women thus provided a provocative new framework for analyzing the social, political and cultural realities of other groups, both disadvantaged and privileged.

When this critical (racial) theory traveled into the academy, the version of intersectionality developed in the context of the critical racial project of advanced by African-American women encountered several factors that changed its form and its function. For one, Women's Studies provided a more favorable home for Black women's studies than that offered by either Black Studies or traditional academic disciplines. At the same time, the Women's Studies agenda of advancing feminist theory as a way to gain legitimacy in the academy and developing a multi-cultural sensibility within feminist theory had the effect of pulling intersectionality away from its social movement roots and recasting it as another theory of truth. For another, the commodi-fication of knowledge within the academy had the unfortunate effect of turning Black feminist theorists and their intellectual projects into commodities. Just because a woman of color writes, especially if her topic is about race, does not mean that she is mindful of a broader critical racial project. Instead, one must ask how women of color enter critical racial theory debates. The overall effect of these trends was that intersectionality became greatly changed when removed from its original context as a critical racial project and recast as a commodified theory (Collins 1998: 147–8).

Recognizing these trends, several scholars aimed to maintain the initial broad scope of intersectionality, legitimate it theoretically and retain its social justice ethos, despite the fact that its initial patterns of production and consumption fall outside the purview of Western theory. My own work on *Black Feminist Thought* examines this space of oppositional knowledge, where critical racial theory may be done not only outside the academy, by organic intellectuals using non-traditional tools of analysis, but also with an eye toward analyzing the world in order to change it (Collins 2000). Similarly, *Racialized Boundaries* by Nira Yuval-Davis and Floya Anthias engages in a similar process of theoretical analysis with an eye toward broader social justice projects (Anthias and Yuval-Davis 1992). Gloria Anzaldua's classic work of intersectional theory engages in critical analysis of Latino perspectives (Anzaldua 1987). Similarly, Rey Chow's *Writing Diaspora* critically engages constructions of Asian-American Studies (Chow 1993).

A second case of a critical racial project emerged within U.S. legal scholarship in the 1990s. Critical Race Theory (CRT) typically refers to a specific set of practices and theories advanced primarily by African-American, Latino, and Asian-American legal scholars (Crenshaw *et al.* 1995; Delgado and Stefancic 2001; Matua in press). CRT constitutes one particular site within a more comprehensive, historically grounded, cross-cultural constellation of critical racial projects that take different form in response to the social conditions that surround them. CRT scholars were among the first to develop compelling arguments of colorblindness as a form of racism in a seemingly post-racial era. Their diagnoses of racism aimed to advance a social justice framework. For example, the corpus of work by Derrick Bell, a founding figure of CRT, illustrates CRT's impetus to use critical racial theory in service of legal reforms. Bell was one of the first scholars to break rank with the consensus that colorblindness, the agenda of the Civil Rights Movement, had in fact benefited African-American children (Bell 2004).

Several distinguishing features of Critical Race Theory illustrate its status as a critical racial project. CRT emerged in response to the limitations of law in a context of colorblindness. Via its efforts to examine and affect racial practices, CRT demonstrates a *dialectical* sensibility that critical theory recognize and take into account its own participation in creating the society that it allegedly studies and an adherence to an *ethical framework* that aspires to better society by transforming it. Critical race theorists also wrote for multiple audiences, namely, legal scholars, practicing attorneys, law students, and academics from several fields, as well as for a wider public. Because CRT addressed multiple audiences and did not meet the disinterested criteria of traditional theory, it was often not immediately recognizable as theory. Yet writing for multiple audiences does catalyze *reflectivity* concerning its own practice, especially how critical theory accounts for change within society and within its own knowledge base; as well as an awareness of how the interdisciplinary and societal power relations affects both the social location of critical race theorists and practitioners and their subsequent intellectual production.

CRT is typically interdisciplinary and embraces multifaceted disciplines and/or research methods. Critical Race Theory tends to be organized around core questions that reach into several disciplines and that require multiple research strategies. Many critical race theorists drew upon the literary and narrative traditions of storytelling from cultural studies, for example, Mari Matsuda's classic analysis of considering the victim's story as a central component of addressing hate speech illustrates the fusion of cultural, social and political phenomena within CRT (Matsuda 1989). In this way, CRT draws from an *interdisciplinary* intellectual world that is also characterized by power relations. Recognizing that race and racism work with and through gender, ethnicity, class, sexuality and/or nation as systems of power, contemporary CRT often relies upon and/or investigates these intersections. Kimberlé Crenshaw's analysis of violence against women argued that race and gender both mattered, illustrates how the construct of intersectionality that permeated African-American women's social movement activism entered into the legal canon. In this way, Crenshaw illustrates the synergy between two seemingly disparate critical racial projects, namely, intersectionality of Black feminism and CRT of the legal community (Crenshaw 1991).

Collectively, these cases point to the ways that critical racial theory that is created within the parameters of critical racial projects is often not recognizable as such to those in more powerful positions. This can be an outcome of its practitioners (people of color; people of African descent; women; or some combination); its mission (the emancipatory impetus of African-American women's intellectual production); its form (the interdisciplinary nature of CRT that makes it difficult for disciplines to recognize it by their established standards); and/or its intended audience (theory written for marginalized people is not valorized by those who are not marginalized). The intellectual production of critical racial projects such as those discussed above may not be recognized as "theory" because of how they are produced and consumed. Because critical racial thinkers wish to address wider publics than academics, many critical race scholars write with multiple audiences in mind and may create different versions of their work for different constituencies. Some versions may meet traditional criteria for theory whereas other versions do not.

Critical racial projects are rarely situated completely within existing social institutions, primarily because such projects often engage in a critique of those institutions. The cases of intersectionality and Critical Race Theory both straddled the boundaries distinguishing academia from varying publics, with different goals and outcomes. This critical posture toward prevailing power relations means that critical racial projects typically risk run of being classified as outside the parameters of what counts as theory and treated accordingly. Yet critical racial projects and their critical racial theory may, by necessity, lie outside the parameters because some sort of outsider positionality strengthens the theoretical substance of critical racial projects. It is important to reiterate that the form of theorizing associated with critical racial theories may not fit within conventions of theory itself, or even the language of race. The irony here is that critical racial theory need not be in forms most recognized as theoretical, nor might they have explicitly racial content to be considered part of a broader critical racial project. For example, Bonaventura de Sousa Santos's claim that *Another Knowledge is Possible*, is not necessarily written as critical racial theory, or even identified as a critical racial project. Yet because Santos reclaims and shares the knowledges advanced by people who are most harmed by global racism, his volume may contribute the kind of "critical" theory that social justice projects need (Santos *et al.* 2007).

These examples suggest that all Western theory can be viewed as part of a broader, overarching *racial* project, primarily because race has been central to shaping modernity, postmodernity, as well as knowledge and social institutions of the West. Criticisms of theory as being abstract, irrelevant, and the like have often been dismissed as part of the anti-intellectualism of marginalized populations if not the public in general. Yet these criticisms of theory are less a rejection of rationality per se, than a critique of how reason, the bedrock of theory, has been placed in service to racial theories that explained, justified and colluded in manufacturing racial inferiority. How does one separate Western theory from this history of collusion? How does one democratize Western theory by bringing in marginalized people and their oppositional analyses of the same social reality without the claims that democratization is watering down theory, because it is becoming more accessible to the public? Questions such as these, as well as the critical racial projects discussed above, ask the very uncomfortable question of the degree to which "theory" remains within the preserve of the West and thus is implicated in relations of domination upheld by the West, in this case, race, but also much broader questions of social injustice.

What is Critical for Critical Racial Theory?

Responding to the question "what is 'critical' about critical racial theory" suggests two meanings of the term *critical*. One meaning references the need to identify epistemological criteria so that theory that is critical can be recognized as such. Specifically, criteria such as those detailed in Table 1 create space to consider a larger swath of intellectual production as part of social theory. Taking a broader view of critical racial theory catalyzes important new questions for theoretical practice. Where do the questions originate? What constellations of social practices legitimate some knowledge as theory and other knowledge as thought? Whose interests are served by the theory?

Yet another meaning of *critical* exists. For people of color and others who have been harmed by historical and contemporary racial projects of racism, critical refers to something that is important, significant, worth doing and/or necessary for survival. Critical racial theories are not simple academic discourses that come and go as academic fads within the far more stable contours of racial inequality. Instead, critical racial projects may not analyze existing social conditions, but also be equally critical for people of color in surviving racism. In this sense, the critical racial theories that infuse critical racial projects may be critical in the sense that they are essential.

Notes

1 Horkheimer spells out what he means by the term *critical*:

> The critical attitude of which we are speaking is wholly distrustful of the rules of conduct with which society as presently constituted provided each of its members. The separation between individual and society in virtue of which the individual accepts as natural the limits prescribed for his activity is relativized in critical theory. The latter considers the overall framework which is conditioned by the blind interaction of individual activities (that is, the existent division of labor and the class distinctions) to be a function which originated in human action and therefore is a possible object of planful decision and rational determination of goals (Horkheimer 1982: 207).

Here, Horkheimer clearly embraces the positive benefits of reason for bettering society – a shared dimension of traditional and critical theory – yet rejects traditional theory's tendency to naturalize and thereby justify existing forms of social organization. For an expansive definition and discussion of critical social theory, see (Calhoun 1995). For a more nuanced discussion of the critical social theory of subordinated groups, see (Collins 1998).

2 Horkheimer contends that critical theory is a dialectical theory of society, originating not in the "idealist critique of pure reason" but rather in a dialectical process that is critical of political economy (Horkheimer 1982: 206). This framework rejects the epistemological stance of traditional theory – that science operates as a mirror of the world – in favor of a dialectical conception of knowledge whereby what counts as theories and/or facts are part of an ongoing historical process in which the way we view the world (theoretically or otherwise) and the way the world is are reciprocally determined.

3 Traditional theory considers the placement of the individual intellectual within a web of group-based social relations (here identified as being of a particular economic class) and the effects that this relationship might have on knowledge (in this case, theory) to be of little concern to knowledge outcomes. Yet, as Horkheimer points out, "since society is divided into groups and classes, it is understandable that theoretical structures should be related to the general activity of society in different ways according as the authors of such structures belong to one or other social class" (Horkheimer 1982: 204–5).

4 This impetus for social transformation is more evident in work by Horkheimer's successors, but the nucleus for a social justice ethos is found within Horkheimer's initial framing of critical theory. In his 1937 essay, Horkheimer mentions social justice, but does not develop ethical standards that might characterize the epistemology of critical theory. However, what he does say is provocative: "For all its insight into the individual steps in social change and for all the agreement of its elements with the most advanced traditional theories, the critical theory has no specific influence on its side, except concern for the abolition of social injustice" (Horkheimer 1982: 242). Horkheimer suggests that grappling with social injustice is a central activity of critical theory: "But the transmission will not take place via solidly established practice and fixed ways of acting but via concern for social transformation. Such a concern will necessarily be aroused ever anew by prevailing injustice, but it must be shaped and guided by the theory itself and in turn react upon the theory" (Horkheimer 1982: 241).

References

Andersen, Margaret L. 2003. "Whitewashing Race: A Critical Review on 'Whiteness'." *Whiteout: The Continuing Significance of Racism*, eds A. Doane and Eduardo Bonilla-Silva. New York: Routledge.

Anthias, Floya and Nira Yuval-Davis. 1992. *Racialized Boundaries: Race, Nation, Gender, Colour and Class and the Anti-racist Struggle*. New York: Routledge.

Anzaldua, Gloria. 1987. *Borderlands/La Frontera*. San Francisco, CA: Spinsters/Aunt Lute Press.

Appiah, Kwame A. 1992. *In My Father's House: Africa in the Philosophy of Culture*. New York: Oxford University Press.

Arendt, Hannah. 1968. *The Origins of Totalitarianism*. New York: Harcourt.

Back, Les and John Solomos. 2000. "Introduction: Theorising Race and Racism." pp. 1–31 in *Theories of Race and Racism: A Reader*, eds Les Back and John Solomos. New York: Routledge.

Balibar, Etienne. 1991. "Racism and Nationalism." pp. 37–67 in *Race, Nation, Class: Ambiguous Identities*, eds Etienne Balibar and Immanuel Wallerstein. New York: Verso.

Balibar, Etienne and Immanuel Wallerstein. 1991. *Race, Nation, Class: Ambiguous Identities*. New York: Verso.

Banton, Michael. 1998. *Racial Theories*. London: Cambridge University Press.

Bauman, Zygmunt. 1989. *Modernity and the Holocaust*. Ithaca, NY: Cornell University Press.

Bell, Derrick. 2004. *Silent Covenants: Brown V. Board of Education and the Unfulfilled Hopes for Racial Reform*. New York: Oxford University Press.

Bonilla-Silva, Eduardo. 2003. *Racism Without Racists: Color-blind Racism and the Persistence of Racial Inequality in the United States*. Lanham, MD: Rowman & Littlefield.

Brown, Michael I., Martin Carnoy, Elliott Currie, Troy Duster, David B. Oppenheimer, Marjorie M. Schultz, and Davie Wellman. 2003. *Whitewashing Race: The Myth of a Color-blind Society*. Berkeley, CA: University of California Press.

Bulmer, Martin and John Solomos. 1999. "Racism." pp. 3–17 in *Racism*, eds Martin Bulmer and John Solomos. New York: Oxford University Press.

Calhoun, Craig. 1995. *Critical Social Theory: Culture, History, and the Challenge of Difference*. Malden, MA: Blackwell Publishers.

Chow, Rey. 1993. *Writing Diaspora: Tactics of Intervention in Contemporary Cultural Studies*. Bloomington, IN: Indiana University Press.

Collins, Patricia H. 1998. *Fighting Words: Black Women and the Search for Justice*. Minneapolis, MN: University of Minnesota Press.

——. 2000. *Black Feminist Thought: Knowledge, Consciousness, and the Politics of Empowerment*. 2nd edn. New York: Routledge.

——. 2009. *Another Kind of Public Education: Race, Schools, the Media and Democratic Possibilities*. Boston, MA: Beacon Press.

Cooper, Anna J. 1892. *A Voice From the South; By a Black Woman of the South*. Xenia, OH: Aldine.

Cox, Oliver C. 1948. *Caste, Class & Race: A Study in Social Dynamics*. New York: Modern Reader Paperbacks.

Crenshaw, Kimberlé W. 1991. "Mapping the Margins: Intersectionality, Identity Politics, and Violence Against Women of Color." *Stanford Law Review* 43(6):1241–99.

Crenshaw, Kimberlé, Neil Gotanda, Gary Peller, and Kendall Thomas, eds. 1995. *Critical Race Theory: The Key Writings That Formed the Movement*. New York: The New Press.

Delgado, Richard and Jean Stefancic. 2001. *Critical Race Theory: An Introduction*. New York: New York University Press.

Du Bois, William E. B. 1969. *Black Reconstruction in America: An Essay Toward a History of the Part Which Black Folk Played in the Attempt to Reconstruct Democracy in America, 1860–1880*. New York: Atheneum.

——. 1979. *The Souls of Black Folk*. New York: Dodd, Mead, & Company.

Duster, Troy. 2003. *Backdoor to Eugenics*. New York: Routledge.

Fanon, Frantz. 1963. *The Wretched of the Earth*. New York: Grove Press.

Foucault, Michel. 1980. *Power/Knowledge: Selected Interviews and Other Writings, 1972–1977*. ed. Colin Gordon. New York: Pantheon.

——. 1990. *The History of Sexuality Vol. I: An Introduction*. New York: Vintage Books.

——. 2003. *Society Must Be Defended: Lectures at the College De France, 1975–1976*. New York: Picador.

Gilman, Sander L. 1985. *Difference and Pathology: Stereotypes of Sexuality, Race, and Madness*. Ithaca, NY: Cornell University Press.

Goldberg, David T. 2002. *The Racial State*. Malden, MA: Blackwell.

Gossett, Thomas F. 1963. *Race: the History of an Idea in America*. Dallas, TX: Southern Methodist University Press.

Gould, Stephen J. 1981. *The Mismeasure of Man*. New York: W. W. Norton.

Grossberg, Lawrence. 1996. "On Postmodernism and Articulation: An Interview with Stuart Hall." pp. 131–50 in *Critical Dialogues in Cultural Studies*, eds David Morley and Kuan-Hsing Chen. New York: Routledge.

Hall, Stuart. 1992. "What Is This 'Black' in Black Popular Culture?" pp. 21–33 in *Black Popular Culture*, ed. Gina Dent. Seattle: Bay Press.

——. 1996. "New Ethnicities." pp. 441–9 in *Stuart Hall: Critical Dialogues in Cultural Studies*, eds David Morley and Kuan-Hsing Chen. New York: Routledge.

Horkheimer, Max. 1982. " Traditional and Critical Theory." pp. 188–243 in *Critical Theory: Selected Essays*, Max Horkheimer. New York: Continuum Publishing.

Lewis, Amanda E. 2004. "'What Group?' Studying Whites and Whiteness in the Era of 'Color-blindness'." *Sociological Theory* 22(4): 623–46.

Loomba, Ania. 1998. *Colonialism/Postcolonialism*. New York: Routledge.

Matsuda, Mari J. 1989. "Public Responses to Racist Speech: Considering the Victim's Story." *Michigan Law Review* 87(August):2380–1.

Matua, Athena D. in press. "Law and Critical Race Theory." *Handbook of Race and Ethnic Studies*, eds Patricia H. Collins and John Solomos. London: Sage.

McClintock, Anne. 1995. *Imperial Leather: Race, Gender, and Sexuality in the Colonial Contest*. New York: Routledge.

Myers, Kristen. 2005. *Racetalk: Racism Hiding in Plain Sight*. Lanham, MD: Rowman & Littlefield.

Omi, Michael and Howard Winant. 1994. *Racial Formation in the United States: From the 1960s to the 1990s*. New York: Routledge.

Said, Edward W. 1978. *Orientalism*. New York: Vintage.

Santos, Boaventura d. S., João A. Nunes, and Maria P. Meneses. 2007. "Opening Up the Canon of Knowledge and Recognition of Difference." pp. xvix–lxii in *Another Knowledge is Possible: Beyond Northern Epistemologies*, ed. Boaventura d. S. Santos. New York: Verso.

Stepan, Nancy. 1982. *The Idea of Race in Science: Great Britain, 1800–1960*. Hamden, CT: Archon Books.

Stoler, Ann L. 1995. *Race and the Education of Desire: Foucault's History of Sexuality and the Colonial Order of Things*. Durham, NC: Duke University Press.

Twine, France W. and Jonathan W. Warren, eds. 2000. *Racing Research, Researching Race: Methodological Dilemmas in Critical Race Studies*. New York: New York University Press.

Van Dijk, Teun A. 1993. *Elite Discourse and Racism*. Newbury Park, CA: Sage.

Zuberi, Tukufu. 2001. *Thicker Than Blood: How Racial Statistics Lie*. Minneapolis, MN: University of Minnesota Press.

Feminist Social and Political Theory

Clare Colebrook

One way of understanding feminism as a movement in general is to see it as a social and political claim for women's justice and equality, and then to see feminist theory as a means for justifying and effecting such claims. (Theory would have the sense of being a second-order or reflective process following on from practice.) Feminism would, on this account, proceed from a certain political grouping or class and may, in turn, provide a specific perspective from which one might evaluate and redefine the nature and proper functioning of the traditional polity. If, for example, one begins from the modern liberal claim that a proper polity is composed of equal and self-legislating persons, then it not only follows that women ought to be included in such an egalitarian state (so that feminism would follow on from liberalism); it may also be the case that feminism adjusts or reconfigures liberalism. Perhaps, one might need to regard political rights as not only those of life, liberty and the pursuit of happiness but also rights to care for others or to determine one's own bodily being (reproductive rights and sexual rights). Feminism would operate in two directions: as a claim of an already existing political body it would *extend* the duties, rights, obligations and norms of the polity – for if women were granted rights suitable to their specific being then rights may have to be modified beyond the classic rights of non-interference. But feminism would also be more than *extension* of already existing social political theories, for it may alter the very nature of political theorizing by asking about both the nature of the subject who theorizes and the nature of the polity.[1] Radical separatist (or second-wave) feminists, for example, deem the liberal paradigm of equality and non-interference to be both inadequate (for women should not be seen as equal *to* men but as bearing their own values and qualities), and also to be implicitly masculine:[2] the ideal of individuals as self-determining subjects who act in their own interests precludes traditional female virtues of care, nurturance, empathy and emotive reasoning (Ruddick 1989). On the one hand, then, feminism is a movement with primarily practical goals – of achieving a better condition for women – and this movement would deploy political and social theory accordingly. On the other hand, it could also be the case that the very nature of women as a group might require new modes of theorizing and new modes of political grouping. I will turn to this second mode of feminism in the final part of this chapter.

Feminist Liberation, Theory and Praxis

For the first part of this chapter I will be considering this initial possibility: that women exist as a group within a polity, that the polity theorizes itself, and that women contribute to and extend this self-constitution of the social whole through their own modes of political engagement. One could therefore begin from various modes of social theory – liberal, Marxist, social-constructivist, communitarian, ecological, postmodern – and these in turn would have feminist variants. We can consider these in turn, for each of these modes of political theory would seem at once to lead inevitably towards the justification of feminism *and* yet also be required to change for the sake of feminist claims. If liberalism begins from the recognition that no single individual possesses power or superior knowledge over any other, then there can be no basis for excluding any subject from the formation and legitimation of law and social forms. It is because there is no divine or eternally prescribed order of the world that law must be constituted; the only justifiable laws would be those that would be agreed upon by any participant whatsoever. Liberalism proceeds from a commitment to reason: one cannot accept any social norm or political arrangement without justification, and the only justifiable social form is one that would appear to be just for any subject whatever (Rawls 1972). It would follow, then, that if the only rational social order were to be one of equality, rights and continued justification and legitimation then women would necessarily be included. To exclude women, or any other group capable of reason, would be to make an irrational exception. This was, indeed, how Mary Wollstonecraft in *Vindications of the Rights of Woman* (1792) argued for female emancipation: she did not present women's claims as being those of a specific interested group, but as the consequence of accepting the norms of a rational humanity.[3] If we are all blessed with reason then it follows that women, too, have the right to education and political involvement; it also follows that any social body (say, of men) that dominated another body of rational individuals (women, slaves) would be impeding its own rational power (Wollstonecraft 1992). For Wollstonecraft, women's rights were human rights, and humanity could not arrive at full rationality as long as it tyrannically (or irrationally) precluded some of its members from participation in political discourse. But if liberalism led to feminism it also seemed to demand, immediately, some from of feminist critique.

The ideal of the liberal individual – a self-determining, self-interested, resource-calculating and ideally disembodied reasoner – would be challenged by later liberal feminists who suggested that the seeming gender neutrality of this liberal self actually privileged a traditionally male subject. If we imagine selves as isolated and self-determining individuals, whose role in the polity is one of self-furthering calculation (limited by the imperative to avoid interfering with others), then we preclude a consideration of those social selves (typically women) who are either biologically or culturally bound to others, through child-rearing and reproduction. The inclusion of women in the liberal polity would at once be demanded by the very principles of liberalism (equality, reason, universalism) and yet would also place pressure upon those very principles: once we include all individuals and grant rights of participation to all, the very definition of an individual may change.

From Practice to Theory

Feminism may begin then by extending a theory – extending liberal rights and freedom to *include* women – but would then have an effect on the theory's inclusive principles. Once women have rights of self-determination and participation then the very concept of self and rights would be modified. The self may have to be expanded, for how else could we consider a pregnant body if we did not revise a concept of autonomy? And how could we consider the rights of a self who is capable of reproduction if we did not somehow render the individual agent more complex than the isolated self? More importantly, the very nature of the political process may also come under pressure. For many liberal feminists, including Mary Wollstonecraft, granting women rights, equality before the law and political participation, did not entail denying women's traditional domestic roles. It did, though, lead to the inclusion of domestic labourers and carers into the polity. This would, in turn, mean the political process could not be as easily split into public and private spheres. If women were granted the rights to reason and education then domestic relations would change, for marriage would not be a relation of possession but one of conversation and negotiation. It is possible that political relations may alter also, if women's orientation towards childcare and reproduction would transform the modes of political conversation. Liberalism's inclusion of women within the polity would therefore follow from liberalism's commitment to universal equality, and yet the way in which equality would be achieved would need to be redefined. One could not, for example, assume a level playing field – that one enters the political arena as a neutral subject – for some subjects (by virtue of biological and cultural inflections) are already entwined with the rights of others.

Nowhere is this more evident than in the one domain in which liberal feminism has had the most practical consequences. In pro-life versus pro-choice debates the discourse of rights operates in two directions, right to life and right to choice or self-determination. This indicates that the very *rights* that allowed women to be included also put the very concept of rights under pressure. For the most part, at the practical and political level, the discourse of rights and liberalism has simply been sustained while harbouring this contradiction. Women who are pro-choice appeal to their rights, and their opponents appeal to rights to life. But these practical problems are, for many post-liberal feminists, indicative of a deeper problem of liberalism. The supposedly neutral political individual, who has no norms or values other than those that are freely chosen, is in actuality neither politically nor sexually neutral. Critics of liberalism in general have suggested that there is a presupposed capitalist norm in the idea of the self who has no qualities other than those that are freely chosen, and who relates to others in the mode of free and unimpeded competition. Liberalism presupposes *possessive* individualism (Macpherson 1962), and assumes that one can be a self without somehow already being defined by shared norms and debts to others (MacIntyre 1981). There are also specifically feminist criticisms of liberalism that follow from Marxist, ecological, psychoanalytic, postmodern and communitarian perspectives. As I have already suggested, such criticisms of the liberal paradigm go beyond feminist corrections of the ideal of the political subject and political process and start to radicalize the very nature of what counts as 'the political' – if such a notion is still sustainable after feminism.

Liberalism, after all, is perhaps the general mode of political theory, proceeding from the modern acceptance that there is no natural and divine order, that social relations are created politically – through the interaction of individuals who are not determined in advance by norms that derive from a transcendent source beyond political life. Various pre-modern paradigms, such as Platonism or Aristotelianism, at least in part proceed by subjecting the political to other criteria: debate among individuals ought to be governed by those who possess wisdom and logic (Platonism) *or* by the processes of human reason that can discern first principles (Aristotle). Modern forms of Aristotelianism, despite first appearances, nevertheless insist that one does not begin with politics (or free and open debate) but must already be part of a community with norms and values, *from which* those norms and values might be evaluated and revised. The notion that politics can be at least thought of as the creation of a social order by individuals begins with modernity, either through the competition among individuals that would lead to the acceptance of a limiting social order (Hobbes) or by the acceptance that individuals have a propensity towards social virtues and justice simply through the demands of living and working in common

(Hume, Rousseau) (Dumont 1986). This modern point of view would then be further intensified and radicalized if one pointed out, critically, that one can never *know* the nature of some supposed pre-social individual and that one must proceed *as if* deprived of any foundation: the choices one makes are always in line with the absence of any knowledge of human nature or ultimate foundations, so that one acts as if one's own choices could be chosen by any imagined other. (This is the modern reading of Kant, put forward by O'Neill 1989 and Korsgaard 1996). One might say that there is a modern ideology of individualism in general, that regardless of one's specific philosophy one nevertheless begins political questioning from the absence of any transcendent or holistic ground or foundation. This seeming neutralization of the political which also makes politics the ultimate ground precisely because all we have is the arena of debate and legitimating, has, as we have seen, two modes of implication for feminism. First, women can no longer be excluded on the grounds of natural hierarchy or nature. Second, feminism may also – having benefited from modernity's commitment to neutrality – question the supposed neutrality of the modern subject. Indeed, one might argue that this supposedly neutral individual, who faces the world with no qualities other than those that are chosen in his relations with others, is not only indebted to the capitalist paradigm of free choice in a market environment (especially, today, when markets include choosing one's lifestyle and personality), he is also far from being gender-neutral. The isolated self-determining individual is associated culturally with masculine values (whereas women are deemed to be tied more to domestic virtues of care, other-directedness, emotional connectedness and feelings of embodiment) (Lloyd 1984).

It would follow, then, that one of the first manoeuvres that might be undertaken by modern feminism is a distinction between sex and gender, with sex being one's natural biological being, and gender being the way in which nature is determined and interpreted by culture (Oakley 1972). The sex/gender distinction is at once a natural consequence of the modern ideology of liberalism: whatever one's natural or pre-social being may be – whatever one's sex – all we can really negotiate politically is one's gender, or the meaning and values one attributes to sex. It would follow from liberalism's suspension of private, partial and inscrutable values – those of one's body – in favour of publically determinable qualities (such as one's role and social identity) that politics can only concern gender, or the ways in which one's body takes on a cultural and political sense. Theorists in the liberal tradition have therefore insisted on a distinction between private norms and values (those of the family, the private sphere, sexuality and one's own taste), and political values, or those that can be discussed and negotiated in common (Elshtain 1981). But the distinction between public and private, and one's natural and social being, is precisely – though crucial for feminist criticism in its early phase – one of the key stumbling blocks for developing a feminist political theory. For the very idea that one's natural and biological being is somehow outside the domain of political negotiation harbours two problematic assumptions: it grants the body or nature a certain apolitical timelessness, and it precludes political discussion from taking hold of issues of the body and private social relations (Gatens 1996).

After Liberalism

Second-wave, radical or post-liberal feminism proceeded from a criticism of the public/private distinction and did so by politicizing the body. Perhaps the most concise way of approaching this intervention was through Kate Millett's claim that the 'personal is political,' which is also to say that the private sphere is already public, and that the way in which one lives one's own supposedly natural body is already determined by history and politics (Millett 1970). Feminists of this second wave went beyond claims for inclusion and equality and aimed to transform the very nature of political formation – no longer assuming the norm of the pre-political individual who subsequently enters politics, and no longer assuming the distinctly public nature of the political arena that would not be already inflected by gendered norms. Such a reaction against, or extension of, liberal feminist demands worked from (and also transformed) other theoretical paradigms. Whereas first-wave or liberal feminism had assumed that political formations and the assumptions of humanism would benefit and emancipate women, second-wave or radical feminism sought to rework political processes and their accompanying norms. Indeed, one might begin to question *the political*, the idea of a domain of ideally free speech where norms are negotiated and legitimated; for one might begin to think of processes beyond the polity – processes of bodies, passions and figures, and timelines beyond those of the an of calculative reason.

Marxism, like liberalism, enables a greater inclusion of women in the political process, and yet (again like liberalism) requires reformulation once women are considered as political individuals. The basic premise of Marxism is that what appears to be natural and universal is ultimately – ideologically – determined by social and economic relations that allow labour to be exploited by those who possess capital or the means of production. It would follow then that the demystification of natural subjection would lead to women's emancipation. If it is the case that social and political formations follow on from the ways in which labour is divided among those who produce and those who own the means of production, then it could no longer be the case that one simply accepts one's position in the social order. For Marxism in its most traditional form it would be workers or the proletariat, precisely because they labour and are responsible for the transformation of the natural world into a cultural world, who would be the best poised to understand that the world is never given simply and naturally but always through the relations of production. On the one hand this basic Marxist criticism of liberalism's notion of the pre-political individual would enable feminism to historicize and politicize myths of nature, so that they could contest the ideal of the competitive, market-oriented, atomized individual from which liberal theory had launched its claims for rights. On the other hand it was because of Marxism's attention to conditions of labour and social production that it would remain blind to sexual exploitation and the conditions of reproduction. Marxism's point of departure for explaining social relations was the labouring individual, working upon a world that had been presented as so much raw material for transformation; it is the worker who, in negating the world as it is, is directly tied to historical materialism.

There are two problems for feminism in such a starting point. First, the worker can only sell his labour and enter the public sphere if there has already been a sexual division of labour (Pateman 1988). Here, women take on domestic labour and reproduction in order to allow men to enter a public sphere where labour is exchanged for money and, in turn, commodities. Second, it is the productive individual, rather than those who reproduce, who becomes the exemplary political agent. Feminists therefore argued that before there could be a political revolution in which workers seized the means of production, creating a communist utopia in which one had a direct relation to production and social relations not mediated by money and commodities, there needed to be a sexual revolution in which reproduction would not be confined to the private sphere and in which women were not assumed to occupy a natural position within the family, subjected to men who would be workers. Carole Pateman argued that before any social contract, where men agree to subject themselves to law for the sake of social stability and efficiency, there would need to have been a *sexual contract* through which men become free and labouring individuals only if women take over the labour of the private sphere (Pateman 1988). Radical feminism in the Marxist tradition, even more than liberal feminism, evidenced the power of feminist thought not only to extend the bounds of a political theory by including women, but also to revolutionize the founding concepts upon which political paradigms were based. Liberal feminists argued that the free individual of modern democracy only appeared as a rational, disembodied and autonomous subject if certain qualities and roles associated with women, such as child-rearing and child-birth, were consigned to a pre-political private sphere (Okin 1989). If liberalism were to continue while taking account of feminist concerns then it would need to take into account that there cannot be an assumed level playing field or neutral subject as long as the private sphere and domestic labour were left out of play. If, however, certain social reforms were to occur – such as adequate child-care and access to employment and education – then the egalitarian ideals and assumptions of liberalism might be achieved.

But liberalism's desire for equality raises the question of 'equal to whom'? And this would also be the (second major) problem for any revolutionary Marxism oriented toward emancipating humanity in general. Should the political sphere be adjusted so that 'we' can all share the same rights and privileges, or do the defining norms of humanity need to be reconsidered to include the differences of women? Marxist feminists, in general, were critical of the norm of labour as defining social individuals – repressing, as it does, the reproductive and domestic labour of women. Other forms of radical feminism suggested that the differences between men and women were not only politically relevant, and needed to be addressed in order to achieve a just polity; such differences may also be irreducible, suggesting an irresolvable split in the polity (Daly 1978).

Perhaps no theory has been more audacious in its claims for the relation between sexual difference and political theory than psychoanalysis. At first glance Freudian theories of sexual difference might appear to be the last place feminists might look for understanding political relations; even Freud himself declared that femininity was a mystery. Freud also argued that women would be less capable of morality (for what threat would castration pose to them?), have less defined ego boundaries (for they would not define themselves in opposition to their mothers so much as identify with the position of mothering), and would be inherently narcissistic having never learned to direct their attention away from the figure of woman towards the social constraints of law (Freud 1965). Freud's model of psycho-social development, in which the child abandons attachment to the mother and submits to the law for fear of castration, makes sense only on a *phallic* model of subjectivity. Either one takes castration literally – where the boy child sees a girl lacking a penis and assumes that there is a threat of castration if he does not obey the social laws that are associated with abandoning his infantile attachment to his (pre-social and unrestrained) oedipal desires; *or* the phallus is symbolic and structural.

The condition of being subjected to law – the brute human condition of being compelled to speak and live in common – leads to the assumption that there *must have been* a point prior to prohibition, and that there is therefore someone who prohibits my enjoyment, along with a prohibited object of enjoyment. This second, structural, notion of psychoanalysis would regard sexual difference less as a literal event – to do with the brute nature of bodies – and would regard the ways in which bodies become sexed through culture as the fundamental question of psychoanalysis. One could, therefore, either dismiss Freud's oedipal account of a subject socialized through the threat of castration as being yet one more way in which women were deemed to be essentially less capable of subjectivity than men, or one could see the Freudian account as descriptive rather than prescriptive, providing – finally – some way of understanding the persistence and resilience of patriarchy.

There has been a long-standing tradition in feminism of seeing Freud as simply and symptomatically sexist. Others have seen Freud's theory of difference as crucial to explaining the long-standing structures of masculine power. Why, one might ask, even after women have been granted rights and suffrage is there continued inequality, and why do women themselves seem to be complicit in the continuation of sexual difference, being less competitive, less directed towards power and domination? This was the question that motivated Juliet Mitchell's (1975) work: only if we see that political subjects are formed through subjection to a law that is figured to be paternal, castrating and *other than woman*, will we begin to be able to negotiate the longevity of sexual difference (and its accompanying injustice). Mitchell's work was deeply indebted to Jacques Lacan whose 'return to Freud' was highly critical of the notion that psychoanalysis should direct itself to helping individuals form healthy egos. The ego, or the idea of the self as a unified individual, was a lure or misrecognition of the subject's necessarily alienated structure. We become subjects only through speech or relation to others; we are, therefore, never self-present wholes who then have either acceptable or unacceptable desires. Rather, in the beginning is our condition of being oriented to an other – the other who is imagined (Oedipally) as being a feminine 'all' who will answer our enjoyment. But that supposed full enjoyment is imaginary, and can be lived only *as prohibited*. Being a subject is, therefore, essentially a predicament of desire, not need. All our speech, all our orientation to objects and others, all our relations even to our own body – all these take place through a system of already articulated differences (language and structure). We are forever displaced from ourselves, forever subjected to desire, and never capable of living at the level of mere need, as mere bodies. This, for Lacanian feminists, means that sexual difference is structural: as subjects subjected to the order of speech we imagine that there must have been a maternal plenitude or Woman from which we are now distanced or prohibited. Sexual difference is not so much a biological fact as a structural symbolic condition; it is the way in which our relation to (and the possibility of) facts is lived. There are, therefore, 'formulas' of sexual difference: either the masculine position, in which I imagine that there must be one object that is outside the domain of possible enjoyment, the prohibited object (Woman) that would answer my desires; or, the feminine position in which there is at least one for whom prohibition does not apply, at least one (mythic) being not subjected to the symbolic order (Copjec 2002). For Juliet Mitchell psychoanalysis, via Lacan, accounted for the inability for liberal or even Marxist reformist approaches to address the predicament of patriarchy. The women's movement would require a consideration of the very structure of the psyche.

One of the challenges, after liberalism and liberal feminism, has been to recognize that feminism is not a question of negotiating sexism or even prejudice but that there may be problems of sexual difference that go beyond, or go deeper, than social and political equality. Psychoanalysis and Marxism have the virtue of allowing us to think of the ways in which the seemingly basic unit of the pre-social individual is not only already determined through political and cultural forces, but also sexually inflected. If individuals are defined through production, then it matters whether their relation to production is direct – in the world of commodities, wages and labour – or indirect, where women maintain the family unity that enables men to compete in a market setting. Psychoanalysis does not only look at the ways in which the structure of the family enables political participation, it argues for the ways in which political and social comportments are determined by the uniquely human predicament of depending upon an other throughout our infancy.

Second-wave or radical feminism in general was, therefore, both an extension and refutation of liberal assumptions; it maintained the practical political force of feminism – a dissatisfaction with the basic units of political theory – and yet argued that liberalism's desires for equality and wider participation would only reinforce, rather than reform, political norms that were not in women's interests.

Liberal and Radical Feminism Today

Contemporary arguments in the popular political domain tend to assume both liberal and psychoanalytic notions: first, that the political sphere is ideally one of equal representation and that there should, therefore, be at least some women in power and government, but also, second, that somehow there is a women's perspective or mode of sociality – less aggressive, more conciliatory, more other-directed – that would alter the mode of political procedures. Some feminists accepted the Freudian model of psycho-social development and suggested that there were indeed different models of psychological development. Nancy Chodorow (1978) and Carol Gilligan (1982) argued that women's orientation to other persons and to morality would be less rule-bound, legislative and calculative and more empathetic, other-directed and mindful of singular nuances. This assumption that women were essentially more attuned to workable models of social cooperation characterized the feminism of the 1970s, which often went as far as separatism, either for feminist utopias, or that women's traditional virtues of care, empathy, embodiment and emotive rather than aggressive approaches provided a better model of sociality in general. This notion has been maintained, more recently, in arguments for ecological forms of feminism, in which the traditionally masculine figuration of the self and its relation to the world (a relationship of subject to object) is replaced by traditionally feminine qualities of care, nurturance, other-directedness and a deep sense of the spirit of *place* (rather than the neutral and calculative attitude to space) (Warren 2000).

The often-narrated three 'waves' of feminism – from demands for equality, to claims for difference, and then to problematizations of the very notion of sexual binaries – is best not thought of as a linear sequence so much as an ongoing enrichment and problematization. Claims for equality (before the law) and difference (or the right to define one's own self, outside models of masculine humanism) have not disappeared or become out-dated. A third wave of feminists pointed out that sexual binaries were themselves problematic and required not so much elimination (liberalism) or justification (radical difference) but complication. Luce Irigaray is perhaps exemplary of French feminism insofar as she accepted the problem of psychoanalytic difference – that subjects come into being in their relation to an other, an other who can only be desired and never known (Irigaray 1996). Yet Irigaray argued for the strong sexual difference of this relation. She did not merely suggest that there were historically and culturally embedded figures of sexual difference – with masculine and feminine qualities being an effect of social and symbolic orders. Such a notion – that we are produced through culture, or that the body is neutral sex that becomes overlaid by gender – is itself a gendered notion. The masculine subject position is that there is a world of passive matter that awaits ordering and synthesis by an active mind, a mind that is subject opposed to object. Irigaray suggests another comportment of sexual difference, one in which the definitive orientation is not subject to object, but subject to subject. This much had already been suggested by Lacan and psychoanalysis more generally, but Irigaray went further and argued that the Lacanian formula for sexual difference – one figured through prohibition of the Woman as Other – was only one side of the equation. In the feminine comportment the relation is not one of representing or mastering an other, but of feeling oneself affected by an other who is also given to me only in their mode of affect. To accept that sexual difference is not about formulae relating to a mythic prohibited Woman, but that there is indeed something like 'Woman' even if her modes of relation are not those of the *subject*, would lead to radical notions of sexuate rights – forming new notions of what it is to be a political subject.

Irigaray's project does not by any means exhaust third-wave feminism, but the way in which she poses the problem of sexuality is exemplary. One needs, her work suggests, to shift the very problem of sexuality away from the subject, away from the self who speaks or acts, towards the potential relations of speaking or acting *from which* subjects are effected. Because Irigaray suggested, also, that different bodies would possess different modes of potentiality (and would be oriented towards otherness differently) her work was at once third-wave, in its demystification of already given male-female boundaries, and *post*-third-wave in its challenging of the very concepts of subject and difference.

For Irigaray, and for many who were influenced by her work, political subjects are sexual subjects: sexual not because they are gendered (or divided between male and female) but because they are who they are through the desiring relations that constitute their being. Such an understanding of politics must, therefore, go beyond the third-wave questioning of sexual structures, in order to question the notion of structure as such. As long as one accepts that the condition for politics is *structural* – that we can speak or act only *as* this or that recognized (sexed, raced) subject – then politics will always be a negative labour. The condition for speaking and acting is (supposedly) that one take part in current systems of sex, gender, race and class, and yet all the while recognize that such systems can be destabilized or challenged from within. But what if the idea of a world or reality given only through structure were itself a sexed model? What if the idea of a mute and passive reality that can be lived only through systems were typical of modern, masculine, heterosexual, white and Oedipal subjects? How, we might ask, did 'we' come to think of ourselves as effects of 'a' system of signification or difference in which 'we' must take up some specific sex or gender? What if this model – of a subject who 'is' only insofar as he speaks in relation to others who are similarly subjected – could be displaced by thinking about a sexuality or difference beyond *the subject*?

This new mode of thinking has taken feminism's deepest and defining problem – of the power of sexual difference – and taken it beyond sexuality. Perhaps the two key figures in this movement were Michel Foucault and Gilles Deleuze, but it is perhaps only through feminism that one can really grasp the force and range of their work (Braidotti 1991). For Foucault the concept of sexuality, far from being a domain of questioning that would (finally) release us from the constitutive prohibition of culture, was itself a normalizing concept (Foucault 1978). The idea that 'we' possess a sexuality that can be read in order to discover the secret of our being is entwined with what Foucault refers to as an 'ethics of knowledge' – where our capacity to read, monitor and interpret our own being would yield some proper politics. At its most normalizing this yields bio-politics: we no longer see politics as a domain of decision and relations among competing forces but seek to ground politics on the truths of life. Politics becomes the management of populations, the maximization of life.

Third-wave feminism, in general, defined itself against the primacy and supposedly binary nature of sexual difference: how could we assume the difference between male and female without a questioning of the genesis of that binary? There were two paths (at least) offered for feminism beyond Foucault's work, both of them resisting any simple assumption of sexual duality and the Freudian assumption of the oedipal family triangle as the ground for explaining life and knowledge in general. It might at first appear as though Foucault's criticism of sexuality as some normalizing ground would preclude any notion of the politics of sexual difference, and that his critique of sexuality would open the politics of identity to other fields of power, such as race, class, ethnicity and queer theory. Certainly, Foucault's emphasis on fields of knowledge and social relations and the *positive* nature of power led to an emphasis on the ways in which selves were made possible, rather than repressed, by the social, cultural and (usually) heterosexual matrices through which they performed as subjects. Judith Butler, whose work was at once influenced by Foucault and Lacan (despite their paradigmatic differences), regarded the notion of 'sex' (as the ground of one's cultural gender) as an effect of social and cultural performance: sex is not the ground of our being, but what appears *as original* after culture and social norms have been performed by individuals who, also, are effects rather than origins of performance (Butler 1990). The distinction between natural/biological sex and cultural gender was, following thinkers like Butler, deemed to be an intensification of the subjection of politics to some normalizing foundation. For Butler the way forward would neither be to do away with constructed genders for the sake of a 'real' sexuality, nor to see identity as nothing more than construction, but to look at the relation between subjectivity and subjection. We become who we are through a process of performance that creates an identity where (we imagine) *there must have been* a self who is other than the systems and signifiers through which action is possible. Materiality, for Butler, is not some prior ground for politics but is a process that splits some supposed material or prior sex, from its supposed social or cultural effect.

Butler's problematization of 'sex' is not, however, the only way in which one can avoid the naturalization of sexual binaries. Another would be to see Butler's theory (that sex is an effect of power, heterosexual norms and systems of signification) as itself part of the modern era of bio-politics and enslavement to familial Oedipalism. Why should we see the relations between bodies and sexed qualities to be one of subjection? Why would the self or body only be individuated through a system or structure that operates by negation, with sex and life being only known as *other than* (or falsely prior to) cultural identity and recognition?

Feminist philosophers, including Luce Irigaray, Julia Kristeva, Elizabeth Grosz and Rosi Braidotti, sought to consider sexual difference beyond the normalizing binaries of the standard male-dyad and as positive. Sexual difference, considered positively, is not – as in Butler – an effect of differential systems. Rather, there are forces or potential *to differ*. These forces are sexual because they take on the identity that they do only *in relation*, and this requires us to rethink – in a way different from Butler – the relation among sex, gender and politics. Political formations and familial structures, including the male-female dyad, are not ways of differentiating a life, materiality or sexuality that can only be known ex post facto. On the contrary, life is anything but a neutral unsexed substance; it is sexual in its capacity to create differences, but to do so – sexually – through encounters among powers that proliferate distinctions (Grosz 2004). Returning to Irigaray's criticism of traditional essentialism and constructivism: it is not that there are two substances (male and female) that come into some relation, nor some blank passive matter that is then represented as male or female by some active and differentiating culture. Sexual difference commits us to differing modes, styles or manners of relation. Any two bodies take on the sex or autonomy that they have only through their encounters with other (different, encountering) bodies. The oedipal figure of the family – that a child takes on its identity in relation to its male and female parents – is a narrowing of a social political, cultural and racial field. Sexual differences are also always racial, cultural, class and political differences – all forces are potentials *to differ* that occur in specific milieu. The idea that there is something like 'humanity' in general with something like 'a' sexuality only belies the complex relations of forces and powers that cannot be reduced to the modern family.

This does not mean, of course, that we are now post-feminist and that race, sexuality, ethnicity and class displace questions of gender. On the contrary, the problem that has always mobilized feminism – which from its beginning was whether something like humanity could really be imagined outside the narrow range of the white, western man of reason – has intensified. It is only if we think of forces *beyond man* that we will arrive at a point beyond the stultifying notion of the polity as nothing more than a gathering of rational selves whose only consideration is life as it is already known and lived.

Notes

1 It was in this respect that Deleuze and Guattari distinguished between majoritarian or 'molar' politics – women as a group, with a range *extending* to include all women – and minoritarian or *intensive* politics, where the inclusion of individuals alters the very nature of what counts as an individual (Deleuze and Guattari 1987: 321).

2 Monnique Wittig's (1975) claim that 'lesbians are not women' aims to think beyond women as they are defined in relation to men, and deploys the category of 'lesbian' as a placeholder for a different mode of subject. Other radical feminists embraced the traditional figure of 'woman' more positively, stressing the value of women's emancipation from male power (Firestone 1970), while deconstructive feminists accepted the term 'woman' while acknowledging its provisional and almost ironic distance from any actual woman (Cornell 1991).

3 Even today if the norms of rationality are extended to include forms of sympathy, imagination and passion that are not those of traditional reason (Nussbaum 2010), it can still be the case that there is one reasoning norm for all humanity that will include men and women – even if the task of discovering this universal humanity will be a distant ideal (Benhabib 1992).

References

Benhabib, Seyla. 1992. *Situating the Self: Gender, Community, and Postmodernism in Contemporary Ethics*. New York: Routledge.

Braidotti. Rosi. 1991. *Patterns of Dissonance: A Study of Women in Contemporary Philosophy*. Trans. Elizabeth Guild. New York: Routledge.

Butler, Judith. 1990. *Gender Trouble: Feminism and the Subversion of Identity*. New York: Routledge.

Chodorow, Nancy. 1978. *The Reproduction of Mothering: Psychoanalysis and the Sociology of Gender*. Berkeley, CA: University of California Press.

Copjec, Joan. 2002. *Imagine There's No Woman: Ethics and Sublimation*. Cambridge, MA: MIT Press.

Cornell, Drucilla. 1991. *Beyond Accommodation: Ethical Feminism, Deconstruction, and the Law*. New York: Routledge.

Daly, Mary. 1978. *Gyn/Ecology: The Metaethics of Radical Feminism*. Boston, MA: Beacon Press.

Deleuze, G. & Guattari, F. (1987) *A Thousand Plateaus: Capitalism and Schizophrenia*. Minneapolis: University of Minnesota Press.

Dumont, Louis. 1986. *Essays on Individualism: Modern Ideology in Anthropological Perspective*. Chicago, IL: University of Chicago Press.

Elshtain, Jean Bethke. 1981. *Public Man, Private Woman: Women in Social and Political Thought*. Princeton, NJ: Princeton University Press.

Firestone, Shulamith. 1970. *The Dialectic of Sex*. New York: Morrow.

Foucault, Michel. 1978. *The History of Sexuality*. Trans. Robert Hurley. New York: Pantheon Books.

Freud, Sigmund. 1965. *New Introductory Lectures on Psychoanalysis*. Ed. James Strachey. New York: Norton.

Gatens, Moira. 1996. *Imaginary Bodies: Ethics, Power, and Corporeality*. London: Routledge.

Gilligan, Carol. 1982. *In a Different Voice: Psychological Theory and Women's Development*. Cambridge, MA: Harvard University Press.

Grosz, Elizabeth. 2004. *The Nick of Time: Politics, Evolution, and the Untimely*. Durham, NC: Duke University Press.

Irigaray, Luce. 1996. *I Love to You: Sketch for a Felicity within History*. Trans. Alison Martin. New York: Routledge.

Korsgaard, Christine. 1996. *Creating the Kingdom of Ends*. Cambridge: Cambridge University Press.

Lloyd, Genevieve. 1984. *The Man of Reason: 'Male' and 'Female' in Western Philosophy*. Minneapolis, MN: University of Minnesota Press.

MacIntyre, Alasdair. 1981. *After Virtue: A Study in Moral Theory*. Notre Dame, IN: University of Notre Dame Press.

Macpherson, C. B. 1962. *The Political Theory of Possessive Individualism: Hobbes to Locke*. Oxford, Clarendon Press.

Millett, Kate. 1970. *Sexual Politics*. New York: Doubleday.

Mitchell, Juliet. 1975. *Psychoanalysis and Feminism*. Harmondsworth: Penguin Book.

Nussbaum, Martha C. 2010. *From Disgust to Humanity: Sexual Orientation and Constitutional Law*. Oxford: Oxford University Press.

Oakley, Anne. 1972. *Sex, Gender and Society*. San Francisco, CA: Harper & Row.

Okin, Susan Moller. 1989. *Justice, Gender, and the Family*. New York: Basic Books.

O'Neill, Onora. 1989. *Constructions of Reason: Explorations of Kant's Practical Philosophy*. Cambridge: Cambridge University Press.

Pateman, Carole. 1988. *The Sexual Contract*. Stanford, CA: Stanford University Press.

Rawls, John. 1972. *A Theory of Justice*. Oxford, Clarendon Press.

Ruddick, Sara. 1989. *Maternal Thinking: Toward a Politics of Peace*. Boston, MA: Beacon Press.

Warren, Karen. J. 2000. *Ecofeminist Philosophy: A Western Perspective on What it is and Why it Matters*. Lanham, MD: Rowman & Littlefield.

Wittig, Monique. 1975. *The Lesbian Body*. Trans. David Le Vay. New York: Morrow.

Wollstonecraft, Mary. 1992. *A Vindication of the Rights of Woman*. New York: Alfred A. Knopf.

Latin American Social and Political Thought

A Historical and Analytical Perspective

José Maurício Domingues and Aurea Mota

Latin American thinkers have been especially concerned with the relation between the subcontinent and the West, in particular with modernity, since the nineteenth century (Zéa 1976). To a great extent the problem remains, since the peculiar position of 'Latin' America – a term problematic in itself – has always been ambiguous: it emerged with Western expansion and is tied to the West in many ways, without being really Western. A question asked by some authors has been also, conversely, how Latin America has been important to the development, institutions and imaginary of modern Europe (Dussel 1996 [1993], 2008 [2006]; Aguilar Rivera 2000).

For a while too, it was as if thought in Latin America was to be immediately practically applicable (Gaos 1943). This issue has been significantly altered. With the development of university life and a 'division of labour' that places intellectuals in specific niches whereas politics is taken over by professionals, a more mixed situation emerged. To a great extent the 'city of letters' – a Platonist ideal republic governing intellectuals in relation to their society and pushing towards social critique and practical engagement (Rama 1984) – is mainly a thing of the past, even though utopian perspectives remain relevant, as we will see throughout this chapter.

This chapter addresses these issues, within a historical perspective and with an analytical approach. We discuss how some themes of modernity have occupied public debate, how liberalism has developed while at the same time suffering a process of attenuation and how, in what may now be called the third phase of modernity, new ideas have emerged that try to deal with the specific aspects of the heterogeneity of social life. We point to some main currents of thought in contemporary Latin America – democratic liberalism and left theories of civil society, plus the ideas underpinning the Bolivian process of social change and the emergence of indigenous peoples movements. Finally, we concentrate on two outstanding thinkers, Enrique Dussel and Roberto Mangabeira Unger.

We show also that universalism and particularism have become even more relevant in recent years. Since its inception the modern horizon has been formative for Latin American social and political thought. Liberalism has been central in the unfolding of this horizon, but the modern imaginary has been broader than that and included several critical traditions, socialism being the main one among them, as well as, more recently, processes of collective identity affirmation that have attenuated the very core elements of liberalism. In this regard, the specific characteristics and social dynamic of Latin America have met and at times opposed, in a search for its own paths in and out of modernity, the configurations that can be found in Europe and the United States.

The emergence and unfolding of modernity

The processes of independence in Latin America in the nineteenth century, sometimes more open, sometimes brutally conservative, established a very restricted sort of modern society in the new nations. But, while liberalism was not realizable in practice in a first moment, it left a *telos* in the collective imaginary that unfolded in the next hundred years and generated several modernizing moves and modernization processes (cf. Fernandes 1975: 33, a thesis about Brazil, applicable to the whole subcontinent). This was no mere copy of the West, especially because Latin American countries belonged to the first wave of nationalism (Anderson 1991). Moreover, Latin America took part in the 'Atlantic constitutional experiments' that marked the early nineteenth century, and stood as a sort of laboratory where liberal institutions were tested (Aguilar Rivera 2000). This period was witness to a number of discussions about which constitutional model was best suited to the region.

The Spanish 1821 Cadiz constitutional matrix (Safford 2001) clashed with the Napoleonic–Bolívarian perspective, although the latter was applied only in the Bolivian and Peruvian 1826 constitutions. Bolívar (2007 [1815]) did not think that the virtues demanded by the liberal–republican model existed in the subcontinent, hence an adapted monarchical matrix would work better. Both matrixes ignored the social plurality of the new countries, a lingering problem until very recently. But only by the 1840s did oligarchic republics triumph and intellectual inactivity set in, with a more centralized state assuming control of the situation and leading some to detect a deep-seated Latin American centralist tradition (Vélez 1984 [1980]).

The very construction of the new nations was complicated. While in Western Europe fierce but long-term state policies allowed for the configuration of rather homogenous nations, in Latin America – with its mix of white ruling classes, black slaves and large indigenous populations, unevenly distributed in the new states – this was much more difficult. Insofar as most of these populations were excluded from the electoral franchise the problem such heterogeneity entailed was brushed aside (Domingues 2006a). In any case, Latin America was seen during this period as belonging to universalizing western civilization – those black, Indian and mixed populations were in this regard basically a nuisance.

As conservative and exclusionary liberalism became dominant, new problems were brewing. The beginning of the twentieth century brought new problems, with working-class militancy, economic crisis due to oscillations in capitalist markets, the increase in the number of people of mixed 'racial' origins, as well as peasant and indigenous unease, and even feminist movements. Similar to processes occurring in Europe, the second phase of modernity in Latin America substituted for its first, too narrow one. Corporatism was established in the more industrially advanced countries (Brazil, Mexico, Argentina), supposedly harking back to the Latin American tradition (Wiarda 1974), labour laws were passed, liberalism contested to some extent, whereas classes were recognized as collectivities, although social rights remained focused on individuals alone and the market was not actually challenged (Vianna 1976). A state ideology which privileged miscegenation spread out (without detriment to white superiority at least in practice), after attempts at whitening the population of most of these countries (cf. Freyre 1987 [1933]). Indeed an 'essence' of each nationality was often pointed out by intellectuals to define the Brazilian, the Mexican and even Latin Americans (see especially Paz 1993 [1950]). A second phase of modernity, state organized, came into being.

A left, socialist and communist perspective emerged in the same period, challenging liberalism. There were socialists of distinct persuasions, while communism was heavily connected to the impoverished ideologies of Third International Marxism–Leninism. Yet, they had a huge impact in Latin America and eventually developed original ideas (Sader 2009). Within the communist left especially José Carlos Mariátegui's (1996 [1928], 1969) indigenist Marxism was of great importance in the 1920s–1930s, stressing both the role of interests and the working class and the importance of the indigenous masses and the need for a myth, recovering a glorious past, that could mobilize them in their struggle. The universalism of socialism and the particularity of those old civilizational forms were thus already underscored.

So-called 'populism', which had a much deeper impact among the popular classes, was a more elusive phenomenon. Since Germani's (1965) identification of a period of transition from 'ascriptive society' to modernity, during which an elite controlled available masses that supported it in exchange for some sort of recognition and freedom, much has been written. Along with corporatism it implied that the state would have a much stronger position in social life. Besides, the developmentalist state, whose programme was loose, it had as its intellectual horizon the theories of the United Nations Economic Commission for Latin America (ECLA), in which Raúl Prebish was the main figure and two issues were especially important: the peripheral role of Latin America as a (primary) commodities exporter and the need to industrialize via import substitution, in which the state had a key part to play (Bielschowsly 2000). One may even suggest that a powerful undercurrent, which was once dominant in 'Iberian' America, resurfaced, namely neo-Thomism, which gave centrality to the state as an organizing and civilizing agent in social life (Morse 1982; Vélez 1984 [1980]). Resuming the ECLA tradition, and mixing it with several variants of Marxism, dependency theory emerged in the 1970s and immediately featured as probably the main contribution of Latin America to an international debate in the social sciences, especially through Cardoso's and Faletto's (1970) book. At the same time, liberation theology, a new way of viewing the relation of Catholic Christianity with the popular classes, the 'poor', slowly developed. It would receive a strong impulse with the emergence of popular masses in the struggle for democracy from the late 1970s onwards (Boff and Boff 1986).

These two periods, the first dominated by a form of restricted liberalism but with its *telos* as the subcontinental horizon of development, the second marked by the increased power of the state, in the search for a more inclusive modernity, with the emergence of middle classes, the urban working classes and the peasantry, as well as attempts at the development of nationalist forms of capitalism, frame most of the modern history of Latin America, the particular manner in which it took part in the two first phases of global modernity. By the end of the second period, though, the unstable, restrictive and highly conflictive democracies of the subcontinent had given way to military dictatorships in the 1960s–1970s. Some tried to carry out 'modernizing moves' that were to some extent attempts to go back to the period when powerful landowners controlled these countries, for example Argentina and Chile. Neoliberalism was instrumental for that. Brazil, however, moved forward in terms of industrialization, while Mexico tried also to build a strong infra-structure. Other countries, such as Colombia and Venezuela, did not quite move. However, the crisis of the second phase of modernity, which was multi-dimensional, implied deep economic problems for all these countries. Meanwhile a powerful democratic movement, a true 'molecular revolution', was played out from the late 1970s, with different rhythms and distinct phases, as well as unequal results, all over Latin America, though this too was overwhelmed by a neoliberal 'transformist' move which was internationally supported as a conservative outcome to the enduring economic crisis. This is how Latin America entered the new, third phase of modernity (Domingues 2008: especially ch. 3).

Socially this implied a much greater level of heterogeneity (see García Canclini (1990), who spoke of a post-modern problematic, though not reality). New, varied perspectives developed and an array of different social movements sprung up on platforms which often diverged from the former concentration on homogeneous nations and a singular, working class, revolutionary force. But the universalizing discourse of rights also became even more important, since the havoc wrought by the dictatorships stressed issues of human rights and democratic freedoms, without detriment to the social agendas suppressed by those regimes. New constitutions have been written across Latin America and new identities crafted (Domingues 2008: chs 1, 3). The complexification of the notion of person, which stems from the idea that the individual subject – the signatory to the whole system of rights and duties, within the overriding conception of the rule of law – is no longer seen as the only 'person' in the play of forces within the legal realm. It has become increasingly common for collective subjects – whether majorities (in Bolivia, for example) or minorities (as in most Latin American countries) – to become the object of specific laws (Mota 2009).

Particularly important to consider is the recent simultaneous ascension and transformation of the left and the attenuation of political liberalism, while neoliberalism seems to carry on in the defensive, yet partly maintaining effective hegemony. The situation of neoliberalism is rather particular: its influence in Latin America has been extremely deep and connected to free markets and open competition, to the dismantling of the developmentalist state and of the idea of social rights, as well as to the introduction of compensatory social policies. But its main spokespersons are actually politicians and especially economists linked to international organizations, with mainly the World Bank and the International Monetary Fund controlling the agenda of economic and social reforms, which also implies a tendency to subdue political democracy within strictly liberal limits (Borón 2003). It has been an intellectually sneaky credo, preaching commodification and personal self-reliance. Right now it is somewhat on the defensive, but by no means dead, since economically and with regard to social policies, its ideas are still dominant (Domingues 2008: ch. 2). An exception to that silence was Soto's (1986) defence of Latin American large popular informal markets as bulwarks, and as deserving of unfettered capitalist development, through the strengthening and simplification of law as well as by rolling back the state; probably the strongest argument made by autochthonous neoliberalism and the numerous liberal institutes that sprung up in the subcontinent in the 1980s. In any case, his attempt to win the popular classes over to the neoliberal project bears witness to the democratization of social life and politics in Latin America.

On the other hand, the context of democratization gave impulse to many new reflections. Initially, with the transitions to democracy, institutionalist analysis prevailed (O'Donnell, Schmitter and Whitehead 1986). Civil society also became an important topic after the early 1980s, via a renewal of Marxism, through the influence of Gramsci (Coutinho 1984). With the development of democracy, beyond many analysts' former commitment to elitist theories the emphasis shifted to enlarging poliarchic institutions, thus privileging the expression of the 'demos' in a renovated 'polis', without detriment to market institutions (Santos 1988), as well as to generating horizontal accountability and the control of citizens over elected politicians, plus strengthening civil rights (O'Donnell 1997). Habermasian theory followed later with its stress on the relation of civil society and public spheres with the state through 'hybrid institutions', receiving a regional configuration called participatory democracy (Olvera 1999; Avritzer 2009). Law issues came to the fore too, with legal pluralism assuming centre stage in the Colombian journal *Otro derecho*, and leading to innovative debates in this regard (cf. Uprimmy, Rodríguez Garavito and García 2006). More recently, emancipation and the questioning of modernity have come once again to the front line, although very often no longer within a Marxist frame

(Santos 2007). Some have spoken of a slow, though as yet restricted, development of post-neoliberalism in the last few years (Sader 2009).

This was simultaneous to a change in social identities and nation building. In Latin America there is no longer room for national essences; indigenous as well as black movements affirm themselves as irreducible particularities, entailing a necessary opening and refashioning of national narratives and identities as well as of state institutions. A more complex and potentially fragmented social life has come about. Democratization was combined with increasing complexification and openings propelled by general processes of globalization, especially at the cultural level. That is why, as argued by García Canclini (2007 [2004]), the most important challenge to Latin America is how to recognize differences, correct inequalities and connect majorities to globalized networks. Universalism has thus been required to become more complex and subtle. Answers vary, but in any case the future is no longer seen as fixed and given. That is, to some extent the de-reification of modernity has also come about.

With respect to the constitutional impact of these new changes in Latin America the phenomenon of attenuated constitutional liberalism is unfolding (Mota 2009). While late-twentieth-century constitutional reforms may be interpreted as questioning the liberal foundations that guided the construction of Latin American constitutions and were highly centred on the individual legal person, they do not actually constitute an absolute challenge to these foundations. The most immediate evidence of this phenomenon is the fact that, in the vast majority of Latin American countries where the process has occurred, we have not seen a broader discussion of how the inclusion of a 'collective person' with both symbolic rights (e.g., recognition of the pluri-national make-up of some states) and material rights (e.g., collective land ownership and bilingual intercultural education) might affect these societies as a whole.

Bolivia has been the country where there is probably a more refined reflection on such topics, starting with a movement by indigenous intellectuals called *Katarismo* (in honour of one of the leaders of a huge late colonial rebellion against Spanish dominium). First of all, there is the identification of distinct civilizations in this internally differentiated and fragmented country. Overall the idea that an 'internal colonization' by white (and *mestizo*) elites has developed over Aymara, Quéchua and other ethnic groups, resuming the colonial legacy, during the whole two hundred years of republican history is widespread. It demands 'decolonization', that is, the substitution of indigenous forms – especially community democracy and justice – for westernized institutions (Tapia 2002, 2007). In fact, most contemporary debates on 'internal colonialism' tend to stress culture and politics, differently from former analysis which denounced capitalism in this connection and pointed to socialist revolutionary strategies (González Casanova 1965).

But this finds expression also in the work of the mathematician, self-taught sociologist, revolutionary Marxist and vice-president of the republic, Álvaro García Linera (2009a [1995], 2009b). His study of Marx led him originally to identify and oppose the 'capital form' and the 'community form', with derivatives which include – as to the working classes in his country – the union, the community and the multitude (implying extended networks of different social movements). His work is closely connected to the substitution of the working class as the spearhead of social change in Bolivia and evolved towards the support for deeper democracy, an Andean sort of popular capitalism and the protection and development of community life (the Andean *Ayllu*) in several dimensions.

While for instance Zapatism in Mexico could be seen under the same logic, its intellectual products are less sophisticated and stress autonomy above anything else (Sader 2009: 141, 146). Implicitly or explicitly these perspectives all tend to refuse liberal multiculturalism and demand what can be named 'interculturality', the cross-fertilization of indigenous and western cosmologies and cultures, although civilizational alternatives are more spoken about than concretely proposed (Walsh 2009).

Reflecting the surge of such sorts of issues, a group of Latin American thinkers, most of whom live mainly in the United States, have been developing what would amount to a programme of intellectual decolonization of 'Latin America' (cf. Escobar 2003). This is the case of Walter Mignolo (2005), who resumes in a more radical and narrow way Dussel's topic of 'exteriority' (to be examined below). But they mostly overstress the indigenous peoples elements and end up with a one-sided picture of the region and a narrow cultural-political programme (for a critical view, see Domingues 2009).

Reflecting social heterogeneity, a tendency towards the fragmentation of topics and objects of study in the social sciences can however be detected, while conceptual issues have receded since the emergence of military dictatorships, meaning that Latin America has not often been theorized. Yet knowledge of social reality has increased, the evolution of university systems has implied that all currents and fads of western academia are reproduced to a greater or lesser extent in contemporary Latin America, from rational choice to Rawlsian approaches, from Marxist to Habermasian debates, from post-structuralism to Luhmmaniann theories (though specifically with a leftist slant, a sample can be found in the large array of books and publications by the Latin American Social Science Council (CLACSO) at www.clacso.edu.ar; for sociology, see Domingues 2006b; for political science, Cansino 2008; for philosophy Dussel 2003). In terms of systematic bodies of work, two main thinkers may be singled-out coming from Latin America at present, although only one of them is actually concerned with the subcontinent as such.

Dussel and Unger: Two Outstanding Thinkers of Contemporary Latin America

Argentine, but due to former exile now living permanently in Mexico since 1975, Dussel has become an outstanding Latin American thinker, as one of the exponents of the 'philosophy of liberation'. Starting with his trip to the old continent as a young scholar well-versed in European philosophy, through the theology of liberation and a moment in which the philosophy of liberation emerges as a possibility to see Latin America as a historically dominated continent by the end of the 1960s, plus his work on exteriority, Dussel arrived at a historical philosophy critical of the 'world-system' asymmetrically structured at the very beginnings of modernity, heralded by the 1492 'invasion' of the Americas by the Europeans (Dussel 1994). He was quite successful in his enterprise, which implied an architectural as well as a content stage for his philosophical system, the latter building upon the former, and should be considered therefore according to a two-phase periodization (against Mendieta's (1996) fourfold one). In his recent work of synthesis Dussel's (2007) proposal to base philosophy on a reflection about concrete reality, casting a framework which follows the political, historical and social displacements lived out by the philosopher, represents a clear, systematic and mature answer to his youthful yearnings (see www.enriquedussel.org).

Initially, the idea to 'look from below' led to the 'philosophy of the oppressed', which drew upon Levinas as well as Heidegger's ontological approach, carrying out a critique of Hegel's philosophy of history and dwelling on the economic ethics of Marx's mature writings (Dussel 1977). Since then, he developed an ethics of liberation based on the concept of 'exteriority' (see Dussel 1996 [1993], especially ch. 8, for his agreement with Levinas and Apel about ethics as *prima philosophia*). At the core of his view is therefore a practical concern with the situation of all oppressed groups whose 'personality construction' is always achieved through a denial of something that they do not possess. One belongs and at once one does not belong, according to this standpoint. This allows also for an analysis of those who, for example, since they are starving, see themselves as the 'not-bread' (as the thinker of peripheral capitalist nations, we may suggest, whose writings, or overlooked knowledge, is usually taken as 'not-knowledge'). Instead, he will propose that the subjugated groups are not different, but the 'other', this leading to a proposal of rupture with the system of 'cynical rationality' through the 'irruption' of the denied presuppositions of the other. However, he has some important criticisms of the ethics of communication especially in its Apelian incarnation, since it must specify the 'other' as the subject of communication, an excluded 'we' (as a 'community of communication') which is the subject of liberation. Latin America, as a periphery, is the focal point of his argument in this respect (Dussel 1996 [1993]: 27ff). As modernity is based on a 'sacrificial myth' rooted in violence against the other and its supposed immaturity and barbarism, and post-modernity would be a poor substitute for modernity in this respect, insofar as it is merely the last moment of western modernity, he opted instead for 'trans-modernity' as a way to achieve liberation beyond the hegemonic western perspective (Dussel 1996 [1993], 2002).

As the denunciation of Eurocentric practices becomes more systematic in Dussel's works published from the 1990s onwards, the philosophy of liberation shows the signs of the 'irruption' that the oppressed groups manage to operate in the horizon of the 'totality', taking to task the systems of domination. His philosophy thus became more sharply historical, tackling the Semitic origins of philosophy as well the philosophy of history born in Europe in the eighteenth century. Contrary to Montesquieu, Herder and Hegel, who, despite huge differences, saw history as something that enables the contemplation of a positive teleology for the development of the modern world, history in Dussel's philosophy mainly plays a critical role. This implied a 'counter-narrative', whose principal task was to search for that which was silenced and for the reasons underlying the specific meanings of the 'exteriority' of the other, of the 'distinct' (Dussel 2002).

The challenge was then, in the first place, to eschew Greece as the cradle of political philosophy, an approach that entirely neglects the Egyptian and Mesopotamian, as well as Phoenician and Semitic, worlds and the origins there of the constructions which were consolidated in the Hellenic civilization. This was aggravated by the 'Occidentalism' that ignored the importance of the Eastern Roman Empire for modern philosophy and the Eurocentric perspective which disregards all the deeds of other cultures, including their impact in the West as such, due to ignorance or purposeful exclusion. Overcoming 'theoretical and mental colonization' included in addition the revision of a periodization based on European patterns (Dussel 2007).

For Dussel (2008 [2006]), a new political theory must not be framed by modern presuppositions. It must take distance from bourgeois liberal positions as well from the concrete instances of real socialism. Paraphrasing Evo Morales, the president of Bolivia, a cultural revolution will be necessary, he thinks, in order that politics in Latin America acquires a content that may take it beyond the exercise of state bureaucratic activities. Possessing a normative view of what must orient 'the political' as a concept and 'politics' as practice, for Dussel contemporary social movements need to have a positively differentiated standpoint of what constitutes power. This would be possible only through the 'will-to-live', universal for the species, that leads to a life in community and makes possible the political as potency, which can move and transform.

Unger's work is quite different. Although Anderson (1992) identified his passionate and sort of messianic work as typically Latin American, this is rather arguable – having perhaps more to do with being an outsider in US academia while in a powerful position in Harvard University. In any event, establishing clear-cut boundaries for the definition of Latin America is pointless. Unger founded the 'critical legal studies movement', as opposed to compensatory legal-activism by judges in search of social justice within merely existing arrangements (Unger 1996). His outlook became increasingly broader, and, although some of his seminal ideas still link up with legal analysis and institutional issues, he has become a general social philosopher and political theorist. Unger developed what he called, against Marx and by and large inherited thought in philosophy and the social sciences, an 'anti-necessitarian' theory, in order to fulfil the programme of modernity of taking society as an 'artefact' (Unger 1997 [1987]: 3–9). The role of pragmatism, imagination and experimentalism, blueprints for reform, the distinction between formative contexts and freedom are central in his outlook.

Unger's (2007) recent work elaborates these points. He argues for a 'radicalized' pragmatism, against its narrow academic and watered-down discursive, quietist versions. We are 'plastic' beings and must make room for this quality to unfold, as godlike creatures, though plagued by finitude and circumstances. This allows for the 'transcendence' of the self over its 'formative circumstances' in 'every department of human existence', implying 'mastery' over the 'terms of our existence' as much as acquaintance with the 'infinite' – although we are powerless towards nature, since we can partly control but not shape its deep structures. Institutional arrangements that can shorten the distance between 'context-preserving' and 'context-transforming' activities are needed, severing the link between crisis and change, socially freeing our imagination and 'experimentalist cooperation', reasserting revolutionary change while overcoming its 'otherworld' connotations. This is true in particular in the domain of politics, with democracy turned into a 'high energy' process, as well as in the legal-institutional organizations of market and free civil society. This may lead to a breakthrough from rigid roles and entrenched forms of inequality, although Unger, in a very liberal mould, stresses that individual freedom and democratized personal heroism are the main values, equality consisting merely in an 'accessory' goal. If absolute equality would pervert that, equality of opportunity offers too little and merely redressing the situation, as did social democracy during the whole twentieth century, is not enough. People must be freed from the constraints that hinder their creative development. Unger is also quite aware of contemporary forms of cooperation-competition, which would be typical of the most advanced firms and economic life, plus some sectors of education, and where innovation is thriving. This should be extended to the whole of social life in the world, where difference and peace might flourish via this process of permanent invention, within a framework of democracies.

In a more politically oriented text, Unger (2005) detailed his proposals to go beyond liberalism and re-found social democracy, leaving behind institutional fetishism and necessitarian Marxism, with its faith in revolution and disastrous election of the proletariat as agent. He elects the petty bourgeoisie and the large masses of (mostly unorganized) salaried workers who yearn for a similar situation to carry out change, energize democracy, find new and nationally varied paths of development, in the US, Brazil, India or China (whose civilizational heritages are of no particular concern, since plasticity is always the key word in his thought). Labour, and not only capital, should become increasingly free to circulate internationally. Heretical models and democratic, context-changing institutions, with greater participation and public debates, as well as mechanisms to overcome deadlocks between distinct branches of the state, are other parts of his blueprint for change. Solidarity should be achieved via state provision of main social rights, but the engagement of every individual in the provision of services and care for each other would greatly enhance it.

Sociologically, much of what he has to say stems from older pieces, especially his *Politics* (Unger 1997 [1987]). Unger does not accept the definition of social forms under encompassing umbrellas such as 'capitalism' in Marxism and the like, since societies are less coherent and solid. He refuses therefore 'deep structure analysis', as well as functionalism, mere variants of the same approach. This means that society is open to experimentation in several domains, although 'formative contexts' – institutional and imaginative – condition social change and creativity, with varying degrees of rigidity and the establishment of routines that suspend conflicts to some extent. A particular way of accomplishing that is through 'destabilization rights', namely, the right citizens must be given to change institutions and practices. They must be protected by immunity rights that guarantee basic freedoms (Unger 1997 [1987]: 386–91).

Unger is a highly sophisticated social, legal and political theorist, but his abstract choice of agents is almost puzzling, understandable only to the extent that he is very much bent on stressing the heroic role of the individual without being prone to give in merely to the powerful. His disconnection from what happens in Latin America is driven home by his total oblivion to social movements in the subcontinent, except for what concerns strong, highly individualist Evangelical sects in Brazil. In fact, in Mexico, Unger allied himself with Vicente Fox's neoliberal government (see www.law.harvard.edu/faculty/unger/). His extremely liberal, westernized, unilateral modernism blinds him to those concrete processes of change, even though we can find plenty of creative ideas, both in interpretative and practical terms, in his large body of work.

Conclusion

In order to conclude, let us start by affirming that social and political thought in Latin America has a strong historical dimension. It could not be simply a universal history, nor rest quietly within a particularistic perspective. The evolution of the subcontinent had its idiosyncrasies explained by contrast with the West, to which it belongs or should belong, but critique has also been based on this historical inclination, which leads beyond abstract theories. Although still grappling with a peripheral or semiperipheral position, and irrespective of the reiteration of perspectives according to which the West should remain the yardstick to judge our trajectories, Latin America has partly gone beyond that. While debates are still very much referred to European and United States authors, implying a sort of 'alopoietic' (versus autonomous) intellectual scene in too many instances, modernity has been nevertheless partly de-reified, that is, it has been to some extent grasped in its specific paths of development. Universalism has assumed more concrete content thereby. This has been facilitated by the recognition of the heterogeneity which inhabits these societies and is a hallmark of the contemporary world, while hegemonic liberalism has become attenuated so as to embrace such particularities. The horizon of emancipation – or 'liberation', as some would prefer – of the subcontinent is therefore still placed within the confines of modernity, even when radical criticism, which includes 'trans-modern' views and an opening to creativity and transformation, occupies centre stage. Political economy, contrary to the period in which ECLA and dependence theory were highly influential, is however absent, and thereby there is indeed a lack of discussion of the position of the subcontinent within global modernity, except in cultural terms.

In this chapter we have searched for an inclusive view of Latin America. We have therefore drawn upon the uneven way in which the most relevant and at times pressing issues that arise in the region have been tackled in different countries at different times, generalizing their specific ways of framing problems and answers. Thereby we hope we have achieved a comprehensive view of Latin American social and political thought, which, despite significant differences, constitutively shares some key issues that have been unfolding in the course of its peculiar history.

References

Aguilar Rivera, J. A. (2000) *En pos de la quimera: Reflexiones sobre el experimento constitucional atlántico*, Mexico: Fondo de Cultura Económica and CIDE.

Anderson, B. (1991) *Imagined Communities: Reflections on the Original Spread of Nationalism*, London and New York: Verso.

Anderson, P. (1992) 'Roberto Unger and the Politics of Empowerment', in *A Zone of Engagment*, London and New York: Verso.

Avritzer, L. (2009) *Participatory Institutions in Democratic Brazil*, Washington, DC: Woodrow Wilson Center Press.

Bielschowsly, R. (ed.) (2000) *Cinqüenta anos de pensamento na CEPAL*, vols 1–2, Rio de Janeiro: Record, Cepal & Cofecon.

Boff, L. and Boff, C. (1986) *Como fazer Teologia da Libertação*, Petrópolis: Vozes.

Bolívar, S. (2007 [1815]) *Carta de Jamaica*, Barcelona: Linkgua.

Borón, A. (2003) *Estado, capitalismo y democracia en América Latina*, Buenos Aires: CLACSO.

Cansino, C. (2008) *La muerte de la ciencia política*, Buenos Aires: Sudamericana.

Cardoso, F. H. and Faletto, E. (1970) *Dependência e desenvolvimento na América Latina*, Rio de Janeiro: Zahar.

Coutinho, C. N. (1984) *A democracia como valor universal e outros ensaios*, Rio de Janeiro: Salamandra, 2nd edition.

Domingues, J. M. (2006a) 'Nationalism in South and Central America', in G. Delanty and K. Kumar (eds), *Handbook of Nations and Nationalism*, London: Sage.

——(2006b) 'A sociologia brasileira, a América Latina e a terceira fase da modernidade', in J. M. Domingues and M. Maneiro (eds), *América Latina hoje: Concietas e interpretações*, Rio de Janeiro: Civilização Brasileira.

——(2008) *Latin America and Contemporary Modernity: A Sociological Interpretation*, New York and London: Routledge.

——(2009) 'Global Modernization, "Coloniality" and a Critical Sociology for Latin America', *Theory, Culture & Society*, 26 (1).

Dussel, E. (1977) *Philosophy of Liberation*, New York, Orbis Books.

——(1994) *1492. El encubrimiento del Otro: Hacia el origen del 'mito de la modernidad'*, La Paz: Plural Editores and Universidad Mayor de San Andrés.

——(1996 [1993]) *The Underside of Modernity: Apel, Ricouer, Rorty, Taylor, and the Philosophy of Liberation*, Atlantic Highlands, NJ: Humanities Press.

——(2002) 'World-system and "Trans-modernity"', *Neplanta: Views from South*, 3 (2).

——(2003) 'Philosophy in Latin America in the Twentieth Century: Problems and Currents', in E. Mendieta (ed.), *Latin American Philosophy: Currents, Issues, Debates*, Bloomington, IN: Indiana University Press.

——(2007) *Política de la liberación: Historia mundial y crítica*, Madrid: Trotta.

——(2008 [2006]) *Twenty Thesis on Politics*, Durham, NC, and London: Duke University Press.

Escobar, A. (2003) 'The Latin American Modernity/Coloniality Program', in G. O'Donnell at al., *Cruzando fronteras en América Latina*, Amsterdam: CEDLA.

Fernandes, F. (1975) *A revolução burguesa no Brasil*, Rio de Janeiro: Zahar.

Freyre, G. (1987 [1933]) *Casa Grande & Senzala*, Rio de Janeiro: José Olympio.

Gaos, J. (1943) 'Significación filosófica del pensamiento hispano-americano', *Cuadernos americanos*, 2 (3).

García Canclini, N. (1990) *Culturas híbridas: Estrategias para entrar y salir de la modernidad*, Mexico: Grijalbo.

——(2007 [2004]) *Diferentes, Desiguais e Desconectados*, Rio de Janeiro: Editora UFRJ.

García Linera, A. (2009a [1995]) *Forma valor y forma comunidad*, La Paz: Muela del Diablo, Comuna and CLACSO.

——(2009b) *La potencia plebeya: Acción colectiva e identidades indígenas, obreras y populares en Bolivia*, Bogotá: Siglo del Hombre and CLACSO.

Germani, G. (1965) *Política y sociedad en una época de transición: De la sociedad tradicional a la sociedad de masas*, Buenos Aires: Paidós.

González Casanova, P. (1965) 'Internal Colonialism and National Development,' *Studies in Comparative International Development*, 1.

Mariátegui, J. C. (1969) *Ideología y política*, Lima: Amauta.

——(1996 [1928]) *Siete ensayos de interpretación de la realidad peruana*, Lima: Amauta.

Mendieta, E. (1996) 'Foreword', in Dussel, E. (1996) *The Underside of Modernity: Apel, Ricouer, Rorty, Taylor, and the Philosophy of Liberation*, Atlantic Highlands, NJ: Humanities Press.

Mignolo, W. D. (2005) *The Idea of Latin America*, Oxford: Blackwell.

Morse, R. (1982) *El espejo de Próspero*, Mexico: Siglo XXI.

Mota, A. (2009) 'A Nova Constituição Política do Estado boliviano: Antecedentes históricos, conteúdo e proposta analítica', in J. M. Domingues, A. Soares Guimarães, A. C. Mota and F. Pereira da Silva (eds), *A Bolívia no espelho do futuro*, Belo Horizonte: Editora UFMG.

O'Donnell, G. (1997) *Contrapuntos: Ensayos escogidos sobre autoritarismo y democratización*, Buenos Aires: Paidós.

O'Donnell, G., Schmitter, P. C. and Whitehead, L. (eds) (1986) *Transitions from Authoritarian Rule*, Baltimore, MD: Johns Hopkins University Press.

Olvera, A. J. (1999) *La sociedad civil: De la teoría a la realidad*, Mexico: El Colegio de México.

Paz, O. (1993 [1950]) *El laberinto de la soledad*, Madrid: Cátedra.

Rama, A. (1984) *La ciudad letrada*, Montevideo: Fundación Internacional Angel Rama.

Sader, E. (2009) *A nova toupeira*, São Paulo: Boitempo.

Safford, F. (2001) 'Política, ideologia e sociedade na América Espanhola do pós-independência', in L. Bethell (ed.) *História da América Latina: Da independência até 1870*, São Paulo: Editora da Universidade de São Paulo.

Santos, B. S. (2007) *Renovar a teoria crítica e reinventar a emancipação social*, São Paulo: Boitempo.

Santos, W. G. (1988) *Paradoxos do liberalismo: Teoria e história*, Rio de Janeiro: Vértice.

Soto, H. (1986) *El otro sendero*, Lima: El Barranco.

Tapia, L. (2002) *La condición multisocietal: Multiculturalidad, pluralismo, modernidad*, La Paz: CIDES, Universidad Mayor de San Andrés and Muela del Diablo.

——(2007) 'Una reflexión sobre la idea de Estado plurinacional', *Revista del OSAL*, 7 (2).

Unger, R. M. (1996) *What Should Legal Analysis Become?* London and New York: Verso.

——(1997 [1987]) *Politics: The Central Texts*, London and New York: Verso.

——(2005) *What Should the Left Propose?* London and New York: Verso.

——(2007) *The Self Awakened: Pragmatism Unbound*, Cambridge, MA, and London: Harvard University Press.

Uprimmy, R., Rodrígues Garravito, C. and García, M. (eds) (2006) *¿Justicia pata todos? Sistema judicial, derechos sociales y democracia en Colombia*, Bogotá: Norma.

Vélez, C. (1984 [1980]) *La tradición centralista de América Latina*, Barcelona: Ariel.

Vianna, L. W. (1976) *Liberalismo e sindicato no Brasil*, Rio de Janeiro: Paz e Terra.

Walsh, C. (2009) *Interculturalidad, Estado, sociedad: Luchas (de)coloniales de nuestra época*, Quito: Universidad Andina Simón Bolívar.

Wiarda, H. (1974) *Politics and Social Change in Latin America: The Distinct Tradition*, Amherst, MA: Massachusetts University Press.

Zéa, L. (1976) *El pensamiento latinoamericano*, Barcelona: Ariel.

Intellectuals and Society

Sociological and Historical Perspectives

Patrick Baert and Joel Isaac

Since its inception, the meaning of the term "intellectual" has shifted over time and across national cultures. This makes a firm definition difficult. In what follows, we designate as "intellectuals" scholars who invoke their expertise to address issues of broader societal or political significance. This definition has a number of implications. First, it draws an analytical distinction between intellectuals and experts. Experts *can* be intellectuals, but only if they tackle issues that go beyond their speciality and are of wider political, cultural, or social significance. Intellectuals are experts, then, just insofar as they are trained and have excelled in one field before dealing with broader issues. Second, intellectuals can, in principle, be found in *any* field of learning or cultural achievement; there is no *a priori* reason why they should be concentrated in the arts and humanities or any other domain. Natural scientists or mathematicians, as we shall see, can and have been intellectuals in the sense we have specified. This means that the study of intellectuals extends to science and to natural scientists, even if the archetypal intellectual is, in fact, usually associated with the arts and humanities. Third, by virtue of the fact that intellectuals address broader social and political issues, they have a predilection to engage with a wider public – either the "general public" or multiple publics outside their specific realm of expertise or authority. It follows from this view that a considerable number of intellectuals can be termed "public intellectuals" because they make a concerted effort to communicate with and influence non-specialist publics, and to shape public policy. Finally, intellectuals do not necessarily work in the academy. To be sure, they often have done so, and, we shall argue below, they are increasingly to be identified within a matrix of academic disciplines. Nevertheless a substantial number of intellectuals operate outside the groves of academe.

Different disciplines and sub-disciplines have studied intellectuals and their role in society. In particular, sociology, science studies, and history have, in recent years, developed methodological toolkits and interpretive frameworks for making sense of intellectuals, expertise, and social order. We assess the contributions and increasingly shared research agendas of each of these fields below. Although there is no question of reducing one field to another or positing a grand synthesis between these scholarly domains, the recent literature, especially in what is called the "new sociology of ideas," suggests a growing convergence of vision and method in the study of intellectuals. Hence we shall begin with a survey of the transformation of the "traditional" sociology of knowledge (and intellectuals) in the hands of post-Kuhnian proponents of the sociology of scientific knowledge and the sociology of academic life. In the second part of the chapter, we turn from these reflections on the history of sociology to the increasingly sociological investigative vocabulary of intellectual history. We conclude with some remarks on the recent reshaping of the persona and institutional location of the "public intellectual."

The Social and Political Theory of Intellectuals

During the first half of the twentieth century, the sociological contribution to the study of intellectuals was limited to the sociology of knowledge. This sub-field of sociology flourished initially in Germany, and dealt with broad questions such as the relationship between knowledge and society, the difference between science and ideology, and the role of intellectuals in the class struggle. It was heavily influenced by Marxism, to which some scholars subscribed and others felt compelled to react. The sociology of knowledge, thus conceived, was primarily a theoretical endeavour without a systematic empirical research agenda. Indicative of this period are Karl Mannheim's theoretical reflections on how social scientific knowledge is influenced by social forces, and how this affects its validity (Mannheim 1936 [1929]). Mannheim was aware of the potentially circular nature of this position, and tried to avoid it by arguing in favour of "relationism" or "perspectivism" rather than "relativism." Whereas relativism questions any sense of truth and is ultimately self-defeating, relationism holds certain theories to be true, but only within the specific context in which they arise. In this context, Mannheim draws on Alfred Weber's *freischwebende Intelligenz* to argue that intellectuals are able to transcend ideology and gain the critical distance that is required to attain objective analysis. Precisely by uncovering the hitherto hidden determinants of their own thinking, intellectuals are able to conduct objective analysis.

Although it is tempting to read Mannheim as presenting an optimistic picture of intellectuals – as social agents uniquely equipped to overcome the ideological forces of their times – his writings also tap into a wider anxiety among his European contemporaries about the extent to which intellectuals *can* be swayed by ideologies and passions of all kinds. For instance, in his highly influential *La trahison des clercs*, Julien Benda (1928 [1927]) argued that intellectuals *ought* to pursue justice, truth, and knowledge for their own sake, but that they had recently gone astray because of the pernicious influence of various "political passions," whether in the name of patriotism, class, or race. Mannheim's account of free-floating intellectuals drew criticisms from Marxists and anti-Marxists alike. Karl Popper famously argued that this form of "socio-analysis" was likely to produce more sophisticated versions of self-deception rather than objective analysis (Popper 1950). Marxists, on the other hand, explored the role of intellectuals in the class struggle and emphasized the self-delusional nature of any notion of intellectuals as autonomous or independent of class interests. For instance, Antonio Gramsci (1971 [1929–35]: 5–23) distinguished between "traditional" and "organic" intellectuals. Whereas the former defined themselves as independent of other classes, developed a distinctive culture, but unwittingly served the interests of the ruling class, the latter were fully aware of the interests of the subordinate class and actively worked with its members to bring about political change.

By the mid-twentieth century, the centre of gravity within the sociology of knowledge moved to the United States and became intertwined with structural-functionalism, as typified by Robert K. Merton's writings on the sociology of science and Talcott Parsons' study of the American university. These American studies were more empirically driven than their German counterparts, and Merton coined the term "theories of the middle range" to refer precisely to the balance required in research between theory and empirical data. Among Merton's contributions to the sociology of science are his doctoral dissertation on science and technology in seventeenth-century England and seminal articles – notably "The Matthew Effect in Science" – about the motivational and institutional structures of modern science (Merton 1968). By the 1960s and 1970s, however, a different strand emerged in the Anglophone sociology of knowledge, one initially centred in Edinburgh, and partly influenced by the later Wittgenstein and by Thomas Kuhn's *The Structure of Scientific Revolutions* (1962). The "strong programme" in the sociology of knowledge adopted the principle of symmetry, according to which not only "false" but also "true" scientific beliefs had to be explained in terms of social causation (see, for instance, Bloor 1991; Barnes, Bloor, and Henry 1996). The strong programme led to accusations of relativism, and subsequent developments within science studies, such as calls for attributing equal causal power to non-human agents, can be seen as attempts to avoid charges of "sociologism" by placing nature and society on the same ontological plane (see, for instance, Latour 2005). From the point of view of the sociology of intellectual life, the strength of both the strong programme and subsequent actor-network theory lies in exploring empirically how scientific activities, rather than corresponding to a methodological algorithm, are embedded in complex networks of social relations, objects, and practices.

In addition to these developments within the sociology of knowledge and the sociology of science, American sociologists in the 1960s and 1970s showed increasing interest in the pivotal role of intellectuals within modern societies. While the term "new class" was initially used to refer to the central position of intellectuals in Easter Bloc bureaucracies, scholars such as Daniel Bell (1973) and Alvin Gouldner (1979) appropriated this concept, first, to hint at a possible convergence between capitalist and socialist societies, and, second, to describe a "post-industrial" setting in which the use of scientific expertise in state planning is the order of the day. In this society, intellectuals are no longer placed in a subservient relationship to a particular class, as Gramsci had thought of traditional intellectuals. Nor, however, were they devoted, as Benda hoped they would be, to the pursuit of other-worldly endeavours. Rather, "intellectuals" had become knowledge-producers who were essential to the functioning of contemporary society. The proponents of this theory were, on the whole, congenial toward the developments they were describing, but they remained concerned about the ways in which these newly empowered intellectuals – both "critical intellectuals" and "technical intelligentsia" – might misuse their position to serve their own interests.

During the course of the 1970s and 1980s, the theory of the new class lost appeal, partly because of the increasing awareness of the lack of empirical support for the theory. More generally, there was a growing literature on the limitations on the impact of intellectuals on society. For instance, Zygmunt Bauman (1991) claimed that the notion of the intellectual as legislator is no longer pertinent. For Enlightenment philosophers, intellectuals developed superior knowledge and ethical and aesthetic judgement because they managed somehow to transcend the culture and language of their age. Bauman argued that this picture is no longer tenable because of widespread doubts about foundationalist philosophy. Instead, in conditions of post-modernity, intellectuals have become mere "interpreters" – skilful in making sense of alien cultures for members of their own. Robert Nisbet (1997) has developed a complementary argument, but focuses on the institutional dimensions of this shift. For him, universities are no longer insulated from society; they have become increasingly intertwined with industry and large-scale organizations. This means that academics no longer have the freedom and the authority that was associated with the era of the ivory tower. We will see in the next section how intellectual historians have treated this question of intellectuals in the era of the corporate university.

From the 1980s onwards, sociologists started to develop detailed empirical methods for studying intellectual life. Michèle Lamont's carefully crafted studies are indicative of this trend, from her study on the diffusion of Jacques Derrida's ideas in France and the US (Lamont 1987) to her recent analysis of the nature of academic judgement in relation to grant-funding bodies and disciplinary norms (Lamont 2009). Three important strands have emerged in what is now a full-fledged sociology of intellectuals: Pierre Bourdieu's reflexive sociology, Randall Collins' sociology of philosophies, and Charles Camic's new sociology of ideas. All three delineate empirical research programmes for the study of intellectual life.

Bourdieu was a remarkably versatile sociologist who wrote on a wide of range of issues, but three recurrent themes stand out. One theme is the need for sociologists to incorporate insights from both "objectivism" and "subjectivism." Although objective social structures have a constraining impact on human agency, any sociological analysis also needs to pay attention to agents' self-understandings of their actions. A second theme concerns the role of non-economic features of the social world in the reproduction of inequality: throughout his life, Bourdieu explored the extent to which differences in cultural, educational, and social resources contributed to the transmission of structures of class domination from one generation to the next. The third theme concerns "reflexive sociology" – that is, a sociology that does not shy away from applying sociological analysis to its own conditions of possibility. In the case of the sociology of intellectuals, the three themes are integrated in so far as Bourdieu explores the power differentials and inequalities within the intellectual arena, whether between academic disciplines, intellectual schools, or individual scholars.

Bourdieu's *Homo Academicus* and *The State Nobility* are among his most cited texts on the sociology of intellectuals (Bourdieu 1988, 1996). Bourdieu acknowledges that, in the past, the intellectual field has been intertwined with other fields, such as the arena of politics. But, in the course of the nineteenth century, the intellectual field managed to acquire a relative autonomy, to such an extent that it now operates more or less according to its own logic. For instance, what is unique about the intellectual field is that the power differentials and inequalities do not manifest themselves, primarily at least, in financial terms, but in terms of symbolic recognition. Bourdieu explores the asymmetries and power struggles between different academic disciplines and faculties, but he is particularly interested in the struggles for symbolic capital *within* disciplines. Depending on their *habitus* and personal "trajectory," some disciplinary practitioners are better equipped than others to compete in the struggle over these scarce symbolic–cultural resources. Successful agents have the right cultural and educational capital and are more likely to gain access to elite schools like, in the French case, the *École normale*; this entry in itself reinforces their dominant position because it provides access to the right kind of teachers and peers.

As Bourdieu himself was the first to admit, his own career raised reflexive problems concerning the place of the intellectual in society. For most of his career Bourdieu focused his energy on academic research and made a concerted effort to avoid taking on Sartre's mantle of the "total intellectual" who intervenes on a wide range of issues in the name of philosophy. But during the 1990s Bourdieu took on an increasingly prominent role as a public intellectual, arguing in particular against the neo-liberal policies of the Juppé government and more generally against the retrenchment of the welfare state. Ironically, around the same time, Bourdieu's *On Television*, which criticized both the medium of television and the media-intellectual that it helps to create, made him particularly well known outside the academy and turned him into something of a celebrity (Bourdieu 1998). This short book, based on two public lectures he gave on television (hence the *double entendre* of the title), warns that this medium undermines the public sphere and turns politics into entertainment. Intellectuals have been complicit in this and should resist the temptation to succumb to the homogenizing features of the journalistic field and its reliance on sound-bites. In the last years of his life, Bourdieu elaborated on the role of the public intellectual, relying to a certain extent on Michel Foucault's notion of the "specific intellectual" who uses his specialized knowledge to help fight local struggles. Bourdieu argued for a "scholarship with commitment" that promotes a "new internationalism" to tackle global issues that transcend national boundaries, and to counteract the ideology of "global competitiveness" (Bourdieu 1999, 2003).

Like the work of Bourdieu, Randall Collins' *The Sociology of Philosophies: A Global Theory of Intellectual Change* is an ambitious attempt to develop an all-embracing sociology of intellectual life. Collins applies it to the history of philosophy (Collins 1998). His theory operates at three levels: first, the macro-level or "economic-political structures"; second, the institutional level which comprises, for instance, universities and publishing companies; and, finally, the micro-level which involves the interactions between intellectuals. But the focus of his theory is primarily on those interactions or "networks" among philosophers. Collins tries to explore which conditions make promising scholars more likely to develop into prominent philosophers. The answer lies, according to Collins, in the networks they manage to forge with other major philosophers. Through connections with prominent mentors, philosophers accumulate "emotional energy" and "cultural capital." Emotional energy gives scholars the necessary motivation and self-confidence to work hard and to be prolific. Philosophy is not a particularly lucrative enterprise and the end products of philosophical activities, in temporal terms, often lie far away, so emotional energy can dwindle quite easily if the right kind of networks are not available. Cultural capital, on the other hand, provides philosophers with a sense of what is important and worth exploring and what are the new trends. In principle, there are no limits to philosophical thinking, but very few philosophical steps are crucial contributions to the field; being connected with other influential philosophers provides the necessary intellectual compass to make the right steps.

Collins is a proponent of what is called "conflict theory" in sociology, an agonistic position that he extends to the sociology of knowledge. Conflict and antagonism imply that, at any point in time, at least two philosophical schools battle it out for supremacy. Collins goes on to argue that there is an upper and lower limit to the number of creative philosophical schools that can co-exist. He proposes the law of small numbers which says that, at any one time, there will be between three and six creative schools of thought. When only two major schools are in play, a third is likely to develop. When the number of co-existing schools surpasses six, it becomes more difficult to recruit new disciples and to secure future generations of disciples. Very quickly some philosophical schools will start losing support until between three and six schools remain.

In contrast with Collins, the "new sociology of ideas" of Charles Camic and Neil Gross (2001) does not aim to develop a general theoretical framework that captures the macro-, meso-, and micro-dimensions of intellectual life. Rather, it focuses on the specific strategies that scholars develop to operate and manoeuvre within the local intellectual contexts in which they find themselves. Hence "contextualism" and "localism" are two key methodological positions in their vision of the field. Camic's analysis of Talcott Parsons' early writings is a clear example of this method in action. In his highly influential article "The Making of a Method: A Historical Reinterpretation of the Early Parsons," Camic carefully reconstructs the academic culture, prejudices, and power relations at Harvard up to the appearance of Parsons' *The Structure of Social Action* in 1937 (Camic 1987). This reconstruction explains why Parsons embraced orthodox neoclassicism rather than institutionalism as his paradigm of economic theory. In comparison with orthodox neoclassical economics, which was well established at Harvard, the more sociological institutionalist tradition in American economics lacked status and institutional recognition in the precincts of Harvard Yard, and the young Parsons had to navigate carefully within this treacherous terrain. The ambition of institutional economists to develop a "science of society as a whole" could potentially undermine any attempt by sociology to carve a niche for itself, just as it would also undermine the separate identity of economics. It is therefore no surprise that Parsons sided with his colleagues in Harvard's Department of Economics to embrace, to a certain extent at least, the methodological principles of neoclassical thinking.

In a subsequent article, Camic (1992) argues against the "content-fit model of predecessor selection," which states that scholars select intellectual predecessors on the basis of how well they tie in with their own project. Instead, Camic argues in favour of the "reputational model" which assumes that scholars select intellectual predecessors on the basis of their "reputational standing" within their local intellectual context. Camic's argument is that Parsons did precisely that: while developing his ideas about sociological theory, he was drawn to authors (Marshall, Pareto, Weber, and Durkheim) who had considerable standing among leading Harvard faculty and gradually abandoned those (such as institutionalists Thorstein Veblen, Walton Hamilton, and Clarence Ayres) who did not. Camic is not arguing that Parsons developed explicit strategies in this regard. Rather, this "crystallization occurred while he was part of a well-signposted intellectual network that warned him of the defectiveness and uselessness of some lines of relevant work while announcing the greatness, brilliance, and fruitfulness of other lines" (Camic 1992: 437).

Neil Gross, Camic's student, has continued this careful historical work on the trajectory and strategies of individual scholars, but he differs from Camic in putting more weight on the role of the "self-concept" of the academic intellectual. By self-concept, he refers to the ideas intellectuals form about themselves and which ultimately guide their work and career. His biography of the American philosopher Richard Rorty examines how Rorty developed a clear sense of himself as a progressive, humanist intellectual and how this self-concept fed into his intellectual and professional trajectory (Gross 2008). We discover how Rorty learned to operate within the contours of an American philosophical profession increasingly dominated by an "analytic" mainstream. Whilst there is undoubtedly a sociological dimension to this analysis – in particular, when Gross investigates the specific intellectual milieu in which Rorty grew up and which helped to form his sense of intellectual identity – Gross' focus on intellectual biography, in conjunction with his notion of self-concept, gives this type of sociology of ideas a particularly social–psychological flavour.

With the new sociology of ideas, the sociology of knowledge has moved remarkably close to intellectual history, but before we elaborate on the latter, it is important to point out that the sociology of sociology has been essential to recent debates within the direction of the discipline itself. This is particularly striking in the recent furore around "public sociology" (Agger 2000; Burawoy 2005). Indeed, Michael Burawoy's arguments in favour of a public sociology rest upon a sociological analysis of the history of the discipline. Burawoy contends that "traditional" forms of public sociology had been prevalent for a long time, and that for half a century the need for professional and academic recognition has turned American sociology into an increasingly inward-looking enterprise. For Burawoy, now that sociology has obtained the recognition it deserves, there is no need to continue along this defensive track. This is not to argue that we ought to resurrect traditional public sociology. We need to move towards what he calls "organic" public sociology – with an obvious hint to Gramsci. Whereas traditional public sociology has an amorphous, passive, and diffuse audience and lacks a clear political agenda, Burawoy's "organic" public sociology focuses on a visible and active audience and has an explicit political message.

Intellectuals in History

We now turn from historical reflections on the development of the sociology of knowledge to sociological perspectives on recent forms of intellectual history. This segue from sociology to history is becoming more and more natural. One of the defining features of the new sociology of ideas has been its invocation of the methods of intellectual history. From Quentin Skinner,

J. G. A. Pocock, and John Dunn, Camic and Gross (2001) learned the contextualist maxim that texts and ideas are "not transparent" but "must be situated in the immediate socio-linguistic contexts in which they were produced – contexts that can be reconstructed by careful examination of the writings of a thinker's contemporaries." "Localism" follows from this contextualist position: by "insisting on the need to reconstruct the context where ideas were produced, new sociologists of ideas generally hold as well that this reconstruction must have a strong local focus" (Camic and Gross 2001: 245–6). The methodological resources, as well as the empirical findings, of intellectual history are therefore directly pertinent to the sociology of ideas. This section of the chapter explores the linkages between these two fields and throws historical light on the place of intellectuals in social and political theory.

Our first observation is that the roots of the new sociology of ideas in contextualist intellectual history run even deeper than Camic and Gross suggest. The shift within the sociology of knowledge from the analysis of *ideas* to the study of *intellectuals* – from bodies of institutionalized knowledge à la Marx and Mannheim to the microsociological activities of knowledge-makers – maps neatly onto the methodological move made by contextualist historians. Famously, Quentin Skinner has inveighed against the notion, common among political theorists and historians of political thought of the post-World War II decades, that political or moral concepts might be detached from the particular arguments in which they were articulated and treated as more or less "coherent" and "perennial" doctrines (Skinner 1969). What was missing in such accounts, Skinner argues, was an appreciation of what the authors in question were *doing* in writing what they did. Invoking the linguistic pragmatism of the later Wittgenstein, and especially the theory of speech acts delineated by J. L. Austin, Skinner has sought to mark out a realm of linguistic action that is integral to the interpretation of texts (Skinner 2002). But this is to move "attention away from 'meanings' and towards questions about agency, usage, and especially intentionality" (Skinner 2002: 2.). In other words, the contextualist turn to speech acts, to what authors self-consciously thought they were doing in making particular claims in particular texts, naturally involves the study of political, social, and moral theorists as *actors* within discrete social contexts: contextualism leads us to the sociology of the knowledge-makers.

In practice, the so-called Cambridge School in the history of political thought has tended to split between those, like Pocock, who prefer to focus on the broad structures of "political languages," and those, like Skinner, who concentrate on the "innovating ideologists" whose rhetorical virtuosity reshapes our normative political languages (Bevir 1999). Nonetheless, the general thrust of contextual intellectual historiography has been to treat canonical figures such as Machiavelli, Hobbes, Locke, and Smith as "theory-politicians" engaged in ideological contests with other such "politicians" over the legitimation of the questionable political and social practices of their day (Palonen 2003). Texts like *Leviathan* or *The Wealth of Nations* are thus read as attempts to extend, retract, or displace the application of normative concepts to contested institutions or practices – as, for example, we see in the attempt by Hobbes to redefine the meaning of "liberty" in the context of his defence of absolute monarchy (Skinner 2008). We should recognize, then, that contextualist historiography in the tradition of Skinner and Pocock vouchsafes an important set of analytical tools for making sense of political and social theorizing *as* political and social practices.

If, however, the new sociology of ideas defines itself, in part, as the study of *intellectuals* in their respective social fields, then there is an element of anachronism in the appeal to the scholarship of the Cambridge School. To explain: it is misleading to speak of Hobbes or Smith as "intellectuals," for this is a term of nineteenth-century Anglophone coinage (Collini 2006: 18), and was perforce most certainly not an actors' category or an intelligible social role in the early modern period. The contextualist approach has in fact been extended by sociologists of ideas and intellectual historians into the nineteenth and twentieth centuries (Camic 1991; Gross 2008). But, in addition to this extension of contextualist method, we must also note a second point of access that intellectual history has provided for the sociology of intellectuals: the history of academic disciplines. This may seem a counterintuitive claim, given our earlier suggestion that intellectuals are those who break the bounds of pure expertise, so let us start with some basic historiographical observations.

Putting a text or a thinker "in context" requires, as we have just noted, the reconstruction of hand-to-hand battles over the application of legitimizing (or delegitimizing) concepts to contested social and political practices; such a task usually entails the mapping of a local network or community in which the terms of dispute were understood and the issues at hand thrashed out. Now, when we deal with "intellectuals" or knowledge-producers in the modern period, such local networks often centre on academic disciplines, the function of which is to train neophytes in the often esoteric practices and problematics of the field in question. Hence another core strand in the intellectual–historical study of intellectuals is the investigation of the formation and dissipation of disciplines, and the cultural capital that accrues from the expertise they provide.

In its earliest phases, the history of disciplines was polarized between "discipline history" and "intellectual history" (Collini 1988), or, in slightly different terms, between "disciplinary history" and "the history of disciplines" (Novick 1988). Pioneers such as the historian of anthropology George Stocking recorded a gulf between the "internal" histories of disciplines that practitioners told themselves and the more contextual histories that those who mined the disciplines for historical insights were apt to write (Stocking 1965). In recent decades, however, two factors have combined to make this dichotomy less salient (Geary 2008). First, practitioners' histories, perhaps unsurprisingly, have profited from an increasingly sophisticated literature on the history of disciplines, and, in some cases, have become reflexive in their treatment of the notions of tradition, conceptual change, and the construction disciplinary boundaries. Volumes on history (Novick 1988), sociology (Calhoun 2007), economics (Mirowski 2002), and political science (Adcock, Bevir, and Stimson 2007) self-consciously tread the line between discipline history and intellectual history, and tend to be produced by figures with allegiances both to history and to the discipline they seek to investigate. Second, historical studies of the nature of discipline formation, pedagogy, and the exercise of specialist expertise have helped make clear what is involved in the reproduction of academic disciplines. The history and sociology of science has been central to these developments, with the suggestive remarks of Kuhn (1962) on the grounds of scientific communal norms and Michael Polanyi (1958) on the "tacit knowledge" required for expert practices inspiring more recent work on experimental and theoretical practices and the "power of pedagogy" in the creation of scientific communities (Warwick 2003; Kaiser 2005a, 2005b).

As a result of these changes, we find more scholars moving back and forth across the formerly sharp divide between internal and external histories of disciplines, and between history and sociology. The University of Chicago sociologist Andrew Abbott is a good example of the new ecumenism. Abbott has contributed both to the history of sociology, in the form of a local history of the Chicago School of sociology (Abbott 1999), and to the formal sociology of disciplines (Abbott 2000). More importantly, the sharpening of our historical appreciation of the structure and reproduction of disciplinary expertise helps to make the analytical category of "intellectuals" somewhat clearer. To return to our earlier distinction, the social role of intellectuals and public intellectuals can be grasped against the background of the possession of expertise. An account of in what "expertise" consists is exactly what the new literature on the history and sociology of disciplines, with its emphasis on pedagogy, training, and research tools, gives us. Many intellectuals are disciplinary experts who speak to publics outside their own discipline.

The historian Stefan Collini invokes a similar "structure of relations" in defining the socio-logical conditions for the performance of the role of the intellectual (2006). One of the fundamental conditions of this role, he has argued, is a "qualifying activity" that "is seen *both* as cultivating mental and imaginative capacities beyond the ordinary *and* as issuing in certain kinds of truths or understanding that exceed what is required for merely technical contributions to the practical and economic life of that society" (p. 54). While such an activity may not always involve the possession of distinction in a scientific or scholarly discipline, being distinguished in academic research is exactly the sort of qualification that has allowed many modern intellectuals, from Raymond Aron to Noam Chomsky, to make their names. A number of recent intellectual biographies of figures such as William James, J. Robert Oppenheimer, and Henry Kissinger zero in on the delicate interplay between expert knowledge and extra-disciplinary claims to political or cultural authority (Thorpe 2006; Suri 2007; Bordogna 2008).

These considerations bring us face to face with more directly historical questions about intellectuals in politics. Needless to say, a comprehensive survey of this issue lies far beyond the remit of this chapter. But we can suggest a central theme or problematic: the increasing difficulty of defining a social group or class of intellectuals and assessing their "impact" upon society and policy. The foregoing reflections on the shared methods and agendas of intellectual history and the sociology of ideas have sought to demonstrate the increasingly wide array of practices and institutions needed to make sense of intellectual life. A set of moving targets is in play: intellectuals, disciplines, and publics. The historical referents of each of these terms, as much recent historical literature attests, have been extremely diverse. Before we fill out this observation, however, we must note that the plasticity of these concepts and the practices they map is sometimes obscured by the persistence of some rigid cultural prejudices about the history of intellectuals.

The first, largely negative, trope centres on the notion that intellectuals betray their vocational commitment to universal, nonpartisan truth when they engage in the messy world of real politics, and that the results of such engagements tend to be politically and intellectually deleterious. This was the guiding theme of Benda's *La trahison des clercs*, but we can find similarly critical judgments of intellectuals in politics in subsequent tracts written by the likes of Raymond Aron (1957), Mark Lilla (2001), and Thomas Sowell (2010). Another view, more positive if also nostalgic, is that the intellectual has the "responsibility" to speak truth to power, but that this public, critical vocation of the intellectual has today, in the era of academic specialization, been lost. This is a position that – in a sign of the ambiguity of Benda's famous text – has been ascribed to Benda himself, and which has found its way into important recent books by figures including Edward Said (1994) and Russell Jacoby (1987).

The difficulty with jeremiads and lamentations of this sort is that they tend to treat one particular historical instantiation of the public intellectual as the normative model for all other times and places. Often, a "Victorian" image of humanist intellectuals such as Zola, Mill, or Emerson is at work, with the "public" in question that of the readership of wide-circulation periodicals or the audiences that gathered in lyceums and public lecture theatres. Undoubtedly, the professionalized disciplinary sociologist, economist, or philosopher of the post-World War II decades would not measure up by comparison, and so one is not surprised to find "autopsies" and epitaphs for the public intellectual in the age of specialization (Jennings 2002; Posner 2001). As Collini has observed, however, we must not take such critiques at face value: the complaint that intellectuals have failed in politics, or the claim that they no longer have a role in public life, has frequently served as the very means by which "intellectuals" have sought to carve out a space in the society and politics of their time (Collini 2006).

Just as important a refutation of the transhistorical vision of intellectuals and society is the recognition that the very meaning of publics, disciplines, and intellectuals has changed, especially during the past half-century. For example, the boom in higher education in the United States after World War II blurred the line between the academy and the public, and between disciplines and national culture. On the one hand, the academic humanities took over the task of preserving and interpreting America's, and the West's, cultural heritage, a function that had previously belonged to men of letters and the "public moralists" of the Victorian era (Hollinger 2006). At the same time, the sheer volume of students attending college and graduate school meant that the academy, with its professors, students, and alumni, became a "public sphere" unto itself (Collini 1994). In an era of mass higher education, disciplines often became expansive institutions that produced the armies of specialists needed to staff the increasingly technical apparatus of America's educational and security infrastructure (Kaiser 2002). A figure such as the economist Walt Rostow could write a best-selling book on economic development and shape national security policy simultaneously (Milne 2008). As the United States battled with the Soviet Union to win the "Third World" for capitalist democracy, social and political scientists became key voices in the promotion of modernization initiatives in Asia, Africa, and Latin America (Latham 2000; Gilman 2003). Finally, scientists in possession of the most esoteric and demanding sorts of specialized technical knowledge, men like the theoretical physicist J. Robert Oppenheimer, became central figures in eminently political debates about security and energy policy. (Schweber 2000; Thorpe 2006).

In such a world, traditional Victorian models of intellectuals, disciplines, and publics were no longer helpful; the lines connecting politics, policy, and expertise required sharper and more varied analytical tools, some of which we have surveyed above. The rethinking of the sociology of ideas, and of the social role of intellectuals, is an ongoing task to which sociology, science studies, and intellectual history can contribute.

References

Abbott, Andrew. 1999. *Department and Discipline: Chicago Sociology at One Hundred*. Chicago, IL: University of Chicago Press.

——2000. *Chaos of Disciplines*. Chicago, IL: University of Chicago Press.

Adcock, Robert, Mark Bevir, and Shannon C. Stimson. 2007. *Modern Political Science: Anglo-American Exchanges since 1880*. Princeton, NJ: Princeton University Press.

Agger, Ben. 2000. *Public Sociology: From Social Facts to Literary Acts*. Lanham, MD: Rowman & Littlefied.

Aron, Raymond. 1957. *The Opium of the Intellectuals*. Trans. Terence Kilmartin. London: Secker & Warburg.

Barnes, Barry, David Bloor, and John Henry. 1996. *Scientific Knowledge: A Sociological Analysis*. Chicago, IL: University of Chicago Press.

Bauman, Zygmunt. 1991. *Legislators and Interpreters: On Modernity, Postmodernity, and Intellectuals*. Cambridge: Polity.

Bell, Daniel. 1973. *The Coming of Post-industrial Society: A Venture in Social Forecasting*. New York: Basic Books.

Benda, Julien. 1928 [1927]. *The Treason of the Intellectuals*. New York: William Morrow.

Bevir, Mark. 1999. *The Logic of the History of Ideas*. Cambridge: Cambridge University Press.

Bloor, David. 1991. *Knowledge and Social Imaginary*. Chicago, IL: University of Chicago Press.

Bordogna, Francesca. 2008. *William James at the Boundaries: Philosophy, Science, and the Geography of Knowledge*. Chicago, IL: University of Chicago Press.

Bourdieu, Pierre. 1988. *Homo Academicus*. Cambridge: Polity Press.

——1996. *State Nobility: Elite Schools in the Field of Power*. Cambridge: Polity Press.

——1998. *On Television*. New York: New Press.

——1999. *Acts of Resistance: Against the Tyranny of the Market*. New York: New Press.

——2003. *Firing Back: Against the Tyranny of the Market II*. London: Verso.

Burawoy, Michael. 2005. "For Public Sociology." *American Sociological Review*, 70: 4–28.

Calhoun, Craig, ed. 2007. *Sociology in America: A History*. Chicago, IL: University of Chicago Press.

Camic, Charles. 1987. "The Making of a Method: A Historical Reinterpretation of the Early Parsons." *American Sociological Review*, 52. 4: 421–39.

——1991. "Introduction: Talcott Parsons before *The Structure of Social Action*." In *Talcott Parsons: The Early Essays*, ed. Charles Camic. Chicago, IL: University of Chicago Press.

——1992. "Reputation and Predecessor Selection: Parsons and the Institutionalists." *American Sociological Review*, 57. 4: 421–45.

Camic, Charles and Neil Gross. 2001. "The New Sociology of Ideas." In *The Blackwell Companion to Sociology*, ed. Judith R. Blau. Oxford: Blackwell.

Collini, Stefan. 1988. "'Discipline History and 'Intellectual History': Reflections on the Historiography of the Social Sciences in Britain and France." *Revue de Synthese*, 101. 3: 387–99.

——1994. "My Public is Bigger than Yours: Professors, Critics, and Other Intellectuals." *Journal of the History of the Behavioral Sciences*, 30. 4: 380–7.

——2006. *Absent Minds: Intellectuals in Britain*. Oxford: Oxford University Press.

Collins, Randall. 1998. *The Sociology of Philosophies: A Global Theory of Intellectual Change*. Cambridge, MA: Harvard University Press.

Geary, Daniel. 2008. "Every Social Scientist Her Own Historian." *Modern Intellectual History*, 5. 2: 399–410.

Gilman, Nils. 2003. *Mandarins of the Future: Modernization Theory in Cold War America*. Baltimore, MD: Johns Hopkins University Press.

Gouldner, Alvin. 1979. *The Future of Intellectuals and the Rise of the New Class*. New York: Seabury.

Gramsci, Antonio. 1971 [1929–35]. *Selections from the Prison Notebooks of Antonio Gramsci*. New York: International Publishers.

Gross, Neil. 2008. *Richard Rorty: The Making of an American Philosopher*. Chicago, IL: University of Chicago Press.

Hollinger, David, ed. 2006. *The Humanities and the Dynamics of Inclusion since World War II*. Baltimore, MD: Johns Hopkins University Press.

Jacoby, Russell. 1987. *The Last Intellectuals: American Culture in the Age of Academe*. New York: Basic Books.

Jennings, Jeremy. 2002. "Deaths of the Intellectual: A Comparative Autopsy." In *The Public Intellectual*, ed. Helen Small. Oxford: Blackwell.

Kaiser, David. 2002. "Cold War Requisitions, Scientific Manpower, and the Production of American Physicists after World War II." *Historical Studies in the Physical and Biological Sciences*, 33: 131–59.

——2005a. *Drawing Theories Apart: The Dispersion of Feynman Diagrams in Postwar Physics*. Chicago, IL: University of Chicago Press.

——2005b. *Pedagogy and the Practice of Science*. Cambridge, MA: MIT Press.

Kuhn, Thomas. 1962. *The Structure of Scientific Revolutions*. Chicago, IL: University of Chicago Press.

Lamont, Michele. 1987. "How to Become a Dominant French Philosopher. The Case of Jacques Derrida." *American Journal of Sociology*, 93. 3: 584–622.

——2009. *How Professors Think: Inside the Curious World of Academic Judgement*. Cambridge, MA: Harvard University Press.

Latham, Michael E. 2000. *Modernization as Ideology: American Social Science and 'Nation-Building' in the Kennedy Era*. Chapel Hill, NC: University of North Carolina Press.

Latour, Bruno. 2005. *Reassembling the Social: An Introduction to Actor-Network-Theory*. Oxford: Oxford University Press.

Lilla, Mark. 2001. *The Reckless Mind: Intellectuals in Politics*. New York: New York Review of Books.

Mannheim, Karl. 1936 [1929]. *Ideology and Utopia*. London: Routledge & Kegan Paul.

Merton, Robert K. 1968. "The Matthew Effect in Science: The Reward and Communication Systems of Science are Reconsidered." *Science*, 159. 3810: 56–63.

Milne, David. 2008. *America's Rasputin: Walt Rostow and the Vietnam War*. New York: Hill & Wang.

Mirowski, Philip. 2002. *Machine Dreams: Economics Becomes a Cyborg Science*. Cambridge: Cambridge University Press.

Nisbet, Robert. 1997. *The Degradation of the Academic Dogma*, 2nd edn. New Jersey: Transaction Publishers.

Novick, Peter. 1988. *That Noble Dream: The 'Objectivity Question' and the American Historical Profession*. Cambridge: Cambridge University Press.

Palonen, Kari. 2003. *Quentin Skinner: History, Politics, Rhetoric*. Cambridge: Polity Press.

Polanyi, Michael. 1958. *Personal Knowledge: Towards a Post-critical Philosophy*. London: Routledge & Kegan Paul.

Popper, Karl. 1950. *The Open Society and its Enemies*. Princeton, NJ: Princeton University Press.

Posner, Richard A. 2001. *Public Intellectuals: A Study of Decline*. Cambridge, MA: Harvard University Press.

Said, Edward. 1994. *Representations of the Intellectual*. London: Vintage.

Schweber, S. S. 2000. *In the Shadow of the Bomb: Oppenheimer, Bethe, and the Moral Responsibility of the Scientist*. Princeton, NJ: Princeton University Press.

Skinner, Quentin. 1969. "Meaning and Understanding in the History of Ideas." *History and Theory*, 8. 1: 3–53.

——2002. *Visions of Politics*, vol. 1: *Regarding Method*. Cambridge: Cambridge University Press.

——2008. *Hobbes and Republican Liberty*. Cambridge: Cambridge University Press.

Sowell, Thomas. 2010. *Intellectuals and Society*. New York: Basic Books.

Stocking, George. 1965. "On the Limits of 'Presentism' and 'Historicism' in the Historiography of the Behaviorial Sciences." *Journal of the History of the Behavioral Sciences*, 1. 3: 211–18.

Suri, Jeremy. 2007. *Henry Kissinger and the American Century*. Cambridge, MA: Harvard University Press.

Thorpe, Charles. 2006. *Oppenheimer: The Tragic Intellect*. Chicago, IL: University of Chicago Press.

Warwick, Andrew. 2003. *Masters of Theory: Cambridge and the Rise of Mathematical Physics*. Chicago, IL: University of Chicago Press.

Part 2
New and Emerging Frameworks

Power, Legitimacy, and Authority

Stewart Clegg

Any sociological discussion of the relations between power, legitimacy, and authority must start with Max Weber, and some vexed issues of translation, for it was Weber who first developed a systematic account of these terms as the cornerstone of his social theory. The chapter will begin with an outline of Weber's views of power, legitimacy, and authority, and the interpretation of these in translation. It will then move to consideration of the functionalist theoretical context into which Weber was translated and its extension in Parsons' work. Finally, the chapter will address the recent centrality of dimensional analysis to debates about power in which it is argued that the most subtle and profound power relations are those where actors assume the legitimacy of systems of belief that do not represent their real interests.

Max Weber

By the dawn of the twentieth century Max Weber was already a minor if not yet significant intellectual in Germany. He had recently completed his essays on the 'protestant ethic' (Weber 1976) and was soon to create most of what we now know as his writings on power, legitimacy, and authority in the early years of the twentieth century. In translation ideas inevitably change. Weber's rugged realism, which was most evident in the centrality of *Herrschaft* or domination to his scheme of thought (see Roth in Weber 1978: lxxxviii) noting in his introduction to *Economy and Society*, that the sociology of domination is the book's core), was invariably translated as if it had the qualifier of legitimacy attached to it.

In the German language, *Autorität* is rarely used to denominate a *process*; in fact, it is almost exclusively used as an *attribute* of a particular person or office. So, one does not usually 'exercise authority' (*Autorität Ausüben*), as one would say in English, but one would only 'exercise power/ domination' (*Macht/Herrschaft*). Hence, someone is more likely to have (possess) *Autorität* rather than exercise (*Ausüben*) it. Also, *Autorität* would be only loosely coupled to legitimacy (someone can have *Autorität* as a person, although the legitimacy of the office is in question and vice versa). So, *Autorität* is more a personal attribute that tends to accompany (if not necessarily so) the exercise of power/domination, at least in German. In English the matters are somewhat different; authority is not merely a positional attribute but can also be something that is observable in process when words and deeds deepen or cheapen the legitimacy of authority, it is not irrevocably attached to positions. While Weber's (1947) translation by Parsons and Henderson emphasized a fair German interpretation it was also one which happened to correspond with the assumptions of functionalist theories. As Cohen, Hazelrigg and Pope (1975a, 1975b) establish, following Gouldner's (1971) tracks, there is every need to 'de-Parsonize' Weber despite Parsons' (1975) objections to the contrary.

Two central Weberian categories, in the original German, were *Macht* and *Herrschaft*. The precise translation of these terms is contested. Initially, they entered into usage as 'power' and 'authority', respectively. Weber defined power in various but related ways in his writings, but his most concise definition is that power is 'the possibility of imposing one's will upon the behavior of other persons' (Weber 1954: 324), and, as he often added, especially where this will is resisted by those over whom it is exercised, regardless of the basis on which the probability of obedience rested (Weber 1978: 53). We may recognize a debt to Nietzsche's (1973) 'will to power' (Schroeder 1987) in the centrality of the notion of will to his conception of power. While there is little controversy surrounding the translation of *Macht* as power (as an active verb rather than a passive noun, although, it should be noted, that 'might' is seen by some scholars as a more appropriate translation), there is considerable dissent surrounding the translation of *Herrschaft* as authority that was initiated by Parsons and Henderson in their edition of *The theory of social and economic organization* (Weber 1947). Later translators do not follow this lead but instead translate it either as 'rule' or 'domination', depending on the context of translation. For one thing, it is necessary in order to recover some sense of the indebtedness that Weber had to German philosophical and literary figures, such as Nietzsche and Goethe (Kent 1983). (On the Nietzsche connections see Fleischmann 1964; Eden 1983; Schroeder 1987; Sica 1988; and Hennis 1988; for the most obvious connection to Goethe see the new edition of his *Elective Affinities* (2005)).

Weber's Domination and Parsons' Authority

Weber introduced the term *Herrschaft* 'as the probability that a command with a given specific content will be obeyed by a given group of persons' (Weber 1978: 53). Where obedience occurs, we have an example of legitimate *Herrschaft*, which Parsons and Henderson appropriately translate as authority. The concept of legitimate *Herrschaft* refers to legitimate, non-coercive rule. Thus, authority is a relationship of legitimate rule, where the meaningfulness of the social relation rests on assumptions accepted without imposition by all parties to that relationship. Both relations of power and legitimate rule must occur within specific spheres, a structure of dominancy conceived as an order 'regarded by the actor as in some way obligatory or exemplary' governing the organization (Weber 1978: 31). The formal structures of dominancy will be experienced as differing substantive types of rule, within which it is probable that there will be willing obedience. Any bureaucracy is an example of a structure of dominancy, although they might vary in their substantive particulars; should it be the case that values infuse its members, binding them with commitments to its rule, then the structure of dominancy may be transformed into a structure of authority, perhaps where the rule is infused with an ultimate value or is taken for granted and accepted as a legally rational basis for constraining action.

In modern organizations, Weber argues, formal rationality would be best institutionalized, and domination most complete, when rationality is accepted as legitimate in its own terms. Such a state of affairs would be what Weber defined as 'authority'. Thus, authority is legitimated domination, one leading to the other. They are not qualitatively different from each other. The differences between them are ones of degree, not of kind. In this regard power and authority are opposed to violence as a mode of dominance, and are themselves specific forms of dominance.

Although Weber is commonly construed as a theorist of authority, in terms of the three types of what Weber refers to as *Herrschaft*, they are, in fact, types of domination. Authority is a social relation that stands at the outer limits of a more probable range of social relations of domination. These relations constitute the normalcy of organization – where there is a probability of resistance – which only shades into authority when the subject owes an allegiance that enables them to legitimate their subjection to an external source of domination. It should be evident that authority derives its legitimacy from the ruled not those ruling. Hence, organizational politics, premised on the necessity of acts of power by putative authorities to counter resistance to their imposition of their will, is something to be expected as normal. It will usually be the case that, despite charisma, tradition, discipline or vocation, situations ensue where there is resistance by some to the will of some other.

Domination

Domination requires organization, concerted action by a body of people employed as staff, to execute commands, and, conversely, all organization requires domination in that the power of command over the staff must be vested in an individual or a group of individuals, in an organization of any scale; hence, the necessity of a division of labor. What is most remarkable about any organization is the way that it shapes superordinate goals that others orient to; in this way, these others will do things that they would not otherwise do and thus will be subject to power. Their social action is constrained and enabled by the manifest will or command of the ruler, rulers, or rules. These are meant to influence the conduct of the rule; that is what they are designed for. Whether or not the rules achieve their purpose is not something to take for granted; the effective legitimacy of rule should never be assumed but is always an empirical matter. Should the rule(r)s positively influence the social action that occurs within the context of organizationally enabled action, it will only be so to the extent that those ruled make the content of the command – its will to power – the maxim of their conduct for its own sake. Of course, the rulers can tilt the probability in their favor by acculturating others to the habitual obedience of commands; they can constitute the others as subjects with a personal interest in seeing the existing domination continue because they derive benefits from it; they can hold out the promise of the pleasures of future rule through participation in domination to the subaltern ranks by dividing some elements of the exercise of functions among them, and they always hold a power of dismissal should these incentives fail.

The power of command can exist irrespective of the sense of duty to obey; when that duty is present then the command may be felt as a legitimate obligation to an authority; with a sense of duty power is transformed into authority, where the legitimacy of rule and rules is accepted. Where power is bereft of that sense of duty it shades into domination, defined as the non-legitimate imposition of will. It should be evident that the judgment of the legitimacy or otherwise of rule – whether it is authority – is not a prerogative of the rulers but of the putatively ruled. It is for this reason that power, as a social relation, will be inherently dynamic. While claims as to power's efficacy are made each time that an organizational action is enacted through command (whether habitual, written, spoken, ruled, or construed in any other way whatsoever) there is always the probability that the command will be met with resistance, either because in the context in which it is interpreted by those subject to it is not construed as being legitimate or, which amounts to the same thing, to resist it fits better with another more highly valued course of action than obedience to rule.

Command may be interpreted quite flexibly. Organizations seek to replace the necessity of frequent interventions into the body politic through a discipline of power that institutionalizes the domination of formal rationality; that is, the probability that a command with a given specific content will be obeyed (Weber 1978: 53). Now it is important not to interpret 'command' too literally; a command is not simply something that is necessarily expressed vocally, as in 'I command you to cease that at once'. A command also encompasses the orders that are received in writing or through other forms of representation, as well as the generalized duties associated with a particular office

The 'Iron Cage' of Discipline

Although Weber's interests were broad and many, the most important types of power discussed by Weber derive from a constellation of interests that develops on a formally free market and from established authority that allocates the right to command and the duty to obey (Weber 1954: 291). According to Weber the modern world increasingly strips social actors of their ability freely to choose the means and ends of their actions, particularly as it organizes through bureaucracy. In modernity institutions rationalize and organize affairs, cutting down on individual choices, replacing them with standardized procedures and rules. Rational calculation becomes a monstrous discipline. Everything and everyone seemingly had to be put through a calculus, irrespective of other values or pleasures. It was a necessary and unavoidable feature of organizing in the modern world.

Weber was pessimistic about the long-term impact of bureaucracy. On the one hand, bureaucracies would free people from arbitrary rule by powerful patrimonial leaders, those who personally owned the instruments and offices of rule. They would do this because they were based on rational legality as the rule of law contained in the files that defined practice in the bureau. On the other hand, they would create an 'iron cage of bondage' (or more literally as translated directly from the original German, a house of hardened steel). The frame was fashioned from the 'care for external goods' (Weber 1976: 181), by which Weber meant if these goods were to come into one's grasp in a market economy then one could gain them only by mortgaging one's life to a career in a hierarchy of offices that interlocked and intermeshed, through whose intricacies one might seek to move, with the best hope for ones future being that one would shift from being a small cog in the machine to one that was slightly bigger, in a slow but steady progression.

The iron cage would be fabricated increasingly from the materialization of abstract nouns such as calculability, predictability, and control, to which one must bend one's will. Thus, power concerned less the direct imposition of another's will on one and more the ways in which the conditions of one's existence were increasingly inscribed in a rationalized frame which one's will had to accommodate as a part of its assent to normalcy. Weber's example is bureaucracy, characterized by rules and regulations, hierarchy of authority, careers, and specialization of roles. The bureaucracy operates in a predictable manner, seeks to quantify, and emphasizes control over people and products through standardized and formalized routines, materializing the will to power.

Where an individual has so internalized commitment to a rational institution, such as the Civil Service, or Science, or Academia, that the commitment shapes their dispositions in such a way that their will knows little or no resistance to its formal rationality, then this represents obedience to an institutionalized will to power. Power, at its most powerful, is a relation that institutes itself in the psyche of the individual. Simmel (1964: 413) explored this when he examined how personality accommodates to the requirements of contemporary urban environments, emphasizing that punctuality, calculability, and exactness become part of modern personalities to the exclusion of 'those irrational, instinctive, sovereign traits and impulses which aim at determining the mode of life from within'.

Increasing self-discipline, meshing with intensified bureaucratization, rationalization, and individualization marked modernity in the social world. External constraint (sovereign power, traditional power) increasingly is replaced by internalization of constraint (disciplinary power, rational domination), assisted by technologies of power. As van Krieken (1990: 353) puts it, 'being modern means being disciplined, by the state [and other organizational forms], by each other and by ourselves; that the soul, both one's own and that of others, became organized into the self, an object of reflection and analysis, and, above all, transformable in the service of ideals such as productivity, virtue and strength'. More recent writers such as Elias (1982) and Foucault (1977) are wholly in accord with Simmel (1971) and Weber (1978) in these respects.

The modern, rationalized person is increasingly disciplined in discourses of power. Simmel saw domination as in part a function of the symbolic content of widely held ideas embedded in everyday practices of life and discourse. These are conceptualized as 'precepts', a term derived from the Latin *praeceptum*, meaning instruction, tutelage, injunction, or command. As Simmel (1971: 119) puts it, one becomes 'habituated' to the 'compulsory character' of these precepts 'until the cruder and subtler means of compulsion are no longer necessary', indeed, until ones 'nature' is so 'formed or reformed' by these precepts that one 'acts ... as if on impulse'. The individual in a situation of formal domination increasingly comes to be subordinated to 'objective principles' which they experience as a 'concrete object' whose necessity takes the form of a 'social requirement ... which must be satisfied for its own sake' (Simmel 1971: 11). Foucault (1977) did not put it better or clearer.

The Further Adventures of Authority

Because the stress in functionalism had been on social order and consensus rather than on contradiction and conflict, it had been widely believed that it lacked a theory of power – until Parsons (1964) provided it with one. That Parsons (1964) developed a theory of power was significant for functionalist analysis. Parsons defined the central problem of social theory as being able to answer how social order is possible and why society exists, rather than there being a bleak and violent war of all against all in a life that is nasty, brutish, poor, and short. In other words, how was it that what Hobbes (1914 [1651]) had conceptualized as a state of nature did not prevail? Parsons sought to show how order was possible on the basis of uncoerced action. He conceived of all forms of social action being organized in terms of four subsystems, two of which were specialized on political and economic rationalization, with the attendant risks of change and conflict, but there were also distinct spheres of integrative and normative processes whose task was to deal with those conflicts that arise.

These four processes were referred to as the conceptual and analytical universe of subsystems of adaptive, goal-oriented, integrative, and normative processes. The latter two subsystems provided a plurality of moral orders which countervail economic and organizational adaptation. Think of religious ethics holding up scientific research on human gene technology, for instance. There is always a gap between the expectations raised by some moral categories and the possibilities created by economic and political rationalities. Power is the medium whereby this gap is narrowed, in either direction, such that, despite moral and other differences, effective goal orientation is facilitated and efficient organization produced, using sanctions if necessary. These sanctions should be authoritative: for instance, shooting abortionists dead might be a sanction of the extreme right-to-life community, but it is not authoritative. What would be authoritative would be to use the law courts to challenge existing rulings and thus change the legislative framework within which abortion is practised. Challenging and changing existing rulings would indicate the sanctioned exercise of power. Thus, power is facilitative in Parsons' schema: it helps create binding obligations. And, if these are not obeyed, then authoritative sanctions can be enacted.

Power is similar to money, says Parsons (1964): both are circulatory media. Just as money functions as a generalized mechanism or means for securing satisfaction of desires within the economy – without money you may want things but one cannot buy them because one lacks 'effective demand' – so does power in political systems. Both power and money are anchored in popular confidence in their currency; it is this which provides them with their legitimacy. Given this legitimacy, power can be deployed in the expectation that others will respect it, and follow its injunctions, because the obligations that it places on those over whom its remit will run, will regard them as binding because of the perception of legitimacy. Symbolic legitimacy is the orderly background within which Parsons' view of power is embedded. Indeed, he theorizes power as the medium of order for social systems, including organizations. Power is defined as a generalized capacity to influence the allocation of resources for attaining collective goals. Members share institutionalized obligations by virtue of being members and within the context of membership certain sanctions as are legitimized through those obligations and institutionalized roles involved in the power system. Power is the legitimate mechanism regulating commitments. Authority, on the other hand, comprises the general rules that govern the making of specific binding decisions.

Parsons' view of power diverges from Weber's formulation of power within a context of domination. Instead, individuals are conceived as moral agents acting within a normative context; they are effectively socialized to be so. Where they are not, then socialization must be amiss. Thus, actors routinely use power not as a form of resistance to domination but as a way of ensuring the reproduction of authority, as a positive force, as a capacity to produce an effect. Thus, when power is exercised organizationally it is always within the context of binding obligations shared both by the power yielder and the power subject, and the sanctions that are threatened for non-compliance are always normatively constrained. One may not agree to consent but one does so in the knowledge of what one can expect the authorities to do in consequence. Deviance and resistance to power, because they call forth the appropriate sanctions, actually strengthen the organizational order, rather than weakening it. Barnes (1988: 26) refers to Parsons' views as normative determinism: it is easy to see why. The assumption is that norms are invariably operative and shared; when they are not then a failure of socialization mechanisms is held responsible. However, this is too strong a line – many forms of social action can flow from authentically held norms that do not happen to be shared by others who hold equally passionately to the authenticity of their norms. Much of life is like this.

Sometimes the public realm within which individual actions are enacted lacks the normative clarity and coherence that Parsons assumes. Consequently, the discursive availability of norms often function to fuel competing calculations of interest by different agents, who make estimates of the probability of sanctioning for the actions that they propose. Whatever normative order ensues is not so much the cause of the power actions that are taken as the result of these actions. Or, as Clegg (1989: 133) put it, 'normative order is the emergent effect of their calculations and differential access to, utilization of and effectiveness in sanctioning resources, just as much as is normative disorder'. We cannot assume a priori that the structures of what Weber termed dominancy will be legitimate and thus function as authority: it is a matter of empirical determination.

Habermas recognizes that 'a person taking orders is structurally disadvantaged in relation to a person with the power to give them' (Habermas 1987b: 271). In trying to make the subject do what is wanted, the ultimate sanction against non-compliance is the threat of withdrawing the continuing condition of membership. The right of withdrawal is clearly not reciprocal. The power-subject in a hierarchical relation lacks the authority to impose this as a sanction: some obligations are more binding than others, and some actors, those whom are hierarchically superordinate, are in a stronger position to impose them. They determine the conditions under which legitimacy is defined and authority dispensed. They can define what is seen to be authority, because it is legitimate, just as they can define what is not taken to be legitimate.

Power may be positive and may serve collective goals but only if one is incorporated within its remit. If one is other to power, if one is the object of its exercise by those who are its subjects, then its authority to do what it wants with one's life chances might seem rather less than legitimate. And this is what usually happens. Discursive participation in consensual goal formation is not a normal condition for most subordinate organization members. I don't need to agree with you to spend my money on something you sell; however, if I sell my labor to you, then there has to be some subjugation of my preferences, dispositions, and attitudes to those that are organizationally defined as legitimate. By accepting the offer of employment the assumption is made that this is a fair exchange; that one *wants* to be in *this* specific position of subordination. It all depends on the alternatives; short of many, most will accept almost anything, no matter how repugnant it may be.

Parsons argued that the creation of power normally 'presupposed consensus on system goals' (Haugaard 2003: 90), thus providing a framework within which facilitative power operated. Power only needed to be coercive when order broke down, periodically, and members needed to be disciplined – in order to reassert the central value system of the normative order. Power flows through the social order as a circulatory medium that positively reinforces authority through creative facilitative episodes as well as being invoked negatively when deviance is punished.

Parsons perceived that power was not the exception which is somehow outside the system. He understood that for power to be effective it had to be a constituting and systemic property and was not totally mistaken in linking it to legitimacy and authority. His crucial error was in the assumption that authority and legitimacy derive 'naturally' from system goals rather than that the consent behind legitimacy and authority will always be constructed through complex means which have nothing to do with the realization of system goals and are very far from a Habermasian ideal speech situation. Legitimacy grounds truth somewhat more than truth grounds legitimacy (Flyvbjerg 1998).

Giddens observed that Parsons' power is 'directly derivative of authority: authority is the institutionalized legitimation which underlies power' (Giddens 1968: 260). At base the criticism is that Parsons neglects 'power over' in favor of 'power to'. In consequence, Parsons is seen to play down hierarchy and division, which give rise to different interests, and thus overstates the degree of authority in the social system (Giddens 1968: 264).

The Dimensions of Power: Legitimacy as a Systematic Delusion

Lukes' (1974) book, *Power: A Radical View*, was a major landmark in the conceptualization of power. It sought to bring what had hitherto been a largely liberal and individualist tradition of theorizing about power as a causal relation into a fruitful dialogue with broader traditions of thought. He shows that each dimension of power rests on a different set of moral assumptions: The one-dimensional view of power is premised on liberal assumptions; the second dimensional view of power is premised on a reformist view, while it is the moral assumptions of radicalism that underlie the third dimensional way of seeing power.

The *one-dimensional view of power* pivots around an account of the different preferences that actors might hold and how these will be settled empirically. It concentrates on observable behavior and concrete decisions that are expressed in overt conflict concerning specific issues, revealed in political participation. The focus was on community power – who was powerful in local communities and what issues were the key ones over which power was exercised. (Clegg's (1989) *Frameworks of Power* contains a good discussion of the community power debate.) It is power as Dahl (1957) saw it. The *two-dimensional view* adds some features to the primary view. It does not focus just on observable behavior but seeks to make an interpretative understanding of the intentions that are seen to lie behind social actions. These come into play, especially, when choices are made concerning what agenda items are ruled in or ruled out; when it is determined that, strategically, for whatever reasons, some areas remain a zone of non-decision rather than decision. What is important is how some issues realize their potential to mature while some others do not; how some become manifest while others remain latent. Given that an issue may remain latent then conflict is not merely overt; it may also be covert, as resentment simmers about something that has yet to surface publicly. One may address these two-dimensional phenomena not so much through discrete political participation as through express policy preferences embodied in sub-political grievances.

From Lukes' point of view, the two-dimensional position is an improvement on that which is one-dimensional – but it could be improved further. Hence, he provides what he calls *a three-dimensional view* – a radical view to be contrasted with liberal and reformist views. While the previous views both define their field of analysis in terms of policy preferences, with the second dimension relating them to sub-political grievances, the radical view relates policy preferences to real interests. Real interests are defined as something objective, as distinct from the interests that people think they have and express themselves as having through their preferences. Whatever preferences people might express can always be charged with being subject to systematic distortion and thus a result of 'false consciousness' – that is, if they do not accord with the preferences that one would expect, analytically. By definition, real interests are what the analyst would have them be: they cannot be judged by the subject who does not express them – because such subjects are systematically deluded about their interests: a condition which he refers to as being subject to hegemony, a term that he borrows from the work of Antonio Gramsci (1971).

Lukes (1974, 2005) suggests that in extraordinary conditions, when routines break down, people may be able to pierce the veil of their everyday hegemonically formed 'consciousness' and grasp their real interests. Or rather, they may grasp their interests in terms of another discourse made available to them, or which they have only glimpsed dimly previously. Lukes (1974) is not explicit about the nature of such alternative discourses. In western society they have usually been identified with various oppositional movements that define their meaning against whatever they determine is the ruling orthodoxy, such as socialism against capitalism, feminism against patriarchy, animal liberation against meat eaters, and so on.

Rather than shaping consciousness positively, through discourse, radical theorists such as Lukes (1974) see power as prohibitory, negative, and restrictive. If it were more really radical it would have to be about what people are *able to articulate and say* and what language *enables them to think and feel*. However, in the second edition of his book, Lukes (2005: 9) cites Przeworski (1985) approvingly to argue a slightly different tack: that hegemony '*does not consist of individual states of mind but of behavioral characteristics of organizations*', noting that when wage-earners 'act as if they could improve their material conditions within the confines of capitalism' they are consenting to capitalism [Lukes 2005: 9, citing Przeworski 1985: 145–6]). Lukes (2005: 10–11) also relates his position to that of Tilly (1991: 594) and, in doing, shows that his fundamental views of 'real interests' have not changed in the intervening 30 years since he first wrote *Power: A Radical View*. In Tilly's (1991: 594) words, with which Lukes concurs, 'subordinates remain unaware of their true interests' because of 'mystification, repression, or the sheer unavailability of alternative ideological frames'.

To suggest that someone is in a state of false consciousness presupposes that there must be a correct or true consciousness as its counterpart (Haugaard 2003: 101). Of course, in some situations it might seem quite unproblematic to say that one is more rational and wise and understands the others real interests better than the other. Where such ideas are applied to deliberate systems of manipulation of knowledge, as, for instance, where cigarette manufacturers mislead their customers about the health-risks associated with their products, then it might be appropriate to speak of a 'false' consciousness. Haugaard (2003: 102) suggests that 'undermining power relations' may be 'a matter of facilitating individuals in converting their practical consciousness knowledge into discursive consciousness knowledge'. This is not a question of some enlightened theorist presenting subject actors with some external truth. Social life presupposes a large tacit knowledge of everyday life and in routine social interaction this knowledge remains practical consciousness. The moment of insight is that moment when what they *already know* in terms of their lived experience and their practical consciousness of it that is articulated discursively for them as an adequate and true account of this experiences is, in fact, false. It doesn't ring true. When this occurs people are facilitated in critically confronting their everyday social practices as part of a system of relations of domination which are reproduced, with their complicity, through everyday interaction. Practical consciousness is a tacit knowledge which enables us to be competent and capable actors in our everyday lives, while discursive consciousness comprises knowledge which we can put into words. These two forms of knowledge are not entirely separate. The relative separateness of the two types of social knowledge is an important element in the maintenance of systemic stability. If practical consciousness has never been critically evaluated, never formed part of discursive consciousness, then it will be reproduced virtually as a reflex.

As Haugaard (2003) argues the case, social critique entails converting practical consciousness into discursive consciousness. Once knowledge of structural reproduction becomes discursive, the actor may reject it or they might simply shrug and accept that this is how things are and there is little they can do to make them otherwise. In this event, it may become apparent that certain structural practices contribute to relations of domination and/or are inconsistent with other discursively held beliefs. What is useful about this approach to the matter of consciousness is that it accommodates arguments about the definition of the situation (Thomas 1923; McHugh 1968). On balance, as the adage has it, if people define situations as real they are real in their consequences, and while interlocutors may try and argue different definitions with different consequences, they rarely have any fulcrum outside of the consciousness of the people whose definitions they are, to do so. Theorizing Lukes' third dimension of power in terms of a form of consciousness-raising through the conversion of practical consciousness knowledge into discursive consciousness knowledge is theoretically consistent and avoids the chief pitfalls of Lukes' analysis – that it requires the theorist to adopt a transcendent position.

Conclusion

No social structuring or ordering exists without being characterized by power relations. Where these are structurally embedded and reproduced we may, with Weber, refer to structures of dominancy in which certain probabilities for command and obedience are lodged and in which resistance, although unlikely to be absent, can be authoritatively represented as illegitimate. Whether these structures of dominancy are regarded by those subject to them as legitimate will always be an empirical matter and not a question of the a priori labeling of such structures as authority; in other words, authority is always a provisional claim and can be contested (viz. the UK Parliamentary expenses scandal of 2009 which undoubtedly tarnished the legitimacy and authority of parliament as an institution). Where authority is ceded there is always the possibility that those ceding it are systematically duped into believing in the legitimacy of that which they support because the existing array of power relations sustains their practical consciousness in a mode in which interpellations of contradictory discursive consciousness are minimized, marginalized, ridiculed and so on. Hence, legitimacy depends on practical consciousness and practical consciousness – as the modes of knowing embedded in everyday social relations – will always be already structured in ways that reflect the dominant institutionalizations of power relations in both material and ideational forms. Consequently, it is usually only at moments of crisis in the reproduction of power's institutionalization as domination that carriers of an alternative discursive consciousness can engage the mass taken-for-grantedness of everyday practical consciousness sufficient to not only de-legitimize these everyday truths but also mobilize organized resources that can supplant their institutionalization. In other words, overall, power relations are very largely conservative, attuned to maintaining the legitimacy of dominancy and thus authority.

References

Barnes, B., 1988. *The Nature of Power*, Cambridge: Polity.

Clegg, S.R., 1989. *Frameworks of Power*, London: Sage.

Cohen, J., Hazelrigg, L.E. and Pope, W., 1975a. De-Parsonizing Weber: A Critique of Parsons' Interpretation of Weber's Sociology. *American Sociological Review*, 229–41.

——, 1975b. Reply to Parsons. *American Sociological Review*, 670–4.

Dahl, R.A., 1957. The Concept of Power. *Behavioral Science*, 20, 201–15.

Eden, R., 1983. *Political Leadership and Nihilism: A Study of Weber and Nietzsche*, Tampa, FL: University of South Florida Press.

Elias, N., 1982. *The Civilizing Process Vol. 2: Power & Civility*, New York: Pantheon.

Fleischmann, E., 1964. De Weber à Nietzsche. *Archives Européennes de Sociologie*, 5, 190–238.

Flyvbjerg, B., 1998. *Rationality and Power: Democracy in Practice*, Chicago, IL: University of Chicago Press.

Foucault, M., 1977. *Discipline and Punish: The Birth of the Prison*, trans. A. Sheridan. London: Allen & Lane.

Giddens, A., 1968. Power in the Recent Writings of Talcott Parsons. *Sociology*, 2(3), 257–72.

Goethe, J.W.V., 2005. *Elective Affinities*. Harmondsworth: Penguin.

Gouldner, A., 1971. *The Coming Crisis of Western Sociology*, London: Heinemann.

Gramsci, A., 1971. *From the Prison Notebooks*, London: Lawrence & Wishart.

Habermas, J., *The Theory of Communicative Action*, trans. T. McCarthy, Cambridge: Polity.

Haugaard, M., 2003. Reflections on Seven Ways of Creating Power. *European Journal of Social Theory*, 61(1), 87–113.

Hennis, W., 1988. The Traces of Nietzsche in the Work of Max Weber, trans. K. Tribe. In *Max Weber: Essays in Reconstruction*, London: Allen & Unwin, pp. 146–62.

Hobbes, T., 1914 [1651]. *Leviathan*, edited by A. D. Lindsay, New York: Dutton.

Kent, S.A., 1983. Weber, Goethe, and the Nietzschean Allusion: Capturing the Source of the 'Iron Cage' Metaphor. *Sociological Analysis*, 44, 297–319.

van Krieken, R., 1990. The Organisation of the Soul: Elias and Foucault on Discipline and the Self. *Archives Européenes de Sociologie*, 31(2), 353–71.

Lukes, S., 1974. *Power: A Radical View*, London: Macmillan.

——, 2005. *Power: A Radical View*, 2nd edition, London: Palgrave-Macmillan.

McHugh, P., 1968. *Defining the Situation: The Organization of Meaning in Social Interaction*, Indiannapolis, IN: Bobbs-Merrill.

Nietzsche, F.W., 1973. *Beyond Good and Evil*, trans. R. J. Hollingdale, Harmondsworth: Penguin.

Parsons, T., 1964. *Essays in Sociological Theory*, New York: Free Press of Glencoe.

——, 1975. On 'de-Parsonizing' Weber (Comment on Cohen *et al.*). *American Sociological Review*, 40, 666–70.

Przeworski, A., 1985. *Capitalism and Social Democracy*, New York: Cambridge University Press.

Schroeder, R., 1987. Nietzsche and Weber: Two 'Prophets' of the Modern World. In *Max Weber, Rationality and Modernity*, London: Allen & Unwin, 207–21.

Sica, A., 1988. *Weber, Irrationality, and Social Order*, Berkeley, CA: University of California Press.

Simmel, G., 1964. *Conflict and the Web of Group Affiliations*, trans. K. H. Wolff and R. Bendix, New York: The Free Press.

——, 1971. *On Individuality and Social Forms: Selected Writings*, Chicago, IL: University of Chicago Press.

Thomas, W.I., 1923. *The Unadjusted Girl*, Boston, MA: Little, Brown, & Co.

Tilly, C., 1991. Domination, Resistance, Compliance … Discourse. *Sociological Forum*, 6(3), 593–602.

Weber, M., 1947. *The Theory of Social and Economic Organization*, New York: Harper & Row.

——, 1954. *Max Weber on Law in Economy and Society*, Cambridge, MA: Harvard University Press.

——, 1976. *The Protestant Ethic and the Spirit of Capitalism*, London: Allen & Unwin.

——, 1978. *Economy and Society: An Outline of Interpretive Sociology*, edited by Roth, G. and Wittich, C., Berkeley, CA: University of California Press.

Modernity

From Convergence and Stability to Plurality and Transformation

Peter Wagner

Has modernity always been or has it recently become a key concern in social and political theory? In the former view, social and political theory emerged in Europe in the aftermath of the great transformations at the end of the eighteenth and the beginning of the nineteenth century. The novel social configuration that was forming as the combined effect of the Industrial Revolution and the French Revolution demanded novel means of analysis and interpretation; and social theory, in particular (without that term yet being coined), was the new intellectual tool to grasp its own present time, that is, its modernity. Proponents of the latter view, in turn, point to the fact that the noun 'modernity' has come into widespread use in social and political theory only since about 1980. A look at this recent development provides us with an angle from which to grasp the longer history and the transformations of the concern with modernity in social and political theory.

In 1979, the French philosopher Jean-François Lyotard published a brief 'report on knowledge', which he had written at the request of the government of Québec, under the title *The Postmodern Condition*. Using data about the rapid diffusion of electronic information and communication technology and building on earlier arguments about the rise of 'post-industrial society', he argued that modern societies were undergoing a new major social transformation and that contemporary social theory was unable to grasp the nature of that monumental change. He criticized both mainstream social theorizing, epitomized by Parsonsian structural functionalism, and its critical alternative, as the exemplar for which he referred to Jürgen Habermas' work, for operating with reductionist and overly homogenizing concepts of the social bond and maintained that contemporary society was instead characterized by a multiplicity of social bonds best captured by the Wittgensteinian idea of a plurality of language games.

The little book contained provocative material for both political philosophy and empirical social research that, though much of it was not entirely new, had never appeared in such a condensed form. It suggested that modernity was neither functionally nor normatively superior to, or more advanced than, earlier social configurations, as almost all Western social and political theory had maintained for one and a half centuries. Furthermore, it denied the commonly held view that modernity undergoes predominantly linear evolution and reaches a stable state at full development. Rather, it was about to undergo a radical social transformation that invalidated many of its promises of human emancipation. And the outcome of this transformation was the co-existence of multiple forms of social bond in the shadow of a diffuse concern with performativity.

In reaction to this provocation, two strands of debate began to form in social and political theory during the 1980s. On the one hand, the foundations of modern reasoning and modern practices were re-assessed in more philosophically oriented debates, with Jürgen Habermas defending a sophisticated understanding of modernity in *The Philosophical Discourse of Modernity* (1985) against critics such as Lyotard, Michel Foucault, and Jacques Derrida, and Richard Rorty moving the pragmatist tradition close to the postmodern agenda in *Contingency, Irony, Solidarity* (1989). More sociologically oriented contributions focused on the question of the existence and nature of that new major social transformation that the theorem of postmodernity entailed. With *Risk Society* (1986), Ulrich Beck was among the first to distinguish a first and simple modernity, in his view rather well captured by sociological debate up to the 1970s, from 'another', 'reflexive' modernity that was about to emerge. In a whole array of writings published between 1987 and 1992, Zygmunt Bauman forcefully distinguished between a modernity obsessed with the creation of order and the elimination of ambivalence from an emerging post-modernity more gently interpreting rather than legislating human relations (*Legislators and Interpreters*, 1987; *Modernity and the Holocaust*, 1989; *Modernity and Ambivalence*, 1991). From a focus on the critique of historical modernity, his more recent writings have turned towards critical assessments of the 'liquidity' of current social life (e.g. *Liquid Modernity*, 2000). Avoiding any strong notions of an epochal break, Alain Touraine (*Critique de la modernité*, 1992) suggested that modernity had always been characterized by the two tendencies towards subjectivation and ratio-nalization, but concern with the former now re-emerged after a long period of predominance of the latter.

These were the debates in which the noun 'modernity' was introduced in social theory and political philosophy, which hitherto had been content with using terms such as 'modern society', 'industrial society', or 'capitalist society' for their main object. The purpose of investigation did not change with the terminology; the analysis of contemporary social configurations and the relations between the human beings that form them remained the major task. However, the change of terminology signaled that there was a need to reassure oneself about the nature of this object and about the purpose of one's investigations.

The doubts about the stability and superiority of Western, 'modern society' were not confined to theoretical reflections during this period. The late 1970s and early 1980s were the years in which: the Iranian revolution brought an end to the idea that non-Western societies were just a bit behind on the same modernizing trajectory on which Western ones had embarked; the rise of the Japanese economy suggested that a capitalism with a non-Protestant cultural background could compete successfully with the allegedly more advanced economies; the rise of neo-liberal ideologies (monetarism and supply-side economics as they were then known) to governing power in the UK and the US and the concomitant failure of economic policy by a socialist-led government in France signaled the end of the optimism that market economies could smoothly be steered by national governments. Furthermore, these years were bracketed by the student, workers, and civil rights movements of the late 1960s that suddenly interrupted the tranquility of the apparent postwar social consensus, on the one side, and by the collapse of Soviet-style socialism between 1989 and 1991, on the other side. There was plenty of everyday evidence at hand that suggested the need to interrogate anew the contemporary human condition.

Against this double background, the adoption of the term 'modernity' expressed the need for a new language for interpreting the contemporary socio-political condition, or at least the need for posing the question whether a new language was required. The new debate clearly drew on and referred to the long tradition of analysis of 'modern society', but aimed at re-assessing that tradition in the light of new experiences that were increasingly being analyzed as a profound transformation of modernity. In the remainder of this chapter, I will first briefly discuss that which is now the 'pre-history' of the modernity debate, that is, the social and political theory of modern and capitalist society in both its affirmative and its critical strands since the great social transformations of the late eighteenth and early nineteenth centuries. This historical look will facilitate the analysis of the outcome of the recent re-assessment of modernity, which will be the second step, presented as the shift from an exclusively institutional to an interpretative analysis of modernity, which more than the former allows for plurality and transformability. Thirdly, this shift has given rise to a new opposition in most recent debate, which sees defenders of (neo-) modernization theory with persistent institutional emphasis reacting to the challenge from interpretative theorists of modernity who are now often lumped together by means of reference to 'multiple modernities', a term introduced by Shmuel N. Eisenstadt. The chapter will conclude with reflections on how this new opposition can fruitfully be overcome.

Modernity as a Set of Institutions and Its Critique

From the early nineteenth century onwards, in works such as G.W.F. Hegel's *Elements of a Philosophy of Right* (1820), social theory and political philosophy worked with the assumption that contemporary Western societies had emerged from earlier social configurations by way of a profound rupture. This rupture, although it could stretch over long periods and occurred in different societies at different points in time, regularly brought about a new set of institutions, most importantly a market-based economy, a democratic polity, and autonomous knowledge-producing institutions developing empirical–analytical sciences. Once such 'modern society' was established, a superior form of social organization was thought to have been reached that contained all it needed to adapt successfully to changing circumstances.

However, a considerable tension between any historical description of a rupture and conceptual understandings of modernity comes immediately to the fore. The conceptual imagery of the institutions of 'modern society' sits in an uneasy relation to historical dates. Were one to insist that the full set of those institutions needs to exist before a society can be called modern, socio-political modernity would be limited to a relatively small part of the globe during only a part of the twentieth century.

This tension between conceptuality and historicity was resolved by introducing an evolutionary logic in societal development. Based on the assumption of a societally effective voluntarism of human action, realms of social life were considered to have gradually separated from one another according to social functions. Religion, politics, the economy, the arts all emerged as separate spheres in a series of historical breaks – known as the scientific, industrial, democratic revolutions, etc. – that follows a logics of differentiation (Parsons 1964; Alexander 1978). A sequence of otherwise contingent ruptures can thus be read as a history of progress, and the era of modernity emerges by an unfolding from very incomplete beginnings. In this view, indeed, modern society came to full fruition only in the US of the post-Second World War era, but 'modernization' processes were moving towards that *telos* for a long time, and continued to do so in other parts of the world.

In conceptual terms, this perspective on modern social life aimed at combining an emphasis on free human action with the achievement of greater mastery over the natural and social world. The differentiation of functions and their separate institutionalization was seen as both enhancing human freedom and as increasing the range of action. Thus, the combination of freedom and reason, known from Enlightenment political philosophy, was transformed and, we may say, sociologized into terms such as subjectivity and rationality (e.g. Touraine 1992).

Without this double concept being explicated in most of the theory of 'modern society', it nevertheless can be identified at the root of this conceptualization of modernity. At the same time, it certainly drew on what may be called the self-understanding of historical modernizers. Proponents of what came to be known as the scientific, industrial and democratic revolutions saw themselves acting in the name of freedom, and they also saw the new institutions they were calling for as providing greater benefits than the old ones.

After the dust of the great revolutions had settled, it became clear that the institutionalization of freedom and reason was a much less straightforward process than had been expected by Enlightenment optimists. A series of major critical inquiries into the dynamics of modernity was elaborated successively from the middle of the nineteenth century up until the 1930s. These critiques identified basic problems in the practices of modernity, but did not abandon the commitment to modernity as a consequence. They all problematized, although in very different ways, the tension between the unleashing of the modern dynamics of freedom and rational mastery, on the one hand, and its, often unintended, collective outcome in the form of major societal institutions.

The first of these critiques was the *critique of political economy* as developed mainly by Karl Marx. In contrast to some of the conservative critics of capitalism, such as the German historical economists who flatly denounced its rationalist individualism, Marx basically adhered to the Enlightenment tradition of individual autonomy. His ideal was 'the free association of free human beings.' In the workings of the 'free' market in capitalism, however, he discovered a societal effect of human economic interaction that asserted itself 'behind the backs' of the actors.

In an economy based on market exchange and forced sale of labor-power, relations between human beings would turn into relations between things, because they were mediated by commodities. Driven by laws of abstract value, markets would transform phenomena with a use value into commodities, the sole important criterion of which was the monetary value against which they could be exchanged. The result of such fetishization of products and money and of the reification of social relations would be the alienation of human beings from their own products, from other human beings, and from themselves. In such an alienated condition, the possibility for autonomy and sovereignty of the economic actors would be completely eradicated, though these actors would indeed constantly reproduce these conditions by their own action.

The second grand critique was the *critique of large-scale organization and bureaucracy*, as analyzed most prominently by Robert Michels and Max Weber. With a view to the enhancement of rational mastery of the world, it postulated the tendency for the formation of stratified bodies with hierarchical chains of command and generalized, abstract rules of action. In the context of a universal-suffrage polity and welfare state, i.e. in 'large' societies in which all individuals had to be included on a formal, i.e. legally equal, basis in all major regulations, such 'iron cages' had emerged as state apparatuses, big industrial enterprises, and mass parties and would spread further in all realms of social life. While such institutions in fact enhanced the reach of human action generally, they limited it to the application of the rules, inside the iron cage so to say, at the same time.

In these terms, a variant of a critique of conceptions of rationality is the *critique of modern philosophy and science*, the third grand critique. Weber, too, was aware of the great loss that the 'disenchantment of the world' through rational domination entailed, still he understood his own social science in rational and value-neutral terms, as he thought no other approach could prevail under conditions of modernity. In contrast, radical and explicit critiques of science were put forward by others in very different forms. In idealist *Lebensphilosophie* the elaboration of a non-scientistic approach to science was attempted as well as, differently, in early-twentieth-century 'Western' Marxism, i.e. by Max Horkheimer and the early Frankfurt School. In some respects, pragmatism in the US can also be ranged under the critiques of science in as much as a new linkage of philosophy, anthropology and social science was proposed against the unfounded separation of spheres of knowledge in the disciplinary sciences. Such linkage would also bring the sciences back to a concern for the fundamental issues of the contemporary social world.

It was in pragmatism in particular – and in Europe in Durkheim's social theory – that a link between moral philosophy, social science, and politics was maintained, or rather recreated with a view to responding to the contemporary problems of societal restructuring. This link gave rise to the fourth critique, the *critique of morality*. The problem may be schematically reconstructed as follows. The development of modern society entailed the risk of moral impoverishment, mainly due to two phenomena. The inevitable decline of unquestioned faith eroded a source that could provide foundations for moral behavior. And if recurring face-to-face interaction is often the basis for the solidarity-supporting insight in the human likeness of the other, such kind of interaction would be decreasingly relevant in mass societies integrated on the scale of a nation. The two questions that arise are, first, how to ground ethics at all, when no foundational criteria are universally accepted, and, second, how to develop adequate standards for morality, when social relations are predominantly 'thin' and at the same time widely extended in space and time, that is, to relatively distant others (Boltanski 1993). The requirements for ethics have been raised, while the likelihood to agree on any ethics at all may have diminished, in such a view. Again, it is the achievement of reflexively questioning any imposed standards of morality that may subvert the possibility of any standard at all.

Synthetically, then, an argumentative figure emerged as follows. In the historical development of modernity as 'liberal' society, the self-produced emergence of overarching structures, such as capitalism and the market, organization and bureaucracy, modern philosophy and science, and the division of labor, is identified. These structures work on the individual subjects and their possibilities for self-realization – up to the threat of self-cancellation of modernity. The more generalized modern practices will become, the more they themselves may undermine the realizability of modernity as a historical project.

Modernity as Experience and as Interpretation

The interpretations of modernity provided by these critiques identified the tension between the modern orientations towards autonomy and towards mastery. They tended to resolve this tension in a clear-cut but also rather one-sided way, namely as the institutionalization of autonomy inevitably leading to forms of mastery that would subject the 'free' human beings. Alienation, atomization, commodification, bureaucratization, and instrumental rationalization would assert themselves as absolutely dominant trends leading to the emergence of 'one-dimensional man' and 'one-dimensional society' (Herbert Marcuse). While this interpretation had some persuasive power, in particular during the first two thirds of the twentieth century, in its totalizing way of reasoning it underestimated the persistence of the ambivalence of modernity and the possible resurgence of the quest for autonomy. Towards the end of the twentieth century, socio-theoretical diagnosis of the present indeed shifted back to an emphasis on individualization, rather than atomization, and reflexivity, rather than rationality (e.g. Anthony Giddens, Ulrich Beck, Alain Touraine).

Although such recent analyses of modernity tend to employ the terminology of a new era (in response to the challenge of 'post-modernity' as discussed at the outset), they indeed draw implicitly on a different concept of modernity altogether. A common view of the history of social life in Europe holds that a 'culture of modernity' spread gradually over the past five centuries. This 'is a culture which is individualist ... : it prizes autonomy; it gives an important place to self-exploration; and its visions of the good life involve personal commitment' (Taylor

1989: 305). Such an emphasis on individuality and individualization is quite alien to the totalizing critiques of modernity but also to the more formalized 'modern' discourses of the individual as in rational choice theory or in liberal political philosophy. And in the affirmative social theory of Parsonsian inspiration, the individual exists and indeed fully emerges only in modern times, but at the same time s/he is well integrated into norm-bound social life and appears 'deviant' when s/he transgresses those norms.

In European intellectual and cultural history, there has long been very little connection between the views of modernity and its inhabitants that praise agency and creativity of human beings, on the one side, and those that see the individual human being as either integrated in or submerged by social forces and structures. Given their interest in institutions and their stability, political philosophy and social theory proceeded predominantly by presupposition and showed little interest in actual human beings, who tend to be taken into account only as disturbances the more they enter the public scene. In literature and the arts, in contrast, the experience of modernity was in the center and, as experience, it concerned in the first place the singular human being and her/his creative potential (Berman 1982). Michel Foucault's lecture 'What is Enlightenment?' very succinctly distinguished between those two readings of modernity. Modernity as an attitude and experience demands the exploration of one's self, the task of separating out, 'from the contingency that has made us what we are, the possibility of no longer being, doing, or thinking what we are, do or think' (Foucault 1984: 46). It is opposed to modernity as an epoch and a set of institutions, which demands obedience to agreed-upon rules. At least in some writers, such as Lyotard, the idea of post-modernity was inspired by such a return to what had been a modern self-understanding since at least the Enlightenment, and much less by the idea of a new era 'after' modernity.

Up to this point, we have identified a double opposition in the ways of theorizing modernity. First, those views that see modernity as the institutionalization of freedom and reason have been opposed by critics that see freedom being undermined by a legislating rationality. Second, both of these views have been criticized for failing to take into account the actual human experience of modernity and their variety. One of the outcomes of the post-1979 re-assessment of modernity stems directly from the analysis of this constellation: If the opposition of affirmative and critical analysis of modernity persists over long periods without resolution, this suggests that modernity is open to a variety of interpretations. And if both approaches tended to neglect experience, then the elaboration of a more comprehensive interpretative approach to modernity should proceed by exploring the variety of experiences of modernity.

Such an interpretative analysis of modernity has gradually been developed since about 1990, and it starts out from the proposed reference to autonomy and mastery that seems to mark, even though the terminology varies, a commonality across all theories of modernity and thus a defining characteristics of modernity itself. Following Cornelius Castoriadis (1990; see also Arnason 1989; Wagner 1994), modernity can be considered as a situation in which the reference to autonomy and mastery provides for a double 'imaginary signification' of social life. By this term, Castoriadis refers to what more conventionally would be called a generally held belief or an 'interpretative pattern' (Arnason). More precisely, the two components of this signification are the idea of the autonomy of the human being as the knowing and acting subject, on the one hand, and on the other, the idea of the rationality of the world, i.e. its principled intelligibility. Conceptually, therefore, modernity refers to a situation in which human beings do not accept any external guarantors – that is, guarantors that they do not themselves posit – of their knowledge, of their political orders, or of their ways of satisfying their material needs.

Earlier social and political theory also recognized the modern commitment to autonomy and mastery, but it thought to derive a particular institutional structure from this double imaginary signification. Thus, it was often inclined to consider a historically specific interpretation of a problématique as a general trait of modernity. This is the case, for instance, when the historical form of the European nation-state is conflated with the solution to, as it was often called, the problem of social order, which was expressed in the concept 'society' (Smelser 1997: ch. 3). When assuming, however, that a modern set of institutions can be derived from the imaginary signification of modernity, it is overlooked that the two elements of this signification are ambivalent each one on its own and tension-ridden between them. Therefore, the recent rethinking takes such tensions to open an interpretative space that is consistent with a variety of institutional forms. The relation between autonomy and mastery institutes an interpretative space that is to be specifically filled in each socio-historic situation through struggles over the situation-grounded appropriate meaning. Theoretically, at least, there is always a plurality and diversity of interpretations of this space.

An interim summary may be useful at this point: The social and political theory of contemporary Western societies has long been based on the idea that those societies emerged through some rupture with the past. In this sense, scholars have long theorized 'modernity', as the attempt to grasp the specificity of the present, even though the term has been used only rather recently. The dominant strand has aimed at capturing this specificity by *structural-institutional analysis*. The modern institutions are here seen as the embodiments of the modern promise of freedom and reason. Against and beyond this dominant strand, three different conceptualizations of modernity have been proposed. First, the *critiques of modernity* have provided an alternative institutional analysis, emphasizing the undermining of the promise of autonomy in and through the workings of the modern institutions. Second, the *interpretative approach to modernity* has demonstrated the breadth of possible interpretations of what is commonly understood as the basic self-understanding, or imaginary signification, of modernity. Third, the conception of *modernity as an ethos and an experience* has underlined the normative and agential features of modernity. In the former sense, it emphasizes the lack of any given foundations and the possibility to push the 'project of modernity' ever further. In the latter sense, it accentuates creativity and openness. In both ways, the experiential understanding complements the interpretative approach by underlining the large, potentially infinite, variety of interpretations of modernity.

Neo-modernization vs. the Plurality of Modernity

The theorem of multiple modernities, which has had the enormous merit of (re-)introducing the idea of a possible plurality of modes of socio-political organization into the analysis of 'modern societies', did not emerge directly out of the theoretical debate as it was sketched above, but rather from concerns of comparative-historical macro-sociology, that is, the study of large-scale social configurations and their transformations over time. Within that field, though, it addressed directly the problem that had been inherited from the theories of modernization of broadly Parsonsian inspiration, namely the assumption of long-term convergence towards a single model of 'modern society'. Significantly, the approach that is central to this opening, pioneered by Shmuel Eisenstadt (see, e.g., 2002, 2003), explained the persistent plurality through 'cultural programmes', thus introducing an interpretative approach, in methodological terms, and some idea similar to the 'imaginary signification' of society, in substantive terms. This approach has been widely received and recognized (see, e.g., *Daedalus* 1998, 2000; some contributions to Hedström and Wittrock 2009); however it has failed to make the strong innovative impact that one could have expected.

This – relative – failure is, among other reasons, due to two weaknesses of the multiple modernities approach: First, the strong idea of 'cultural programme' suggests considerable stability of any given form of modernity. Indeed, many contributors to the debate now reason in terms of civilizations, and 'classical' civilizations like the Chinese, Japanese, or also the Indian one have been key objects for the identification of multiple modernities (see Arnason 2003 for the most nuanced contribution). As a consequence, considerable limitations to the applicability of the approach are introduced, as it is difficult to conceive of South Africa, Brazil, or even the USA or Australia in terms of deep-rooted, rather stable cultural programmes that merely unfold in the encounter with novel situations.

Second, the approach is based on only two main concepts: the characteristic (common and inevitable) features of modernity, on the one hand, and the (variety of) cultural programmes, on the other. This dichotomy limits the possibility of comparison since all difference between modernities needs to be explained in terms of the specific underlying programme. In this light, this approach either does not move far away from standard institutional analysis that permits surface cultural variation in terms of mores and customs or, alternatively, any supposed incomparability across cultural programmes raises the spectre of normative relativism, a key concern of political theorizing committed to modernity

Indeed, the absence of a controversy between proponents of the multiple modernities concept and those who continue to work with a modernization approach, now sometimes referred to as neo-modernization to signal the reception of, and response to, earlier criticism, is striking. There is a profound opposition in at least two respects: the view of the dynamics of historical transformation, cultural resources on the one hand, a functional logic on the other; and the outcome of this dynamic, convergence towards a single institutional set-up on the one hand, persistent diversity on the other. Rather than giving rise to debate and exchange, though, this opposition seems to be seen as unresolvable by both sides and work concentrates on each side on the further elaboration of the own research programme (for a rare explicit confrontation, see Schmidt 2010, heavily biased towards modernization theory though).

Both theoretical considerations and empirical findings have led the current author to side with an agency-oriented, interpretative understanding of modernity that makes the possible plurality of modern forms identifiable and analyzable. At the same time, however, too many deficiencies exist in the multiple modernities approach and too many valid issues are raised by modernization-oriented scholars to make the avoidance of communication a viable strategy. The concept of modernity has rightly been criticized as often being both too comprehensive and too imprecise to allow operationalization for research and clarifying communication in scholarly exchange (see Yack 1997). Thus, a most fruitful next step should be the disentangling of the concept with a view to separating out researchable aspects of modernity that can be compared across the dividing lines of recent scholarship. Furthermore, such disentangling should be done with a view to making all contemporary societies amenable to analysis in terms of the specificities of their modernity (or lack of it) under current global conditions, not only either Western societies or their counterpart in the classical civilizations with their apparently stable cultural programmes.

Social and Political Theory Confronted with the Comparative–Historical Sociology of Global Modernities

Starting indeed out from the deficiencies of the multiple modernities debate, the requirements for true innovation in the analysis of contemporary societies and their historical trajectories stand out clearly: For most current cases, *first*, the self-understanding of societies has not been stable for centuries but has undergone significant transformations, often even and especially in the recent past. Thus, there is no underlying cultural programme but rather an ongoing process of – more or less collective – interpretation of one's situation in the light of crucial experiences made in earlier situations (for the theorem of 'successive modernities', Wagner 2010a). *Second*, rather than separating 'culture' from the institutional girders of modernity, one needs to demonstrate if and how re-interpretations of a society's self-understanding have an impact on institutional change or, in other words, how cultural–interpretative transformations are related to socio-political transformations (Sewell 2005).

For most cases, *third*, an interpretative approach should take as its object something smaller than a 'cultural programme'. The modern imaginary signification of autonomy and mastery is not only inherently ambivalent, as was shown above. It also may be applied in different walks of life in different ways. Investigating the variety of socio-historical interpretations of the double imaginary signification of modernity and the resources such interpretations draw on and mobilize, one will find that those resources are much richer and much more varied than earlier research has been able to identify – already within Western Europe (e.g. between France and Germany; see Zimmermann *et al.* 1999) or within the more broadly defined 'West' (e.g. between Europe and the US; see Lamont and Thévenot 2000). Both richness and variety increase considerably further as soon as one focuses on the so-called non-Western societies (see Larrain 2000 and Domingues 2008 for Latin America; Kaya 2004 for Turkey, for instance).

While broad evidence of the plurality of modern forms now exists, much research is idiosyncratic and does not lend itself easily to comparison with other findings. To systematically grasp the main features of the modernity of a given socio-political configuration, one may want to start by selecting those elements that concern a *limited set of basic problématiques* that all human societies need to address, such as the questions: (a) as to what certain knowledge a societal self-understanding is seen to rest upon; (b) as to how to determine and organize the rules for the life in common; and (c) as to how to satisfy the basic material needs for societal reproduction (Wagner 2008; for a related attempt at disentangling, see Domingues 2006). To say that a society embraces a *modern* self-understanding, furthermore, implies that all these questions are truly open; that answers to them are not externally given but need to be found; and that, therefore, contestation of the validity of existing answers is always possible.

The distinction of these problématiques creates a focus on societal features that then can be systematically compared. In brief: the fact that societies need to effectively address these problématiques by searching for their own answers is what is *common* among all 'modernities'; the fact that the questions are open to interpretation; that there is not any one answer that is clearly superior to all others (even though one answer can certainly be better than others and societies will search for the better ones and/or those that are more appropriate to them) and, thus, that several answers can legitimately and usefully be given constitutes the *possible plurality* of modernity (for more detail, Wagner 2010b).

References

Alexander, Jeffrey C., 1978 'Formal and Substantive Voluntarism in the Work of Talcott Parsons: A Theoretical and Ideological Reinterpretation', *American Sociological Review*, 43, 177–198.

Arnason, Johann P., 1989 'The Imaginary Constitution of Modernity', in *Autonomie et autotransformation de la société: La philosophie militante de Cornelius Castoriadis*, Giovanni Busino *et al.*, Geneva: Droz, 323–37.

——2003 *Civilizations in Dispute*, Leiden: Brill.

Berman, Marshall, 1982 *All That Is Solid Melts into Air. The Experience of Modernity*, New York: Simon & Schuster

Boltanski, Luc, 1993 *La souffrance à distance*, Paris: Métailié.

Castoriadis, Cornelius, 1990 *Le monde morcelé: Les carrefours du labyrinthe III*, Paris: Seuil.

Daedalus, 1998 'Early Modernities', 127, 3, summer.

——2000 'Multiple Modernities', 129, 1, winter.

Domingues, José Mauricio, 2006 *Modernity Reconstructed*, Cardiff: University of Wales Press.

——2008 *Latin America and Contemporary Modernity: A Sociological Interpretation*, London: Routledge.

Eisenstadt, Shmuel Noah, 2002 *Multiple Modernities*, Piscataway, NJ: Transaction.

——2003 *Comparative Civilizations and Multiple Modernities*, Leiden: Brill.

Foucault, Michel, 1984 'What is Enlightenment?' in *The Foucault Reader*, ed. by Paul Rabinow, London: Penguin, 32–50.

Hedström, Peter, and Björn Wittrock, eds, 2009 *Frontiers of Sociology*, Leiden: Brill.

Kaya, Ibrahim, 2004 *Social Theory and Later Modernities: The Turkish Experience*, Liverpool: Liverpool University Press

Lamont, Michelle, and Laurent Thévenot, eds, 2000 *Rethinking Comparative Cultural Sociology: Polities and Repertoires of Evaluation in France and the United States*, New York: Cambridge University Press.

Larrain, Jorge, 2000 *Identity and Modernity in Latin America*, Cambridge: Polity.

Lyotard, Jean-François, 1979 *La Condition postmoderne*, Paris: Minuit (trans. G. Bennington and B. Massumi, *The Postmodern Condition*, Manchester: Manchester University Press, 1994).

Parsons, Talcott, 1964 'Evolutionary Universals in Society', *American Sociological Review*, 29, June.

Smelser, Neil, 1997 *Problematics of Sociology*. Berkeley, CA: University of California Press.

Taylor, Charles, 1989 *Sources of the Self*. Cambridge, MA: Harvard University Press,

Schmidt, Volker H., 2010 'Modernity and Diversity', *Social Science Information*, 49, 4, 511–538.

Sewell, William H. jr., 2005 *Logics of History: Social Theory and Social Transformation*, Chicago, IL: University of Chicago Press.

Touraine, Alain, 1992 *Critique de la modernité*, Paris: Fayard.

Wagner, Peter, 1994 *A Sociology of Modernity: Liberty and Discipline*, London: Routledge.

——2008 *Modernity as Experience and Interpretation: A New Sociology of Modernity*, Cambridge: Polity.

——2010 'Successive Modernities and the Idea of Progress', *Distinktion*, Scandinavian Journal of Social Theory, 21, 9–24.

——2011 'From Interpretation to Civilization – and Back: Analyzing the Trajectories of non-European Modernities', *European Journal of Social Theory*, forthcoming.

Yack, Bernard, 1997 *The Fetishism of Modernities*. Notre Dame, IN: University of Notre Dame Press.

Zimmermann, Bénédicte, Claude Didry, and Peter Wagner, eds, 1999 *Le travail et la nation: Histoire croisée de la France et de l'Allemagne*, Paris: Editions de la Maison des Sciences de l'Homm.

Social and Political Trust

Karen S. Cook and Brian D. Cook

Trust has become a major focus of many social scientists since the early 1990s following large political, social, and economic changes in the world after 1989. During this period of transition, risk and uncertainty increased in part as a result of the growth of globalization, the rapid inter-nationalization of business, and the increased interdependence of nation states. As Sztompka (2006) notes, the significance of trust has been fueled by changes in the quality and nature of the social structures and social processes in later modernity with the shift to democracy in many sectors and an attendant increase in human agency and interconnectedness. Along with these changes come increases in uncertainty inherent in the "unfamiliar, non-transparent and distant linkages" entailed by these new forms of connectedness. In addition, reasons for distrust have not declined. Highly publicized failures of transparency and integrity in the world of business (e.g. Enron in the United States) have eroded public trust in enterprise. Declining trust in public officials and professionals (e.g. lawyers, physicians, politicians, and ministers, etc.) has also fueled concern over decreasing social trust and the demise of civil society in general (e.g. Putnam 2000). Rising concerns about terrorist activity, civil wars, and other forms of violence continue unabated in many parts of the world fanning the flames of distrust and fomenting disorder. A large part of the increasing interest in trust, therefore, is centered on understanding what factors facilitate cooperation under varying conditions and help to produce social order and reduce disorder. Given these concerns, in this chapter we focus our discussion on current research trends in social and political trust within an international context.

Social Trust

In the mid-1990s, the social historian Frances Fukuyama (1995), among others, focused on comparing levels of social trust in a number of countries. He argued that social trust varied by culture; comparing the more familistic societies such as China, France, Italy, and South Korea with more individualistic societies such as the United States and Germany, where sociability is more likely to be centered around nonkinship-based communities. Japan in his view is more like the United States than China, though research on general trust is not consistent on this point (Buchan, Croson, and Dawes 2002). For Fukuyama, interpersonal trust arises where those who interact have relatively complete knowledge about their interaction partners either through direct personal experience or indirectly through networks in which reputational information easily flows. Social trust for Fukuyama is the kind of general trust in others that exists in the *absence* of this type of direct interpersonal or particularized trust. In the General Social Survey for several decades general trust has been measured by several questions including the main indicator: "Generally speaking, would you say that most people can be trusted, or that you can't be too careful in dealing with others?"[1] Responses to this item are assumed to reflect a general sense that others can be trusted (even those we do not know) or a general sense of optimism in dealing with others, implying that the risk of exploitation or harm is not perceived to be high.

There are a number of other conceptions of trust in the social science literature. Sociologists and political scientists often focus on trust as a relational or social phenomenon, not as a psychological state as reflected in Rousseau's (1998) widely cited definition of trust as making oneself vulnerable to another party. Hardin's (2002) treatment of trust as "encapsulated interest" is relational. It defines trust in terms of a belief that the trustee in the two-party relationship between a trustor and a trustee will take the interests of the trustor into account and honor them to the extent that she values the continuation of the relationship. A trusts B with respect to x (a particular domain of activity) when A believes that her interests are included in (or encapsulated by) B's utility function. In this case B values what A desires because B wants to maintain a relationship with A or wants to maintain a good reputation with respect to A. Psychologists tend to define trust as the belief that the trustee will not take advantage of the trustor's vulnerability. In either case, psychological or relational definitions of trust presuppose risk. That is, it is the existence of uncertainty and risk that makes the act of trusting another significant. If there is no risk of exploitation or harm there is no real need for trust in the situation. The act of trusting another party, person, or institution places one at risk and does make one vulnerable to the other party's actions. The relational view of trust articulated above simply clarifies the nature of the risk; its source is the action of the trustee with respect to the trustor.

Robert Putnam (1993, 2000), a political scientist, put social trust on the social science agenda by popularizing the term *social capital*, which he used to refer to the "networks, norms, and trust" that exist to make transactions easier and to foster civil society. High social capital leads to the formation of strong civil society. Low social capital impedes it. And social capital is related to economic growth as well as the production of collective goods for society. In general the extent to which Americans say they trust most people has been in decline since the late 1950s. For both Paxton (1999) and Putnam (2000) analyses of the General Social Survey items reflecting what has been termed "general social trust" indicate a decline of around twenty percent in forty years or so, most notably in the extent to which respondents say "most people can be trusted." Even more disturbing to those who track trends in general trust is the fact that there are large racial differences in responses to this question with African-Americans reporting low levels of trust in "most people" in every time period, with a decline over time as well. Smith (2010) reports that in a number of surveys Blacks have very low levels of trust, high levels of distrust, and a general propensity to view others as unfair and unhelpful. She also reports even lower levels for Hispanics in the 2007 Pew Research Center report on trust. As Smith notes, these findings demonstrate that general trust measures seem to be picking up trust of those in the majority group, in this case, whites in the U.S. When specifically asked about trust in others "like them," however, blacks report much higher levels of trust. These findings reflect the deep divide between racial groups in the United States that still persists.

Trustworthiness

Other scholars such as Gambetta (1988), a sociologist, and Luhmann (1979), a social theorist, treat trust as an important lubricant of social life. Gambetta's (1988) edited volume brought together the work of a number of social scientists from varied disciplines (including philosophy) to analyze the role of trust and its meaning for society. Gambetta and Hamill (2005) later published an interesting study of taxicab drivers in Northern Ireland and New York City empirically identifying the "signs" that drivers use to lower their own risk and to assess the likely trustworthiness of their clients. Gambetta has subsequently developed a more complete theory of signaling that builds on his earlier work on the Mafia to clarify how and when individuals and groups can maintain trust networks especially in high-risk contexts in which distrust rather than trust may best characterize the surrounding culture or environment. This research dovetails nicely with the writings of Hardin (2002) and others (Cook, Hardin, and Levi 2005) that attempt to refocus some of the work on trust, making trustworthiness more central to the research agenda. As Hardin (2002) points out, it is often not wise to trust others in many contexts given the risks that are involved, thus to trust others in a general way may not be the right thing to do. Instead of generalized trust in others, focusing on whether or not people live up to our expectations of trustworthiness provides an empirical basis for assessing whether or not trust is warranted in a given situation. What this simple point suggests is that the focus on the positive role of trust in the social science literature is often overstated and some of the sweeping theoretical claims about the role of trust in society are unsubstantiated by straightforward logic if not empirical evidence. If we want anything, it is likely more trustworthiness.

It is important, therefore, as Hardin (2002) and Cook, Hardin, and Levi (2005) have argued, to distinguish between the concepts trust and trustworthiness. To the extent that one can judge trustworthiness accurately trusting can be merited, but trust in the absence of signs or clear assessments of trustworthiness, as we have argued, is not wise and thus can not be said to be the "right" or moral action. This distinction is at the center of the debates concerning the overly normative claims about trust. In general, there are at least two dimensions to the assessment of trustworthiness: competence and motivation. In the case of competence the judgment that is made reflects the extent to which the party involved has the capacity to carry out the actions required for trust to be merited. For example, when we say "I trust my physician" a prime component of the judgment of her trustworthiness is her competence to perform the duties of a physician to the best of her ability (and our capacity to judge it). A second component of the judgment of her trustworthiness is a separate assessment of her motivations with respect to us. How much does she care about me and, more precisely, the effectiveness of my treatment? Will she treat me as if my health really matters to her? Or in encapsulated interest terms, will she take my interest to heart in her decisions concerning what is in my best interest and what would be the proper course of treatment?

Given the risks involved in many situations, there are numerous alternatives to reliance on trust (Cook, Hardin' and Levi 2005). These include formal mechanisms for ensuring reliability such as rules and procedures that are established as legitimate in the organizational or institutional setting in which the interactions occur. Other mechanisms include efforts to monitor and sanction behavior that is untrustworthy to enforce norms of proper behavior in a specific context – a group, organization, or community setting. Even efforts to control professional behavior through enforcement of proper codes of conduct are meant to reinforce trustworthiness and reliability and foster trust. These codes of conduct are common in professions such as the ministry, law, medicine, and education, especially when it is difficult to observe behavior with clients who are often very dependent thus creating situations in which trust is required. It is the frequent failure of some professionals to live up to these codes of conduct (e.g. priests or doctors) that result in organizational intervention, increased monitoring and new forms of regulation. This was a common reaction to medical malpractice when PSROs (professional standards review organizations) were initially established. In other cases, as in the situation in which priests have been discovered to abuse parishioners, often children, the courts have had to intervene to provide protection and recompense to those who are vulnerable or whose trust has been violated. Often it is these alternatives to trust that we rely on, especially when the risks of failed trust are too high. The degree of reliance on trust, however, varies not only across contexts but also across countries.

Cross-cultural differences

Various researchers have attempted to identify the unique characteristics of different cultures and nationalities that are revealed in responses to survey questions on the General Social Survey or the World Values Survey which are presumed to measure general social trust. Delhey and Newton (2005), for example, investigate variations in the level of generalized social trust in sixty nations, demonstrating that there is a complex of factors that predicts (but not necesarrily explains) generalized trust. Countries high in trust tend to have greater ethnic homogeneity, higher gross domestic product per capita, more income equality, and Protestant religious traditions. Exemplars include high-trust Nordic countries such as Norway, Sweden, Iceland, and Finland. The opposite holds for low-trust countries such as Turkey, South Africa, the former Soviet states, and Brazil, among others.

Experimental work has also addressed cultural differences in trust by assessing responses to games meant to elicit cooperative or trusting behavior as measures of variations in trust. Buchan, Croson, and Dawes (2002), for example, report that in their experiment the Chinese and American participants were more trusting than the Korean and Japanese subjects. This research supports previous results obtained by Yamagishi and his collaborators (1988, 1994, 1998) suggesting that in Japan general trust is lower than in the United States because their cooperative behavior is driven more by expectations of reciprocity and the assurance of cooperation by others given that monitoring and sanctioning for non-cooperation is common. Buchan, Croson, and Dawes (2002) conclude that there are many conflicting results concerning national and cultural differences in trust and further research is needed to delve into the causes of these variations including religious, political and social factors.

Organizations and the economy

Trust is often viewed as important in many organizational and economic relations. For economists Kenneth Arrow (1974) and Douglass North (1990) market relations are facilitated by trust since it is simply not possible for an economy to function well with constant monitoring, sanctioning, and lack of cooperation. Arrow emphasized the role of trust in reducing transaction costs in complex economies. Another economist, Oliver Williamson (1993), focuses more on the role of trust in organizations in which transaction costs are reduced when the parties involved have confidence in each other and in the background institutions that enforce contracts. In such formulations trust seems to fill in where contracts and organizational rules and routines fail to supply adequate safeguards. In the world of management theory and research, Dirks and Ferrin (2001) have conducted a meta-analysis of a large number of focused empirical studies. They conclude that trust is often a mediator rather than a direct cause of a range of organizational behaviors, including individual and team performance, organizational citizenship behaviors, and reactions to the exercise of authority. In another organizational arena, reports on physician–patient trust relations (e.g. K. S. Cook et al. 2004) reveal that higher trust is associated with higher levels of compliance and satisfaction among patients, and with fewer procedures performed by physicians and greater confidence in their ability to help diagnose and manage the patient.

Fukuyama (1995) argues that it is social trust that generates the conditions under which specific forms of organization emerge that facilitate competitive economic enterprise. It is the lack of general social trust that Fukuyama identifies as the reason why organizations adopt a more hierarchical form (including networks of organizations created by contracting). The more flexible networks of smaller firms that engage in exchange require trust. In Fukuyama's words:

> A "virtual" firm can have abundant information coming through network wires about its suppliers and contractors. But if they are all crooks or frauds, dealing with them will remain a costly process involving complex contracts and time-consuming enforcement. Without trust, there will be strong incentive to bring these activities in-house and restore old hierarchies.
>
> *(1995: 25)*

Economic development requires the kind of trust that facilitates flexible transactions and nimble organizational strategies, as his case studies reveal. Cultures that fit this motif are poised for economic success in the global economy. Ironically, he argues that it is precisely those cultures with strong and large families that have lower social trust and national prosperity. Fukuyama (1995) refers to this claim as the "paradox of family values."

Various economists have attempted to analyze the link between trust and economic performance, building on the insights provided by Fukuyama (1995), whose work was more suggestive than conclusive. Knack and Keefer (1997), for example, use the World Values Survey to investigate the association between interpersonal trust (the level of trust in others) with economic growth, finding a significant positive correlation even though the mechanisms producing this effect are not clearly spelled out. Alesina and LaFerrara (2002) extend this work by including community-level variables in addition to individual-level factors such as level of trust in others, education, income, gender, ethnicity, and religious affiliation. Consistent with earlier findings they discover that belonging to a group previously discriminated against (i.e. blacks in the United States), being disadvantaged in terms of income and education, as well as living in a more heterogenous commmunity with respect to ethnicity and income disparity, decrease trust in others. They also focus on differences in confidence in institutions related to economic growth. Strong economic performance requires the type of trust or confidence in institutions that supports growth and reduces transaction costs. We turn now to the related topic, trust in government.

Political Trust

Political trust can focus on government, politicians, or state-level actors. We address primarily the debates surrounding trust in government. One of the earliest views of trust in relation to government was put forward by Tocqueville (1840 [1838]), though his work has been cited as supportive of several different arguments. A key argument is that stable government creates the grounds for trusting relationships between people in a society. Legal scholars and some economists also adopt this view of the link between trust and government. Much of the current work on economic and political transitions is also based on this view, focusing on the need for stable, predictable, and transparent instruments of governance (e.g. constitutions, legal apparti, and enforcement mechanisms).

A separate and not necessarily contradictory view is that the trust of citizens in government is essential to stable government. Here the work on social capital and civil society, cited above, is most relevant. Central to the well-functioning of any government is the good will and trust of the governed, which legal and constitutional scholars argue arises from procedural fairness and the perceived legitimacy of those who govern and the institutions they populate. Beyond these separable claims is the standard view of many in the classical liberal tradition that trust in government can be problematic and that what we want is a healthy skepticism, even passive distrust of those in positions of power in order to keep government from abusing its power. In fact Madisonian scholars focus on the perils of too much trust in government. Distrust is actively built into the construction of many constitutions, in order to provide checks and balances on the potential abuse of power. In the case of the U.S. constitution it takes the form of the separation of powers assigned to the executive, judicial and legislative branches of government.

In addition to these theories, political trust has been defined and measured in many different ways. In this section we address three prominent areas of research on political trust. First we discuss the general relationship between trust and government and the various ways in which scholars have addressed the role of trust among and between citizens and government officials and institutions. We then move to contexts in which political trust has been shown to play an important and debated role. Second we look at the importance of political trust in the causes and consequences of inequality, ethnic fragmentation, and assimilation. We conclude by discussing the role trust has played in countries involved in political and economic transitions.

Trust and government

Some political theorists view trust as a key to the smooth functioning of government. Dunn (1988), for example, treats the foundation of government in social contract theory as based on trust of the governed more so than on consent. Trust in government is often treated as a key factor in the stability of a society. But what precisely trust in government refers to is not always clear. For some theorists trusting a government allows citizens to engage in trusting relationships with others since they can rely on government to provide or support the institutions that produce stability, legal enforcement for failures to fulfill relevant obligations, and contractual relations. In this case trust in government is mainly about support for adequate enforcement mechanisms that provide the grounds for the types of cooperation that are central in a productive society.

Others view trust in government as based on the trust of citizens in one another. Authors such as Putnam argue that high levels of trust among members of a society lead to a vibrant and engaged citizenry or civil society that produces cooperation and stability. From this perspective, social capital produces cooperation among citizens as well as good governance at all levels. Without such social capital societies are politically unstable, citizens are less cooperative and less engaged, and governance is continually problematic. Trust among citizens, according to Putnam, leads to more civic engagement and better governance. A number of mechanisms have been discussed that lead to such results including the mobilization of particular constituencies by political leaders to support government policies, strong leaders that take the interests of the governed as primary and thus appear trustworthy to the citizenry, and active membership and engagement in effective civic associations. The precise nature of the role of these various mechanisms in producing better governance is the subject of much theoretical and empirical debate. Levi (1997; and Levi and Stoker 2000) notes, for example, that it is only under specific conditions that citizens comply with the demands of government. She studies both conscription and taxation as cases in which the legitimacy of government based on perceived procedural fairness and the capacity to govern effectively mediates the degree of compliance.

Another aspect of scholarly debate surrounding political trust is the distinction and relationship between interpersonal trust and trust in political institutions and their impact on democracy. For scholars such as Fukuyama (1995), Putnam (2000), and Uslaner (2002) interpersonal trust is an important determinant of trust in political institutions and citizen involvement in political life. Similarly, Keele (2007) argues that, while government performance contributes significantly to trust in political institutions, social capital appears to be the force that accounts for the decline in trust in the government in the U.S. since the 1950s and 1960s. However, Hardin (2002) has shown that declining trust between individuals is not correlated with declining trust in government, and that the two are independent. Similarly, Mishler and Rose (2001; and Mishler 2005) challenge the view that trust in political institutions is an extension of interpersonal trust. Using data from post-Communist countries in Eastern and Central Europe and the former Soviet Union, they show that perceptions of corruption and macroeconomic performance are far more important determinants of trust in political institutions than levels of interpersonal trust.

A somewhat different view of political trust has arisen from the survey-based research in political science. In some studies, generalized social trust is seen not so much as the property of individuals, but as a collective feature of society. In this research, respondents answering questions about trust tell us less about themselves and their personal inclinations, and more about how they evaluate the trustworthiness of the people in the world around them (Newton 2007). According to this conception of trust, authors such as Kaase (1999) and Newton (2001, 2007) note that political trust and confidence do not seem to overlap much, if at all, with social trust. This research finds that social trust is independent of political confidence, and the politically trusting are, if anything, even more randomly distributed among social groups than the socially trusting. These scholars argue that political trust is better explained by political variables such as support for the governing party or coalition, national pride, interest in politics, and belief in open government (Anderson and Lo Tempio 2002). Ultimately, however, it remains unclear how much these findings reflect a fundamental difference between social and political trust or whether instead they are an artifact of the types of survey data used to measure the concepts.

Migration, assimilation, and inequality

A number of studies report that those who are high in social trust are those who Putnam (2000) refers to as the "winners" in society – those with more money, education, status, and higher levels of satisfaction in life and in work. Those who reside in the slums and the economically disadvantaged in our ethnic enclaves and inner cities simply do not have the same experiences that would foster general social trust (Newton 2007). There are many reasons for this, but one of them is the role that assimilation, or the lack of it, plays in providing individuals and communities the resources they need to succeed. On-the-ground experiences of many immigrants are such that disillusionment is likely to set in once the difficulties of making it in a new cultural setting sink in and greater knowledge of the weaknesses of a previously idealized version of democracy are acquired. In fact, Michelson (2001, 2003) shows that assimilation has an adverse effect on political trust for several groups migrating into the United States. For example, Michelson finds that Mexican-Americans who were born or have become citizens are less trusting of government than people of Mexican decent living in the U.S. that have not yet become citizens. Similarly, she also finds that Puerto Ricans born in Puerto Rico and living in the U.S. are more trusting than Puerto Ricans born in the United States. Michelson argues that these findings suggest that the process of assimilation is "corrosive of poltical trust" (2001: 232). In other words, it appears that attitudes about trust in government in this case reflect ideology and optimism rather than serve as an actual assessment of the performance of governmental institutions, though clearly experience tempers trust.

The migration of people to the more advanced capitalist societies is one of the major consequences of increasing economic interdependence in the global economy. Portes and Sensenbrenner

(1993) analyze the role of trust in economic outcomes for immigrants demonstrating empirically the impact of what Granovetter (1985) calls the embeddedness of economic activities in social relations. In particular, trust plays a big role in the informal economy in which immigrants are able to barter and trade services with individuals they deem trustworthy in their personal networks. They also use these networks as a kind of social capital to provide access to critical resources such as educational and training opportunities, entry-level jobs, and the provision of food and shelter until they can become established on their own terms. These networks provide the social capital immigrants need to get started on a new path to economic self-sufficiency, but under some circumstances they serve to lock-in immigrants with too much indebtedness to those who offered favors in the beginning. Some of their network-based relations, often with co-ethnics, are based on trust and provide social support, but some do not. Closed networks may result, which lock the employees into low-wage jobs with little time to develop the human capital that would be needed to move up and out of the enclave in which they live and work.

Victor Nee and Jimy Sanders (2001) look at this flow of human capital across national boundaries as one of the major social movements of our time. Problems of trust arise in the host societies as a byproduct of this flow of labor mainly into urban centers. Immigrants arrive and need to find both economic and social support. The incorporation of recent immigrants into the U.S. economy is a major determinant of economic development since it provides labor that is not available in certain job categories (especially in a service economy). It also creates stresses and strains in the receiving social context. Nee and Sanders look at the diverse paths immigrants take in their efforts to establish economic viability. They identify the family as the "key" institution that provides a basis for trust and for collective action among contemporary immigrants. The family becomes a source of social capital providing a multidimensional array of resources that facilitate incorporation into the larger society. In an empirical investigation of samples of Chinese, Filipino, and Korean immigrants in the Los Angeles area these investigators demonstrate how different modes of incorporation tend to be adopted by various immigrant groups. These differences are a function of differential access of these group members to social, financial, cultural, and human capital. Based on residential and job histories obtained from extensive interviews they examine the transition into various forms of ethnic entrepreneurship and self-employment. They find, for example, that the probability of owning an ethnic enterprise increases when the former employer is a co-ethnic, suggesting that these employers offer valuable experience and personal ties facilitative of future self-employment. Working for a relative, however, is inversely correlated with the rate of transition into owning one's own ethnic enterprise. Several reasons are explored including slower accumulation of capital due to unpaid or under-compensated labor and the likelihood that one moves into the family business over time rather than striking out on one's own.

The findings reported by Nee and Sanders (2001) support what they call a family capital model of incorporation that places great emphasis on the social capital generated by the family system (intra-family, kinship, and ethnic ties). Lack of access to family-based capital yields less desirable jobs in the low- and semi-skilled labor sectors. One major reason for the reliance on family capital is that for immigrants these relations form the basis of both interdependence and trust in settings in which, at least initially, they are in a world of strangers without access to the resources they need to enter the mainstream. This type of research focuses primarily on the individual-level transitions of immigrants and the role of trust and networks and the types of capital provided by each in their eventual success in the host society. But trust has also been treated as a factor in the transitions at the state-level in economic systems and governance structures as a result of political upheaval and transformation.

Trust in transitions

As we indicated in the introduction, one of the factors that has fueled the research on political as well as general social trust is the wave of political, economic, and social transitions that began in the early 1990s and has continued since then. Some of these transitions such as the one in Russia have been so fraught with corruption that confidence in all financial and political institutions became extremely low. Russia's transition from a central planned economy to a decentralized market economy created so much uncertainty and risk that for some time there was a retreat to closed social networks (some based on trust) and informal barter. This informal barter economy of exchange persists in response to banking failure and is reported to represent about half of all transactions (Rock and Solodkov 2001) in addition to perpetuating what is called the banking development trap in development economics. Zak and Knack (2001), among others, have discussed the role that generalized social trust plays in economic prosperity. While the mechanisms are not always clear, one major argument is that general social trust may reflect confidence in the institutions that support widespread cooperation and a reduction in the types of risks that make economic development possible.

Recent research from transitional societies outside of the United States and Europe has emphasized the importance of government performance, particularly in terms of corruption and macro-economic development, in fostering generalized trust in political institutions. In South Africa, increasing dissatisfaction with government delivery of socio-economic development has led to decreasing levels of trust in political institutions and a significant growth in anti-government social movements (Ballard 2005). A number of authors have suggested that this relationship between government performance and political trust is an important factor for the consolidation of democracy in transitional societies (e.g. Diamond 1999). However, Cleary and Stokes (2006) caution that the link between trust in any form and democracy is tenuous at best. Assessing a variety of theories and empirical evidence on trust and democracy, Cleary and Stokes argue that neither interpersonal nor institutional trust should be viewed as a *cause* of democratization, democratic consolidation, or improved democratic institutional performance (2006: 129–30). Thus it appears that the specific role of political trust in contrast to general social trust in these matters is still up for debate.

Conclusion

The rise in the reported significance of trust in social, organizational, and international relations has paralleled the increase in risk and uncertainty that has accompanied massive changes in the global economy. What happens in one small corner of the world can have large repercussions for those in places once viewed as distant. Along with increased interdependence and interconnectedness comes the need for new social structures and forms of collective action and governance that move beyond national boundaries. It has been argued by many scholars that general social trust is correlated with a productive economy. But it is not clear why. Cook, Hardin, and Levi (2005: 196) argue that: "Societies are essentially evolving away from trust relationships toward externally regulated behavior," due to changes in the nature of our relationships. Over long periods of time we have moved away from thick relations of trust and normative control in small, sometimes isolated or closed communities to larger open networks of thin relations of trust and cooperation with many people spread out in geographic space. This has altered the fundamental ways in which everyday business is accomplished and has important implications for the potential for the emergence of trust relations, accurate assessments of trustworthiness, and alternative modes of cooperation. It also has implications for our capacity to know enough to "trust" any institution. What is important is that we, at the least, gain confidence that these institutions are being given proper oversight and that there is legal recourse for those who are the victims of corruption or exploitation.

Confidence in institutions supports the growth of the types of transactions that result in economic development. Often what individuals mean when they say they have trust in government is that they are confident in the reliability and legitimacy of government. Political trust refers mainly to this domain. Social trust seems to reflect not only confidence in the institutions and organizations in which social exchanges are embedded, but also trust in other individuals, typically those we do not know and whom we can take a risk on because there are safeguards. But in some networks, such as those facilitated in the online world of interaction and transactions, the risk of exploitation remains high. It appears that social trust and political trust are quite distinct. Future research should examine more carefully the relations between the various forms of trust as well as move beyond correlational evidence to examine their causes and consequences. While we know a great deal about trust in specific domains we still do not have a clear conception of the linkages between trust at various levels. Finally, there is much less work on distrust and the ways in which it can be mitigated (but see Hardin 2004 and Kramer and Cook 2004). Efforts to investigate settings in which distrust is the norm should allow us to understand more about the role of trust in others and in institutions.

Note

1 The General Social Survey asks a number of questions that have been used in the past as indicators of generalized trust. In addition to this item the others typically used in a general social trust scale include: 1) Do you think most people would try to take advantage of you, or would they try to be fair? 2) Would you say that most of the time people try to be helpful, or that they are mostly looking out for themselves?

References

Alesina, A. and E. La Ferrara. 2002. "Who Trusts Others?" *Journal of Public Economics* 85 (2): 207–234.

Anderson, C.J. and A.J. LoTempio. 2002. "Winning, Losing and Political Trust in America." *British Journal of Political Science* 32 (02): 335–51.

Arrow, Kenneth J. 1974. *The Limits of Organization.* New York, NY: Norton.

Ballard, Richard *et al.* 2005. "Globalization, Marginalization and Contemporary Social Movements in South Africa." *African Affairs* 104 (417): 615–34.

Braithwaite, Valerie A. and Margaret Levi eds. 1998. *Trust and Governance.* New York: Russell Sage Foundation Publications.

Buchan, Nancy R., Rachel T. A. Croson, and Robyn M. Dawes. 2002. "Swift Neighbors and Persistent Strangers: A Cross-cultural Investigation of Trust and Reciprocity in Social Exchange." *American Journal of Sociology* 108 (1): 168–206.

Cleary, Matthew R. and Susan Carol Stokes. 2006. *Democracy and the Culture of Skepticism: Political Trust in Argentina and Mexico.* New York, NY: Russell Sage Foundation.

Cook, Karen S. 2005. "Networks, Norms, and Trust: The Social Psychology of Social Capital 2004 Cooley Mead Award Address." *Social Psychology Quarterly* 68 (1): 4–14.

Cook, Karen S., Russell Hardin, and Margaret Levi. 2005. *Cooperation without Trust?* New York, NY: Russell Sage Foundation.

Cook, K.S., R. Kramer, D. Thom, S. Bailey, I. Stepanikova, and R. Cooper. 2004. "Physician–Patient Trust Relations in an Era of Managed Care," in *Trust and Distrust in Organizations,* edited by R. Kramer and K.S. Cook. New York, NY: Russell Sage Foundation.

Cook, K.S., E.R.W. Rice, and A. Gerbasi. 2004. "The Emergence of Trust Networks Under Uncertainty: The Case of Transitional Economies – Insights from Social Psychological Research," in *Problems of Post Socialist Transition: Creating Social Trust,* edited by S. Rose-Ackerman, B. Rothstein, and J. Kornai. New York, NY: Palgrave Macmillan.

Delhey, Jan and Kenneth Newton. 2005. "Predicting Cross-National Levels of Social Trust: Global Pattern Or Nordic Exceptionalism?" *European Sociological Review* 21 (4): 311–27.

Diamond, Larry Jay. 1999. *Developing Democracy: Toward Consolidation*. Baltimore, MD: Johns Hopkins University Press.

Dirks, Kurt T. and Donald L. Ferrin. 2001. "The Role of Trust in Organizational Settings." *Organization Science* 12 (4): 450–67.

Dunn, J. 1988. "Trust and Political Agency," in *Trust: Making and Breaking Cooperative Relations*, edited by D. Gambetta. Oxford: Blackwell.

Fukuyama, Francis. 1995. *Trust: Social Virtues and the Creation of Prosperity*. New York, NY: Free Press.

Gambetta, Diego. 1993. *The Sicilian Mafia: The Business of Private Protection*. Cambridge, MA: Harvard University Press.

——. 1988. *Trust: Making and Breaking Cooperative Relations*. New York, NY: B. Blackwell.

Gambetta, Diego and Heather Hamill. 2005. *Streetwise: How Taxi Drivers Establish their Customers' Trustworthiness*. New York, NY: Russell Sage Foundation.

Granovetter, Mark. 1985. "Economic Action and Social Structure: The Problem of Embeddedness." *American Journal of Sociology* 91 (3): 481–510.

Hardin, R. 2004. "Distrust," in edited by Anonymous. New York, NY: Russell Sage Foundation.

——. 2002. *Trust and Trustworthiness*. New York, NY: Russell Sage Foundation.

Kaase, M. 1999. "Interpersonal Trust, Political Trust and Non-Institutionalised Political Participation in Western Europe." *West European Politics* 22: 1–21.

Keele, L. 2007. "Social Capital and the Dynamics of Trust in Government." *American Journal of Political Science* 51 (2): 241–54.

Knack, Stephen and Philip Keefer. 1997. "Does Social Capital have an Economic Payoff? A Cross-Country Investigation." *Quarterly Journal of Economics* 112 (4): 1251–88.

Kramer, R.M. and K.S. Cook. 2004. "Trust and Distrust in Organizations: Dilemmas and Approaches," in edited by Anonymous. New York, NY: Russell Sage Foundation.

Levi, Margaret. 1997. *Consent, Dissent, and Patriotism*. New York, NY: Cambridge University Press.

Levi, Margaret and Laura Stoker. 2000. "Political Trust and Trustworthiness." *Annual Review of Political Science* 3 (1): 475–507.

Luhmann, Niklas. 1979. *Trust and Power: Two Works*. New York, NY: Wiley.

Malhotra, Deepak and J. Keith Murnighan. 2002. "The Effects of Contracts on Interpersonal Trust." *Administrative Science Quarterly* 47 (3): 534–59.

Michelson, Melissa R. 2003. "The Corrosive Effect of Acculturation: How Mexican Americans Lose Political Trust." *Social Science Quarterly* 84 (4): 918–33.

——. 2001. "Political Trust among Chicago Latinos." *Journal of Urban Affairs* 23 (3): 323–34.

Mishler, W. 2005. "What are the Political Consequences of Trust? A Test of Cultural and Institutional Theories in Russia." *Comparative Political Studies* 38 (9): 1050–78.

Mishler, W. and R. Rose. 2001. "What are the Origins of Political Trust? Testing Institutional and Cultural Theories in Post-Communist Societies." *Comparative Political Studies* 34 (1): 30–62.

Nee, V. and J. Sanders. 2001. "Trust in Ethnic Ties: Social Capital and Immigrants," in *Trust in Society*, edited by K.S. Cook. New York, NY: Russell Sage Foundation.

Newton, Kenneth. 2001. "Trust, Social Capital, Civil Society, and Democracy." *International Political Science Review* 22 (2): 201–14.

North, Douglass Cecil. 1990. *Institutions, Institutional Change, and Economic Performance*. New York, NY: Cambridge University Press.

Paxton, Pamela. 1999. "Is Social Capital Declining in the United States? A Multiple Indicator Assessment." *American Journal of Sociology* 105 (1): 88–127.

Portes, Alejandro and Julia Sensenbrenner. 1993. "Embeddedness and Immigration: Notes on the Social Determinants of Economic Action." *American Journal of Sociology* 98 (6): 1320–50.

Putnam, Robert D. 1995. "Bowling Alone: America's Declining Social Capital." *Journal of Democracy* 6: 65–78.

——2000. *Bowling Alone: The Collapse and Revival of American Community*. New York, NY: Simon & Schuster.

——. 1993. *Making Democracy Work: Civic Traditions in Modern Italy*. Princeton, NJ: Princeton University Press.

——. 1995. "Tuning in, Tuning Out: The Strange Disappearance of Social Capital in America." *PS: Political Science and Politics* 28 (4): 664–83.

Radaev, V. "How Trust is Established in Economic Relationships: When Institutions and Individuals are Not Trustworthy," in *Problems of Post Socialist Transition: Creating Social Trust*, edited by S. Rose-Ackerman, B. Rothstein, and J. Kornai. New York, NY: Palgrave Macmillan.

Rock, Charles P. and Vasiliy Solodkov. 2001. "Monetary Policies, Banking, and Trust in Changing Institutions: Russia's Transition in the 1990s." *Journal of Economic Issues* 35 (2): 451–8.

Rousseau, Denise M. *et al.* 1998. "Not so Different After All: A Cross-Discipline View of Trust." *Academy of Management Review* 23 (3): 393–404.

Smith, Sandra. 2010. "Race and Trust." *Annual Review of Sociology* 36.

Sztompka, P. 2006. "New Perspectives on Trust." *American Journal of Sociology* 112 (3): 905–19.

Tocqueville, Alexis de. 1840 [1838]. *Democracy in America*. London: Saunders & Otley.

Uslaner, Eric M. 2002. *The Moral Foundations of Trust*. New York, NY: Cambridge University Press.

Uslaner, Eric M. and Mitchell Brown. 2005. "Inequality, Trust, and Civic Engagement." *American Politics Research* 33 (6): 868–94.

Williamson, Oliver E. 1993. "Calculativeness, Trust, and Economic Organization." *Journal of Law and Economics* 36 (1): 453–86.

Yamagishi, Toshio. 1988. "The Provision of a Sanctioning System in the United States and Japan." *Social Psychology Quarterly* 51 (3): 265–71.

Yamagishi, Toshio and Karen S. Cook. 1993. "Generalized Exchange and Social Dilemmas." *Social Psychology Quarterly* 56 (4): 235–48.

Yamagishi, Toshio and Midori Yamagishi. 1994. "Trust and Commitment in the United States and Japan." *Motivation and Emotion* 18 (2): 129–66.

Yamagishi, Toshio, K. S. Cook, and M. Watabe. 1998. "Uncertainty, Trust, and Commitment Formation in the United States and Japan." *American Journal of Sociology* 104 (1).

Zak, Paul J. and Stephen Knack. 2001. "Trust and Growth." *The Economic Journal* 111 (470): 295–321.

Zucker, L.G. 1986. "Production of Trust: Institutional Sources of Economic Structure, 1840–1920," in *Research in Organizational Behavior*, edited by B.M. Staw and L.L. Cummings. Greenwich, CT: JAI Press, Inc.

Environment and Risk

Timothy W. Luke

Risk and the environment offer many opportunities for social and political theorists to probe serious and unstable uncertainties, which today's major cultural, economic, and state institutions should face in the twenty-first century. For those who scrutinize the threats involved, risk can, in fact, be both routinely regarded, and cynically constructed, as an inescapable component of complex contemporary capitalist exchange. Whether one considers the varying probabilities of experiencing a local nuclear meltdown (like Chernobyl or Three Mile Island), weathering a national financial meltdown (like the collapse of Bear Stearns or Long Term Capital Management), or surviving a global market meltdown (like the financial panics of September 2008 in the North Atlantic or July 1997 in South Asia), it is plain that recognizing risk must be regarded as another unavoidable aspect of coping with freedom and necessity. Indeed, risks are now a quite ordinary conditions of human beings interoperating with complex institutions, machineries, and systems; and, in turn, theorizing about the conditions of risk brings it into the collective cultural consciousness of the overall environment as a rather normalized abnormality (Beck 1992; Cairncross 1992; Durning 1992).

Certainly, no one wants accidents, catastrophes, or disaster to disrupt the natural, built, or information environments that global economies and societies rely upon (Casimir 2008). Yet, these abnormal disruptions will occur. Accepting the fact that these risks are foreseeable, manageable and even predictable is part of making them, in turn, acceptable practical preoccupations in policy-making via more disciplinary permutations in the discourse of risk (Lash, Szerszynski, and Wynne 1996).

Risk and the Environment

Risk typically is understood as a quantifiable assessment of either less-than-optimal returns and/ or more-than-expected losses (Douglas 1983; Beck 1992; Lupton 2005). This characterization can be seen as too matter-of-fact, if not ideological, in its simplicity. Confining this brief discussion only to risk and the natural environment is plenty to consider cautiously as an engagement for social and political theory, even though one can find many other varieties of risk in global markets or sophisticated technologies. Taken together, these intertwined domains of activity unfold in the still ongoing modernization and development of already modern and developed life, or what Beck (1992) goes so far as to label as "second modernity." Beck's risk society analyses have been questioned (Strydom 2002), but Beck's analysis is one widely used approach to the social construction of both risk and the analysis of the risk (Eder 1996) found in the equally social constructions of Nature. Even though Beck's characterizations are contestable, accepting the benefits of this alleged second modernity in the twenty-first century apparently demands that many human beings must both endure and enjoy the creation of continuous chaos and occasional catastrophes as normal attributes of everyday life under conditions of affluence (Galbraith 1958). Of course, many more might have to endure the costs, while only a few enjoy the benefits. While Eder perhaps goes too far in claiming that risk populations constitute a new postindustrial class structure, given the many cross-cutting parameters of risk that rip across these classes, he is correct to observe how far the recognition of, mobilization against, and protection from greater risk are used "to reproduce a public image of a class of people at risk" (Eder 1993: 13) by professional–technical experts and the populations they believe to be, or actually are, at risk. Yet this reality of risk is made ordinary through the matrices of power/powerlessness, prestige/obscurity, privilege/deprivation that normalize varying qualities of individual existence. Their frequency and severity vary by location, differ in timing, and fluctuate in duration, but everyone anywhere at any time in this second modernity usually at some point accedes that risk is as salient as prosperity as an environmental condition for their being (Douglas 1983; Brown 1981). At the household, firm, and national level of calculation, every individual essentially has new duties imposed upon his or her existence, namely the state expects them to be aware of "the potential for catastrophe of modern large-scale technologies and industries," which, in turn, allows both the elites and masses in society to "estimate and legitimate" (Beck 1995: 32) the necessity of living in this fashion. As Sunstein (2002a: xiv) asserts, "risk reduction has become a principal goal of modern governments."

Risk, then, is a perfect discourse for conjuring moral equivalents of fear, hate, or loss within the creative destruction of market exchange by professional–technical experts. Because the enemy is not truly a foreign outsider or insurgent insider marked by sufficient otherness to be an existential foe, the politics of risk must identify and substantiate often more fictive foe-like surrogates in the hazards of everyday existences unfolding along with large machinic systems, unknown environmental disruption, unanticipated structural dangers, or unintended lifestyle harms. Here expert scientific and technical knowledge discovers, or at least validates, the reality of risk, and the basis is found for organizing multiple programs of risk politics. Once organized, these political programs can be ignored by all, turned into an institutional basis for lobbying corporations, governments, and NGOs, or adopted by local, provincial, or national state agencies to orient their official policies.

Actuarial statistics are plain on this count. To take one example, with now 310 million people in the U.S.A., it is the case that around 6,700 will die every day (Campos 2010). Close to 4,800 of these deaths will be individuals 65 and older, whose deaths are typically deemed "natural." To live on Earth is to risk death, and these individuals mostly exceeded, met, or slightly missed their life expectancies from surviving in this planet's environment. So about 1,900 of those who die each day are less than 65. Nearly 140 or so are children, around 120 are auto accident victims, about 85 will be suicides (usually half due to a handgun), around 50 will be murders (Campos 2010). Each cluster of deaths, then, constitutes, as Eder suggests "an empirical class of people at risk" (1993: 13) of death by some socially identifiable, representable, and assessable cause of death that the many basically ignore until a few mobilize some to gain attention.

An awareness of the need to anticipate existential risk for humanity and the entire environment undoubtedly was first seriously sparked during July 16, 1945 when the world's inaugural nuclear test was conducted outside Alamogordo, New Mexico. After working for nearly a decade on the engineering challenges posed by creating and controlling nuclear fission, the U.S.A. was ready to ignite humanity's first atomic explosive device. Some Manhattan Project scientists had speculated for years that such a nuclear event on the planet's surface might set afire its entire atmosphere. The White House and the Pentagon deemed the risks involved worth taking, so the firing button was pushed. The Trinity site atomic test experiment worked, and the Earth's skies did not burst into flames during the experiment. It also was deemed worth the risk to use the device in war within three weeks. Two operational bombs – Little Boy and Flat Man – were then exploded respectively over Hiroshima and Nagasaki, Japan. These risky, but also rewarding decisions for Washington initiated a new era of nuclear warfare, but they also ended the last phase of the big conventional world military conflicts of World War II that began when Tokyo risked so much for Japan by attacking Pearl Harbor four years before.

With the invention, testing, and deployment by 1953 of thermonuclear weapons, which had immensely greater destructive potential, the U.S.A. and U.S.S.R. did put some scientists to work studying the risks of destroying the Earth's biosphere should an all-out thermonuclear war occur. There arguably were not the requisite numbers of bombs, delivery systems, and targets developed, deployed, and designated truly to hazard that prospect until 1970, but the initiation of the Strategic Arms Limitation Talks in November 1969 (and then later Treaties in May 1972 and June 1979) in the Nixon/Ford/Carter era implicitly underscored how seriously both Washington and Moscow regarded the raw reality of these environmental risks. With over 50,000 deliverable warheads in the American and Soviet arsenals carrying a combined destructive potential in the multigigatons range, most experts were certain all life on Earth could end, at least for some decades if not centuries, within weeks after a full-scale thermonuclear exchange. The "crisis of science" as modernity took full hold well before 1914 (Husserl 1970), but it became a constant crisis for society when this uniquely unpredictable second modernity blossoms after 1945.

The embeddedness of risk in this problematic second modernity is all the more an ineluctable aspect of life once one realizes how, like the system of nuclear deterrence, complexly accidental everyday life is organized. Following Perrow (1984: 3), advanced standards of living develop as "we create systems – organizations, and organizations of organization – that increase risk for the operators, passengers, innocent bystanders, and for future generations." Perrow is fascinated with the regularity with which "normal accidents" with "catastrophic potential" (Perrow 1984: 3) in the organized complexity of an organizational society. Still, this focus on systematicity, organization, engineering, and design stresses the elements of extraordinary intentional rationality, which all signal that risks always are anticipated and checked. In fact, the normal accident is a marker of accidental normality all tacitly acknowledge as background conditions for modern life. Its manifold ordinary unintended irrationalities generate routinized risks one rarely considers until, like today's excessive levels of greenhouse gassing, threaten the ways of existence that greenhouse gases make possible through intensive fossil fuel energy consumption. Routinizing risk in the accidental normality organized of built and unbuilt environments is critical for modernity, but it is rarely identified fully as being another standpoint to articulate a full-blown critique of modernity.

Strangely enough, from initial studies of the Earth's atmosphere during the 1950s to assess the prospects for a nuclear end of life on Earth, scientists confirmed, and then began to systematically monitor, a trend first detected in 1824 by Joseph Fourier, namely a rising concentration of greenhouse gases, such as nitrous oxide, carbon dioxide, methane, and carbon monoxide. Measured effectively first in the atmosphere by Svante Arrenius in 1896, and then later in the planet's oceans, this side-effect of industrialization initially was regarded as a positive, if unanticipated, outcome of industrialization as the Earth experienced a Little Ice Age into the nineteenth century. While it was known that the concentration of these greenhouse gases has varied widely over geological time, a significant new spike began to rise considerably in the nineteenth century, especially in the Northern Hemisphere, as the Industrial Revolution began. From the 1780s on, their levels steadily have increased; but it has been the institutional emplacement of accurate measurement sites, beginning in the darker days of the Cold War during the 1950s, which have enabled scientists to track a truly intense and rapid concentration of these compounds as the post-World War II global economy boomed. While greenhouse gas levels have been varied from year to year, an upward trend in their concentrations has been relentless since 1959. Some scientists saw the greenhouse effect as positive, but others regarded this phenomenon as negative. Either way, these human industrial activities apparently have been putting the Earth's environment, and thus humanity, at risk through inadvertent anthropogenic alterations in the planet's biosphere.

Risk and Inequality

Because environmental risks are characterized by many cross-cutting contradictions, society's customary inequalities frequently color many people's considerations of the upsides and downsides of acting with alacrity to mitigate risk in the environment (Hudson 2003). As Strydom (2008: 5–22) observes, the process of risk identification and communication is one of "world creation" in conditions of contingent complexity by multiple learning collectives. While many risk calculations often only scan initial primary effects rather than more mediated secondary, tertiary, or even quaternary implications of endangerment, they are nonetheless what many experts and most people confine themselves to consider in calculations of risk (Lupton 2005). Some groups, for example, still believe global warming trends linked to rising concentrations of carbon dioxide in the atmosphere from generating more fossil fuel energy can be checked at 350 parts per million, keeping average temperatures at no more than 2°C above preindustrial levels and then even reversed back to those less contaminated levels. Others, however, doubt the prospects of either halting these trends in contaminating pollution or seeing much immediate positive benefits from any containment of greenhouse gas increases.

As a result, this sense of environmental risk is leading many to look beyond mitigating further increases in greenhouse gas levels to anticipate and then adapt to the widespread environmental damage already sure to occur. As many plan for such things to come, the environmental risks of greenhouse gases are becoming a major theme behind steering future social and economic development. Those who continue to reside in existing coastal cities and regions now do so at their own hazard, since the risks of rising sea levels, extraordinary storm damage, and unprecedented weather patterns make many human settlements of the past century or more entirely unsustainable in their current forms. Beck pays less attention to the class inequalities in second modernity, but here, of course, the poor are left with few options but to remain in place, hoping for the best. The middle classes can risk ruin in the long run, while having short-run emergency contingency plans for surviving infrequent severe emergencies. And, finally, the wealthy are able to stay in place until perhaps forced to retreat to the probable new coastal zones made predictably by risk assessment. The rising water, varying weather, and changing climate to come are the risks all are invited to anticipate. By and large, however, few are changing their current energy-use behaviors in any truly radical manner (McDonough and Braungart 2002). The poor still use very little energy, the middle classes might shift their home lighting over to compact fluorescent from incandescent bulbs, and the rich can invest in carbon credit swaps, but few believe their individual risks truly can be reduced by shrinking their ecological footprint, carbon intensity, or resource use (Lyall and Tait 2005).

The varieties of programmatic risk politics are quite diverse in scale, scope, and success, but they have been particularly successful in many areas where basic human needs already are mostly satisfied for the majority of the population. By the 1950s and 1960s, then, one sees risk-mitigating campaigns to curtail smog, limit urban sprawl, stop tobacco smoking, improve automobile safety, increase physical fitness, halt nuclear power, change medicine containers, ban pesticides, outlaw certain food additives, etc. in wealthy societies. In each case, the element of risk varies, but cadres of experts mobilize anxieties about personal safety and security to bring these matters into public debate, if not ongoing corporate practices and continual state regulation.

Since fossil fuel will be burned, automobiles will be built, and packaged foods will be produced, risk managers calculate the numbers of deaths per 100,000 or 1,000,000 in the population for doing business as usual, and then mount their moral equivalents of permanent war on GHG emissions, unsafe automobile/road design, and industrial agriculture's pesticide-, preservative-, and packaging-intensive means of bringing products to market that also then may promote heart disease, cancer, autoimmune disorders, obesity, or other debilitating health effects. In staging their symbolic politics of "populations at risk," actuarial science is mobilized as the decision technics for risk assessment, comparison, and response. When it finds out of any 100,000 or 1,000,000 people that X or Y number will on average definitely die a year, the basis of individual and/or collective responses perhaps can be sought, if not even found, depending upon the nature of the threat, who is threatened, and how effectively the public image of the classes of people at risk represent their endangerment.

When a risk factor in the social environment, such as radical Islamic terrorists or aging nuclear plants, is fairly specific, tangible, and point-specific, experts often quickly organize responses, however ineffectual and perhaps counterproductive they might be. When risk factors, such as greenhouse gas emissions or automobile crashes, are more general, attenuated, or dispersed, getting serious countermeasures in place, however necessary and productive they might be, typically proves difficult. Here there are many ironies. Closing down nuclear power plant growth in the U.S.A. since 1979 has only made it more necessary to import gas and oil from the unstable Islamic Mideast, but this dependence on the region has served to enflame Islamic terrorist attackers. Billions have been spent in the U.S.A. since the attacks of 9.11.01 on counterterrorist measures, but the risk of a passenger on an American commercial airliner during the 2000s being killed was 1 in 25 million ("this high" only due to the 9.11 attacks when all of the fatalities were incurred) versus 1 American out of 500,000 being struck by lightning a year (Silver 2010). And no Americans are known to have been harmed by any commercial nuclear power plant mishap outside the facilities experiencing the accident. Even the infamous March 28, 1979 Three Mile Island reactor accident released only an average radioactive dose equivalent to a chest x-ray for those within 10 miles of the plant (see: <http://www.ans.org/pi/resources/sptopics/tmi/whathappened.html>). With 310 million people, the U.S.A. has around 255 million automobile vehicles on the road, (see: http://www.bts.gov/publications/national_transportation_statistics/html/table_01_11.html), according to the U.S. Department of Transportation. These human and machine populations help to make the nation the world's second largest emitter of greenhouse gases. Yet, it is still hard to specify in 2010 how many deaths are somehow attributable now (or in the past two decades of its growing concern) to global warming, even as humanity puts another 8.2 tons of carbon dioxide into the atmosphere each year (Hodges 2010: 17). At the same time, 120 Americans typically die every day in traffic accidents (Campos 2010), or about 44,000 a year. Of course, insurance companies, auto manufacturers, and traffic organizations continue to highlight the risks of automobile crashes, but these most common, numerous, and deadly annual losses are viewed as tolerable costs for the immense benefits of automotive ways of life.

There are pernicious dilemmas at play in these knowledge-driven calculations (Gibbons *et al.* 1994). Most environmental disasters are localized, infrequent, and short-lived, so doing anything generally in the long run to forestall their occurrence seems unnecessary: maintaining the might behind "the system of objects" (Baudrillard 1996) trumps any search for security for subjects as such. Until an environmental catastrophe becomes more universal, frequent, and long-lasting, few react with dispatch. Hardly any individuals, few firms, and not many governments have done anything with any radical scope or true importance. To do so would entail other risks. Doing something significant, as many risk-management experts note, would have to be based upon still contested scientific analysis, incomplete technical developments, and high-cost/limited effectiveness countermeasures (Briden and Downing 2002). Yet, once something significant must be done, all existing countermeasures believed to be effective now might have no effect, would involve unbearable costs, could use maladapted technology, and rest upon still problematic, if any, sound scientific certainty in existing evidence. At that point, adaptation may well require more than retreating inland from existing coastal areas, building more weather-resistant structures, or changing familiar consumption patterns. Survival itself might be in question; and, once again, those who are likely to survive will shift through customary triage patterns. That is, the poor will be victimized, suffer, and die first, more, and sooner at the local, national, and global level. The rich will be able to cope more effectively but, like the middle class, they will not be able to live the same ways as before the risks foretold of global warming caused by greenhouse gases got out of control.

Once fixed upon a sort of solutions by the calculi of risk, it is clear that the managerial elites at the top of states, companies, and non-governmental organizations increasingly tend to mobilize risk-management scenarios as the discipline they require "to manage a population" not only as a "collective mass of phenomena, the level of its aggregate effects" on macro-level scales, but also to focus "the management of population in its depths and details" (Foucault 1991: 102) in micro-level settings. The environment, then, serves well as a polyvalent focus for states in such calculations, but national loyalties often will fade, or maybe even fail, for those initiating campaigns to launch global interventions against risk. If one appraises environmental risk management against the costs and benefits incurred by the most successful fraction of individuals who are "risk makers" against those of the least successful majority of individuals who suffer as risks are taken, then its imperatives for success are high. In the "order of things" (Foucault 1970), one finds the imperatives of political economy eclipsing the needs of biology and humanity as the losses of greater energy use are counterbalanced against their economic benefits. Risk makers rarely are the real risk takers, so the overall taken risks soon fall hardest and soonest on those beyond the risk-making minority. In somewhat glib liberal fashion, Sunstein concurs in this regard. He argues that even though nations everywhere seem to be responding "to reduce risks, to improve safety, and to extend lives. … Nations do not place sufficient emphasis on science. Rather than investigate the facts, they tend to react on the basis of intuition or in response to temporary fears" (Sunstein 2002a: xiii).

In his brief epistemic meditation, "What is Enlightenment?" as Foucault observes, Kant appears to be, "looking for a difference: What difference does today introduce with regard to yesterday" (1984: 34). Foucault (1984: 34) suggests Kant finds his decisive difference for humanity in accepting the merits of "knowing as empowering." Fear of loss, anxiety over injury, and want of benefit often come from powerlessness (Virilio 1995). To the extent that knowing the risks of loss, harm, or cost are calculable, power would then come from realizing the level and nature of risk as systematic knowledge. For Foucault, Kant assigns the project of enlightenment "a motto, an instruction that one gives oneself and purposes to others. What, then, is this instruction? Aude Sapere: 'dare to know,' 'have the courage, the audacity to know'" (Foucault 1984: 34–35).

A good bit of this courage under conditions of Beck's second modernity is meant to steel oneself for risk, and the audacity of knowing is the willingness to know more clearly the percentages of hazarding greater gain against the chances of great loss (Virilio 1996, 1997).

Coping with "environmental problems" on what are believed commonly to be sound scientific and technical grounds is often regarded as the paramount risk management exercise of this century. Professional–technical experts propound disciplinary expressions of different "knowledges" to anchor operations of "power" over, but also within and through, the flow of events that are worked-up actuarially as calculable risks of either disaster or development by modern economies and societies. Technoscientific power over the environment, however, is, and always has been, evolving with changing interpretive fashions, shifting epistemic agendas, and developing technical advances coming from knowledge about "the nature" of Nature (Mangun and Henning 1999). To manage risk in an environment still under development is to have "a will to knowledge that is anonymous, polymorphous, susceptible to regular transformations" (Foucault 1977: 200–1).

Risk arguably, then, is a polymorphous unstable combination of knowledge and power born from a ceaseless quest for great performativity (Lyotard 1984). As Foucault indicates, it "traverses and produces things," but its calculi needs to be considered as another productive network which runs through the whole social body (Foucault 1980: 119). Because of its potential negative effects, the level and intensity of risk in the environment must be recognized, and then some quantifiable measurements of it have to be produced, but who produces it, how it is done, why it becomes what it is, and where it happens are critical concerns.

From risk discourse, one can define, for example:

> the way in which individuals or groups represent words to themselves, utilize their forms and meanings, compose real discourse, reveal and conceal in it what they are thinking or saying, perhaps unknown to themselves, more or less than they wish, but in any case leave a mass of verbal traces of those thoughts, which must be deciphered and restored as far as possible to their representative vivacity.
>
> *(Foucault 1994: 353)*

Where life, labor, and language conjoin in discourses of risk and environmental hazard, one finds those formations of power/knowledge about greenhouse gases that disclose "how man, in his being, can be concerned with the things he knows, and know the things that, in positivity, determine his mode of being" (Foucault 1994: 354). Risk, therefore, is now, a historical artifact of restrictive expert management that is constructed in nation states, corporate entities, and scientific analyses by professional technoscientific interventions as the armature for Beck's "risk society" (1992). In this network of technoscientific activity, the identification of risk and the strengthening of controls over them can be linked together as "the empirical realm" of policy management (Foucault 1994: 362–3).

Such flexible and fluid codes of risk are used to constitute a new worldwide regimen for managing economic resource scarcities and social reward systems as the costs and benefits of greenhouse gas emissions are measured against greater economic growth. It is not just risk that matters but rather "the human skill and social organization which lie behind it. ... it is the professional experts who have constructed the system, which in turn has created them" (Perkin 1996: 1). As Sunstein argues, the main operation logic of expertise in risk society is cost/benefit analysis (Sunstein 2002b). That these forces of administration emerged at the dawn of the Cold War from the stark realities of the nuclear deterrence regime is telling.

Risk calculi reveal sites where "truth," or "a system of order procedures for the production, regulation, distribution, circulation, and operation of statements" (Foucault 1984: 133), can arise within legitimate social formations, such as the decision-making bureaux of liberal democratic states and capitalist firms (Fischer 1990). As Foucault asserts:

> [T]here are manifold relations of power which permeate, characterize and constitute the social body, and these relations of power cannot themselves be established, consolidated nor implemented without the production, accumulation, circulation and functioning of a discourse. There can be no possible exercise of power without a certain economy of discourses of truth which operates through and on the basis of this association.
>
> *(Foucault 1984: 95)*

The economy of discourses behind the truth needed for risk and environment managerial actions are vital cycles of conceptual cogeneration. In these exchanges, power re-energizes knowledges with truthfulness even as these knowledges mediate power through the expertise of calculating costs and benefits (Denney 2005). Risk environmentalism, then, simply rearticulates the same modernist paradigms of all control-centered positivist science. Through risk analysis, as Argyrou (2005: x) would maintain, envisioning the environment as always "at risk" reaffirms the inherent inequities in "the ability of a group of societies to define and redefine, construct and reconstruct the order of the world and the world order," which empowers the few to negotiate their views on the conditions of life for the many.

Conclusion

To make the political or social analysis of risk matter in social theory, then, one must ask, "Where are we going?" (Flyvbjerg 2001: 612). What is regarded usually as acceptable is just too simple a response: to trust scientific experts and business owners to do what is best for the common good in accord with prevailing scientific and business practices is the policy that had used apparently to the brink of disaster. Liberal democratic assumptions about science and capital typically trust those with the control of technology (or the "know-how") and/or those who have ownership of capital (or the "own-how") in the economy and society (see Yanow 1996) with unwarranted power (Chertow and Esty 1997). These same assumptions, however, occlude how fully most economic and social relations are structured to assure that most members in society cannot acquire the know-how or accumulate the own-how (Luke 2003) needed be equal players in the policy process. Certainly, current arrangements of risk management structurally ensure that most individuals will never know-how or own-how the modes of production operate, because the subpolitical impulse of risk management (Beck 1992) has mostly displaced political will as the driving force in most economies and societies. Thus, to ask "where we are going" deflects attention from the experts who speak for us, where we have headed, and how it is going.

As Beck asserts, the momentum embedded in big technological systems, like cybernetic networks, national economies, or logistical chains, are the material basis of risky outcomes from the policy process as social space and time shrink in globalization (Luke 1996). Within their mystified workings,

> The political institutions become the administrators of a development they neither have planned for nor are able to structure, but must nevertheless somehow justify. ... Lacking a place to appear, the decisions that change society become tongue-tied and anonymous. ... What we do not see and do not want is changing the world more and more obviously and threateningly.
>
> *(Beck 1992: 186–7)*

Quite problematically, therefore, individual choices made by engineers and experts are built into collective choices about how to structure the economy and society. As a result, the overall development of human society is now organized around "subpolitical systems of scientific, technological, and economic modernization."

(Beck 1992: 186)

Major systems are, explicitly and implicitly, manipulated mostly by a tiny minority, which can reconfigure shared risk without much, if any, decisive civic legitimation (Beck 1997) beyond the dictates of ordinary economic rationality. Sunstein, for example, does not see risk reduction as an unchecked set of practices. On the contrary, his social theory of risk oversight easily justifies a new governmentalization of the state via the practices of actuarial science. For him, the U.S.A. is rapidly evolving into "a cost-benefit state" in which "government regulation is increasingly assessed by asking whether the benefits of regulation justify the costs of regulation" (Sunstein 2002b: ix). The 1997 Kyoto protocol and 2009 Copenhagen accords basically enjoin all to "take note" of the risks in greenhouse gassing on the environment, but there are no binding constraints on the costs entailed. Certainly, as more gain the benefits of greater fossil fuel use, there is a lessened willingness to check their growing gain even though many more potentially will lose most of the advances of energy-intensive development as the natural environment deteriorates. While such international accords are more than just empty talk, they do not point towards making substantial serious changes in either policies or practices.

Nonetheless, at this juncture in contemporary global affairs, these emergent trends in risk management have acquired great significance, because the capillaries of control where social forces or political theorists might possibly make a difference in the calculations of risk regarding the environment are diffuse. Social and political theory must continue to tussle with the hard realities at work in this challenge. Avoiding future losses, as well as protecting the already realized gains from the modern forms of life already constructed since the nineteenth century, are the key goals for risk assessment, but the relevant columns for calculating gain and loss in these accounts truly are difficult to map over existing social divides. That is, most policy-driven calculations of risk regarding the environment in most economies and societies today usually

> lie across the distinction between theory and practice, across the borders of specialties and disciplines,across the specialized competencies and institutional responsibilities, across the distinction between value and fact (and thus between ethics and science), and across the realms of politics, the public sphere, science and the economy, which are seemingly divided by institutions.
>
> *(Beck 1992: 70)*

While their arcane mechanisms are complex, the ethical and economic criteria supporting such risk assessments are all the more important, because they unfold at these creaky intersections of power, position, and prestige.

Stuck at these conjunctures, which cross-cut so many other social and technical structures embedded in the natural and artificial environment, the contestable exercise of quantifiable assessment about either less-than-optimal returns or more-than-expected losses underscores how risk managers ride atop the normalization of undesired abnormalities. When it comes to the environment and risk, no one wants to lose his or her present ecological benefits, but few are genuinely willing to limit the current economic costs of preserving these natural environments for the future use of humans and nonhumans alike. Having become ready "to dare to know," the risks involved in making further economic advances today leave those willing to face the facts that they now must "know they dare" ecological collapse. On these precarious prospects of risk for the natural environment, despite their many troublesome dimensions, much of what is seen as second modernity's everyday life rests.

References

Argyrou, V. (2005) *The Logic of Environmentalism: Anthropology, Ecology and Postcoloniality*, New York: Berghan Books.
Baudrillard, J. (1996) *The System of Objects*, London: Verso.
Beck, U. (1997) *The Reinvention of Politics*, Oxford: Polity Press.
——(1995) *Ecological Politics in an Age of Risk*, Cambridge: Polity Press.
——(1992) *The Risk Society*, London: Sage.
Briden, J. C. and T. E. Downing (2002) *Managing the Earth: The Lineacre Lectures*, Oxford: Oxford University Press.
Brown, L. R. (1981) *Building a Sustainable Society*, New York: Norton.
Cairncross, F. (1992) *Costing the Earth*, Boston, MA: Harvard Business School Press.
Campos, P. (2010) "Undressing the Terror Threat," *Wall Street Journal* (January 9–10): W3.
Casimir, M. J. (2008) *Culture and Changing Environment: Uncertainty, Cognition, and Risk in Cross-cultural Perspective*, New York: Berghan Books.
Chertow, M. R. and D. C. Esty (1997) *Thinking Ecologically: The Next Generation of Environmental Policy*, New Haven, CT: Yale University Press.
Denney, D. (2005) *Risk and Society*, London: Sage.
Douglas, M. (1983) *Risk and Culture: An Essay on the Selection of Technological and Environmental Dangers*, Berkeley, CA: University of California Press.
Durning, A. (1992) *How Much is Enough? The Consumer Society and the Future of the Earth*, New York: W. W. Norton.
Eder, K. (1996) *The Social Construction of Nature: A Sociology of Ecological Enlightenment*, London: Sage.
——(1993) *The New Politics of Class: Social Movements and Cultural Dynamics in Advanced Societies*, Sage: London.
Fischer, F. (1990) *Technocracy and the Politics of Expertise*, London: Sage.
Flyvbjerg, B. (2001) *Making Social Science Matter: Why Social Inquiry Fails and How It Can Succeed Again*, Cambridge: Cambridge University Press.
Foucault, M. (1994) *The Order of Things: An Archaeology of the Human Sciences*, New York: Vintage.
——(1991) *The Foucault Effect: Studies in Governmentality*, ed. G. Burchell, C. Gordon, and P. Miller, Chicago, IL: University of Chicago Press.
——(1984) *Power/Knowledge: Selected Interviews & Other Writings, 1972–1977*, New York: Pantheon.
——(1980) *The History of Sexuality, Vol. I*, New York: Vintage.
——(1977) *Language, Counter-memory and Practice*, Ithaca, NY: Cornell University Press.
——(1970) *The Order of Things: An Archaeology of the Human Sciences*, New York: Vintage.
Galbraith, J. K. (1958) *The Affluent Society*, Boston, MA: Houghton Mifflin.
Gibbons, M. *et al.* (1994) *The New Production of Knowledge: The Dynamics of Science and Research in Contemporary Societies*, London: Sage.
Hodges, J. (2010) "Global Warming Made Easy," *The Roanoke Times* (January 7): 17.
Hudson, B. (2003) *Justice in the Risk Society*, London: Sage.
Husserl, E. (1970) *The Crisis of European Science and Transcendental Phenomenology*, Evanston, IL: Northwestern University Press.
Lash, S., B. Szerszynski, and B. Wynne (1996) *Risk, Environment and Modernity: Towards a New Ecology*, London: Sage.
——(2003) "Real Interdependence: Discursivity and Concursivity in Global Politics", in F. Debrix (ed.) *Language, Agency and Politics in a Constructed World*, Armonk, NY: M. E. Sharpe, 101–120.
Luke, T. W. (2002) 'The Property Boundaries/Boundary Properties in Technoculture Studies: 'Inventing the Future',' in D. F. White and C. Wilbert (eds.) *Technonatures: Environments, Technologies, Spaces, and Places in the Twenty-First Century*, ONT: Wilfrid Laurier University Press, 193–213.
——(1996) "Identity, Meaning and Globalization: Space–Time Compression and the Political Economy of Everyday Life', in S. Lash, P. Heelas, and P. Morris (eds) *Detraditionalization: Critical Reflections on Authority and Identity*, Oxford: Blackwell, 109–33.

Lupton, D. (2005) *Risk and Sociocultural Theory: New Directions and Perspectives*, Cambridge: Cambridge University Press.

Lyall, C. and J. Tait (2005) *New Modes of Governance: Developing an Integrated Policy Approach to Science, Technology, Risk and the Environment*, Burlington, VT: Ashgate.

Lyotard, J.-F. (1984) *The Postmodern Condition: A Report on Knowledge*, Minneapolis, MN: University of Minnesota Press.

Mangun, W. R. and D. Henning (1999) *Managing the Environmental Crisis: Incorporating Competing Values in Natural Resource Administration*, second edn, Durham, NC: Duke University Press.

McDonough, W. and M. Braungart (2002) *Cradle to Cradle: Remaking the Way We Make Things*, New York: North Point Press.

Perkin, H. J. (1996) *The Third Revolution: Professional Elites in the Modern World*. Routledge: London.

Perrow, C. (1984) *Normal Accidents: Living with High Risk Technologies*, Princeton, NJ: Princeton University Press.

Silver, N. (2010) "Crunching the Risk Numbers," *Wall Street Journal* (January 9–10): W3.

Strydom, P. (2008) "Risk Communication: World Creation Through Collective Learning Under Complex Contingent Conditions," *Journal of Risk Research*, 11, 1/2: 5–22.

——(2002) *Risk, Environment and Society: Ongoing Debates, Current Issues and Future Prospects*, London: Open University Press.

Sunstein, C. R. (2002a) *Risk and Reason: Safety, Law, and the Environment*, Cambridge: Cambridge University Press.

——(2002b) *The Cost Benefit State: The Future of Regulatory Protection*, Chicago, IL: American Bar Association.

Virilio, P. (1997) *Open Sky*, London: Verso.

——(1996) *Speed and Politics*, New York: Semiotext(e).

——(1995) *The Art of the Motor*, Minneapolis, MN: University of Minnesota Press.

Yanow, D. (1996) *How Does a Policy Mean? Interpreting Policy and Organizational Acts*, Washington, DC: Georgetown University Press.

Networks

The Technological and the Social

Amelia Arsenault

The digitization of information into the universal language of electronic binary code has blurred the boundary between technological and human interaction. Contemporary social processes are increasingly mediated via a labyrinthine web of Internet and mobile communication networks and supplemented by increasingly elaborate search tools and social networks such as Google, Baidu, MySpace, and Facebook. Technology, of course, emerges out of specific human contexts. But once facilitated, technological networks influence and compel human-centered networks. Not surprisingly, particularly since the birth of the World Wide Web in 1994, social scientists have turned their attention to the ways in which computer networks have facilitated radical changes to societal practices and organization, and the implications of these transformations for culture, economics, and politics.

This chapter considers the importance of networks as a social and political phenomenon. In the following pages, it explores the theoretical debate surrounding how to define networks, how to study them, and their implications for both the individual and society as a whole. While scholars across disciplines increasingly turn their attention to the subject of networks, there is not a singular approach, nor even preliminary agreement about what networks are, what they mean, or how they should be studied. Catalonian sociologist Manuel Castells (1996, 1997, 1998, and 2009) puts forward the idea of a 'network society', a contested, but highly influential meta-theory that networks are the defining social structure of the information age. In the field of communication, Peter Monge and Nosh Contractor (2003) have presented a multi-theoretical, multilevel framework (MTML) theory of communication networks. They suggest using network analysis to uncover network principles at the levels of the individual, the organization, and society. Actor-Network-Theory (ANT), most closely associated with the work of Bruno Latour (1991, 1996, 2001, and 2005), maintains that, while technology has intensified the importance of looking at network associations, the social has always been organized around networks. Social theorists have as yet failed to account for this fact. Therefore, sociology should be redefined as the tracing of network associations (Latour 2005: 5). But before moving into a closer consideration of these approaches, it is important to establish at least a baseline definition of networks as a subject of inquiry.

Defining a Network

While representing a variety of approaches, theories, and methods, the study of networks is, in essence, the study of relationships. We may identify network associations between a small group of individuals, at the level of society, and between or within organizations. Relationships between different social actors are, of course, integral to many facets of social and political theory. However, networks as a subject of academic analysis are bounded by the overarching consideration of who is (or is not) associated with whom, why, and to what social effect. Those concerned with networks generally take the perspective that one-to-one or many-to-many associations *only* take on meaning when contextualized against the broader *structure* of the network.

In the simplest terms, a network refers to a set of relationships between objects (i.e. nodes). Depending on the network and/or the theoretical approach taken, nodes within a particular network are typically heterogeneous, consisting of such varied elements as inanimate objects, humans, machines, and organizations. Network nodes are linked according to associations, also described as linkages or messages. These associations may take many forms, including: interpersonal interactions, strategic corporate alliances, flows of information between and within groups, and computer-mediated-communication between humans or machines. The protocols, what Castells (2000a [1996]) terms the 'programs', governing these associations between nodes can also assume many guises, including: cultural customs; machine code; or the rules of engagement surrounding a particular economic, social, or political project.

Networks may also be formal or informal. Formal networks are solidified by official arrangements between nodes. For example, a multinational corporation may have multiple offices (nodes) around the world that are connected by legal contracts, exchanges of money, and assigned responsibilities reflected through an organizational chart. Paralleling these formal networks are informal networks sometimes referred to as 'emergent networks'.[1] In emergent networks, nodes are connected by a joint project or a common identity rather than a formal mandate. Loosely networked organizations such as Al Qaeda or the Anti-Globalization Movement may be characterized as emergent networks. In another example, Monge and Contractor (2003) suggest that informal grapevine communications along interpersonal networks are potentially as influential, if not more influential than formal networks associations.

Networks may also be understood as building blocks. Different nodes can belong to multiple networks. An individual may serve as a node in a corporate network as well as in an otherwise separate political network. A network may also function as a node in a larger network. For example, a multilateral institution such as the United Nations operates as an organizational network comprised of formal nodes (e.g. UNESCO, UNDP, UNHCR, and its 192 country representatives). The UN simultaneously function as a node in a larger multinational political network comprised of many formal and informal organizations (e.g. the UN, the United States government, NATO, the World Bank). The internal functioning (or malfunctioning) of the UN's organizational network may influence the larger international political network within which it serves as a node, and vice versa. Because networks can be constructed out of many smaller networks, it is generally more instructive to think of networks as embedded within a network of networks rather than one or several separate networks. It is for precisely this reason, that some theorists (most notably Castells [1996]) have posited the emergence of a 'network society'.

Just as networks are typically heterogeneous, so too is the study of networks. Levels of analysis range from small communities or individuals, to corporations, to entire global systems. According to Castells (2000c), sociologists should consider the network, not the nodes or the association between nodes, as the unit of analysis. Of course, those nodes and associations are constituent elements of the network, but their specific characteristics are made relevant or redundant according to the program (i.e. goals) of the network at hand. Network analysts, on the other hand, often focus on the level of the individual or dyad (i.e. a pair of nodes) rather than the network level (Wellman 1999). Monge and Contractor (2003) posit that networks are inherently multi-level constructs made up of macro, micro, and meso (i.e. organizational) levels; therefore their proper study requires a multi-level analysis. Latour (1996, 2005) and other proponents of ANT consider the associations between different monads (i.e. individual nodes) as the critical subject of investigation.

In the presence of ubiquitous networking technology, the consideration of networks as social constructs also raises the question of the chicken or the egg. Did the rise of technological networks facilitate networked forms of social organization? Or do technological networks mirror pre-existing social networks? As with any foundational question, the answer is probably somewhere in the middle. Early computer and Internet engineers adopted natural metaphors such as nodes and hubs to describe the building blocks of computers. Similarly, network analysis is rooted in the study of humans rather than machines. During the 1950s and 1960s, anthropologists developed and expanded upon the concept of a social network through a series of analyses of changing community practices in the face of global migration. In these early studies, a network referred to a set of ties linking social system members across social categories and bounded groups.[2] Callon and Latour (1981) laid the foundations for ANT in their study of baboons and EDF's (Electricity of France) attempt to launch an electric car. But despite the non-technical roots of network analysis and network theory, considerable confusion remains about networks as a subject of study vis-à-vis electronic networks.

The physical manifestations of computer networks have ignited the study of networks; and computing terminology often provides useful metaphors with which to identify the social, political, and economic processes accompanying network associations. Readers with even a passing familiarity with computer terminology may find the language surrounding the academic study of networks familiar. Not surprisingly, the shared terminology between the physical technology and networks as social constructs causes definitional confusion, often leading to problems of specificity. Latour (1999), for example, argues that equating networks with electronic networks implies that information is transported without 'deformation', which is the opposite of what Actor-Network-Theory suggests.

How then is technology understood in the context of theories and approaches about networks? For some, such as Benkler (2006) writing on the *Wealth of Networks*, network is mainly a descriptive term referring to the array of humans connected to digital devices such as mobile phones and computers. For others, a network may refer to a more complex set of interactions between man, machine, and nature. For Castells, 'technology as a material tool, and meaning as symbolic construction, through relationships of production/consumption, experience, and power, are the fundamental ingredients of human action – an action that ultimately produces and modifies social structure' (2000b: 9). Technology is not merely technology; but, following Fischer (1992), it is a culturally embedded process rather than an exogenous variable (Castells 2000c: 693). Networking technology has become inseparable from the human actors that use it, leading to the rise of a network society. Proponents of ANT similarly define technology and society as mutually constitutive. Each is embedded within the other. But ANT takes the social conditions of technology a step further. Technological networks do not mirror or complement human-centered networks; they are one in the same. A computer user is connected to his/her computer, which is in turn connected via micro-electronic networks to other servers, hosts, hubs, and ultimately to other humans. Latour (1996) passionately champions the extension of the concept of agency to non-human objects, arguing that humans and machines often fulfil the same functions within networks. Associations condition machine operations, and their proper or improper functioning may destabilize or stabilize power relationships. Humans rely upon technology in much the same way that they rely upon other humans. Your computer may crash or your lover may leave you – both occurrences may have broader effects on the networks within which you might be embedded.

As Latour cautions: 'now that the World Wide Web exists, everyone believes that they know what a network is' (1999: 15). The great challenge for those concerned with network theory is to find a common definition of a network in the context of the social that accounts for technological networks but is not subsumed by them. The theoretical foundations for the study of networks both predates and extends beyond the technological transformations of the Internet. Yet too often, academics fail to distinguish whether they are referring to networks as social constructs or network technology. Because of this definitional and theoretical confusion, what different scholars mean by the term 'networks' is often lost in translation.

Over the first part of this chapter, I have referenced multiple competing approaches and theories about networks. Questions about how they should be studied and what role technology plays in their construction are just the first in a long line of divisions separating these approaches. In the subsequent sections, I examine the major schools of thought on the subject in greater detail.

Actor-Network-Theory

Actor-Network-Theory, commonly referred to as ANT, is most closely associated with the work of anthropologist Bruno Latour, a leading figure in the study of science, knowledge, and technology. Callon and Latour (1981) laid the foundations for ANT in 'Unscrewing the Big Leviathan: How Actors Macro-structure Reality and How Sociologists Help Them to Do So'. In this seminal article, they consider the implications for sociology of Hobbes' claim that the Leviathan is the people itself in another state. Following Hobbes, they argue:

> There are of course macro-actors and micro-actors, but the difference between them is brought about by power relations and the constructions of networks that will elude analysis, if we presume a priori that macro-actors are bigger than or superior to micro actors.
>
> *(Callon and Latour 1981: 280)*

Although ANT is commonly described as a theory (not surprisingly given its name), its proponents argue that it is not a foundational theory but a descriptive set of assumptions guiding empirical research of the social (Latour 2005; Law 2009). It suggests focusing on associations rather than individuals, organizations, or society. It starts with the premise that nothing natural or man-made has any meaning outside those associations. Everyone and everything is relational, embedded within networks. Humans, objects, and institutions are joined together into networks by associations. Each node is linked to other nodes through a complex and heterogeneous geography of these associations (Hinchcliffe 2000). The social is thus constructed out of connections and relations rather than discrete subjects and objects. Because no animate or inanimate object exists free from associations, networks are the defining organizing principle of society. It is therefore the researcher's job to identify how networks form, function, and malfunction rather than why they exist in the first place. Guided by the perspective that associations not actors are the critical subject of analysis, ANT champions two main arguments.

First, society and nature are inextricably intertwined (Latour 2002). This first argument, referred to as the 'principle of generalized symmetry', is the most controversial element of the ANT approach. It implies that in a world of associations, inanimate objects functionally exhibit as much agency as humans. Associations connect humans, inanimate objects, nature, and machines. The division between nature and technology is thus arbitrary. ANT in general and Latour (2002) in specific owes a debt to the work of nineteenth-century theoretician, Gabriel Tarde (1999 [1893]), who argued that society is formed by associations between monads whether they be animate or inanimate; 'What is a monad? It is the stuff out of which the universe is built' (p. 119). Latour (1996) interprets this to mean that because there is nothing necessarily unique about humans, the study of the social could be applied to a study of the associations between concepts, solar systems, or computers as easily as communities or nation-states. For this reason, ANT is sometimes described as a material-semiotic approach rather than a unified theory.

ANT's second foundational argument is that micro-level and macro-level distinctions are counterproductive. The object of study is the relationship between monads, which come in all shapes and sizes. When analyzing the social, a researcher must give equal weight to individuals and to organizations. It is not that ANT does not recognize the existence of micro and macro actors, only that the difference between them is power relations and network associations. These are fundamental features that will elude analysis if a researcher starts with a preconceived notion of big and small. For ANT, the significant division is between intermediaries and mediators. Intermediaries are actors with little or no ability to affect network functions and as such can be ignored. They are merely transporters for the will of another entity. Mediators, on the other hand, transform or 'translate' the will of others. Whether actors transport or translate associations is another important concept behind ANT. Translation refers to 'a relation that does not transport causality but induces two mediators into co-existing ... the tricky word "network" being defined ... as what is traced by those translations in the scholars' accounts' (Latour 2005: 108). Translation might be thought of as the codes or programs assigned to the network that help to negotiate its formation and functions.

Michael Callon (1986) has identified four 'moments of translation' that he believes are fundamental to the study of networks and of power:

(1) *Problematization*: During this process an actor or actors identify the problem to be solved and seek to become indispensable to other actors 'by defining the nature and the problems of the latter and then suggesting that these would be resolved if the actors negotiated the 'obligatory passage point' of the actor's solution to the problem' (Callon 1986: 196);
(2) *Interessement* describes a series of processes by which the actor seeks to lock the other actors into their network roles;
(3) *Enrollment* refers the strategies through which an intermediary gets other actors to accept the roles that have been assigned to them;
(4) *Mobilization* is a set of methods used by the initiating actor to expand support and identify potential allies for his/her/its proscribed solution to the problem in question.

Again, the actors involved in this translation process may be animate or inanimate. ANT takes the perspective that sociology has tended to treat too much of the world as intermediaries. Machines and other inanimate objects can play an important role in mediating associations between actors.

ANT studies commonly focus on mapping the associations between different actors and noting these processes of translation versus transportation. These studies generally rely on two approaches: ethnography and textual analysis. A researcher might conduct an ethnographic study of associations, following an association from actor to actor. For example, if one wanted to trace the associations surrounding the launch of a new product, a researcher might follow the lifecycle of the product from engineers, to management, to marketing, to users, including all the inanimate and animate actors involved in the process. They might also examine the texts (physical evidence) that document different associations. However, because ANT studies have no predetermined limits, they have often been criticized for being overly descriptive and including associations that are irrelevant or at least cursory to social processes.

The Network Society

Castells' conception of the network society is best understood as an alternative set of explanations, or rather a more precise explanation for the move from an industrial to an 'information society'.[3] He first began to consider the issues of the information society in earnest in the late 1980s when he developed a theory of a 'space of flows', referring to the fact that network flows increasingly define meaning in the material manifestations of society (Castells 1989). He also recognized the rise of 'timeless time' as opposed to locally based clock time. In the information age, time is compressed; networked forms of communication allow nodes, regardless of place, to work together in real time. Time is also de-sequenced; traditional stages of human growth, production, and work are upended. However, while Castells initially utilized the term 'information society', he began to see it as 'unspecific and misleading' because knowledge and information have always played a pivotal role in society (2000b: 10).

What is new is that society has entered a new technological paradigm: the network society. Castells first put forward a detailed analysis of the network society in a three-part trilogy: *The Rise of the Network Society* (1996), *The Power of Identity* (1997), and *End of Millennium* (1998). In these volumes, he argues that

> Dominant functions and processes in the Information Age are increasingly organized around networks. Networks constitute the new social morphology of our societies … while the networking form of social organization has existed in other times, the new information technology paradigm provides the material basis for its pervasive expansion throughout the entire social structure.
>
> *(Castells 2000a: 500)*

The network society is not solely the product of technological innovation. He attributes its rise to four concurrent historical occurrences during the 1960s and 1970s: (1) a move towards economic deregulation and liberalization; (2) the failed reform of the nation-state and a corresponding political crisis of legitimacy; (3) the embrace of libertarianism by the counterculture movements; and (4) the reconfiguration of the media and information systems shaped around a global/local electronic hypertext (Castells 2000a). He has conducted a series of case studies on a range of phenomenon, from emergent fundamentalist networks, to the Zapatistas, to environmental movements, to East Asian business practices to demonstrate the breadth and depth of networked forms of organization.

The supremacy of networked forms of organization is associated with several interrelated social transformations (see Castells 2000a, 2004a, 2007, and 2009). First, who is allowed to participate in a network and why is largely a product of the codes and programs that define that network. These programs and codes are articulated via the information sphere: thus 'informationalism' is the currency of power in the network society (Castells 2004b). Under this new informational paradigm 'the capacity for any communicating subject to act on the communication network gives people and organizations the possibility of reconfiguring the network according to their needs, desires, and projects' (Castells 2004b: 12). In recent years, Castells has applied his study of networks to that of the communication sphere, conducting several empirical investigations into global media and communications businesses (Arsenault and Castells 2008a, 2008b), political projects (Arsenault and Castells 2006), and social movements (Castells *et al.* 2006).

Second, because electronic hypertext has become the main purveyor of meaning, there are more opportunities for 'autonomous mass self communication' and mass communication. As a result, there are fewer and fewer common cultural codes, which has led to cultural fragmentation and the rise of non-traditional networked organizations built around identity issues and formed largely through the use of new communication technologies (Castells 2009). Third, informationalism has had a decisive influence on work and commerce. Because the new economy relies on informationalism 'the capacity of generating knowledge and processing/managing information determine the productivity and competitiveness of all kinds of economic units, be they firms, regions, or countries' (Castells 2000b: 10). The diffusion of information technology also means that the new economy is global, and that corporate activities often take place on a planetary scale and operate in real time (i.e. timeless time).

As a result of these changes, Castells (2000c) argues that twenty-first-century social scientists must expand their analysis beyond specific social networks to considerations of the entire social structure. Because society is increasingly organized around networks, processes of inclusion and exclusion from networks should supersede studies of centers and hierarchies. This is due to the fact that networks as units are not controllable by one individual or actor. For example, central banks, no matter how hard they try, never successfully control the value of their currency (Castells 2000a). In order to understand its functions, we must contextualize the central bank in the context of the networks within which it operates. In view of the fact that social, economic, and political activities are now fully immersed in networked forms of organization, the network not the actors should be the primary unit of analysis.[4]

Network Analysis

Network analysis can better be understood as a broad approach rather than a body of theory or methods. Canadian sociologist Barry Wellman (with Paul Craven) first unveiled the concept of the 'Network City' in 1973, and put forth the idea that communities were best conceived of and studied as networks. Wellman (1973), Granovetter (1973), and Fischer (1992) were some of the first to conduct quantitative social network analyses of specific communities. Today, network analysis remains highly quantitative. Particularly in the last decade, there has been a movement towards the construction of network modelling, which measures the density and frequency of interactions between different nodes. The focus is generally on structure (i.e. the network) rather than on individual action. In other words, network analysts focus on the structural constraints upon individual and collective action rather than the specific reasons for individual actions: associations supersede attributes. This often takes the form of measuring network linkages. Network analysts may examine a particular network in terms of the following: links, indirect links (i.e. mediated or linked through others), frequency, length, multiplexity (i.e. how many associations link two nodes), strength (i.e. intensity), direction, and symmetry (Monge and Contractor 2003: 31–3). Alternatively, they may analyze particular actors within a network in terms of their links to other nodes, the diversity of their associations, and the extent to which they are central or peripheral to the functioning of the network. Network analyses underscore that not all actors are created equal. Tracking who communicates or has associations with whom may uncover whether an actor is central or peripheral to a network. For example, a low-level bureaucrat responsible to one immediate boss and working in isolation may function on the periphery of a network, while a CEO may have linkages across the network, or vice versa.

Some scholars draw upon a network typology based upon common computer network configurations. They note that human interactions are commonly computer-mediated and, even when they are not, exhibit similar attributes to electronic networks. In a chain (aka line or bus) network, associations link a series of sequential actors. Those at the ends of a line network must communicate through intermediate nodes. A ring network is similar, but the associations flow in a circle rather than a line. In a star (aka hub) network, all nodes are linked through a central actor. Nodes connect only to the central hub and not to one another. In a fully integrated (aka mesh) network, all nodes are linked to or capable of linking with all other nodes. Some argue network structure has important social and political ramifications. For example, Arquilla and Ronfeldt (2001) posit that the information revolution has facilitated the rise of 'Netwars' as the main type of conflict in the international arena. Criminal, terrorist, and other non-state actors have adopted networked forms of organization to challenge traditional power structures. The strengths and weaknesses of these networks are dependent upon the network configuration. Traditional state military and diplomatic responses are no longer effective because they are predicated on fighting a hierarchically organized enemy. Netwars are won or lost based on identifying and tailoring responses to the structure of the networked actor in question. For instance, terrorist networks organized into a star configuration are difficult to demolish unless the hub is neutralized. A fully integrated mesh network linked through common principles or religious values may prove more prolific because even though individual actors may be captured, the network will easily reconfigure itself and continue on its mission.

Most network analysis takes place at the micro-level and relies on static cross-sectional analysis (Monge and Contractor 2003: xiii). The debate remains whether it is useful to map network connections without a consideration of the content circulating between those connections. Therefore, in recent years, there have been growing calls for more multi-level analysis and a greater integration of theory into network analyses.[5] Network analysis, Castells' conception of a network society, and ANT take different approaches, but they all agree that structure is decisive. However, whether this structural configuration is potentially liberating or controlling is a subject of debate. As the following section will demonstrate, some see the end of territoriality wrought by new communication technologies as liberating while others see it as a new agent of structural domination.

Network Effects

While most theorists agree that the rise of networks has altered traditional power dynamics, where power lies in networks and how it is exercised is subject to multiple interpretations. Networks by definition operate according to a principle of exclusion/inclusion. If everything were part of the same network, then the network construct would cease to have meaning. Latour (2005) maintains that ANT does not mean that everything is connected to everything; however, the focus is on the associations rather than the nodes and thus the principle of exclusion/inclusion takes second seat. Castells, on the other hand, posits that the network society is equally defined by who is included within the network as well as who is excluded. The implications of networks have implications for those outside of as well as within the network. Continuing network participation is predicated on the node's ability to contribute to the network's goals. Networks are mercenary, 'they kill or kiss, nothing personal', depending on whether the node fulfils the needs of the network (Castells 2004b: 32). Networks are thus, flexible, scalable, and survivable because they constantly adapt to changes in the environment, deleting and adding nodes while maintaining a unity of purpose—the survival of the network. In this sense, we may say that ANT focuses on the associations while Castells is particularly interested in who is included and who is excluded from particular networks and to what effect.

So how then is power exercised in networks? Castells identifies the importance of communication as a sphere of power negotiation: 'The key point is that electronic media (including not only television and radio, but all forms of communication such as newspapers and the Internet) have become the privileged space of politics' (Castells 2004a: 369). In his most recent work, Castells (2004b, 2009; Arsenault and Castells 2008b) has put more weight behind the importance of 'switchers'. Because contemporary society depends on networks, a 'switcher', or a connection point between media, political, and economic networks 'that ensures their cooperation by sharing common goals and resources', is particularly situated to govern the programs by which different networks operate (Castells 2004b: 32).

While questions of power are central to Castells' concept of a network society, ANT has been criticized for failing to account for power imbalances because all actors in a network are considered to have equal weight. However, while specific ANT studies might not focus on questions of power, the ANT approach evolved out of considerations of power. Callon and Latour (1981) laid the foundations of ANT drawing upon Hobbes and the question of the Leviathan, positing that Hobbes was mostly right, but that translation rather than the presence or absence of a social contract constrained or aided micro-level actors from growing into macro-level actors. As a subject of analysis, micro-level actors are the same as macro-level actors; the difference between them is wrought by power relations and the construction or failure to construct associations (Callon and Latour 1981: 280).

Then what does this mean for traditional institutions? Networks have not replaced traditional institutions; rather they propel traditional institutions to enter a phase change. Networks pre-date the introduction of electronic networking technologies, but before these technologies were available, hierarchies trumped networks in their ability to mobilize resources around particular projects. By undermining the importance of spatial proximity, new technologies helped to facilitate the triumph of networked organization over centralized hierarchies. According to Castells, political institutions are no longer the locus of power (2000b: 23); power is in the instrumental flows of power along networks.

The traditional nation-state, which previously may have operated as a hierarchy, now operates as a networked state. The media have shifted towards multi-modal and multinational organizations. Time Warner, News Corp., Disney, etc. are no longer hierarchical sites of cultural production, but formulate the backbone of the global network of media networks (Arsenault and Castells 2008a). Even the smallest newspapers now incorporate content, formats, or media practices programmed by this global core of companies. Similarly, nation-states trade hierarchy for networked power in the global arena. States still exert instrumental power via military engagement, but frequently exercise power through their ability to program the network of political networks. For example, as a superpower the United States' political agency acts as a key programmer – wielding a disproportionate influence over the rules and regulations governing international relations.

Given this whirlwind of social consequences attributed to networks, what are the implications for the individual? The consequences vary depending on whether the focus is on the network or the node as a unit of analysis. Urry (2000, 2003, 2005) argues that the social is now organized around mobility. Relationships between mobile and immobile elements of a global networked society rather than between people are what is important. According to Hampton and Wellman (2003), the sociability of individuals/nodes varies not according to their attributes (e.g. gender, race, etc.) but according to their position relative to other nodes in the network. The network is thus greater than the sum of its parts. However, scholars who focus on the node rather than the network identify a greater potential if not actual ability for individuals to achieve greater autonomy. Benkler (2006) documents the potential 'wealth of networks' which has unleashed a new battle for the ecology of the digital world. Individual producers freed from the constraints of needing great material wealth are in a position to challenge traditional relationships of production and politics. On the other hand, traditional power centers are reformulating new rules and laws and arrangements of capital to reassert power.

Conclusion

This chapter has presented conflicting interpretations of networks. Unfortunately, there is little interaction between these different bodies of thought. The left hand makes little reference to what the right hand is doing. Latour and Castells present different interpretations of networks, but, as of yet, neither has directly addressed the others work in any considered way. Similarly, network analysis and network theory largely remain divorced from one another. Monge and Contractor (2001, 2003) raise the criticism that empirical research of networks are either largely a-theoretical or rely heavily on single theories rather than testing multiple possible explanations. Conversely, work on ANT and the network society would benefit from wider empirical study utilizing the tools of network analysis. This atomization of network theory is arguably due to disciplinary boundaries, but is more likely because macro-level theories are often difficult to engage with at the level of the node and vice-versa. The question remains: how can we integrate theories about networks as subjects of analysis with studies of nodes embedded within those networks? At the risk of abusing the terminology, this chapter underscores that academics studying networks need to strengthen their networking skills.

Notes

1 See also Monge and Contractor (2003: 8–16).
2 See Wellman (1983) for a comprehensive overview of the early roots of social network analysis.
3 The 'information society' as theoretical subject of interest first emerged in the early 1960s surrounding a series of conferences around the work of Tadao Umesao (1963). In the ensuing years – particularly following the growth of the personal computing industry and the Internet in the 1980s and 1990s – the 'information society' and similar terms arose to identify a paradigm shift in society characterized by globalization (another critical buzzword of the 1990s) and the digitization of commerce, governance, work, play, and person-to-person interactions.
4 While Castells is the best-known proponent of the Network Society, there are alternate conceptions of the Network Society. Dutch sociologist Jan van Dijk first coined the term 'network society' in 1991 in his book *De Netwerkmaatschappij* (1991). However van Dijk's vision of a network society is more modest. He still sees the primary unit of social organization as individuals, institutions, and communities, but notes that they are more information driven and densely linked via formal and informal communication systems. Van Dijk criticizes Castells' approximation as technologically deterministic and containing a one-dimensional view of technology that leaves very little room for individual agency.
5 See Monge and Contractor (2003) on MTML.

References

Arquilla, J. and Ronfeldt, D. F. (2001). *Networks and Netwars: The Future of Terror, Crime, and Militancy*, Santa Monica, CA: Rand.
Arsenault, A. and Castells, M. (2008a). 'The Structure and Dynamics of Global Multi-media Business Networks', *International Journal of Communication*, 2(1), 707–48.
——. (2008b). 'Switching Power: Rupert Murdoch and the Global Business of Media Politics: A Sociological Analysis', *International Sociology*, 23(4), 488.
——. (2006). 'Conquering the Minds, Conquering Iraq: The Social Production of Misinformation in the United States – a Case Study', *Information, Communication, and Society*, 9(3), 284–307.
Benkler, Y. (2006). *The Wealth of Networks: How Social Production Transforms Markets and Freedom*, New Haven, CT: Yale University Press.

Callon, M. (1986). 'Some Elements of a Sociology of Translation: Domestication of the Scallops and the Fishermen of St Brieuc Bay', in J. Law (ed.), *Power, Action and Belief: A New Sociology of Knowledge*, London: Routledge & Kegan Paul.

Callon, M. and Latour, B. (1981). 'Unscrewing The Big Leviathan: How Actors Macro-Structure Reality and How Sociologists Help Them to Do So', in K. D. Knorr-Cetina and A. V. Cicourel (eds), *Advances in Social Theory and Methodology: Toward an Integration of Micro and Macro Sociologies*, Boston, MA: Routledge.

Castells, M. (2009). *Communication Power*, New York: Oxford.

——. (2007). 'Communication, Power and Counter-power in the Network Society', *International Journal of Communication*, 1(1), 238–66.

——. (2004a). *The Power of Identity*, Malden, MA: Blackwell.

——. (2004b). 'Informationalism, Networks, and the Network Society: A Theoretical Blueprint', in M. Castells (ed.), *The Network Society: A Cross-cultural Perspective*, Cheltenham, UK: Edward Elgar.

——. (2000a). *The Rise of the Network Society* (2nd edn), Malden, MA: Blackwell.

——. (2000b). 'Materials for an Exploratory Theory of the Network Society', *British Journal of Sociology*, 51(1), 5–24.

——. (2000c). 'Toward a Sociology of the Network Society', *Contemporary Sociology*, 29(5), 693–9.

——. (1998). *End of Millennium*, Malden, MA: Blackwell.

——. (1997). *The Power of Identity*, Malden, MA: Blackwell.

——. (1996). *The Rise of the Network Society* (1st edn), Malden, MA: Blackwell.

Castells, M., Fernández-Ardèvol, M., Qiu, J. L., *et al.* (2006) *Mobile Communication and Society: A Global Perspective*, Cambridge, MA: MIT Press.

Craven, P. and Wellman, B. (1973) 'The Network City', *Sociological Inquiry*, 43(3–4), 57–88.

van Dijk, J. (1991). *De Netwerkmaatschappij: Sociale Aspecten van Nieuwe Media [The Network Society, Social Aspects of the New Media]*, Netherlands: Bohn Stafleu van Loghum.

Fischer, C. (1992). *America Calling: A Social History of the Telephone to 1940*, Berkeley, CA: University of California Press.

Granovetter, M. (1973). 'The Strength of Weak Ties', *American Journal of Sociology*, 78(6), 1360–80.

Hampton, K. and Wellman, B. (2003). 'Neighboring in Netville: How the Internet Supports Community and Social Capital in a Wired Suburb', *City and Community*, 2(4), 277–311.

Hinchcliffe, S. (2000). 'Entangled Humans: Specifying Powers and Their Spatiality', in J. Sharp (ed.), *Entanglements of Power: Geographies of Domination and Resistance*, London: Routledge.

Latour, B. (2005). *Reassembling the Social: An Introduction to Actor-Network-Theory*, Oxford: Oxford University Press.

——. (2002). 'Gabriel Tarde and the End of the Social', in P. Joyce (ed.), *The Social and its Problems*, London: Routledge.

——. (1999). 'On Recalling ANT', in J. Law and J. Hassard (eds), *Actor Network Theory and After*, Oxford: Blackwell.

——. (1996). *Aramis, or, The Love of Technology*, Cambridge, MA: Harvard University Press.

——. (1991). 'Technology Is Society Made Durable', in J. Law (ed.), *A Sociology of Monsters: Essays On Power, Technology and Domination*, London: Routledge.

Law, J. (2009). 'Actor Network Theory and Material Semiotics', in B. Turner (ed.), *The New Blackwell Companion to Social Theory*, Malden, MA: Routledge.

Monge, P. R. and Contractor, N. S. (2003). *Theories of Communication Networks*, New York: Oxford University Press.

——. (2001). 'Emergence of Communication Networks', in F. M. Jablin and L. L. Putnam (eds), *New Handbook of Organizational Communication* (2nd edn), Newberry Park, CA: Sage.

Tarde, G. (1999). 'Monadologie et sociologie', in *Euvre de Gabriel Tardes*. Collection Les Empecheurs de Penser en Rond. Paris: Institut Synthelab.

——. (1893). 'Les monades et la sociologie', *Revue Internationale de Sociologie*, 1(1) 157, 231–46.

Umesao, T. (1963). 'Jôhô Sangyô Ron [Theory of Information Industries]', *Hoso Asahi*, March 46–58.

Urry, J. (2005). 'The Complexities of the Global', *Theory, Culture, Society*, 22(5), 235–54.

——. (2003). *Global Complexity*, Malden, MA: Polity.

——. (2000). *Sociology Beyond Societies: Mobilities for the Twenty-First Century*. London: Routledge.

Wellman, B. (1999). 'The Network Community', in B. Wellman (ed.), *Networks in the Global Village: Life in Contemporary Communities*, Boulder, CO: Westview.

——. (1983). 'Network Analysis: Some Basic Principles', *Sociological Theory*, 1, 155–200.

From Linguistic Performativity to Social Performance

The Development of a Concept

Moya Lloyd

From its earliest formulation in the work of philosopher J. L. Austin through to its contemporary uses in the fields of anthropology, literary studies, sociology, economics, cultural studies, film and media, and politics, performativity has become one of the most important theoretical approaches of recent times. As an approach, however, it is far from uniform. In the hands of diverse thinkers too many to name, the concept of performativity has been interpreted and reinterpreted in a range of distinct ways, with the result that what it means and the theoretical ends to which it is put often diverge significantly. Moreover, these assorted theorizations of the performative have, themselves, been turned in plural directions. Since it would be impossible to trace all these competing articulations in a single chapter, this one will concentrate on those that, to date at least, have been the most influential in terms of social and political thought. As many of these take their theoretical bearings from Austin and as language continues to be one of the focal points for discussions of performativity, this is where we will begin.

Performativity and Language

The concept of performativity originates in a series of lectures by Austin that were published posthumously as *How To Do Things With Words* (1962), and is a part of the speech act theory he develops therein. His interest is ordinary language use and, in particular, the *pragmatics* of speech: language as action upon, rather than a description of, the world. Where analytic philosophy was concerned with what Austin called constative utterances, assertions that could be evaluated as true or false, pragmatics focused on a different category of utterance: the performative. By this Austin meant speech that performs the action it describes: as in 'I bet' or 'I name this ship'. This idea that words could do things – that communication is a mode of action – was to prove hugely influential. It was also to give rise to one of the main fault-lines dividing contemporary theories of performativity: between those treating performativity as a formal property of language and those treating it as a social or cultural practice.

The immediate prompt for this difference of opinion is Austin's explanation of what it is that determines the success or failure of an utterance in enacting what it says. In particular, it is the argument that an utterance derives its 'force' from its adherence to a series of conventional procedures. So, the successful performance of a marriage ceremony requires the utterance of an approved sequence of words by parties who are in a legal position to wed; it must take place in a licensed venue; be conducted by someone authorized to do so. If any of these conditions is breached – if an unauthorized person conducts a marriage ceremony, say – the performative will fail; it will be 'infelicitous'.

An important account in elaborating the view that performativity is a quality of language is that offered by French philosopher Jacques Derrida in 'Signature Event Context' (1988 [1972]). What concerns him is the stress Austin places on the conventionality of performative utterances, instead of on the formal properties of language *per se*. In particular, it is Austin's construal of failure as *extrinsic* to those utterances that is the problem. Even though Austin notes that all performatives have the capacity to fail, he errs, according to Derrida, in not pursuing this insight to its logical conclusion, which would be to acknowledge that performative failure is structurally inherent in language itself as a feature of its iterability (see also Loxley 2007). Consequently, Derrida reorients the concept of performativity away from a focus on specific kinds of linguistic utterance towards performativity understood as an innate quality of language in general. Influential as Derrida's thinking is in its own right, particularly in literary theory, it is the uptake of this idea by American feminist Judith Butler (discussed later) that is perhaps most noteworthy from a political and social thought perspective.

The genesis of the idea of performativity as a social phenomenon, by contrast, owes much to the thinking of French social theorist Pierre Bourdieu. As part of his wider theory of language and power, Bourdieu also turns to Austin. Where Derrida had criticized the latter for over-emphasizing factors external to language, Bourdieu takes the opposite standpoint. He argues that his stress on the *formal* qualities of language means Austin fails to acknowledge that, in fact, 'authority comes to language from outside' (1991: 109). In reconfiguring performativity as a specifically sociological concept, Bourdieu thus extends Austin's discussion of convention to take wider account of its social and political dimensions. In *Language and Symbolic Power* (1991), Bourdieu reconceives the force Austin attributes to performative utterances as a force deriving from the institutions (broadly understood) that endow particular agents with the publically recognized authority, resources, and symbols (ceremonial regalia and the like) to perform particular acts. When a police officer declares 'You are under arrest', his/her utterance has performative force because s/he is institutionally authorized to perform arrests. When an unauthorized person – an 'imposter' – does the same, her/his utterance will fail because of the lack of institutional validation behind it. Performative success is thus reconceptualized by Bourdieu as a function of social power, dependent upon the 'symbolic capital' of a particular actor, and performative failure of their lack. At the same time, the concept of performativity is transformed from a purely linguistic phenomenon into one concerned with the social conditions, including gender and class, that impact on language use.

There are, however, other features of Austin's work that have been equally important in terms of the development of linguistic theories of performativity, including his distinction between locutionary, illocutionary, and perlocutionary acts, and, though we won't pursue it here, his typology of illocutionary acts (built on by, amongst others, German philosopher and social theorist Jürgen Habermas). Austin defines the three different aspects of the speech-act just noted in the following way: a locutionary act is simply 'the act *of* "saying something"' (1962: 94, my emphasis); an illocutionary utterance involves the 'performance of an act *in* saying something' (1962: 99, original emphasis) – so a saying that is a doing; while perlocutions are utterances that 'will often, or even normally, produce certain consequential effects' on others (1962: 101) – where an effect is produced *by* saying something, in other words. The last two, as we will see later, are the most noteworthy from the perspective of the development of speech pragmatics (Loxley 2007: 18).

Austin's speech-act theory provides the inspiration for a number of important accounts of linguistic normativity, including those of American philosophers John Searle and Stanley Cavell. Undoubtedly the most important from a political and social theory viewpoint, however, is the version of universal pragmatics advanced by Habermas. This account of performativity, influenced not just by Austin but also by Noam Chomsky's discussion of communicative competence and Karl-Otto Apel's speculations about the transcendental–pragmatic conditions of communication, emerges as Habermas expounds his theory of communicative action. It is thus is central both to his discourse ethics and the analysis he furnishes of modern society and modernization (though neither is discussed here).

Performativity and Communication

Habermas's so-called 'linguistic turn' began in the mid-1970s, with essays in universal pragmatics (see Outhwaite 1994). It is given its fullest expression, however, in the two-volume *Theory of Communicative Action* (1984 [1981], 1987 [1981]) where Habermas sets out his own unique account of rationality, understood as 'how speaking and acting subjects acquire and use knowledge' (1984 [1981]: 11). The theory of communicative action thus depends on an examination of linguistic communication. The goal of this theory is to 'identify and reconstruct universal conditions of possible understanding' (Habermas 1996 (1976): 118). Following Austin, therefore, Habermas is concerned with the pragmatics of speech. His is not, however, an 'empirical pragmatics' concerned with the actual language used in specific contexts (as, for instance, in a linguistic exploration of a particular text or a sociological analysis of conversations). It is what he initially terms a 'universal' and then later a 'formal' pragmatics, focusing on the universal features of language that speaking subjects acquire and deploy in order to communicate successfully (Habermas 1996 [1976]: 129n.1; and 1984 [1981]). Indeed, we might say, it is precisely a version of the form of linguistic analysis that Bourdieu discerned and disclaimed in Austin.

The principal purpose of speech, for Habermas, is to coordinate the action of multiple participants. Language is able to do this because the 'telos' of human speech is 'reaching understanding' (Habermas 1984 [1981]: 287). Habermas's starting point, therefore, is what he calls the 'performative attitude' adopted by participants (speakers and interlocutors) in communication oriented to mutual understanding (which he opposes to the 'objectivating attitude' adopted by those deploying language for personal strategic or instrumental ends). Both his theory of communication and of rationality endeavour, thus, to reconstruct the practical knowledge required by participants in order to communicate successfully.

Habermas's fundamental idea is that communication is able to generate mutual understanding (or 'consensus'), because the meaning of utterances depends on 'the validity basis of meaning' (1984 [1981]: 9). These are necessary features of communication, present in *all* speech. There are three such types of validity claims: that speech is sincere, normatively right, and factually true. All three are open to contestation and justification: a claim, that is, might be rejected as (variously) insincere, illegitimate, or erroneous or may be accepted once reasons have been given to support it. Although this aspect of Habermas's work has come in for intense scrutiny, not least for occluding the social and institutional character of language use (Bourdieu 1991: 107; Ingram 1987: 40) the important point to note is that by linking speech acts to reason-giving, Habermas was able to generate two very influential theories: a discourse ethics grounded in a dialogical principle of universalizability and a theory of democracy grounded in deliberation.

A discussion of performativity in the work of Habermas would not be complete, however, without a discussion of the distinction he endeavours, somewhat controversially, to draw between communicative action (that is, action oriented to mutual understanding) and other types of language use, including most notably strategic action (action oriented to ulterior ends). Not content simply to differentiate between these competing types of action, Habermas also seeks to demonstrate that communicative action is the 'original mode of language use' (1984 [1981]: 288), upon which all other forms are parasitic. To do so he refashions Austin's distinction between locutionary, illocutionary and perlocutionary speech acts. It is the latter two performative and pragmatic aspects of language, in particular, that Habermas homes in on.

Recall, both illocutionary and perlocutionary acts refer to the effects that utterances are able to produce in the world. According to Habermas, in *The Theory of Communicative Action*, illocutionary speech acts produce mutual understanding (or rationally driven consensus) while perlocutionary speech acts, by contrast, are tied to instrumental or strategic goals. That is, they aim to bring about certain consequential effects, specifically effects that are not made explicit in the speech act itself. In order to generate strategic effects, however, perlocutionary acts rest on illocutionary success – the fact that what is said has been understood (even if the motivations behind it may have been hidden from the auditor). Habermas's purpose in making this distinction is to establish that strategic action is dependent on communicative. Whether or not his argument is ultimately successful is a moot point. Critics (e.g. Alexander 1985; Culler 1985) were quick to point out the flaws with it, and although Habermas made various qualifications and adjustments in response to these criticisms (such as allowing that perlocutionaries might be either strategic or non-strategic), significant questions still remain about the viability of his basic position – that there is action oriented to mutual understanding – and about what it is that motivates individuals to set aside an 'objectivating attitude' in favour of a 'performative' one (Outhwaite 1994). Whatever reservations and objections linger, and there are several, it must be noted that his exploration of language enabled Habermas to produce what was to be one of the foremost social, ethical and political theories of recent times, the significance of which continues to resonate across multiple disciplines. In the process, the concept of performativity was remade yet again.

So far the discussion has concentrated on performativity as an aspect either of language (formal or social) or of communication. This does not yet capture, however, the extent or full reach of its applications and interrogations in contemporary theoretical work. In particular, it does not reflect the deployment and remodelling of the concept in the work of American feminist author, Judith Butler. The influence, both within and outside the academy, of Butler's argument that gender is performative cannot be underestimated. It has crossed numerous disciplinary boundaries, stimulating thinking in subject areas from politics and sociology, through cultural studies, anthropology, gender studies and queer theory, to cultural studies and literary theory to name just a few. It has helped to shape both queer theory *and* queer politics. And it has inspired others to endeavour to translate the idea of performativity into their analyses of race, ethnicity, and disability. What, though, does it mean to claim that gender is performative?

Performativity and Gender

In *Gender Trouble*, the text that introduced the concept of gender performativity to a wider public, Butler describes gender as a '*stylized repetition of acts*' (1999: 179, original emphasis). Drawing on Victor Turner's idea that ritual social drama depends on performances that are *repeated*, Butler initially described gender as a 'ritualized, public performance' (1988: 526n.9). The effect of gender, that is, is produced by the repetition of particular bodily gestures, activities, and movements. Where Austin uses performativity to denote linguistic utterances that are also enactments; Butler uses it to describe a corporeal repertoire, the replication of which produces gender. Hers is thus a conception of performativity refigured as a 'style of the flesh'. This fleshy style is one that is historically and culturally sedimented; the acts and gestures that comprise it have accrued social meaning over time. It is also normalizing (in Michel Foucault's sense of that term). As the product of 'the regulatory fiction of heterosexual coherence' (Butler 1999: 173), where biological sex is assumed to flow naturally from gender and gender from sexuality, and where the male body expresses masculinity and heterosexual desire for a woman while the female body expresses femininity and heterosexual desire for a man, it is the basis on which gender performances are judged and, if found wanting, gendered bodies disciplined.

There are, at first glance, parallels with earlier dramaturgical accounts of social performance, such as that elaborated by Canadian sociologist Erving Goffman (1959, 1976). Here individuals are construed as actors playing a particular part, according to certain socially scripted codes and behavioural conventions, in order to create a certain impression of gender on a given audience. In essence, gender is a form of social drama, constructed through interaction with others. Unlike Goffman, who regards the actor as being able consciously to manage their own gendered performances, with those performances regarded as forms of expressive behaviour that reveal something about the individual's 'essential' nature, Butler takes a different tack: she argues, first, in Nietzschean fashion that gender is a 'doing' (1999: 33) but without the constituting role of the doer. The repetition of acts and gestures that generates gender is not performed *by* a gendered subject who directs what they do; the repetition alone constitutes the subject as gendered. She thus puts a new spin on Simone de Beauvoir's famous statement that 'one is not born, but rather becomes, a woman', and by so-doing challenges traditional accounts of both the subject and agency, challenges that were to bring her critics out in force. Second, she rejects the idea of gender as expressive of an interior truth (an essence) about the (sexed) self. Gender identity, for Butler, does not pre-exist the acts that make that identity known to others; what gender *is* (its ontology) is recast rather as an effect of its constitutive acts (1999: 136).

Understanding gender as performative has a number of radical implications. It gives rise to the idea that all gender performances (straight or gay, masculine or feminine) are parodic or imitative. They are all forms of impersonation because they are all modes of corporeal enactment, all the effects of specific practices. Drag, which in *Gender Trouble*, Butler suggests exposes the fiction of gender thus offers just as 'real' a performance of gender, in this regard, as the straight woman performing femininity. Plus, allied to her argument that binary sex is itself a construct of the gender apparatus (a reversal of the normal sex-gender logic found in feminism, which sees sex as prior to gender), it draws attention to the *norms* that regulate and constrain gendered existence.

Readers were, however, divided by her thesis. In particular, despite Butler's insistence throughout *Gender Trouble* that there is no performer behind the performance, many still took her discussion of drag to imply that by electing to dress differently an individual could intentionally and knowingly refashion its gender in any way it wanted. In *Bodies That Matter* (1993), Butler restates her understanding of performativity, this time resorting to Derrida's notion of iterability to clarify. Derrida outlines this idea in his critique of Austin's distinction between serious and non-serious uses of language set out in *How To Do Things With Words*; the latter referring to words spoken by actors or in poems, words Austin describes as both 'parasitic upon' on and as 'etiolations of' ordinary language use (Austin 1962: 22). What Austin characterizes in this way, Derrida construes as a property of language itself: namely, its citationality. Performative utterances succeed, Derrida commends, precisely because just like fictional speech ordinary language (as Austin has it) 'repeat[s] a "coded" or iterable utterance' (1988: 18). The words used to launch a ship are recognizable as such only because they cite a given series of words.

Gender, Butler proposes, has a similar citational structure. Behaviour is identifiable as feminine precisely because it reiterates the corporeal styles (acts, gestures, movements) that have come historically to signify femininity. But this process of gender iterability is based on the compulsory repetition – and thus reproduction – of a specific range of normalized practices. Gender is a mode of citation that is socially constrained and regulated and this is why drag is not necessarily a radical or transformative practice. Although seeing a man enact femininity might lead people to question the idea that gender flows naturally from sex, there is no guarantee that it will. Indeed, the performance might be read simply as evidence that he is not a 'proper' man. Does this mean, therefore, that the gendered subject can never subvert gender norms because they are so thoroughly determined by them? Butler argues that it does not. This time she turns to another aspect of Derrida's argument to explain: that no sign is ever tied indelibly to any particular context but has, instead, an infinite faculty to split from one situation to be recited in any number of others, with its meaning altering in the process. The implication for gender norms is clear: they too can be repeated in ways that resignify them and thus be reworked.

Without a doubt, the notion that gender is performative is the most path-breaking element of Butler's work. It is not, however, her only discussion of performativity to have made an impact. To end this section, therefore, I briefly consider her study of linguistic performatives in *Excitable Speech* (Butler 1997). Here Butler outlines her approach to hate-speech, a debate that had engaged feminists and critical race theorists in the US throughout the 1980s and 1990s. There is much that could – and, indeed, should – be said about this debate in general, about Butler's contribution to it, and about the subsequent work that it has given rise to (see e.g. Freccero 1997; Wright 2002). For our purposes, however, two observations will have to suffice.

First, returning to but revisioning Austin's distinction between illocutionary and perlocutionary utterances, Butler proposes that although illocutionary speech-acts enact their effects as they are uttered, their force (their capacity to succeed), like that of perlocutionary utterances, rests on their prior usages. In terms of hate-speech, this means that words that wound do so, directly or indirectly, not because their speaker intends them to wound (no one can control meaning) but because of their repetition over time – their coding, to paraphrase Derrida – as wounding words. Their performative force, in other words, is an effect of the particular history of meaning accreted through their reiteration.

Second, the need for injurious language to be repeated in order to sustain it is, for Butler, precisely what renders it vulnerable to political contestation. Taking from Derrida the idea that failure inheres structurally in all language (because of *différance*: that each time a term is used a difference is introduced), and that, as such, any term can be potentially wrested away from its context, and allying this to Louis Althusser's idea of interpellation (meaning that hailing – or calling – someone produces them as a subject), Butler argues against censoring hate-speech (as her opponents proposed) and in favour of resignification. Politically, resignification – talking back – is more effective and more democratic, she proposes, because it allows both for the recitation of noxious words in ways that counter their historical associations and for persons so-addressed both to refuse subordinating interpellations and thus to defuse hate-speech of its pernicious potential. Since it is language, not the individuals that use it, that is the means of injury (needless to say, not an uncontroversial position), far better, she argues, that language also be the means of resistance.

Although some critics were worried that Butler appeared to be absolving those deploying hate-speech of any legal culpability and others registered concern that she underestimated the degree of difficulty of resignifying certain particularly entrenched forms of racial or gender slur (see Lloyd 2007 for further discussion), it is clear that hers is not a formal account of linguistic performativity as advanced by Derrida. Like Bourdieu's, it is an approach explicitly focused on linguistic performativity as a social and political practice. It is not authorized or ritual discourses that interest Butler. It is 'ordinary' language use.

In the final section, we turn to an account of performativity that has been particularly influential, if not a little controversial, within sociology. This is the theory of social performance developed by Jeffery Alexander and others at the Centre for Cultural Sociology, at Yale University, a theory that has brought debates about the nature of culture to the fore within that discipline.

Culture and Performance

The performative turn in sociology is part of the so-called 'strong program in cultural sociology' championed by Alexander (2003) and others. Sociological interest in culture is not new; what Alexander proposes, however, is. As one critic has described it, it entails a 'paradigm formation' that is 'nothing less than an argument for the refounding of the American sociological undertaking by "culturalizing" it through and through' (Kurasawa, 2004: 54). Against the sociology *of* culture, where culture is treated as dependent on, even epiphenomenal to, other social structures (particularly, the economic), Alexander advocates *cultural sociology* based on an understanding of social action as cultural performance and combining structuralist approaches with cultural hermeneutics. Culture, in this perspective, ceases to be conceived of as a dependent variable and is reconceptualized as (relatively) autonomous from other structures – an 'independent variable' – the distinctiveness of which ought to be analysed in its own right. This is sociology *as* the examination of culture and meaning. It is not always clear, however, if the implication of this switch of focus is that the social is cultural through and through or only that it may be studied using the same methodologies and theoretical approaches as deployed in the study of culture. (A recent essay implies the latter: Reed and Alexander 2009: 33.)

The methodology developed to address social action as cultural performance is cultural pragmatics. Its direct antecedents include Austin's speech pragmatics, though as with other theories of performativity, cultural pragmatics develops in part out of a critique of Austin. In this case, it is his inattention to cultural context in determining the felicity conditions of speech that is at issue. That is, Austin's neglect of the specific cultural codes actors deploy, often unthinkingly, in their daily lives (Alexander, Giesen, and Mast 2006: 3–4). Cultural pragmatics is not concerned with speech alone, however; it is, rather, concerned more broadly with the variety of actions deployed by determinate social actors in the communication and construction – the *performance* – of meaning. Thus Alexander also draws on theories of theatrical performance, including the work of Professor of Performance Studies, Richard Schechner (commonly credited with initiating the discipline of performance studies), and anthropologists Clifford Geertz and Victor Turner; as well as on dramaturgical theory (for instance, as advanced by Goffman); and even on Stanislavski's system of Method acting to promote the argument that social performances are analogous to theatrical performances.

To understand a cultural performance – such as the 9/11 terrorist attacks on New York and the American response to them (Alexander, Giesen, and Mast: 2006a) – it is, Alexander argues, necessary to identify the basic elements that constitute it. These are: 'systems of collective representation' (Alexander, Giesen, and Mast: 2006b: 33), which include the 'scripts' that are used in the performance, as well as the background narratives and codes against which the action is played out; the actors who perform; the audience for (or observers of) the performance, who may variously identify with what is happening or be uninterested in or unpersuaded by it; the 'means of symbolic production' (Alexander, Giesen, and Mast: 2006b: 35), including the clothing and props required for the performance and the venue in which to perform; the *mise-en-scène* or staging of the performance, how actors move and when, their positioning and other aspects of what might be thought of as direction; and, finally, social power – who may act, who may attend a performance, what might be included in a script and what must be excluded from it, how a performance will be interpreted and by whom. It is the combination of these elements that ensures the performativity – the illocutionary and perlocutionary force – or otherwise of a specific performance (see also Alexander 2007).

To suggest that certain events may be understood as akin to theatre seems a relatively unremarkable claim to make. Cultural pragmatics is not simply a method for studying empirical examples, however. As an ingredient of the strong programme, it is part of a wider theory designed to illuminate the historical transformations that have occurred in the nature of symbolic action from the Greeks to modern times; from 'ritual' as symbolic performance in simpler societies (tribal, band) to 'social drama' as symbolic performance in complex societies. One of the features of this transition is that the probability of performative success (that recurring theme in theories of performativity) diminishes. The question is why.

A successful performance is one that produces authentic acting; has a script (generally organized around the binary: sacred and profane, and here, of course, Alexander is reworking Durkheim), which is believed both by the actors who perform it and the audience that watches it; draws on – reiterates – background cultural representations that are familiar to its viewers; and where the audience identifies (emotionally, psychologically, and so on) with what is being played out in front of it. On such occasions, fusion between the diverse components constituting the performance has been achieved. In simpler, less socially differentiated societies, cultural fusion occurs more readily as performances become ritualized. As Alexander has it, this is not just because such societies are smaller in size but because of the more 'mythical and metaphysical nature of their beliefs' and because their institutions, culture, and social structures are more integrated (Alexander, Giesen, and Mast 2006b: 38). Collective representations apply to society as a whole; the community as a whole participates in rituals (such as initiation rites); and the fit between social roles and sacred texts is tight. Here cultural performances – rituals – operate performatively to generate particular social relationships directly.

In post-ritualistic society, however, as a result of various social and political processes, society has become more complex and more highly differentiated, with the result that the components of performance have become de-fused. Because all societies, indeed all organizations, need to support collective beliefs, the task becomes how to produce performances capable of re-fusing these performative elements. In such societies, social drama takes the place of ritual. As the belief in authority and hierarchy that characterized earlier societies wanes, so culture becomes increasingly critical and social processes more subject to dispute. In this context, Alexander notes, what appears is not the public sphere (as Habermas charges); it is the public stage, upon which actors, of all varieties, have a greater freedom than available to them in previous times to produce performances designed to appeal to the specific audiences (Alexander, Giesen, and Mast 2006b). This means, of course, that a larger number of performances are vying for verisimilitude; it also means a larger number will fail to achieve it.

A re-fused performance is thus one that manages to combine its diverse elements into a convincing whole. To do this, it has to ensure that this performance is the only one to grab the attention of the audience; and to do this it has to be able to surmount the fragmentation that characterizes modern society by, for instance, presenting history in such a way that it overcomes the divisions created by the past. A fascinating example of this process at work is offered by Tanya Goodman (2006) in her exploration of the work of the South African Truth and Reconciliation Commission (TRC). She shows how the hearings it organized throughout South Africa managed to re-fuse a divided society by producing performances of apartheid as a cultural trauma in need of recognition and reparation, that appealed to multiple audiences (both domestic and international), in ways that both separated the new democratic South Africa from its racist past *and* that helped to reintegrate a society divided by apartheid.

In short, the performances orchestrated by the TRC performed – performatively invoked – the new nation.

Conclusion

Performativity clearly means different things to different writers. It connotes a category of speech; a property of language; a corporeal style; and a mode of cultural performance. As part of its circulation within social and political theory it has been used to explain the perpetuation of relations of domination and subordination *and* the means for challenging such; tied to the possibility of justice and deliberative democracy; and linked to the refocusing of a discipline. If it is to operate as an effective social and political theory, however, a theory of performativity has to be capable of explaining *both* the reproduction and perpetuation of relations of power (gendered, capitalist, racial, and so on) *and* how those relations can be contested, given that it is precisely because it is understood to produce effects in the world that the theorists addressed in this chapter turn to it. Suffice to say that few explain both aspects equally well.

Those that do demonstrate how performativity propagates structures of inequality or normalizing frameworks that differentiate adversely between populations take in Bourdieu and Butler (in her account of gender performativity, at least). Those that do not address this question include Alexander, who largely ignores the intersections between culture and other stratifying structures, and Habermas in his formal pragmatics, where the focus is on language. (Habermas, of courses, addresses power in his social theory, which is not examined here.) The risk in these latter cases, however, is that performance and performativity appear to operate entirely independently of all other forces (social, political, and economic), which is patently not the case. The capacity of actors to reshape their environment and of that environment to be reshaped is both enabled *and* constrained by the multiple forms of power relations that underpin it – including those present within culture, something Alexander is charged with not addressing (Emirbayer 2004).

A social and political theory of performativity should also be able to show how social and political change is made possible. Here it is not sufficient to focus on the *abstract* potential for change inherent in language or signification (Derrida and Butler, in her discussion of hate-speech), in re-fusion (Alexander), or even in communicative action (Habermas), though such a potential for change is clearly necessary. Attention needs to focus too on the historical, political, and social conditions of possibility that facilitate that change, which might include particular institutions, forms of political rationality, the activities of nascent groupings, or changing political circumstance. This is where empirical case studies of the kind developed by Alexander and colleagues are important (e.g. Alexander 2006a, 2007; Goodman 2006), provided – and this is not always the case – they are able to explain both *how* meanings become embedded socially and politically and *how* cultural codes are reworked (de- and re-contextualized in Derrida's sense) therein. The absence of any account of change, as in Bourdieu, ultimately undercuts the potential explanatory power of any discussion of performativity. It tells only half the story.

References

Alexander, J.C. (1985) 'Habermas's New Critical Theory: Its Promise and Problems', *American Journal of Sociology*, 91 (2): 400–24.
——(2003) *The Meanings of Social Life: A Cultural Sociology*, New York: Oxford University Press.
——(2006a) 'From the Depths of Despair: Performance, Counterperformance and "September 11"', in J.C. Alexander, B. Giesen, and J.L. Mast (eds) *Social Performance: Symbolic Action, Cultural Pragmatics, and Ritual*, Cambridge: Cambridge University Press.

——(2006b) 'Cultural Pragmatics: Social Performance between Ritual and Strategy', in J.C. Alexander, B. Giesen, and J.L. Mast (eds) *Social Performance: Symbolic Action, Cultural Pragmatics, and Ritual*, Cambridge: Cambridge University Press.

——(2007) 'Power and Performance: The War on Terror between the Sacred and the Profane', Robert Schuman Centre for Advanced Studies Distinguished Lectures, European University Institute, RSCAS DL 2007/01.

Alexander, J.C., B. Giesen, and J.L. Mast (eds.) (2006) *Social Performance: Symbolic Action, Cultural Pragmatics, and Ritual*, Cambridge: Cambridge University Press.

Austin, J.L. (1962) *How To Do Things With Words*, Oxford: Oxford University Press.

Bourdieu, P. (1991) *Language and Symbolic Power*, Cambridge: Polity.

Butler, J. (1999) *Gender Trouble: Feminism and the Subversion of Identity (Tenth Anniversary Edition)*, London: Routledge.

——(1993) *Bodies That Matter: On the Discursive Limits of 'Sex'*, London: Routledge.

——(1997) *Excitable Speech: A Politics of the Performative*, London: Routledge.

——(1988) 'Performative Acts and Gender Constitution: An Essay in Phenomenology and Feminist Theory', *Theatre Journal*, 40 (4): 519–31.

Culler, J. (1985) 'Communicative Competence and Normative Force', *New German Critique*, 35: 133–44.

Derrida, J. (1988 [1972]) 'Signature Event Context', in *Limited Inc.*, Evanston, IL: Northwestern University Press.

Emirbayer, M. (2004) 'The Alexander School of Cultural Sociology', *Thesis Eleven*, 79 (1): 5–15.

Freccero, C. (1997) 'Historical Violence, Censorship, and the Serial Killer: The Case of "American Psycho"', *Diacritics*, 27 (2): 44–58.

Goffman, E. (1959) *The Presentation of Self in Everyday Life*, Harmondsworth: Penguin.

——(1976) 'Gender Display', *Studies in the Anthropology of Visual Communication*, 3: 69–77.

Goodman, T. (2006) 'Performing a 'New' Nation: The Role of the TRC in South Africa', in J.C. Alexander, B. Giesen, and J.L. Mast (eds), *Social Performance: Symbolic Action, Cultural Pragmatics, and Ritual*, Cambridge: Cambridge University Press.

Habermas, J. (1984 [1981]) *The Theory of Communicative Action*, volume 1. London: Heinemann.

——(1987 [1981]) *The Theory of Communicative Action*, volume 2. Cambridge: Polity.

——(1996 [1976]) 'What is Universal Pragmatics?', in W. Outhwaite (ed.) *The Habermas Reader*, Cambridge: Polity.

Ingram, D. (1987) *Habermas and the Dialectic of Reason*, New Haven, CT, and London: Yale University Press.

Kurasawa, F. (2004) 'Alexander and the Cultural Refounding of American Sociology', *Thesis Eleven*, 79: 53–65.

Lloyd, M. (2007) *Judith Butler: From Norms to Politics*, Cambridge: Polity.

Loxley, J. (2007) *Performativity*, London: Routledge.

Outhwaite, W. (1994) *Habermas: A Critical Introduction*, Cambridge: Polity.

Reed, I., and J.C. Alexander (2009) 'Social Science as Reading and Performance: A Cultural–Sociological Understanding of Epistemology', *European Journal of Social Theory*, 12 (1): 21–41.

Wright, C. (2002) 'Speaking out of the Blue? September 11th as Hate Speech', *Situation Analysis*, 1: 26–39.

Nationalism and Social Theory

The Distinction between Community and Society

Steven Grosby

During the last 25 years approximately, an enormous amount has been written on nations and nationalism, largely in response to the recognition, at times grudging, that the so-called "age of nationalism", once thought by many as a designation of the nineteenth century, persists with vigor into the twenty-first. Hardly a year passes without numerous books and articles on these subjects appearing – too many for any one scholar to read. There are seven journals devoted exclusively to the study of nationality, the most prominent of which is *Nations and Nationalism*, edited by Anthony Smith; and one finds articles on nationality in many other journals of the most diverse areas of scholarship. Despite this flood of publications that includes myriad investigations of putatively theoretical scope, the study of nationality remains curiously isolated from the modest contributions of social and political theory to the clarification of human conduct. In fact, the majority of the analyses of nationality are theoretically primitive, confined to the antiquated schema of a sharp historical disjunction between status and contract, as formulated by Henry Sumner Maine in *Ancient Law*, or between *Gemeinschaft* ("community") and *Gesellschaft* ("society"), as formulated by Ferdinand Tőnnies in *Gemeinschaft und Gesellschaft*. Thus, social theory and political theory have pressingly important contributions to make in clarifying both this significant social phenomenon of our time, nationality (a term I shall use to designate the character of otherwise historically and constitutively diverse nations), and the uncivil ideology of nationalism; however, in order to do so, this historically simplistic disjunction must be put aside.

The Burden of an Analytical Tradition

Tőnnies (1940 [1887]: 119–73) posited two, distinctive types of action: *Wesenwille* ("natural" or "essential" will) and *Kürwille* ("rational" or "arbitrary" will), corresponding respectively to two forms of social relations – *Gemeinschaft* and *Gesellschaft*. The actual, but often overlooked merit of Tőnnies' contrast between *Gemeinschaft* and *Gesellschaft*, each characterized by a form of action distinctive to it, is that it conveys a pluralism of orientation of human conduct. To be sure, that pluralism subsequently required careful differentiation and refinement, as one sees in, for example, the different types of understanding and action, and heterogeneous "life-spheres" throughout Max Weber's work; the pattern variables in Talcott Parsons' and Edward Shils' *Toward a General Theory of Action* (and especially in Shils' (1975 [1957]) recognition of qualitatively different orientations of the mind); the mediating associations in Robert Nisbet's *The Quest for Community*; and the distinction between civil and enterprise associations in Michael Oakeshott's *On Human Conduct* (Grosby 2002a).

Despite this merit and subsequent refinement, Tőnnies' analytical contrast between these two categories of action has all too often been wrongly simplified by numerous analysts through a crude historicism that isolates the appearance of one type of action and its corresponding social relation from that of the other. Thus, it is often argued that *Gemeinschaft* and its corresponding action of *Wesenwille* are only to be found in the local societies of the distant past, while *Gesellschaft* and its corresponding action of *Kürwille* are exclusively constitutive of modern times. In doing so, these analysts eschew the insight of those refinements of Tőnnies' analytical contrast, that is, the co-existence of qualitatively heterogeneous orientations of human action, even though, it must be admitted, they have done so with justification from Tőnnies' initial formulation of the contrast (but by avoiding Tőnnies' (1971 [1926]) own, later complication of his analysis, especially in the aftermath of World War I, when he rightly could not avoid coming to terms with the modern, yet nonetheless *gemeinschaftliche* attachment of patriotism to the nation). That historicism has had a baneful influence on both the understanding of human action, for example, the currently fashionable, doctrinaire expression of the theory of rational choice that, in economic theory, wrongly reduces all knowledge and its interpretation to information capable of utilitarian calculation, and, for our purposes, the study of nationality.[1]

Tőnnies' distinction between these two types of action turns on the character of deliberation: on the one hand, *Wesenwille*, where thinking is an integral and immediate part of action, hence "natural" or "essential", and, on the other, *Kürwille*, where thinking directs action, hence "rational" or "arbitrary" in the sense that a calculation takes place as to whether or not to engage in action. The former, *Wesenwille*, is, according to Tőnnies, characteristic of both impulsive action, for example, courage or habit and, more generally, where conduct conforms to traditional patterns of activity. Thinking is by no means absent in the action of *Wesenwille*, as the reception of tradition is always in varying degrees critical because, one among a number of reasons, the tasks and challenges facing one generation differ from those of another.

There are from antiquity many confirmations of the modification (one could even say "manipulation") of tradition through its critical reception. I mention here only in passing the writings of the legalist Shang Yang (fourth century BCE), Wang Ch'ung (first century CE), Carneades (second century BCE), and works like the pre-axial age, so-called "Babylonian Theodicy" (c. 1000 BCE) and the theologically challenging, monotheistic *Ecclesiastes*. To take another example, one finds, as is well known, in the first five books of the Bible the commandment that the Israelites are to circumcise the foreskin of the penis of their male children. However, Deuteronomy 10:16, 30:6, and Jeremiah 4:4 call upon the Israelites to circumcise the foreskin of their hearts. The latter commandment is such a strikingly odd metaphor that it can only be a critical commentary on, and modification of, the evidently earlier tradition of the circumcision of the penis. The significance of the example of this modification is that the critical evaluation of tradition in antiquity was by no means confined to the works of putatively isolated individuals like Wang Ch'ung and Carneades; rather, this heightened, self-conscious reflection is potentially part of public discourse, as was the case for Shang Yang's legalism and the Bible in antiquity and the Middle Ages. The very existence of Christianity is yet another example of the critical reception of tradition with manifestly broad public consequences in antiquity; and it was acknowledged as such, that is, the "new" covenant or testament – already called for by Jeremiah – in contrast to the "old". Many other historical examples from antiquity of the public, critical reception of tradition can be alluded to, ranging from the public performance of Euripides' *Orestes*, with its absurd, even self-described idiotic conclusion that could have only conveyed a tragic skepticism about Greek tradition and its gods, to the acute religious turmoil throughout the Roman Empire (Stoicism, Christianity, Manichaenism, the cults of Isis and Mithra, Julian's pagan revival, etc.). Too often historical sociology and social and political theory evaluate the distant past as if its societies were nothing more than isolated, small villages of unthinking brutes who are mindlessly captive to an all encompassing tradition; that is, as if those societies were merely homogeneous *Gemeinschaften* with one uniform form of thought and action. But this is not so.

Insofar as there are any secure insights into the nature of human conduct from social theory, one surely is the rejection of a "group mind" through affirmation of the principle of methodological individualism, that is, thought and action are individually centered; and this is so for all historical periods. Thus, it is not surprising that we have from antiquity abundant historical evidence of not only the critical reception of tradition, but also contracts, partnerships for trade, private property, and the rule of law (for one example, see Veenhof 1997). What is of lasting theoretical value to Tönnies' categories of *Wesenwille* and *Kürwille* is that both, to be sure in varying degrees, are found in all historical periods. However, given the principle of methodological individualism, the problem arises how both *Wesenwille* and *Gemeinschaft* should be understood. It is precisely here where the study of nationality ought to make a contribution to political and social theory and vice versa.

At least this much should be clear: *Wesenwille* should not be historically relegated to an earlier period; rather, it is to be understood as a type of deliberation and corresponding action infused with the intimacy of, or undertaken with reference to, the social relation, for example, the attachment of patriotism to the homeland – an attachment found throughout all historical periods. Accordingly, it is with this type of action where, as formulated by Tönnies, one finds sympathy and self-sacrifice, for example, on the part of the parent for his or her child. The prototypical social relation of this form of action is the "existential" collectivity of the family, where one's actions are bound up with the thought of gratifying or promoting the ends of other members of the family with little or no calculation of the costs involved to oneself. The prototypical cognitive referents – the recognized objects of significance – of this form of action are kinship and the actor's immediate environs of the home, that is, the tradition-bound village.[2] However, as Schmalenbach (1977 [1922]) convincingly argued, those *gemeinschaftliche* referents are susceptible to expansion, transformation, and even wide variation beyond their prototypical, parochial scope, as one observes in, for example, the *Wesenwille* of the patriotic attachments to the territorially extensive nation.

Kürwille, in contrast, is a type of action motivated by the thought (thus, prior to action) of satisfying one's own need, hence, the prototypical social relation is that of the exchange of the market, or *Gesellschaft* ("society"). Characteristic of *Kürwille* is the individual's motivation to attain what is desired by that individual. As such, *Kürwille* does not, according to Tönnies, encompass a "positive" or philanthropic attitude towards fellow human beings, because the sympathetic attachments arising out of shared resemblance of one kind or another, for example, kinship, putatively no longer exist or, if they do exist, they are clearly subordinated to the self-interest of the individual – self-interest understood as where the benefits of action accrue directly to the acting individual. However, if one views modern society as dominated by *Kürwille*, then the problem arises as to how this modern, territorially extensive association is held together, or as Simmel famously formulated the problem, "How is society possible?"

Tönnies' categorial and historical contrast between *Gemeinschaft* and *Geselllschaft* had an enormous influence on the early development of social and political theory, for example, on

Durkheim's distinction, as presented in *The Division of Labor*, between "mechanical" and "organic" solidarity. The accuracy of this distinction for societies of the past was taken for granted, as those societies were of little interest to social and political theorists who were more concerned with modern life, often characterized by them as the "crisis of modernity". It did not occur to them and still does not occur to many that the merit of the historical contrast between these two forms of social relation also rests upon the accuracy of Tönnies' (or earlier Maine's and subsequently Durkheim's) understanding of the societies of antiquity. But only a moment's reflection forces one to conclude that something is analytically awry; for there is no place in Tönnies' conception of the historically early *Gemeinschaft* for such ancient metropolises as Babylon, Alexandria, and Rome.

The influence of the historical contrast between *Gemeinschaft* and *Gesellschaft* on social and political theory continues today, even if largely unacknowledged, as can be seen in the shared assumptions of such otherwise diverse works as F.A. Hayek's *The Fatal Conceit* and James Coleman's *Foundations of Social Theory*, and, for political theory, the widely accepted understanding of the state as a social contract. But, once again, only a moment's reflection forces one to conclude that something is analytically awry; for even if one rightly acknowledges a significant degree of social integration arising from the division of labor and the market, as writers such as Durkheim and Hayek have argued, the conception of the putatively voluntaristic, overly individualistic, anomie-ridden modern *Gesellschaft* cannot account for a singularly important fact: the patriotic outbursts of World War I and World War II. Furthermore, as many scholars have recently observed, early in the twenty-first century, the significance of nationality persists. Thus, it is remarkably curious that many of the influential theoretical analyses of nationality remain burdened by Tönnies' dichotomy, as if, in the twentieth century, *Wesenwille* were merely residual. Ernest Gellner's *Nations and Nationalism* is a case in point.

Gellner's argument for the emergence of nations in modern Europe is straightforward. Its starting point is the development of industrial capitalism and its corresponding requirement of a mobile, culturally uniform workforce. This "industrial variation" of the "human situation" – to use Gellner's terms – is described by him as "an anonymous, impersonal society, with mutually substitutable atomized individuals" (1983: 57). Clearly, Gellner's description of modern society has much in common with Tönnies' understanding of the *Kürwille*-constituted *Gesellschaft*. Gellner proceeds by posing a variation of Simmel's question. Given this mass of substitutable, atomized individuals necessary for modern industrial society to function, how does this otherwise disaggregated society hold together?

His answer to this question is that society is "held together above all by a shared culture" that is diffused through "a school-mediated, academy supervised idiom, codified for the requirements of reasonably precise bureaucratic and technological communication" (Gellner 1983: 57). This culture – called by Gellner "high culture" – holds together these mobile, atomized individuals "in place of a previous complex structure of local groups" each of which had once been sustained by their own "low", folk culture. For Gellner, the nation is the imposition of this high culture on these previously isolated low cultures – an imposition necessary for industrial capitalism. Thus, in the parlance of the social anthropology of Bronislaw Malinowski and A.R. Radcliffe-Brown, Gellner's analysis of nationality is a "functionalist" argument: in order for industrial capitalism to exist (or function), it requires a culturally uniform population. The analysis rests upon two assumptions: 1) a historical disjunction between the high culture of the modern, industrial nation and the low cultures of previously isolated, local groups – a disjunction that is little more than a slight variation of Tönnies' distinction between *Gesellschaft* and *Gemeinschaft*; and 2) the beliefs constitutive of nationalism are derivative of industrial capitalism, that is, the high culture of nationalism – a functional requirement for the economic organization of modern society – forms the sociological uniformity of the nation.

Many of the well known analyses of nationality share these assumptions of Gellner's analytical framework, albeit with shifts in emphasis. Thus, for Benedict Anderson's (1983: 42–3) *Imagined Communities*, the focus is the technology of "print capitalism" necessary for the shared communication constitutive of the emerging cultural cohesiveness of the nation; that is, nationalism is, in effect, the formation of an imagined community of the politicization of language. John Breuilly's *Nationalism and the State* concentrates on the centralizing modern state that, in turn, requires the cultural justification of nationalism. In other words, for Breuilly (1982: 2, 55–64, 398–401), the ideology of nationalism is exclusively a modern, political vehicle in support of the state's requirement of allegiance.

For all of these analyses, the intellectuals' political ideology of nationalism creates the modern national state (Delanty and O'Mahony 2002: 7, 18, 30, 87). There is nothing artificial or conspiratorial in the existence of this ideology, as is implied by the category "false consciousness" of the Frankfurt School; for, according to these analyses, modern life – the centralizing bureaucratic state, democracy, forms of communication, industrial capitalism – requires beliefs that distinguish one group of human beings, organized as a national state, from another. Even for Eric Hobsbawm (Hobsbawm and Ranger 1983, Hobsbawm 1990), with his emphasis on the "invention of tradition", that invention is necessary as a political requirement for the modern national state, or at least it was necessary as today, so Hobsbawm (1990: 181–3) wrongly claimed, national states are being pushed aside in favor of new, supranational, political structures.

While more should be said about these analyses, it will suffice for our purposes to observe that they all view nationality as exclusively modern and as a predominately political phenomenon, that is, the modern ideology of nationalism creates nations. None of them draws a clear distinction between, on the one hand, the nation as an always historically complex and highly differentiated collectivity and, on the other, the often competing views – various nationalisms – about what the nation has been, is, and should be. There have always been competing views within any nation about that nation, as John Hutchinson (2005) so convincingly argued. These analyses have no place for what factually has always been the case: the existence of these competing views and the differentiated, even fragmented character of any nation. They all labor under the burden of the tradition of Tönnies' contrast between the putatively homogeneous, pre-modern *Gemeinschaft* and the putatively homogeneous, modern *Gesellschaft* in their view of nationality as primarily or even exclusively a temporally flat and constitutively seamless vehicle for either the formation of modern culture or as a political means to justify the modern state.

An Alternative Approach

There should be no doubt that there is a degree of merit in the arguments of the above mentioned analyses. Surely, modern means of communication and state-supervised public education have contributed significantly to the formation of a common culture, as Anderson and Gellner argued. It is also clear that the centuries-long process of the consolidation and expansion of the authority of the modern state has facilitated greatly the deference of its citizens such that a spatially extensive, political community exists. Nonetheless, it is noteworthy that various and sometimes intense expressions of regionalism persist, thereby complicating the view of the putatively homogeneous *Gesellschaft*. It is not clear how, if at all, this regionalism can be accounted for in these previously mentioned analyses. Moreover and importantly, the functionalism of these analyses, however analytically appealing, does not address a crucial question. Why should nationality, with its significance of a bounded territory and a form of kinship, have proved to be and continues to be so receptive to individuals? In other words, why are there not merely states, but *national* states? Thus, despite some merit to these analyses, one concludes from their inability to address satisfactorily the problems raised by these questions that their philosophical anthropology is inadequate for our understanding of modern society. Despite the coherence of, for example, Gellner's argument, his understanding of culture is too simplistic, as the ideas constitutive of culture are consequences of the mode of production. As such, his analysis displays an impoverished, restrictive conception of the mind, with little or no place for the relative independence of tradition, and a historicist infatuation with the putatively dramatic plasticity of human conduct. The questions central to our interest in nationality remain. Just why does it matter to many human beings today where they were born and the location where they live? And why do they often view those born and dwelling within what they understand to be their country as being in some way related such that those born and living elsewhere are not? Tönnies' original formulation of *Gesellschaft* and all the subsequent analyses that share its assumptions avoid these and similar problems. Obviously, one cannot in good conscience dismiss the attachments raised by these questions as being today merely residual or irrational, as Walker Connor (1993) rightly argued.

To be sure, not all humans attribute significance to the relations of territorial kinship constitutive of nationality, not only today but also in antiquity: for example, Paul's assertions in Galatians 3:28 and Romans 10:12. It remains to be seen if recent supranational structures, as Hobsbawm observed, for example, the European Union and its Court of Human Rights, and other developments that are usually described today under the rubric of "globalization" more pervasively and lastingly undermine relations of territorial kinship than in the past. Recall that the most significant alternative to territorially parochial societies – nations or otherwise – was the Roman Empire with its empire-wide citizenship, begun under the reign of Caracella (211–17 CE). In our attempt to understand what may or may not be distinctive about modern society, one should acknowledge that there have historically always been supranational structures and developments, for example, respectively, empires and the world religions – both realistic alternatives in antiquity – for how individuals organize and understand themselves. This is factually obvious, or should be if, once again, political and social theorists would pay more attention to the history of the past in their analysis of human conduct. Thus, the theoretical schema of a sharp, historical contrast between *Gemeinschaft* and *Gesellschaft* is exposed to two important criticisms: one of philosophical anthropology, the second historical. And the problem of how to understand nationality is at the axis of both.

After all, honesty to the historical record forces recognition of further complications to the theoretical framework of those analyses that share Tönnies' assumptions, and its derivative categories, for example, that of "modernity".[3] Take, for example, language. One finds clearly in the biblical Genesis the following classificatory schema, "These are the descendants of Japheth by their lands – each with its language – their clans (or families) and their nations" (Genesis 10:5; see also 10:20, 31–2).[4] There are numerous, similar classifications that conflate language, territory, and its inhabitants throughout history, for example, medieval Poland (Grosby 2005: 70). The origin of this kind of classification – what writers like Anderson, Gellner, Breuilly, and Hobsbawm would call the politicization of language – is by no means modern as John Armstrong (1982) noted; it required neither "print capitalism" nor the modern state, even though, as already observed, modern means of communication and a modern state bureaucracy, so intrusive in all spheres of life, have clearly been factors in the stabilization and politicization of language.

The modern state was also not necessary for the sharp cultural demarcation between one group and another. To take only one among a plethora of examples, Shi'ism has been the national religion of Iran since the beginning of the Safavid period (1502 CE), earlier as a Persian vehicle of opposition to Sunni Arabs ruling from Syria, then as emblematic of the re-emergence of Persian collective self-consciousness in contrast to the Sunni Ottoman Empire (Gallagher 1967). Even if one were to follow the logic of Breuilly and Hobsbawm by accepting the seductively simplistic explanation for the Safavid embrace of Shi'ism as merely an opportunistic exploitation of religious differences in the service of consolidating state power, one would still have to account for the gradual adoption of Shi'ism since the ninth century and the re-awakening of attachments to the image of Persia as distinct within the otherwise universalistic Islamic *ummah*. Both that earlier adoption and that re-awakening were prerequisites for the success of the Safavid policy; for it is likely impossible for a state-directed initiative to gain acceptance if there are not already existing attachments to which an appeal, however opportunistic and transformative, can be made.

These latter observations open up a properly more complicated and accurate understanding of the temporally deep, symbolic cross-currents in the formation of any nation, as found in John Armstrong's *Nations and Nationalism* with his rich discussion of territorial identity, religion, and myth; Adrian Hastings' *The Construction of Nationhood* (1997: 1–65) with his examination of the influence of the Old Testament on the development of England as a nation; especially the arguments of Anthony Smith's *The Ethnic Origins of Nations* (1986), *The Nation in History* (2000), and *Ethno-symbolism and Nationalism* (2009) that have been largely responsible for productively re-orienting the study of nationality through their emphasis on the symbolic bearers of memory and ethnicity; and recently Aviel Roshwald's *The Endurance of Nationalism* (2006). All of these works have rightly brought into the foreground the place of tradition – of the past in the present while not ignoring the present in the understanding of the past (that is, the critical reception or even manipulation of tradition) – in the formation of nationality. In doing so, they have reminded social and political theorists that to avoid tradition, however knotty a problem, is a grave mistake.

The kind of complications briefly alluded to above are good reasons to put aside aspects of Tönnies' contrast between *Wesenwille*-dominated, pre-modern community and *Kürwille*-dominated, modern society as being heuristically unproductive. The merit of the analytical contrast between two types of action remains, although requiring both differentiation and recognition that these two forms of action co-exist, influencing one another in a variety of ways. What is to be rejected is the unequivocal historical distinction between pre-modern and modern, as one finds in Heidegger's (1977 [1938]) factually unsupported "The Age of the World Picture", for there is abundant evidence in antiquity for carefully delineated territorial boundaries, albeit without the geographical precision of degrees of latitude and longitude. This rejection is not to deny that in one historical period in contrast to another, one type of action is more prevalent than another; but to note such an ascendancy must be only the beginning of an analysis, not a conclusion that forecloses engagement with factually obvious complications: for example, today, restrictions on immigration that compromise the *gesellschaftliche* market of free labor. To proceed otherwise results in a misevaluation of both past societies, for example, Routledge's (2003) criticisms of Gellner's distinction between low and high culture viz. ancient Egypt, and modern societies, hence the often found theoretical confusion over the character of nationality. When one puts aside the putative, historical disjunction between pre-modern and modern, a number of problems of pressing theoretical significance emerge.

Given the diverse complexity of factors and temporally deep processes in the constitution of any nation, it is heuristically appropriate to have a relatively expansive *definition of the nation as an extensive, yet bounded community of territorial descent*. There is obviously much that is implied in this definition that requires elucidation, some of which will be addressed below. Furthermore, there are methodological problems concerning the formation of categories that I note but will not take up here. What is relevant here is how various theorists of nationality avoid this complexity; for example, the largely unavoidable – except during those necessarily brief periods of patriotic outburst – distinction between center and periphery, and divisions within the center so manifest since the development of the universal, world religions, the existence of which challenges the attachments to the parochial nation. Here, too, an examination of Gellner's analysis will prove useful as an example of such an avoidance.

One observes a conceptually mischievous sleight of hand in Gellner's understanding of nationality, evidently motivated to exclude the multitude of historical facts that would undermine his analysis that the modern ideology of nationalism creates the homogeneous high culture that pervades an entire population (1983: 55). Gellner makes clear that he is concerned with "genuine" cultures and "genuine" nations. However, one wonders what would be a "counterfeit" or "pseudo" culture and nation. The use of this adjective reveals that Gellner's analysis does not rest upon the examination of facts of an always complicated reality; rather, he has a theoretical schema which, because of his fidelity to it, must run roughshod over those facts. There is no such thing in reality as a "genuine nation". In contrast, the definition of nationality offered above is predicated upon the recognition of the historical facts of the complex character of nations. It, thus, allows one to group together, for especially comparative purposes, such otherwise diverse societies as ancient Israel, Persia/Iran of the sixteenth century, Canada with its pronounced regionalism, and linguistically diverse India. While the sample of these societies displays a marked heterogeneity among them and within each of them, all are nonetheless different from empire or city-kingdom. However tenuous and conflict-ridden, the culture or collective self-consciousness of these societies revolves around the significance of a territory believed to be unique to its respective people.

These observations present social and political philosophy with the following problem. How are the attachments to the nation to be understood? The problem can be reformulated. How is the relation between individuals, as members of the nation, to be accounted for? It is obvious enough that we are dealing with a form of recognition, of the conception of the self – self-consciousness – that is unevenly shared in some way among a bounded group of individuals – collective self-consciousness – such that a *Gemeinschaft* exists. There may be, indeed always are, numerous factors, actually tension-ridden historical processes, constitutive of this recognized, only relatively stable boundary, for example, common language, common religion, or belief in a common ancestry; but for a nation to exist, for the category of nationality to have heuristic specificity, the recognition of a common territory which, as such, unites those individuals' self-conceptions to one another, must be ascendant, or at least have the potential to become so.

To draw attention to this collective self-consciousness poses a complication for the principle of methodological individualism because it is predicated upon recognition of a shared property in the image of the individual that has a bearing on action. More precisely, it is not merely the existence of that shared property, for example, speaking a common language or having been born in the same land, but the individual's evaluation – the attribution of significance – of that property such that a classification is made, distinguishing one individual and one group from another individual and group. To be sure, deliberation and action remain individually centered in that evaluation; nonetheless, various kinds of groups are recognized, membership in which conveys preferences and obligations, thereby influencing the individual's decisions and conduct. These observations are merely to acknowledge what is often taken for granted: the wide use of "we", one example of which is a nation (with its preference for familiarity and the fellow national, and the patriotic obligation to defend it). Thus, while the principle of methodological individualism retains its validity, it must be qualified so that these facts of human existence are accounted for. Doing so remains a task of social and political philosophy.

It will not suffice to account for our use of "we" as either the result of the individual's pursuit of a perceived advantage or a ubiquitous tendency to social life, even though both are operative. As to the former, it is precisely the self-sacrifice elicited by "existential" collectivities like the family and nation that arouse our theoretical curiosity; as to the latter, it is analytically unproductive to bring together the intense, integrative attachments characteristic of a family or village with those of a religious sect or a friendship. The former, as noted above, raises a problem for the principle of methodological individualism; the latter forces the theorist to distinguish the various modes of attachments that individuals form with one another by differentiating the incommensurable objects or referents of those attachments. This leads us to another task facing social and political philosophy.

One of those incommensurable objects of significance centers on vitality; this is what was implied by the phrase "existential collectivities", that is, kinship. Now, it used to be assumed and is still widely assumed that there is a categorically pure, developmentally and historically, form of kinship that is narrowly gentilic, that is, kinship understood as a relation of descent based on the perceived "tie of blood". It is this form of kinship that one generally means when one uses the term "family", irrespective of whether the relation is traced matrilineally or patri-lineally. This assumption should be put aside, because the anthropological and historical evi-dence indicates that kinship is constituted around the recognition of not only familial descent but also through the image of a shared territory, specifically, descent in – being "native to" – that territory. There are, thus, two lines of descent, neither one precluding the other; they are often intermingled. Another task for social and political philosophy is to clarify "territorial kinship" that has been obscured by the contrast between *Gemeinschaft* and *Gesellschaft* (and status and contract) but which is key to nationality.

Conclusion

There are several paradoxes of human existence that are clearly manifested in nationality. The nation is a structure of collective self-consciousness, and yet it has no mind of its own. This first paradox is a reformulation of a long-standing problem of social philosophy: the clarification of what is meant by "culture". Even though by no means new, this problem remains in need of further analysis; and it has been brought into sharper focus by the work of the last twenty-five years on nationality. One expression of this problem is the need to qualify carefully the principle of methodological individualism.

The nation necessarily contains meaningful references to the past, and yet is constituted in the present. Here, social and political philosophy face the problem of temporal depth in the formation of collectivities and, in fact, human consciousness. It is, more generally formulated, the problem of tradition and the reception of tradition.

The nation is a structure of kinship constituted by the significance attributed to the location of one's birth (a territorial collectivity of nativity); and yet, especially insofar as it becomes a national state, it is a bearer of the rationalization of custom and law. Here again, social and political philosophy face the problem of clarifying our understanding of kinship. Moreover, these concluding remarks bring into focus the necessity to distinguish analytically nation from the Manichean-like ideology of nationalism, and nation from state. The way forward for social and political philosophy to clarify productively these problems, thereby achieving a more accurate understanding of human action and nationality, requires that the limitations of the distinction between *Gemeinschaft* and *Gesellschaft* be recognized.

Notes

1 The classic formulation of the reduction of knowledge to information is Stigler 1961. For how this historicism has influenced the study of nationality, see Smith 1998.
2 Following Shils 1975 [1957], I (Grosby 1995, 1996, 2001) have designated these cognitive referents of the significance of nativity as "primordial".

3 One gets a sense of these complications by S.N. Eisenstadt's (2003: 493–571) recourse to "multiple modernities" (or is it an avoidance of the complications?).

4 The translation of the ancient Hebrew *goy* as nation has long been defended by biblical scholars (see Grosby 2002b).

References

Anderson, Benedict. (1983) *Imagined Communities: Reflections on the Origins and Spread of Nationalism*, London: Verso.

Armstrong, John. (1982) *Nations Before Nationalism*, Chapel Hill, NC: University of North Carolina.

Breuilly, John. (1982) *Nationalism and the State*, Chicago, IL: University of Chicago Press.

Conner, Walker. (1993) "Beyond Reason: The Nature of the Ethnonational Bond", *Ethnic and Racial Studies*, 16(3): 373–89.

Delanty, Gerard and O'Mahony, Patrick. (2002) *Nationalism and Social Theory: Modernity and the Recalcitrance of the Nation*, London: Sage.

Eisenstadt, S.N. (2003) *Comparative Civilizations and Multiple Modernities*, Leiden: Brill.

Gallagher, Charles F. (1967) "The Plateau of Particularism: Problems of Religion and Nationalism in Iran", in K.A. Silvert (ed.) *Churches and States: The Religious Institution and Modernization*, New York: American Universities Field Staff.

Gellner, Ernest. (1983) *Nations and Nationalism*, Ithaca, NY: Cornell University Press.

Grosby, Steven. (2005) *Nationalism: A Very Short Introduction*, Oxford: Oxford University Press.

——(2002a) "Pluralism in the Thought of Oakeshott, Shils and Weber", *Journal of Classical Sociology* 2(1): 43–58.

——(2002b) *Biblical Ideas of Nationality: Ancient and Modern*, Winona Lake, IN: Eisenbrauns.

——(2001) "Primordiality", in A. Leoussi (ed.) *Encyclopaedia of Nationalism*, New Brunswick, NJ: Transaction.

——(1996) "The Category of the Primordial in the Study of Early Christianity and Second Century Judaism", *History of Religions*, 18(2): 211–26.

——(1995) "Territoriality: The Transcendental, Primordial Feature of Modern Societies", *Nations and Nationalism*, 1(2) 143–62.

Hastings, Adrian. (1997) *The Construction of Nationhood*, Cambridge: Cambridge University Press.

Heidegger, Martin. (1977 [1938]) "The Age of the World Picture", in *The Question Concerning Technology and Other Essays*, New York: Harper & Row.

Hobsbawm, Eric. (1990) *Nations and Nationalism since 1780: Programme, Myth, Reality*, Cambridge: Cambridge University Press.

Hobsbawm, Eric and Ranger, Terrence (eds). (1983) *The Invention of Tradition*, Cambridge: Cambridge University Press.

Hutchinson, John. (2005) *Nations as Zones of Conflict*, London: Sage.

Roshwald, Aviel. (2006) *The Endurance of Nationalism*, Cambridge: Cambridge University Press.

Routledge, Bruce. (2003) "The Antiquity of the Nation: Critical Reflections from the Ancient Near East", *Nations and Nationalism*, 9(2): 212–32.

Schmalenbach, Herman. (1977 [1922]) "Communion: A Sociological Category", in Günter Lüschen and Gregory P. Stone (eds) *Herman Schmalenbach on Society and Experience*, Chicago, IL: University of Chicago Press.

Shils, Edward. (1975 [1957]) "Primordial, Personal, Sacred and Civil Ties", *British Journal of Sociology*, 7, 13–45.

Smith, Anthony D. (2009) *Ethno-symbolism and Nationalism*, London: Routledge.

——(2000) *The Nation in History*, Hanover, NH: University Press of New England.

——(1998) *Nationalism and Modernism*, London: Routledge.

——(1986) *The Ethnic Origins of Nationalism*, Oxford: Basil Blackwell.

Stigler, George. (1961) "The Economics of Information", *Journal of Political Economy*, 63(3): 213–25.

Tönnies, Ferdinand. (1940 [1887]) *Gemeinschaft und Gesellschaft*, New York: American Books.

——(1971[1926]) "The Individual and the World in the Modern Age", in Werner J. Cahnman and Rudolf Heberle (eds) *Ferdinand Tönnies On Sociology: Pure, Applied and Empirical*, Chicago, IL: University of Chicago Press.

Veenhof, Klaas. (1997) "'Modern' Features in Old Assyrian Trade", *Journal of the Economic and Social History of the Orient*, 40(4): 336–66.

Empire and Imperialism

Krishan Kumar

The world has seen many empires – indeed the recorded history of the world can fairly be said to be a history of empires. But imperialism, as an ideology and calculated policy, is relatively recent, not much earlier than the mid-nineteenth century. The relation between empire and imperialism must therefore be one principal strand of our inquiry. The other must be to trace the career of the concept of imperialism, as it worked its way out in the world of the nineteenth and twentieth centuries. Have we reached the "end of empire", or are we witnessing novel forms, imperial in character if not in name?

Empire has had two main meanings over the centuries (Koebner 1961; Koebner and Schmidt 1964). Deriving – in the West at least – from the Latin *imperium*, it has first meant absolute rule or authority, beyond which there is no appeal. The term was originally applied to Roman magistrates and commanders in the field. Later it was applied to the authority of the emperor, the *imperator* (itself too originally a military term). A famous example in English history of this meaning of empire is the declaration of Henry VIII's Act in Restraint of Appeals (1533) that "this realm of England is an empire, entire of itself" – in other words, that the English ruler was sovereign in his own land, and that no appeal beyond his rule, as for instance to the Papacy, was possible.

This old and original meaning of empire, as sovereign authority, has continued into our own times, though often in more metaphorical terms – e.g. "the empire of nature", "the empire of modernity". But already in Roman times it was accompanied by an additional meaning: as rule over an extensive territory containing many and diverse peoples. Of such a character was the *imperium Romanum*, the Roman empire – for most Europeans the defining instance of empire, and the one they most aspired to imitate. It is this meaning of empire that has gradually, in both popular and scholarly use, come to overlay and to some extent displace the earlier uses. When we speak of the Habsburg Empire, the Ottoman Empire, the Russian, British, and French Empires, it is generally this meaning that we have in mind. Emperors remain more or less absolute of course – though there have been republican empires, such as those of Venice or the French Third Republic – but what is more important is their command over vast territories, often overseas, in which there are peoples many of whom differ in race and culture from the ruling peoples.

This situation then throws up the leading concerns of empires: their need to protect their far-flung frontiers, and their relation to other empires; the relation between centre and periphery, "metropole" and "colony", in the empire; the challenge of ethnicity and nationalism; the question of citizenship and assimilation (Doyle 1986). For many of these questions, Rome remained a continuing point of reference through the centuries. The fact of its decline and fall – at least in the West – also suggested that ultimately empires were doomed, however long they might last. A certain melancholy has nearly always accompanied speculation on empire, seen often as an expression of human vanity and pride, a hopeless striving for lasting greatness (Maier 2006).

One last point by way of introduction. Empires have always striven to be universal. In principle, there is, or should be, only one empire in the world (Münkler 2007). The existence of other empires is acknowledged in practice, but the aspiration is to be the only empire, the one that informs the world with its values. Empires usually see themselves as the carriers of certain "missions" which are meant to incorporate the whole of humanity. Frequently these missions have been seen in religious terms, as with the Christian and Islamic Empires. But, taking their cue again from Rome, the imperial mission can also be seen in a more secular guise, as a mission to "civilize", the *mission civilisatrice*, as the French expressed it in the nineteenth century (Baumgart 1982). In recent times most empires have seen themselves in some such terms – whether, as with the Soviet Union, to spread the system of communism around the world or, as with the Americans, to "make the world safe for democracy". But religious imperialism has not entirely disappeared. The recent resurgence of Islam has revived the old aspiration of the Caliphate to carry Islam – by force if necessary – to all the corners of the globe.

The universal striving of empires is responsible for the concept of the *translatio imperii*, the transfer or passing on of empire. Empires can see themselves as existing within a chain of transmission that keeps the imperial purpose or mission alive, whatever the fate of particular empires as the carriers of the mission. Thus when the Roman Empire in the West collapsed, the Catholic Church continued its mission, eventually embodying it in the form of the Holy Roman Empire. Later the Spanish Empire took on the mission of Christianizing the world. Other empires have at various times also seen themselves as the continuations of an imperial purpose that may be said to have been most decisively initiated – in both East and West – by the empire of Alexander the Great in the fourth century BCE. In a real sense, all empires strive to be Alexandrian, to cover the world in a cosmopolitan culture that would allow everyone to move freely across the face of the earth as part of a single *ecumene*.

Land and Sea Empires

The accomplishments of the Roman Empire, its spreading of a unitary civilization that stretched from Hadrian's Wall in the north of Britain to the Euphrates in the east, and from north Africa to the Rhine and Danube in the north, made it seem for centuries that the only acceptable form of rule, the only one to aspire to, was empire. After the fall of Rome in the West, a succession of empires struggled to recreate the unitary civilization it had brought into being. Chief of these was the Holy Roman Empire, which maintained an existence until 1806, though with severely restricted power in its last centuries (Muldoon 1999). For much of its history the Holy Roman Empire was headed by the Habsburg dynasty which, first in Spain, then in Austria, drew together an astonishing range of European regions, East and West. This enterprise was also long-lasting, ending only with defeat in the First Word War. In the case of the Spanish Habsburgs, the European land empire was accompanied by a vast overseas empire, incorporating much of the Americas. The Portuguese too constructed an extensive overseas empire, linking Europe decisively to Africa, India, China, and south-east Asia (Pagden 1995; Aldrich 2007).

The key to real power would turn in the end on overseas empires (Osterhammel 2005). This was shown by the Dutch, French, and British. Latecomers to the field of empire, they rapidly made up for lost time. The Dutch faltered in the eighteenth century, but the French and British went on to conquer large tracts of the world. At its height in the early twentieth century the British Empire occupied a quarter of the earth's land surface and included a quarter of the world's population – the largest empire the world has ever known. The French, though thwarted by the British in India and North America, established themselves strongly in North Africa and south-east Asia. By comparison with the British and French, the Portuguese and Spanish lost out, though they managed to hang on to their empires until the nineteenth century and, in the case of Portuguese Africa, even later.

The overseas empires of the Europeans were the first standard-bearers of real globalization. With the exception of Alexander's empire, none of the ancient empires had extended much beyond their heartlands. Even Rome remained basically a Mediterranean empire. With the Portuguese, Spanish, Dutch, French, British, and Belgian Empires, European religion, ideas, and institutions began that global diffusion that has never been halted (and which was continued by that European off-shoot, America). Not of course that the traffic was all one way. Europe too was decisively influenced by the flow of goods and ideas that came from all parts of the world, not excepting religion. But the dynamic force was undoubtedly European. The Chinese had created a strong land empire, and in the late Middle Ages embarked on great sea-going voyages that could have led to an overseas empire. But for reasons still not properly understood, early in the sixteenth century the Chinese destroyed their large fleets and abandoned overseas ventures. The field was left to the Europeans, an advantage which they eagerly seized.

But though in territory and resources the overseas empires generally exceeded the land empires, the European land empires were powerful and extensive enough to dominate their surrounding regions and sometimes well beyond. The Russians from the seventeenth century onwards created a great continuous Eurasian empire, stretching from the Baltic all the way across Asia to the Pacific. The Habsburg Empire at various times included territories in a swath of lands from the Low Countries of northern Europe to the Balkans in the south-east and Poland in the East. Equally dominant in its region, and for several centuries posing a special threat to the other empires, was the Ottoman Empire. The other European empires were Christian, and in the early centuries saw the propagation and extension of Christianity – whether in Catholic, Protestant, or Orthodox forms – as their central mission. The Ottoman Empire was Muslim; and from the time of the conquest of Constantinople in 1453, the Ottomans – continuing the earlier effort of the Arab empires, especially in Spain – carried the Muslim religion right into the heart of Europe, on two occasions coming close to taking Vienna, the imperial capital of the Habsburgs. Ottoman power declined from the eighteenth century onwards; but the Empire lasted until, like the Habsburg and Russian Empires, it went down in the First World War. Throughout its existence the Ottoman Empire acted as both a challenge and a foil to the other European empires, a mirror in which Christian Europe could see both its strengths and its failings.

Though land and overseas empires shared several structural features, they differed significantly in the way and to the extent that these features were expressed. Most important was the relation between centre and periphery, metropole and colony. With the overseas empires, the distance and difference between metropole and colony were, for fairly obvious reasons, a palpable fact. In the French, British, Dutch, and other overseas empires, a "core ethnicity" made up of white Europeans ruled over many, mostly non-European, peoples of different colour, culture, and customs. Questions of citizenship, and of assimilation and integration, were hotly debated issues. The French tended towards an assimilationist strategy, the British preferred on the whole to leave local cultures intact and to rule indirectly. But in both cases, as in that of the Dutch and Belgians, awareness of the differences between the ruling people and the vast mass of their subjects was keen throughout the history of their empires. The great physical distance between the metropole and its colonies was matched by a consciousness of racial and cultural differences, even when the physical distance came to be mitigated by developments in transport and communications.

Land empires did not have so strong a consciousness of the separation of core from periphery. Land empires, like overseas ones, grew by expansion from a metropolitan core. But the expansion was not to distant regions broken by oceans but generally to contiguous territories (though dynastic marriages, as famously with the Habsburgs, could join lands that were not necessarily neighbouring). The "core" and the "periphery" might merge insensibly into one another, so that one would not be sure where the one ended and the other began. What was the "core" of the Austrian Habsburg Empire, and what the "periphery"? Vienna eventually became the imperial capital, to be sure, but at various times Prague had served as capital, and cities such as Budapest vied with Vienna and Prague for cultural and economic primacy. Eventually, in the *Ausgleich* ("Compromise") of 1867, Hungary actually achieved parity with Austria in what came to be called the Austro-Hungarian Empire. Moreover, although the German language was the official imperial language for much of the time, Germans themselves were not necessarily preferred at the Habsburg court. Poles, Italians, Bohemians, Hungarians, and Croatians could all achieve high office, in the army and bureaucracy.

The Russian and Ottoman Empires showed similar characteristics. Although Russians clearly predominated in the Empire, and Russian was the preferred language, conversion to Orthodoxy was normally all that was necessary to open the path to a career in the state. Baltic Germans for instance were disproportionately represented in the higher echelons of the army. In the case of the Ottomans, it is difficult even to speak of a dominant ethnicity. It was certainly not the "Turks", generally looked down upon as Anatolian peasants. Conversion to Islam was sufficient to allow former Christians, such as Greeks and Serbs, to rise to the very top of the Ottoman hierarchy.

These differences between land and overseas empires have important consequences when empire is no more. For overseas empires, the break between the metropole and the colonies can be painful and difficult but may not leave a long-lasting legacy. Physical and cultural distance once more makes the separation easier to absorb. For land empires, where the populations are more mixed together and share much more in the imperial culture, the rupture can be more severe. For the metropole especially the loss of empire means also loss of identity, since imperial rule was its mainstay. The British and the French may feel that they have faced great difficulties in coming to terms with the loss of empire, and one would not want to minimize the problems. But arguably they have managed better than the Russians and Austrians; while in the case of the Ottomans, the break-up of empire involved an orgy of violence and the forcible separation of peoples whose consequences are still with us today.

Imperialism and Nationalism

In the nineteenth century, all European empires came under the pressure of nationalism. The multiethnic, multinational, character of empires offended against the nationalist principle that states should be based on nations, that ideally there should be one state, one nation.

Empires responded differently to the challenge. For the land empires, with populations of different nationalities living in close proximity, it was an especially difficult problem. The Habsburgs attempted to stamp out nationalism, notably during the 1848 revolutions. Eventually however they had to concede to a limited extent, in agreeing to share power with the Hungarians, though simultaneously denying the national aspirations of Czechs and other Slavic nations. Russia too reacted sternly to the nationalist challenge, especially among its Poles; but it also went in for a certain amount of "Russification", to assuage its own nationalist movement. The

Ottomans tried to head off nationalism by re-articulating and re-emphasizing "Ottomanism", an imperial strategy that proclaimed the near-equality of all its subjects, of whatever religious persuasion. It was the failure of Ottomanism, especially in the face of Balkan nationalism, that encouraged the growth of Turkish nationalism, which became one of the forces that led to the downfall of the Ottoman Empire.

For the overseas empires of the British, French, and Dutch, nationalism was a more containable threat. Limited concessions could be made to nationalists, allowing for a certain amount of power-sharing at lower levels, as the British did in India. But, with the backing of home populations, military force was generally sufficient to ensure that nationalism did not seriously threaten the integrity of the empire. It took defeat by another empire, the Japanese, in the Second World War, to weaken and discredit the British, French, and Dutch sufficiently to allow nationalists the opportunity to challenge European rule.

This fact can be generalized and applied to the relation of nationalism and imperialism in all the empires. It was not usually nationalism that brought down empires; it was other empires (Kumar 2010). The Habsburg, Ottoman, and Romanov Empires collapsed in the First World War because of their defeat by the imperial powers of France, Britain, and, in the early stages of the war, Germany (until the German Empire too succumbed to defeat by the Western imperial powers). The British, French, and Dutch Empires came to an end following their humiliation by the imperial power of Japan in the Second World War (and later the Japanese Empire in its turn was put down by the imperial power of the United States). Nationalism creates problems for empires, and concessions of some kind generally have to be made. But by itself nationalism is not generally a sufficient force to bring down empires. Only the countervailing force of other empires can do this.

The legitimacy of nationalism in recent times – enshrined in President Woodrow Wilson's enunciation of the doctrine of "self-determination" at the 1918 peace settlement, and re-affirmed in the United Nations Declaration of Human Rights Nations of 1948 – served to hide the persistence of empires well into the twentieth century. Nation-states lived in the shadow of empire for much of this time. The leading powers of the twentieth century were imperial – Britain, France, America, the Soviet Union, Japan, China. Fascist Italy and Nazi Germany constructed short-lived empires. Even after the European overseas empires were wound up in the 1950s and 1960s, the imperial powers of the United States and the Soviet Union continued their rivalry on a world stage, dominating and manipulating supposedly independent nation-states. Only with the collapse of the Soviet Union – the "last empire"? – in 1991 can imperialism really be said to have reached a certain terminus; though that still leaves America, and other possible contenders for imperial rule.

There are other ways in which nationalism and imperialism did not so much oppose each other as live off each other, symbiotically. In the later nineteenth century, European states engaged in a ferocious competition for imperial possessions, the "scramble for Africa" being the best-known. The term "imperialism" came into vogue at this time precisely to describe this phenomenon (Lichtheim 1974; Hobsbawm 1987; Semmel 1993). Previously pejorative, to describe the despotic systems of Napoleon I and III, in the hands of statesmen such as Benjamin Disraeli imperialism came to mean a definite policy of acquiring and expanding empire. Far from being something to fear, imperialism was now embraced as the duty and destiny of every great power, on pain of being relegated to subordinate and dependent roles (Bell 2007).

Given the context of competitiveness, and the growing popularity of the national principle, it proved possible to present imperialism as a species of nationalism, as a kind of super-nationalism, a "great power nationalism". In France and Germany especially, in the face of British dominance, imperialism was harnessed powerfully to nationalism, as the assertion of a rightful claim to an influential place in the world, based on national strength. In America, in the course of the Spanish-American war of 1898, vital national interests were trumpeted as the ground for acquiring Spanish territories (Go 2007). Every nation, it was asserted, had the right to empire, if it could prove its claim by its success in the competitive struggle. Imperialism was thus carried by the national principle, which in turn reacted back on it, intensifying the rivalry between states for possession of greater and greater portions of the globe.

Imperialism and Its Critics

What to its proponents could pass as legitimate nationalism, could, to the critics of imperialism, appear as hyper-nationalism, a dangerously inflated or hypertrophied from of nationalism (Mommsen 1982). Such was the charge of the English Liberal writer J. A. Hobson, whose book *Imperialism* (1902) became the inspiration of a powerful current of anti-imperial thought in the first half of the twentieth century. Hobson provided the analysis of imperialism that became the mainstay of most accounts of imperialism on the left. Imperialism, he argued, was the more or less inevitable product of "underconsumption" – the lack of purchasing power due to the poor living standards of the working class in the industrialized societies. This had led the capitalists to search out the undeveloped areas of the world for the investment of their "surplus capital", the capital that could not find profitable investments at home. In theory, that search did not require direct political rule over such areas – and indeed there developed a type of "informal imperialism", practised especially by the British in such areas as Latin America, in which powerful capitalist interests controlled the development of states without taking over formal power. In practice, however, the machinations of rivals together with conflicts between native groups often meant forcible intervention and the assumption of formal sovereignty over particular territories. In any case though it was economic motives, specifically the needs of the capitalist class, that were the driving force of modern imperialism – replacing the aristocratic passion for power and glory that had been the mainspring of traditional empire.

Hobson's theory of imperialism achieved international fame when it was taken up by Lenin in his *Imperialism, the Highest Stage of Capitalism* (1917). From then on it had more or less canonical status on the left (Wolfe 1997). In addition Lenin drew on Rudolf Hilferding's *Finance Capitalism* (1910) for the additional point that imperialism was not simply, as Hobson thought, an off-shoot of capitalism, and hence remediable by reform, but an intrinsic part of capitalism's development. This was bound, Hilferding thought, to lead to war between the imperial powers, and so to the collapse of capitalism. Lenin found the confirmation of the first part of Hilferding's prediction in the First World War but not, alas, that of the second part, the collapse of capitalism, despite the success of the Bolshevik Revolution. Also disappointed were the hopes of Rosa Luxemburg, whose powerful work *The Accumulation of Capital* (1913) followed Hobson closely in its analysis of imperialism but, unlike him, thought remedial measures would be hopeless and that an imperialist war between capitalists would offer the proletariat the best chance to overthrow the system.

It is a curious fact that, ever since imperialism's appearance on the scene in the late nineteenth century, it has been dominated by critical approaches, most of which have been Marxist in one form or another (Kemp 1967; Hetherington 1982). There were one or two exceptions. The Austrian economist and sociologist Joseph Schumpeter published a characteristically provocative essay, "The Sociology of Imperialisms" ([1919] 1974), in which he argued that contemporary imperialism was a rearguard action on the part of a still-persisting and powerful warrior aristocracy, and was driven by its traditional concerns of glory and honour. Imperialism was hence an atavism, and would disappear once the bourgeoisie secured full control of society. This was an ironic comment on Hobson's view that it was the bourgeoisie that was responsible for imperialism. But it shared Hobson's conviction that imperialism was not intrinsic to capitalism – that it was an aberration, brought about, as Hobson saw it, largely through the influence of a particular group of capitalists, the bankers and financiers.

Later in the century, as Mussolini attempted to establish his new Roman Empire, and Hitler his new German Empire, there were fascist theorists – including Hitler and Mussolini themselves – who provided a rationale for empire. But most accounts were simply echoes of nineteenth-century "social Darwinism" and race theory, with their ideas of the necessary inequalities among humankind and the right of the stronger to rule the weaker. With the defeat of both the short-lived fascist empires, right-wing theories of empire were thoroughly discredited, leaving the field once more to critics of empire.

The Hobson–Lenin theory and critique provided the basis for most radical accounts of empire in the first half of the twentieth century (Kiernan 1974). It was vigorously debated by Western Marxists, and it became the credo of most Third World nationalists and communists, such as Mao Tse-Tung. Little was added to the terms of the analysis; anti-imperialist theory mainly functioned as a call to action, in the form of what were increasingly called anti-colonial struggles. For the critics, colonialism rather than imperialism became the preferred term, perhaps reflecting the fact that with the fall of so many land empires at the end of the First World War, what remained to be dealt with were rather the overseas empires with their many distinct colonies.

The Return of Empire?

With the exception of a relatively brief period at the end of the nineteenth and the beginning of the twentieth centuries, empire and imperialism have been largely on the defensive for the past hundred years or so. This is despite the continuing massive presence of empires on the world scene for much of the twentieth century. It is as if empire is the thing that "dare not speak its name". Empire was assailed from the left, as the brutal expression of class rule, and the means for "paying off" the industrial working class, thus making it complicit with the bourgeoisie in the exploitation of Third World societies. It was also attacked by liberals and democrats who saw it as denying the legitimate national aspirations of all peoples. It offended against the principle of self-rule proclaimed at the Peace of Versailles in 1918. The aptly-named League of Nations, and its successor, the United Nations, both upheld this ideal of the independent nation-state as the bedrock of the international community. In such a world what room was there for empires? What could they be but archaic hangovers, desperately clinging on to power against the surging currents of the time?

In what to many people seemed a hypocritical flourish, it was the United States that often seemed to offer ideological support to the enemies of empire. The American War of Independence could fairly be represented as one of the first, if not the first, anti-colonial "liberation struggles" of modern times. During the Spanish-American War of 1898, opponents of the move to take over the Spanish colonies of Cuba, Puerto Rico, and the Philippines – and in the face of Rudyard Kipling's urging that America take over the role of Europe in shouldering the "White Man's Burden" – invoked America's anti-colonial past in support of their position, with considerable success. In the First World War, President Woodrow Wilson emerged as the champion of nationalism, especially the nationalism of small nations, and was mainly responsible for the setting up of independent nation-states in Central Europe and the Balkans. In the 1930s and 1940s, American statesmen often referred disparagingly to the British and French Empires – not to mention the Soviet Empire – as contrary to all principles of democracy and self-rule.

Franklin Delano Roosevelt was particularly hostile to empire, and did much to ensure that the British would wind up their empire as soon as possible after the defeat of Hitler. As late as the 1950s, America was offering support to liberation movements in Cuba, Africa, and elsewhere (though enthusiasm was later dampened when it turned out that many of the new states were of a distinctly socialist, if not actually communist, character). Later still when, in the wake of the invasions of Afghanistan and Iraq, America itself was accused of being an empire, the retort was often couched in the terms expressed by a former Secretary of Defense, that, with its own anti-colonial origins, "America doesn't do empire".

In the debate over whether or not America is or has been an empire, sceptics of the anti-colonial argument have often pointed to America's own very imperial development in the nineteenth century. Starting from a handful of colonies on the east coast, America expanded gigantically westwards, in the process not simply dispossessing the native American Indians wholesale but also seizing large tracts of territories from the Mexicans, especially in the 1840s. Moreover, America may not in the end have gone in much for overseas possessions – to that extent it kept faith with its anti-colonial past – but it has been highly effective in practising "informal colonialism" worldwide, through the operations of its foreign policies, its multi-national corporations, and the strategic placing of American military bases in over a hundred countries. Whether or not America is an empire remains a moot point (Mann 2003; Steinmetz 2005; Maier 2006; Calhoun *et al.* 2006). But it hard not to say that it has often acted imperially, not least in recent years when it has occupied the role of "the lonely superpower", the one remaining superpower following the demise of the Soviet Union.

It was indeed around the concept of "informal" imperialism or colonialism that debates about empire revived in the second half of the twentieth century. With the rapid and massive de-colonization of the European empires in the 1950s and 1960s, it might have seemed that there were no empires left to reflect on (the United States and the Soviet Union being special cases, both in fact formally anti-colonial). But to many observers of and in the Third World, empire seemed to be alive and well, even if not so-called. A powerful group of "dependency" theorists, many of them Latin America, such as Andre Gunder Frank (1967) and Fernando Henriques Cardoso (Cardoso and Faletto 1979), argued that the West had given up formal empire only to continue or retake it informally, through close control over the development – or "under-development" – of formally free nation-states in Africa, Asia, and Latin America. Colluding with local elites and setting up or supporting "puppet" regimes, Western capitalists were able to ensure that development took place in accordance with their own interests, at the cost if necessary of the welfare and liberty of the local population, and the creation of an independent indigenous economy.

Dependency theory generally regarded itself as working within Marxist theories of imperialism. But in many ways the most original formulation of their position was given not by Marxists but by two non-Marxist historians of the British Empire, John Gallagher and Ronald Robinson, in an influential article of 1953, "The Imperialism of Free Trade". They pointed out that the British had always been pragmatic about how far their interests were served by formal empire, and how far by less direct forms of influence and pressure. Informal "control" was always an alternative, often cheaper and more effective, to formal "rule". In Latin America informal methods sufficed; in Africa and many parts of Asia and the Middle East, the British were forced to intervene in local quarrels, often fuelled by European rivalries, and in many cases had to assume formal rule. One further consequence of this approach was to displace the usual concentration on the metropolis, the focus hitherto of Marxist and non-Marxist studies alike, and direct our attention to the colonial peripheries, as the source of many of the concerns that brought about European rule (Robinson *et al.* 1968; Robinson 1986; Louis 1976).

The approach of Gallagher and Robinson could be employed by dependency theorists, if they so wished, as it provided a clear path towards understanding the "imperialism of decolonization", or the continuation of Western imperialism by other means (Louis and Robinson 1994). If they preferred to work within a Marxist paradigm, this was largely because they wished to retain its critical edge and the eventual prospect of liberation. Other more academic scholars however were stimulated by the work of Gallagher and Robinson to open up a rich vein of studies of empire in a more dispassionate way, and to launch what was in effect a veritable renaissance of interest in empire. Other influences in this direction included the work of the so-called "post-colonial theorists", such as Edward Said (1979, 1993), and behind them the seminal writings of the French-Algerian psychologist Franz Fanon, in such books as *The Wretched of the Earth* (1967). What interested Fanon and the post-colonialists were the emotional and psychological scars of colonialism, its lasting effect on the culture and personality of both the colonized and the colonizers. While some commentators were proclaiming that the age of imperialism was dead, to these thinkers imperialism had to be seen as having a long after-life, in the hearts and minds of individuals.

Is imperialism in fact dead? The very debates over the "American empire", the idea that the European Union might also be thought of as a revived Holy Roman or Habsburg empire, are enough to suggest that this may be a premature judgement (Zielonka 2007). The revival of interest in empire has more than just academic fashion behind it. It must surely reflect the sense that empires have something to teach us, that they speak in some way to our current condition. The most obvious aspects of that condition are all that go under the heading of "globalization", together with the associated feeling that the contemporary nation-state is in crisis. There is also the challenge of multiculturalism, the realization that all states are made up of varying groups of people who have to find a mode of living with each other without retreating into their own separate communities. The popularity of works such as *Empire* by Michael Hardt and Antonio Negri (2000) lies not so much in the actual analysis of empire – in truth there is not much of that, as empire is simply for them a synonym for global capitalism – as in the invocation of a form that seems somehow congruent with our current hopes and anxieties.

The depiction by Hardt and Negri of a headless, de-centred global empire certainly looks very different from any previous empire. But the variety of imperial forms has been one of the features of imperial history, and it is not inconceivable that we are seeing the emergence of a new kind of global empire which will demand an analysis that departs radically from the standard account in terms of metropole and colony, centre and periphery. Science fiction, rather more than academic theorizing, is currently playing imaginatively with some such theme, as in the *Matrix* trilogy of films (1999–2003), which builds upon the earlier tradition of imperial fiction established by Isaac Asimov in the *Foundation* trilogy (1942–50). Given the importance of new kinds of information technology and communications in the current world order, it is hardly surprising that imaginative fiction has been the first to try to outline its contours. But what unites all accounts, fictional and other, that use the imperial theme today is the overriding sense that the old world of nation-states, with its claims of sovereignty and autonomy, has had its time. Overlapping and mixed sovereignties, regions and protected enclaves, even perhaps some sort of world government, will be the order of the day. The future world order will not necessarily be very orderly; but it will look more like the imperial system of the sixteenth century than the national-state system of the nineteenth and twentieth centuries.

Empires have been long-lived experiments in managing diversity. They have not all managed it equally well, and there have been episodes of cruelty and brutality (though perhaps no worse than in the case of nation-states). But there is a wealth of experience to be examined as we confront our own attempts to manage societies in which difference and diversity are central features. There is something also in the aspirations of empires to be universal, to encompass the whole *ecumene* in a single civilization. Again, we have had reason to be wary of these attempts. But we are now conscious as perhaps at no other time in human history of the need for the world to act together, as one. Nothing less than the survival of the planet, and all that lives on it, is at stake. If empires can teach us something about our common humanity, and of some of the ways to achieve our common goals, they will have immeasurably repaid our attention.

References

Aldrich, Robert (ed.). (2007). *The Age of Empires*. London: Thames & Hudson.

Baumgart, Winfried. (1982). *Imperialism: The Idea and Reality of British and French Colonial Expansion, 1880–1914*. New York: Oxford University Press.

Bell, Duncan. (2007). *The Idea of Greater Britain: Empire and the Future of World Order, 1860–1900*. Princeton, NJ: Princeton University Press.

Calhoun, Craig, Cooper, Frederick, and Moore, Kevin W. (eds) (2006). *Lessons of Empire: Imperial Histories and American Power*. New York: The New Press.

Cardoso, F., and Faletto, E. (1979). *Dependency and Development in Latin America*, translated by M. M Urquidi. Berkeley, CA: University of California Press.

Doyle, Michael W. (1986). *Empires*. Ithaca, NY: Cornell University Press.

Fanon, Franz. (1967). *The Wretched of the Earth*, translated by Constance Farrington. Harmondsworth: Penguin Books.

Frank, Andre Gunder. (1967). *Capitalism and Underdevelopment in Latin America*. New York: Monthly Review Press.

Gallagher, John, and Robinson, Ronald. (1953). "The Imperialism of Free Trade", *Economic History Review*, 6 (1): 1–15.

Go, Julian. (2007). "Global Fields and Imperial Forms: Field Theory and the British and American Empires", *Sociological Theory*, 26 (3): 201–29.

Hardt, Michael, and Negri, Antonio. (2000). *Empire*. Cambridge, MA: Harvard University Press.

Hetherington, Norman. (1982). "Reconsidering Theories of Imperialism", *History and Theory*, 21(1): 1–36.

Hobsbawm, E. J. (1987). *The Age of Empire, 1875–1914*. London: Weidenfeld & Nicolson.

Kemp, Tom. (1967). *Theories of Imperialism*. London: Dobson.

Kiernan, V. G. (1974). *Marxism and Imperialism*. London: Edward Arnold.

Koebner, Richard. (1961). *Empire*. Cambridge: Cambridge University Press.

Koebner, Richard, and Schmidt, Helmut Dan. (1964). *Imperialism: The Story and Significance of a Political Word, 1840–1960*. Cambridge: Cambridge University Press.

Kumar, Krishan. (2010). "Nation-states as Empires, Empires as Nation-states: Two Principles, One Practice?", *Theory and Society*, 39: 119–43.

Lichtheim, George. (1974). *Imperialism*. Harmondsworth: Penguin Books.

Louis, Wm. Roger (ed.). (1976). *Imperialism: The Robinson and Gallagher Controversy*. New York: New Viewpoints.

Louis, Wm. Roger, and Robinson, Ronald. (1994). "The Imperialism of Decolonization", *Journal of Imperial and Commonwealth History*, 22 (3): 462–511.

Maier, Charles S. (2006). *Among Empires: American Ascendancy and Its Predecessors*. Cambridge, MA: Harvard University Press.

Mann, Michael. (2003). *Incoherent Empire*. London: Verso.

Mommsen, Wolfgang J. (1982). *Theories of Imperialism*, translated by P. S. Falla. Chicago, IL: University of Chicago Press.

Muldoon, James. (1999). *Empire and Order: The Concept of Empire, 800–1800*. Houndmills: Macmillan.

Münkler, Herfried. (2007). *Empires: The Logic of World Domination from Ancient Rome to the United States*, translated by Patrick Camiller. Cambridge: Polity Press.

Osterhammel, Jürgen. (2005). *Colonialism: A Theoretical Overview*, translated by Shelley L. Frisch. Princeton, NJ: Markus Wiener Publishers.

Pagden, Anthony. (1995). *Lords of All the World: Ideologies of Empire in Spain, Britain and France c. 1500-c.1800*. New Haven, CT: Yale University Press.

Robinson, Ronald. (1986). "The Eccentric Idea of Imperialism, With or Without Empire", in Wolfgang J. Mommsen and Jürgen Osterhammel (eds), *Imperialism and After: Continuities and Discontinuities*. London: Allen &Unwin, pp. 267–89.

Robinson, Ronald, Gallagher, John, with Denny, Alice. (1968). *Africa and the Victorians: The Climax of Imperialism*. New York: Anchor Books.

Said, Edward W. (1979). *Orientalism*. New York: Vintage Books.

——(1993). *Culture and Imperialism*. London: Vintage.

Schumpeter, Joseph. (1974). *Imperialism* and *Social Classes: Two Essays by Joseph Schumpeter*, translated by Heinz Norden. New York: New American Library.

Semmel, Bernard. (1993). *The Liberal Ideal and the Demons of Empire: Theories of Imperialism from Adam Smith to Lenin*. Baltimore, MD: Johns Hopkins University Press.

Steinmetz, George. (2005). "Return to Empire: The New U.S. Imperialism in Comparative Historical Perspective", *Sociological Theory*, 23 (4): 339–67.

Wolfe, Patrick. (1997). "History and Imperialism: A Century of Theory, from Marx to Postcolonialism", *American Historical Review*, 102 (2): 388–420.

Zielonka, Jan. (2007). *Europe as Empire: The Nature of the Enlarged European Union*. Oxford: Oxford University Press.

Cosmopolitanism's Theoretical and Substantive Dimensions

Fuyuki Kurasawa

Over the last decade or so, cosmopolitanism has become one of the most significant and disputed concepts in social and political theory. Indeed, it acts simultaneously as an analytical nodal point through which several key theoretical questions are intersecting and as a normative horizon that fosters new lines of thought. If the idea of being a citizen of the world has lengthy historical antecedents, its return to prominence is attributable to a number of developments: accelerating and intensifying processes of globalization and transculturalism, challenges to the Westphalian state system, the search for alternatives to the thesis of a clash of civilizations, the hegemony of neoliberal capitalism, the prevalence of discourses of universal human rights, and the reproduction of global injustices, *inter alia*. Cosmopolitanism, then, has been at the core of a massive rethinking of the modern human sciences' implicit nation-state-centrism, whether in methodological (what is the proper unit of analysis?), sociological (what are the boundaries of societies and the social?), political (what kinds of postnational institutional configurations are possible?), or ethical (what are the limits to our moral communities?) terms.

What is Cosmopolitanism?

While the multiplicity of uses to which cosmopolitanism is put and its contested nature are inescapable (Pollock *et al.* 2000), at least three principal meanings emerge out of the large body of literature devoted to it. In its most literal and basic sense, cosmopolitanism refers to a worldview according to which human beings conceive of themselves as citizens of the world, in contradistinction – or in addition – to belonging to territorially or socio-culturally delimited communities (city-states, nations, religious or ethnic groups, etc.).[1] Yet this formulation transcends strictly political membership to encompass a second meaning, that of a sense of the world being one's proper home or dwelling-place. To that extent, cosmopolitanism refers to a certain experience of and quest for worldliness (Terence: 'I am human, and therefore nothing human is alien to me') and a consequent rejection of parochialism or nativism, fostered by familiarity and dexterity with a plurality of ways of thinking and being in the world. Although this worldly sensibility prevails among certain segments of global cultural and economic elites, it is also the outgrowth of a long-standing 'vernacular cosmopolitanism' (Diouf 2000) grounded in the realities of ordinary persons and groups whose everyday social interactions are conducted in several languages, with others of different backgrounds and persuasions (e.g. inhabitants of global cities). Hence, to be cosmopolitan in this way involves less a strategy of distinction per se than an ethos of multi-perspectivism, whereby subjects undertake the work of trying to understand specific belief-systems or socio-cultural practices from several situated vantage-points (and thus denaturalize or relativize their own habituated understandings and modes of social action) (Hannerz 1990).

Cosmopolitanism is employed in a third way, to designate a belief in the moral primacy of human unity and an attachment to, even love of, humankind as a whole (Tagore 1997). Underpinned by a humanist universalism valuing the diverse contributions of all peoples and civilizations to the human condition, this cosmopolitan iteration integrates forms of knowledge and practice from varied societies, while seeking to overcome socio-cultural divisions and relations of domination that hamper the realization of human potential in all its expressions.[2] As such, it seeks to problematize longstanding, historically constituted categorical distinctions and discourses supporting assumptions of incommensurability between humankind's varied manifestations. Thereby radically put into question are essentialized civilizational dichotomies (e.g. 'East' and 'West'), but also religious fundamentalism, 'cultural separatism' (Sen 2005) and ethno-racial nationalism – with their visions of discrete, clearly demarcated groups and their xenophobic hostility via-à-vis those constructed as different (the non-believer, the foreigner, the racialized 'other', etc.). Relatedly, this line of cosmopolitan thinking is anti-ethnocentric and anti-nativist, being deeply suspicious of the false universalization of cultural specificities and of the presumed superiority, or the intrinsic privileging, of familiar or indigenous modes of thought and action. In this third sense, cosmopolitanism advances what its proponents believe to be a foundational and unconditional normative principle, that of the moral equality of all human beings (Nussbaum 2002b; Benhabib 2006).

Despite the fact that these three characterizations of cosmopolitanism appear to be relatively straightforward, their political and ethical implications are disputed. Most strikingly, the concept of being a citizen of the world contains a paradox akin to that noted by Arendt in her celebrated analysis of the condition of the stateless in postwar Europe (Arendt 1968): the formal polis of which persons are members may well be the world *in toto* – with participation in this political community being unrestricted, thus making all human beings bearers of universal rights in principle – yet the concrete institutional recognition of these rights (and thus the substantive capacity to exercise them and have them enforced) is conditional upon membership of a limited number of powerful, restrictive, and territorially bound political units (ranging from rich nation-states to the European Union). To paraphrase Orwell, all citizens of the world are equal, but some citizens of the world are more equal than others.

Hence, imbedded in all three meanings of cosmopolitanism is a tension between their normative (*de jure*) and analytical (*de facto*) dimensions, principally attributable to the gap between the ideals of world citizenship, worldliness, and human unity and their actual implementation. For liberal cosmopolitans, implementing these ideals can be done by reforming the existing world order, to grant certain rights to foreigners within the current state system and to promote tolerance toward cultural diversity. Critical theorists of cosmopolitanism, however, assert that such liberal formulations are too readily subsumed under the aegis of neoliberal capitalism, with its agenda of deregulation of national borders (to facilitate the circulation of commodities and capital), multiculturalism as a strategic means to open up new markets for goods and services, and sophisticated consumption by dominant groups; in other words, cosmopolitanism can become the 'class consciousness of frequent travellers' (Calhoun 2003). If all human beings are to have the substantive capacities to treat the world as a meaningful polis, in which they feel at home and part of an indivisible human community, cosmopolitanism should address systemic sources of domination at the global scale: exclusionary and punitive immigration and citizenship regimes; socio-economic inequalities between persons and groups; and forms of civil and political violence within and between countries (Balibar 2004; Harvey 2009).

Analytical Paradigms

The debates noted above are refracted through what can be designated as formalist, ethicist, and materialist analytical orientations. Formalism focuses on intersubjective procedures of public deliberation to entrench norms of universal moral equality, building upon Kant's vision of a pacified domain of international relations secured through a world federation of states and peoples, as well as his seminal concept of hospitality, according to which strangers enjoy a right of temporary residence in foreign lands (and thus to not to be treated with hostility there). Formalists seek to bring such Kantian ideals to fruition by arguing for their institutionalization through an enforceable, legally binding regime of global governance, thus putting forth proposals for the juridification of cosmopolitan norms via international law and constitutional mechanisms (Held 1995; Bohman and Lutz-Bachmann 1997; Habermas 1998a). Consequently, in addition to regulating all actors in global politics, cosmopolitan legality would substantively erode the hitherto sacrosanct principle of absolute and undisputed sovereignty by states over territorial units and their populations. Furthermore, by virtue of being grounded in discourse ethics, formalism employs cosmopolitan norms to critically interrogate the argumentative justifications for various socio-political arrangements – particularly exclusionary practices of constitution of the membership of political communities (chiefly, national citizenship regimes), which prevent some human beings from enjoying rights available to others and rule them out from participation in decision-making processes (Benhabib 2006).

The second, ethicist orientation in the literature on cosmopolitanism is principally concerned with the ethics of alterity – that is to say, how the ontological primacy of being-for-the-other, as an infinite and unconditional cosmopolitan responsibility, can be realized without spatial or socio-cultural restrictions. For this strand of thought, human rights signify that we are ethically responsible for the rights of the other human (Levinas 1999; Douzinas 2007), for the stranger whose radical difference cannot be assimilated or domesticated into sameness. On the one hand, this leads ethicists to underscore the need for a perpetual interrogation of the implicit bounds of humanity in Euro-American discourses of cosmopolitanism, and to question whom these discourses constitute as human (and thus as others to whom we are responsible) and whom is considered outside of humanity's limits (abject others to whom we do not understand ourselves to be responsible) (Butler 2004). On the other hand, the ethicist perspective attempts to reconstruct cosmopolitanism by grounding it in a radicalization of the aforementioned Kantian principle of hospitality, which is translated into an a priori and unrestricted responsibility to welcome and be with and for the other in her or his alterity (Derrida 2001). For ethicists, what binds us together as members of humankind is this responsibility to others, as well as recognition of common experiences of loss and mourning that expose our shared state of interdependence and vulnerability vis-à-vis others (Butler 2004).

Materialism represents the third of cosmopolitanism's analytical frameworks, since it is concerned with what its proponents believe to be formalists' and ethicists' idealist bias, namely, their positing of abstract and reified ideas severed from socio-economic structures and political relations of domination (Calhoun 2003). Specifically, materialists assert that their two analytical counterparts neglect the ties that bind cosmopolitanism to capitalism, whether by virtue of elective affinities with the borderless ideology of neoliberalism or the neglect of questions of structural violence, global inequality, and control of the means of production (Harvey 2009).

When devoid of a critique of capitalist forces, cosmopolitan ideology can complement the most recent global regime of exercise of power, a totalizing, deterritorialized and decentred network of economic and political relations designated as 'empire' (Hardt and Negri 2000). By contrast, the materialist perspective is interested in the cultivation of socially thick bonds of solidarity between human beings through political practices and public discourse, including the identification of forces of resistance to neoliberal capitalism and collective agents of universal emancipation capable of enacting cosmopolitanism's egalitarian principles (e.g. progressive social forces and elements of global civil society).

Substantive Dimensions

For heuristic purposes, cosmopolitanism can be divided into its political, economic, and cultural dimensions. The theme of cosmopolitan democracy embodies its most prominent and dynamic political theorization, through its imaginative proposals for the organizational transformation of the current system of global governance. Key among these is the strengthening of international public law to juridify cosmopolitan principles and regulate interstate relations via an enforceable regime of 'legal pacifism' (Falk 2000; Archibugi 2008), as well as the reform of multilateral decision-making organizations in order to curb state sovereignty and hold national and transnational actors accountable to global institutions or legal regulations (e.g. the International Criminal Court). The democratization of processes of global governance is another major preoccupation, with the putting forth of proposals for a global parliament or peoples' assembly within the structure of the United Nations to serve multiple functions: providing representation for civil society groups; forming an executive counterweight to the Security Council; and creating a space for deliberation and decision-making about matters of global significance. Furthermore, advocates of cosmopolitan democracy aim to loosen the nation-state's monopolistic grip over the legitimate exercise of sovereignty and determination of citizenship, by promoting the creation of a complex architecture of democratic oversight, regulation, and rights on the part of self-governing groups at subnational and transnational scales (Held 1995; Sassen 2006).

For their part, analysts of global civil society have drawn attention to the roles of transnational activist networks, social movements, and non-governmental organizations in the political institutionalization of cosmopolitanism from below (Kumar 2009). Indeed, this cosmopolitanism from below is being generated through the proliferation and growing integration of supranational political coalitions of 'rooted cosmopolitans' (Tarrow 2005), who pursue campaigns tackling global problems across territorial borders: environmental damage, war, women's and indigenous rights, crimes against humanity, neoliberal capitalism and its international organizational infrastructure (the International Monetary Fund, the World Bank, the World Trade Organization, etc.), and so on (Kurasawa 2007). Such transnational networks frequently employ a distinctive 'boomerang pattern' (Keck and Sikkink 1998) of spatially nested political activism, initially bypassing hostile or unresponsive domestic governments to mobilize external resources and allies within global civil society, which, in turn, can exercise 'rebound' pressure on these governments.

Framed through the lens of global distributive justice, economic cosmopolitanism is producing key contributions. Particularly notable are discussions surrounding the moral justification for the redistribution of material resources along North–South lines, as a way to alleviate extreme poverty for much of the world's population and address gross planetary discrepancies in the living conditions of human beings. Although public opinion mostly accepts the legitimacy of redistributive obligations to fellow citizens within a country because of the modern constitution of moral communities along national lines (e.g., in the form of the postwar welfare state in the Euro-American world), the challenge for economic cosmopolitanism is to unbind this logic from its territorial specificity to become applicable to humankind as a whole. Utilitarianism strives to do so by contending that the redistributive privileging of compatriots over foreigners is a type of arbitrary discrimination that cannot be impartially justified and, furthermore, that it contradicts the cosmopolitan belief in the equal worth of all human beings. According to utilitarian theory, then, we should prioritize the reduction of the number of persons living in absolute poverty through taxation and targeted donations, relatively modest and thereby widely attainable measures for a largest possible number of materially secure persons in rich regions of the world (Singer 2002).

The transnational extension of social contractarianism is another approach undergirding economic cosmopolitanism, as Rawlsian political theorists (Beitz 1999; Pogge 2002) assert that the restriction of norms of justice to the domestic sphere represents an egregious double standard that, in effect, ignores responsibilities to the poor around the world. Global distributive justice, then, is made necessary by transnational economic integration and interdependence, which have created bonds and responsibilities akin to those existing between persons entering into a domestic social contract with each other. Additionally, the global economy is a non-voluntary contractual arrangement, given that the dependence and vulnerability of poor countries render them powerless to set the conditions of their participation in it; it is an asymmetrical and unjust system that reproduces the subordinate positions of these countries, from which inhabitants of the rich world derive unjust benefits by virtue of their random winning of the planetary 'birth lottery' and a set of systemically-reproduced structural privileges (Pogge 2002). This leads directly to the need for a cosmopolitan application of Rawls' famed 'difference principle' (Rawls 1971), whereby inequalities in the distribution of resources are legitimate when they are to the greatest benefit of the least advantaged human beings (Beitz 1999), and for a 'global resource dividend' extracted from states that use and sell natural resources located on their territories in order to ensure that the basic needs of all human beings are met (Pogge 2002). Critical theory constitutes a third approach through which to formulate moral justifications for economic cosmopolitanism, with Habermas's universalistic egalitarianism and Fraser's notion of 'participatory parity' being applied to condemn global distributive injustices. For critical theorists, the continued existence of such injustices (in the form of domestic and transnational class structures and status orders) poses structural obstacles to the ideal of equal moral worth of all human beings, as well as to their symbolic and material capacity to participate on a par with others in public and social life (Fraser 2008; Kurasawa 2011). Without addressing these obstacles, the world economy will reproduce types of maldistribution or misrecognition that violate cosmopolitan norms of global justice.

The cultural facets of cosmopolitanism have sustained theoretical exchanges animated, among other things, by the task of developing an intercultural universalism that captures humankind's common values. Hence, cosmopolitan theory eschews the tendency toward the ethnocentric universalization of particular societies' or civilizations' worldviews, which are often assumed to be 'generalizable' to the rest of the world through imposition or diffusion (e.g. in modernization theory). Conversely, cosmopolitanism is wary of the most common response to the critique of ethnocentric universalization, the embrace of an absolute relativism that couples radical context specificity (the exclusively internalist validation of moral systems) with cross-cultural incommensurability (the necessary incompatibility between different moral systems). By contrast, cosmopolitan theorists underscore the essential nature of intercultural dialogism to the uncoerced formation of a pluralistically inclusive constellation of universal norms. In its discourse–ethical formulation, public deliberation across societies and civilizations is directed toward the attainment of mutual understanding and the creation of agreement between parties, bound by a principle of egalitarian reciprocity (Benhabib 2002; Delanty 2009). Kögler specifies three reflexive capabilities that represent necessary pre-conditions among parties participating in the construction of such a dialogical universalism: a post-conventional sense of normative commitment (the capacity to potentially commit oneself to norms that challenge or transcend one's own traditional socio-cultural context); interpretive perspective-taking (the capacity to understand another party's perspective from within her or his own context of meaning); and social self-reflexivity (the capacity to gain critical distance from one's self-evident background assumptions) (Kögler 2005).

Dialogical interculturalism can yield a cosmopolitanism structured around notions of human unity and equality, a 'pluralist universalism' whose normative substance is specified compara-tively, that is, less by virtue of the intrinsic superiority of entire moral systems than the relative worth of certain values in relation to others (Parekh 1999). Furthermore, rather than repre-senting a uniform or homogeneous whole, cosmopolitan universalism fosters a diversity of modes of operationalization and institutionalization of this normative substance. Nevertheless, cosmopolitan theorists have not resolved the matter of determining the extent to which implementation of universal values can vary contextually or, to put it differently, how thick or thin the 'overlapping consensus' (Rawls 1993) can be across various parts of the world in order to adapt to historical and institutional differences among socio-cultural settings.

The aforementioned idea of 'vernacular' (Diouf 2000) or 'banal' cosmopolitanism (Beck 2006) is a vital component of its cultural dimension. Theorists have examined how cosmopo-litanism exists not solely as an abstract ideal, but as a lived condition that characterizes the everyday experiences of persons and groups in transcultural settings. Cosmopolitan culture is defined by its syncretism, its blending or collage of different and seemingly disparate socio-cultural formations into an entity that is intrinsically polyvocal and heterogeneous. In this sense, cosmopolitanism is defined by thick engagement with difference as well as 'social promiscuity' – that is to say, the transgression and blurring of boundaries between cultural groups that surpasses the multicultural model of tolerant yet mutually indifferent communities living in proximity to each other while remaining self-contained (and thus with limited social interaction) (Zubaida 2004). Terms such as 'contamination' (Appiah 2006) and 'impurity' (Gilroy 2000) are employed to sharpen the cosmopolitan critique of the widespread conception of 'cultures' as discrete, pure, and self-enclosed entities. Instead, vernacular cosmopolitanism favours transcultural, inauthentic, and hybrid amalgams produced out of the interpenetration of a multiplicity of forces and influences.

Just as importantly, analysts argue that socio-cultural syncretism is a phenomenon whose existence precedes its recent recognition within the human sciences. In several regions of the world, versions of cosmopolitan culture are long-standing features of social life, which have been brought about by contact between civilizations and groups, whether through travel, edu-cation, commerce, migration, or empire. Hence, major cities are featured prominently in the history of vernacular cosmopolitanism, from major portuary gateways for trade routes and refugees (Shanghai, Marseilles, New York, etc.) and great centres of learning (Alexandria, Dakar, Baghdad, etc.) to contemporary global cities where experiments with cultural hybridity are part of the fabric of daily existence (Istanbul, Los Angeles, Mumbai, etc.) (Pollock et al. 2000; Zubaida 2004). Likewise, much writing has been devoted to carrier mechanisms of banal cosmopolitanism: education designed to broaden students' horizons by gaining an understanding of unfamiliar or distant societies and ways of life (Tagore 1997; Nussbaum 2002b) and music, in the form of jazz or contemporary hybrid genres combining several styles (bhangra, rai, etc.) (Gilroy 2000).

Equally significant for theories of everyday cosmopolitanism are studies of specific commu-nities that cultivate cosmopolitan practices as part of their habitual lifeworlds. Here, one can refer to cases of dominant diasporic groups who have adopted strategies of 'flexible citizenship' whereby they envisage the latter less as a sense of collective belonging to a territory than a regime of rules to be negotiated to facilitate capital accumulation and their mobility between countries of residence. This global elite has acquired a postnational worldview, incorporating several national identities without being attached to any one in particular (Ong 1999). Nonetheless, cultural cosmopolitanism is also generated by subaltern groups, such as immigrant communities in global cities, whose social interactions are marked by processes of adaptive flexibility and selective appropriation of traits from varied sources (or from their 'home' and 'recipient' settings). Subaltern cosmopolitan culture, then, is neither a strict preservation of traditions nor a complete assimilation into host societies, but the invention of syncretic customs and beliefs (Diouf 2000; Appiah 2006).

Zones of Contention

Cosmopolitanism is filtered through several theoretically contentious topics, with human rights standing out amongst these because of they are widely recognized and institutionalized expressions of the cosmopolitan outlook. Hence, liberal cosmopolitans hold that human rights express a universal ensemble of humanity's core values shared or aspired to by all persons and societies; liberal conceptions of human rights are organized around a minimalist, negative conception of liberty (namely, freedom from domination) and the protection of individuals against institutional abuses limiting their capacity to choose the kind of life that they want to lead (Ignatieff 2001). However, postcolonial and critical theorists point out that liberal individualism and the monadic conception of the self contained therein sustain a historically and culturally contingent formulation of human rights, one that is tied too closely to the imperatives of the capitalist market and the specificities of Euro-American intellectual traditions to be genuinely universal in design or scope (Pollock *et al.* 2000; Brown 2004). For these theorists, a thickly cosmopolitan version of human rights would decentre the liberal emphasis on individualistically conceived civil and political rights, to incorporate socio-economic rights in addition to collective rights to self-determination and development for the peoples of the global South (Cheah 2006). The sort of intercultural cosmopolitanism can sidestep the trap of cultural relativism, evoked by authoritarian regimes promoting the exceptionalism of so-called 'Asian values' as a means to deflect or neutralize criticisms of the violations of their own citizens' basic rights.

Controversies surrounding the universal applicability of human rights highlight another contentious question, the peril of cosmopolitan imperialism. Indeed, critical analysts contend that the rhetoric of human rights is not, in and of itself, immune to being utilized as 'swords of empire' (Bartholomew and Breakspear 2004), ideological devices selectively applied to legitimate the use of military force against countries or groups perceived to threaten global Euro-American hegemony (Chandler 2003). The rise of humanitarian interventionism and of the 'responsibility to protect' populations against their own governments erode the principle of national sovereignty for weaker states in the global order, thus clearing the way for the possible instrumentalization of cosmopolitan discourses to justify Western invasion and occupation of some of these weaker states. According to a Schmittian logic, the moralization of human rights politics leads to the identification of certain peoples as non-cosmopolitan enemies who must be destroyed in the name of humanity itself. Opposed to this, a critical cosmopolitanism utilizes the aforementioned dialogically constructed, universalist conception of human rights to resist their conversion into imperialist tools. This anti-imperialist buffer can be realized by developing a transnational regime of cosmopolitan law based on multilateralism, a commitment to the 'right to have rights' (Arendt 1968) of all human beings, and a redistribution of power in the system of global governance through the empowerment of progressive forces within global civil society (Held 1995; Habermas 1998a).

On a different front, the fraught relationship of cosmopolitanism to nationalism has generated a lively space of theoretical exchange. Within the literature on cosmopolitanism, a general consensus exists about the need to overcome 'methodological nationalism' (Beck 2006), the tendency to take the nation-state as the self-evident unit of analysis in the social sciences (e.g., the sociological equation of a society with a certain territory demarcated by national borders). Despite this rejection of methodological nationalism, theorists of cosmopolitanism have not, for the most part, been prompted to conceive of the world as a borderless entity; the significance of nation-states as political actors and of territorial boundaries in shaping global affairs remain. Nevertheless, political nationalism is understood as anathema to cosmopolitanism by many of the latter's advocates, for whom nationalist ideologies are suspected of fomenting ethno-culturally-, racially-, or religiously-driven forms of chauvinism. For several cosmopolitan theorists, patriotism itself is a troubling phenomenon whose fostering of pride in and primary devotion to one's country militates against the possibility of widening one's moral community beyond national borders, or of envisaging one's country through cosmopolitanism's interculturally comparative – and thus relativizing – lens (Habermas 1998c; Nussbaum 2002b).

A second cluster of authors argues that cosmopolitan critics of nationalism overlook its revolutionary, anti-colonial, and secular republican forms, which underlie civic nationalisms born out of resistance to modes of domination and serving emancipatory, universalist ambitions (such as liberation from colonialism and self-determination, or popular sovereignty against authoritarian monarchical and religious rule). In other words, civic nationalism may be entirely compatible with – and perhaps even a necessary condition for the advent of – cosmopolitanism (Appiah 1998; Calhoun 2002; Cheah 2006). Two specific types of civic nationalism are considered relevant in this capacity: 'constitutional patriotism' (Habermas 1998b), an attachment to a set of universal principles (e.g. liberty, equality, and solidarity) institutionalized through nationally based republican structures or symbolically meaningful legal-constitutional mechanisms, which need to be broadened to encompass the whole of humanity; and multiculturalism, the promotion and belief in the legitimate co-existence of a plurality of ethno-cultural groups within the same society (Kymlicka 1995; Tully 1995), which is neither nationally specific nor territorially bound (and may thus facilitate the advance of cosmopolitan norms of interculturalism). Hence, far from being the negation or overcoming of nationalism, cosmopolitanism co-exists with it in the contemporary world. In fact, the implicit narrative of teleological progression from national to cosmopolitan worldviews is belied by historical reality, as cosmopolitanism's intellectual origins in classical Greece preceded nationalism's emergence in the modern age rather than evolving from it (Holton 2009).

Whereas certain writings on cosmopolitanism theorize a condition of rootlessness, of having no patriotic feelings or social ties to any particular group (nation, ethnicity, religion, etc.), others focus on the more pervasive phenomenon of 'rooted cosmopolitans,' whose identities are nested in various communities of belonging (from the local to the global) and who seek to translate their specific socio-cultural attachments into cosmopolitan ideals – and vice versa (Appiah 2006). From this perspective, it is less a matter of an either/or identitarian logic than one of both/and, whereby subjects undertake processes of negotiation and articulation between cosmopolitan and particularized discourses to inform their sense of self and their collective belongings. In political terms, rooted cosmopolitans are activists grounded in local or national settings, yet taking aim at global opponents or building transnational coalitions with external actors; they orient simultaneously to the inside and outside of the nation-state, based upon the effectiveness of the scale of action of specific tactics (Tarrow 2005).

Finally, discussions of cosmopolitanism have not yielded an overarching agreement about how to understand 'cosmopolitanization' (Beck 2006), the social processes that are making human beings cosmopolitan in their outlooks and everyday lives through increasing bonds of interdependence and, importantly, reflexivity about such interdependence among increasing segments of the world's population. For Beck, the determining force driving cosmopolitanization is the coming into being of a series of risks (chiefly among these, environmental degradation and terrorism) without specific territorial limitations, for which responses can only be global because exposing all human beings to grave perils. Another significant factor is the appearance of a highly globalized 'space of flows' (Appadurai 1996), the acceleration and intensification of movements of all kinds (people, commodities, images, etc.) across national borders, leading to an increasing awareness of planetary interconnectedness.

A different framing of cosmopolitanization insists on the importance of identifying sources of human commonality. The first of these is human reason, which, aside from sheer cognitive abilities shared by all human beings, entails moral reasoning – that is to say, the capacity to recognize certain universal and absolute moral duties (e.g. the categorical imperative), as well as the commitment to reciprocity and mutual understanding in the pragmatics of discursive communication (Habermas 1990). Sentiments and the moral imagination comprise a distinctive source of cosmopolitanization, for certain thinkers claim that our shared capacity to experience pain and to imagine others' suffering via representational means (first-person testimonials, fictional narratives, etc.) is what humanizes them and binds us to them (Rorty 1998; Laqueur 2001). On the basis of the capabilities approach, one can also argue that cosmopolitanization is engendered by recognition of common human capabilities, which involve not only a formal set of skills, but the ability of persons to develop and exercise those skills in their social lives (Nussbaum 2002a).[3] Thus, whether cosmopolitanization is explained via structural processes of planetary interdependence and interconnectedness or a subjective turn to a philosophical anthropology emphasizing humankind's collective traits, it posits a working through of seemingly intractable divisions between human beings.

Conclusion

Because of cosmopolitanism's definitional ambiguity and thematic elasticity, it functions simultaneously as an epistemological approach, a normative stance, an institutional design, and a description of social life. In all these forms, its theoretical prominence is attributable to the degree to which it corresponds to the current reconfiguration of the global order, which is characterized by a disarticulation of nationally based organizational and experiential configurations without their corresponding rearticulation into clearly defined postnational or supranational assemblages (Sassen 2006). Furthermore, theories of cosmopolitanism must confront the fact that, to date, its normative and institutional elaborations far surpass its empirical manifestations; when contrasted to the thickness of national, ethnic, or religious communitarian affiliations, cosmopolitanization continues to be a relatively thin social dynamic and identitarian discourse for human subjects.

Thus, our age is marked less by the triumphant sweep of cosmopolitanism than its confrontation with strong counter-tendencies, ranging from restrictive migration and citizenship regimes to neoliberal capitalism and the guarding of national sovereignty by traditional and new superpowers. In the upcoming years, the task will be to observe how cosmopolitan beliefs and practices fare in the face of such forces, and the extent to which socio-political agents and processes will participate in realizing these beliefs and practices by reducing the gap that separates them from the exigencies of everyday life for ordinary human beings around the world.

Notes

1 The term itself originated with the ancient Greek Cynics (Diogenes: 'I am a citizen of the world'' [*kosmou polites*]) and the Greco-Roman Stoics (e.g. Seneca) (Nussbaum 2002; Douzinas 2007: 151–9).

2 Santiniketan (in West Bengal, India), the educational institution founded by Rabindranath Tagore in 1921, represents one of the institutional embodiments of these cosmopolitan ideals – notably because of its emphasis on the integration and universality of human knowledge.

3 The capabilities approach proposed by Sen and Nussbaum specifies ten core human capabilities: life; bodily health and integrity; senses, imagination and thought; emotions; practical reason; affiliation; other species; play; and control over one's environment (Nussbaum 2002: 129–30).

References

Appadurai, A. (1996). *Modernity at Large: Cultural Dimensions of Globalization*. Minneapolis, MN: University of Minnesota Press.

Appiah, K. A. (1998). 'Cosmopolitan Patriots'. In *Cosmopolitics: Thinking and Feeling Beyond the Nation*, ed. P. Cheah and B. Robbins. Minneapolis, MN: University of Minnesota Press, pp. 91–114.

——(2006). *Cosmopolitanism: Ethics in a World of Strangers*. New York: Norton.

Archibugi, D. (2008). *The Global Commonwealth of Citizens: Toward Cosmopolitan Democracy*. Princeton, NJ: Princeton University Press.

Arendt, H. (1968). 'The Decline of the Nation-state and the End of the Rights of Man'. In *The Origins of Totalitarianism*. New York: Harcourt Brace, pp. 267–302.

Balibar, E. (2004). 'Outline of a Topography of Cruelty: Citizenship and Civility in the Era of Global Violence'. In *We, the People of Europe? Reflections on Transnational Citizenship*. Princeton, NJ: Princeton University Press, pp. 115–32.

Bartholomew, A. and J. Breakspear (2004). 'Human Rights as Swords of Empire'. In *Socialist Register 2004: The New Imperial Challenge*, ed. L. Panitch and C. Leys. New York: Monthly Review Press, pp. 124–45.

Beck, U. (2006). *The Cosmopolitan Vision*. Cambridge, UK: Polity.

Beitz, C. (1999). *Political Theory and International Relations*. Princeton, NJ: Princeton University Press.

Benhabib, S. (2002). ' "Nous et les Autres" (We and the Others): Is Universalism Ethnocentric?' In *The Claims of Culture: Equality and Diversity in the Global Era*. Princeton, NJ: Princeton University Press, pp. 24–48.

——(2006). *Another Cosmopolitanism*. Oxford: Oxford University Press.

Bohman, J. and Matthias Lutz-Bachmann, eds (1997). *Perpetual Peace: Essays on Kant's Cosmopolitan Ideal*. Cambridge, MA: MIT Press.

Brown, W. (2004). ' "The Most We Can Hope For … ": Human Rights and the Politics of Fatalism.' *South Atlantic Quarterly* 103 (2/3): 451–63.

Butler, J. (2004). 'Violence, Mourning, Politics'. In *Precarious Life: The Powers of Mourning and Violence*. London and New York: Verso, pp. 19–49.

Calhoun, C. (2002). 'Constitutional Patriotism and the Public Sphere: Interests, Identity, and Solidarity in the Integration of Europe'. In *Global Justice and Transnational Politics*, ed. P. De Greiff and C. Cronin. Cambridge, MA: MIT Press, pp. 275–312.

——(2003). 'The Class Consciousness of Frequent Travellers: Towards a Critique of Actually Existing Cosmopolitanism'. In *Debating Cosmopolitics*, ed. D. Archibugi. London and New York: Verso, pp. 86–116.

Chandler, D. (2003). 'International Justice'. In *Debating Cosmopolitics*, ed. D. Archibugi. London and New York: Verso, pp. 27–39.

Cheah, P. (2006). *Inhuman Conditions: On Cosmopolitanism and Human Rights*. Cambridge, MA: Harvard University Press.

Delanty, G. (2009). *The Cosmopolitan Imagination: The Renewal of Critical Social Theory*. Cambridge, UK: Cambridge University Press.

Derrida, J. (2001). *On Cosmopolitanism and Forgiveness*. London and New York: Routledge.

Diouf, M. (2000). 'The Senegalese Murid Trade Diaspora and the Making of a Vernacular Cosmopolitanism.' *Public Culture* 12 (3): 679–702.

Douzinas, C. (2007). *Human Rights and Empire: The Political Philosophy of Cosmopolitanism*. Oxford and New York: Routledge-Cavendish.

Falk, R. (2000). *Human Rights Horizons: The Pursuit of Justice in a Globalizing World*. London and New York: Routledge.

Fraser, Nancy (2008). 'Abnormal Justice.' *Critical Inquiry* 34: 393–422.

Gilroy, P. (2000). ' "Race" ', Cosmopolitanism, and Catastrophe'. In *Between Camps: Nations, Cultures and the Allure of Race*. Harmondsworth: Penguin, pp. 279–326.

Habermas, J. (1990). *Moral Consciousness and Communicative Action*. Cambridge, MA: MIT Press.

——(1998a). 'Kant's Idea of Perpetual Peace: At Two Hundred Years' Historical Remove'. In *The Inclusion of the Other: Studies in Political Theory*. Cambridge, MA: MIT Press, pp. 165–201.

——(1998b). 'Struggles for Recognition in the Democratic Constitutional State'. In *The Inclusion of the Other: Studies in Political Theory*. Cambridge, MA: MIT Press, pp. 203–36.

——(1998c). 'The European Nation-State: On the Past and Future of Sovereignty and Citizenship'. In *The Inclusion of the Other: Studies in Political Theory*. Cambridge, MA: MIT Press, pp. 105–27.

Hannerz, Ulf (1990). 'Cosmopolitans and Locals in World Culture.' *Theory, Culture and Society* 7: 237–51.

Hardt, M. and A. Negri (2000). *Empire*. Cambridge, MA: Harvard University Press.

Harvey, D. (2009). *Cosmopolitanism and the Geographies of Freedom*. New York: Columbia University Press.

Held, D. (1995). *Democracy and the Global Order: From the Modern State to Cosmopolitan Governance*. Stanford, CA: Stanford University Press.

Holton, R. J. (2009). *Cosmopolitanisms: New Thinking and New Directions*. Houndmills: Palgrave Macmillan.

Ignatieff, M. (2001). 'Human Rights as Idolatry'. In *Human Rights as Politics and Idolatry*, ed. A. Gutman. Princeton, NJ: Princeton University Press, pp. 53–98.

Keck, M. E. and K. Sikkink (1998). *Activists Beyond Borders: Advocacy Networks in International Politics*. Ithaca, NY: Cornell University Press.

Kögler, H.-H. (2005). 'Constructing a Cosmopolitan Public Sphere: Hermeneutic Capabilities and Universal Values.' *European Journal of Social Theory* 8 (3): 297–320.

Kumar, A. *et al.*, eds (2009). *Global Civil Society Yearbook 2009: Poverty and Activism*. London: Sage.

Kurasawa, F. (2007). *The Work of Global Justice: Human Rights as Practices*. Cambridge, UK: Cambridge University Press.

——(2011). 'Putting the Social Back into the Transnational Public Sphere'. In *Transnationalizing the Public Sphere*, ed. K. Nash. Cambridge, UK: Polity.

Kymlicka, W. (1995). *Multicultural Citizenship: A Liberal Theory of Minority Rights*. Oxford: Oxford University Press.

Laqueur, T. W. (2001). 'The Moral Imagination and Human Rights'. In *Human Rights as Politics and Idolatry*, ed. A. Gutman. Princeton, NJ: Princeton University Press, pp. 127–39.

Levinas, E. (1999). 'The Rights of the Other Man'. In *Alterity and Transcendence*. New York: Columbia University Press, pp. 145–50.

Nussbaum, M. C. (2002a). 'Capabilities and Human Rights'. In *Global Justice and Transnational Politics*, ed. P. De Greiff and C. Cronin. Cambridge, MA: MIT Press, pp. 117–49.

——(2002b). 'Patriotism and Cosmopolitanism'. In *For Love of Country?* ed. J. Cohen. Boston, MA: Beacon Press, pp. 2–17.

Ong, A. (1999). 'The Pacific Shuttle: Family, Citizenship, and Capital Circuits'. In *Flexible Citizenship: The Cultural Logics of Transnationality*. Durham, NC: Duke University Press, pp. 110–36.

Parekh, B. (1999). 'Non-ethnocentric Universalism'. In *Human Rights in Global Politics*, ed. T. Dunne and N. J. Wheeler. Cambridge, UK: Cambridge University Press, pp. 128–59.

Pogge, T. (2002). *World Poverty and Human Rights*. Cambridge, UK: Polity.

Pollock, S. *et al.* (2000). 'Cosmopolitanisms.' *Public Culture* 12 (3): 577–89.

Rawls, J. (1971). *A Theory of Justice*. Cambridge, MA: Belknap/Harvard University Press.

——(1993). *Political Liberalism*. New York: Columbia University Press.

Rorty, R. (1998). 'Human Rights, Rationality, and Sentimentality'. In *Truth and Progress: Philosophical Papers, Vol. 3*. Cambridge, UK: Cambridge University Press, pp. 167–85.

Sassen, S. (2006). *Territory, Authority, Rights: From Medieval to Global Assemblages*. Princeton, NJ: Princeton University Press.

Sen, A. (2005). *The Argumentative Indian: Writings on Indian Culture, History and Identity*. London: Penguin.

Singer, P. (2002). *One World: The Ethics of Globalization*. New Haven, CT: Yale University Press.

Tagore, R. (1997). *Rabindranath Tagore: An Anthology*. New York: St Martin's Press.

Tarrow, S. (2005). *The New Transnational Activism*. Cambridge, UK: Cambridge University Press.

Tully, J. (1995). *Strange Multiplicity: Constitutionalism in an Age of Diversity*. Cambridge, UK: Cambridge University Press.

Zubaida, S. (2004). 'Cosmopolitans, Nationalists and Fundamentalists in the Modern Middle East.' Inaugural Lecture, Birkbeck College.

Nature and Society

Byron Kaldis

Recent developments in the biological sciences and the neurosciences (see Gunnell's chapter in this volume) have been perceived as either drastically altering the disciplinary landscape within which the social sciences are located or as altogether threatening the very epistemic standing of the social sciences. In some cases such developments have been explicitly posited as attempts to usurp the role of the social sciences as distinct discourses dealing with human beings and their social and political action. It is noteworthy, from a sociological point of view, that such attempts have not only been obviously controversial ever since their inception but also, interestingly, they have met with opposition coming from where one would least expect: their most vehement opponents have come more from the ranks of fellow life scientists and rather less from practitioners of the social sciences (though we should mention feminist critics, and in particular feminist biologists, being also the most vociferous; cf. Fausto-Sterling 1997). Another point regarding the epistemological aspect of the dispute and the relative status of disciplinary dichotomies must be underlined at the outset: it has to do with scientific language. A central part of the terminology, having at first been inherited by biology from social sciences and bearing anthropomorphic marks, is then lent back to the human domain as part of the social-scientific explanations that the life sciences offer.

This chapter charts the epistemological and social-theoretic standing of human sociobiology in particular: what its progenitor called, in an unguarded early moment, the "discipline of anthropological genetics". Sociobiology in general is the study of the evolution of social behaviour in certain gregarious animals that exhibit sociality. Human sociobiology specifically is sociobiology's extension into human sociality: in the phrase of the eminent primatologist Frans de Waal human beings are even more social, they are "obligatorily gregarious". Obviously animal gregariousness – as we know early on from Malinowski when social anthropology as a field was forming its separate identity – must not be identified with human sociality. Yet evolutionary-adaptationist theories of both animal and human cognition have not heeded Malinowski's warning. This is especially so because increased knowledge gained about genes has added scientific confidence to such explanations (at the detriment of philosophical argumentation).

Lack of space precludes discussing a kindred development, evolutionary psychology and its position about the "adaptive mind", its thesis of the "modularity of the mind" and its provocative characterization of our current psychological and mental make-up as being appropriate for a Stone Age mind. In addition both sociobiology and evolutionary psychology have advanced theses – related to those about society but not exclusively so – regarding the evolutionary origin of ethics, something we shall not be touching on directly. The repercussions for social theory are obvious and have of course been drawn. The gist of all such attempts is their common employment of Darwinian evolutionism. Related attempts at a scientistic reduction of the study of human thought and action, forming a continuous thread with all such studies privileging the biological basis of human cognitive abilities and social arrangements, such as naturalistic ethics or naturalized epistemology, cannot be discussed here.

The new developments in biology, evolutionary psychology, and their attendant paradigms extended even to economic behaviour together with the politicization of the debate regarding our freedom to technologically re-fashion our bodies and minds by "enhancing evolution" in ways that would fuse us with computers, animals, or whatever, have altered the nature-society controversies in two principal and interrelated ways: (a) on the one hand, the debate is not merely or not so much any more a debate about the autonomous status of social sciences as explanatory vehicles independent of the natural sciences, but mainly one about *normative* social theory waging a political war against normative claims being made in the name of "genes"; and (b) on the other hand, the familiar twin worries, *determinism* and *reductionism*, have acquired subtle aspects thanks to advances in biology (notably, mathematical models have played a crucial role).

Put in a nutshell the force of the two theses combined, (a) and (b), adds up to the assertion that the biological reduction of the social life of human beings to their genetic causes determining the form such social life has taken, thereby *necessitates* in addition certain normative claims (moral, social, political) to which evolutionary biology is entitled as a new version of social theory: namely, evaluations about the particular form human societies or political institutions have taken (normative claims, for instance, about racism, incest, competition, or these sexual division of labour or economic inequality, etc.) are now phrased as claims stemming irrevocably from scientific descriptions of how evolution has affected our gene pools. Therefore these evaluations or normative claims here hold a peculiar status: their objects, to which they refer, i.e. social and political institutions, cultural values, and the like being entailed, as we said, by evolutionary forces, acquire their evaluative approval in the sense of being the best possible – or "fittest adaptations". Therein lies their being normatively embraced, but deriving an "ought" from an "is" amounts to the well-know naturalistic fallacy opponents of biological reductionism never tire pointing out. It should not however be seen as a paradox that the defenders of the biological basis of human sociality claim for the themselves, too, the ambitious accomplishment of having furnished scientific foundations to normative claims, far from covert ideological partispris or speculative wishful-thinking, that is all those anti-scientific stigmata borne by classical social and political theories. In a sense, such an evolutionary biology of sorts becomes a social and political theory in its own right. The same goal is also aimed at in the kindred field of evolutionary ethics (Barkow 2006; Boniolo and De Anna 2006; Farber 1994; de Waal *et al.* 2006; Wright 1994). While to deny that human nature is an integral part of our moral views, a kind of silly "anthropodenial" in de Waal's terminology, since having the kind of biological make-up we happen to have affects what kinds of pain we feel etc., to claim that all our ethical responses and our moral theories must trace their origin to evolution is not outright self-evident and hence it is heavily contentious (among the first philosophers to embrace it was Mackie 1985 and to combat it Midgley 1979; cf. Singer 1982). For a punchline of the original hard line, read: "Morality has no other demonstrable ultimate function (other than survival of, and by, the genetic material)" (Wilson 1978).

Sociobiology and Human Sociality

Sociobiology's main claim is to subsume *all* forms of behaviour, whether animal or human, under the study of that field of biology that examines the behaviour of the so-called social animals, especially the social insects and non-human mammals. It is this assimilation that has been anathema to its retractors (see a balanced introduction in Ruse 1979). Before we go on with some of the details regarding the sociobiological study of human social behaviour (notice, though, the terminology of "behaviour" as opposed to "action" which is the normal term used by the social sciences) it is worth underlining at the outset the stages through which the nature–society disciplinary matrices have gone: they moved from simple ethology to human sociobiology and on to the more recent evolutionary psychology. The common core of the latter two is their allegiance to the Darwinian idea of evolution by means of natural selection. More recently a further stage has been added: the study of neuronal structures in the brain and their agitation patterns. This line of research is utilized so as to move from the study of animal cognition or animal motor cognition to human social cognition.

A helpful initial succinct picture of what the two principal evolutionsit–adaptationist programmes of sociobiology and evolutionary psychology combined would say about human sociality boosted by some recent findings about neuronal activity in the brains of primates when motor action is involved (i.e. a kind of acting) would go roughly like this: humans "have a faculty of social cognition" composed by mental building-blocks geared to specific tasks and all operating in an organized pattern to "guide thought and behavior with respect to the evolutionary recurrent adaptive problems posed by the social world" (Cosmides and Tooby 1992: 165). Let us look into sociobiology in particular.

Edward O. Wilson, the eminent zoologist at Harvard and world expert on insects, was the first to define sociobiology "as the systematic study of the biological basis of all social behavior" (Wilson 2000 [1975]) – Wilson elsewhere says that the term "sociobiology" was coined by John Scott in 1946. He published his now famous or infamous voluminous book *Sociobiology: The New Synthesis* in 1975, containing a first and last chapter expressly added to stir a controversy. The first chapter was entitled "The Morality of the Gene". These enveloping chapters extended the biological study of the behaviour of social animals into human societies and morality while placed in between them was a huge number of pages of run-of-the-mill animal sociobiology and population genetics. On the provocative side we read that "sociology and the other social sciences, as well as the humanities are the last branches of biology, waiting to be included in the Modern Synthesis". There is accordingly, for Wilson, a single "thread" that unites the sociality of insects like termites, of non-human mammals like turkeys as well as the social behaviour of humans. At the same time Wilson makes large predictive claims perilously against the grain of social sciences which, traditionally, have been self-consciously non-predictive: "The principal goal of a general theory of sociobiology should be an ability to predict features of social organization from a knowledge of … population parameters combined with information on the behavioral constraints imposed by the genetic constitution of the species" (Wilson 2000 [1975]: 5). Notice that all the ingredients are there.

The furore over Wilson's expressly provocative views sandwiching an otherwise ordinary scientific presentation of sociality among animals started immediately and went on for quite some time or, depending on how debates are timed, even for some decades (Segerstråle 2000, the best sociological history of the debate; Kay 1986). It is fair to say that since then the landscape has changed: some of sociobiology's initially provocative views or its general tendency to use evolution as its main analytical tool have been widely accepted now but dissociated from their supposedly automatic entailment of certain other views regarding human ethics and so forth, i.e. simplistic applications to the human case that have definitely been demolished. Most of the forefathers have moved into new areas of investigation (Wilson, e.g., has turned into a passionate critic of evolutionary degradation and a scientifically acute supporter of biodiversity) and the hard core of its proponents (who actually work in strictly animal behaviour and evolution) have either watered down the initial aggressive claims about humans or speak of the "triumph of Sociobiology" (see Alcock 2001) but in a diluted or defensive version that does not extrapolate heavily from animal behaviour seen from an evolutionary perspective to identical claims being applicable, allegedly, to human societies. Yet others have continued with the application of sociobiological analyses at the level of genes (e.g. Dawkins 1977; Alexander 1979, 1987) with softened yet explicit anthropological applications.

The furore also had the effect of calming down Wilson's initial hyperbolic goals and unmeasured declarations (see his immediate first reaction in Wilson 1976). In his 1979 Tanner Lecture we read: "man's social behavior has unique qualities unlikely to be predicted from a general, animal-based sociobiology" (Wilson 1979: 54), but also "social theory can be regarded as continuous with evolutionary biology". Yet he proposes still: "A new perspective on the human condition, extending beyond the species and through evolutionary time, requires the cultivation of *comparative social theory:* the deduction of principles that define the evolution of social life in intelligent, culture-transmitting species wherever they might occur. And similarly, a transspecific *comparative ethics* is both feasible and desirable" (Wilson 1979: 62).

Interestingly the twin bones of contention we touched on above, determinism and reductionism, threatening the independence of social theory, have either been claimed to have been unfairly attributed to sociobiologists of the initial stock or have gained increasingly nuanced analysis avoiding vulgar positions asserting the opposition between environment and genetic inheritance. Yet the problems persist, as we shall see below. In addition it is worth underlining that the perceived social and political dangers of sociobiology were first raised by colleagues of Wilson (even from his own department) and, tellingly, by those biologists and life scientists who spoke in the name of Marxism[1] and relatively less by philosophers (Stuart Hampshire was one of the first philosophers to make a contribution in the *New York Review of Books* focusing on the epistemological pitfalls) or by social theorists (with the exception of cultural anthropologists such as Sahlins or Marvin Harris) The economist Paul Samuelson was also one of the first negative commentators in *Newsweek* in 1979.

Irrespective of the particular academic provenance of each critic, one common theme used as criticism is more or less the same line of criticism used against Darwin himself and even against his precursors, in particular his grandfather Erasmus Darwin. In the case of the latter it has been claimed that when he or his like-minded progressivists were enunciating evolutionist ideas that brought nature and society into close contact (though without jeopardizing religion) they were all in favour of ideas of social and economic progress mingled with the Industrial Revolution's success: in doing so, it is claimed, theirs was just a classic case of ideology – in this instance the ideology of the Industrial Revolution – being read into nature (Ruse 2008). The same type of argumentative strategy has been used by Wilson's Marxist detractors: namely, reading one's favoured social and political beliefs or ideologically deformed views that reflect a certain stage of capitalist production into biological nature and back again in reflection, that is, extrapolating from the contingent into the inevitable, from the social to the natural and back to the social. Here is Sahlins' similar diagnosis: "Since the seventeenth century we seem to have been caught up in this vicious cycle, alternately applying the model of capitalist society to the animal kingdom, then reapplying this bourgeoisified animal kingdom to the interpretation of human society" and "What is inscribed in the theory of sociobiology is the entrenched ideology of Western society: the assurance of its naturalness, and the claim of its inevitability" (Sahlins 1976: 101).

It is pertinent to note in connection to this line of criticism that, historically speaking, social and political beliefs started to be noticed as such and codified by ancient organized societies only after these beliefs had been unconsciously projected first onto nature itself, and in particular the starry firmament in Mesopotamia, and then brought back (or down) from nature to society in the guise of laws of natural justice, or gods' justice, rather that societies must abide by (missing in this travelling around their all-too-human origin). It can therefore be said fairly accurately that the contemporary sociobiological debate and the fought-over issue of the opposition between "culture *vs.* genes" recapitulates the ancient Sophists' distinction between "physis" and "nomos": what remains, in its modern version, as a similar core defining the relationship of social and political theory to naturalistic explanations of human affairs is this common strategy of accusing the opponent of ignoring the fact that so-called natural inevitabilities are in reality latent social constructions. And, what is more, that leaving them as latent is the error of all naturalistic explanations of human social and political life, while making them explicit is the task of social theories. We shall come back to this in the next section.

The sociobiological programme insists on drawing an epistemological distinction on which it defends its distinctive character while avoiding attacks. It distinguishes between explanations on the basis of cell or molecular biology or on the basis of neurophysiology on the one hand and the study of population phenomena due to evolution on the other. Claiming the latter as its own field, it insists on the distinction between studying the anatomy or the physiology of animals or their ethological behaviour and the study of evolutionary trends on the basis of gene heritability and adaptation to environmental pressures of the natural environment on populations, the latter being gene pools on which natural selection operates. It is the latter field of study that sociobiology carves out for itself, honouring orthodox Darwinian principles of individual-selection (not group-selection) while answering questions about "ultimate" causes, not about "proximate" ones. Proximate causes are the actual mechanisms, anatomical or neurophysiological, that lie behind divergent evolutionary adaptations, but these are not the questions that concern sociobiology. Rather it is "ultimate" questions – or what in other contexts we would call roughly "teleological" ends – that form the core of any evolutionary disciplinary. What it is after is not the internal neurophysiology of a trait or behaviour pattern but its adaptive value, i.e. what kind of past evolutionary problem it was meant to be a solution to, allowing the survival and further propagation of the organism that carried the relevant trait and its background genetic basis. So in this sense, and in this sense alone, there can be a connection between studying the internal mechanism responsible for a trait or behaviour (proximate cause) and the latter's fitness value (ultimate cause). The primary goal is always finding the best, testable hypothesis explaining the evolutionary adaptive value carried by a trait or behaviour. This goal is served, methodologically, by drawing *analogies* between humans and animals – though such analogical reasoning rests on the fallacy of not distinguishing between what in biology are called *homologies* and what *analogies* (see Gould 1979: 240–1). As feminist life-scientist and critic Anne Fausto-Sterling has said, referring to the phalaropes, with their reversed sex roles "You name your species and make your political point" (cited for ridicule, though, in Wright 1996 [1994]).

It is fair to say that sociobiology has become more sophisticated but perhaps less interesting because less controversial and more guarded when it comes to explaining human constants by hedging its bets. Another way of putting a similar distinction, though one that does not entirely agree with mine, is that between "pop sociobiology" and respectable "narrow theories of animal sociobiology" found in Kitcher's masterful critique (1985: passim), one of the most profound and detailed criticisms in the field. One point respectable or narrow sociobiology has by now made clear is that it does not admit total generic determinism. What is more, even if genetic determinism held true, that would be no guarantee that all kinds of determinism should follow suit. Given that not all events in the world are exclusively biological in their composition, containing constituents not belonging to the biological aspect of things, such as e.g. climate change or other environmental factors being rather the effects of non-biological causes, it follows that even if human beings were subject to genetic determination, their participation in events that were clearly more than simply biological demolishes any position in favour of the exclusively biological determinism of everything. And since the social life into which such allegedly genetically determined human beings would enter falls under the multi-variance of events being themselves not exclusively biological, any insistence on social life being the outcome of biology is simply logically flawed. Early sociobiologists such as Wilson were relatively careless, talking loosely of "biological basis", and incurring the wrath of their opponents when they mixed carefully guarded terms with outright exaggerations: talking of genes as "hidden masters", while at the same time (Wilson 1978) explaining e.g. sexual activity and family organization in terms of the need for bonding, not unlike functionalist sociologists. Others were more adamant about explaining human social life in purely biological language (e.g. parental behaviour towards one's sons and daughters as a biological cost–benefit analysis of gene-propagation). As things progressed they learned to be more cagey and sophisticated, yet the problems remained. No sociobiologist would claim that in theorizing about human societies they see human beings as genetically determined. No one is as bad a biologist as this. We know that there is no one-to-one genotype–phenotype correspondence even at the same chromosome loci of the same allele. What is more, genotypes may be inherited (not entirely) but, even so, that does not make identical phenotypes inheritable. For two reasons genetics recognizes the impossibility of total correspondence between genes and character: (1) due to "pleiotropy" one and the same gene may affect more than one external characteristics of an organism; and (2) due to "polygeny" one and the same behavioural trait or characteristic may be the effect of more that one genes. It is now a common stance of both the sociobiologists and their opponents that simplistic determinism has given its place to different views of gene–environment interdependence. This comes in two principal varieties.

This can best be seen in a contrast drawn by Lewontin (Lewontin 2000: 8–9, 42, 48–9, and passim). On the one hand, the environment can be seen as an independent relatum against which genetic mutations, i.e. biological variations, the other relatum, are tested. Even if the environment is itself changing the changes are held independent of the gene variations. The organism is a kind of "plaything" tossed around by "evolutionary forces" whereby the environment is a (changing) "niche" to which the organism must either settle or not. Another metaphor here would be the one that has become prominent in evolutionary psychology and the modularity of the mind: the organism or mind responds to problems thrown at it by altering itself to accommodate the necessary solutions to those problems. In this original Darwinian view, the environment changes on its own due to several causes that remain independent from what happens to the organism, and the organism then has to "respond" accordingly – either adapts ("fits") or not to this environment. "Fitness" and "adaptation" are thus numerical markers. In Lewontin's own more subtle version the two relata co-vary dynamically in the sense that there is a holistic understanding of the erstwhile outside-inside dichotomy: environments are not niches but co-constructions. Hence the beloved metaphor in these debates: Lewis Carroll's Red Queen image of organism and environment chasing each other.

In an attempt to develop a more subtle version of the effects of the "biological basis" of human behaviour that avoids total genetic determinism which is admittedly false, later versions of sociobiological thinking opted for the strategy of genetic causation "in the last analysis" or "culture held on a leash" (Wilson 1978; cf. criticism of "culture evolving" in Fracchia and Lewontin 1999): i.e. allowing for cultural variability to shape human action and beliefs but only up to a point, that point being as far as it can go before genetic properties identified by our biology kick in, barring any further cultural variation. The cultural–social–political superstructure is allowed to have elbowroom to manoeuvre, or margins of polytropism are admissible, but the genetic infrastructure holds the primary causal role in the last analysis: you cannot defy the genetic base too much without paying the consequences awaiting such maladaptive cultural choices, namely evolutionary extinction. There may well be cultural variation in forms of religion, educational schemes, political electoral practices, styles of government, legal codes, economic systems, and agrarian policies, but the genetic code holds the leash, the length of which defines the kind of liberty allowed to cultural variation. In what sense then genes have become central to sociobiology?

Sociobiologists always took pride in their neo-Darwinism reminding us that theirs is a call back to orthodox Darwinian explanation in terms of individual selection and away from the mistaken views of those who see natural selection acting on groups, i.e. against whole species selection banned by Darwin himself. What Darwin realized but remained a puzzle for him to explain can now be fully explainable by means of the knowledge we have gained about how the genes work, in particular the knowledge and corresponding theories plus mathematical models in genetics that were developed in the late 1950s and in the 1960s. Orthodox neo-Darwinism asserts the primacy of the twin forces of evolution by natural selection through which species originate and change. But the unit on which the mechanism of selecting operates is the *individual* organism, and in some more recent versions the gene within the organism. The lever of evolution by natural selection operating on the genes transforms organisms – in the words of Dawkins, the principal advocate of this gene-centred version – into simple "vehicles" through which genes propagate after passing the natural selection test. Genes therefore struggle not just for existence but also for multiplication in the same sense that the well-known analogous Malthusian process demanded and was adopted by Darwin himself before the (re)discovery of the genes and their mechanism (something that Darwin missed). For Dawkins these are primarily "selfish genes" working "opportunistically" to propagate their numbers in the next generations of each organism in which they find themselves (Dawkins 1977; cf. Hardin 1978). Additional theoretical support for these views has come from complicated mathematical modelling, game-theoretic applications of cost–benefit analyses similar to rational choice explanations used in some social-scientific explanations. It should come as no surprise then that in the field of economics such a neo-Darwinism was more than welcome (see Rosenberg 1981: 67ff; Becker 1976; Koslowski 1996) or even linking evolution to properties rights (Krier 2010).

The puzzle perplexing Darwin was what in a sense has become the spur of developing sociobiology from its animal version to its human one. How could obviously altruistic behaviour in favour of a group be explained in the face of the equally obvious self-induced catastrophic consequences for the individual organism concerned? How could such a self-suicidal behaviour be explained if the genes responsible for such self-sacrificial acts would find no outlet to propagate? The vehicle itself gets eliminated and with it the relevant genes. So sooner or later there will be no such genes left and, naturally, selection would have weeded out all forms of such behaviour. Yet altruism persists. How is this possible? Only if we stop talking of groups and focus on *kin*. Solving the puzzle in the case of social insects has inspired sociobiologists to extend it via the gene-centred route to the human case. Parallel puzzles concern similar behaviour that is apparently self-annihilating in terms of the genes' future, e.g. homosexuality, or not fully adaptive or maximizing in evolutionary gain, e.g. some forms of religion, etc. – all these being the primary targets awaiting explanation by sociobiology, the proponents of which hail them as even better explanations than the corresponding social-scientific ones (for representative criticism of the overall programme see Lewontin 1976; Symons 1989). Now obviously non-egoistic, genuine, or non-calculating, or non-reciprocal, altruism is hard to explain in the context of evolutionary theory in which natural selection operates. This would be so if one chooses to remain at the wrong level of analysis. Looked at as an act of an organism one misses the fact that behind the individual there lies a whole self-perpetuating strategy carried out by the genes. What is needed to make the argument is what has come to be known as "inclusive fitness" and the haplodiploid type of genetic make-up found in certain insects and not in others. As an equivalent example to the types of human beings whose social behaviour should have eliminated them long time ago, yet paradoxically they are still around, here there are self-sacrificing insect-workers which should have been extinct, yet they are not. Given the mathematics of the case regarding which and how many alleles are found in the chromosomal bodies of relatives, plus certain environmental constraints, and the crucial point here is that if the probability of a gene's self-multiplication lies in its copies being perpetuated side-ways to the individual's relatives, i.e. more of the same would come if one organism helps its kin produce offspring rather than the organism itself trying to give birth to its own offspring, then that gene would follow a cost–benefit maximizing strategy to that effect.

Such strategies have been shown by mathematical modelling to be "evolutionary stable strategies". The full force of the meaning of such a phrase characterizes all sorts of behaviours that follow particular strategies of maximizing fitness in the face of adversaries doing the same, as we have learned from game-theory. Here is an excellent example warning against oversimplification, and a case from which to draw social analogies. Birds seen as behaving in an apparently "dupe" way obviously being manipulated by other subspecies which force on the former their own offspring to be raised by the "dupes", thus increasing the burden on the former to invest in both their own offspring and in those of the "free-riders" are actually not losers: what happens once we follow the algorithms of population genetics is that the apparent paradox evaporates and the "dupe" strategy may appear under suitable circumstances to be the benefit-maximizing strategy that evolution has favoured for both subspecies. Try to extrapolate such benevolent free-riding to the case of human societies and you have theories by early sociobiologists (without the benefit of game-theory) on differential parental-offspring investment or on human sons and daughters maximizing their own fitness by being 'cocky' to their parents or behaving as rebels with overall beneficial effects even for the parents. Or try even further to claim that all sorts of economic free-riding might have a game-theoretic effect on particular occasions that rewards the practitioners with economic benefit that maximizes all round, for the whole society, and you have landed with a controversial social theory in your hands. The line of thought on evolutionary stable strategies that grew out of the first insights of what I present in the next paragraph as a veritable scientific revolution was carried out in what later became a flourishing research programme linking genetic evolutionary strategies with game-theory modelling that clearly eschews the vagaries of popular human sociobiology (see Maynard-Smith 1982; Axelrod 1984; Axelrod and Hamilton 1981). Actually the game-theoretic approach was parallelled by the same kind of analysis of all sorts of social settings, principally international relations, where the dominant model based on Hobbesian prisoner-dilemma games was evidently similar even if applied to beetles or to nations: what gets counted is the relative genetic cost of sociality/cooperation.

The turn away from the erroneous "group-selection", understood as favouring species or as natural selection having species as its unit of selection, and back to Darwin's own viewpoint privileging *individual* selection but with the additional sideways favouring the individual's *kin*, i.e. "kin selection", and even more gene selection is owed to two pioneers: the American G. Williams and the British W. C. Hamilton (Hamilton 1964). Their work inspired a whole u-turn in the analytical model of evolution. George C. Williams' emblematic – even in terms of the words in its title – *Adaptation and Natural Selection* (Williams 1966) opened the door to re-Darwinizing in an orthodox fashion the field that eventually led to the rise of sociobiology.

In a sense that is not metaphorical one could say in a teleological vein that the prey "attracts" the predator "on purpose" in an act of self-sacrifice, saving its own flock, so that the whole chain of genetic manipulation could be activated and natural selection operate on the evolutionary process – only that strictly speaking it is the genes that "do" this, not the animal, and certainly, as sociobiologists are quick to point out, no anthropomorphism is being intended – no conscious or intentional acting on the part of genes actually takes place.

Armed with this development from population genetics we can augment our sociobiological social theory of the "culture on the leash" we saw above. Certain types of families or education and the like can be seen as falling within the leash's slack yet others cause its being taut, held tightly by the 'selfish genes". The genes would themselves put a stop to any kind of social arrangement that would contravene their algorithmically expressed evolutionary fitness: there would simply be none left to carry on those reformed detrimental institutions. No cultural artifact, social arrangement, or political institution (something, by the way, that Montesquieu realized in pre-genetic terms) could develop or vary in such a way that – ceteris paribus – the gene pools would end up being totally depleted. The survival of the genes would put an end to this. The fact therefore that certain social arrangements or political systems have not been selected while others prove sustainable despite superficial variegation of their form entails that the former are "unnatural", hence impossible, given the gene stock we happen to have as human beings, while the latter prove to be natural and hence "unchangeable". But if the latter contain forms of domination and inequality amongst human beings, unjust societies, or forms of social arrangements that appear rigidly to favour one of the sexes, then the normative claim inherent in this sociobiological analysis of what is "natural" is obviously going to generate controversies.

Let us remember that most of the early passionate reaction to sociobiology was placed explicitly within an ideologically loaded framework of what science "really" is or ought to be recognized to be: that scientific explanations have social determinants and are embedded in social matrices; that scientific knowledge is structured by the social world or that there is a "bourgeois view of nature" evolutionary theory being its apotheosis (e.g. Lewontin *et al.* 1984: passim; cf. Lewontin 1991; cf. Dupré 1992, 1993).

Critique of Human Sociobiology

Human sociobiology in its development has had to take into account the social environment as we have seen either in the form of the "leash" principle or in the form of the "gene-culture co-evolution" (Lumsden and Wilson 1981, 1983). In either case the non-genetic socio-cultural superstructure plays only a collaborative role, sometimes taking on as its task the assisting of genes: laws, customs, education, artistic production could boost collaterally what the genes allow. This is the case with another social phenomenon, the prohibition of incest, that sociobiologists are both at pains to explain and at the same time happy to showcase as an instance of their being unjustly accused of being determinists and reductionists. On the one hand, if incest leads to genetic deterioration then no laws or socially imposed sanctions are needed since nature could automatically take care of itself (Trigg 1985: 156–84; Rosenberg 1981: 178ff). On the other hand, socially enforced regulations (prohibiting by law) are seen as necessary additional force injected into nature in certain kinds of societies. It becomes obvious at this point that sociobiology cannot claim scientific status as a social-scientific theory if it remains at the level of vague assertions such as the ones we have examined about gene-culture synergy of sorts. Deciding in which types of societies the genetic base is sufficient and in which it is in need of the cultural–legal superstructure to reflect back on the genetic base demands being clear about the kind of causal relationships between naturalistic infrastructure and cultural superstructure across the board. Otherwise it sounds as if sociobiologists avail themselves of convenient ad hoc distinctions: sometimes the gene-base is sufficient, sometimes the social–cultural superstructure must legislate social action. In extreme versions of genetic determinism, sometimes encountered in biological theories of incest special "lethal recess" genes are stipulated. In addition, whenever the genetic base is admitted as sufficient, then sociobiology runs the risk of losing sight of the distinction it needs to keep alive with respect to the cultural superstructure which seems to implode or collapse into the base: should there be no distinct cultural superstructure with respect to which the genetic base stands in causal relation, thereby affecting it, then there is no causal relation, period. The cultural superstructure becomes just a name of a part of the genetic infrastructure. Charting a way to distinguish these two amounts to a pluralist methodological programme needed for social sciences perhaps best encapsulated in the title of one of Sahlins' *NYRB* contributions, "Culture as Protein and Profit" (1978).

This is a logical point usually missed between proponents and opponents: once the social relatum evaporates there is no causal relation and hence no dispute to begin with. In this sense, literature, social norms, political behaviour, and the like would turn out to be an extension of the genetic logistics as far as the human species is concerned, as photosynthesis is in the case of the plants. In fact this logical point can be, and has been, exploited in an ingenious way so as to yield a more sophisticated version of animal sociobiology and at the same time a more methodologically suspect human sociobiology. It can turn the whole neo-Darwinian synthesis based on evolution into a gigantic network of interconnected behaviour where circles of increasing radius can represent the whole natural world throughout which one's organism's genotype is extended (a version of this is Dawkins 1982). Every other segment of nature could then be seen as the phenotype that promotes the genotype of an organism. Everything could count as one's own phenotype, even another whole organism. In this sense where and how this advanced version of sociobiology cuts up the world – since it turns out to be a seamless whole distinguishing one organism from its survival list, possibly another organism – is clouded in obscurity. It parallels our criticism above of losing track of a separately identifiable cultural superstructure (here phenotype) needed by the genetic base in order for the latter to exercise its causal relatedness. What is worse in such a case everything is explained by everything else and in the case of human societies this amounts to the worst types of wishful functionalist explanations that social anthropology was wise enough to avoid early on. It appears that once we accept the critical point made here then the "way-out" sociobiologists invented in terms of gene-culture co-evolution as allowing the parallel development of social sciences and biological sciences does not hold. One of the main points of this chapter is that the co-evolution thesis does not lead where its proponents wished it to take us. It does not exonerate suspect sociobiological epistemology.

At various points throughout we encountered one of the earliest and most repeated accusations hurled constantly against sociobiology as social theory: its *reactionary* character. This links up with what we said about its normativity. The principal accusers have been S. J. Gould and R. Lewontin and their allies of either Marxist pedigree or of similar sort, scientists like Steven Rose, Leon Kamin, or Jon Beckwith. The criticism takes the form of sociobiology furnishing us with "just-so-stories" as its critics call sociobiological explanations, borrowing Kipling's phrase. Adopting the evolutionary process of the species, the critics claim, sociobiology cannot but embrace as natural the status quo of injustice (Ruse 2008: 237ff, 506ff; Ruse 1984; Ruse and Wilson 1986). The obvious precursor here is the despicable forms of social-Darwinism, especially in its Spencerian theory that also coined the famous phrase "struggle for the survival of the fittest", touting the natural elimination of the less adaptable members of society as increasing overall maximum fitness. It is worth pointing out that just about when Darwin's second magnum opus appeared in 1871 a breath's away from the Paris Commune perverse forms of Social-Darwinism were ready to justify by a just-so-story, even the abominable housing tenements in nineteenth-century London or New York as promoting fitness by forcing energetic young men who couldn't stand the wretched squalor to get out and struggle for success in the economic arena.

Furthermore the claim that we cannot fight against nature holding the leash, admitting there is a limit to what human invention, cultural variability, flexibility, and creative abilities can bring about in reforming unjust social differences that seem to resist reform as being coagulated after a certain limit, (differences, for example, between the sexes) has led critics like Gould to baptize sociobiology and kindred theories "Limit Theories" as if evolutionary Darwinism imposes nat-ural limits to biological change: limits to enhancing IQ or smoothing out differences in IQ, or differences in how the sexes invest in emotions, etc. Admitting this amounts to capitulating to the uncritical acceptance of the injustice of inequalities, misery, and permanent sorrow. For this reason it is crucial that for those critics like Gould who wish to attack the social theory behind sociobiology it is imperative to attack first the biotheoretical basis at the foundation: i.e. evo-lutionism. And so they have done. Though admitting the operation of natural selection and evolution, they reject total adaptationism pointing to both "punctuated equilibria" (Eldredge and Gould 1972) and unintended consequences, thus promoting the decoupling of adaptation from selection. At the same time they reject a social theory based on one-sided adaptationist socio-biology: for example, seen through the lens of sociobiology a cultural practice such as Aztec human sacrifice is re-interpreted as a solution to an environmental pressure/problem (chronic shortage of meat) and then this is used as an explanation of an adaptive, genetic predisposition for carnivory in humans (Gould and Lewontin 1979: this classic paper itemizes all the gambits, argumentative tactics, and subterfuge utilized by sociobiologists to explain human societies by means of adaptationism). By explaining everything in a "Panglossian" mode, the hyper-adaptationist programme ends up explaining nothing (a classic charge in falsificationist tactics).

A crude determinism would claim that it is the genes themselves, camouflaged as "higher culture or civilized benevolence", that are behind any social or political reform such as, for instance, the equality of the sexes. However, neither is crude determinism admitted by socio-biologists nor its twin reductionism as we saw. (All early accusations, especially by Gould or Lewontin, that Wilson had committed the fallacy of stipulating specific "genes *for*" this or that trait were unfair – they exist only in the case of some debilitating diseases.) Yet Darwinian explanations, even if reductionist, should not be feared as entailing genetic determinism (Rosenberg 2006: ch. 8). The problem is not even a matter of limited technical knowledge not being able yet to manipulate genetic alterations. We should rather say, in defending sociobiology here, that the issue is both normative and epistemological: normative because it should first be argued why the abolition of sexual inequalities and the like is a valuable state to be pursued, and to the extent such an argument is not forthcoming, we have a normative lacuna; it is also an epistemological issue because making a decision in favour of such a social reform must be shown (by the critic of sociobiology) not to be a matter of genetic causation which the critic wishes to combat. Carrying on their defence further, one could point out that the critics of sociobiology accuse its practitioners for not "wishing" to interfere with the possible progress of societies towards less unequal or more democratic ones because the cost, according to sociobiologists, would be unendurable. But not only some sociobiologists are down as all for progress, it is also unfair to accuse them for not "wishing' such social changes, for according to their theory they are bound to always take into account cost-benefit analyses of evolutionary progress. At the same time it sounds unfair for these critics to also accuse sociobiologists at a later phase of the opposite: i.e. for being unduly optimistic about the beneficial effects of evolution and its unobstructed path to progress. In contrast, critics, like Gould, point out that evolution should make us show humility in the face of evolution's unpredictable paths as far as what we would like to hope for in terms of unfettered technological and scientific progress is concerned.

A further critical point that links up with its epistemological counterpart regarding structuralist–functionalsit explanations in social studies, is the charge of *relativism* that reappears here. In both versions – the social as well as its cousin (functionalist anthropology and teleological biology), the biological what is examined is the role or function that is being carried out by social/biological structures ignoring variations in the form of such structures. In that respect sociobiology eschews relativism: to the extent that diverse social formations have the same "beneficial" effects; their apparent or morphological differences (e.g. endogamy as opposed to some other form of sexual economic arrangement) are disregarded as far as the explanation of their persistence is sought for. What matters is their evolutionary gained functionality. In addition, the "leash" keeps in containment the gamut of possible cultural variability, keeping "wild" kinds of relativism checked. Moreover, for Wilson and others geographic, political, or economic reasons (such as population movements) throughout the ages keep the gene pool on average in an almost steady state, i.e. as far as content and proportionate mix are concerned, preventing in this way the formation of special pockets of special super genes – thus avoiding the charge of racism.

Lewontin, in his criticism, has identified as a particular target the manner in which sociobiology understands or even "defines" human nature. The first point is that such "definitions" (i.e. "man is[gullible, spiteful, easy to … , or whatever]" given by Wilson in the early days) are arbitrary or thinly disguised extrapolations of ideologically held stereotypes. In saying this, the critics underline the social role of the deceptively value-free or "purely scientific" sociobiology – what we identified above as its normative element that makes it into a social theory. But at the epistemological level we should now add more recent discussions regarding such definitions: the suspicion with which definitions of "natural kinds" or "biological species" as reflecting how reality in itself is supposedly cut up "at its joints" omitting the fact that "kinds" or even "subatomic" particles or kinds of "disease" may be, from a non-realist point of view, constructed in a sense to be specified (even socially constructed from quartz to autism). Close to this charge is the reification criticism that sociobiology "freezes" some traits as if they were "things", turning their properties into substances and baptizing them as if they were self-existing independent entities that we must only discover out there in the natural world. Whereas in reality these are sets of characteristics that we decided to put together (this echoes an longstanding headache in biology ever since Linnaeus and Buffon regarding classification, now coming back as a debate on how to define biological taxa, as individuals or not). Neither "intelligence" or "tendency to take care of offspring" *names* an autonomously existing rigid "kind" any more than "corporation" would name a legal entity unless it was identified as such by the corresponding social meanings defining the terms involved. In an extreme Kuhnian interpretation sociobiology sees only what it itself can see, being a prisoner of its own epistemological filtering. "Aggressiveness" must be approached as what it "means" or what the concept involves, not as what it "is". If it is a matter of what it "means" or is socially perceived as, then "aggressiveness" cannot be a matter of simply genetic determination (assuming of course that the critics are not drawn into the quagmire of endless spirals of genetic determination). However, it should be pointed out that the "Kuhnian move" is equally applicable to both sides: each may be barricaded behind its own scientific language determining its distinctive ontological domain. Critics of sociobiology commit the same sin if they forget that they have to engage in defining too. The point that this chapter wishes to draw out is the lesson learned from Locke – and forgotten by both sides in the sociobiological debate – regarding the construction of nominal essences as opposed to the (unattainable) real essences of substances as well as from Locke's discerning account of how the mind goes about in building those essences out of elements that do not necessarily correspond to real properties of substances. Lewontin himself, a vehement critic of biological determinism, commits the fallacy of talking in terms of fixed essences (Lewontin 2000: 10).

"Cultural evolution" despite being for some a misnomer may represent the autonomous changes that human sociality can go through in a quite different mode from our parallel biological evolution: thus driving a wedge between nature and society and also between social and political theory and biological theory. This may be one of the promising routes at securing the independence of the two. Has Descartes won? Should there be a separate science of the body contrasted to one of the mind? Or Vico, in terms of which of the two we can really know? Critics never tire of pointing out that cultural and social changes are exponential and, what is more, located within relatively short time periods compared to genetic changes that take an enormous amount of time and would thus fall behind, proving that the two processes are out of step; hence reductionism is false. Yet to state that increasing complexity can be discerned in the case of social and cultural change bearing a clearly evaluative mark of progress towards better or morally enhanced societies (unlike genetic evolution whose unfolding does not necessarily guarantee a progressive complexity) commits the same fallacy of begging the question that detractors of sociobiology accused its proponents of. The promise of carrying on with Descartes' separation between mind and body has survived many waves and keeps coming back: but increasing sophistication as far as the natural side of the antithesis is concerned – i.e. being more knowledgeable about biology and in particular cognitive neuroscience – does not necessarily make us any wiser regarding the mental–cultural side and certainly no more secure in our judgments that the social–cultural side is independent of the genes, any more than those maintaining their necessary connection.

Conclusion

Theodosius Dobzhansky – the patriarch of modern biology – admonishes steering soberly between outright genetic determinism and the Enlightenment myth that we are born *tabula rasa*, i.e. steering a middle ground between the two extremes of each type of science, in a brusque phrase: "Biological racism and 'diaper anthropology' are just aberrations of scientific thought" (Dobzhansky 1956: conclusion).

For reasons of space this chapter could not expand on other recent attempts in which the natural basis of human beings becomes both a negotiable issue to be interfered with technologically and at the same time an item that acquires a social and political value, itself vehemently contested ideologically. I have in mind the futurist human enhancement of our up-to-now limited biological make-up – for non-therapeutic reasons, it must be emphasized – by means of drastically altering ourselves, fusing with uploadable computer-programs or by means of high-tech implants; or even by radically altering our germline thus affecting future generations, who have not been asked for their consent, thereby altering the kinds of societies that future post-human species will be designing (not to mention the non-predictable transformations in ethical systems to be adopted). These issues have brought back into prominence a new form of eugenics, though unlike the one that plagued all forms of social Darwinism, both with the best and worst of intentions as we bitterly learned from recent history. It was Darwin's cousin, Francis Galton (1822–1911), who first coined and defined the term eugenics in 1883 for scientific purposes. Eugenics crusades in different countries lasted between the last quarter of the nineteenth century and the first half of the twentieth. At the other extreme, deserving at least mention, is the infamous Lysenko affair and its orchestrated appropriation for the benefit of a pseudo-Marxist caricature of human biology by Stalin in his own book, as a peculiar episode in the history of nature meeting society: it should be pointed out that Lysenkoism is best understood as a kind of voluntarist progressivism whereby naturalistic reductionism is placed in the service of a kind of extreme voluntarism – total change even of biological iron processes being brought about by, as it were, a Soviet will power. Equally interesting is the different history of Marxist reception and eventual rejection of sociobiology in China (Jianhui and Fan 2003; cf. Zhang 1994)

It should be stressed, though, that both in the case of the older eugenics movement as well as in the case of sociobiological explanations based on the propagation of genes acting independently of the conscious actions of the individual who bears them, being Marxist does not necessarily amount to an opposition to either. J. B. S. Haldane is a classic case in point: anecdotal stories have him calculate on the back of a beer-mat at a pub the differential mathematical ratios of (the probability of) his genes (or copies of alleles strictly speaking) being present at the same chromosomal loci in his siblings depending on the degree of kin-relation, i.e. brothers/sisters, cousins, etc., in an attempt to determine which ones he should be prepared to sacrifice himself for (and for how many precisely). Though his reply may have been facetious, his calculations were nevertheless correct and serious as Hamiltonian genetic mathematics of "inclusive fitness" would later show in identical fashion.

But this new type of self-induced and freely decided eugenics in our days, operated on one's own self (leaving society out) and as a form of total reproductive freedom inscribed as a human right can, and must, be the subject of political theories and political defence, too, in the name of political liberalism, for instance. By sticking to the natural evolutionary processes and not going over into "enhancing evolution technically", orthodox sociobiology or recent evolutionary psychology may be immune to charges of being ideologically prone to positions in favour of eugenic manipulation. At least in their case the manipulation is natural. Furthermore, coupled with contemporary eugenics of human enhancement is the culture of medicalization afflicting social thinking again in terms of the natural–social antithesis: namely, the dominant intrusion of medicine into all aspects of life, beyond therapy, and into the cyberspace as well, repositioning medicine at centre-stage, redefining and empowering it socially and politically.

Art and literature have of course flirted with social Darwinism. But, more importantly, modern literary classics – Zamyatin's *We*, Huxley's *Brave New World*, and Orwell's *Nineteen Eighty-four* – have played an important historical role in making futurist visions along with didactic warnings vividly present in everyone's imagination: their legacy, certain names and titles synonymous to nightmarish dystopias, persist as the public vernacular of such themes, acting as hackneyed metaphors. However, what is usually forgotten or mistaken is that, unlike what preceded them, namely the classic *Frankenstein* or *Erewhon*, these twentieth-century texts portray a radically changed social, political, or natural environment, not radically altered humans or conscious machines as contemporary transhumanism envisages. It is ironic, though important from the viewpoint of cultural history and a testimony to the symbolic utility of literary notions affecting social and political imagination, that they are still being used so confusingly.

Some of the arguments against drastically altering our nature are socio-political, others bio-political, while others stem from an opposite avant-garde cultural critique that wants to redraft what counts as the nature vs. culture or society divide or what counts as "humanity" shattering uniform notions that privilege humans as we are today. These contemporary alternative voices are also forms of alternative social and political theory.

One of the most interesting suggestions amongst the former is Rabinow's widely used concept of "biosociality" meant to invert the dependence of society to nature: "If sociobiology is culture constructed on the basis of a metaphor of nature, then in biosociality nature will be modeled on culture … A crucial step in overcoming the nature/culture split will be the dissolution of the category of 'the social'" (Rabinow 1996: 99). Patients, e.g. with an identifiable set of specified chromosomes responsible for their debilitating condition will form social communities named by, and around, that chromosome. Similarly (e.g. Rheinberger 2000: 27) there is an "irreversible transformation" of all sorts of beings, including humans, towards "deliberately engineered beings" so that the opposition between biology and culture will be collapsing.

Amongst the latter, namely those who overturn the concept of being "human", certain cultural critics sometimes argue against cyborg mania from within transhumanism, i.e. supporting at the same time the artificial transgression of constraints imposed by natural evolution. So sometimes a "posthuman" future is feared from a religious or a conservative ethico-political standpoint while at other times it is positively judged from a cultural standpoint, not because of the wonderfully enhanced future beings it promises and the biological benefits accrued, but as pointing to a welcome end of hegemonic conceptions of humanness.

Notes

1 See Lewontin *et al.* (1984) voicing this extreme orthodoxy in the early part of the debate: "As working scientists in the field of evolutionary genetics and ecology, we have been attempting with some success to guide our own research by a conscious application of Marxist philosophy. ... There is nothing in Marx, Lenin or Mao that is or that can be in contradiction with the particular physical facts and processes of a particular set of phenomena in the objective world" (Rose and Rose 1976: 34, 59).
2 For a direct link between the biological and even endocrinological study of human nature, see the works of R.D. Masters (1991, 2001) and Schubert (1989, 1991).

References

Alcock, J. (2001) *The Triumph of Sociobiology* Oxford: Oxford University Press.
Alexander, R. (1979) *Darwinism and Human Affairs* Seattle: University of Washington Press.
——(1987) *The Biology of Moral Systems* New York: Aldine de Gruyter.
Axelrod, R. (1984) *The Evolution of Cooperation* New York: Basic Books.
Axelrod, R. and Hamilton W. D. (1981) "The Evolution of Cooperation" *Science* 211 (4489): 1390–6.
Barkow, J. H. (ed.) (2006) *Missing the Revolution: Darwinism for Social Scientists* Oxford: Oxford University Press.
Becker, G. (1976) "Altruism, Egoism and Genetic Fitness: Economics and Sociobiology" *Journal of Economic Literature*, 14 (3): 817–26.
Boniolo, G. and De Anna, G. (eds) (2006) *Evolutionary Ethics and Contemporary Biology* Cambridge: Cambridge University Press.
Cosmides, L. and Tooby, J. (1992) "Cognitive Adaptations for Social Exchange", in J. Berkow *et al.* (eds) *The Adapted Mind* New York and Oxfrod: Oxford University Press.
Dawkins, R. (1977) *The Selfish Gene* Oxford: Oxford University Press.
——(1982) *The Extended Phenotype: The Long Reach of the Gene* Oxford: Oxford University Press.
Dobzhansky, T. (1956) *The Biological Basis of Human Freedom* New York: Columbia University Press.
Dupré, J. (1992) "Blinded by 'Science': How Not to Think about Social Problems" *Behavioral and Brain Sciences* 15: 380–1.
——(1993) "Sexism, Scientism and Sociobiology: One More Link in the Chain" *Behavioral and Brain Sciences*, 16: 292.
Eldredge, N. and Gould, S. J. (1972) "Punctuated Equilibria: An Alternative to Phyletic Gradualism" in T. Schopf (ed.) *Models in Paleobiology* San Francisco: Freeman, Cooper & Co.
Farber, P. (1994) *The Temptations of Evolutionary Ethics* Berkeley, CA: University of California Press.
Fausto-Sterling, A. (1997) "Feminism and Behavioral Evolution: A Taxonomy" in P. A. Gowaty (ed.) *Feminism and Evolutionary: Boundaries, Intersections and Frontiers* NewYork: Chapman & Hall.
Fracchia, J and Lewontin, R. (1999) "Does Culture Evolve?" *History and Theory* 38 (4): 52–78.
Gould, S. J. (1979) *Ever Since Darwin* New York: Norton.
——(1996) *Life's Grandeur: The Spread of Excellence from Plato to Darwin* London: Jonathan Cape.
Gould, S. J. and Lewontin, R. (1979) "The Spandrels of San Marco and the Panglossian Paradigm: A Critique of the Adaptationist Paradigm" *Proceedings of the Royal Society of London* B (205): 581–98.
Hamilton, W. D. (1964) "The Genetical Evolution of Social Behavour", I and II, *Journal of Theoretical Biology* 7: 1–52.

Hardin, G. (1978) "Nice Guys Finish Last" in M. S. Gregory *et al.* (eds) *Sociobiology and Human Nature* San Francisco: Jossey Bass.

Jianhui, L. and Fan, H. (2003) "Science as Ideology: The Rejection and Reception of Sociobiology in China", *Journal of the History of Biology* 36: 567–78.

Kaye, H. (1986) *The Social Meaning of Modern Biology*, New Haven, Yale University Press.

Kitcher, P. (1985) *Vaulting Ambition: Sociobiology and the Quest for Human Nature*, Cambridge, MA: MIT Press.

Koslowski, P. (1996) *The Ethics of Capitalism and the Critique of Sociobiology* Berlin: Springer.

Krier, J. (2010) "Evolutionary Theory and the Origin of Property Rights" *Cornell Law Review* 95: 139–59.

Lewontin, R. (1976) "Sociobiology – A Caricature of Darwinism" *PSA Proceedings* 2: 22–31.

——(1991) *Biology as Ideology: The Doctrine of DNA* West Concord, MA: Aransi Press.

——(2000) *The Triple Helix: Gene, Organism, and Environment* Cambridge, MA: Harvard University Press.

Lewontin, R., Rose, S. and Kamin, L. J. (1984) *Not in Our Genes* New York: Random House.

Lumsden, C. J. and Wilson, E. O. (1981) *Genes, Mind, and Culture: The Coevolutionary Process* Cambridge, MA: Harvard University Press.

——(1983) *Promethean Fire: Reflections on the Origin of Mind* Cambridge, MA: Harvard University Press.

Mackie, J. L. (1985) *Persons and Values: Selected Papers*, Vol. II, ed. John Mackie and Penelope Mackie, Oxford: Oxford University Press.

Masters, R.D. (1990) "Evolutionary Biology and Political Theory", *The American Political Science Review*, 84: 195–210.

——(2001) "Biology and Politics", Annual Review of Political Science, 4: 345–369.

Maynard-Smith, J. (1982) *Evolution and the Theory of Games* Cambridge: Cambridge University Press.

Midgley, M. (1979) "Gene-Juggling", *Philosophy* 54 (210): 439–58.

Rabinow, P. (1996) "Artificiality and Enlightenment: From Sociobiology to Biosociality", in P. Rabinow, *Essays On the Anthropology of Reason* Princeton: NJ, Princeton University Press.

Rheinberger, H.-J. (2000) "Beyond Nature and Culture: Modes of Reasoning in the Age of Molecular Biology and Medicine", in M. Lock *et al.* (eds) *Living and Working with the New Medical Technologies* Cambridge: Cambridge University Press.

Rose, H. and Rose, S. (eds) (1976) *The Radicalization of Science* London: Macmillan.

Rosenberg, A. (1981) *Sociobiology and the Preemption of Social Science* Oxford: Blackwell.

——(2006) *Darwinian Reductionism: or How to Stop Worrying and Love Molecular Biology* Chicago, IL: University of Chicago Press.

Ruse, M. (1979) *Sociobiology: Sense or Nonsense* Boston, MA; Reidel.

——(1984) "Is the New Biology a Tool of Social Oppression?" *The Hastings Center Report* 14 (16): 42–4.

——(2008) *The Evolution Wars: A Guide to the Debates* Millerton, NY: Grey House Publishing.

Ruse, M. and Wilson, E. O. (1986) "Moral Philosophy as Applied Science" *Philosophy* 61 (236): 173–92.

Sahlins, M. (1976) *The Use and Abuse of Biology: An Anthropological Critique of Sociobiology* Ann Arbor, MI: University of Michigan Press.

——(1978) "Culture as Protein and Profit" *The New York Review of Books*.

Schubert, G. (1989) *Evolutionary Politics*, Carbondale: Southern Illinois University Press.

Schubert, G. and Masters, R.D. (eds) (1991) *Primate Politics*, Carbondale: Southern Illinois University Press.

Segerstråle, U. (2000) *Defenders of the Truth: The Sociobiology Debate* Oxford: Oxford University Press.

Singer, P. (1982) "Ethics and Sociobiology" *Philosophy and Public Affairs* 11 (1): 40–64.

Symons, D. (1989) "A critique of Darwinian Anthropology" *Ethology and Sociobiology* 10: 131–44.

Trigg, R. (1985) *Understanding Social Science* Oxford: Blackwell.

de Waal, F. with Wright, R., Korsgaard, C. M., Kitcher, P., and Singer, P. (2006) *Primates and Philosophers* Princeton, NJ: Princeton University Press.

Williams, G. C. (1966) *Adaptation and Natural Selection* Princeton, NJ: Princeton University Press.

Wilson, E. O. 2000 (1975) *Sociobiology: The New Synthesis* Cambridge, MA: Harvard University Press.

——(1976) "Academic Vigilantism and the Political Significance of Sociobiology" *Bioscience* 26: 187–90.

——(1978) *On Human Nature* Cambridge, MA: Harvard University Press.

——(1979) "Comperative Social Theory", The Tanner Lectures, The University of Michigan.

Wright, R. (1994) "Feminists, Meet Mr Darwin" *The New Republic* 28: 34–46.

——1996 [1994] *The Moral Animal: Why We Are the Way We Are: The New Science of Evolutionary Psychology* London: Abacus.

Zhang, B. (1994) *Marxism and Human Sociobiology: The Perspective of Economic Reforms in China* Albany, NY: State University of New York Press.

The Cognitive and Metacognitive Dimensions of Social and Political Theory

Piet Strydom

In this chapter[1] I am charged with explicating the contribution of a relatively new departure, the cognitive approach, to contemporary social and political theory as well as its potential for coming to grips with the problems with which this theory has to grapple today. After some preliminary remarks, accordingly, I propose to open with a brief consideration of the nature of modern society in order to pinpoint the problems stimulating social and political theory. This is followed by a cognitively inspired analysis in terms of the dialectical processes of the constitution and organization of society. It provides the opportunity to introduce some central cognitive theoretical concepts and to indicate both their meaningfulness and usefulness. Finally, this account allows a restatement of the task of contemporary social and political theory and the identification in a practically meaningful way of a core aspect of the contemporary problematic situation: the formation of a subject appropriate to the emerging world society.

As regards contemporary social and political theory, its central concern is closely related to the nature of modern society as a functionally differentiated class society which involves normative claims pointing far beyond its systemic and stratified organization. The contradictory institutionalization characteristic of modern society was since the early modern period economically, politically, and culturally exacerbated in the nineteenth and twentieth centuries, and in the late twentieth century it became writ large through being transposed to the transnational level. The global problems following this evolutionary spurt currently provide the focal issues of social and political theory.

As regards the cognitive approach as such, Gunnell's (in this volume) excellent account of the history of the relations between cognitive science and social science and the different directions pursued in their articulation gives me the opportunity to start from a less complicated point of departure.[2] For present purposes, I assume that the widespread volatility, disagreement, and contestation in cognitive science indicate that the contemporary state of the art in this field is most fruitfully captured by the expression 'weak naturalism' (Habermas 2003, 2005; Strydom 2002, 2007). It is neither a matter of the naturalization of the mind in the strong sense of the reduction of mental terms such as intention, belief, and memory and, by extension, social and cultural phenomena to processes and states in the brain, or of the nominalist presupposition that every term and phenomenon has to have an ostensive or physiological reference (e.g. Damasio 1999; Churchland 1995; Sperber 1996; Turner 2001). Nor is it a matter of the diametrically opposed anti-naturalist strategy of regarding the mind as a social construction or purely socioculturally – for instance, narratively – constituted text abstracted from every natural and biological substrate (e.g. Zerubavel 1999) and thus in its ineffable symbolicity in principle closed to scientific investigation (e.g. Hałas 2002). Instead, I take it that the appropriate location of the cognitive approach in the case of social and political theory is between these two extremes (e.g. Goffman 1986; Dennett 1991; Searle 1995; Conein 2005). By contrast with strong naturalism and anti-naturalism, weak naturalism allows two things at one and the same time: ontological continuity between nature and sociocultural life, within the framework of which an evolutionary explanation of the grounds of human sociality is certainly possible; and epistemological discontinuity according to which the sociocultural world, without denying the interference of natural or biological factors and the need to take such restraints into account under certain conditions, must be studied in the irreducible terms pertaining to it as the special world in which social actors become involved.

Central Theoretical Concerns

The core concern of contemporary social and political theory stems from the problematic nature of modern, particularly late modern, society. The latter presents the internally fractured picture of a global, functionally differentiated, ecologically endangered, class society that, at least partially, gives rise to normative claims which point far beyond its overwhelmingly functionalist, risk-generating, and asymmetrical organization in the tension-laden field between the national and the transnational or global constellation. On the one hand, modern society is based on egalitarian presuppositions manifest in expectations about a similar dependence of all on, as well as equal chances of access to, function systems and their products. But, on the other, the mode of organization of this society is characterized by a disturbingly unequal distribution of both dependency and access. At a deeper level still, there is the presupposition of a philosophically appropriate, scientifically correct, and hence collectively beneficial relationship of society to nature which, likewise, is contradicted by the increasing level of societal self-endangerment, self-injury, and potential self-destruction and the highly unequal distribution of manufactured or scientifically and technologically based ecological risk. This fractured and tension-laden nature of society is finally refracted and focalized in the typical yet historically varying ontological insecurity of the modern individual.

Faced with this multi-levelled problematic situation, social and political theory is required today, at least to begin with, to find a theoretical point of articulation of these different apparently disparate dimensions: the gap between function systems and normative claims; the typical modern problems of individualization and social exclusion following this lack of coordination; the globalization of these very problems which are now manifest in the form of the global risk society, world poverty, and intercultural clashes; and the failure of globalization to mature into adequate worldhood. Such a theoretical means of mediation would entail mitigating long-standing internal divisions – e.g. micro and macro, lifeworld and system or agency and structure, and in particular immanent social obligations and context-transcending normative guidelines – and concurrent tendencies toward one-sidedness. There is no doubt that social and political theory can neglect or ignore any aspect of the diverse range of significant phenomena and developments characteristic of our time only at its peril. The question of how social theory could be brought, for instance, to adopt a more consistent global and cosmopolitan perspective or to recognise its own normative poverty, or how one version of political theory could be encouraged to reconsider, for example, its national fixation or ethnocentrism and another opened up so as to acknowledge its ecological blindness, is of central theoretical importance.

Cognitive theory has an important part to play in contributing to a fulfilment of this theoretical desideratum. This is apparent from the rationale for the adoption of the cognitive approach in social science and its quite remarkable growth during the past two decades or so. As regards the history of ideas, Gunnell (in this volume) points out that, beyond the displacement of behaviourism by the cognitive revolution, the contemporary interest in the cognitive approach is impelled by a complementary declining attachment to rationalist positions and an increasing concern with the role of social interaction, judgement informed by emotion, and other subconscious factors (e.g. Varela *et al.* 1991; Carassa *et al.* 2009) – a range of concerns, to recall, which are covered by a weak naturalistic understanding of the cognitive. The rationale of this approach, however, is not only to be found in the dynamics of intellectual history and the development of science. It turns also on developments in social reality itself. Central here is the obvious lack of coordination and increasingly visible vulnerability of late modern society and, hence, the mounting uncertainty about macro-processes and their outcomes in the wake of rapid and pervasive societal transformation. Such lack of coordination, vulnerability, and uncertainty compelled social scientists to take a more penetrating look at processes and structures and to de- and reconstruct macro-phenomena. This required more attention being paid to modes of perception, modes of schematization, classification, or framing, processes of construction of cognitive structures of different levels and scope, and the discursive processing and actual use of cultural models of reality.

A glimpse of the central concern of social and political theory as well as the form the latter is taking having been given, it is now possible to offer a cognitively inspired analysis of modernity and its problems in terms of the dialectical processes of their constitution and potential resolution. As a reflexive exercise, the analysis is simultaneously a reconstruction of social and political theory with the aim of focusing its contemporary status. The three major phases in the development of modern society are first briefly reconstructed to provide a basis for the analysis which is then embarked upon to make visible the principal constitutive mechanisms and both their positive and negative impacts on the creation and organization of society.

Unfolding Modernity as Object Reference

The early modern period was characterized by princely, capitalist, and religious violence, Hobbes' 'the war of all against all'. Theories of sovereignty and of rights emerged gradually since the sixteenth century, yet the prevalence of disorder indicates the absence for a considerable time of a normative framework on the scale required by the situation. Absolutism's defeat of the church and pacification of the religious factions, incorporation of capitalism in its mercantilist form, and the monopolization of science provided an initial solution. That it was only a partial one, however, is borne out by the vehement opposition of the classical emancipation movements against absolutist domination. The confrontation and conflict between these forces gave rise to an intensifying process of increasingly unbridled normative communication. Rights claims-making increased dramatically and actions were taken toward establishing an institutional framework to secure the normative demands. Eventually, revolutionary events generated by the rivalry culminated in a framework capable of domesticating the unchecked exercise of administrative power, primitive accumulation practices, and resort to violence through the constitutionalization of the state, emancipation of civil society from the state, and constitutional and legal regulation of the economy. A new level of normative commitment beyond kinship, traditional ties, estates, and sectarian factions now became possible. It was directed by the *focus imaginarius* of a self-constituting, self-organizing, self-legislating, and self-governing society – the societal self-understanding which became embodied in and secured by the constitution. A completely new situation was thus opened, but the subsequent outcome was as yet undetermined. It would take shape under conditions of modernity.

Once an institutional framework was established, the communicative process was embedded in the constitutional nation-state, liberal associational society, and the public sphere, and as a consequence underwent a significant change. The nation-state, liberal society, and the public sphere now operated as constraints which had a civilizing effect on communication, claims-making, and the associated action. The unbridled conflict between society and state was replaced by tension, coordination, mutual constitution, and co-evolution, with only occasional frame-breaking by civil society actors such as the labour, suffragette, and civil rights movements. The normative commitment made possible by the initial situation – i.e. a self-constituting, self-organizing, self-legislating, and self-governing society – could now be pursued immanently by social and political means. Nevertheless, counter-pressures deriving from the economy and state as well as, ironically, from civil society itself weighed rather heavily on the outcome of these efforts to realize and give effect to the leading normative vision. But conditions would once again drastically change.

Due to evolution, development, change, and transformation on a variety of levels, a globalizing transnational thrust re-contextualized modern society in the late twentieth century which weakened the nation-state as capsule of liberal society. The communicative process originally set in train in the early modern period and then embedded in modern society was now to a significant degree abstracted and disembedded from the national context. Simultaneously, it was and today still is hesitantly and as yet inadequately being re-embedded in the emerging world society. As a result, the dynamics of the communicative process became altered and the mechanisms constituting society are required to operate under completely new conditions. For some time now, the outlook is uncertain and unpredictable, but considering the process and operative mechanisms a number of possible lines of development can be envisaged.

Cognitive Theoretical Reconstruction

Facing the problems deriving from early modern contextual forces, communication increased and gave rise to effects which became consolidated in the form of the public sphere as a social space for focused communication. Its emergence motivated individuals, however different due to sociocultural position, to conceive of themselves as possessing the competence to engage in constructive communication. The engagement of a plurality of individuals on the basis of the generation of ideas and claims-making from a variety of positions and perspectives allowed civic interaction and issue-related discourse. This process brought together individuals and allowed them to encounter each other as socio-political beings in the sense of potentially free and equal members of society and citizens of the state who, however different, are nevertheless able to freely associate. Communication about common issues, or discourse, and the resulting association led to collective value- and will-formation which, in turn, involved collective learning. The latter is a process in which a network of competing and conflicting ideas brings individuals to learn through self-contradiction, to adjust their views, and to develop cooperative relations. The collectively achieved outcome of this learning and cooperation was the establishment of a normative framework for self-constitution, self-organization, self-legislation, and self-governance embracing the principles of freedom or participation, equality or deliberation and solidarity.

From a theoretical perspective it is crucial to isolate the principal mechanisms operative in this reconstructed sequence of events (Miller 1986, 2002; Eyerman and Jamison 1991; McCarthy 1993; Eder 1999, 2007; Strydom 2002, 2008; Benhabib 2008). For present purposes, four types stand out. The first is a micro-cognitive generative mechanism. It is responsible for the generation of variety and involves the ability of individuals self-reflexively to construct an identity, to frame the problem situation, to create new ideas and to engage in claims-making through both strategic communication and communicative action. The second is a meso-cognitive relational mechanism which takes the form of association or the forging of associational relations among a plurality of individuals and collective agents. The third is a meso-cognitive transformative mechanism which produces both macro and micro effects. It is the mechanism of collective learning which, in successful cases, entails the transformation of structures on the social level, with an impact on both the cultural and subjective levels. Finally, there are the macro-cognitive and structural or causal context-setting mechanisms. Most important among them are the state and economy which lay down broad structuring parameters, but there is also another instance of this mechanism, namely schemes of perception, classification, and interpretation operating in civil society which become codified in culture. The state and economy themselves are of course to a significant degree directed and guided by cultural models of this kind.

It should be noted here, as suggested by Habermas' compositional concept of culture, that rather than the traditional narrow sense of the intellectual and the rational, the cognitive must be understood in terms of a range of dynamic knowledge enabling and bearing structures which indeed includes intelligence – i.e. empirical–theoretical knowledge – but embraces also conscience – i.e. moral–practical knowledge – as well as emotivity or conativity – i.e. aesthetic–practical knowledge. In turn, this structural view only apparently has static implications since the cognitive is understood in relation to pragmatics, including interaction, discourse, and action. Above and beyond the mentioned mechanisms, therefore, communication in the sense of interaction and discourse needs to be emphasized (Habermas 1979; Harré and Gillett 1994). Communication is the medium of the formative process, including the activation and operation of mechanisms. It provides a social constitution context, makes a problem situation visible, and is a context of discovery of differences and commonalities. It furthermore allows intersubjective reflexion, social construction, structure formation, the incorporation of intramental in intersubjective social and cultural structures, collective learning, and the coordination of micro, meso, and macro cognitive structures.

It should be noted that the situational context made available by communication is one of *possible* intersubjectivity or mutual understanding and agreement and, therefore, has a context-transcending normative reference – a reference to social relations which could be achieved, rational norms which ought to be observed, and performative consistency which ought to be maintained. This reference is not a purely normative one, however, but a cognitive or, more precisely, a metacognitive[3] one in so far as it entails reflexivity regarding the use of knowledge as well as the role of the emotions and normative rules.

Since every social situation, including the early modern one, possesses an objective structural possibility it is open to any of a number of eventualities – not only positive, but also negative outcomes. The decisive question is how the mechanisms are related, the configuration of generative (ideas and claims-making) and associational (relation-forming) mechanisms (Strydom 2000; Eder 2007). Such a configuration depends on the context-setting mechanisms, particularly the state, economy, and even civil society, representing opportunities and constraints facilitating or blocking the operation of the other mechanisms. On the basis of the early modern achievement, it was possible for the outcome to be democratic self-constitution, but it could alternatively also turn out to be skewed in a more or less pathological – for instance, an authoritarian, ideological, marketized, instrumental, repressive, or obfuscating – direction, or some combination of these. Such a mixed result became characteristic of modern society.

The embedding of the communicative process in the constitutional nation-state and liberal associational society represented a new situation. It was marked by a threefold system of intermediation consisting of state/economy, political intermediaries, and citizens. In this context not only the communicative process changed, but the mechanisms also started operating in a new way. As regards context-setting mechanisms, civil society and state/economy were now coordinated in a relation of mutual constitution through the newly emergent public sphere with its institutional supports, rules and guiding normative principle. With this development, the public was transformed into an internal third point of view, an observing, evaluating, judging, and commenting public, and became a constitutive feature of the liberal-national situation. The generative and relational mechanisms were now subjected to civilizing constraints which were mediated through the threefold communicative relation of active governing and oppositional politically relevant civil society agents, on the one hand, and the monitoring public in accordance with whom the active agents must conduct themselves affectively and morally or ethically and normatively.[4] Under these changed conditions the collective learning mechanism was no longer confined to doubly contingent social relations, but took a form which allowed the possibility of 'triple contingency learning' (Trenz and Eder 2004; Eder 2007; Strydom 2008) – i.e. socially engaged agents, for instance the state and a social movement, learning not just through competition, contestation, and conflict, but rather with reference to the public's ethical incarnation of the normative vision.

Central to social and political theory is the question of the nature and quality of the outcome of the changed process of constitution and organization of society under modern conditions. Constitutionalization and the liberal associational society could now be taken for granted and claims-making and action could concentrate on the self-production of society, constitutional refinement, democratization, broadening of the public sphere, inclusion, and welfare arrangements. In the best case scenario, this drive towards the immanent social and political realization of the context-transcendent counterfactual normative guideline took the form of a cooperative process of democratic self-constitution. It presupposed the free flow of communication and the constructive configuration of the mechanisms such as the free generation of new ideas and claims, free and equal association and relation-formation, collective learning, and inclusive self-organization, self-legislation, and self-governance. But pressures and counter-forces deriving from the context-setting mechanisms weighed heavily on both the process of communication and the configuration of mechanisms, so that in certain respects the outcome took a pathological form. The efficacy of these interfering mechanisms depended on partial or one-sided normative commitments or metacognitive deficits which constituted pathological effects (Miller 1986, 2002; Eder 2007; Strydom 2000). Among these were: authoritarianism (e.g. fascism) generated by a commitment to the state as structure and/or agent; ideologization (e.g. nationalism or racism) produced by a commitment to a unitary ethnic people or to the reproduction of a reified cultural scheme; marketization (e.g. *laissez faire* liberalism) stimulated by a commitment to a mode of organization serving individual or particular group self-interests; and instrumentalism (e.g. exploitation of nature; Holocaust) deriving from a commitment to bureaucracy, science, and technology. Often forming part of these pathological manifestations were repression or the silencing of need articulation and participation, and obfuscation in the sense of distorting communication, manufacturing public opinion, or manipulating the relation between active agents and the monitoring public.

Pathological deformations attest to failing collective and hence individual learning processes. Typically, a metacognitive failure or deficient normative commitment to context-transcendent rational norms or reasons is responsible: either a fixation on something immanent to the exclusion of the context-transcendent, or a distorted context-transcendent reference. Such problems led to a deformation of the social functions of communication, including assertion, relation building, expression, explication, and validation, which has problematic consequences both socially and politically. The cooperative process of democratic self-constitution, self-organization, self-legislation, and self-governance, by contrast, demands reflexive or metacognitive commitment to a context-transcendent normative guideline (e.g. principles of participation, deliberation, solidarity) and its more or less successful immanent realization under historically specific conditions. This was patently not the case under conditions of modernity. It is a pressing question, therefore, to what extent such a metacognitive failure can be avoided under currently emerging transnational or global conditions.

The globalizing transnational thrust that followed World War II and gained increasing momentum with the abandonment of the Bretton Woods exchange rate regime, the intervention of the Chicago School, and the promotion of neo-liberalism rendered modern liberal-national self-constitution problematic. The boundaries of the nation-state as container of liberal society became porous as the communicative process to a significant degree simultaneously became disembedded from this context and re-embedded, even if only hesitantly and hence still inadequately, in the emerging world society. The picture becomes a little clearer if one considers how the dynamics of the communicative process and the operation of the mechanisms were altered.

As regards context-setting mechanisms, the system of intermediation diversified due to the entry of new collective agents – i.e. new social movements – between political agents and the public, and the globalization of economics, politics, law, civil society, social movements, culture, the public sphere, and the public. Accordingly, the set of triple contingency relations is tendentially pushed beyond the national constellation and rendered more complex, involving potentially transnational or global agents and public. As a consequence, the generative and relational mechanisms are required to operate under completely new conditions, while transformative collective learning processes of the triple contingency type at the transnational level now become a possibility. Indeed, instances of success at this level are already in evidence in the health, human rights, and environmental areas (Therborn 2000). Overall, then, the demand for self-constitution has shifted to the global transnational level. The as yet undetermined position we find ourselves in between the national and the transnational constellation, however, leaves the outlook today decidedly uncertain and unpredictable.

Given the serious problems arising in liberal–national society and the shift beyond it, however, a number of distinct ideas of reason have emerged from the communicative process, became consolidated into cognitive cultural models, and thus are candidates for metacognitive normative guidance in the emerging transnational situation. Among them are cultural models such as: a 'responsible society' directed and guided by a 'planetary macro-ethic of co-responsibility' instead of a 'risk society'; 'ecology' instead of depleted organic foundations of life; 'intercultural communication' instead of a 'clash of civilizations'; a 'politically constituted world society' instead of a 'Hobbesian security state'; an 'international legal order' instead of a 'private law society'; 'global governance' instead of 'world government'; 'cosmopolitanism' instead of closed particularistic, ethnocentric, or theocratic communities; an ecologically and socially 'domesticated capitalism' instead of an unbridled 'global free market'; 'global justice' instead of 'world poverty', and so forth.

As normative principles, reflexive rules, or metacognitive devices these cultural models harbour promising potentials for immanent structure formation and, therefore, the possibility of a cooperative self-constituting, self-organizing, self-legislating, and self-governing world society cannot summarily be ruled out of court. But in its realization of these principles the world society will necessarily take some historically specific manifestation or other. Context-setting mechanisms will have an impact and the generative and relational mechanisms will take a corresponding configuration. It is likely, therefore, to assume one of a number of more specific forms, any of which could tend towards pathogenesis or even become pathological in the full sense of the word. With the political system as a context-setting mechanism that prioritizes a hierarchical rule-based mode of constitution and organization there arises the possibility of a pathological form of authoritarianism. If the economic system, together with science and technology, has a decisive structure forming impact on the emerging world society instead rather than being domesticated ecologically and socially, then its opportunity-oriented and instrumentalist market mode of constitution and organization is likely to lead to a reproduction of the pathological form of marketization which not only contributed to the ecological crisis and world poverty, but also culminated in the recent financial, economic, and social crisis. Finally, civil society, particularly by way of some reified cultural scheme or other, could equally well lead to a pathological form of ideologization, despite its inherent civic-oriented social mode of constitution and organization.

Tasks of Contemporary Social and Political Theory

The above-mentioned negative potentials leave contemporary social and political theory with the question of what normative commitment would be appropriate under currently emerging transnational conditions to help avoid pathogenesis or, worse still, a full-blown pathological outcome in the course of the twenty-first century.

From a social scientific perspective to which the creation and organization of society is central, particularly one informed by cognitive theory, it is certain that a whole range of different commitments are entering the process and contributing to it. These commitments are carried, for example, by increasingly cosmopolitan states, transnational corporate actors, transnational organizations, and global civil society actors as well as the monitoring global public. All these agents and monitors play some generative and relation-building role or other in the constitution of the emerging world society. The first task of a cognitive social and political theory is to ascertain the generative variety, their discursively mediated interrelations, and the resulting structure formation which are visible in micro, meso, and macro level outcomes. All the contributors, further, should be critically evaluated.

The positive aspects of their contributions should be registered as such and, if need be, the negative subjected to critique, to be sure, in a social scientifically self-critical manner. Candidates for critique include the ideas the contributors generate, the way they communicate, the claims they advance, the configuration of constitutive mechanisms they intentionally or operatively promote, the relational complex they form together, the quality of collective learning, and the nature and quality of the outcome they collectively produce. Above all, however, the cognitive approach is interested in the degree to which the commitment of each contributor comes to grips with the dialectical – i.e. the immament–transcendent or cognitive–metacognitive – nature of the normative problematic. The standard for such a critical evaluation is provided by the cognitive core of society: a set of relations of free and equal association and cooperation which is capable of constituting, organizing, legislating and governing itself – including, it should be noted, not only the relations among human beings but also its relation to nature. The critical question here, therefore, is whether a contributor reflexively or metacognitively recognises the cognitive core of society and allows its context-transcendent moment to have a structuring effect on social life immanently, from the micro through the meso to the macro level. Such critical analysis, strictly speaking a cognitive type of critique (Strydom 2002),[5] thus veers over cognitive structuration taking place in the head, in organizations, and in social relations and culture.

Critique of this kind typically correlates with a new spurt of subject formation and the emergence of a collective agent, such as an association, a social movement, or even a range of cultural and social movements, who introduces a normative innovation. And a normative innovation, whether in the form of an initial idea generated at the micro level or a later stage cognitive cultural model at the macro level, represents of course a more or less potent metacognitive world disclosure.[6] In successful cases, such an innovation or disclosure has the effect of making people experience the world, their relations to others and themselves in a new and different light. It instigates a change of existing conditions and cultural and institutional frameworks, thus allowing the process of constitution and realization of cognitive cultural models in situated social life to continue under a new normative guideline – until further notice. Here is located the very core of the challenge facing the emerging transnational, global, or world society: the problem of the formation of a subject appropriate to this currently emerging constellation (Touraine 2000; Honneth 2003; Dubet 2004). Being a vital issue of the times, it is also a central concern of contemporary social and political theory.

The need for the formation of an appropriate subject for our times is widely recognized by contemporary social and political theorists. Some agree that we are witnessing the emergence of a global society, but at the same time stress that we are not yet bringing it into being and transforming it into a humanly inhabitable society by way of our collective will (e.g. Giddens 1999; Beck 2009). Others acknowledge the need for transnational will-formation borne by global powers to get to grips with the maelstrom of an accelerating modernization process left to its own devices, but emphasize the more basic requirement of citizens and social movements introducing normatively innovative perspectives from below, transforming their value orientations, and developing new forms of consciousness to alter the frameworks within which governments, global powers, and transnational organizations have to make decisions (e.g. Habermas 2006). Yet others focus on the still more basic need for the constitution of autonomous agency which is necessary not only for the ethical incarnation of normative principles but also for the creation of cultural forms and institutions capable of safeguarding freedom as well as communicative relations (e.g. Touraine 2000; Honneth 2003). Precisely as in the early modern period, individuals are encouraged to conceive of themselves as possessing the competences – especially metacognitive ones – demanded by the emerging transnational situation. This is the case since such self-transformation stands in a dialectical relation to the formation of collective actors as well as their impacts on social and political relations and cultural forms and models (Snow *et al.* 1986; Eyerman and Jamison 1991; Eder 1996).

The advantage of the cognitive approach is that it directs attention to the interaction among these different levels and the resulting dynamics in terms of the micro, meso, and macro cognitive structure formation taking place in the course of the communicatively mediated process. The analytical focus on such structure formation is further sharpened by the adoption of a broad conception of the cognitive, as intimated earlier, which focuses not just on intelligence or purposive rationality (theoretical–empirical schemes and knowledge) but incorporates also conscience or normative rationality (moral–practical schemes and knowledge) and emotivity/conativity or aesthetic rationality (aesthetic–practical schemes and knowledge). It is interesting and encouraging to see that cognitive scientists are at present hard at work to correct the traditional rationalistic bias by investigating the role of social interaction, the emotions and other subconscious or infra-individual factors (e.g. Varela *et al.* 1991; Sperber 1996; Carassa *et al.* 2009), but what is remarkable is the neglect of the normative moment. At best, it makes its appearance under the title of 'deontic normativity' (Carassa *et al.* 2008) which is shorn of any moral connotations. Such an incomplete conception is inimical to the central commitment of social and political theory. Only when the full scope of the cognitive – including its metacognitive penumbra – is acknowledged, can the threefold concern of social and political theory – namely problem solving, world creation, and subject formation – be adequately attended to.

Conclusion

Having been opened with an argument for a weak naturalistic rather than either a strong naturalistic or a strong idealistic conception of the cognitive approach, this chapter sought to clarify this approach by identifying the principal mechanisms operative in the process of constitution and organization of society. The mechanisms were illustrated by way of a cognitive reconstruction of social and political theory as it reflexively ran parallel to the unfolding of modernity through its major historical phases up to the currently emerging transnational constellation. Central to the account is the dialectical conception of the cognitive immanent in social life and the metacognitive reflexively available in context-transcendent cultural models. It allowed a critical analysis of the way in which context-transcendent normative guidelines – for instance, the idea of a democratically self-governing society – can and do play a positive role in structuring immanent social orientations and relations, but are often deformed or even blocked by the interference of context-setting political, economic, and cultural factors which themselves, to be sure, have a significant cognitive component. The major task of cognitively inspired contemporary social and political theory is precisely to critically analyse the process of the constitution and organization of the emerging world society so as to contribute to the mitigation, if not avoidance, of such interferences and their undesirable consequences.

Notes

1 The first version of this chapter was presented at the 'Social Commitments' workshop held at the Université de Provence, Aix-en-Provence, France, 24–26 June 2009. I owe a debt of gratitude to Alban Bouvier who organized the event, and I also wish to thank him, Paul Roth, Jesús Zamora-Bouilla and Sylvie Thorou for searching comments on some of the central ideas.
2 For a more comprehensive overview, see Strydom 2007.
3 According to Brinck and Liljenfors: 'Metacognition concerns the subject's implicit and explicit access to his or her own cognitive states, in judgments of knowing and learning, feelings of knowing, uncertainty monitoring, categorization, evaluation, decision-based action, etc.' (Carassa *et al.* 2009: 17). Here I give this cognitive psychological concept a social and political theoretical twist.
4 See Strydom 1999 on 'triple contingency'.
5 As regards critical theory, the proposed cognitive approach cuts deeper than both Habermas' language philosophical and Honneth's anthropological positions.
6 Although conventionalist, see e.g. Boltanski and Thévenot 1991 on cognitive cultural models.

References

Beck, U. (2009) *World at Risk*, Cambridge: Polity Press.

Benhabib, S. (2008) *Another Cosmopolitanism*, New York: Oxford.

Boltanski, L. and Thévenot, L. (1991) *De la justification*, Paris: Gallimard.

Carassa, A., Colombetti, M., and Morganti, F. (2008) 'The Role of Joint Commitment in Inter-subjectivity', in F. Morganti, A. Carassa, and G. Riva (eds) *Enacting Intersubjectivity: A Cognitive and Social Perspective on the Study of Interaction*, Amsterdam: IOS Press.

Carassa, A., Morganti, F., and Riva, G. (eds) (2009) *Enacting Intersubjectivity*, Proceedings of international workshop on cognitive science, social cognition, and neuroscience, Lugano, Switzerland.

Churchland, P. (1995) *The Engine of Reason, the Seat of the Soul: A Philosophical Journey into the Brain*, Cambridge, MA: MIT Press.

Conein, B. (2005) *Les sens sociaux: Trois essays de sociologie cognitive*, Paris: Economica.

Damasio, A. (1999) *The Feeling of What Happens: Body and Emotion in the Making of Consciousness*, New York: Harcourt Brace.

Dennett, D. (1991) *Consciousness Explained*, Boston, MA: Little, Brown.

Dubet, F. (2004) 'Between a Defence of the Subject and a Politics of the Subject: The Specificity of Today's Social Movements', *Current Sociology*, 52(4): 693–716.

Eder, K. (1996) *The Social Construction of Nature*, London: Sage.

——(1999) 'Societies Learn and Yet the World is Hard to Change', *European Journal of Social Theory*, 2(2): 195–215.

——(2007) 'The Public Sphere and European Democracy: Mechanisms of Democratisation in the Transnational Situation', in J. E. Fossum and P. Schlesinger (eds) *The European Union and the Public Sphere*, London: Routledge.

Eyerman, R. and Jamison, A. (1991) *Social Movements: A Cognitive Approach*, Cambridge: Polity Press.

Giddens, A. (1999) *Runaway World*, London: Profile Books.

Goffman, E. (1986) *Frame Analysis*, Boston, MA: Northeastern University Press.

Gunnell, John G. (2010) 'Cognitive Neuroscience and the Theory and Practice of Social and Political Inquiry' (in this volume).

Habermas, J. (1979) *Communication and the Evolution of Society*, London: Heinemann.

——(2003) *Truth and Justification*, Cambridge: Polity Press.

——(2005) *Zwischen Naturalismus und Religion*, Frankfurt: Suhrkamp.

——(2006) *The Divided West*, Cambridge: Polity Press.

Hałas, E. (2002) 'Symbolism and Social Phenomena', *European Journal of Social Theory*, 5(3): 351–66.

Harré, R. and Gillett, G. (1994) *The Discursive Mind*, London: Sage.

Honneth, A. (2003) 'The Point of Recognition', in N. Fraser and A. Honneth, *Redistribution or Recognition?* London: Verso.

McCarthy, T. (1993) *Ideals and Illusions*, Cambridge, MA: MIT Press.

Miller, M. (1986) *Kollektive Lernprozesse*, Frankfurt: Suhrkamp.

——(2002) 'Some Theoretical Aspects of Systemic Learning', *Sozialer Sinn*, 3: 379–422.

Searle, J. (1995) *The Social Construction of Reality*, New York: Free Press.

Snow, D. A., Rochford, E. B., Worden, S. K., and Benford, R. D. (1986) 'Frame Alignment Processes, Micro-Mobilization and Movement Participation', *American Sociological Review*, 51(4): 464–81.

Sperber, D. (1996) *Explaining Culture*, Oxford: Blackwell.

Strydom, P. (1999) 'Triple Contingency: The Theoretical Problem of the Public in Communication Societies', *Philosophy and Social Criticism*, 25(2): 1–25.

——(2000) *Discourse and Knowledge*, Liverpool: Liverpool University Press.

——(2002) *Risk, Environment and Society*, Buckingham: Open University Press.

——(ed.) (2007) Special Issue: 'Social Theory after the Cognitive Revolution: Types of Contemporary Cognitive Sociology', *European Journal of Social Theory*, 10(3).

——(2008) 'Risk Communication: World Creation through Collective Learning under Complex Contingent Conditions', *Journal of Risk Research*, 11(1–2): 1–22.

Therborn, G. (2000) 'Globalizations: Dimensions, Historical Waves, Regional Effects, Normative Governance', *International Sociology*, 15(2): 151–79.

Touraine, A. (2000) *Can We Live Together?* Cambridge: Polity Press.

Trenz, H.-J. and Eder, K. (2004) 'The Democratizing Dynamics of a European Public Sphere: Towards a Theory of Democratic Functionalism', *European Journal of Social Theory*, 7(1): 5–25.

Turner, S. (2001) *Brains/Practices/Relativism*, Chicago, IL/London: University of Chicago Press.

Varela, F., Thompson, E. and Rosch, E., eds (1991) *The Embodied Mind*, Cambridge, MA: MIT Press.

Zerubavel, E. (1999) *Social Mindscapes: An Invitation to Cognitive Sociology*, Cambridge, MA: Harvard University Press.

Cognitive Neuroscience and the Theory and Practice of Social and Political Inquiry

John G. Gunnell

"So, then, if political science is not psychology, what is it?"

Horace Kallen (1923)

In 2001, a cognitive scientist claimed that "social science as a whole is in a position something like biology before the theory of evolution", and that although it was important to study what Clifford Geertz referred to as the "thick" dimension of social meanings, it was as essential to go even further and grasp the "neurocognitive level at which these meanings emerge" as it had been to apply Darwin's theory to an explanation of biological speciation. He claimed that social science and cognitive science share a concern with "mental events" and that the "deep play" of social interaction could only be explored by the "founding of cognitive social science" in which the two fields would "converge" (Turner 2001: 11–12, 151). The question, however, of whether cognitive science is to contemporary social science as Darwin's theory was to mid-nineteenth-century biology raises some persistent significant issues.

The Attractions of Psychology

From the beginning of the human sciences, there has been a search for laws and underlying causes of social action, and this was perpetuated as the social science disciplines emerged as distinct enterprises during the later part of the nineteenth century. Psychology dealt with mental phenomena such as belief, intention, and attitude, and whether or not it was categorized as a social science, it seemed to offer a deeper and more naturalistic basis for achieving social science's perennial dream of achieving scientific status and, in turn, the kind of epistemic authority that would facilitate practical purchase and provide a vehicle of social transformation and control. All of this was represented, for example, during the early twentieth century, in the work of many Progressive intellectuals such as Walter Lippmann as well as in the Chicago school of social science and the program of individuals such as Charles Merriam in political science. Merriam early on turned to psychology for a paradigm, and his protégé Harold Lasswell, with his commitment to Freudian theory, perpetuated this quest and contributed significantly to the subsequent social scientific adoption and adaptation of psychological theory (Simon 1985).

There have been several fundamental shifts in the history of psychology. We might project this field as far back as Aristotle's account of *psyche* as the life force animating human action. This was followed by a neo-Platonic and Christian dualism of soul and body which was structurally perpetuated in Descartes' influential account of mind as an invisible immaterial substance which was the seat of consciousness and causally related to bodily events. The perplexities that attended the heritage of Cartesian dualism, such as the problems of access to other minds and of how there could be an empirical science of psychology, led, by the early twentieth century, in the work of individuals ranging from J.B. Watson to B.F. Skinner, to the theory of behaviorism which was predicated on explaining human behavior in terms of the causal impact of external factors which conditioned actions. The mind was left out as unobservable, or even unreal, and consequently not accessible to experimental science.

Freud's account of the unconscious as an explanation of conscious thoughts and actions involved a return to dualism. Behaviorism was also called into question in the last quarter of the twentieth century by the influential work of Jerome S. Bruner, who sought to develop models which explained the states and processes of the unobservable functions of the mind. This was followed by what is often called the computational theory of the mind and the concept of artificial intelligence. Much of the work in the most recent stage in the practice and philosophy of cognitive science assumes that the mind is the brain and that behind cognitive functions there are brain processes which can be computationally modeled. Extreme versions of this view would entail what is called eliminative materialism or the reduction of the reference of mental terms to states and processes in the brain, but other versions suggest that the mind is still something real and distinct even though it is a product of the brain.

One immediate impetus behind the contemporary interest in cognitive science has been a declining attachment to rational choice approaches to inquiry and, as a consequence, increased attention to the role in social interaction and judgment of emotion and other subconscious factors. Although enthusiasm for "naturalizing the mind" (Dretske 1995) and expanding the domain of "the mind's new science" (Gardner 1985) is hardly new, variations on this theme and the idea of the possibility of a cognitive social science have now become quite widespread (e.g., Strydom 2007). Contemporary literature in cognitive science, and apposite material in the philosophy of mind, relate to the persistently anomalous status of mental concepts in political and social theory and research as well as to other unresolved theoretical and methodological issues in these fields. Cognitive science, however, is a diverse and highly contested field (Harré 2002), and the manner in which social scientists have accessed this literature has often been highly selective, conceptually problematical, and designed to support prior commitments.

Many of the general difficulties that attend the current interest of social scientists in cognitive science were characteristic of past involvements with psychology. Not the least of these difficulties has been a tendency to draw somewhat narrowly and uncritically from the literature of psychology and to take certain elements of this material as authoritative. There has often been insufficient first-hand knowledge of the literature and of internal differences and controversies. What social scientists find most accessible is often less the content of actual research in cognitive neuroscience than hybrid claims which emanate either from neuroscientists engaging in philosophical speculation or from philosophers seeking support for certain philosophical theories.

One of the difficulties in borrowing from, or attempting to expand the applicability of, cognitive science is the lack of consensus within the field on both issues and findings (Lepore and Pylyshyn 1999). Despite the prevalence, and even dominance, of certain broad positions, such as various, but sometimes conflicting, versions of the computational theory of the mind, the field is far from paradigmatic, or even free from ideology, Although cognitive science has been generically defined as "the study of the mind as machine" or "how a brain thinks" (Boden

2006), it includes a number of different research areas. These have been variously specified, sometimes in terms of subjects such as perception, memory, affect, and higher cognitive functions and sometimes in terms of areas of research such as computational intelligence, culture, cognition and evolution, linguistics and language, neuroscience, philosophy, and psychology (Wilson and Keil 1999). Furthermore, the questions and answers that dominate these research programs "change on almost a daily basis" (Hardcastle 2007: 295).

Minding the Brain

One of the most dominant, but still controversial, approaches in cognitive science is connectionism which seeks to explain a wide range of primate capacities by modeling the brain's neural networks and the strength of synaptic connections that link neurons and store information. This research has resonated in the philosophy of mind in part because it presents a challenge to some aspects of the computational model of the mind but particularly to what the philosopher Daniel Dennett has dubbed "folk psychology" or the assumptions embedded in everyday human practices. One of the philosophers who has relied heavily on connectionist research is Paul Churchland (1995; McCauley), 1996).

Churchland argues that "each distinct set of religious, moral, and scientific convictions, and that each distinct cultural orientation resides" in "myriad synaptic connections" which are "steadily adjusted to a configuration that allows it to behave as a normal member of the community." Much like early associational psychologists, he claims that the "world" causally determines each individual's experience by producing a trained network in the brain. He maintains that what is characteristically referred to as the mind is the brain and that despite the assumptions of folk psychology and its philosophical analogues there is no "self" or agent manifesting intentions and purposes. For Churchland, the mind is the brain functioning as a computer, but the "style" of computation that takes place in the brain is parallel distributed processing, which is different and far more powerful than the typical computer.

Much of human cognition, Churchland argues, is beneath the threshold of language and other conventions. He claims that in effect there are " 'social areas' in the brain", but he presents this directly in opposition to arguments such as those of Noam Chomsky and similar claims about a universal grammar and innate rules embedded in a special language module. He claims that experimental modeling has demonstrated that connectionist architecture can account for the complexities of grammatical structure and syntactic compositional abilities. In the case of the conventional dimensions of life such as morality, he claims that behavior is primarily a matter of applying "learned prototypes" which determine "what social skills will make one the maximally successful social agent". He rejects arguments that view consciousness as something irredeemably subjective and ultimately ineffable. Although he subscribes to the notion that individuals have a certain first-person authority and unique perspective with respect to what they are experiencing at any particular time, he insists that this does not mean such phenomena are nonphysical and impervious to third-person scientific examination. His goal is the "scientific reduction" of all everyday mental concepts to "an exquisite neurocomputational dance".

Churchland accepts the thesis that an electronic machine could in principle be conscious, but he rejects an identification of consciousness with language and other symbolic cultural units. He nevertheless claims that the "contents of consciousness … are profoundly influenced by the social environment" and that this in turn shapes the networks of the brain and "constitutes a form of extrasomatic memory, a medium of information storage that exists outside any individual's brain". This provides a way for "human cognition to be collective" and for groups of people to be transformed into what is functionally a "single brain". Churchland, however, denies any theoretical autonomy to symbolic forms, and he claims that his vision promises a brave new world of "public policy" and the "prospect of major cognitive growth for entire societies." He suggests that it is even possible to underwrite a new basis of "moral realism" by grounding ethical principles on "genuine knowledge". For Churchland, and his collaborator and spouse Patricia Churchland, it will be possible even in practical life to dispense with folk psychology and the explanation of human behavior in terms of concepts such as intention and purpose.

The Churchlands have insisted that the human sciences cannot remain theoretically independent. They argue that a connectionist understanding of things such as emotions "will give us a much more penetrating expectation of how any person's daily mental life will unfold, and a much more effective practical grip on the manifold factors that will influence it". Although they once associated their views with eliminative materialism, they have more recently urged for their position the label of "good-guy materialism", since they claim that work such as that of Antonio and Hanna Damasio has demonstrated that emotion is "an essential ingredient in what we call rational deliberation". And they maintain that in the end, "moral knowledge must be just one species of scientific knowledge, since the social world is a subset of the natural world" and "social reality is just one aspect of natural reality".

Antonio Damasio's attack on "Descartes' error" and the "abyssal separation between body and mind" is based on his experimental studies of how brain damage affects reasoning and behavior. Damasio (1994, 1999) claims that sensory experience creates "somatic markers," which give rise to emotions which in turn are evolutionary predecessors and unconscious determinants of more advanced forms of cognitive processing. For Damasio, the "mind" is really "neural processes" in the brain which is a special receptor registering other states of the body, and he defines the self as "a perpetually re-created neurological state". The main thrust of his argument is against the idea that reason and emotion are separate and distinct processes, and his emphasis is on evidence suggesting, for example, that brain injuries which impair practical reason are related to an inability to "experience feelings". Damasio insists that feelings are not some "elusive mental quality" but something with a "neural substrate" and that their "essence" can be seen by any individual "through a window that opens directly onto a continuously updated image of the structure and state of our body". For Damasio, emotion is "the collection of changes in body state that are induced in myriad organs by nerve cell terminals, under the control of a dedicated brain system which is responding to the content of thoughts relative to a particular entity or event". Like Churchland, Damasio claims that there are significant policy applications of neuroscience and that its relevance extends to explaining and formulating ethical principles.

Borrowing and Lending

One of the most visible social scientific applications of cognitive science was George Lakoff's explanation of the success of conservatives and the failure of liberals in recent American elections (1996; Lakoff and Johnson 1999). This was advertised as "the first full-scale application of cognitive science to politics". Lakoff relied significantly on the work of Churchland and Damasio, and he argued that his own field of "cognitive linguistics" revealed the "unconscious" basis of the "conceptual metaphors and categories" that constitute "common sense" political judgments. According to Lakoff, conservatives were able to exploit "categories and prototypes" dealing with matters such as the family and to deploy metaphors that were grounded in "cognitive constructions" rather than in "objective features of the world". Lakoff maintained that even though he could not "hide" his "own moral and political views", which he admitted were decidedly liberal, "cognitive science was, itself, apolitical" and that this knowledge, devoted to the study of the "embodied mind", would significantly contribute to understanding moral and political life (Lakoff and Johnson 1999).

The sociologist Stephen P. Turner (2001) has drawn upon Churchland's connectionist philosophy in defense of an individualist social ontology and as a response to what he identified as relativist trends in social theory which contribute to an idea of the mind as a social construction and product of the practices in which individuals engage. Turner, who had earlier criticized the emphasis on practices in social theory (1994), claimed that Churchland had demonstrated that "every mind is the product of a distinctive and individual learning experience," rather than of the "downloading" and "sharing" of a collective mental object. Consequently, it was necessary for social science to undertake "a revised understanding of a great many of our core concepts" such as practice, rules, habit, tacit knowledge, and paradigms which imply the existence of collective consciousness and an irreducible relativity of perspectives. Similarly, concepts such as belief, which are elements of everyday language as well as a central part of the vocabulary of much of social scientific research, and assumed to play a causal role in human behavior, are "appropriate candidates for the most drastic sort of elimination". These, he asserted, are epiphenomenal constructs and can be replaced by references to "nodes" in a neural network.

The first person to refer to "neuropolitics" was Timothy Leary (1977), but the political theorist William E. Connolly (2002) has employed the term in his attempt to integrate cognitive science with social and political theory by stressing the interaction, and basic unity, of physiology and culture as well as of emotion and reason. Connolly noted that his interest in this material was "hitched to an agenda to advance a political pluralism", and he suggested that it might support the idea of a "deep pluralism" which would take account of the "layered character of thinking" and of "how biology is mixed into thinking and culture" through affective primary responses that are situated below the level of logical thought. He argued that "the contemporary revolution in neuroscience offers the possibility of opening up a new discipline" which could bridge the gap between empirical social science and interpretive social theory. Building on Damasio's work, Connolly suggested that research in neuroscience pointed to a connection between conscious and pre-conscious aspects of perception and judgment and that it indicated support for a postmodernist and poststructuralist anti-universalist ethic which would call into question rationalist theories such as those associated with the concept of deliberative democracy.

Political scientists George Marcus, Russell Newman, and Michael Mckuen (2000) also relied on Damasio in claiming to present "a theory about how emotion and reason interact to produce a thoughtful and attentive citizenry" and to explain why the American political "system works as well as it does given the limited attentiveness and knowledge of the average citizen." Although emotion, they suggested, is usually viewed as inhibiting reasoned decision and is depreciated in political science by the dominant "rational choice model," the tendency "to idealize rational choice and to vilify the affective domain is to misunderstand how the brain works." They claimed that, by "drawing on extensive sources in neuroscience, physiology, and experimental psychology", they were led "to conceptualize affect and reason not as oppositional but as complementary" and to develop a model of "Affective Intelligence" which is methodologically "commensurate with rational choice approaches". They claimed that "emotional evaluation not only precedes "conscious awareness" but constitutes the basis of much judgment that never reaches the conscious level. These authors admitted, however, that "we have yet to fully work out how the neurological specifics translate into political life" and that the "array of methods available to neuroscientists to study the brain is not as yet generally suitable for political science research" and that political scientists interested in emotional response would have to rely on such things as survey research.

Rose McDermott (2004) made a case for what she claimed to be the "meaning of neuroscientific advances for political science," and once again a principal source was the work of Damasio. McDermott's focus was on how "emotion can provide an alternative basis for explaining and predicting political choice and action" and how "emotion theory can enhance our understanding of decision-making" rather than being construed as a hindrance to an optimal model of rationality. McDermott claimed that this "promises the unfolding of the first major theoretical innovation in the social sciences of the twenty-first century: the new neurological revolution is upon us". She argued that because emotion is "part of rationality itself", studies of emotion have important implications for rethinking or amending rational choice theory as well as for engaging matters of public policy and achieving public happiness by creating something like a neo-Benthamite felicific calculus.

These selective examples of the recent uses of cognitive theory are part of a growing literature which advances arguments to the effect that political judgment is divided between, yet shares elements of, conscious action and a primal unconscious which is located in neural processes (e.g., Thiele 2006). The turn to cognitive science is apparent in fields ranging from economics (e.g., McCabe 2005) to moral philosophy (e.g., May, Friedman, and Clark 2006) and in special areas such as feminist theory (e.g., Wilson 1998). The equation of mind and brain is, however, not without challenges.

Re-minding the Brain

Jerry Fodor has remained one of the strongest philosophical supporters of the "nativist" assumption that the human ability to acquire and utilize language is lodged in an innate mental capacity which cannot be physiologically located (1975, 1983, 1990). Although Fodor is prominently associated with the computational theory of the mind, he is a strong opponent of artificial intelligence, and he rejects the idea that consciousness can be explained on a naturalistic basis. He not only dismisses connectionism as an account of "how the mind works" (Fodor 2000) but has argued that the computational model can be neither extended globally to all forms of cognition nor integrated with evolutionary biology. Fodor's work has been devoted to a defense of the basic coherency of folk psychology. He claims that language and actions are causal products of thought and real intentions, which gain their meaning from corresponding mental states which in turn can be physically realized in multiple ways but which both represent and are caused by external phenomena. These mental representations are, Fodor claims, cast, through a computational process, in symbols of a syntactically structured universal "language of thought" or "mentalese". Part of Fodor's program, however, like that of some of his opponents, is to combat what he believes to be the relativistic implications of a social theory of the mind.

Probably more than anyone else Steven Pinker, a psychologist and cognitive scientist, has attempted to speak to a wide audience with his claims about the existence of universals in human culture and particularly of a "language instinct", which he advances as the core of the "mind" and the seat of the human capacity to "attach words to the world" (1994, 1997, 2002). He is adamant in his rejection of what he characterizes as the image of the mind as a "blank slate" and the assumption that there is no "human nature". Pinker also is intent on combating relativism and what he views as its current manifestations in trends such as social constructivism. Unlike Fodor, and Chomsky who is their mutual mentor, Pinker insists that language, in the sense of embedded rules which precede a learned lexicon of words, is an "evolutionary adaptation", but, like Fodor, he argues that language does not determine thought, which is ontologically prior. There is, he claims, "nonverbal thought", which, again like Fodor, he speaks of as "mentalese", and a "single computational design of universal grammar", which exists before and without conventional languages and which transcends the cultural variations.

The philosopher John Searle has explicitly attempted both to counter the growing tendency to reduce mental states to brain states and to combat any line of argument that suggests that the mind is a social construction (1992, 1995). Although he goes to great lengths to reconcile the physical and mental domains, his ultimate goal is to defend the autonomy of mind and consciousness. Searle designates his position as "biological naturalism" which entails that while all mental states are ultimately caused by neurobiological processes in the brain, conscious states and processes involve a higher, but not experimentally accessible, level of the biological system. They are distinguished by a first-person ontology which gives rise to a sense of self and the capacity for intentionality which is expressed in human behavior. For Searle, mental causation is a basic fact of the world and the ground of the explanation of speech and action, and in this respect he implicitly gives support to folk psychology as well as to the underlying assumptions and conceptual repertoire that inform much of social science and social theory.

Despite how far Searle's position is from that of someone such as Pinker, they both agree on the intellectual and social dangers of relativism and the idea of the mind as a socially constituted text. Searle has undertaken an extensive analysis of the logical structure of what he calls "institutional facts", but although he claims that culture is part of the "real world", he maintains that cultural facts ultimately rest on, and are constructed from, the "brute facts" of nature which "are totally independent of us". What is especially important for Searle is to account for "collective intentionality" or "we-intentions" which characterize institutional facts but which, he claims, are nevertheless "biologically innate" and located, like all agency, in the minds of individuals. For Searle, "language is essentially constitutive of social reality" and the move from brute to institutional status is a "linguistic move", but he stresses that there are thoughts which are independent of and prior to language. He also places great weight on what he terms "the background", which he describes as an unconscious "preintentional" causal realm of "capacities" that, while functionally equivalent to embedded rules and conventions, such as those posited by Chomsky and Fodor, are not actually linguistic or rule-governed.

The Challenge of the Discursive Mind

What is apparent in most of this literature, in both social science and philosophy, is that despite disagreements about concepts of mind and the nature of mental phenomena, much of it, like earlier attempts of social science to draw upon psychology ranging from behaviorism to Freudianism, is in part inspired by a concern with establishing the epistemic and critical authority of these disciplines. It involves an attempt to question the theoretical autonomy of conventional phenomena and reach beneath to something deeper and firmer on which to base explanation and judgment and combat what is viewed as the relativistic implications of certain social theories.

Despite the often conflicting, and sometimes questionable, claims of experimental research in cognitive science, there are few who challenge the basic validity of this line of research. What is pointedly challenged, however, are some of the philosophical premises and extrapolations. An article in a scientific journal titled "Neuropolitics Gone Mad" castigated neuroscientists for jumping on the bandwagon of claiming that the field can contribute to explaining phenomena such as elections and for giving credibility to such claims (Butcher 2008). One very prominent source of both criticism and an alternative concept of mind and the meaning of mental concepts has been the work of Ludwig Wittgenstein (Racine and Müller 2009) who is also viewed by many adherents of cognitive science as one of the principal inspirations for the positions they wish to combat. Wittgenstein famously stated that "no supposition seems to me more natural than that there is no process in the brain correlated with … thinking; so that it would be possible to read off thought processes from brain processes" (1967: 608), and he ended his most important work with the statement that "the confusion and barrenness of psychology is not to be explained by calling it a 'young science' … for in psychology there are experimental methods and *conceptual confusion*" (2001:195).

Although much of cognitive science has been devoted to challenging dualism, some critics have argued that it is still a prisoner of the Cartesian legacy. This claim has been extensively pursued in the joint work of a neuroscientist and a Wittgensteinian philosopher who argue that the reduction of mind to the brain as the bearer of psychological attributes is actually a new form of dualism. M.R. Bennett and P.M.S. Hacker (2003) claim that what many neuroscientists, such as Damasio, ascribe to the brain are properties and powers which are properly attributed to whole human beings rather than to particular organs of the body. These critics, no more than Wittgenstein, deny that there are physiological and neural correlates of psychological concepts such as intention, belief, remembering, and emotion, but they insist that there is a conceptual mistake involved in seeking to explain these attributes in terms of functions of the brain or, alternatively, to conceive of the mind and consciousness as a supervenient entity or inner eye with which we view our private experience. To have a mind is to have a certain range of characteristic human capacities. They argue that emotions, for example, are, despite claims ranging from William James to Damasio, neither brain states nor somatic reactions but symbolic manifestations. Much of the conceptual difficulty, they suggest, stems from the continuing assumption, which Wittgenstein attempted to dispel, that there must be an ostensive reference for all terms and that mental concepts such as intention and emotion imply a physiological reference when in fact they are simply terms that have a place in the human practices in which they are embedded.

Wittgenstein claimed that although the vocabulary of mental terms does have uses in our language, "the psychological verbs to see, to believe, to think, to wish, do not signify phenomena" (1967: 471) either inner or outer, and that it is important not to be seduced by the illusion that mental terms such as "intention" must refer to some state or process which lies hidden behind language and action. Wittgenstein posited intentionality as a function of language and "embedded in its situation, in human customs and institutions", that is, in what he referred to as the "forms of life" that are "given" and manifest in social practices. The idea of the inner world of the mind, he maintained, is just "part of the mythology stored in our language" (Wittgenstein 1993: 133). With respect to claims about factoring emotion into an explanation of social action, correlations between brain states and what is categorized as emotional behavior, even if such correlations could be achieved, are not, in some obvious manner, explanations of that behavior. The philosopher Charles Taylor, for example, noted that "our language is constitutive of our emotions" and is the medium in which they are "experienced" and "articulated" (1985: 74), and the philosopher Rom Harré (1986) argues that emotion is a "social construction." The more positive dimensions of what has been referred to as a "discursive" theory of the mind and an approach to psychology based on Wittgensteinian premises have been developed by Harré and others (Harré 1986; Harré and Gillett 1994; Harré and Tissaw 2005; Racine and Müller 2009).

What could be viewed as an alternative to the sometimes dichotomous choices of naturalism and conventionalism has been advanced by the philosopher Daniel Dennett who, while fully accepting many of the claims of neuroscience, provides an argument that supports of the theoretical autonomy of social phenomena (1991, 1995). His position is, in one fundamental respect, distinctly reductive and materialistic in that he rejects any form of dualism that assumes that consciousness involves "qualia" or subjective experiences which cannot be studied in a naturalistic manner from a third-person stance. He maintains, however, that the *contents* of consciousness are products of culture and must be understood and explained accordingly.

Dennett drew heavily upon Richard Dawkins' account of how the "selfish gene" ultimately gave rise to trans-organic "systems of representations" or "memes" which eventually parasitized the brain and had a recursive effect upon the organic system as a whole (1989). Dennett claims that the content of human consciousness is in effect a huge complex of memes or basic but diverse ideas and conventional units of culture. Although Dennett does not accept folk psychology as an explanation of how the mind works, this is not because, any less than folk physics, it is a bad model or heuristic for accounting for and predicting human behavior. But, explicitly following Wittgenstein, he wishes to refute the often entailed idea that minds are entities that operate in some private inaccessible space under the control of a subject or ego that functions like a homunculus in a Cartesian theater. Dennett, again relying on Dawkins, defends a kind of universal Darwinism and suggests that memes eventually transform the architecture of the brain and that they themselves evolve in a manner somewhat analogous to genes as they seek their own advantage and can even override biological imperatives.

Final "Thoughts"

Many of the issues surrounding the relationship between cognitive science and social science are manifest in recent discussions about "mirror neurons". In the last quarter of the twentieth century, research that began in Italy claimed to discover in the brain physiology of macaque monkeys a class of neurons that fire both when such an animal acts and when it observes the same behavior in other animals. The claim has been extended to research on human behavior dealing with imitation, empathy, and even language acquisition (Rizzolatti 2006; Iacoboni 2008). The idea that imitation is at the root of human interaction has been advanced from a number of perspectives (Hurley and Chater 2005), and the claim, which dates at least back to Adam Smith's *Theory of Moral Sentiments*, that empathy is an aspect of human nature and constitutes a fundamental basis of society has gained new attention (Steuber 2006; Decety and Ickes 2009). It has been argued that this research also speaks more generally to simulation theory (Goldman 2006) and claims about the capacity of humans both to relate to each other and to represent mental states and engage in "mind-reading". Some have argued that mirror neurons lend support to the theory that humans are endowed with an innate "theory" of the mind which is at the root of folk psychology.

If humans do possess mirror neurons, their presence would be important for explaining various capacities, but this would not necessarily entail the conclusion that studies of brain processes would replace or provide a theory of social phenomena in which such things as empathy and "mind-reading" are attributed to sharing in human practices and conventions. But another problem with the literature on mirror neurons is recent evidence that both cognitive scientists and social scientists may have been somewhat precipitous in speculations about the implications of this research, particularly since there is now even some doubt about the existence of such neurons (e.g., Dinstein 2008; Hickok 2009).

If we return to the question posed at the beginning of this essay, the first problem with suggesting an analogy between something such as Darwin's theory of evolution and cognitive science is that the latter is not characterized by any such distinct theory. Even if one of the theories within cognitive science, such as connectionism, became paradigmatic, comparability with what Dennett spoke of as "Darwin's dangerous idea", would not necessarily entail the reduction of social phenomena to appearances but only a biological explanation of the grounds of human conventionality. But maybe such a hasty analogy might more closely resemble the saga of social Darwinism's misplaced application of a scientific theory.

References

Bennett, M.R. and Hacker, P.M.S. (2003) *Philosophical Foundations of Neuroscience*, Oxford: Blackwell.
Boden, M. (2006) *Mind as a Machine: A History of Cognitive Science*, 2 vols, Oxford: Clarendon Press.
Butcher, J. (2008) "Neuropolitics Gone Mad," *The Lancet Neurology* 7 (4).
Churchland, P. (1995) *The Engine of Reason, the Seat of the Soul: A Philosophical Journey into the Brain*, Cambridge, MA: MIT Press.
Connolly, W. (2002) *Neuropolitics*, Minneapolis, MN: University of Minnesota Press.
Damasio, A. (1994) *Descartes' Error: Emotion, Reason, and the Human Brain*, New York: Putnam & Sons.
——(1999) *The Feeling of What Happens: Body and Emotion in the Making of Consciousness*, New York: Harcourt Brace.
Dawkins, R. (1989) *The Selfish Gene*, Oxford: Oxford University Press.
Decety, J. and Ickes, W. (2009) *The Social Neuroscience of Empathy*, Cambridge, MA: MIT Press.
Dennett, D. (1991) *Consciousness Explained*, Boston, MA: Little, Brown.
——(1995) *Darwin's Dangerous Idea*, New York: Touchstone.
Dinstein, Ilan (2008) "Human Cortex: Reflections on Mirror Neurons," *Current Biology* 18 (20).
Dretske, F. (1995) *Naturalizing the Mind*, Cambridge, MA: MIT Press.
Fodor, J. (1975) *The Language of Thought*, Cambridge, MA: Harvard University Press.
——(1983) *The Modularity of the Mind*, Cambridge, MA: MIT Press.
——(1990) *A Theory of Content and Other Essays*, Cambridge, MA: MIT Press.
——(2000) *The Mind Doesn't Work that Way*, Cambridge, MA: MIT Press.
Gardner, H. (1985) *The Mind's New Science: A History of the Cognitive Revolution*, New York: Basic Books.
Goldman, A. (2006) *Simulating Minds: The Philosophy, Psychology, and Neuroscience of Mindreading*, New York: Oxford University Press.
Hardcastle, V. (2007) "The Theoretical and Methodological Foundations of Cognitive Science," in P. Thagard (ed.) *Philosophy of Psychology and Cognitive Science*, New York: Elsvier.
Harré, R. (ed.) (1986) *The Social Construction of Emotion*, New York: Oxford University Press.
——(2002) *Cognitive Science: A Philosophical Introduction*, Thousand Oaks, CA: Sage Publications.
Harré, R. and Gillett, G. (1994) *The Discursive Mind*, Thousand Oaks, CA: Sage Publications.
Harré, R. and Tissaw, M. (2005) *Wittgenstein and Psychology*, Aldershot: Ashgate.
Hickok, G. (2009) "Eight Problems for the Mirror Neuron Theory of Action Understanding in Monkeys and Humans," *Journal of Cognitive Neuroscience*, Jan 13.
Hurley, S. and Chater, N. (2005) *Perspectives on Imitation: From Neuroscience to Social Science*, vols 1, 2, Cambridge, MA: MIT Press.
Iacoboni, M. (2008) *Mirroring People: The New Science of How We Connect with Others*, New York: Farrar, Straus, & Giroux.
Lakoff, G. (1996) *Moral Politics: What Conservatives Know that Liberals Do Not*, Chicago, IL: University of Chicago Press.
Lakoff, G. and Johnson, M. (1999) *Philosophy in the Flesh: The Embodied Mind and its Challenge to Western Thought*, New York: Basic Books.
Leary, T. (1977) *Neuropolitics: The Sociology of Human Metamorposis*, Los Angeles, CA: Starseed/Peace Press.
Lepore, E. and Pylyshyn, Z. (eds) (1999) *What is Cognitive Science?* Oxford: Blackwell.
Marcus, G., Newman, W., and Mackuen, M. (2000) *Affective Intelligence and Political Judgment*, Chicago, IL: University of Chicago Press.
May, L., Friedman, M., and Clark A. (eds) (2006) *Mind and Morals: Essays on Ethics and Cognitive Science*, Cambridge, MA: MIT Press.
McCabe, K. (2005) "Neuroeconomics," in L. Nadel (ed.) *Encyclopedia of Cognitive Science*, New York: Macmillan.
McCauley, R. (ed.) (1996) *The Churchlands and Their Critics*, Oxford: Blackwell.
McDermott, R. (2004) "The Feeling of Rationality: The Meaning of Neuroscientific Advances for Political Science," *Perspectives on Politics* 2.
Pinker, S. (1994) *The Language Instinct*, New York: William Morrow.
——(1997) *How the Mind Works*, New York: W.W. Norton.

——(2002) *The Blank Slate: the Modern Denial of Human Nature*, New York: Viking Penquin.

Racine, T. and Müller, U. (eds) (2009) "Mind, Meaning, and Language: Wittgenstein's Relevance for Psychology," *New Ideas in Psychology* 27.

Rizzolatti, G. (2006) *Mirrors in the Brain: How Our Minds Share Actions, Emotions, and Experience*, New York: Oxford University Press.

Searle, J. (1992) *The Rediscovery of the Mind*, Cambridge: MIT Press.

——(1995) *The Social Construction of Reality*, New York: Free Press.

Simon, H. (1985) "Human Nature in Politics: The Dialogue of Psychology with Political Science," *American Political Science Review* 79 (2).

Steuber, K. (2006) *Rediscovering Empathy: Agency, Folk Psychology, and the Human Sciences*, Cambridge, MA: MIT Press.

Strydom, P. (ed.) (2007) "Social Theory after the Cognitive Revolution: Types of Contemporary Cognitive Sociology," *European Journal of Social Theory* 10 (3): 339–496.

Taylor, C. (1985) *Human Agency and Language*, Cambridge: Cambridge University Press.

Thiele, L.P. (2006) *The Heart of Judgment: Political Wisdom, Neuroscience, and Narrative*, Cambridge: Cambridge University Press.

Turner, M. (2001) *Cognitive Dimensions of Social Science: The Way We Think About Politics, Economics, Law, and Society*, New York: Oxford University Press.

Turner, S. (1994) *The Social Theory of Practices: Tradition, Tacit Knowledge, and Presuppositions*, Chicago, IL: University of Chicago Press.

——(2001) *Brains/Practices/Relativism: Social Theory after Cognitive Science*, Chicago, IL: University of Chicago Press.

Wilson, E.A. (1998) *Neural Geographies: Feminism and the Microstructure of Cognition*, London: Routledge.

Wilson, R.A. and Keil, F.C. (eds) (1999) *Encyclopedia of the Cognitive Sciences*, Cambridge, MA: MIT Press.

Wittgenstein, L. (1967) *Zettel*, Berkeley, CA: University of California Press.

——(1993) *Philosophical Occasions: 1912–1951*, Indianapolis: Hackett, 133.

——(2001) *Philosophical Investigations*, Oxford: Blackwell, 355, 337.

Feminist Border Thought

Elena Ruiz-Aho

In Latin America, one of the ways in which Amerindian and *mestizo* (mixed-race) peoples have come to experience themselves as marginalized, both in their concrete public dealings and in history, concerns the ways in which the interpretive traditions of their indigenous communities have been covered-over and forced into concealment by European colonialism. In this regard, one of the greatest impacts of colonization has been a sense of inarticulacy (or discursive limitation) due to the loss of prior social contexts and the interpretive alternatives they made possible, particularly with regard to conceptions of selfhood and cultural identity. This is especially important given that, as colonialism introduced new gendered, ethnic, and racial categories not native to Mesoamerica (Quijano and Wallerstein 1992; Quijano 2000; Lugones 2007), it simultaneously instituted exclusionary practices on the basis of those categories. The need to theorize identity based on new social, historical, and epistemic realities thus marks the starting point of Latin American social and cultural theory in general (Sarmiento 1946; Vasconcelos 1948; Zea 1953; Paz 1961; Mariátegui 1971; Kusch 1973; Retamar 1974).

In the 1980s, the emergence of neoliberal economic policies, hyperinflation, increased migration of Latin Americans into the U.S., along with the shifting paradigms of globalization, resulted in a need to develop cultural analyses that took these new circumstances into account. The discourse of 'hybridity' came into being as a way to theorize the complex constellation of these factors in Latin American culture (Canclini 1995 [1989]). More specifically, the term was originally used by Argentine-born cultural anthropologist Néstor García Canclini as an explanatory paradigm for social processes and identity formations in Latin American culture that reflected 'more modern forms of cross-cultural contact' than the racial mixture of European colonization (thereby absorbing the older paradigms of 'mestizaje' or cultural 'syncretism' within hybrid discourses) (Canclini 1995: xxxii).

More recently, however, the discourses of modernity that gave rise to models of hybridity in the social sciences – and the hyphenated, transnational identities they helped theorize – have once again undergone significant shifts. As Linda Martín Alcoff and Mariana Ortega argue in *Constructing The Nation* (2009), in the twenty-first century, the post-9/11 geopolitical realignment of ethnic territories and the rhetorical construction of national identity based on the concept of 'homelands' have brought new issues into the mix (1–12). Among these are the pressing concerns of racial prejudice, anti-immigrant sentiment, and the privileging of identities based on cultural and linguistic assimilation into the dominant North American, U.S. culture. As a result of this shift, social and political life becomes characterized by the *exclusion* of difference in the name of abstract universals like freedom, steadfastness and unity, rather than the inclusion of plural, multicultural identities and social perspectives (Anzaldúa 2009b: 308). One place this tension is particularly visible, moreover, is at the borderland regions between the U.S. and Mexico (Gracía 2010).

Given these developments, it is not surprising that in recent years a new turn has also taken place in Latin American social theory, this time towards *pensamiento fronterizo*, or 'border thought'. Border thinking can be very broadly understood as a socio-political perspective or organizing concept around which complex narratives of displacement associated with multi-ethnic identity, migratory life, and multicultural citizenship can be theorized. It not only emerges from academic discourses of formally trained social scientists but from the cultural and artistic production of multicultural women of color, as well as from 'the critical reflections of (undocumented) immigrants, migrants, bracero/a workers, refugees, campesinos, women, and children on the major structures of dominance of our times' (Saldívar 2006: 152). In this chapter I will introduce this emerging field of research by way of the borderland theories of 'U.S. Third-World feminists' (Anzaldúa and Moraga 1981; Sandoval 1991), or what I call 'feminist border thought' (*pensamiento fronterizo feminista*). I do so, both as a way to cast emphasis on the complex intersections of race, gender, and ethnicity that are so central to contemporary discourses of citizenship and rhetorical constructions of national identity, as well as to shed light on the remarkable reach of influence border feminisms are experiencing across a broad range of disciplines today. Although she is by no means the sole or even principal architect of this field, the work of Gloria Anzaldúa (1942–2004) stands out in particular for its widespread critical acclaim and interdisciplinary reception. For this reason, it will serve as the primary example in this chapter.

Border Thought vs Border Feminisms

It is important to differentiate Anzaldúa's feminist border thought from Walter Mignolo's influential analysis of the 'modern/colonial world system' as producing new forms of knowledge that call for 'border thinking' or 'border gnosis' (2000: 9, 11). Although not mutually exclusive to each other (Mignolo, for example, often draws on Anzaldúa's work to help dismantle Eurocentric knowledges or practices), the two branches of thought are informed by different intellectual traditions and by different methodological approaches to the problem of colonization. While both can be seen as pursuing a 'decolonizing' agenda, Mignolo's program is primarily responsive to the problem of Eurocentrism in modern thought, as well as to lacunae left in Anglophone postcolonial theory (or occidental thought) with respect to Latin America (Said 1978). For this reason, Mignolo advances a form of, what he calls, '*post*-occidental reason' (2000: 91) with the basic aim of 'decentering theoretical practices' through 'the politics of geohistorical locations', meaning by taking into account the specificities of regions (like Latin America and the Caribbean) that, due to European colonialism, are historically marked by a convergence of knowledge/power systems at all levels of culture (107; Foucault 1980).

Because modern capitalism has only intensified the relations set up by colonialism, the goal, for Mignolo, is to produce a more perspectival standpoint epistemology (or 'pluritopical hermeneutics') based on one's position outside, or at the border of, what the Peruvian sociologist Anibal Quijano calls 'the modern/colonial world system' (Quijano and Wallerstein 1992; Mignolo 2003 [1995]:11, 2000: 52). Although dynamic in its range and pluralized through its use of Quijano's notion of 'the colonial difference', the primary model by which Mignolo understands 'border thought' remains rooted in the conceptual framework of world-system analysis (2000: 18, 2006; Wallerstein 1974; Wallerstein and Hopkins1982). Through groundbreaking empirical research programs on Mesoamerican literary practices and subaltern knowledges (Mignolo 2003 [1995]), Mignolo's project can thus be seen as an applied effort towards epistemic decolonization, one that is methodologically grounded on the peripheral locations of marginalized social actors and world-views. In this respect, it is a scholarly effort to bring the anti-colonial theoretical successes of South Asian Subaltern Studies to Latin America (see Rodríguez 2001).

By contrast, feminist border thought originated in Mexican-American (or Chicano/a) involvement in the U.S. progressive social movements of the 1960s (Sandoval 1980; Segura and Pasquera 1992; Gracía 1997; Hurtado 1998), has strong roots in social activism, and is primarily concerned with articulating the complex workings of intersectional oppressions such as race, class, gender, and ethnicity on women of color.

Unlike their counterparts in the Anglophone feminist movement or the African-American civil rights movement, the difference lies in that Chicanas' identities were inscribed with added layers of differences that further marginalized them within these movements, and in society at large. These included their legal or immigration status, indigenous heritage, spiritual practice, or language (whether it was heavily accented English, Spanish, Spanglish, Tex-Mex, or a hybrid of all these infused with indigenous dialects). Because of these layered differences, Chicanas not only faced class and raced-based discrimination, but also suffered a continual erasure or muting of their voices, regardless of which group identities and affiliations they attempted to organize around. Even in their own communities, where sexist, paternalist, and machistic attitudes prevailed, their status as women or lesbians threatened their ability to feel fully integrated or 'at home' in any one place.

For these reasons border feminism emerged out of a particular social context favorable to the development of what W.E.B. Du Bois called 'double consciousness' (1983 [1903]), only in their case it was a tripled, even quadrupled (or in Anzaldúa's case, as Chicana lesbian woman of color with a disability, quintupled) consciousness.[1] Chicana writers' positionality in multiple cultural and social realities enabled them to shift perspectives more easily and to ground their methodologies on destabilizing practices, that is to say, by persistently 'finding absences and exclusions and arguing from that standpoint' (Hurtado 1998: 135).

But Chicanas' multiple perspectives also meant that their lived-experiences were particularly difficult to theorize, as they often fell outside the dominant cultural constructions of selfhood or normative identity. In this regard, through their landmark anthology, *This Bridge Called My Back: Writings by Radical Women of Color* (1981), Gloria Anzaldúa and Cherríe Moraga began taking steps towards a more robust articulation of the unique experiences that arise out of multicultural life, and to develop context-dependent tactics for successful coping in the absence of social, institutional, and cultural inclusion. In its wake, border feminists began not one, but a series of conversations and overlapping political, literary, scholarly, and artistic movements that together constitute Chicana literary, academic, and artistic production since the 1980s. (See Moraga 1983; Anzaldúa 1987; Alarcón 1990; Hurtado 1996; Gracía 1997; Sandoval 2000; Saldívar-Hull 2000; Cantú and Nájiera-Ramirez 2002.) Arguably, the most significant publication to arise from this vibrant cultural production has been Gloria Anzaldúa's *Borderlands/La Frontera* (1987).

Confronting Contradictions: Anzaldúa's *Borderlands/La Frontera*

According to Anzaldúa, postcolonial life in general, and borderland life in particular, give rise to a unique set of contradictory cultural experiences that result from inhabiting multiple yet conflicting frames of reference. In her most celebrated work, *Borderlands /La Frontera* (1987) Anzaldúa gives a first-hand account of how being 'a border woman' can result in heavy costs, both to one's sense of self and political agency, as the experience of being caught between multiple cultural norms and standards (or 'worlds') makes it very difficult to effectively address the numerous oppressions that affect one's life.

For Anzaldúa, borderlands exist 'whenever two or more cultures edge each other, where people of different races occupy the same territory' (1987: preface). However, because she uses this term in two ways that often overlap, they are easily and often confused. On her account, borderlands are concrete, geospatial, cultural, and political formations that define territories, such as the physical border separating the United States and Mexico. But in a wider sense, they are also psychic spaces that develop out of an experience of exclusion or marginality, from being outside a cultural norm or dominant cultural formation. A borderland is, on this alternate use of the term, 'a vague and undetermined place created by the emotional residue of an unnatural boundary' that is constantly changing due to challenges from both sides of the exclusion (25).[2]

As a psychological state, the experience of borderlands is endemic to what she calls 'los atravesados,' as in those who continually 'cross-over' or transgress the boundaries of proscribed normative identities in culture, like gays and lesbians or the illegal alien. Because this category can apply to such a wide range of social groups and actors across cultures, including those unaffected by the markers of race or ethnicity, it should not be lost that Anzaldúa's formulation of the borderlands arises out a specific need to theorize the complex experiences of women of color living in the wake of Spanish colonization. Thus, as Anzaldúa describes, 'to live in the Borderlands means you are neither *hispana india negra española ni gabacha, eres mestiza, mulata,* half-breed caught in the crossfire between camps/ while carrying all five races on your back' – an image of which she is painfully reminded by living at the edge of the U.S.– Mexico border (216). It is through this context-specific lens that she writes *Borderlands*.

Borderlands is a hybrid text, a 'mosaic' of genres (poetry, history, testimony, creative non-fiction) that, in its polyphonic structure, is also an allusion towards the assumptions of a unified, stable self that Anzaldúa tries to dismantle throughout her writings. Continually shifting in and out of English, Spanish, and Nahuatl (a native Amerindian language), she begins by tracing the history of the southwestern United Sates and the creation of the Chicano people as an artificial political category rooted in imperialism and social prejudice. The 1848 Treaty of Guadalupe Hidalgo that ended U.S. occupation of Mexican territories, for example, resulted in more than the loss of over half of Mexico's lands (through the annexation of what is now Texas, Arizona, New Mexico, Colorado, and California); beyond the loss of physical terrains, it left Mexicans and indigenous peoples residing in these areas (now Mexican-Americans, or 'Chicanos') with a government, national language, and culture that was not their own (28–9). Because this is a general outcome whenever political borders are redrawn, Anzaldúa is careful to also chronicle the racial rhetoric and discursive strategies used in the justification of western expansion in the U.S. (28–35).

As Anzaldúa argues, the history of Chicano cultural identity is further complicated by the fact that this political remapping of homelands was not a first, but second conquest. It followed sixteenth-century Spanish colonization of Mesoamerican Aztlán, out of which the new racial mixture of Indian and Spanish blood, the *mestizo*, or *mexicano*, was created (27). Because, as earlier suggested, Spanish colonialism introduced new categories of racial purity and hierarchical social systems based on these categories, Chicanos faced the difficult experience of being multicultural in a social context where certain aspects of one's identity were seen as inferior, not only in relation to Spanish, but now also Anglo-American cultural norms and standards:

> Cradled in one culture, sandwiched between two cultures, straddling all three cultures and their value systems, *la mestiza* undergoes a struggle of flesh, a struggle of borders, an inner war. Like all people, we perceive the version of reality that our culture communicates. Like

others having or living in more than one culture, we get multiple, often opposing messages. The coming together of two self-consistent but habitually incompatible frames of reference causes *un choque*, a cultural collision (100).

This multicultural 'struggle of borders' is especially pernicious for women given that colonization was also 'a twofold process of racial infeiorization *and* gender subordination' (Oyewume 1997: 124), a type of double oppression that has, historically, been neglected in favor of national-populist constructions of the oppressed subject (as in the collectivity, *el pueblo*) in anti-colonial movements (Schutte 1993). Gender, in this regard, adds a unique layer of epistemic violence or oppression multicultural subjects such as Anzaldúa face, so that 'alienated from her mother culture, alien in the dominant culture, the woman of color does not feel safe within the inner life of her Self' (1987: 42).

Because the dominant Western philosophic and humanist paradigms for understanding selfhood in the modern era have relied on a conception of the self that is unified, stable, coherent, and whose inner workings as a rational mind can be made transparent through introspective reflexivity, subjects whose lived-experience is structured by flux, change, and cultural discontinuity have a sense of selfhood that does not map on to, or 'feel safe' within these dominant frameworks. In fact, the multicultural subject herself feels muted by these frameworks because they do not account for her sense of ruptured subjectivity that comes as a result of being straddled in multipe, yet asymmetrically valued cultural contexts (such as the Anglo, the Mexican, and the Indigenous). It is this constant clash of differently-positioned cultural norms that make lived-experience painful for postcolonial subjects because one is never fully able to engage tacitly or pre-reflectively with one's own worldly context, having to stop frequently to negotiate the various social standards encountered though everyday activities (Ortega 2001).

Moreover, this loss of narrative continuity in the experience of selfhood means that, to maneuver in different cultural contexts (whether successfully or not) one often has to frequently shift states, thus suffering from a form of 'psychic restlessness' (78) or psychological exertion. In this regard, the experience of being multicultural in the sense described here is homologous to border-line states of consciousness, where one is neither neatly situated in one state nor the other, but rather finds oneself 'caught between *lost intersticios*, the spaces between the different worlds' one is forced to inhabit due to legacies of conquest and imperialism (42).

The problem, from a political perspective, is that this new hybrid, multicultural self has the added burden of reconciling different strands of one's identity at the same time she is forced to address pressing issues of oppression and social violence, which generally require one to speak, make claims, or advocate for particular interests or on a group's behalf. To put it simply, in contexts of domination, 'we need to voice our needs' (Anzaldúa 1987: 107). This is particularly difficult, as Anzaldúa herself suggests, if one's voice is constantly under erasure, or if the normative categories in which social and political demands are publicly articulated do not accommodate certain realities or experiences of oppression.

The task, then, is to produce bodies of work that can speak to the complex, multiplicitous experiences that emerge from borderland life, forming what Cherrie Moraga aptly calls a 'theory in the flesh' (1981: 23). This theme of finding (or creating new) resources of expression for giving voice to lived-experience runs through all of Anzaldúa's writings, whether it takes the form of phenomenological descriptions, fictional narratives, children's stories, poetry, drawings, or theoretical constructs:

> We need *teorías* that will enable us to interpret what happens in the world ... Necesitamos teorías that will rewrite history using race, class, gender, and ethnicity as categories of analysis,

theories that cross borders, blur boundaries … And we need practical applications for those theories. We need to de-academize theory and to connect community to the academy.

(Anzaldúa 1990: xxv)

To this end, many of the concepts used to rethink difference and identity in *Borderlands* have had a profound impact on contemporary feminism and gender studies, as well as in applied contexts of coalition work and grassroots organizing (Saldívar-Hull 2000, 2006; Alarcón 2002; Castillo and Córdoba 2002; González 2003; Barcinski and Kalia 2005; Segura and Zavella 2008; Falcón 2008; Blackwell 2010).

The first of these is the notion of the 'New Mestiza,' which, simply put, formally posits a need for new conceptions of gender and race (*mestizaje*) that can accommodate the unique lived experience of multicultural, postcolonial subjects like Anzaldúa. Thus, in her view, 'the *new mestiza* is a liminal subject who lives in the borderlands between cultures, races, languages, and genders' but is not totally incapacitated or silenced by this complex positioning: 'in this state of in-between-ness' the new mestiza can also 'mediate, translate, negotiate, and navigate these different locations' (Anzaldúa 2009b: 209). Although the force of this concept seems to be merely descriptive, it rests on the insight that social and political liberation will require the preparatory act of visualizing that liberation, of concretely conceiving the possibilities for transforming 'living in the Borderlands from a nightmare into a numinous experience' (Anzaldúa 1987: 73).

This is important because the barriers that stand in the way of such liberation are often significant when considering the historical contexts in which borderland women of color theorize. Anzaldúa, for example, is very aware that in order to decolonize, the postcolonial subject is faced with the daunting task of mobilizing projects of liberation against Anglo-Eurocentric and colonial thinking using the very language which originally constrained one – a problem which has been powerfully articulated by Audre Lorde's concern of whether 'the master's tools' can ever 'dismantle the master's house' (1981: 98).

One possible remedy, as Anzaldúa sees it, is to try and decolonize the tools and categories by which one comes to understand and describe one's lived-experience in the first place. Anzaldúa pursues this strategy but with a heavy emphasis on still being able to communicate with the dominant culture in order to voice one's needs, as well as to build bridges and pathways for solidarity with other marginalized groups and social actors. In this sense, a powerful strategy for postcolonial 'theorists-of-color' is to formulate 'marginal theories that are partially outside and partially inside the Western frame of reference' (Anzaldúa 1990: xxvi). Anzaldúa contributes to this effort by creatively deploying pre-Colombian, indigenous thought and imagery at the same time that she pursues social and political projects rooted in the liberal, Western-democratic frameworks of inclusion, social justice, freedom, and emancipation.

It is in the service of this liberational, inclusive, *mestiza* politics that Anzaldúa formulates several of her most important theories. Alongside the 'New Mestiza', these concepts include 'autohistoria-teoría', 'El Mundo Zurdo', 'Nepantilism' (or 'Nepantla'), 'mestiza consciousness', the 'Cuatlicue state', 'La Facultad', the 'Coyolxauhqui imperative', 'conocimiento', and, in her later writings, 'Nos/Otras', 'spiritual activism', and 'new tribalism'. Although many of these theories are interrelated, they have often been received in ways that do not reflect this linkage (Keating 2006). Thus, without severing them from one another, two of the most influential concepts to come out of *Borderlands* (along with the 'New Mestiza') are 'nepantla' and 'mestiza consciousness'.

The word *nepantla* is a Nahuatl word signifying a type of process or activity that palaces things between categories, a type of 'middling' or 'thirding' quality that rests on native

Mesoamerican principles of ambiguity, reciprocity, and change (Maffie 2007). Anzaldúa uses the term 'mental nepantlism' to describe the sense of being caught in between cultures rather than within them (1987: 100). Henceforth, she uses 'nepantla' to 'theorize liminality' in such a way that she is able 'to shift from one world to another' with a bit more ease (2009d: 248). Through 'nepantla', old epistemic frameworks are called into question, particularly those that depend on exclusionary dualisms for the construction of identity, and which make thinking about being 'middled' or simultaneously situated in multiple cultural realities very difficult.

This is related to what Anzaldúa calls 'mestiza consciousness' (1987: 102). In Anzaldúa's view, 'uprooting dualistic thinking' (80) is one of the most important tasks of mestiza consciousness, especially for removing some of the harmful weight of Anglo-Eurocentric thought and social practices on the lives of postcolonial women.

Take the experience of gender, for example. In *Ancient Maya Gender Identity and Relations*, Karen Bassie-Sweet describes how, 'in the male/female principle, a human being was considered to be both male and female, with the right side of the body male and the left side female' – a concept which can be found throughout Mesoamerica and in Uto-Aztecan cultures such as the Hopi Indians (2002: 169; Williams 1986; Allen 1992). This is continuous with anthropological accounts of balanced oppositions and reciprocal dualisms in pre-Columbian thought (Maffie 2007). Now, consider Anzaldúa's assertion that 'what we are suffering from is an absolute despot duality that says we are able to be only one or the other,' either male or female but not both (1987: 41).

As a lesbian woman, when growing up, Anzaldúa suffered deep prejudices and alienation form her own community on account of her sexuality. 'The people of Hargill, in south Texas,' she comments, 'believed that if you were a lesbian, you were a woman for six months of the year and had periods, and for the other six months, you were a man and had a penis' (Anzaldúa 2009c: 90). It would seem to be the case that, given the apparent continuation and resilience of (at least some aspects of) the male/female principle, so-called 'half and halfs' would not be normatively devalued to the extent that Anzaldúa recounts.

But when we recall that European colonialism imported a system of *exclusionary* logic (which would include the laws of identity and non-contradiction) that was reinforced through, among other things, gendered articles (in Spanish) and subject-predicate grammar, we see that for beings caught 'between and betwixt' these categories, the resources of expression necessary to describe and do justice to such experience are no longer at arm's length.

Instead, due to the logical rules built into the language we use to describe experience, what falls outside these categories or cannot be assimilated through them becomes devalued as Other, as outside the norm. Thus, we see here a vivid example of the internal clashes, the 'choque' Anzaldúa talks about when referring to the multiple, but *asymentrical* contexts of reference borderland subjects must inhabit, and which often lead to experiences of being 'an outsider' at multiple levels – of being 'always the outside of the outside of the outside' (Anzaldúa 2009c: 90).

'Mestiza consciousness' can, in this respect, be a powerful tool of analysis for thinking through the 'subject-object dualisms' that keep the mestiza woman of color 'a prisoner' with regard to possibilities for understanding and conceptualizing identity (Anzaldúa 1987: 102).

Finally, the criticisms that have arisen in response to *Borderlands* center on possible essentializing tendencies of border women's experiences and Anzaldúa's idealized renditions of pre-Colombian, indigenous deities (Yarbro-Bejarano 1994). With regard to the latter, in the absence of a thick background of pre-conquest Amerindian cultural norms and practices to situate native Nahuatl concepts in more appropriate, context-dependent ways, Anzaldúa makes strategic use of indigenous images and metaphors; in this way she combats what she sees as marginalizing and oppressive Anglo-European cultural practices, and can be read as an example of what Spivak calls 'strategic essentialism' (Anzaldúa 1987: 205). The resources of expression available to postcolonial women of color like Anzaldúa must therefore be considered in the context of the 'extraordinary *possibilities* wiped out by' colonialism (Césaire 2000: 43).

Wirth regard to the charge of essentializing experience, although Anzaldúa, by her own account, attempts to theorize 'the unarticulated dimensions of the experience of mestizas living in between overlapping and layered spaces of different cultures' (2000: 176), she insists that her methodology is grounded in the phenomenological insights of her own concrete, bodily lived-experience (Anzaldúa 2002). In this sense, she limits her discourse by producing vivid descriptions of everyday life and complex experience which other mestizas may (or may not) relate to; in either case, what she offers the mesitza is a new vision for understanding her identity as plural and multiplicitous, while also postulating concrete strategies for building her own pathways for change.

Future Directions: Conclusion

At the moment, Anzaldúan cultural theory is experiencing a surge in interest across a wide array of fields. These range from well-known areas of influence such as Chicano, feminist, LGBT, and ethnic studies, where her works have been included in over 100 anthologies (Keating 2006), to now (more general) areas such as political science (Burke 1999), anthropology (Behar 1993), social psychology (Ayala and Torre 2009), sociology (Lamont and Molnár 2002; Martinez 2005), philosophy (Ortega 2001, 2008), and theology (Grant 2010), to name only a few. One particular developing topic that is of interest for social scientists in general is the use of Anzaldúa's theories of multiplicitous subjectivity and multiethnic cultural identity to recast notions of cosmopolitanism and (Will Kymlicka's notion of) multicultural citizenship (Burke1999, 2004).

As a leading figure in what I have here called *pensamiento fronterizo feminista*, or feminist border thought, Anzaldúa's influence on contemporary discourses of cultural diversity, citizenship studies, identity politics, and minority studies should grow even further in the coming years, particularly on account of the post-9/11 historical realities facing ethnic groups and immigrants in the U.S. and abroad. As it does, one should keep in mind both the specific context in which her theories emerged as well as the latticed network of Chicana and Latina feminisms that helped initiate, sustain, and disseminate the discourse of 'borderlands' that her work (along with Mignolo's) is now beginning to make mainstream. The danger, it should be noted, is in abstracting the border-crossing experience of the mestiza the point of covering over the differences marked by its specificity and original context of use (Yarbro-Bejarano 1994). If one keeps this in mind, it is possible to see how 'Anzaldúa's theories have much to offer social scientists – especially those scholars interested in combining cutting-edge theory with social justice' (Keating 2006: 7).

As a socio-political theory that articulates the barriers towards inclusiveness and recognition of cultural differences in multiethnic societies, feminist border thought can be seen as an emerging paradigm for understanding and revising disciplinary discussions that center on identity-based issues such as class, race, gender, and ethnicity, as well as for formulating new methods of cultural analysis that can respond to the complex needs of cultural and ethnic minorities in multicultural democracies.

Notes

1 Along with suffering from diabetes and life-long chronic pain, Anzaldúa was also born with a rare hormonal imbalance that resulted in 'precocious menses,' or the onset of puberty at the age of six. Her first period was at only 3 months of age (Anzaldúa 2000: 34).

2 One way to spot the difference is by noting the case used in the word, whether it is a capital 'B' or lower case 'b'. With vey few exceptions, the lower-case use corresponds to the physical state of a geographic borderland, while the other corresponds to the psychic domain.

References

Alarcón, N. (1990) 'Chicana Feminism: In the Tracks of "the" Native Woman', *Cultural Studies*, 4(3): 248–55.

——(2002)'Anzaldúa's Frontera: Inscribing Gynetics', in A. Aldama and N. Quiñonez (eds) *Decolonial Voices: Chicana and Chicano Cultural Studies in the 21st Century*, Bloomington, IN: Indiana University Press, 113–26.

Alcoff, L.M. and Ortega, M. (eds)(2009) *Constructing the Nation: A Race and Nationalism Reader*, Albany, NY: SUNY Press.

Allen, P.G. (1992) *The Sacred Hoop: Recovering the Feminine in American Indian Traditions*, Boston, MA: Beacon Press.

Anzaldúa, G. (1987) *Borderlands/La Frontera: The New Mestiza*, San Francisco, CA: Aunt Lute.

——(ed.)(1990) *Making Face, Making Soul / Haciendo Caras: Creative and Critical Perspectives by Feminists of Color*, San Francisco, CA: Aunt Lute Books.

——(2000) *Interviews/Entrevistas*, A.L. Keating (ed.), New York: Routledge.

——(2002) 'Now Let Us Shift', in A.L. Keating (ed.) *This Bridge We Call Home: Radical Visions for Transformation*, New York: Routledge, 540–78.

——(2009a [1992]) 'The New Mestiza Nation: A Multicultural Movement', in A.L. Keating (ed.) *The Gloria Anzaldúa Reader*, Durham, NC: Duke University Press, 203–16.

——(2009b [2002]) 'Let Us Be the Healing of the Wound: The Coyolxauhqui Imperative/ La Sombra y el Sueño', in A. L. Keating (ed.) *The Gloria Anzaldúa Reader*, Durham, NC: Duke University Press, 303–17.

——(2009c [1983]) 'Spirituality, Sexuality, and the Body: An Interview with Linda Smuckler', in A. L. Keating (ed.) *The Gloria Anzaldúa Reader*, Durham, NC: Duke University Press, 74–94.

——(2009d [2002]) '(Un)natural Bridges, (Un)safe Spaces', in A. L. Keating (ed.) *The Gloria Anzaldúa Reader*, Durham, NC: Duke University Press, 243–8.

Anzaldúa, G. and Moraga, C. (eds)(1981) *This Bridge Called My Back: Writings by Radical Women of Color*, Watertown, MA: Persephone Press.

Ayala, J. and Torre, M.E. (2009) 'Envisioning Participatory Action Research Entremundos', *Feminism & Psychology*, 19(3): 387–93.

Barcinski, M. and Kalia, Y. (2005) 'Extending the Boundaries of the Dialogical Self: Speaking from within the Feminist Perspective', *Culture and Psychology*, 11(1): 101–9.

Bassie-Sweet, K. (2002) 'Corn Deities and the Male/Female Principle', in L. Gustafson and A. Trevelyan (eds) *Ancient Maya Gender Identity and Relations*, Westport, CT, and London: Bergin & Garvey, 169–90.

Behar, R. (1993) 'Expanding the Boundaries of Anthropology: The Cultural Criticism of Gloria Anzaldúa and Marlon Riggs', *Visual Anthropology Review*, 9(2): 83–91.

Blackwell, M. (2010) 'Líderes Campesinas: Nepantla Strategies and Grassroots Organizing at the Intersection of Gender and Globalization', *Aztlán*, 35(1): 13–47.

Burke, J.F. (1999) 'Reconciling Cultural Diversity with a Democratic Community', *Citizenship Studies*, 3(1): 119–40.

——(2004) *Mestizo Democracy: The Politics of Crossing Borders*, College Station, TX: Texas A & M Press.

Canclini, N.G. (1995 [1989]) *Hybrid Cultures: Strategies of Entering and Leaving Modernity*, Minneapolis, MN: University of Minnesota Press.

Cantú, N. and Nájiera-Ramírez, O. (eds) (2002) *Chicana Traditions: Continuity and Change*, Urbana, IL: University of Illinois Press.

Castillo, D. and Córdoba, M.S.T. (eds) (2002) *Border Women: Writing from La Frontera*, Minneapolis, MN: University of Minnesota Press.

Césaire, A. (2000 [1955]) *Discourse on Colonialism*, New York: Monthly Review Press.

Du Bois, W.E.B. (1983 [1903]) *The Souls of Black Folk*, New York: Penguin.

Falcón, S. (2008) 'Mestiza Double Consciousness: The Voices of Afro-Peruvian Women on Gendered Racism', *Gender and Society*, 22(5): 660–80.

Foucault, M. (1980) *Power/Knowledge: Selected Interviews and Other Writings, 1972–1977*, New York: Pantheon.

González, D.J. (2003) 'Gender on the Borderlands: Re-textualizing the Classics', *Frontiers: A Journal of Women Studies*, 24(2): 15–29.

Gracía, A. (ed.) (1997) *Chicana Feminist Thought: The Basic Historical Writings*, New York: Routledge.

Gracía, M.T. (2010) 'La Frontera: The Border as Symbol and Reality in Mexican-American Thought', in I. Stavans (ed.) *Border Culture*, Santa Barbara, CA: Greenwood Press, 3–26.

Grant, K. (2010) 'Living in the Borderlands: An Identity and a Proposal', *Dialog: A Journal of Theology*, 49(1): 26–33.

Hurtado, A. (1996) *The Color of Privilege: Three Blasphemies on Race and Feminism*, Ann Arbor, MI: Michigan University Press.

——(1998) 'Sitios y Lenguas: Chicanas Theorize Feminisms', *Hypatia*, 13(2): 134–61.

Keating, A.L. (2006) 'From Borderlands and New Mestizas to Nepantlas and Nepantleras: Anzaldúan Theories for Social Change', *Human Architecture: Journal of the Sociology of Self-Knowledge*, 4: 5–16.

Kusch, R. (1973) *El Pensamiento Indígenista y Popular en América*, Buenos Aires: Hachette.

Lamont, M. and Molnár, V. (2002) 'The Study of Boundaries in the Social Sciences', *Annual Review of Sociology*, 28: 167–95.

Lorde, A. (1981) 'The Mastern's Tools Will Never Dismantle the Master's House', in G. Anzaldúa and C. Moraga (eds) *This Bridge Called My Back: Writings by Radical Women of Color*, Watertown, MA: Persephone Press, 98–101.

Lugones, M.(2007) 'Heterosexualism and the Colonial/Modern Gender System', *Hypatia*, 22(1): 185–209.

Maffie, J. (2007) 'The Centrality of Nepantla in Conquest-Era Nahua Philosophy', *The Nahua Newsletter*, 44 (Nov.): 11–31.

Mariátegui, J.C. (1971) *Seven Interpretive Essays on Peruvian Reality*, Austin, TX: University of Texas Press.

Martinez, T.A. (2005) 'Making Oppositional Culture, Making Standpoint: A Journey into Gloria Anzaldúa's Borderlands', *Sociological Spectrum*, 25(5): 539–70.

Mignolo, W.D. (2000) *Local Histories/Global Design: Coloniality, Subaltern Knowledges, and Border Thinking*, Princeton, NJ: Princeton University Press.

——(2003 [1995]) *The Darker Side of the Renaissance: Literacy, Territoriality, and Coloniazation*, Ann Arbor, MI: University of Michigan Press.

——(2006) 'El Desprendimiento: Pensamiento Crítico y Giro Descolonial', in C. Walsh, W.D. Mignolo, and G. Linera (eds) *Interculturalidad, Descolonización del Estado y del Conocimiento*, Buenos Aires: Ediciones del Siglo, 9–20.

Moraga, C. (1981) 'Theory in the Flesh', in G. Anzaldúa and C. Moraga, C. (eds) *This Bridge Called My Back: Writings by Radical Women of Color*, Watertown, MA: Persephone Press.

——(1983) *Loving in the War Years/Lo que Nunca Paso Por Sus Labios*, Boston, MA: South End Press.

Ortega, M. (2001) ' "New Mestizas," "World-Travelers," and "Dasein": Phenomenology and the Multi-voice, Multi-cultural Self', *Hypatia*, 16(3): 1–29.

——(2008) 'Wounds of Self: Experience, Word, Image, and Identity', *Journal of Speculative Philosophy*, 22(4): 235–47.

Oyewumi, O. (1997) *The Invention of Women: Making an African Sense of Western Gender Discourses*, Minneapolis, MN: University of Minnesota Press.

Philosophy, Princeton, NJ: Princeton University Press, 116–36.

Paz, O. (1961 [1950]) *The Labyrinth of Solitude: Life and Thought in Mexico*, New York: Grove Press.

Quijano, A. (2000) 'Coloniality of Power, Eurocentrism, and Latin America', *Nepantla: Views from the South*, 1(3): 533–80.

Quijano, A. and Wallerstein, I. (1992) 'Americanity as a Concept, or the Americas in the Modern World-System', *International Journal of Social Science*, 134: 549–59.

Retamar, R.F. (1974) *Calíban: Apuntes Sobre la Cultura de Nuestra América*, Mexico D.F.: Diógenes.

Rodriguez, I. (ed.) (2001) *The Latin American Subaltern Studies Reader*, Durham, NC, and London: Duke University Press.

Said, E. (1979) *Orientalism*, New York: Vintage Books.

Saldívar, J.D. (2006) 'Border Thinking, Minoritized Studies, and Realist Interpellations: The Coloniality of Power from Gloira Anzaldúa to Arundhati Roy', in L. Alcoff, M. Hames-García, S. Mohanty, and P. Moya (eds) *Identity Politics Reconsidered*, New York: MacMillan, 152–70.

Saldívar-Hull, S. (ed.) (2000) *Feminism on the Border: Chicana Gender Politics and Literature*, Berkeley, CA: University of California Press.

Saldívar-Hull, S. (2006) 'Women Hollering: Transfronteriza Feminisms', in A. Chabram-Dernersesian (ed.) *The Chicana/o Cultural Studies Reader,* New York: Routledge, 448–57.

Sandoval, C. (1980) 'First Hispanic Feminist Conference Meets' *La Rázon Mestiza/Union Wage*, June 20–22: 1–6.

——(1991) 'U.S. Third World Feminism: Theory and Method of Oppositional Consciousness in the Postmodern World', *Genders*, 10 (Spring): 1–24.

——(2000) *Methodology of the Oppressed*, Minneapolis, MN: University of Minnesota Press.

Sarmiento, D.F. (1946) *Conflicto Y Armonía de las Razas en América*, Buenos Aires: Editorial Intermundo.

Schutte, O. (1993) *Cultural Identity and Social Liberation in Latin American Thought*, Albany, NY: SUNY.

359

Segura, D. and Pasquera, B. (1992) 'Beyond Indifference and Antipathy: The Chicana Movement and Chicana Feminist Discourse', *Aztlán*, 19(2): 69–93.

Segura, D. and Zavella, P. (2008) 'Gendered Borderlands', *Gender and Society*, 22(5): 537–44.

Vasconcelos, J. (1948) *La Raza Cósmica*, Mexico City: Espasa-Calpe Mexicana.

Wallerstein, I. (1974) *The Modern World-System I: Capitalist Agriculture and the Origins of the European World-Economy in the Sixteenth Century*, New York: Academic Press.

Wallerstein, I. and Hopkins, T. (1982) *World-Systems Analysis: Theory and Methodology*, Beverly Hills, CA: Sage.

Williams, W. (1986) *The Spirit and the Flesh*, Boston, MA: Beacon Press.

Yarbro-Bejarano, Y. (1994) 'Gloria Anzaldúa's Borderlands/La Frontera: Cultural Studies, Difference, and the Non-Unitary Subject', *Cultural Critique*, 28 (Fall): 5–28.

Zea, L. (1953) *América en la Historia*, Mexico City: UNAM.

Contemporary Chinese Social and Political Thought

Guanjun Wu

In the last three decades, Chinese intellectuality has developed new outlooks. It is very easy for one to tell that there is a radical break between the intellectuality of the Maoist time (1949–78) and that of the post-Maoist era (1978–the present). Indeed, one salient difference between the two periods is that the latter saw the rise of intellectuals as a leading group in Chinese society. Whereas it was the Party leadership that had previously set the tone of cultural and intellectual life, academics and independent scholars now guide the production of Chinese social and political thought. The post-Maoist intellectuality as it has developed since the 1980s is the object of critical examination in this chapter.[1]

The Socio-political Background of Contemporary Chinese Intellectuality

The intellectual activities of post-Maoist China have been observed and studied in diverse ways in both mainland Chinese and Western scholarship (for example, Xu Jilin *et al.* 2007; Davies 2007; Deng Zhenglai *et al.* 2008). A key feature of the post-Maoist era is the development of critical independence that enabled intellectual discourse to flourish after the strict ideological control of the Maoist era.

It can be said that the post-Maoist intellectual discussions on socio-political practices and theories were enabled by the sudden shift from the revolutionary doctrine of the Maoist era to Deng Xiaoping's post-Maoist paradigm of "modernization construction" – following Deng's seizure of power in 1978 from Mao's alleged chosen successor, Hua Guofeng. Deng's slogan that "practice is the sole criterion for evaluating truth" (*shijian shi jianyan zhenli de weiyi biaozhun*), along with his pragmatic, utilitarian approach towards socialism, provided Chinese thinkers with the political legitimacy to create new spaces for intellectual activities in the early to mid-1980s. To distinguish this new post-Maoist era from the Cultural Revolution (*wenhua da geming*, 1966–76), the 1980s came to be widely known in the state-owned media as the "new era" (*xin shiqi*).

Deng Xiaoping regarded science and education as the key to national development and Chinese intellectuals were keen to reflect this new direction in their discourse. The most important institutional change that occurred in 1977 was the reintroduction of nationwide college and university entrance examinations, after these examinations had been halted for almost a decade. In 1978, graduate schools were reopened. Most participants in the post-Maoist intellectual movement known as the "New Enlightenment movement" (*xin qimeng yundong*, which was also called *wenhua re*, the "Culture Fever") in the mid-to-late 1980s were beneficiaries of this policy of revitalizing high education. The discussions over "the humanistic spirit" and "postmodernism" in the mid-1990s, the debate between "liberalism" and the "New Left" in the late 1990s, the rise of "new Confucianism" in the 2000s, and so on, can be seen as further developments out of the New Enlightenment movement.

However, although intellectual independence was a key goal of the 1980s, the Chinese government maintained a careful ideological control. The Anti-Spiritual Pollution Campaign that lasted for three months between November 1983 and January 1984 reflected the effectiveness of state censorship over intellectual activities. Nonetheless, economic development also expanded the space for cultural expression and the development of a cultural marketplace in the 1980s resulted in the production of a large variety of journals, books, films, TV series as well as fee-paying courses of study conducted by independent groups of intellectuals.

The (re-)emergence of an intellectual sphere and the normalization of intellectual life in China in the mid-1980s is a product of the "complex process of transformations" China has undergone since Deng took power.[2] Regarding the new relationship between Chinese intellectuals and the state, it is also important to note that the new space for intellectual activities flourished in the 1980s because intellectuals were able once again to regard themselves as playing an important role in the work of government and in society. Though often employing various translated scholarly jargon from the discourses of Western humanities and social sciences in their writings, contemporary Chinese intellectuals, primarily the new generation of scholars who resumed their education in the late 1970s and entered graduate school, do not confine themselves to the academic realm. They also see themselves as leaders of social change who are engaged in producing a social blueprint for China's transformation. In this sense, with the resumption of higher education, the establishment of a cultural market, and some freedom of expression in post-Maoist China, many prominent intellectuals regard themselves as agents of social change. They portray their writings as works that are carrying out the task of solving "Chinese problems" (*Zhongguo wenti*) and guiding China's transformation.

As Gloria Davies points out, although there is an evident diversity in the intellectual discourse of post-Maoist China, with many intellectuals disagreeing with each other about what changes are needed, nonetheless the arguments on offer all "share one thing in common":

> They all point to the strength of the belief held by many Chinese intellectuals in the power of intellectual labor to shape and change social life. More specifically, this belief is informed by a certain assumption that the individual intellectual laborer is – within a post-Maoist idiom – the *zhe* (the "one") or *fenzi* (element) who can remake society by harvesting from the *jie* (fields) that he or she oversees the appropriate knowledge items to produce a social blueprint.
>
> *(Davies 2001: 3)*

Although it is produced largely by academics and graduate students, contemporary Chinese intellectual inquiry is nonetheless not purely academic discourse. Intellectual debates are, by the same token, much more than just an exchange of ideas. The ambition of producing a social blueprint is the larger task that Chinese intellectual discourse assumes. The topics of contemporary debates and discussions among Chinese scholars and intellectuals are therefore tightly intertwined with the ongoing socio-political changes of post-Maoist China.

The New Enlightenment Movement of the 1980s

During the 1980s Culture Fever, intellectual inquiry reflected a largely univocal style. This was why it was termed as the New Enlightenment movement. "May Fourth Enlightenment" was used as the model because this movement of the late 1910s and early 1920s was widely perceived as having a common anti-Confucian purpose. In the 1980s, however, it was Maoism (especially the radical ideas of the Cultural Revolution of the 1960s and 1970s) that was being opposed, not Confucianism. Hence, the various New Enlightenment intellectual projects were unified by a common anti-Maoist purpose.

The idea of "enlightening" China was, very often, synonymous with "modernizing" China in the 1980s New Enlightenment discourse. The project of China's modernization had two aspects. The Party-state's official campaign of "Four Modernizations" was accompanied by the campaign for "cultural modernization" proposed by the participants of the New Enlightenment movement. From the late 1970s onwards, the post-Mao Chinese Communist Party launched an official project of modernization (*xiandaihua jianshe*) which includes four aspects – the modernization of agriculture, industry, national defense, and science-technology. Having replaced Maoist socialist construction with modernizing China through market reform, the post-Maoist state allowed and encouraged Chinese intellectuals to pursue "cultural modernization" as well. In Chinese, the idea is regarded as complementary to the official campaign of the "Four Modernizations". Although there were many different proposals for modernization, these generally proceeded along one of two directions – either towards the goal of a fully Westernized culture, or towards the achievement of a "creative transition"[3] of traditional Chinese culture. Thus, despite their differences, New Enlightenment thinkers were still united under the same banner of "cultural modernization." Even though they differed with regard to the "imagined" content of "modern Chinese culture," they had this "shared belief" that through "(cultural) modernization" they could effectively improve the quality of the Chinese Thought and Life. The term "modernization" was the organizational theme of the New Enlightenment intellectual movement.

The appearance of "unity" allowed intellectuals to imagine that there was a "homogeneity of attitude"[4] among them. One can thus say that in the 1980s, the differences in terms of the "picture" of China's ultimate perfection among Chinese intellectuals was concealed by the ostensibly unified intellectual movement that called for an act to enlighten China's vision. Hence, an *ultimate truth* is presupposed by the intellectuals who identify with the New Enlightenment: they do not necessarily agree with each other about the actual content of this ultimate truth, but they *all* assume that there *is* an ultimate truth out there that will enable people to discover the answer to restoring China as a great civilization.

During the May Fourth era of the 1910s and 1920s, "Westernization" was one of the central proposals in order to regain China's greatness. In the 1980s, the project of modernization took its place. By describing the Maoist era as the obstacle to cultural modernization, the New Enlightenment discourse of the 1980s conforms to the official economic project of modernization to provide a new way of seeing China's historical past and the present-day reality using a new set of concepts (that are opposed to the revolutionary rhetoric of the Maoist era) such as "rationality", "industrialization", "market", "democracy", "science", "enlightenment", "human rights", and so on and so forth. The New Enlightenment discourse of the 1980s became known as "Culture Fever" because it elevated intellectuals to new social heights. In fact, it was also referred to as a "fever for intellectuals" (*zhishifenzi re*). By claiming that they were working to resolve the antagonism between socialism (China) and capitalism (the West) and that China's modernization would be realized through overcoming the obstacles of undesirable aspects of Chinese tradition, leading intellectuals in the New Enlightenment movement saw themselves as heroic figures who were working to discover the *ultimate truth* so that they might lead the nation towards a bright future.

The New Enlightenment intellectual movement was indeed socially and politically influential. In many scholars' view, the New Enlightenment intellectual movement of the 1980s not only led directly to the production of popular mass-media products such as the famous 1988 TV series *River Elegy*,[5] but also contributed to the emergence of the 1989 student movement and hence the June Fourth *Tiananmen* event. New Enlightenment intellectuals not only influenced students in their thinking and provided inspiration for the social movement, but became themselves involved in numerous demonstrations and protest activities. (See for example Chen Fong-ching 2001: 81–2.) The June Fourth incident – the killings in the streets of Beijing – was a traumatic event for most mainland intellectuals and halted the 1980s New Enlightenment movement. Some New Enlightenment thinkers such as Liu Xiaobo were severely punished by the authorities; others such as Bao Zunxin, Jin Guantao, Liu Qingfeng, and Gan Yang were fortunate enough to flee the mainland but were prevented from returning for many years. Most of them, however, visited China in the late 1990s. The intellectual discourses of the 1990s and 2000s that became known as "Post-New Enlightenment," featuring new concepts such as postmodernism, the "humanistic spirit", liberalism, the "New Left", "new nationalism", "new Confucianism", etc., can be also regarded as various intellectual attempts of coping with the trauma caused by state violence in 1989. The presumed "homogeneity of attitude" of the New Enlightenment could no longer be imagined in the post-*Tiananmen* intellectual world.

New Intellectual Developments after Tiananmen

After the 1989 purge of the *Tiananmen* student protest, the government-led modernization project lost its credibility in the intellectual circles. The optimistic 1980s imaginings of the imminent arrival of democracy collapsed. There was relative silence in the Chinese intellectual world from 1989 to 1992. This period of "aphasia" (*shiyu*), as it was subsequently called, is an indication that the passion with which intellectuals desired modernization in the 1980s was vaporized by their traumatic encounter with the violence of the Party-state. Since then the phrase *Tiananmen* (or "June Fourth") has become discussed by many Chinese intellectuals as the moment that modernization toward democracy turned out to be an illusion.

In the early 1990s, the control over intellectual writings was much tighter than in the late 1980s. Under such an ideological atmosphere, some participants of the New Enlightenment movement started to reflect upon the proximity of intellectual work to socio-political transformations which have been featured in New Enlightenment writings, and suggested a separation of scholarly works from "vacuous" (*kongshu*) proposals for socio-political change, and correspondingly that intellectuals should withdraw themselves from contemporary debates over China's path or China's problems and concentrate instead on the pursuit of scholastic research and the establishment of the system of "academic norms" (*xueshu guifan*), in order to "join rails" (*jiegui*) with the institutionally established model of Western intellectual inquiry. During the first few years of the 1990s, a series of scholastic journals was successively founded in mainland China. As this trend of professionalization of intellectual life was not a natural outcome of the development of Chinese intellectuality, it thus did not last very long.

After Deng Xiaoping's "Tour of the South" (*nanxun*) in 1992, intellectuals embraced a gradual loosening of political controls, and the space for expression was reestablished. Although the topic of "June Fourth" was banned, there were heated discussions and debates over topics related to "Chinese problems", China's reality and its perfection, and others such as the "loss of the humanistic spirit", "postmodernism", "globalization", and "liberalism". There was also a call for academic standardization, and some reacted to it by describing the tendency as weakening intellectual life. For instance, the prominent New Enlightenment thinker Li Zehou claimed that "thinkers fade out when academicians come to prominence" (*sixiangjia danchu, xuewenjia tuchu*). Especially, intellectuals who publicly identified themselves as "liberals" (*ziyouzhuyizhe*) or "liberal intellectuals" (*ziyou zhishifenzi*) in the late 1990s openly appealed for "bearing the torch of Enlightenment" and claimed that their intellectual endeavor was to carry on the unfinished project of Enlightenment and China's modernization.

The discussions over the "loss of the humanistic spirit" (*renwen jingshen de shiluo*), initiated by several Shanghai-based intellectuals in 1994, already manifested a strong reaction against academic professionalization, as well as the related current of cultural commercialization. As the Shanghai-based historian Xu Jilin remarked in a 2003 essay, this discussion signifies an attempt "to reestablish the publicness of the intellectual and to reassert the intellectual's responsibility for guiding society". (quoting from Davies 2007: 90). Thus, embedded deeply in the self-understanding of contemporary Chinese thinkers, is the notion that intellectual works are not just mere knowledge production that can be developed into an industry in an institutionalized academic marketplace, but are also burdened with the urgent task of finding proper solutions to China's problems and shedding a light on the picture of a better future for the Chinese people. It is this unique intellectual tradition running deep over centuries in China which highlights a moral dimension of intellectual works that held back any trend of "joining rails" with the professionalism featured in Western humanities and social sciences and thus from blossoming in the Chinese intellectual world. After this short debate over what Xu Jilin called "the rift between 'the engaged' and 'the academic'" had happened in the early 1990s, it is apparent that Chinese intellectual inquiry of the 1990s followed its own highly engaged tradition, though, after the "homogeneity of attitude" was out the picture, took a completely different outlook from that of the 1980s.

In post-*Tiananmen* China, the question of which path China should take became much more urgent, because to comply with the Party-state's establishment was seen in the Chinese intellectual sphere after 1989 as a shameful moral corruption.[6] The blood in the square made many participants of the New Enlightenment unable to keep their support to the official ideology of modernization. Quite a few intellectuals started to reflect the New Enlightenment project of China's modernization. For them the urgent questions were: Where will this ongoing "transformation" and official modernization campaign lead China to? What is the picture after China fully "modernizes" itself?

With this context, some intellectuals started to employ "postmodern" terms and jargons to depict the picture and claim an "end of modernity". In the view of Chinese postmodernists such as Zhang Yiwu and Chen Xiaoming, with the emergence of postmodern discourse in the Western intellectual world, the "myth of modernity has been deconstructed", and consequently, for Chinese intellectuals, "stepping out of 'modernity' means a new path of development and the emergence of a new cultural strategy" (Zhang Yiwu 2000 [1994]: 230). This "new cultural strategy" is the thriving popular commercial culture: the cultural and value shifts caused by commercialization, which quickly developed after Deng Xiaoping's statement "to get rich is glorious" unleashed a tidal wave of commercial euphoria in China, were depicted by those Chinese advocates of postmodernism as the emergence of a promising postmodern culture and the end of modernity; and they saw the emergence of postmodern culture as a "new path of development" (231).[7]

Also around the mid-1990s, many intellectuals sought to redefine modernization in much clearer and liberal-flavored terms, openly appealing for constitutional rule, representative democracy, and human rights.[8] For these Chinese liberals, the New Enlightenment failed because it focused too much on "cultural" modernization instead of *political* modernization. In other words, the New Enlightenment thinkers did not target CCP's authoritarian rule as the primary object of their critique. In 1999, ten years after the June Fourth event, the leading figure of Chinese liberal intellectuals, Li Shenzhi (1923–2003), who was a party official (Vice-President of the Chinese Academy of Social Sciences until 1989) and accompanied Deng Xiaoping on his visit to the U.S. serving as adviser to the delegation, even wrote a public letter to the General Secretary of CCP Jiang Zemin immediately after the grand ceremony at *Tiananmen* Square celebrating the fiftieth anniversary of the People's Republic, urging him to be a "clear-sighted man" (*mingbai ren*) and use his power to install parliamentary democracy in China, as well as to allow non-party owned newspapers and opposition political parties to form. (Li Shenzhi 1999).

Rising as opponents of Chinese liberals in the late 1990s, a group of intellectuals (some also active participants of the 1980s New Enlightenment movement) started to turn their attention to various contemporary leftist or Marxist discourses and suggested alternative paths to embracing and merging into today's capitalist-inflected globalization. These intellectuals, because they all held a critical attitude towards liberal-flavored modernization and appealed for noncapitalist reform, were labeled by their detractors as "New Leftists". In the historical and ideological context of mainland China, the term "New Leftist" implicates a compliance with Party theory, and thereby for those labeled by it, this term is associated with a strongly pejorative connotation. In order to avoid being simply discredited as a return to Maoist politics, some of those intellectuals such as the Beijing-based philosopher Wang Hui thus employed another term to refer to their group – "critical intellectuals" (*pipan de zhishifenzi*).

Labeled as a leading representative of China's "New Left", Wang Hui has been at the centre of intellectual debates since the late 1990s and began to gain international reputation in the 2000s. Part of his work has already been translated into English and published by prominent academic publishers (for example, Wang Hui 2006, 2010). Wang starts his intellectual project by criticizing the "New Enlightenment thinking".[9] He affirms that the New Enlightenment movement was once a critical discourse against Maoist ideology. However, with the rapid social change and the rise of Chinese capitalism in Deng's era, it started to lose its "critical potential" (*pipan qianneng*) and joined the chorus with the Party-state's official ideology (the socialist reforms). Thus the New Enlightenment discourse failed to function as a powerful critical voice in the post-*Tiananmen* context: it was incapable of providing a persuasive critique of the inter-related forces of the global capitalist market system and the "dictatorial state". More importantly, for Wang, the fundamental limitation of the New Enlightenment was its reliance on the tradition/ modernity dichotomy. He claims that this dichotomy framework handicapped New Enlightenment thinkers and confined them to thinking about "modernity" from a falsely universal (but actually Eurocentric and capitalist) perspective. In Wang's view, the post-Maoist language of New Enlightenment canceled out the uniqueness of China's approach to modernity, or "Chinese modernity". By emphasizing what he calls the "question of modernity". Wang attempts to challenge the liner narrative of modernization that liberal intellectuals have advocated since the 1980s New Enlightenment movement (Wang Hui 1998).

Wang's magnum opus, *The Rise of Modern Chinese Thought* (four volumes in total), appeared in 2004; its primary object is the search for the "seeds" of an alternative modernity in intellectual legacies of the "premodern" Chinese past, a "native modernity" rooted in China's traditional culture before it was polluted and shaped by "modern institutions". The presupposition of Wang's intellectual project is that the rich intellectual dynamics embedded in China's premodern thought that Western-style modernity arrogantly refuses can in fact open up radical possibilities, and thus be able to serve as intellectual resources in overcoming the crisis of modernity. For Wang, many moments in China's history of thought can provide resources for us to transcend the present Western model of modernity. The aim of Wang's *Rise* can be seen as an intellectual search for a new theoretical framework to present socio-political critique in an age when global capitalism is generally regarded as the only path (Wang Hui 2004). Though Wang's work may not impress his worldwide readers as a striking alternative project,[10] his lengthy historical elaboration of "Chinese modernity" nonetheless has successfully earned him an international reputation as a prominent leftist thinker from China.

In recent years, the economic rise of the People's Republic has brought a rapid resurgence of national pride at popular as well as intellectual levels. A new trend of "nationalism" emerged as a powerful discourse. Though post-Maoist Chinese intellectual inquiry, generally speaking, is structured around a strong nationalistic longing – a longing for the ultimate achievement of China's perfection – the term "nationalism" on the contemporary China intellectual scene refers specifically to a type of discourse that attributes the causes of contemporary "Chinese problems" solely to the bullies from the West (primarily the U.S. and Japan). Intellectuals who publicly identify themselves with "Chinese nationalists" generally hold a vehemently hostile attitude towards the 1980s New Enlightenment intellectual enterprise as well as the discourse of liberalism of the 1990s, and characteristically advocate the empowerment of China from the angle of military (instead of cultural or political) modernization. Many extremely violent and vulgar expressions can be found in this trend of what Peter Gries terms "China's new nationalism" (Gries 2004). This trend of nationalist discourse has also triggered social events such as the large-scale anti-foreign demonstrations of the last decade, among which the 1999 anti-U.S. demonstrations in Beijing and the 2005 anti-Japanese demonstrations in over twenty major cities of mainland China are the most salient.

In parallel to this rather vulgar trend of "new nationalism", there also emerged an "elite" discourse of "new Confucianism" (see Bell 2008), an intellectual mixture of various attempts to resuscitate classical Confucian ideas.[11] Wang Hui's late work on the search for new resources in China's intellectual history for the reconstruction of "Chinese modernity" is also very often seen as a pivotal endeavor of this trend. Jiang Qing, another leading scholar in this intellectual current, advocates a specific project termed as "political Confucianism". In Jiang's view, Chinese intellectuals in the last 150 years have searched for modernization in the wrong place: they all believed that in order to achieve China's modernization, Chinese people had to implement social and political reforms in accordance with knowledge learnt from the West. This is for Jiang a false belief shared by Chinese liberals and Chinese Marxists alike. He also accuses the representatives of Hong Kong- and Taiwan-based "Neo-Confucians" such as Tang Junyi (1909–78), Xu Fuguan (1904–82), and Mou Zongsan (1909–95), of having been equally mistaken in their insistence on liberal democracy as the only path of political modernization for China. Rejecting all such propositions, Jiang claims that the Chinese people already possessed a highly developed political system that was perfectly suited for China's modernization. He called this "the system of rites and law" (*lifa zhidu*), which refers actually to various specific institutions, regulations, and customs which were effective in imperial China since Han dynasty (Jiang Qing 2003). By proposing a "tricameral" (instead of bicameral) representative system and a Chinese-style "Confucian system of constitution" as an alternative to Western models, Jiang avers that his work is "an attempt to 'Confucianize' contemporary Chinese political order" and he sees it as "the modern form of Dong Zhongshu's 'reform through returning to the ancient' (*fugu genghua*) in Han dynasty". Similar to Dong Zhongshu (179–104 BC), who convinced Emperor Wudi to accept his suggestions and elevated Confucianism as the sole official ideology, Jiang attempts to convince the top leaders of the Party to resuscitate the former status of Confucianism as "the learning of kings and officials" (*wangguan xue*) (Jiang Qing 2005). Some other prominent scholars such as Liu Xiaofeng and Gan Yang, two influential figures in contemporary Chinese landscape since the 1980s New Enlightenment movement, called for a thorough re-evaluation and re-interpretation of the Chinese classics in recent years by introducing Leo Strauss's obscure technique of "esoteric" reading. Although these scholars did not directly offer their readers any clearly stated political project, they nonetheless imply, following the path paved by Straussian political philosophy, that ancient wisdom contains intellectual recourses to overcome the crisis of modernity. (See, for example, Liu Xiaofeng 2002; Gan Yang 2003a; Gan Yang and Liu Xiaofeng 2006.)

At this juncture, it is worthwhile noting the Party's attitude towards these post-*Tiananmen* intellectual discourses. While strongly suppressing the discourse of liberalism, it is nonetheless quite tolerant towards the discourses of "new nationalism", "new Confucianism", and, to some extent, that of the "New Left". In fact, the Party-state leadership has been actively advocating the discourse of nationalism for many years. Nationalism and patriotism have been used to *produce political legitimacy and social solidarity* in post-Maoist China, especially in the post-*Tiananmen* era. Also, the government has nurtured some specific anti-foreign sentiments (especially anti-American sentiment) in order to tackle the increasing difficulties of "information-control" (*xinxi kongzhi*): in the age of the Internet they cannot totally stop information from coming in, they thus turn to the task of *shaping how the people think about what they learn from abroad*. Also, since 2005 the Hu Jintao-Wen Jiabao leadership of the Communist Party (i.e. the fourth generation of CCP's leadership) has taken a special interest in reviving Confucian ideas in order to legitimize its authoritarian rule in mainland. In betrayal of its own history of anti-Confucian practices in the Maoist time, the Party in fact has already started in recent years to consciously praise Confucian ideas such as "harmony" (*hexie*) as one of its newest ideological slogans – the official campaign advocated in the last several years is the construction of a "harmonious society".[12] As to the discourse of the New Left, the Party holds an ambivalent attitude: while being quite tolerant towards those intellectual searches for Chinese model of modernity (modernity with "Chinese characteristics"), it nonetheless suppresses the concerns voiced by the New Left figures such as Wang Hui regarding domestic socio-economic injustices caused by ruthless marketization and massive corruption.

To sum up, those various post-*Tiananmen* intellectual discourses are best understood as offering competing projects for China's future path, which are quite contrary to the optimistic scenarios of future success produced in the 1980s. In short, the unified (at least at an ostensible level) New Enlightenment movement of the 1980s was replaced in the following two decades by various, often mutually hostile arguments: liberal intellectuals attempt to repair the old broken modernization enterprise by filling in a series of clearly-stated "liberal elements", such as constitutional rule, parliamentary democracy, market economy, etc.; by praising the emerging commercial culture in the post-*Tiananmen* era as a new cultural strategy and a new path of development, postmodernist intellectuals attempt to "end the project of modernity", and to negate "grand narratives" of enlightenment, revolution, liberation, etc.; the intellectual group labeled by its critics as the "New Left" tries to reinvent the idea of China's modernity as an alternative to global capitalist marketization, aiming in general at creating different new socio-political projects to achieve China's national or civilizational perfection; the recent trend of new Confucianism also moves in this direction, with explicit efforts to resuscitate classical Chinese thought. One can thus say that Chinese intellectuality of the post-*Tiananmen* era is characterized by antagonistic projects engaging in a fierce struggle for hegemony.

Assuming Personal Responsibility for Social Change

The characteristic proximity of intellectual works to practical projects for socio-political transformations has deep cultural-intellectual roots. In today's Chinese language there are two common understandings of the term *zhishifenzi* (intellectuals): the broader understanding of *zhishifenzi* tends to include all educated people who are well-educated professionals, whereas the narrower understanding links *zhishifenzi* to the *shi* (or scholar) and the Confucian moral mandate of "assuming personal responsibility for all under Heaven" (*yi tianxia wei jiren*). The literal translation of *zhishifenzi* is "knowledgeable elements" but it is in terms of the Confucian *shi* that post-Maoist intellectuals regard as its ideal model.

In dynastic China, Confucian *shi* were privileged and highly respected in society not only as imperial officials or *shi dafu* (often translated as "scholar-official"), but also due to their commitment to assure the welfare for "all under Heaven" (*Tianxia*). Tu Wei-ming characterizes the pursuits of Confucian scholars and intellectuals into these three categories: *Dao* (the ontological Truth, the literal translation of which is "way"), *xue* (learning), and *zheng* (politics). As Tu argues, Confucian intellectuals are indeed political activists, and the primary goal of their endeavors is to shape the existing political order from the inside out (Tu Wei-ming 1993: 10–1). In the system of orthodox Confucian doctrine, intellectual "learning" (*xue*) was structured around a moral–political purpose (*zheng*), that is, to rectify the existing order in accordance to *Dao*. In this sense, Confucianism can be said to privilege an instrumentalist approach towards knowledge: intellectual ideas are perused in the services of grasping the truth and establishing an ideal order.[13] "Politics" in classical Confucian understanding refers to an act of "rectifying" (*zheng*) the existing order in accordance with *Dao*; thus, in pursuit of revealing *Dao* via their scholarship ("learning"), Confucian *shi* endeavored to find the correct way through which an ideal political order can be established.

Hence, Confucian scholars were, as Tu Wei-ming argues, also *political activists*. It is not only because they endeavor to present the Confucian classics of past sages as aimed at unveiling the meaning of *Dao*, but, and more importantly, because they do so in an attempt to shape social life and establish an ideal political order – and in thoroughly proper Confucian terms, that is, to *ping Tianxia* (establish peaceful and harmonious order everywhere under Heaven).[14] In traditional China the socially privileged status of the *shi* was based on the authority of those who had acquired "learning" (or "thought", "theory", etc.) to determine what is a peaceful and harmonious order.[15]

In their desire to play a leading role in social reform, post-Maoist intellectual works reflected the depth of Confucian cultural influence in twentieth-century China: by adopting ideas presumed to have the power to change "reality", contemporary Chinese intellectuals, just like the Confucian *shi* before them, assume their *personal* responsibility for China's transformations. Thus, it is appropriate to consider the modern Chinese term "intellectual" as having a strong moral and political connotation.

In the Maoist era, intellectuals were officially defamed as the "stinking ninth" (*chou laojiu*) – the lowest group of society, which was in stark contrast with the tradition of China where intellectuals were regarded and revered as the top elite. As the thesis of "returning to the centre" in the 1980s "fever for intellectuals" presupposes that intellectuals once again occupy the central spot of the political stage, this call implies an attempt to bring about a contemporary revivification of the old Confucian privileging of *shi*. By such an attempt to return to the centre of the nation's "socio-political life", post-Maoist intellectuals once again aimed at establishing an ideal order in accordance with the *Dao* of Heaven (*Tian-Dao*) in China. Through their new, Western-inspired learning, intellectuals view the projects they propose respectfully as the correct "way" for China's transformation. It is in this sense that they regarded guiding China's socio-political transformation as their *personal* mission. Through their engagement in leading China's transformation, intellectuals in turn re-identified themselves with "social elite". This desire of Chinese intellectuals for social recognition also reflected a Confucian assumption of moral and intellectual leadership.

One consequence of the Confucian idea of "assuming personal responsibility for all under Heaven" is an *instrumentalist* approach toward knowledge. Similarly this instrumentalist approach persisted during the "Chinese Enlightenment movement" of the May Fourth (*wusi*) era of the 1910s and 1920s, even as that intellectual movement claimed to be radically anti-traditional and thoroughly modern. In fact, May Fourth discourse emphasized the need for useful and effective knowledge. The call for "appropriatism" (*nalaizhuyi*) by Lu Xun (1881–1936), one of the best known May Fourth thinkers, is a case in point.[16] Thus, despite the many differences of view among May Fourth thinkers, they shared a common desire for producing a social blueprint for China.

In the broadest terms, the practical emphasis of Confucian learning on finding solutions to social, economic, and political problems has persisted throughout the twentieth century and since. What is common between the May Fourth Enlightenment of the 1910s and 1920s and post-Maoist intellectual praxes is such an attitude towards knowledge – it is regarded as an instrument for strengthening and perfecting the nation. Clearly, this is in accordance with the Confucian motto that "Everyone has a share of responsibility for achieving the welfare for *Tianxia*" (*Tianxia xingwang, pifu youze*).[17]

Conclusion

Contemporary Chinese intellectuals commonly work under the unspoken presupposition that their writings can *make a difference* to social transformations of post-Maoist China. They regard their intellectual works as carrying the great mission of providing an "enlightened" vision via which they are able to change the national status quo and improve the quality of Chinese culture and the welfare of the people. Gloria Davies employs the phrases "worrying about China" and "voicing concerns" (in the titles of her books) to highlight this feature of contemporary Chinese intellectual engagement. The usual procedure that resonates powerfully in the writings of many contemporary Chinese intellectuals contains the following two steps: (1) to identify "Chinese problems" (whether social, political, cultural, historical, or economic); and (2) to solve perceived problems in accordance with a stated argument serving as a blueprint for change and reform. As a consequence the strong moral tone of this instrumentalist approach indeed, makes Chinese inquiry significantly and strikingly discordant with the "decidedly non-nationalistic tenor of self-reflexive EuroAmerican critical inquiry"(Davies 2007: 7).

One should therefore bear in mind that when contemporary Chinese intellectuals engage in intellectual discussions and debates, in which various terms and jargon imported from Anglophone critical inquiry are employed, they are also competing with each other for intellectual authority in determining the correct path ahead for China's perfection. In the 1980s, this endeavor was embodied in the New Enlightenment project of China's modernization. Various intellectual groups "united" themselves in the "homogeneity of attitude": they shared a common attitude toward the necessity of Western-style modernization, believing that this was the only way forward for China. In contrast, the post-*Tiananmen* Chinese intellectuality is characterized by competing intellectual discourses, though participants in contemporary Chinese intellectual discussions face the same question – the question of "whither China".[18] In this sense, despite the fact that intellectuals in the post-*Tiananmen* era are often locked in fierce debate, they nonetheless fundamentally share an instrumentalist attitude towards knowledge: the shared aim of their intellectual enterprises is to achieve China's national or civilizational perfection.

Notes

1 My grateful thanks go to Gloria Davies for her illuminating comments on a draft version of this chapter.
2 The Shanghai-based historian Xu Jilin is right when he observed that the intellectual movements of post-Maoist China were initiated from the top downwards by the Party's reformist ideology. It is "[i]n

keeping and in tandem with this complex process of transformations," wrote Xu, that "the intellectual world of China experienced constant splits and realignments" (Xu Jilin 2000: 169).

3 This term is used by the Beijing-based philosopher Gan Yang in his various texts written in the 1980s; see, for example, Gan Yang 1987: 18. Emerging as a prominent New Enlightenment thinker in the 1980s, Gan also remains very active in the Chinese intellectual arena in the post-*Tiananmen* era.

4 This phrase was first coined by Wang Hui in his early studies on the May Fourth movement. Later Xu Jilin borrowed it to characterize the 1980s New Enlightenment movement. See Xu Jilin 2000: 177.

5 This socially influential six-episode television series was directly approved by Zhao Ziyang's administration, and produced by several New Enlightenment intellectuals including Su Xiaokang, Wang Luxiang, and Xie Xuanjun. Leading New Enlightenment figures such as Jin Guantao, Liu Qingfeng, Li Yining, etc. were invited to serve as consultants and some directly appeared in the show as interviewees. *River Elegy* was aired on CCTV (China's Central TV) twice in June and August of 1988. After the *Tiananmen* event, some of the people who worked on *River Elegy* were arrested and others fled mainland China.

6 During the debate between "liberals" and "New Leftists" in the late 1990s, both camps were keen to accuse their "discursive enemies" (*lundi*) as defenders of the existing order.

7 Because the 1980s is often called the "new era" in the post-Maoist official as well as intellectual discourses to demarcate the Party-state's new agenda of modernization from its Maoist past, the post-1989 era was labeled by Zhang Yiwu and other Chinese postmodernists as the "post-new era." By this they meant an era that embraces the end of modernity.

8 What should be noted here is that after Deng Xiaoping's death in February 1997, there was a temporary relaxation of state censorship. Thus, in the late 1990s and early 2000s, intellectuals were able to publish more freely and this encouraged renewed debate on China's future. After Hu Jintao took total power from Jiang Zemin in 2004, this space was severely narrowed. Many mainland Chinese intellectuals have difficulties in voicing their concerns, and even encounter indirect or direct political oppression.

9 What should be noted is that though Wang claims that he started his critical reflection on Western modernity in the 1980s, he nonetheless obviously shared the sentiments of most New Enlightenment thinkers at that time, and in fact was one of the protesters on *Tiananmen* Square who withdrew from the spot in the last minute (i.e. the early morning of June Fourth).

10 Wang Hui's theorization of "Chinese modernity" is rather ambiguous and, to some extent, still left "unfinished," since what he provides in *Rise* is nothing close to a clearly stated normative project, but instead, to borrow Zhang Yongle's phrasing, basically "an epistemological reconstruction of the successive systems of knowledge, or belief, that dominated China from the Song to the early Republic." As Zhang writes in his book review, "[T]he modernity or 'early modernity' [Wang] seeks in Chinese history is an open possibility rather than a structured project. The only thing we know about its meaning is that it involves the emergence of new pathways, not the replication of any version of modernity confected in the West" (Zhang Yongle 2010).

11 In Jiang Qing's view, the trend of China's new nationalism is merely a "rootless nationalism." Jiang in turn advocates a "sustentative nationalism based on Confucian culture." Also, Gan Yang proposes that China should shift itself "from nation-state to civilization-state" (Jiang Qing 2003: 396–415; Gan Yang 2003b). According to these scholars, China's nationalism cannot truly flourish without resuscitating its civilizational core – Confucianism.

12 Harmony is one of the central ideas of classical Confucianism. However, as Geremie Barmé observes, in today's China, "[i]t is a kind of harmony that is policed with overt rigour. So much is 'harmonized' (*hexie diao*) in the process of creating a quiescent socio-economic environment in which authoritarianism and plutocracy hold sway, that 'to harmonise' has become a common verb in colloquial Chinese meaning 'to censor,' 'elide' or 'expunge'" (Barmé 2010).

13 Suffice it to recall the famous four-sentence motto written by Song-dynasty Confucian scholar Zhang Zai (1020–77), which very well summarizes the Confucian-dominated intellectual tradition of China: (To be a Confucian scholar proper is) to reveal the core essence of nature for Heaven and Earth (*wei tiandi li xin*), to ascertain the mandate of life for the people (*wei shengmin li ming*), to continue the lost learnings of sages past (*wei wangsheng ji juexue*), and to establish universal peace and harmony for ten thousand generations to come (*wei wanshi kai taiping*).

14 The others, from the lowest, are *xiu shen* (to cultivate oneself), *qi jia* (to regulate properly one's family), and *zhi guo* (to improve state governing). This is the primary teaching of the *Great Learning* (*Da xue*), one of the most essential texts of Confucianism.

15 The Chinese Communist Party also presents its history as organized around the system of thought (*sixiang*) of Party leaders. Thus, from Mao Zedong to Hu Jintao, persons who occupy the highest position (as the Party's General Secretary) are implicitly accorded the role of not only a political leader but also as an intellectual leader as well. Theoretically at least, their "thought" (or "theory", "doctrine", etc.) is presented as the "blueprint" for the nation's development. This unique contemporary phenomenon of Chinese intellectual life – the persistent representation of the Party's top leaders as intellectual leaders (i.e. people whose ideas constitute the nation's blueprint for the future) – can also be read as a heritage of Confucianism. The emphasis on intellectual leadership is an important part of Chinese political culture. It is this Confucian inheritance that has led both officials and critical intellectuals to share in common the privileging of intellectual authority.

16 I use Gloria Davies's translation of Lu Xun's term which has also been translated as "grabism" and, the English translation of Lu Xun's *Selected Works*, as "the take-over policy" (Davies 2007: 250).

17 When the Party-state in the 1950s started to preach the concept of the "great Self" (*da wo*) as a reference to the Chinese nation, and encouraged people to devote themselves (the lower self) into the service of improving the great Self, it also invoked the traditional moral teaching of "assuming personal responsibility for all under Heaven".

18 In 2001, Xudong Zhang edited a book on "intellectual politics in contemporary China" (including translations of essays by Wang Hui, Gan Yang, Cui Zhiyuan, Wang Shaoguang, etc.) published by Duke University Press, whose very title is "Whither China". In 2005, another book on contemporary Chinese intellectuality published by Verso – a collection of post-*Tiananmen* intellectual discourses including essays by Wang Hui, Gan Yang, Zhu Xueqin, Qin Hui, and many others – also has a title that is quite emblematical: *One China, Many Paths* (Xudong Zhang 2001; Chaohua Wang 2005).

References

Barmé, Geremie (2010) "The Harmonious Evolution of Information in China", in *The China Beat*, available at <http://www.thechinabeat.org/?p=1422> (accessed 18 June 2010).

Bell, Daniel A. (2008) *China's New Confucianism: Politics and Everyday Life in a Changing Society*, Princeton, NJ: Princeton University Press.

Chaohua Wang (ed.) (2005) *One China, Many Paths*, London: Verso.

Chen Fong-ching (2001) "Popular Cultural Movement of the 1980a", in Gloria Davies (ed.) *Voicing Concerns: Contemporary Chinese Critical Inquiry*, Lanham, MD: Rowman & Littlefield.

Davies, G. (2001) "Introduction", in Davies (ed.) *Voicing Concerns: Contemporary Chinese Critical Inquiry*, Lanham, MD: Rowman & Littlefield.

——(2007) *Worrying About China: The Language of Chinese Critical Inquiry*, Cambridge, MA: Harvard University Press.

Deng Zhenglai (*et al.*) (2008) *Zhongguo renwen shehuikexue sanshi nian* (Chinese Humanities and Social Sciences in the Last Three Decades), Shanghai: Fudan daxue chubanshe (Fudan University Press).

Gan Yang (1987) "*Bashi niandai wenhua taolun de jige wenti*" (A Few Issues Concerning the 1980s Cultural Discussion), in *Wenhua: Zhongguo yu shijie* (Culture: China and the World)1, Beijing: Sanlian shudian (Joint Publishing House).

——(2003a) *Zhengzhi zheren shitelaosi* (Leo Strauss as a Political Philosopher), Hong Kong: Oxford University Press.

——(2003b) "Cong 'minzu-guojia' zouxiang 'wenming-guojia'" (From Nation-State to Civilization-State), available at <http://www.chinese-thought.org/zwsx/007497.htm> (accessed 18 June 2010).

Gan Yang and Liu Xiaofeng (2006) "Zhengzhi zhexue de xingqi" (The Rise of Political Philosophy), in *Nanfang zhoumo* (Southern Weekly), 12 January 2006.

Gries, P.H. (2004) *China's New Nationalism: Pride, Politics, and Diplomacy*, Berkeley, CA: University of California Press.

Jiang Qing (2003) *Zhengzhi ruxue: dangdai ruxue de zhuanxiang, tezhi, yu fazhan* (Political Confucianism: The Turn, Characteristics, and Development in Contemporary Confucianism), Beijing: Sanlian shudian (Joint Publishing House).

——(2005) "Guanyu chongjian Zhongguo rujiao de gouxiang" (Thoughts on the Reconstruction of Chinese Confucianism), available at <http://culture.people.com.cn/GB/27296/3969429.html> (accessed 18 June 2010).

Li Shenzhi (1999) "Fengyu canghuang wushi nian" (Fifty years in Wild Wind), available at <http://www.chinaelections.org/NewsInfo.asp?NewsID=140662> (accessed 18 June 2010).

Liu Xiaofeng (2002) "Editorial Preface", in Liu (ed.) *Shitelaosi yu gudian zhengzhi zhexue* (Leo Strauss and Classical Political Philosophy), Shanghai: Shanghai sanlian shudian (Shanghai Joint Publishing House).

Tu Wei-ming (1993) *Way, Learning, and Politics: Essays on the Confucian Intellectuals*, New York: State University of New York Press.

Wang Hui (1998) "Contemporary Chinese Thought and the Question of Modernity", translated by Rebecca Karl, in Xudong Zhang (ed.), *Intellectual Politics in Post-Tiananmen China*, Durham, NC: Duke University Press.

——(2004) *Xiandai Zhongguo sixiang de xingqi* (The Rise of Modern Chinese Thought), 4 vols, Beijing: Sanlian shudian (Joint Publishing House).

——(2006) *China's New Order: Society, Politics, and Economy in Transition*, ed. and trans. Theodore Huters, Cambridge, MA: Harvard University Press.

——(2010), *The End of the Revolution: China and the Limits of Modernity*, London and New York: Verso.

Xu Jilin (2000 [1998]) "The Fate of an Enlightenment: Twenty Years in the Chinese Intellectual Sphere (1978–98)", trans. Geremie R. Barme and Gloria Davies, *East Asian History*, 20.

Xu Jilin (et al.) (2007) *Qimeng de ziwowajie: 1990 niandai yilai Zhongguo sixiang wenhua jie zhongda lunzheng yanjiu* (The Self-destruction of Enlightenment: Studies on the Important Debates in the Chinese Intellectual World since the 1990s), Changchun: Jilin chuban jituan youxian zeren gongsi (Jilin Publishing Company).

Xudong Zhang (ed.) (2001) *Whither China: Intellectual Politics in Contemporary China*, Durham, NC: Duke University Press.

Zhang Yiwu (2000 [1994]) "'Xiandaixing' de zhongjie: yige wufa huibi de keti" (The End of 'Modernity': An Unavoidable Topic), in Luo Gang and Ni Wenjian (eds), *Jiushi niandai sixiang wenxuan* (The Intellectual Anthology of the 1990s), Vol. 1, Nanning: Guangxi renmin chubanshe (Guangxi People's Publishing House).

Zhang Yongle (2010) "The Future of the Past: On Wang Hui's Rise of Modern Chinese Thought", *New Left Review*, 62.

Part 3
Emerging Problems

The Limits of Power and the Complexity of Powerlessness

The Case of Immigration[1]

Saskia Sassen

My concern here is exploring the limits of power and the complexities of powerlessness – the direct or mediated resistances that the powerless can deploy knowingly or not.[2] Immigration policy enforcement is one institutional domain for exploring these issues, especially in the case of powerful countries and undocumented workers, among the most vulnerable subjects in those same countries. We can think of this case as representing an instance of highly formalized power (the US state) and an instance of extreme powerlessness (undocumented immigrants). To gain some closure on this vast subject, I will focus on the tensions between current policies for controlling immigrants and what we can think of as new elements in the immigration reality. The particular policies that stand out involve the weaponizing of border control. The particular changes in the immigration reality can be thought of as bits, as in digital bits, that are being assembled into a somewhat novel reality constituted through both well-established conditions and emergent bits whose status is often unclear – they may or may not support that long-standing reality. Here I confine myself to certain bits in a multi-bit reality in-the-making which are unsettling basic alignments on which immigration policy rests. They also reveal the limits of even the most powerful state in the world to get its way, and they show that in certain settings powerlessness becomes complex. Let me illustrate with two recent cases.

Mexico's (former) President Fox's decision to meet with undocumented Mexican immigrants during his visit to the US in Spring 2006 amounted to the making of a new informal jurisdiction. His actions did not fit into existing legal forms that give sovereign states specific types of extra-territorial authority. Nonetheless, his actions were not seen as particularly objectionable; indeed, they were hardly noticed. Yet these were, after all, unauthorized immigrants subject to deportation if detected, in a country that is now spending almost US$2 billion a year to militarize border control. But no INS or other police came to arrest the undocumented thus exposed, and the media barely reacted. Further adding to the novelty was the fact that Congress was considering making illegal immigration a felony, mandating imprisonment. And yet, not even in this political atmosphere did any arrest take place. Nor did the press comment on the juxtaposition of elements.

A second case is the large demonstrations on the streets of Chicago, Los Angeles, and other US cities in March and April of 2006, which included many self-declared undocumented claiming the right to have citizens' rights. Whether some of these may have been actually legal immigrants or citizens is beside the point. We do know that many were indeed unauthorized. At a time when the US Congress was discussing legislation to criminalize illegal immigrants, these undocumented individuals responded by going onto the streets and protesting in very public ways. Their faces appeared on hundreds of front pages and television screens, but no one was arrested – again, against a backdrop of militarized borders and a policy aimed at apprehensions.

Beyond the fact of the lack of intention to arrest these undocumented immigrants, the events point to a second – and perhaps more significant – bit of a reality in the making. There were signs that the claim-making was more about the right to have rights than about the desire to become American citizens per se. American citizenship becomes a channel for becoming a (generic) rights-bearing subject, a more foundational condition than American citizenship per se. There are multiple instances in other countries of an emerging claim for a similar sort of *denationalized* citizenship.

Both instances also signal that although undocumented immigrants are powerless and highly vulnerable, in certain settings they gain a measure of autonomy from powerful actors that intend to control them, and that they even can reshape the policies of powerful countries. Some of the most powerful countries in the world have re-geared their public bureaucracies to control these powerless vulnerable actors. In this process, they have been willing to sacrifice their standing as states following the rule of law and compliant with human rights norms. In the long run, this is a very high price for "liberal democracies" to pay – and all in order to control powerless and vulnerable people who want only a chance to work. In the process, these powerful states have also lost credibility and revealed the limits of their power, no matter how weaponized their borders.[3]

This emergent multi-bit reality does not fit neatly under transnationalism nor under post-nationalism. It does not necessarily extend beyond the territory of the nation-state nor does it presume the end of the state. And even in cases where it might fit, we lose something when we explain it in those terms. Perhaps it is more helpful to see this reality as a variety of micro-processes inside the nation-state which are beginning to denationalize the national as historically constructed. They are not confined to immigration, although this essay utilizes that regime as its lens. Their partial and fragmented character means these processes can coexist with a renationalizing of policy and of political discourse in multiple domains, including immigration.[4]

The Limits of Militarized Border Controls Given New Realities

Against this larger context, the increasingly militarized US–Mexico border is a sort of natural experiment to examine the interaction of great material power and great human vulnerability. Even as the US government seeks to further weaponize the border with Mexico to control undocumented immigration, the bits of this new immigration reality multiply. This multi-bit reality functions within specific settings insofar as migration flows are far more institutionally and geographically structured than is often assumed.[5]

The border itself is a good case to make legible the fact of multiple bits within which we need to situate government border control policy. There is a strong contrast, and possibly contradiction, between the project of militarizing border control and the reality of the border zone. In 2004, the latest year for which we have comprehensive figures on all the following variables, 175,000 legal immigrants entered the US from Mexico, along with 3.8 million visitors for pleasure, 433,000 visitors for business, 118,000 temporary workers and dependents, 25,000 intra-company transferees and dependents, 21,000 students and dependents, 8,400 exchange visitors and dependents, and 6,200 traders and investors.[6] On the other hand, it is estimated that there are approximately 3 million Americans living in Mexico, mostly undocumented; 19 million Americans travel there each year as visitors. US foreign direct investment in Mexico now totals US$62 billion annually; and trade with Mexico grew by a factor of eight from 1986 to 2006, before the economic and financial crises began More difficult to measure, but still very real, are the multiple cross-border networks connecting people from each side of the border which go beyond physical border crossings. These include the variety of transnational processes extensively described in the literature with terms such as transnational households and communities,[7] as well as digital transactions that begin to constitute a cross-border electronic space.

Thus the reality of the border is not quite a line that divides but a partly denationalized fuzzy zone. It binds as much as it divides, and perhaps more so. Thereby it enters in tension with the explicit aims of US immigration policy, and the latter in turn enters in tension with other major US policies, notably trade, off-shore manufacturing, and tourism. The US has indeed the resources and the power to insert a militarized barrier and to ensure night vision to border patrols in cars and helicopters. We are left, however, with a significant subsequent question. Can this powerful government willing to go all the way to control that border ensure that it will work as it wants it to?[8]

Many of the facts are by now familiar, but some are not. After 15 years of increased militarizing of the border, we have an all-time high in the estimated unauthorized immigrant population (ca. 11 million). The annual INS budget rose from US$200 million in 1996 to US$1.6 billion in 2005.[9] The number of Border Patrol officers increased from 2,500 in the early 1980s to 18,000 by 2008 (Overmeyer-Velaquez 2011). In *Backfire at the Border* (Massey 2005) reports a sharp increase in the costs per arrest and falling arrest rates. Before 1992, the cost of making one arrest along the US–Mexico border stood at US$300; by 2002, that cost had grown by 467% to US$1,700, and the probability of apprehension had fallen to a 40-year low, despite massive increases in spending on border enforcement. Finally, the escalation of border control has raised the risks and costs of illegal crossing, which in turn has changed a seasonal circulatory migration – with workers leaving their families behind – into a family migration and long-term stays. The *Border* study established that in the early 1980s, about half of all undocumented Mexicans returned home within 12 months of entry. By 2000, the rate of return migration stood at just 25 percent. In brief, the results were the opposite of what the government aimed at: border militarization did not reduce the probability of illegal crossings on the US–Mexico border, and forced unauthorized immigrants to stay longer than they wanted and to bring their families even when they would rather not.

There are three peculiar absences in the enforcement effort in the US which are also part of the larger ecology within which militarization has failed to achieve its aims. One is the absence of a parallel "escalation" in the visa application process: because of understaffing it can still take ten years for a lawful applicant to get processed and we know that many are constrained, often for family reasons, to enter illegally because they cannot wait for years. Second, the budget for inspections of workplaces suspected of violating the law remains minimal and employers sanctions are rare.[10] Third, the budget for tracking visa over-stayers remains minimal and apprehensions are few. At least part of the reason for these absences seems to me rather straightforward. There are four critical differences between these three options and investment in border control. They concern jobs, buying material, lobbies, and propaganda.

On jobs, regardless of political party, the US government has repeatedly shown a strong reluctance to create more jobs for inspecting workplaces, for tracking visa-overstayers, and for processing green-card applications. Over the last 20 years especially, none of these efforts has seen the sharp budgetary increases allocated for controlling the border with Mexico. On buying material, the sharp increases in the INS budget have benefited the makers and sellers of armaments and surveillance technology. A third difference concerns lobbying efforts in Congress. Armament makers and large corporate employers in agri-business, meat-packing, and other sectors known to employ significant numbers of unauthorized immigrants operate powerful lobbies. INS inspectors and green-card processors, and large sectors of the workforce, do not. Finally, there is the electoral-and-public opinion machinery: weaponizing a border makes for better footage and a better media story than does hiring more INS inspectors and green-card processors.

There are winners and losers in this policy framing. The winners include armament makers, some large corporate employers in particular sectors of the economy, various types of lobbies, employers of undocumented immigrants generally insofar as employers' sanctions are not seriously enforced, and the growing numbers of smugglers whose fees and whose business have increased sharply as US policies have made border crossing more difficult and risky.

The losers include citizens whose taxes are paying for a far larger and costlier border control operation that is not even reducing illegal crossings – the intended policy outcome for supporting all those Congressional authorizations for budget increases. The losers also include the migrants themselves whose crossings have become far more difficult, dangerous, sometimes deadly, as well as costly given the greater need for using a smuggler. They also include the INS inspectors who have not seen sharp increases in their numbers and resources to enforce employers' sanctions, and the overworked and understaffed processing units at the INS.

But the problems go deeper. The emergent multi-bit immigration reality briefly and only partially described earlier is an increasingly active socio-political ecology[11] that undermines traditional notions of border control. Further, this emergent reality is partly fed and strengthened by the fact that the estimated 500 annual deaths among illegal crossers due to current US border control policy are becoming unacceptable on normative grounds – whether social justice norms, human rights, or religious values.

The State Itself Has Changed

While the state continues to play the most important role in immigration policy making and implementation, the state itself has been transformed by the growth of a global economic system and other transnational processes, such as the institutional thickening of the human rights regime, and EU institutions in the case of the EU. Three particular changes in the positioning of national states could have a potentially significant impact on the role of the state in immigration policy making and implementation.

One is the relocation of various components of state authority to supranational organizations, including the institutions of the European Union, the newly formed World Trade Organization, or the newly instituted International Criminal Court with its potentially universal jurisdictions. In the specific case of migration there is also the renewed role of the International Organization for Immigration (IOM) in managing migration and refugees flows, and to some extent the OECD.

Strictly speaking we should include a whole series of other actors as well. One instance is the financial and banking sector that handles immigrant remittances. This sector is not an insignificant actor if we consider that worldwide immigrant remittances reached US$230 billion in 2005 and US$318 billion in 2007; after 2008 they declined markedly due to the financial and economic crises (World Bank 2006, 2009).[12] While most of this money goes to developing countries, almost a third went to highly developed countries, principally through the remittances of the transnational professional class. Further, the *Inter-American Development Bank* (IADB) estimates that in 2003, immigrant remittances generated US$2 billion in handling fees for the financial and banking sector on the US$35 billion sent back home by Hispanics in the US.[13] I mention this mostly as a way of illustrating the extent to which what we call immigration is a larger assemblage of elements embedded in multiple domains of the host society – in this case, even in high finance. This is one of many little (and large) facts that tend to be excluded from the typical analysis of immigration, one characterized by a narrow delineation of the object for research and for policy-making.

Second, the privatization and deregulation of public sector activities has brought with it a type of *de-facto* (rather than formally explicated) privatization of various governance functions that were once in the public bureaucracy.[13] This privatization of governance is particularly evident in the internationalization of trade and investment. Corporations, markets, and free trade agreements are now in fact "governing" an increasing share of cross-border flows, including the regimes for cross-border professionals described earlier.

Third, the numbers and kinds of political actors involved in immigration policy debates and policy making in Europe and the US are far greater than they were two decades ago: the European Union; anti-immigrant parties; vast networks of organizations in both Europe and North America that often represent immigrants, or claim to do so, and fight for immigrant rights; immigrant associations and immigrant politicians, mostly in the second generation; and, especially in the US, so-called ethnic lobbies. The policy process for immigration is no longer confined to a narrow governmental arena of ministerial and administrative interaction. Public opinion and public political debate have become part of the space wherein immigration policy is shaped. Whole parties position themselves politically in terms of their stand on immigration, especially in some of the European countries.

The emerging realities about immigration and the state described in these two first sections amount to a larger ecology within which border controls function. That larger ecology can unsettle, if not undermine, the foundations of border controls.

When Bits of the National are Denationalized

There is more movement towards a novel approach in handling immigration than the statements and speeches of national politicians in the US and Europe imply. US immigration policy, with its overwhelming focus on border control, rests precisely on not factoring in that emergent immigration reality and the particular state transformations described in the first two sections. Here I can only limit myself to the narrowest definition of these issues.

One particular angle into this matter is to understand whether the renationalizing of the politics of membership precludes the denationalizing of a growing set of components of the larger immigration reality. The partial denationalizing of the national is to be distinguished from transnationalism and from post-nationalism because it does not happen beyond the realm of the national or in more than one country. Its distinctive character is that it happens deep inside the thicket of the national. It may at times intersect with or be one moment in a larger transnational dynamic. In that sense, identifying this denationalizing multi-bit reality adds to, rather than replaces, the types of processes identified in the rich literatures on trasnationalism and post-nationalism.

Some of the developments in the EU can be interpreted as an instance of denationalized portable rights. It might be interesting to provide some detail because it may well signal the beginning of a process of which we see elements in the US. At the heart of this process is the shift of rights to individuals as individuals rather than as citizens of a specific country. Immigrants are incorporated into various national and EU-level systems of rights as a result of EU law. This EU-level format for rights shifts the question of "immigrant integration" away from an emphasis on the "foreignness" of immigrants and what to do about it (such as the requirements for learning the language and the culture of the host country increasingly demanded by national governments of EU member states), and begins to move towards the work of mixing EU level law/policy (such as the *ECHR* and the *Social Charter* of the Council of Europe) with the decisions of national judiciaries, that is to say with a particular component of the state rather than "the" state as such (see Jacobson and Ruffer 2006). One possible outcome is that integration (including the necessity to learn the language of the country of residence) shifts from being *the* requirement for acquiring rights to a responsibility for a rights-bearing immigrant.

A far thinner version of denationalized rights can be seen in the portable mobility rights given to top-level professionals through the major free trade agreements as part of the globalization of trade and investment in services. These are rights inscribed in WTO, NAFTA, and dozens of other trade agreements shaped by the new realities launched in the 1990s. There is a mini-immigration policy in each of the major chapters in these treaties (chapters on a broad range of services, notably, finance, business services, telecommunications, particular types of engineering, and so on). Professionals in each of the specific sectors are given the right to reside in any signatory country for at least three years and enjoy various rights and protections. Staff from major supranational organizations such as the IMF and WTO also enjoy special protections that will hold even in their own country of citizenship.[14]

While the fact of such portable mobility rights is rarely a focus in the migration literature, these professionals are a class of "migrant workers" who are formally endowed with multiple rights. This fact is obscured by the placement of these mobility rights in the treaties under specific economic sectors and descriptions that avoid the language of migration. These are rights that originate in international agreements and require signatory states to fulfill them. Their fulfillment entails a partial denationalizing of the national state's power to grant rights.[15]

The filtering of supranational norms into national law can take many forms.[16] The fact that national systems are critical for the implementation of non-national types of rights (whether those inscribed in free trade agreements or in the human rights regime) is not the only mechanism. A different type of filtering is the growing weight of international norms in national courts and in national law, and, more generally, in domains once reserved to the exclusive authority of national states. While this does not amount to postnationalism or trans-nationalism, the filtering of non-national norms does involve a partial denationalizing of at least some components of national law.[17] It all happens within the state apparatus and often remains coded in the language of the national.

Positing matters as an either/or (as in either national or global) is far less valid today than it was even 10 years ago. The last decade has seen significant changes, not only in the EU but also in a country like the US, one of the most closed and "nationalist" in the world. Even the US Supreme Court has in the last few years acknowledged that it needs to consider not only international but also foreign law in its interpretations and decisions. Specifically, when it comes to human rights norms, the US has seen sharp growth in the use of these norms in national courts, and it has seen the federalizing of these norms through rather informal processes that make these norms part of customary practice, eventually enabling their federalization – their becoming national law (Koh 1997).

Any Policy Bits to Match the New Immigration Reality?

Accepting the fact of a new emergent immigration reality and the serious limitations and even unsustainability of militarized borders does complicate governments' efforts to control immigration. The EU offers some interesting options, even though EU member states are foundationally different from the US in their political culture.

Over the last two decades, the EU has actually accumulated a series of innovations that move it towards governing, rather than controlling, immigration *inside* the EU. This move towards governing is gaining strength even as national governments in the EU continue to speak of unilateral control. Yet when it comes to immigration from outside the EU, strengthening control is what the EU has been gearing up to for the last decade. We can learn something positive from the EU's internal efforts, and, in a way, the EU can learn something negative from the US border control policy – how not to do it.

One foundational outcome from years of EU negotiations that can illustrate the specificity of the EU approach and its contribution to notions of governing rather than controlling immigration is the *Treaty of Amsterdam* (2003). It formally allows a shift of immigration policy and its coordination out of the third pillar (where it is handled as part of justice and home affairs), and into the first pillar, whose legal provisions become part of European Community law and are binding on each member state. Further, it is possible to argue that since individuals will have the legal capacity to invoke first pillar laws and bring them to bear against member states, the changes of the *Amsterdam Treaty* may give the judiciary, here the European Court of Justice, more authority over immigration too. The *Treaty* calls for enforcement of non-discrimination principles within member states, with enforcement through the European Court of Justice (ECJ). The *Treaty*'s formal commitment to human rights could strengthen the ECJ's authority over member states and contribute to strengthen the notion of rights-bearing individuals who can move across the member states with their portable rights.

More generally, beyond human rights there is a far larger case to be made: multiple different types of international law are becoming part of the fabric of national law, both through legislative law making and through use in judges' interpretations. This contributes to partly denationalize aspects of national law. Thus one of the foundational transformations lies in the extent to which a good part of the EU's project inhabits and gets structured inside the complex institutional apparatus of the state. Similarly, in the case of the US much of globalization is structured inside the state. In both cases, this often happens in the language of the national – national law, national economic regulations, national monetary policy, and so on. We need to decode this language of the national rather than take it at face value: though formulated as national, these structurations may they have little to do with the national as historically constructed.

Finally, we need a few words on borders given their increasingly ambiguous character. Borders are institutions, and as such they are undergoing change and stress. In my research I have tried to track the formation of a whole range of novel types of bordering capabilities – types of controls that are not embedded in the notion of geographic borders as produced in the historic process of nation-state formation.[18] These bordering capabilities do not pivot on geographic border controls. They are highly technical capacities which have multiple institutional locations beyond the "border" *per se*. For instance, in global finance, there are multiple such bordering capabilities (many inside financial institutions rather than in government offices) that have replaced the older traditional national borders. Free-trade agreements certainly open up countries, but multiply processes of certification at point of production, again not the typical border. When "borders" are looked at through these lenses one can see a wide range of possibilities. The sharpest and most developed case at this time regarding these new bordering capabilities and people flows, are the portable rights of the new transnational professional class. These rights are derived from free-trade agreements, discussed earlier, as well as the IMF and other institutions deeply engaged in global processes; as rights they become operative inside the countries that are signatories. There is no similar regime for working-class migrations today, but it is one possible regime in the future, perhaps as part of a flexibilizing of migration flows (which would enable return and circular migrations).

Conclusion

This paper has examined the institutional insertions of the immigration question in a far larger and complex map than current immigration law can fathom. We need more such close examinations in order to understand the micro shifts that are amounting to a new immigration reality. This new immigration reality comprises a variety of bits. These include changes in the position of the state in a world that is not only increasingly interdependent but also one where the national is itself being partly denationalized through state action. This begins to unsettle the distinction national-foreign, as epitomized by Fox's visit described earlier and by more foundational shifts, such as the institutionalizing of the human rights regime and claims for rights made by unauthorized immigrants in all major immigration countries. Immigration is beginning to play on a far broader register than that represented by the "immigrant" in her relation to immigration policy narrowly defined. This opens up a whole new research agenda that is not concerned with the familiar issues of geographic border controls and the binaries of inside/outside. Such analysis dislodges the immigration question from narrow national versus foreign dimensions as made emblematic in militarized border control. It helps expand the analytic and policy terrain within which to examine the question of immigration, immigrant rights, and the governing of immigration.

Notes

1 For a full development of the issues raised in this paper beyond the case of immigration, see Sassen 2008.
2 Power and powerlessness are, clearly, complex categories subject to diverse forms of theorization. This essay in a way can be seen as an exploration of the limits of the Weberian notion of power – power as an actor's or institution's capacity to impose its will. Elsewhere (Sassen 2008: chs 3, 4, 8, and 9) I have elaborated on the work of constructing the condition we call power, and thereby emphasized the variable success and effectiveness of that work of constructing power and the durability of its results. There (2008: chs 2, 6, 7, and 8) I have also elaborated the notion that powerlessness is constructed and hence variable; from there, then, comes the possibility that at one end of that variable, powerlessness can be elementary, and at another end, complex. This variability does not simply depend on the individuals: for instance, the powerlessness of a specific undocumented immigrant wil be quite elementary in the context of a California commercial farm, but can become complex in a city like New York, Los Angeles, or Chicago.
3 In using "weaponized" I seek to emphasize a particular component of the militarized border – the materiality of border control. Militarized is aform of control which includes but cannot be reduced to the weapons being used. One reason for making the distinction is the role of the armaments industry in this shift, a subject I briefly address later in this essay.
4 See here Benhabib 2004, and my response to Seyla Benhabib in Sassen 2007a.
5 A few basic figures help illustrate this geographic structuring; I develop the institutional aspect in Sassen 2007b: chapters 5 and 6). About 30 countries account for over 75% of all immigration; 11 of these are developed countries, with over 40% of all immigrants. More generally, the latest estimate is of a worldwide immigrant resident population of 185–192 million in 2005. This is under 3% of global population, but up from the 2.1% of world population in 1975; and up from the 175 million or 2.9% of world population estimated for 2000 (IOM 2006).
6 Please find sources for these various items in Massey 2005; for continuous updates see http://www. inci.ox.ac.uk
7 This literature is particularly vast in the case of North American scholarship on Western Hemisphere immigration. I discuss it briefly in Sassen 2007b: ch. 6. For an excellent analysis of the Mexico-US border see Mark Overmyer-Velázquez (ed) Beyond la Frontera : The History of Mexico-U.S. Migration. Oxford: Oxford University Press 2011.
8 On the question of control as a political choice, see Andreas1998. See also generally Cornelius, Wayne Controlling 'unwanted' immigration: Lessons from the United States 1993–2004." *Journal of Ethnic and Migration Studies*, 31 (4): 775–794.
9 As of 2007, the INS function is part of the Department of Homeland Security.
10 Historically, only about 2% of the INS budget was allocated to employer sanction enforcement ,and few sanctions were imposed after the passing of the legislation as part of the 1984 Immigration Reform

and Control Act (IRCA). In 2005, US Immigration and Customs Enforcement, which succeeded the INS, strengthened enforcement efforts: it won 127 criminal convictions in 2005, up from 46 in 2004, and won US$15 million in settlements from Wal-Mart and 12 subcontractors for violations. To address the failure of employer sanction enforcement, the government has started the Basic Pilot Program, part of Homeland Security. It is an electronic search machine that combines Social Security and immigration databases to verify an employee's status. While today's program is small and voluntary, with about 6,000 employers enrolled, it can be extended to each of the country's approximately 8 million employers. Violations of the law would subject employers to stiff fines, with jail sentences for repeat offenders. However, the program is problematic in technical and legal terms. This combination has created a mixed opposition – from civil rights organizations to big business. A Government Accountability Office report issued in August 2005 criticized the program for its inability to identity fraud, for flaws in the databases, and for the possibility that employers will abuse the system.

11 In using this term I am partly playing off a concept that is today much used in analyses of the new interactive communication technologies: the notion is that these technologies become performative (deliver their "goods") in the context of social systems or configurations that go well beyond the technology itself (Sassen 2008: ch. 7). In the context of the border I seek to emphasize that the border can be activated into diverse specific formations, not only the one that has to do with dividing and closure.

12 The IADB also found that, for Latin America and the Caribbean as a whole, in 2003 these remittance flows exceeded the combined flows of all foreign direct investment and net official development assistance.

13 Elsewhere I have examined how when public sector firms are privatized, and, more generally, when economies are deregulated, regulations do not simply disappear. Rather, they are transformed into private corporate specialized services (accounting, legal, etc.), and oriented towards the private interests of the firms and markets at issue (see Sassen 2001).

14 For a development of this aspect, see Sassen 2007b: ch.6.

15 A detailed examination of these issues can be found in Sassen 2007b:chs 5, 6, and 9).

16 See, for example, Spiro 2008 and Koh 1998.

17 For instance, to mention just one of the more recalcitrant EU members, in 2000 the UK incorporated the bulk of the European Convention of Human Rights into domestic law. The British Parliament adopted the Human Rights Act of 1998 in November of 1998; it became effective in the UK in October 2000.

18 For more detail, see Sassen 2008: ch. 9.

References

Andreas, P. (1998) "The Escalation of U.S. Immigration Control in the Post-NAFTA Era", *Political Science Quarterly*, 113(4): 591–615.

Benhabib, S. (2004) *The Rights of Others: Aliens, Residents, and Citizens*, Cambridge: Cambridge University Press.

Cornelius, W. (2005) "Controlling unwanted immigration: Lessons from the United States 1993–2004", *Journal of Ethnic and Migration Studies*, 31(4): 775–794.

——International Organization for Migration (IOM) (2006) *World Migration 2005: Costs and Benefits of International Migration*, Geneva: IOM.

Jacobson, D. and G. B. Ruffer (2006) "Social Relations on a Global Scale: The Implications for Human Rights and for Democracy", in M. Giugni and F. Passy (eds) *Dialogues on Migration Policy*, Lanham, MD: Lexington Books, pp. 25–44.

Koh, H. H. (1997) "How Is International Human Rights Law Enforced?" *Indiana Law Journal*, 74: 1379.

——(1998). "The 1998 Frankel Lecture: Bringing International Law Home", *Houston Law Review*, 35: 623.

Massey, D. S. (2005) *Backfire at the Border: Why Enforcement without Legalization Cannot Stop Illegal Immigration*, Washington, DC: Center for Trade and Policy Studies, Cato Institute.

Overneyer-Velázafuez, M. (ed.) Beyond la Frontera: The History of Mexico–US Migration, Oxford: Oxford University Press.

Sassen, S. (2001) *The Global City: New York, London, Tokyo*, 2nd edn, Princeton, NJ: Princeton University Press.

——(2007a) "Response to Seyla Benhabib", *European Journal of Political Theory*, 6(4): 431–44.

——(2007b) *A Sociology of Globalization*, New York: Norton.

——(2008) *Territory, Authority, Rights: From Medieval to Global Assemblages*, Princeton, NJ: Princeton University Press.

Spiro, P. J. (2008) *Beyond Citizenship: American Identity After Globalization*, Oxford: Oxford University Press.

World Bank (2006) *Global Economic Prospects: Economic Implications of Remittances and Migration*, Washington, DC: World Bank.

Sovereignty, Security, and the Exception

Towards Situating Postcolonial *homo sacer*

Sheila Nair

The US "war on terror" has led liberal democracies to openly voice their disavowal of due process, basic human decencies, and civil liberties (selectively applied in the best of times); a disavowal that is rationalized in the name of justice. The messy complexities of a post 9/11 world have thus been reduced to conventional aphorisms – an epic struggle against good and evil. In this narrative collateral destruction of whole neighborhoods and villages in Iraq and Afghanistan is rendered an unfortunate, but unavoidable, consequence of a just war. Retribution accompanies a reinterpretation and reformulation of mid-twentieth-century international humanitarian and human rights laws, foundational in their conception and application. But acts of retribution also highlight the "privileged – and lazy – immunity" of intellectuals and scholars whose abstract inquiries into the constitution of sovereign violence and power are troubled by vulnerable bodies marked in the unleashing of this power (Gregory 2004: xiii). The exception, specifically the *state of exception*, has much currency in this context of neo-liberal rationalizations of violence.

The execution of the US-led war in Iraq and Afghanistan, the resulting violence and deaths, detention and torture of "enemy combatants" in Guantanamo Bay, Abu Ghraib, as well as other war on terror hotspots, and state impunity in the face of it all have combined to make more visible critiques of sovereign power. Yet, while 9/11 and its aftermath have led to a more careful exploration of the scope of sovereign power, anti-immigrant backlash in the West, refugees, deepening global inequality and poverty, and racism have also clearly contributed to study of the exception. Interrogating how sovereign power is produced and exercised has led to an explosion of interest, especially on the left, in the writings of Giorgio Agamben and Carl Schmitt. This chapter explores how the notion of the exception – its relevance and meanings – has enabled us to inspect more carefully the constructs of sovereign power, and its diffuse and authorizing gaze in contemporary international relations. It also addresses how other associated key concepts have framed the debates round the scope of sovereignty, sovereign power, and their implications especially for postcolonial exception. This chapter draws in the main from Agamben and, to some extent, Schmitt's notions of the political, "friend-enemy" distinction, and sovereignty.[1]

The Question of the Exception

In locating Schmitt's statement that the sovereign is "he who decides on the exception", Agamben provides an important corrective on power, one that is not confined to the workings of the sovereign state (Biswas and Nair 2010: 5). For Agamben,

> [The] paradox of sovereignty consists in the fact that the sovereign is, at the same time, inside and outside the juridical order. If the sovereign is truly the one to whom the juridical order grants the power of proclaiming a state of exception and, therefore, of suspending the order's validity, then "the sovereign stands outside the juridical order and, nevertheless, belongs to it, since it is up to him to decide if the constitution is to be suspended *in toto*".
>
> *(Agamben 1998: 15)*[2]

What does this mean? Sovereign power and sovereign law depend upon, and are constituted by, this inclusive exclusion. The sovereign is, in short, captured inside the exception, just as the exception is itself a clear expression of the extent and limits of sovereign power. It has to be emphasized that sovereign power can only be grasped in relation to its negation or suspension in the state of exception. Therein lies the paradox. Sovereign power relies on and is constituted by what it silences or erases in the exception; sovereign authority stands outside and in opposition to the exception, but is also simultaneously embedded in it.

Agamben argues that this fundamental contradiction underlies the production of sovereign law. Indeed, according to Agamben,

> Law is made of nothing but what it manages to capture inside itself through the inclusive exclusion of the *exceptio*: it nourishes itself on this exception and is a dead letter without it … The sovereign decision traces and from time to time renews this threshold of indistinction between outside and inside, exclusion and inclusion, *nomos* and *physis*, in which life is originarily excepted in law.
>
> *(Agamben 1998: 27)*

The state of exception, while suggestive of the suspension of the law or the norm, does not imply the abolition of the law or norm (Agamben 2005: 23). On the contrary, "the state of exception is neither external or internal to the juridical order, and the problem of defining it concerns precisely a threshold, or a zone of indifference where inside and outside do not exclude each other but rather blur with each other" (Agamben 2005: 23). This point is critical to understanding how the exception embeds sovereignty within it in even as it is alienated from it, just as the logic of sovereignty relies on the exception for its foundational, lawful authority in international relations.

The concept of the "ban"[3] illustrates how the exception has become the rule in the managing and staging of crises such as 9/11. Agamben argues that the "relation of exception is a relation of ban. He who has been banned is not, in fact, simply set outside the law and made indifferent to it but rather *abandoned* by it, that is exposed and threatened on the threshold in which life and law, outside and inside, becomes indistinguishable"[4] (Agamben 1998: 28). The logic of sovereignty is thus a logic that is inverted, and is sustained not by any contractual shift away from the state of nature (as in a Hobbesian frame), but by its production in the exception and the ban. The ban is embodied in the figure of the *homo sacer* (sacred man) – "a life that may be killed but not sacrificed" – who represents bare life that stands in contrast to *bios* or politically qualified life. Here is where Agamben's interchangeable use of *zoe* ("natural reproductive life") with *homo sacer* (bare life) elsewhere in his work is countered by his assertion that *homo sacer* – distinct from natural life – occupies a zone of indistinction and the state of exception it embodies. It is thus not a social contract that establishes the formal structure of sovereignty, but the ban. *Homo sacer* is quite simply he who is abandoned by the law (Agamben 1998: 109). In short, "what the ban holds together is precisely bare life and sovereign power" and thus all "representations of the originary political act as a contract or convention marking the passage from nature to the State in a definite and discrete way must be left wholly behind" (109). Caldwell situates this distinction between bare life and *zoe* or natural, "sweet" life in contemporary political discourse. So, in essence, "[H]omo sacer, regardless of whether it lives a life of happiness or misery, is defined by its dependence upon sovereign power for its status. This nexus, in which sovereignty emerges by capturing life in the exception, defines the nature of political belonging in the West" (Caldwell 2004: 20). If we set aside the sovereignty mythologeme, what are we left with? We have a critique of sovereignty and sovereign power whose very structure and logic is exposed as presupposing the ban, the camp, and *homo sacer*.

As Agamben puts it, the construction of this mythologeme deflects our gaze away from the inclusions, exclusions, and exceptions of sovereign power (Agamben 1998: 109–10), and in undoing it we redirect our attention to sovereignty's hidden power and demarcations. The zone of indistinction implicit in contractual sovereignty is thus exposed by the blatant assertion of sovereign authority in the production of the modern camp. It is to the camp that bare life in the form of *homo sacer* must be relegated. But it is also in the camp "that the 'juridically empty' space of the state of exception … has transgressed its spatiotemporal boundaries and now, overflowing outside them, is starting to coincide with the normal order, in which everything again becomes possible" (Agamben 1998: 38), and the exception becomes permanent.

Following Agamben and Schmitt, some scholars have used the exception and the ban to illustrate the workings of the modern camp as the "new biopolitical *nomos* of the planet" while situating its analysis in the context of imperial and neo-colonial projects (Gregory 2006: 406). Reid-Henry, for example, explores the imperial histories that have shaped the production of "enemy combatants" and "battlefield detainees" as bare life in the detention camp. He argues that this is the case with the camp at Guantanamo Bay, Cuba, where "American (extra) territoriality and Cuban (pseudo) sovereignty" render Guantanamo as a grey area "as indeterminate as the variously described 'enemy combatants' and 'battlefield detainees' being held there" (Reid-Henry 2007: 628). The indeterminate status of Guantanamo prisoners cannot merely be located in the context of the US war on terror but, as Reid-Henry argues, is closely indexed to the territory's imperial past (Reid-Henry 2007: 628). This indexing of Guantanamo to imperial practices resurrects it as an indistinct space, a state of exception that has been in the making for some time. It refers us back to policies of earlier US administrations and to a time when Guantanamo served as a detention centre for Haitian refugees among others, whose existence on the periphery of international politics marked them as so many *homines sacri*.

The spatial boundaries of the state of exception, it should be remembered, are coterminous with the boundaries of the politically qualified life of the sovereign. But Guantanamo demonstrates the "process by which the *exception everywhere becomes the rule*,[5] the realm of bare life – which is originally situated at the margins of the political order – gradually begins to coincide with the political realm, and exclusion and inclusion, inside and outside, *bios* and *zoe*, right and fact, enter into a zone of irreducible indistinction" (Agamben 1998: 9). Guantanamo, thus, comes to exemplify the permanency and emergency of the exception, one where the very applicability or relevance of law is not in question since it has essentially been suspended in this space of indistinction. In fact its suspension is not merely a reflection of the non-legal status of detainees but also of the referral of sovereign, international law. Notably, the state of exception embodied in

Guantanamo (and elsewhere) accompanies US rationalization of its sovereign authority through legal machinations and justifications that suspend due process and international human rights. The US has drawn from the legal arguments of then Deputy Assistant Attorney-General Patrick Philbin and conservative legal scholar John Yoo to ground its claims. These arguments in the infamous Torture Memos outline the grounds for denying habeas corpus, the Geneva Conventions, and the Convention Against Torture to prisoners at Guantanamo, Abu Ghraib, and elsewhere.[6] In Guantanamo we find a "carefully constructed legal absence", which functions as "the geographical articulation of a more generalized juridico-political 'state of exception'" (Reid-Henry 2007: 630). While Reid's emphasis is on the "geographical mechanisms behind the production of bare life," Gregory (2006) draws attention to the legal and para-legal architectures of Guantanamo as "a staging post for the contemporary 'war on terror'" and suggests that a reverse Euro-American exceptionalism has marked the production and management of Guantanamo and the camp's inhabitants as bare life, where international and sovereign laws may not exist.

Rearticulating Security and Sovereignty

> At once excluding bare life from and capturing it within the political order, the state of exception actually constituted, in its very separateness, the hidden foundation on which the entire political system rested.
>
> *(Agamben 1998: 9)*

Sovereignty and doctrines of security are so intimately related it is often difficult to dis-entangle one from the other. Security has consistently been at the forefront of realist arguments about power in international relations. In this view, the sovereign state exercises power and agency in defense of security and the national interest. It is thus not difficult to see why Agamben concludes that security is embedded and implicated in the "birth of the modern state", and that it is today the principle activity of the state (Agamben 2002). The politics of western liberal democracies, according to Agamben, produce and rely on emergencies, making it unlikely that the paradigm of security will disappear anytime soon. Security measures are always articulated in relation to a state of exception, and "work towards a growing depoliticization of society" (ibid.). Security and sovereign power are thus inseparable logics that shape a range of exclusionary, globalized discourses. Such exclusions – militarized, gendered, subalternized, and racialized – reflect civilizational and cultural anxieties. Anti-immigration policies underscore "racial, cultural, and civilizational superiority" (Persaud 2002: 19), which mark undocumented migrants as bare life and the detention camps in which they are held as so many zones of indistinction (Rajaram and Grundy-Warr 2004). Representations of the immigrant "other" make it acceptable to imprison migrants, to deny them basic legal rights and due process, and deport them whenever possible.

After 9/11 the US border was reinscribed in civilizational terms, and in the "popular American imagination … fears of an external threat and danger usually embodied by the alien, barbaric Other" became once again core referents (Agathangelou and Ling 2004: 525). Yet this binary inscription is grounded in the articulation of sovereignty and security. Campbell explains how "the constitution of identity is achieved through the inscription of boundaries which serve to demarcate an 'inside' from an 'outside', a 'self' from an 'other', a 'domestic' from a 'foreign'" (Campbell 1992: 8). But the inside/outside opposition, or in Schmitt's terms the "friend/enemy" opposition,[7] functions to obscure the zone of indistinction in which this opposition is embedded. In short, the sovereign decision to exclude or except encapsulates what is projected as external (threats to security), within it. What is at stake is identifying how "the limit concept of the doctrine of law and the state, in which sovereignty borders (since every limit concept is always the limit between two concepts) on the sphere of life and becomes indistinguishable from it" veils the constitution of sovereign power and its deployment (Agamben 1998: 11). And further, how the logic of sovereignty obscures the indeterminate political status of those inhabiting the grey areas of Guantanamo and other exceptional spaces.

So if, as Gregory (2006) suggests, Agamben's "metropolitan predilections" hide the "architecture of colonial power", what does this mean for how we understand postcolonial sovereignty? Is sovereign power expressed differently in postcolonial sites? I turn now to these questions.

The postcolonial exception

Sovereign power, in Agamben's view, generates a "zone of indistinction" or "zone of anomie" in international life, such that the state of exception has become "the *nomos* of our present". But he has little to say about how or whether colonial and imperial modalities of sovereignty matter in the way the exception is conceptualized and contextualized. Although Agamben insists that sovereign authority and power do not reside centrally in the Westphalian or the liberal state, but rather, following Foucault, in a biopolitical regime that exemplifies modernity, we cannot assume that this is universally the case. His insight that the sovereign and biopolitical are not separate and opposing realms, but instead constitutive of one another may well yield similar insights into operations of sovereign power in the postcolonial world. But even if we grant that sovereignty, *homo sacer, et al.* are universal in their application it is still useful to inquire into how postcoloniality generates different understandings and meanings associated with these terms.

In this vein, colonial and postcolonial sovereignties cannot be seen as "deformed or incomplete, but as polymorphous and yet vital to the so-called Westphalian system of nation-states by constituting almost permanent zones of exception" (Hansen and Stepputat 2005: 18).[8] But postcolonial sovereignties look different from the *sui generis* sovereignty attributed to the Westphalian system. The former is captured by Mbembe's notion of *commandement*, a term "used to denote colonial authority, that is, insofar as it embraces the images and structures of power and coercion, the instruments and agents of their enactment, and a degree of rapport between those who give orders and those who are supposed to obey them, without, of course discussing them" (Mbembe 1992: 30). Postcolonial sovereignty thus appears as an imitation or mimicry of the forms of rule and order enacted by colonial power and equally repressive. Sovereign rule is experienced in the exercise of sovereign power through coercive and violent colonial and postcolonial policies, institutions and laws. It is also implicated in the assertion of postcolonial statehood and sovereignty (in the Hobbesian contractual sense). However, the insistent regulation of third world spaces and their production as crisis-prone, terror-ridden, disease-bearing, anarchic, corrupt, non-rational, and ungovernable reaffirms the postcolonial exception.

Agamben's work has been faulted, as noted above, for its reluctance to engage colonial and imperial histories in theorizing the exception, but this does not mean that the concept itself is suspect. Mbembe has shown how a critique of the exception yields insight into the workings of sovereign power in postcolonial Africa, where the exception mirrors the spectacular violence of colonialism and imperialism even as it stands in some opposition to them. Such is the case in the display of the "grotesque and obscene" as essential elements of the postcolonial regime's affirmation of its domination (Mbembe 1992: 4). The performance of sovereignty, or as Mbembe puts it, the *fetish* of postcolonial legitimacy, is evident in the elaborate rituals and spectacles staged for public consumption, although the postcolonial exception is made only more evident in the production of such excess. These performances also underscore that the exercise of sovereign power in the postcolony is also at its core a relation of violence, which excludes many from the state's legal protections, and reduces them to an exceptional and marginal existence. However, this exclusion is not hidden or obscured by the way sovereign power sets outside the law those who are not subject to politically qualified life. Rather, the reproduction of bare life in these contexts is a principal and obvious object and outcome of sovereign power.

The history of colonization and imperialism frames a different trajectory of postcolonial sovereignty than the liberal version projects. The destruction of pre-Westphalian "sovereignties" – if such a term may be applied to pre-colonial state formations – means any recuperation of situated understandings of that term is not very helpful. More to the point, Gregory argues that "modalities of colonial violence" continue to bear on the "colonial present", and "international law bears the marks of those colonial predations: its locus is drawn not only through relations of sovereign states, but also through what Peter Fitzpatrick calls 'the colonial domination of people burdened by racial difference'" (Gregory 2006: 410). The exception thus has a particular structure of meaning in relation to the civilizational and racialized discourse embedded in the "war on terror". The "barbarians at the gate" suffer a double exclusion not only as those set outside the law – *homo sacer* – and hence not entitled to the rights and privileges extended to citizens, but as an enemy who is "beyond the human" (Gregory 2006: 410). As Cesaire decries, the colonizer sees the "other man as *an animal*, accustoms himself to treating him like an animal, and tends objectively to transform *himself* into animal" (2001: 41). This relationship is quintessentially a relationship of violence. Being denied even the status of one who may be killed but may not be sacrificed raises other questions about how the constitution of the exception depends upon the specific emergencies being declared. And how those emergencies are mapped around bodies that may not even be entitled to the "bareness" of *zoe*, thus revoking the operative distinction between natural and politically qualified life so integral to the making of sovereign power.

The assertion of sovereign power evident in the enactment, but perhaps even more significantly in the suspension, of international law by the production of enemy combatants, terrorists *et al.* may also be related to a colonialism that places whole peoples and communities beyond, but also simultaneously within, the spectral violence of the sovereign state. But where is this double exclusion of *homo sacer* in the colonial and postcolonial exception located? Colonial sovereignties were structured around exceptions to the norms of citizenship and its inclusions, and the subjection of the colonized to techniques of surveillance and repression that were not universal in scope, but were spatially, geopolitically, and culturally constructed and organized. The attendant spatial, geopolitical, and cultural exclusions involved the setting off internal frontiers,[9] or the zoning off of selves and others not only in the demarcation of settlements for natives and their colonial rulers, but also throughout a complex administrative apparatus, in the punishment of *metissage*,[10] and in the production of cultural identity.[11] Without a doubt law itself was reinvented through a colonial administration that "took place as a permanent, tropical exception from common law applicable in Europe" (Hansen and Stepputat 2005: 24). Colonial authorities disregarded normal metropolitan rules of governance in the application of law. In any case, the production of the colony as a space of inexplicable brutality, wildness, and "otherness" meant that (sovereign and colonial) power "was 'circular' … (seeking) 'absolute submission'" Mbembe cited in Hansen and Stepputat (2005: 24).

In demonstrating the constitution of this otherness embedded in sovereignty in Africa, Mbembe writes that: "we are interested in a specific form of *domestication*[12] and mobilization of space and resources: the form that consists in producing boundaries, whether by moving already existing ones or by doing away with them, fragmenting them, decentering or differentiating them" (2000: 261). Consistent with such boundary marking practices, exclusions embedded in racialized and patriarchal systems of rule are further regulated and ordered through the fictional embrace of colonial governance. For Mbembe then, "the colonies are the location par excellence where the controls and guarantees of judicial order can be suspended – the zone where the violence of the state of exception is deemed to operate in the service of 'civilization'. That colonies might be ruled over in absolute lawlessness stems from the racial denial of any common bond between the conqueror and the native" (Mbembe 2003: 14). To kill or to "let live" – by the exercise of sovereign power – will thus have qualitatively different meanings in colonial sovereignty (and in their postcolonial progeny) than in the metropolitan, "civilized" states.

But the lack of subtlety involved in the extension and exercise of power in colonial and postcolonial sovereignty, are attenuated by the workings of biopower and governmentality. Colonial sovereignty normalized the regulation of people through managing sexual reproduction, while governmentality was infused throughout the socio-economic and political apparatus of the colonial state although perhaps less obvious given its use of naked force. Postcolonial governmentality bears traces of its violent colonial origins, which prompts comparisons to governmentality in spaces such as Guantanamo where metropolitan powers exercise their sovereign authority more openly. Spivak's argument that imperial expansion secured the new mechanisms of (bio) power that began to emerge in Europe in the seventeenth and eighteenth centuries worth recalling here (Spivak 1999: 279). She faults Foucault, whose work on biopower and governmentality have critically informed Agamben's theorization of the exception – for producing "a miniature version of that heterogeneous phenomenon: management of space – but by doctors; development of administrations – but in asylums; considerations of the periphery – but in terms of the insane, prisoners, and children. The clinic, the asylum, the prison, the university – all seem to be screen allegories that foreclose a reading of the broader narratives of imperialism" (Spivak 1999: 279). Such imperialist narratives more fully express the complex reworkings of sovereign power and authority in, as well as in relation to, the postcolonial world. If, as Butler (2004: 51), suggests governmentality itself is being revitalized through the state, then it would be useful to consider how particular forms of state and sovereignty are generative and expressive of different modes of governmentality and biopower.

The relationship between colonial and imperial tropes, and postcolonial difference also surfaces in discussions and debates around development. At the critical "moment when imperialism has come more to the fore in both critical and conservative literatures about globalization, the meanings and configurations of development and sovereignty are also undergoing flux" (Sidaway 2007: 345). Development has, after all, been one of the "central organizing concepts" in and through which imperialism "produces particular landscapes; territories of 'development space'" (Sidaway 2007: 347). Informed by the core precepts of modernization theory, development discourse positions marginality as an outcome of third-world maladies rather than as integral to the consolidation of a global economy, where capital accumulation and sovereign authority are seen as increasingly fused (e.g. Hardt and Negri 2000). In this global economic order, development discourse is overwritten by colonial imaginings of "race, progress, and civilization" (Sidaway 2007: 346). Escobar critiques the development discourse as projecting a political and economic universe "coded by a tale of three worlds" and sees development as resting "on a traffic of meanings that mapped new domains of being" (in Sidaway 2007: 346). The critical significance of colonialism and imperialism in these mappings is evident in the exceptions to the sovereignty norm invoked in development discourse.

As Ong puts it, these exceptions to the norm of sovereignty are "graduated" (2000). She argues that "graduated sovereignty" is a mode of "governing segments of the population who relate to or do not relate to global markets", and is visible in "the different mixes of legal compromises and controls tailored to the requirements of the special production zones" scattered throughout the developing world (Ong 2000: 55). Viewed from this perspective, graduated sovereignties reflect zonal exclusions, which are bounded and exceptional, and the assertion of sovereign power in such spaces does not reflect any singular logic of the state or sovereign power but rather the demands of capital mobility, which are especially predatory in the developing world. Such "differentiated spaces of the political" call for different regulatory and disciplinary practices. The postcolonial exception – the idea embedded in the notion of *commandement* – is situated in relation to graduated sovereignties in which "petty sovereigns" (borrowing Butler's usage) relay governmentality and sovereign authority, and where decisions (on the exception) presume an existential "lawlessness". This is especially the case when it comes to undocumented or irregular migrants who are often at the mercy of petty sovereigns, many of whom may be private contractors running detention camps, or employers and thus beyond even the regulative reach of state authorities. The reluctance of postcolonial state authorities, for example, to intervene and impose as it were the "law" in such situations, or hold accountable those who violate it, underscores the exceptional fragility and vulnerability of whole populations in the global economy.

Conclusion

This chapter revisits some of the arguments associated with the state of exception, and in doing so references Agamben's critical discussion of the ban; the camp and the zone of indistinction. It draws attention not only to how the state of exception expands our understandings of contemporary sovereign power and its modalities, but also its restrictiveness. For example, Agamben's theorization of the state of exception in the camp as the *nomos* of the present must take into account, at the very least, the coerciveness of colonial power and postcolonial authority, and their distinctive permutations. Agamben's injunction that we are in a phase where the state of exception has become the norm and where we are all *homines sacri* forces us to seriously ask how this moment is taking shape. But it should mean addressing why bare life and states of exception emerge through the violence of imperialism (and colonial rule), and how the asymmetries reflective of this violence generate alternative modalities of sovereignty in time and space.

Notes

1 Schmitt's influence on contemporary political thought has not been without controversy given his associations with the Nazi regime. For an excellent assessment of Schmitt's resurrection in contemporary social and political theory as well the debate he has triggered, see the foreword by Tracy B. Strong to Schmitt's *Concept of the Political* (Schmitt 1996). This debate while illuminating does not, in my view, detract from the arguments he advances on the exception and Agamben's reformulations of this concept.

2 Agamben quotes from Schmitt's *Politische Theologie* in the second sentence of this passage.

3 In using the notion of the *ban* Agamben introduces "the old Germanic term that designates both exclusion from the community and the command and insignia of the sovereign" (1998: 28).

4 Emphasis in the original.

5 Emphasis added.

6 Available at <http://www.aclu.org/national-security/memo-regarding-torture-and-military-interrogation-alien-unlawful-combatants-held-o>.

7 See Schmitt's extended discussion of this relation in *The Concept of the Political* (1996).

8 Similarly, Hansen and Stepputat argue: "The traces of the colonial state, or the culture of colonialism, have not withered away, however. Sovereignty in the postcolonial world has in many ways remained provisional and partial, despotic and excessively violent" (Hansen and Stepputat 2005: 27).

9 Fanon (1967) refers to the internal frontier as the "division of space into compartments", which were marked by the colonial state's police apparatus and segregated native settlements. For a discussion of Fanon's arguments on the internal frontier, see Mbembe 2003: 27–8.

10 In Stoler's analysis of *metissage*, the cultural basis of European colonialism appeared, from the perspective of the colonizer, to be threatened or subverted by inter-racial mixing. The "purity" of the races was to be maintained not only by keeping the natives physically in their place, but also by ensuring that the psychology and ideology of colonial rule were preserved. *Metissage*, according to Stoler, emerges as "a powerful trope for internal contamination and challenge, morally, politically, and sexually conceived" (Stoler 1994: 130).

11 Said's (1993) critique of the culture of imperialism captures these contradictions well.

12 Emphasis added.

References

Agamben, G. (1998) *Homo Sacer: Sovereign Power and Bare Life*, trans. Daniel Heller-Roazen, Stanford, CA: Stanford University Press.

——. (2002) 'Security and Terror,' trans. Carolin Emcke, *Theory and Event*, 5: 4.

——. (2005) *State of Exception*, trans. K. Attell, Chicago, IL: University of Chicago Press.

Agathangelou, A. and L.H.M. Ling (2004) 'Power Borders, Security, Wealth: Lessons of Violence and Desire from September 11', *International Studies Quarterly*, 48: 517–38.

Biswas, S. and S. Nair, eds (2010) *International Relations and States of Exception: Margins, Peripheries and Excluded Bodies*, London and New York: Routledge.

Butler, J. (2003) *Precarious Life: The Powers of Mourning and Violence*, New York: Verso.

Caldwell, A. (2004) 'Bio-sovereignty and the Emergence of Humanity', *Theory & Event*, 7 (2).

Campbell, D. (1992) *Writing Security: United States Foreign Policy and the Politics of Identity*, Minneapolis, MN: University of Minnesota Press.

Cesaire, A. (2001) *Discourse on Colonialism*, trans. Joan Pinkham, New York: Monthly Review Press.

Fanon, F. (1967) *Black Skin, White Masks*, trans. C. Markmann, New York: Grove Press.

Gregory, D. (2004) *The Colonial Present*, London: Blackwell Publishing.

——(2006) 'The Black Flag: Guantánamo Bay and the State of Exception', *Geografiska Annaler: Series B, Human Geography*, 88 (4): 405–27.

Hansen, T.B. and F. Stepputat (2005) *Sovereign Bodies; Citizens, Migrants, and States in the Postcolonial World*, Princeton, NJ: Princeton University Press.

Hardt, M. and A. Negri (2000) *Empire*, Cambridge, MA: Harvard University Press.

Mbembe, A. (1992) 'Provisional Notes on the Postcolony', *Africa: Journal of the International African Institute*, 62 (1): 3–37.

——. (2000) 'At the Edge of the World: Boundaries, Territoriality, and Sovereignty in Africa', *Public Culture*, 12 (1): 259–84.

——. (2003) 'Necropolitics', trans. Meintjes, L., *Public Culture*, 15 (1): 11–40.

Ong, A. (2000) 'Graduated Sovereignty in South-East Asia', *Theory, Culture & Society*, 17 (4): 55–75.

Persaud, R. (2002) 'Situating Race in International Relations: The Dialectics of Civilization Security in American Immigration', in G. Chowdhry and S. Nair (eds), *Power, Postcolonialism and International Relations: Reading Race, Gender and Class*, London, UK: Routledge.

Rajaram, P.K. and C. Grundy-Warr (2004) 'The Irregular Migrant as Homo Sacer: Migration and Detention in Australia, Malaysia and Thailand', *International Migration*, 42 (1): 33–64.

Reid-Henry, S. (2007) 'Exceptional sovereignty? Guantánamo Bay and the Re-colonial Present', *Antipode*, 39 (4): 627–48.

Said, E. (1993) *Culture and Imperialism*, New York: Vintage Books.

Schmitt, C. (1996[1932]) *The Concept of the Political*, trans. G. Schwab, Chicago, IL: Chicago University Press.

——. (2005) *Political Theology: Four Chapters on the Concept of Sovereignty*, Chicago, IL: University of Chicago Press.

Sidaway, J.D. (2007) 'Spaces of Postdevelopment', *Progress in Human Geography*, 31 (3): 345–61.

Spivak, G. C. (1999) *A Critique of Postcolonial Reason: Toward a History of the Vanishing Present*, Cambridge, MA: Harvard University Press.

Stoler, A.L. (1994) 'Sexual Affronts and Racial Frontiers: European Identities and the Cultural Politics of Exclusion in Southeast Asia', in S. Cooper and R. Cooper (eds) *Tensions of Empire: Colonial Cultures in a Bourgeois World*, Berkeley, CA: University of California Press.

The Future of the State

Georg Sørensen

Many observers are too optimistic when they consider processes of political change; the outcome of such processes may not always be political development; it might as well be political decay, a point emphasized by Samuel Huntington (1968) more than forty years ago but often forgotten in recent deliberations. The end of the Cold War installed a profound optimism in many people; the emblematic formulation of liberal hopes was 'the end of history' thesis by Francis Fukuyama (1989). The liberal belief in rapid progress and fast transitions to liberal democracy in many countries of the world dominated the 1990s; this was a period of political transformations and humanitarian interventions, animated by the desire to bring the universal values of democracy and human rights to all people.

Recent years have seen another mood; *Time Magazine* celebrated Vladimir Putin as 'Person of the Year' in 2007. A man of 'steely confidence and strength', he allegedly moved Russia away from the 'rudderless mess' that prevailed under Boris Yeltsin, towards order and stability. A year later, the World Public Opinion survey (2009) found that 'the world now seems to have more confidence in undemocratic than democratic leaders'. The change of mood reminds us that the optimism about progress was never as strong in the liberal tradition as it was claimed to be in the 'end of history' version. During the Cold War, leading liberal voices – including Karl Popper, Raymond Aron, and Isaiah Berlin – were much more cautious and defensive, concerned with 'avoiding the worst rather than achieving the best' (Müller 2008: 48).

We do well to bear in mind these skeptical voices in discussing the future of the state. History, said Berlin, has 'no libretto'; it is not predetermined (Herzen, quoted in Berlin 1979: 92). There is no inbuilt guarantee of progress. For Immanuel Kant, progress was predicated on the existence of a pacific union among republics (democracies). But no such union would emerge automatically; it would be formed in a slow process where earlier results of cooperation would eventually lead to further cooperative efforts. The pacific union is a possibility rather than a certainty; Kant speaks of 'an infinite process of gradual approximation' (1992: 30).

Political decay is as likely a possibility as is political development. A discussion of the future of the state should be guided by this more open view and not by a definite belief in progress. An important point follows: the advanced states in Europe, North America, and a few other places, are not necessarily frontrunners for everyone else; they are the result of unique and peculiar processes of development that cannot easily be repeated elsewhere. Similarly, the very weak states in sub-Saharan Africa and elsewhere are the result of particular historical developments which make it extremely difficult for them to embark on a process of modernization. They might not succeed; history contains no guarantee that modernity awaits everyone.

In order to discuss the future of the state we need a baseline: some notion of what the state looks like today. At the same time, we want to avoid descending into pure description where every state is unique. Weberian ideal types are a way forward; they define the core features of present modalities of statehood. On the basis of these, we may discuss the future of the state.

Not All the Same: Three Types of State in the Present International System

I want to suggest three major modalities of state in the present international system: they are the postmodern states in the OECD-world, the weak post-colonial states mostly in sub-Saharan Africa, and the modernizing states, mainly in Asia, Latin America, and parts of Eastern Europe. Postmodern states have developed due to the changes that modern states have undergone since the end of World War II, sparked by the combined processes of economic globalization and political integration. The 'post'-prefix is a way of emphasizing that we are not quite clear about the shape and form the postmodern state will eventually take but we do know that it will be different from the modern state. The reader should be warned that the label 'postmodern' is used in several different ways by scholars, some of which do not at all correspond to the way it is used here (for a comparison of my usage with Robert Cooper's, see Sørensen 2008: 17–20). Weak, post-colonial states emerged in the process of decolonization. The normative framework around colonies changed dramatically in the post-World War II period. Before the war, the possession of colonies was considered legitimate and even necessary given the backward condition of the colonized areas. After the war, colonialism came to be considered fundamentally wrong, even 'a crime' (Jackson 1993). Pre-colonial patrimonial structures and colonial 'divide-and-rule' dominance were of course also significant elements defining the nature of weak statehood.

Modernizing states combine features of the modern, postmodern, and weak statehood ideal types in different mixtures. Some of them (e.g. China) were never weak states; others (e.g. India, Brazil) were weak once but have developed modern and some postmodern features as well. Table 1 portrays the modalities of statehood discussed here. Four major aspects of statehood are in focus: the political level (government); the level of national community (nationhood); the economic basis (economy); and the institution of sovereignty. The modern state is the conceptual basis for many observers in the fields of comparative politics and international relations, but this will clearly not do in assessing sovereign statehood in the twenty-first century.

Let us then look at the prospects for these major types of state in the present system.

New Patterns of Violence and Conflict

We are used to think of large-scale war between states as the major security problem but this is changing. Postmodern states are consolidated liberal democracies; they make up a security community (Adler and Barnett 1998) which can no longer be classified under the traditional notion of sovereign states in an anarchical environment. Processes of integration mean that patterns of legitimate international and supranational authority have replaced anarchy. This is most developed in context of the EU but these developments involve the other postmodern states as well (Sørensen 2007). In a security community states no longer resort to force as a means of conflict resolution. This means that the security dilemma is eliminated: states do not fear each other in the classical sense of fear of attack, and war between them is not a possibility.

Table 1 Four types of states

State dimensions	Modern state	Postmodern state	Weak postcolonial state	Modernizing state
Government	A centralized system of democratic rule, based on a set of administrative, policing and military organizations, sanctioned by a legal order, claiming a monopoly of the legitimate use of force, all within a defined territory.	Multilevel governance in several interlocked arenas overlapping each other. Governance in context of supranational, international, transgovernmental and transnational relations.	Inefficient and corrupt administrative and institutional structures. Rule based on coercion rather than the rule of law. Monopoly on the legitimate use of violence not established.	The modernizing states combine features of the modern, the postmodern and the weak, postcolonial state.
Nationhood	A people within a territory making up a community of citizens (with political, social and economic rights) and a community of sentiment based on cultural and historical bonds. Nationhood involves a high level of cohesion, binding nation and state together.	Identities less exclusively national. Collective identities 'above' and 'below' the nation reinforced. Transformation of citizenship. Less coherent 'community of citizens'.	Predominance of local/ethnic community. Weak bonds of loyalty to state and low level of state legitimacy. Local community more important than national community.	Brazil, China, India, and Russia are major examples of modernizing states.
Economy	A segregated national economy, self-sustained in the sense that it comprises the main sectors needed for its reproduction. The major part of economic activity takes place at home.	National economies much less self-sustained than earlier because of 'deep integration'. Major part of economic activity embedded in cross-border networks.	Heterogeneous combination of traditional agriculture, an informal petty urban sector, and some fragments of modern industry. Strong dependence on the global economy.	Additional examples include Argentina, Mexico and Venezuela in Latin America, as well as Indonesia, Malaysia and Thailand in Asia.
Sovereignty	National authority in the form of constitutional independence. The state has supreme political authority within the territory. Non-intervention: right to decide without outside interference.	From non-intervention towards mutual intervention. Regulation by supranational authority increasingly important.	Constitutional independence combined with 'negotiated intervention' (donor control of aid, supervision by international society). 'Non-reciprocity' (special treatment of weak states because they cannot reciprocate).	Each of these countries contains a unique mixture of different types of statehood.
Country Example	OECD-states circa 1955	OECD-states today	Most countries in Sub-Saharan Africa	See above

Modernizing states may become part of this security community provided they become consolidated democracies; Brazil and India are on that path, Russia and China are certainly not for the time being. But even these latter states know that the road to greatness involves focus on manufacture upgrading and deep involvement in economic globalization; by no means does it involve territorial conquest and militarization. In this sense, they are following the 'trading state' path set by Japan and Germany after World War II (Rosecrance 1986). Furthermore, there is increasing respect for the 'territorial integrity norm', that is, 'the proscription that force should not be used to alter interstate boundaries' (Zacher 2001: 215). According to the detailed analysis by Mark Zacher, that norm emerged in the context of the League of Nations after World War I; it was generally accepted as an element in the UN Charter in 1945 and it has been strengthened since the mid-1970s.

These normative and substantial developments have all but eradicated the occurrence of interstate war (defined as armed conflict between governments in which at least 1,000 people are killed, or killed yearly, as a result of the fighting). Few such wars have taken place since the end of World War II and fewer still since the end of the Cold War (Harbom and Wallensteen 2009).

But violent conflict has not gone away. It has been moved to the domestic realm of weak states. Self-seeking elites in weak states lacked legitimacy from the beginning and faced populations divided along ethnic, religious, and social lines. They created 'captured states' that benefited the leading strongman and his select group of clients. The majority of the population was excluded from the system and faced a state that was sooner an enemy and a mortal threat than a protector and a champion of development (Sørensen 2001). Challenges to elites are often met with repression and that opens to violent conflict. Paradoxically, then, weak states are surrounded by an international system of relative order and with fairly secure protection of borders and territories. But the population is not safe because the government makes up the greatest potential threat to people within its boundaries.

The international community has been concerned with domestic conflict in weak states for some time. Its efforts probably culminated by the late 1990s; a 'responsibility to protect' was acknowledged at the UN World Summit in 2005. It contained a commitment to intervene 'where a population is suffering serious harm' (UNGA 2005) as a result of domestic conflict. But there is a long way from principle to implementation. Intervention is bound to be selective, belated, and short of resources in terms of troops and money. And even with substantial involvement, external actors cannot easily address the root causes of weak statehood as defined in Table 1.

Meanwhile, postmodern states face new challenges even when old-fashioned war is no longer on the agenda. The growth of all kinds of relations across borders not only brings transnational goods; it also brings transnational 'bads': pollution, disease, economic crisis, crime, unwanted migration, and, in recent times, international terrorism. None of these would appear to be existential threats on par with the apocalyptic Cold War scenario of nuclear conflict; but they are serious enough and the advanced states have not so far found effective answers to most of them. In sum, large-scale violent conflict is now within weak states while advanced states must address an increasing number of transnational bads.

Politics: Democracy Challenged

Postmodern states are consolidated liberal democracies but they are also increasingly integrated systems characterized by multilevel governance. That is a challenge to democracy because the whole idea of liberal democracy is based on the assumption that the relevant political unit is the sovereign state; according to Will Kymlicka, 'the only forum within which genuine democracy occurs is within national boundaries' (Kymlicka 1999: 124). Multilevel governance challenges mainstream democratic theory in two ways. The first concerns the overlap between the political community of citizens within a defined territory on the one hand and the group of people affected by the political decisions taken by those citizens' representatives on the other (Held 1995: 16). The second concerns the room for manoeuvre of the sovereign, democratic state; the assumption is that such states enjoy a high degree of national autonomy, allowing them to substantially be in control of their own future. The first assumption is challenged because a large number of 'national' decisions in one state have significant implications for citizens in other states due to the high level of interdependence. The second assumption is challenged because economic and other integration significantly narrows the policy options of individual states.

There is no agreement on the severity of these challenges. Robert A. Dahl simply claims that international organizations cannot be democratic because they do not provide citizens with 'opportunities for political participation, influence, and control roughly equivalent in effectiveness to those already existing in democratic countries' (Dahl 1999: 31); he recommends that states retain as many decisions at home as possible, a difficult posture in an increasingly globalized world.

Others are more optimistic. International cooperation can also be seen as a democratic gain because forces outside the control of any single country are now being regulated in a multilateral setting. That increases output legitimacy (Scharpf 1997) because the political system is better capable of regulating the forces that shape people's lives. Joseph Nye argues that the democratic legitimacy of multilevel governance can be safeguarded if international institutions are designed in such a way that they 'preserve as much space as possible for domestic political processes to operate' (2001: 3). This can be combined with measures that increase the transparency of international organizations, including better access for NGOs and more open procedures.

But in cases of supra-national cooperation, such as the EU and parts of the WTO, where organizations can define rules for member states, Nye's recommendations appear much less effective. If that is the future of more intense international cooperation, what then? There are different views, depending on the underlying theory of democracy (McGrew 2000). David Held has formulated a model of 'cosmopolitan democracy' (Held 1995) which foresees a new ensemble of organizations at different levels from local to global, all bound by a common framework of cosmopolitan democratic law. That is surely an ambitious scheme; postmodern states have so far not come up with effective answers to the democracy challenge posed by multilevel governance.

In weak states, the democracy-problem is straightforward. Is democracy at all possible in systems with defect economies, ineffective institutions, corrupt bureaucracies, self-seeking elites, and populations divided along ethnic and other lines? The early answer after the end of the Cold War, informed by liberal optimism, was a resounding 'yes'. Lack of convincing success has led to a much more skeptical stance today. What began as democratic transition is today rather a democratic 'standstill'. A very large number of regimes are situated in a gray area between fully democratic and outright authoritarian. They are likely to remain semi-authoritarian or semi-democratic with little prospect of further democratization. Western democracy-promoters have tended to focus too much on elections as core elements in a process of democratization. But elections have taken place in many systems, including sharply authoritarian states such as the old Soviet Union or present-day North Korea. 'Free and fair elections', says Robert Dahl, are 'the culmination of the [democratic] process, not the beginning … Unless and until other rights and liberties are firmly protected, free and fair election cannot take place' (Dahl 1992: 246).

Elections appear 'the wrong place to start' (Ottaway 1995: 235) when it comes to democratizing weak and conflict-ridden states. This has led towards a recent discussion about the need for 'stateness first': that is, the precondition for democracy is a fairly effective state (Fukuyama 2005). The problem is of course that it is extremely difficult to conduct effective state-building over a short span of time, as currently demonstrated in Afghanistan, Iraq, and elsewhere. Underlying social and cultural factors are not easily changed in the short and medium term; and any successful change must be accomplished by insiders, not by outsiders. We must expect problems of state weakness to persist in many countries for the foreseeable future. State weakness makes it less likely that countries can escape from the gray zone. In the worst cases, countries have moved toward state failure and complete breakdown.

Modernizing states would appear to be in better shape as regards basic conditions for democratization; they are economically much more robust and they have relatively effective political systems compared to weak states. But even in India, a modernizing state with a long democratic tradition, the system is plagued by communal violence, corruption, elite dominance, and the persistence of several hundred million people in abject poverty. China has introduced capitalism and seeks involvement in the international society but one should not assume that this amounts to an embrace of liberal values. Integration into an international order is seen as necessary for the promotion of national greatness and power; it is not at all connected to a liberalism emphasizing individual freedom and rights. In China, the emphasis is on a project of nation-building where the value of individual liberties is 'assessed in terms of their compatibility with the task of achieving freedom for the state as an actor in international society' (Hughes 2002: 98). Put differently, what is embraced is capitalism whereas individual liberty and democracy are emphatically rejected because they threaten fragmentation and chaos. Singapore is the role model, not Taiwan.

In sum, modernizing states are not all on a secure path towards stable democracy; they might develop capitalist models more compatible with some form of authoritarian or semi-authoritarian rule. Weak states lack the preconditions for stable democratic rule. Postmodern states are democratic but they face a number of new democratic challenges emerging from cross-border integration.

The Economy: No Prospect for a Stable Order

The end of the Cold War was also a period of economic optimism. There was now almost universal support for a liberal–capitalist free market arrangement; only very few countries have not adopted this model in some form or another. Near universal support for free markets 'strengthens the foundation for a liberal world order' (Buzan 2004). But two decades later, there is a global financial and economic crisis. It is not an existential crisis of capitalism but it is sufficiently severe to question whether there will be a stable global economy based on liberal principles that can make up the cornerstone of a liberal world order.

In the advanced states, the crisis began with a burst housing bubble in the United States. That led to extensive mortgage defaults; as a consequence, financial institutions had to incur heavy losses. Lack of capital forced them to decrease investment and tighten credit; with substantial reductions in demand, asset prices declined leading to further losses. Furthermore, the crisis marks the culmination of a long period of development where financial markets have become increasingly more complex, offering a number of products (derivatives) the real value of which is difficult or impossible to ascertain. The financial sector's share of total economic activity has grown dramatically, making advanced countries more dependent on that sector. And even if the financial system is so globalized today that it acts as a real-time, 24-hour integrated organism where exchange rates, interest rates, and asset values are determined in the context of the global market, there is no cooperating political centre, no common global, or even Western institution of financial governance that could adequately respond to the crisis. The financial system is deeply integrated on a global scale but regulation and control remain almost purely national; it was thus left to national governments to respond to the crisis, with different national 'packages', only thinly coordinated.

Worse still, there are no indications of impending institutional reform that will prevent a new crisis. The international financial institutions, even the G20, continue to place their confidence in perfect markets; the task is to 'restore confidence' in those markets. An increasing number of commentators see this as a case of 'regulatory capture', that is, state regulators are dominated by the mindsets of those economic interests that they are meant to supervise (Morris 2008).

Modernizing states, especially China, have fared better in the economic crisis, but they face severe problems of their own. The larger question is whether their economic progress is based on sustainable models of growth. Both China and India have sweatshop factories with poor working conditions, low job security, low wages, and long hours of work. In the Pearl River and Yangtze River delta regions in China, for example 'migrant workers routinely work 12 hours a day, 7 days a week; during the busy season, a 13–15 hour day is not uncommon' (Wen 2005: 3). This is not economic upgrading; it is sooner 'downgrading' with deteriorating conditions for labour. At the same time, there are serious environmental problems. Some sixty percent of China's major rivers are 'unsuitable for human contact' (Wen 2005: 10). Desertification has halved habitable and usable land over a period of fifty years. Seven of the ten most polluted cities in the world are in China. More than one-third of industrial wastewater enters waterways without any treatment.

In weak states, economic conditions are even worse. Large parts of the population are outside the formal sectors, living in localized subsistence economies. Exports consist of a few primary products and the economies are highly dependent on imports. Weak states are not attractive sites for foreign investment. There is no dynamic domestic market, no adequate supply of skilled labour, no developed physical infrastructure, and they do not offer stable, market-friendly conditions of operation. In other words, the circuits of global capital do not include the weak states in any major way. While heavily dependent on foreign aid, they are marginalized bystanders in the process of economic globalization.

In sum, global capitalism is not in existential crisis, but a stable liberal economic order with benefits for all will not emerge sometime soon.

Nationhood and Community: Identity on the Move towards Common Values?

Many people hoped that intensified globalization and the end of the Cold War would strengthen the support for universal liberal values as they have been expressed in human rights declarations, the UN Millennium Declaration, and the Charter of the United Nations. It is true that the post-Cold War world pays more attention to human rights. States that do not ensure the political and civil rights of their citizens run the risk of losing legitimacy in the society of states. Among the liberal postmodern states there is a 'Western civic identity' which is distinct from national identities. It is a consensus around a set of common norms and principles, including 'political democracy, constitutional government, individual rights, private property-based economic systems, and toleration of diversity in non-civic areas of ethnicity and religion' (Deudney and Ikenberry 1999: 193). The liberal hope is that the support for these values will continue to grow with the progress of democratization in many more countries around the world; the claim is that in the long run, 'modernization brings democracy' (Inglehart and Welzel 2009: 35).

But even if modernization is conducive to the strengthening of liberal values, it is no deterministic relationship, neither in the advanced countries nor anywhere else. In postmodern states, the processes of integration have also bolstered support for regional movements that vie for increased national autonomy or even secession. Another response to globalization is nationalistic movements that stress a very exclusive definition of national identity. They perceive stronger interdependence as a two-pronged threat. First, it threatens the social and economic wellbeing of 'original' citizens because of the new claims made on the state by immigrants. Second, it threatens a historically specific, narrow conception of national identity in which there is no room for newcomers. So the situation in postmodern states is much more mixed than liberal optimists think. National identities are not dissolving; they are sooner being transformed in a complex and heterogeneous manner. On the one hand, national identities increasingly contain supranational elements. What it means to be German or French, for example, now includes a commitment to European cooperation and common values. On the other hand, more divisive 'resistance identities' (Castells 1998: 60) are growing stronger as well and that includes a much more skeptical view of cooperation and interdependence.

In modernizing states, processes of economic modernization are combined with more, rather than less, commitment to a nationalist definition of identity. The Communist Party (CCP) in China uses nationalism as a legitimating ideology. The CCP lacks democratic legitimacy and traditional communist ideology has collapsed. Therefore, the CCP 'is increasingly dependent upon its nationalist credentials to rule' (Bajoria 2009:2). But nationalism is a double-edged sword for the government. Domestically, it seeks to suppress ethnic nationalism in Tibet, Taiwan, and elsewhere; in the international sphere, the claim of 'peaceful rise' of China can be harmed. China is certainly joining the world, but only reluctantly, and it remains a highly self-seeking player (Deng 1998). In India, with its stronger liberal democratic tradition, Hindu nationalism has grown under the Bharatiya Janata Party (BJP) and several other, more extremist organizations (Basu 2001). That has led to a new trend towards political decentralization, threatening a significantly more fragmented polity.

In weak states, nationhood has not taken on the significance that it has elsewhere; ethnic affiliations remain of crucial. When the state does not deliver, ethnic communities become focal points for a 'moral economy' (Ndegwa 1997). Early processes of democratization had promoted ethnic cleavages in the population because more political openness increases the possibilities for different ethnic groups to present their views and formulate their demands; and state elites actively enforce links with ethnic groups in their attempt to stay in power.

Overall, there is no strong trend towards the emergence of common liberal values on a global scale. Both processes of modernization and processes of decay can help produce more nationalistic or more fragmented and divisive responses in terms of identity.

The End of Sovereignty?

We come to the foundational institution of sovereignty, the rules that define the locus of political authority and set the context for relations between states. There is a large debate about the possible 'end of sovereignty' in the context of intensified globalization. But sovereignty has not ended; the institution is, however, being transformed in response to new circumstances (Sørensen 2001).

The juridical core of sovereignty is constitutional independence. It means that the sovereign state stands apart; other entities have no political authority within the state's territory and the sovereign state is legally equal to other sovereign states. In addition to this juridical core, sovereignty is also a set of rules regulating how states go about playing the game of sovereignty.

In the classical game of sovereignty, played by modern states, two such rules are of special significance: *non-intervention* and *reciprocity*. Non-intervention means that states have a right to choose their own path, to conduct their affairs without outside interference. Reciprocity means giving and taking for mutual advantage. States make deals with each other as equal partners; a game based on reciprocity is a symmetric game where the players enjoy equal opportunity to profit from bi- and multilateral transactions.

What has then changed in the institution of sovereignty? The juridical core of sovereignty, constitutional independence, remains in place. It continues to be the one dominant principle of political organization in the international system. In that sense, sovereign states 'have all remained recognizably of the same species up to our time' (Ruggie 1998: 191). The regulative rules of the sovereignty game, however, have changed considerably, responding to the changes in statehood depicted in Table 1. Postmodern states, especially the EU-members, have been compelled to modify the rule of non-intervention. That is because the whole idea of multilevel governance is based on *intervention* by the EU in the affairs of member states. Modern states playing the classical game of sovereignty jealously guarded their sovereign right of non-intervention. EU member states are doing exactly the opposite: they agree to accept rules made by outsiders (i.e. fellow members) as the law within their own jurisdictions. This is 'regulated intervention' rather than non-intervention. Some international organizations, e.g. the WTO, contain examples of this as well.

Reciprocity is also modified within the EU. The old game is one of equal treatment of competing players. The new game is *unequal* treatment according to special needs or cooperative reciprocity; poor regions in the EU get special, preferential conditions because of their special needs. The game on 'non-reciprocity' is even more developed in the case of *weak states* because they cannot reciprocate: they need, and demand, economic aid from the advanced states. In that respect, they demand to be treated as *unequals* (i.e. qualified for aid) and *equals* (i.e. enjoying recognition on par with everybody else), at one and the same time. Aid donors, in contrast, want to supervise any aid in order to see it is put to proper use; that leads to *negotiated intervention* rather than non-intervention.

In sum, the regulative rules of the sovereignty game are changing while constitutional independence stays in place. That leads to tensions in the institution of sovereignty. Postmodern states are simultaneously segregated (constitutional independence) and integrated (regulated intervention, cooperative reciprocity). Weak states are simultaneously segregated (constitutional independence) and associated (non-reciprocity, negotiated intervention). In the case of postmodern states, future developments towards integration will strengthen the pressure in favour of federation which spells the end of constitutional independence. In the case of weak states that fail to develop so that they can stand on their own feet, the pressure will be for international society to end segregation and adopt some form of protectorate (e.g. Kosovo, East Timor, Afghanistan).

Modernizing states must live with both types of pressures: they would like aid in order to develop faster but will not give up on the principle of non-intervention. They want integration in the international society and participation in globalization, but they will not abandon constitutional independence and will not allow outsiders to set rules for them. The institution of sovereignty remains in place, but it is being transformed in ways that exposes it to significant challenges.

Conclusion

States never stand still; they continue to change. The modern, Westphalian state as it had emerged mainly in Western Europe and in North America around 1950 took a very long time to mature, but once it had, a new process of transformation immediately began. I have diagnosed that transformation as a transition from modern to postmodern statehood.

Weak, postcolonial states are qualitatively different; they were never modern in the first place. They emerged from a process of colonization and decolonization. Leading states carry major responsibility for this entire process, but domestic conditions are also important for explaining the emergence of weak states. Modernizing states are different again.

In conclusion, the sovereign state is alive and well. By no means has it been obliterated by the forces of globalization. But it has been transformed in significant ways and it will continue to change. These changes may not always be for the better. The major types of state discussed here all face considerable challenges to which they have so far not found very good answers.

References

Adler, E. and M. Barnett (eds) (1998). *Security Communities*, Cambridge: Cambridge University Press.

Bajoria, J. (2009). 'Nationalism in China', Council on Foreign Relations, at: <http://www.cfr.org/publication/16079/nationalism_in_china.html>, accessed 14 October 2010.

Basu, A. (2001). 'The Dialectics of Hindu Nationalism', in A. Kohli (ed.), *The Success of India's Democracy*, Cambridge: Cambridge University Press.

Berlin, I. (1979). *Russian Thinkers*, Harmondsworth: Penguin.

Buzan, B. (2004). *From International to World Society*, Cambridge: Cambridge University Press.

Castells, M. (1998). *The Power of Identity*, Oxford: Basil Blackwell.

Dahl, R.A. (1992). 'Democracy and Human Rights Under Different Conditions of Development', in A. Eide and B. Hagtvet (eds) *Human Rights in Perspective: A Global Assessment*, Oxford: Blackwell.

——(1999). 'Can International Organizations be Democratic? A Sceptic's View', in I. Shapiro and C. Hacker-Cordón (eds) *Democracy's Edges*, Cambridge: Cambridge University Press.

Deng, Y. (1998). 'The Chinese Conception of National Interests in International Relations', *The China Quarterly*, 154: 308–29.

Deudney, D. and G.J. Ikenberry (1999). 'The Nature and Sources of Liberal International Order', *Review of International Studies*, 25 (2): 179–96.

Fukuyama, F. (1989). 'The End of History', *The National Interest*, 16 (Summer): 3–18.

——(2005). ' "Stateness" First', *Journal of Democracy*, 16 (1): 84–8.

Harbom, L. and P. Wallensteen (2009). 'Armed Conflicts, 1946–2208', *Journal of Peace Research*, 46 (4): 577–87.

Held, D. (1995). *Democracy and the Global Order*, Cambridge: Polity Press.

Hughes, C. (2002). 'China and Global Liberalism', in E. Hovden and E. Keene (eds) *The Globalization of Liberalism*, Basingstoke: Palgrave Macmillan.

Huntington, S.P. (1968). *Political Order in Changing Societies*, New Haven, CT: Yale University Press.

Inglehart, R. and C. Welzel (2009). 'How Development Leads to Democracy', *Foreign Affairs*, 88(2): 33–49.

Jackson, R. (1993). *Quasi-states: Sovereignty, International Relations and the Third World*, Cambridge: Cambridge University Press.

Kant, I. (1992). *Kant's Political Writings*, ed. H. Reiss, Cambridge: Cambridge University Press.

Kymlicka, W. (1999). 'Citizenship in an Era of Globalization', in I. Shapiro and C. Hacker-Cordón (eds) *Democracy's Edges*, Cambridge: Cambridge University Press.

McGrew, A. (2000). 'From Global Governance to Good Governance: Theories and Prospects of Democratizing the Global Polity', Copenhagen: Workshop on the Global Polity.

Morris, C.R. (2008). *The Two Trillion Dollar Meltdown*, New York: Public Affairs.

Müller, J.-W. (2008). 'Fear and Freedom: On "Cold War Liberalism"', *European Journal of Political Theory*, 7 (1): 45–64.

Ndegwa, S.N. (1997). 'Citizenship and Ethnicity: An Examination of Two Transition Moments in Kenyan Politics', *American Political Science Review*, 91 (3): 599–617.

Nye, J.S. (2001). 'Globalization's Democratic Deficit', *Foreign Affairs*, 80 (4): 2–6.

Ottaway, M. (1995). 'Democratization in Collapsed States', in W.I. Zartman (ed.) *Collapsed States: The Disintegration and Restoration of Legitimate Authority*, Boulder, CO: Lynne Rienner.

Rosecrance, R. (1986). *The Rise of the Trading State: Commerce and Conquest in the Modern World*, New York: Basic Books.

Ruggie, J.G. (1998). *Constructing the World Polity*, London: Routledge.

Scharpf, F.W. (1997). 'Introduction: The Problem Solving Capacity of Multi-level Governance', *Journal of European Public Policy*, 4 (4): 520–38.

Sørensen, G. (2001). *Changes in Statehood: The Transformation of International Relations*, Basingstoke: Palgrave Macmillan.

——(2007). 'After the Security Dilemma: The Challenges of Insecurity in Weak States and the Dilemma of Liberal Values', *Security Dialogue*, 38 (3): 357–78.

——(2008). 'The Case for Combining Material Forces and Ideas in the Study of IR', *European Journal of International Relations*, 14 (5): 5–32.

United Nations General Assembly (UNGA) (2005). 'World Summit Outcome 2005', Assembly Resolution A/RES/60/1, 24 October.

Wen, D. (2005). *China Copes with Globalization*, San Francisco, CA: International Forum on Globalization.

WorldPublicOpinion (2009).'Survey' at: <www.asianoffbeat.com/default.asp?Display=1841>, accessed 14 October 2010.

Zacher, M.W. (2001). 'The Territorial Integrity Norm: International Boundaries and the Use of Force', *International Organization*, 55 (2): 215–50.

Modern Constitutionalism and the Challenges of Complex Pluralism

Paul Blokker

The abstract idea of a written constitution as the foundational basis of modern democratic societies is a largely undisputed element in much of social, political, and legal theory. At the same time, the nature, form, and distinct functions of the constitution in – and increasingly also beyond – modern democratic societies is an evermore frequent object of dispute. As will be discussed in this chapter, this is not least because of the profound changes that affect constitutional democracies and constitutionalism as a result of processes of globalization, sub-state empowerment, as well as internal transformations of the modern polity and of democratic politics, and a related diversification of democratic imaginaries.

In the two centuries of 'reign' of modern constitutionalism, a general, minimal consensus has emerged on the nature and functions of the constitution. As Michel Rosenfeld argues, '[t]here appears to be no accepted definition of constitutionalism but, in the broadest terms, modern constitutionalism requires imposing limits on the powers of government, adherence to the rule of law, and the protection of fundamental rights' (Rosenfeld 1992: 497). Modern constitutionalism corresponds largely with the Westphalian idea of a state system of separate and homogeneous nation-states, and, in this, it comprises a tendency to 'presuppose the uniformity of a nation state with a centralised and unitary system of legal and political institutions' (Tully 1995: 9). In a slightly different formulation, the 'understanding of a constitution and its assigned role as the guardian of the political process is commonly associated with modern constitutionalism and builds on institutionalised and mythical links with statehood that had been forged over centuries' (Wiener 2008: 23).

In this, modern constitutions tend to share a number of generic features (the following list is not meant to be exhaustive). First, a modern constitution is regarded as a 'structure of law' that is in important ways separate from its subjects. Whereas the modern constitution is ultimately dependent on the people for its legitimation, once constituted, it becomes a relatively autonomous set of meta-norms and rules that constitutes social and political interaction. James Tully calls this relative autonomy or externality the 'formality' of modern constitutions (Tully 2008). Second, one of the essential ideas behind the constitution is to channel and express popular sovereignty. In this, popular sovereignty has been widely understood in a monist way, i.e., as the expression of a singular people. At any rate, the act of the constitution transfers this sovereignty from the *pouvoir constituant* to the *pouvoir constitué*. Third, the singular understanding of the people presupposes a shared civic or ethno-cultural identity, which is symbolically reflected in the constitution, either implicitly or explicitly so (cf. Weiler 2003). Fourth, modern constitutions are understood as coherent and non-contradictory, contractual structures, in which 'constitutional essentials are unambiguously settled and made binding into the future' (Chambers 1998: 149). Fifth, while many of the dimensions noted above invoke a limitative, and foundational perception of constitutions, constitutions also provide for a positive, democratic dimension, including civil and political rights which enable citizens and political actors to set their own rules, even if within the limits set by the very same constitution.

Modern constitutionalism is, however, increasingly under strain. Notwithstanding the global trend, of the last half century or so, of convergence to an 'amplified' form of modern constitutionalism around a form of 'democracy by judiciary' or 'new constitutionalism' (Arjomand 2003; Stone Sweet 2008), more recent trends of pluralization seem to provoke profound changes in modern constitutionalism. Constitutionalism appears now increasingly contested, and anachronistic in some of its key features. One way of describing and evaluating such changes is by focussing on the two imperatives or legitimatory principles of modern constitutionalism, which in a way condense the five generic features. The two imperatives are popular sovereignty (democracy) and the limitation of sovereignty (constitutionalism) (Loughlin and Walker 2007: 1; cf. Tully 2008: 91–2).

The first principle is that of constitutionalism or the rule of law. In the light of this principle, the constitution, in order to be legitimate,

> requires that the exercise of political power in the whole and in every part of any *constitutionally* legitimate system of political, social and economic cooperation should be exercised in accordance with and through the general system of principles, rules and procedures, including procedures for amending any principle, rule or procedure.
>
> *(Tully 2008: 92)*

The emphasis is on the rule of law and the provision of an orderly process of politics. A second principle is the principle of democracy, which

> requires that, although the people or peoples who constitute a political association are subject to the constitutional system, they, or their entrusted representatives, must also impose the general system on themselves in order to be sovereign and free, and thus for the association to be *democratically* legitimate.
>
> *(Tully 2008: 93)*

The second principle is then about (collective) autonomy or self-rule, in which people give themselves their own laws, rather than being subject to some form of 'heteronomy'.

The rest of the chapter will engage with recent pluralistic trends that put modern constitutionalism under strain. After a brief discussion of the post-Second World War, reinforcing trend of modern constitutionalism in the form of legal, 'new constitutionalism', I will argue that the significance of this trend needs to be qualified by a range of pluralistic tendencies that, while in some ways amplifying legalistic and monistic tendencies in constitutionalism, also involve strong corrosive and diversifying implications for the modern constitutional template. These pluralistic tendencies comprise the fragmentation of sovereignty, cultural pluralism, and substantive or interpretative pluralism. The argument is that the challenges of complex pluralism undermine many of the constraining features of modern constitutionalism, but, while in some cases forms of autonomy and democratic participation are strengthened, in many others, constitutional pluralism tends to further compromise the democratic dimension of constitutionalism. In a normative sense, the chapter critically discusses a number of theoretical reflections on these challenges, and in particular emphasizes those approaches that search for the potential reinforcement of democratic, participatory, and inclusive dimensions in the current constitutional predicament.

New Constitutionalism

Since the Second World War, and more prominently so since the end of the 1980s, the modern constitutional form has not only enjoyed its finest hour in terms of its widespread adoption in 'new democracies' (cf. Haberle 1992), or even elicited 'enthusiasm about the global rule of law' (Koskenniemi 2007: 3), but has also experienced a distinct turn in terms of a re-interpretation and rebalancing of some of its key dimensions, particularly so in the context of democratic transition. By the early twenty-first century, this 'new constitutionalism' (Arjomand 2003; Stone Sweet 2008, 2009) has allegedly become predominant, even if not uncontested. The emphasis is on written constitutions with an entrenched 'catalogue of rights', and a 'system of constitutional justice to defend those rights' (Stone Sweet 2008: 219). The novelty is that the constitutional court as an independent institution is not only the ultimate guardian and interpreter of the constitution, but equally so of fundamental rights.

In terms of the generic features of modern constitutionalism, new constitutionalism prioritizes the higher law status of the constitution and of fundamental rights, as well as normative coherence and legal certainty, and takes an amplified understanding of the rule of law. The latter is part of post-authoritarian and post-totalitarian transitions to 'new democracies', such as those in Central and Eastern Europe. It includes a constitutional politics that comprises both the 'judicialization of politics' – which encompasses the reconstruction of the normative basis of the state – and the political activism of judicial actors (Arjomand 2003). The emphasis in democratic transition is on legal formalism and coherence, and constitutionally entrenched democratic preconditions, while democratic participation is largely confined to 'normal politics'. In this, the shift is towards legal constitutionalism, while, '[w]ith very few exceptions, legislative sovereignty has formally disappeared. The new constitutionalism killed it, paradoxically perhaps, in the name of democracy' (Stone Sweet 2008: 218).

If new constitutionalism amplifies some of modern constitutionalism's main dimensions, it at the same time seems difficult to deny that a number of its key features have become increasingly untenable (in a normative, democratic sense), and unrealistic or anachronistic (in terms of correspondence with political, social, cultural, and economic reality). Below, I will argue that with regard to at least three recent pluralistic tendencies, modern constitutionalism – including its new, amplified form – is subject to a variety of corrosive trends that seem difficult to reverse, and that are bound to fundamentally change its nature.

The Fragmentation of Sovereignty

Even if 1989 has entailed modern constitutionalism's finest hour, Westphalian-type constitutionalism is at the same time increasingly confronted with powerful, corrosive trends, in an empirical sense, and critical contestation and reinterpretation, in a theoretical sense. Constitutional and legal, as well as social and political theory increasingly attempt to deal with the (contested) observation that modern, state-centred constitutionalism is subject to modification, and even marginalization, in the context of a complex set of trends regarding globalization and particularization. These include the emergence of alternative (transnational, international, non-state) authorities that claim constitutional capacity and some hold of sovereignty, beyond or parallel to the traditional sovereign nation-state; the European Union is the most significant and evolved example of this (other such phenomena include the World Trade Organization and human rights charters). But constitutionalization beyond the state equally includes private, economic actors that engage in the production of 'self-validating contracts' and 'closed circuits' that differ from state legal orders not only in terms of geographical site but also in terms of the novel, self-referential quality of the norms themselves (cf. Teubner 1997). A concomitant, but not altogether overlapping, trend is that of a devolution and differentiation of democratic sovereignty towards sub-state levels. This trend is related to processes of post-state constitutionalization, but is much more importantly inspired by political resistance to imposed, Western forms of majoritarian constitutionalism and by political projects for cultural recognition, regional autonomy, and self-government.[1]

While the move away from the traditional state order in terms of post-state constitutional norms challenges the monistic, unitary, and exclusionary nature of modern constitutionalism, post-state constitutionalism does not in any obvious way resolve pressing normative problems of a 'demo-cratic deficit', or disputed trends of the juridification of politics and legal constitutionalization. To the contrary, it can often be argued that many of the alleged forms of constitutionalization beyond the state tend to rely on closed, expert-based, juridical, and self-contained under-standings of constitutionalism (cf. Cohen 2004), in which democratic or civic-participatory dimensions are of less or no concern. The emerging post-state constitutional regimes bind modern states in many ways, but mostly without being subject to any type of significant democratic control, i.e., control by those that are affected by these new constitutional structures. With regard to the sub-state level, shifts away from the traditional level of national sovereignty tend to further weaken an overall sovereign capacity within formally sovereign states, even if shifts to the local level potentially offer prospects for the democratic enablement of local actors.

In social and political theory, much attention is on the constitutionalization of an emerging European polity as a potential answer to increased fragmentation and democratic erosion, and the implications of such a supranational constitutional form for social integration, collective identity, and civic participation. One of the more prominent normative appraisals of a potential European polity can be found in the work of Jürgen Habermas, who proposes a polity grounded in post-national 'constitutional patriotism' (e.g. Habermas 2001). The upshot is clearly that it is in principle possible to overcome fragmentation by reconstructing a political community on the European level. But others point to the difficulties of such a move, and the impossibility of lifting specific dimensions of constitutional democracy to the supranational level. Well-known forms of critique include the democratic dimension – the absence of a European demos (indicating the lack of a constituent people that might constitutionally ground the new European polity), the want of a European-wide public sphere, and the elitist, closed nature of supranational politics, and the symbolic or cultural dimension – the conundrum of how to reflect the plurality of cultural traditions in a singular European identity (cf. Priban 2007; Weiler 2001). A promising attempt to overcome some of these problems is suggested in the theory of 'reflexive con-stitutionalism', which is explicitly formulated against the problem of juridification or legal domination, and proposes a novel understanding of constitutionalism (Bohman 2004). Significantly, the reflexive constitutional order is to include multiple demoi (rather than a European People-As-One), which might hold a plurality of substantive perspectives, and is to be based on ongoing (constitutional) deliberation, rather than on a foundational moment.

In legal and political theories of 'constitutional pluralism' (Walker 2002; for a recent over-view, see Avbelj and Komarek 2008) and 'legal pluralism' (Teubner 1997; Stone Sweet 2009), the focus is on a range of post-state constitutional experiences, first on the European, but also on the global level. The focus is on an emerging plurality of constitutionally relevant sites and actors, with distinct (territorial, functional, sectoral, multi-functional) pretensions to sovereignty that 'escape the template of the state'. This plurality is taken to imply that the 'homology of territory, community and political capacity which was the historical project of the national or plurinational state of the Westphalian state has come to an end' (Walker 2002: 320).

Overall, there is no consensus then on the classificatory status of post-state constitutional developments, nor on their normative implications. In the expanding literature, two approaches are particularly worth mentioning, one legal-taxonomic, the other political-normative. Both engage with normative vicissitudes but also explicitly use a sociological lens to analyse post- and sub-state legal pluralism. One of the more comprehensive legal approaches is the above-mentioned 'constitutional pluralism' (Walker 2002; 2008). In Neil Walker's understanding, constitutional pluralism entails a way of 'charting the post-Westphalian order' (2002: 348). To this end, he suggests an elaborated set of criteria (i.e. constitutive, governance, as well as societal criteria) that are to provide us with a conceptual grasp of a variegated range of constitutional experiences, as well as with a structural grasp of the practical significance of, and relationships, conflicts, and overlaps between, novel constitutional forms (Walker 2002: 339–40). In this, constitutional pluralism – even if acknowledging a potentiality for emancipation in pluralism's anti-monolithic thrust – is primarily concerned with providing a taxonomy of new phenomena.

In 'democratic constitutionalism', in contrast, a critical, radical-democratic dimension is at the forefront. On James Tully's rather unorthodox view, contemporary state and global legal forms, despite their fragmentary and pluralistic nature, can nevertheless be understood from within their common basis in the logics and biases of 'modern constitutionalism'. Rather than an erosion of modern constitutionalism's significance in a novel and fragmented post-state order, Tully observes its continuation in 'informal imperialism'. The latter refers to the diffusion and imposition of modern constitutional forms – including state-based 'constitutional democracy' and 'systems of law beyond the state' – over the globe (Tully 2008: 199). Democratic constitutionalism consists then of a critical, normative suggestion of how to radically rebalance the legal and democratic dimensions in the contemporary situation in favour of the democratic-participatory dimension. The approach builds on a rehabilitation of non-modern, alternative experiences of constitutionalism (such as those of aboriginal communities) and grass-roots struggles 'in the most effective forums' against inequalities and heteronomy that are continued through informal imperialism (Tully 2008: 103).

Cultural Pluralism

In recent decades, various disciplines in the social sciences have shifted attention to issues of collective identity, multi-cultural society, and cultural plurality in constitutional democracies, and struggles for recognition and sub-national self-government. In political theory, the issues of multi-national democracy, multi-culturalism, and recognition have become salient foci of debate (cf. Kymlicka 2001; Taylor 1994; Tully 2001), while in social theory, nationalism and collective identity have (re-)turned to prominence (Calhoun 2007). Recently, also legal studies and constitutional law have incorporated collective identity and sub-national self-government as core problématiques of constitutionalism (cf. Rosenfeld 1992; Priban 2007; Tierney 2004).

The emerging concern is that traditional 'monistic' ideas of a singular collective identity, a supposed neutrality of liberal-democratic polities towards cultural identity, and allegedly 'thin' forms of collective identity are deeply problematic. The general idea is that the strong affinity of modern constitutionalism with an idea of 'national identity' has become difficult, if not impossible, to uphold in increasingly pluralistic democratic societies. The homogenizing logic of modern constitutionalism can be seen to imply that – even if put here in somewhat strong terms – 'human experience must be decontextualized and diverse personal identities extirpated in order to create a single national legal identity for each State' (MacDonald 2005: 2).

The relation between national identity and constitutional democracy is now commonly understood as less straightforward and unproblematic than in the past. As aptly put by Stephen Tierney, in a discussion on the recent return of attention for nationalism in political philosophy,

> liberal philosophers over the past two decades have found the relationship between the state and the nation to offer very fertile soil within which to cultivate wide-ranging and fundamental challenges to widely held assumptions about the nature of the democratic state and the nature of the *demos* within the state: assumptions which for centuries have underpinned – it now seems in many respects mistakenly – so much grand theorising about the nature of the *polis* and the relationships of identity and loyalty between citizens and their respective states.
>
> *(Tierney 2008: 130)*

Tierney goes on: 'these stateist assumptions came to be characteristic also of constitutional ideology, with states presenting their constitutions as neutral on cultural and societal matters when in fact they reflect, and serve to entrench, cultural particularisms'.

In a cultural-sociological vein, then, the liberal idea of state neutrality is not only considered a myth, but the explicit recognition of some kind of common cultural identity is deemed indispensable in order for modern law to be integrative. The idea is that a modern constitutional order cannot merely be a formal structure, independent of society, but would need to reflect a symbolic dimension which encourages cohesion and allegiance for legal subjects. Rosenfeld claims that '[i]ndeed, without some predominant identity such as that of the sovereign nation or of the constitutional self, it is difficult to imagine how one could justify the imposition of a constitutional order' (Rosenfeld 1992: 498–9).

A symbolic dimension or shared identity is then often understood as grounded in some notion of commonality, referring to a common language, ethnicity, and/or religion. In the case of, for instance, the new constitutional democracies in Central and Eastern Europe,

> the constitution-making process also reflected the new political identity of the emerging democratic nations. In this sense, constitution-making was a process of self-reflection, clarification and codification of what constitutes a sovereign *people*. The process of constitution-making significantly contributes to the symbolic creation of the people as one nation.
>
> *(Priban 2007: 72)*

The theorization of modern constitutionalism, if not necessarily the practice of constitutional democracies, can then largely be said to have been exposed as insensitive to questions of cultural identity and diversity, not least because of an implicit assumption of a majority identity. Traditional notions of constitutional democracy have been shown to be largely indifferent to, assimilationist towards, or even unaware of, cultural diversity within its borders (cf. Tierney 2004, 2008: 130–1). There is thus a clear need to rethink modern constitutionalism, in that the current historical period, in which cultural plurality and sub-state demands for recognition are evermore prominent (the most discussed cases are Canada, Spain, the United Kingdom, and Belgium), increasingly shows the problematic nature of assumptions of neutrality regarding issues of culture, religion, gender, and ethnocultural identity, as well as the failing nature of modern constitutionalism to provide cohesive force on its basis.

But the explicit recognition of a cultural–sociological dimension to constitutionalism is evidently in tension with cultural plurality. Three problems stand out with regard to cultural pluralism: first of all, the monistic, statist view of constitutional democracy or 'monistic demos thesis'; second, the definition of cultural identity, and related assumption of its decreasing relevance in modern constitutional democracy; and, third, the understanding of the relation between collective identities and democracy. Different resolutions to cultural plurality in modern constitutional democracies have been offered. In the probably most well-known reconceptualization of constitutional democracy in the light of cultural pluralism – 'liberal nationalism' – the (constitutional) recognition of multiple nations is made explicit. Stephen Tierney's work (2004) on constitutionalism and national pluralism builds on this view, showing that constitutional solutions are increasingly the focus of sub-state nationalists, whose search for constitutional change involves increased recognition of multiple nations, increased representation on the central state level, and calls for higher levels of autonomy. There is, however, a risk in liberal nationalist approaches that cultural pluralism is understood in a rather narrow and static sense, and, consequently, that the emphasis in constitutional reform is largely on formal-constitutional arrangements and accommodation.

From a more radical-democratic and pluralistic view, as in the earlier mentioned 'democratic constitutionalism', a more drastic shift in perceptions of constitutionalism would be needed. While the focus here is equally on forms of 'multinational democracy' and constitutional resolution, the argument goes against the search for definitive, formal solutions and favours ongoing 'struggles of recognition' as an intrinsic part of modern politics, and as enhancing legitimacy and stability. In this view, constitutionalism needs to endorse 'the freedom of the members of an open society to change the constitutional rules of mutual recognition and association from time to time as their identities change' (Tully 2001: 5, 6).[2]

Substantive or Interpretative Pluralism

In addition to the tensions caused by post-state constitutional pluralism, and by sub-state nationalism, modern constitutionalism is exposed to increasing forms of substantive, interpretative pluralism or 'pluralism-in fact' (Rosenfeld 1998, 2008). The fact of an increasingly prominent ideational pluralism in modern democratic societies, and the equally increasing acknowledgement of different (national) constitutional traditions, as well as legal pluralism *within* national legal orders (in particular as emerged in the debate on the European Constitution), have invoked significant attempts at rethinking some of the main principles of modern constitutionalism.

Arguably, the main debate in the context of interpretative pluralism is that regarding the nature of the relationship between constitutionalism and democracy. Here, a first distinction can be made between those that endorse a form of 'legal constitutionalism' (Dworkin 1995; Rawls 1993), and continue to estimate the modern constitutional tradition as the only answer to questions of increasing ideational and value pluralism, and those that are in favour of some form of 'political constitutionalism', 'democratic liberalism', or 'democratic constitutionalism' (Bellamy and Castiglione 2000; Bellamy 2007; Tully 1995, 2008; Waldron 1999; Colon-Rios 2009), in which irreducible value pluralism is allowed to democratically emerge through political participation.

The legal–constitutionalist view in principle endorses liberal constitutionalism, i.e., 'as a normative framework that sets limits on and goals for the exercise of state power' (Bellamy and Castiglione 2000: 172). In this view (akin to 'new constitutionalism'), the constitution is seen as providing the preconditions for democracy. Democracy can only function as such if democratic politics abides to the constitutional limitations set to it. The constitution, and increasingly so the idea of an included set of entrenched fundamental rights, provide then an independent and superior law that secures the working and outcomes of democracy.

One of the key assumptions of legal constitutionalism is that it is in principle possible to reach a reasonable consensus on what such preconditions of democracy ought to be, and how to translate them into a language of rights and fundamental law (Bellamy 2007: 3). In other words, it is possible to arrive at a set of 'essential preconditions for democracy', the 'right' abstract principles (Dworkin 1995) or 'best answers' (Bellamy 2007). One of the most well-known formulations of such an idea is that of an 'overlapping consensus' (Rawls 1993). The idea is further that once a higher law with the right basic norms is formulated, it should be regarded as a 'constitutional structure that a majority cannot change' (Dworkin 1995: 2). Since a consensus on the right norms has been found, there is no need to change such norms in the future, only to ensure the correct implementation of such norms. The view of the constitution emerging is a static, permanent framework, which is only to a very limited extent open to amendment. In this, the legal-constitutionalist view in essence understands the constitution as a 'meta-norm', which is not implicated in, as it transcends, substantive views on the common good, and in this provides a 'neutral framework that rests on a separation of the right from the good' (Bellamy and Castiglione 2000: 174–5). The type of societal and substantive pluralism that is guaranteed through such a consensus is, however, best designated as one of 'limited pluralism', in that only those views that ultimately are compatible with liberal individualism are included (Rosenfeld 1998).

The political–constitutionalist conception takes a wholly different view of the role and substance of the constitution, and its relation to democratic politics. Its dispute with legal constitutionalism is based on the observation that the

> need for [an] alternative and more political approach arises from the contested nature of rights. Despite widespread support for both constitutional rights and rights-based judicial review, theorists, politics, lawyers and ordinary citizens frequently disagree over which rights merit or require such entrenchment, the legal form they should take, the best way of implementing them, their relationship to each other, and the manner in which courts should understand and uphold them.
>
> *(Bellamy 2007: 16)*

Rather than understanding the constitution as a 'right basic norm', it is understood as providing a basic framework for resolving disagreements over the right and the good. This also means that foundational norms should always be subject to reconsideration and reformulation. In other words, the constitution is not seen as an entrenched set of fundamental principles, but rather as the framework for the articulation of and deliberation over conceptions of self-government and the common good. As Bellamy aptly expresses it: 'we could see constitutions not as constraints imposed upon democracy but as the limits that a mature democracy places upon itself' (Bellamy 2007: 91).

Political constitutionalism starts from the idea that reasonable disagreement is part and parcel of democracy. The critique of legal constitutionalism is that a 'failure to acknowledge the disagreements that surround constitutional values, and the resulting need for political mechanisms to resolve them, can itself be a source of domination and arbitrary rule that impacts negatively on rights and the rule of law' (Bellamy 2007: 145; cf. Waldron 1999). The attempt is then not to transcend pluralism, but to include the widest range of substantive views possible. Political constitutionalism points to a continuously evolving process of politics, including constitutional politics, in terms of political debate grounded in the principles of mutual recognition and *audi alteram partem.* The political view of the constitution arguably endorses a more comprehensive and inclusive view of pluralism, in that it emphasizes the negotiation of differences and a continuous quest for mutually agreeable conditions. In sum, political constitutionalism does not attempt to sever democratic politics from questions of justice and right, but, in full acknowledgement of the impossibility of settling constitutional questions and rights issues once and for all, it makes the relation between politics, and rights and legality visible by means of a continuous political engagement with acceptable interpretations.

But theoretical pluralism does not end here. The shift towards a re-evaluation of democratic politics in political constitutionalism goes quite some way, but, according to more critical and radical-democratic constitutionalists, it falls short of obtaining its own, self-set ultimate aim. From one point of view, it can be argued that political constitutionalism supports the *status quo ante* of liberal representative democracy. A radical democratic view of constitutional democracy, in contrast, claims that democracy would need to entail a more direct and substantive participation of citizens in the democratic process, including constitutional politics. This second challenge to legal constitutionalism (but in part also to political constitutionalism) has been identified variously as 'democratic constitutionalism' (Tully 1995, 2008), 'weak constitutionalism' (Colon-Rios 2009), or 'participatory constitutionalism' (Hart 2003). Here, I will refer to this broad strand as 'civic constitutionalism'.

Civic constitutionalism shares with political constitutionalism an emphasis on the open-endedness of the democratic process, and the ultimately open-ended nature of rights. But for civic constitutionalism this means the nature of the constitution itself is understood in a radically different way from modern constitutionalism's foundationalism. That is, whereas modern constitutionalism understands 'constitution making as an "act of completion", the constitution as a final settlement or social contract in which basic political definitions, principles, and processes are agreed, as is a commitment to abide by them', civic constitutionalism entails a 'conversation, conducted by all concerned, open to new entrants and new issues, seeking a workable formula that will be sustainable rather than assuredly stable' (Hart 2003: 2–3; cf. Chambers 1998).[3] While the foundational nature of modern constitutionalism is not dissolved completely, the idea of a 'final act of closure' is replaced by one of flexibility and a 'permanently open process' (Hart 2003: 3). This derives from an unwillingness to tie down democracy to choices made by previous generations, the recognition of the continuously changing nature of society and identity, as well as the realization of the ultimate impossibility of grounding foundational principles once and for all.

Civic constitutionalism departs significantly from political or republican constitutionalism in that it judges representative constitutional politics as insufficient. Indeed, according to the latter, the 'democratic arrangements found in the world's established working democracies are sufficient to satisfy the requirements of republican non-domination' (Bellamy 2007: 260). Instead, civic constitutionalism endorses a more open democratic settlement which aims at the 'extension of democratic process to include, free, open, and responsive discussion of the constitutional settlement'.[4] The latter provides the framework under which 'diverse and disagreeing groups can live, while continuing to engage in a freely accessible debate about that settlement itself' (Hart 2003: 5, 3). If then both political and civic constitutionalism understand the constitution not as fully entrenched and pre-political, but as an outcome of the continuous political process itself, it is only in the latter that democratic politics is understood in its radical sense as the 'rule of people extended to all matters … , including the creation and recreation of the fundamental laws' (Colon-Rios 2009: 23). In civic constitutionalism, the democratic dimension of constitutional democratic legitimation clearly has the overhand, even if the constitutional ordering type of legitimacy is not abandoned. To this effect, civic constitutionalism is potentially open to a much wider range of pluralistic influences.

Conclusion

The argument of the chapter has been that while a sustained trend of 'new constitutionalism' indicates a global convergence on legal understandings of constitutionalism – in this, amplifying distinct aspects of modern constitutionalism – the three pluralistic trends outlined problematize convergence as well as some of modern constitutionalism's key features. The trend of a fragmentation of sovereignty menaces the core of modern constitutionalism, i.e., the idea of sovereignty as rooted in a singular, central site of authority, and the coincidence of jurisdiction, sovereignty, and constituent power. The trend of cultural pluralism and diversity, in particular in multi-national democracies, problematizes modern constitutionalism's alleged neutrality and the background assumption of a singular identity. In this, it problematizes the formalistic reading of constitutionalism in much of legal and political theory, and shifts attention to the constitution's sociological, symbolic dimension. The trend of interpretative pluralism further reveals the deeply problematic nature of an understanding of constitutionalism and rights as uncontested and politically neutral concepts, and the impossibility of formulating incontestable meta-norms. It suggests that democratic politics needs to comprise its own foundations if pluralism-in-fact is to be included comprehensively.

Modern constitutionalism is evidently in flux, and, in this, the post- and sub-state pluralization of constitutional orders, and proliferation of multiple layers and segments, seem inarrestable trends. But while the theoretical evaluations of the three pluralistic trends illustrated in this chapter indicate, on the one hand, the undeniable erosion of modern constitutionalism's centralizing, homogenizing, legalistic, and exclusionary dimensions, on the other, the possible openings for more inclusionary, pluralistic, and democratic forms of constitutional politics and constitutionalisms – identified in particular by critical, radical-democratic accounts – seem much less assured.

Acknowledgement

The author acknowledges a three-year post-doctoral fellowship provided by the *Provincia Autonoma di Trento*, held at the department of Sociology, University of Trento, Italy.

Notes

1 Below, cultural diversity and its implications for understandings of constitutionalism are discussed more at length.
2 The archetypal case is that of Canada, see Tully 2001; Chambers 1998.
3 Some dimensions of the afore-mentioned reflexive constitutionalism – deliberation, participation, conversationalism – clearly fall within this participatory strand.
4 Important constitutional innovations in this regard can be found not only in established democracies, but also in some more recent Central and Latin American as well as African constitutions (see Colon-Rios 2009; Hart 2003).

References

Arjomand, S.A. (2003). 'Law, Political Reconstruction and Constitutional Politics', *International Sociology*, 18 (1): 7–32.
Avbelj, M. and J. Komarek (2008). 'Four Visions of Constitutional Pluralism – Symposium Transcript', *European Journal of Legal Studies*, 2 (1): 325–70.
Bellamy, R. (2007) *Political Constitutionalism: A Republican Defence of the Constitutionality of Democracy*, Cambridge: Cambridge University Press.
Bellamy, R. and D. Castiglione (2000) 'Democracy, Sovereignty and the Constitution of the European Union', in Z. Bankowski and A. Scott. (eds) *The European Union and Its Order: The Legal Theory of European Union Integration*, Oxford: Basil Blackwell, 169–200.

Bohman, J. (2004). 'Constitution Making and Democratic Innovation: The European Union and Transnational Governance', *European Journal of Political Theory*, 3 (3): 315–37.

Calhoun, C. (2007) *Nations Matter: Culture, History, and the Cosmopolitan Dream*, London/New York: Routledge.

Chambers, S. (1998). 'Contract or Conversation? Theoretical Lessons from the Canadian Constitutional Crisis', *Politics and Society*, 26: 143–72.

Cohen, J. (2004). 'Whose Sovereignty? Empire Versus International Law', *Ethics and International Affairs*, 18 (3): 1–24.

Colon-Rios, J.I. (2009). 'The End of the Constitutionalism–Democracy Debate', CLPE Research Paper, 03, 5 (1).

Dworkin, R. (1995). 'Constitutionalism and Democracy', *European Journal of Philosophy*, 3 (1): 2–11.

Haberle, P. (1992). 'Verfassungsentwicklungen in Osteuropa – aus der Sicht der Rechtsphilosophie und der Verfassungslehre', *Archiv des öffentlichen Rechts*, 117 (2): 169–211.

Habermas, J. (2001). 'Why Europe Needs a Constitution', *New Left Review*, 11: 5–26.

Hart, V. (2003). 'Democratic Constitution Making', Special Report, United States Institute for Peace, available at <http://www.usip.org>, accessed 14 October 2010.

Koskenniemi, M. (2007). 'The Fate of Public International Law: Between Technique and Politics', *Modern Law Review*, 70 (1): 1–30.

Kymlicka, W. (2001). *Politics in the Vernacular: Nationalism, Multiculturalism, and Citizenship*, Oxford: Oxford University Press.

Loughlin, M. and N. Walker (2007). 'Introduction', in M. Loughlin and N. Walker (eds) *The Paradox of Constitutionalism: Constituent Power and Constitutional Form*, Oxford: Oxford University Press, 1–8.

MacDonald, R.A. (2005). 'Legal Republicanism and Legal Pluralism: Two Takes on Identity and Diversity', in M. Bussani and M. Graziadei (eds) *Human Diversity and the Law*, Brussels: Bruylant, 43–70.

Priban, J. (2007). *Legal Symbolism: On Law, Time and European Identity*, Aldershot, UK/Burlington, VT: Ashgate.

Rawls, J. (1993). *Political Liberalism*, New York: Columbia University Press.

Rosenfeld, M. (1992). 'Modern Constitutionalism as Interplay Between Identity and Diversity', *Cardozo Law Review*, 14: 497–531.

——(1998). *Just Interpretations: Law Between Ethics and Politics*, Berkeley, CA: University of California Press.

——(2008). 'Rethinking Constitutional Ordering in an Era of Legal and Ideological Pluralism', *International Journal of Constitutional Law*, 6 (3/4): 415 –455.

Stone Sweet, A. (2008). 'Constitutions and Judicial Power', in D. Caramani (ed.) *Comparative Politics*, Oxford: Oxford University Press, 217–39.

——(2009). 'Constitutionalism, Legal Pluralism and International Regimes', *Indiana Journal of Global Legal Studies*, 16 (2): 621–45.

Taylor, C. (1994). *Multiculturalism: Examining the Politics of Recognition*, edited and introduced by Amy Gutmann, Princeton, NJ: Princeton University Press.

Teubner, G. (1997). 'Global Bukowina: Legal Pluralism in the World Society', in G. Teubner (ed.) *Global Law Without a State*, Dartmouth: Aldershot, 3–28.

Tierney, S. (2004). *Constitutional Law and National Pluralism*, Oxford: Oxford University Press.

——(2008). 'Review Article. Beyond the Ontological Question: Liberal Nationalism and the Task of Constitution-Building', *European Law Journal*, 14 (1): 128–37.

Tully, J. (1995). *Strange Multiplicity: Constitutionalism in an Age of Diversity*, Cambridge/New York: Cambridge University Press.

——(2001). 'Introduction', in A.-G. Gagnon and J. Tully (eds) *Multinational Democracies*, Cambridge: Cambridge University Press, 1–34.

——(2008). *Public Philosophy in a New Key*, Cambridge: Cambridge University Press.

Waldron, J. (1999). *Law and Disagreement*, Oxford: Clarendon Press.

Walker, N. (2002). 'The Idea of Constitutional Pluralism', *Modern Law Review*, 65 (3): 317–59.

——(2008). 'Taking Constitutionalism Beyond the State', *Political Studies*, 56: 519–43.

Weiler, J.H.H. (2001). 'In Defence of the Status Quo: Europe's Constitutional Sonderweg', in J.J.H. Weiler and M. Wind (eds) *European Constitutionalism beyond the State*, Cambridge: Cambridge University Press, 7–26.

——(2003). *Un'Europa cristiana: Un saggio esplorativo*, Milano: BUR Saggi.

Wiener, A. (2008). *The Invisible Constitution of Politics: Contested Norms and International Encounters*, Cambridge: Cambridge University Press.

Reflexive Integration

A Perspective on the Transformation of Europe

Erik O. Eriksen

Europe has been transformed from an order of largely independent nation-states with their divergent identities and interests to a supranational order with some capacity to rule in the name of all. Hence, the transformation of Europe not only testifies to Europeanization of the nation-states but also to new forms of political rule emerging beyond the international system of state relations. Europe has been integrated within *the multi-level constellation* that makes up the European Union (EU). While international affairs traditionally are conducted through diplomacy and intergovernmental bargaining between the executive branches of government, we are now witnessing problem-solving in policy networks and transnational institutions as well as collective goal attainment and conflict-resolution in supranational institutions such as the European Parliament (EP), the European Court of Justice (ECJ), and the European Commission. The EU has emerged beyond that of international regime and is a major force in the reorganization of political power in Europe. It constitutes a new type of political order that does not fit into the traditional dichotomy of intergovernmental versus nation-state regulation.

There is confusion and disagreement about the core characteristics of the EU as well as about its future design. Currently, there are different notions of what the EU is (or should be) and there are different theories of how to explain the integration process. This chapter deals first and foremost with the latter problem. Integration is a process where actors shift their loyalties and activities towards a new centre with the authoritative right to regulate interests and allocate resources. How to explain that supranational institutions circumscribing the autonomy and sovereignty of the nation-states have been established? Supranationalism entails the consolidation into multi-lateral institutions with the potential to override the preferences and interests of the nation-states and to transform identities (Schmitter 1969: 166; Haas 1968).

That powerful supranational institutions have been established represents an explanatory problem for conventional approaches because they would require either the presence of force or (bargaining) power in order for some to impose their will or a common identity strong enough to override particular (national) interests. Power-based explanations do not suffice as voluntarism prevails. Compliance is always optional on the part of the member states (Weiler 2003). Also the other requirement, that of a collective European identity, is widely held to be missing. How to account for the voluntary relinquishment of sovereignty when a collective identity is lacking? To approach this puzzle I suggest a pragmatist approach which revolves around problem-solving through deliberation and experimental inquiry. It depicts cooperation as a response to *problematic situations*, and institution formation as a response to the indirect consequences of such. In this perspective democracy is a condition for intelligent problem solving as well as for alleviating legitimacy problems.

I start by outlining the characteristics of European integration processes, the move beyond intergovernmentalism and the ensuing legitimacy problem. Thereafter I spell out some elements of a pragmatist approach to the integration process and a provisional solution to the puzzle that integration can take place absent of a collective identity. This endeavour requires also attention to the nature of the EU.

Integration and the Problem of Legitimacy

The EU has sustained a rapid expansion of political regulation in Europe and has over a period of 50 years transformed the political landscape in a profound manner. Integration has deepened as a wide range of new policy fields have been subjected to integrated action and collective decision-making. This has taken place not only with regard to trade, monetary and business regulation, fishing and agriculture but also with regard to foodstuff production, gene- and biotechnology, labor rights, environmental protection, culture, tourism, immigration, police and home affairs, and now also with regard to foreign and security policy. The EU has succeeded in entrenching peace and it has established a Single Market, a Monetary Union (the Euro), a European citizenship, and a Charter of Fundamental Rights. The EU has widened and has successfully managed to include new members, by 2010 a total of 27. Even though the powers of the Union in many policy areas – such as social and tax policy – are severely restricted, a significant amount of laws and amendments in the nation-states emanate from the binding EU decisions.

The present supranational state of affairs is due to a protracted process of integration since its inception with the Paris (1951) and Rome (1957) Treaties, through the Single European Act (1986), Maastricht (1992), Amsterdam (1997), Nice (2000), up to the Laeken declaration (2001) and the work on forging a Constitutional Treaty (2002–5), and the Lisbon Treaty (2007). The supranational character of the Union's legal structure started with the constitutionalization of the Treaty system, which transformed the EC from an international regime into a quasi-federal legal system based on the precepts of higher law-constitutionalism. All legal persons, and not just states, have now judicially enforceable rights. Further, the progressive strengthening of the *doctrines of supremacy and direct effect* is coupled with the growth of the number of EU provisions and Court rulings, where the Court acts as a trustee of the Treaty and not as an agent of the member states. The EU differs from the nation-state hierarchical structure of representation and power. The non-hierarchical, multilevel constellation that makes up the EU reflects a peculiar separation of powers: Under the regulation of the *acquis communautaire* (and the authority of the ECJ) legislative power is shared between the Commission (which has the right of initiative), the Council, and the Parliament; executive power between the Commission, the Council, and the member states; and judiciary power between the European Court of Justice, the Court of First Instance (CFI), and member-state courts.

Not only does this peculiar form of powers' separation pose legitimacy problems, so does the fact that the EU cannot be boiled down to a distinct type of international organization. As long as the EU is only an instrument for the nation-states to realize their mutual interests, it would leave the integrity and the identity of its constituent parties intact. It would be the lowest common denominator politics that do not challenge state sovereignty or core national interests. However, when the EU is a power-wielding system which establishes *domination relations*, the electoral authorization of ministers at the national level, and their accountability to national parliaments, cannot provide for democratic legitimacy. The EU's legal basis is international treaties, but its competence and law-making power reaches so deep into the working conditions of the member states, that the EU cannot be legitimized on this basis alone. G. Majone, who advocates delegating policy-making power to non-majoritarian institutions – not directly elected or accountable agencies – acknowledges the ensuing questions of accountability and legitimacy but maintains that these could be solved by sectioning off particular policy areas. He argues:

> Delegation is legitimate in the case of efficiency issues, that is, where the task is to find a solution capable of improving the conditions of all, or almost all, individuals and groups in society. On the other hand, redistributive policies, which aim to improve the conditions of one group in society at the expense of another, should not be delegated to independent experts.
>
> *(Majone 1996: 5)*

This is problematic, first of all because the decision to institutionalize certain issues as technical, subjected to efficiency considerations only, is essentially a political one. An issue is never merely technical and 'output oriented legitimation', as Scharpf (1999) famously coined it, is not neutral. To leave, for example, the monitoring of free trade and competition, of currency stability, to agencies withdrawn from the control of affected parties, is a political decision of vital importance. Second, the European Union has emerged, from humble beginnings into an entity whose policies cover virtually all areas of public policy. The EU does not merely regulate. It also re-regulates and performs some market-redressing functions, through standard-setting and rule-making. The EU has become a polity which performs functions that affect interests and identities all over Europe. It establishes domination relations: its decisions impinge on national priorities, influence the domestic allocation of resources, and constrain the sovereignty and autonomy of the states. Hence, the level and scope of European integration indicates that there is something to be legitimized at the European level beyond what efficiency can provide for.

Less than a State

The EU has supranational dimensions but does not fit the customary concept of state, as it does not possess the required means, such as monopoly of violence and taxation, and a well developed collective identity necessary for majority vote, to enforce its will. It is not sovereign within a fixed, contiguous, and clearly delimited territory. There are no European jails, no army, and no police force. Clearly the EU is something less than a federal state but more than an international organization, where the member states are the contracting parties. To the latter, democratic criteria do not apply. It is the states and not the citizens that make up the 'constituencies'; states are the sole sources of legitimacy and they act internationally on indirect and delegated powers on governance functions. Here, 'constitutions' are *contracts*; and contractually based orders do not put up normative criteria of political legitimacy (Frankenberg 2000: 260–1).

The EU, in contrast, puts up normative criteria of political legitimacy and is based on a *status contract* aiming at changing the identity of the contracting partners – from nation-states to member states. The EU is a particular kind of order, which originated through treaties, and which not only created a 'distinct political entity – a union or *Bund* – but which at the same time transformed the political status of the parties to this treaty' (Offe and Preuss 2007: 192).

The supranational character, the democratic vocation, the status contract, and the *organized capacity to act* are what make the European form of cooperation stand out in marked contrast to international cooperation in general.

This also means that the requisite legitimacy cannot be provided by deliberative, transnational structures of governance that the so-called neo-madisionans put their trust in. (see Bohman 2005; see further Bohman 2007; Cohen and Sabel 1997; Gerstenberg 2002). According to them, policy networks consisting of private actors, interest groups, NGOs, and governmental actors constitute a kind of *transnational civil society*; and deliberation in spontaneous and horizontally dispersed polyarchies can deter legal domination and solve problems rationally. However, such cannot possibly provide for democratic legitimacy as there is no chance of equal access and popular control (see Schmalz-Bruns 1999; Eriksen 2009: 155ff). Rather, the new structures of governance mystify and confuse authority lines so that the citizens may be left in baffling wilderness with regard to who exercises control and influence. In legitimacy terms, such an order is clearly deficient, as popular sovereignty is not brought to bear on the processes. It is steering without democracy, and governance without government. There is a marked difference between the kind of legitimacy and accountability that possibly can be provided for by policy networks and the type of legitimacy required by the domination relations of the EU, which to a certain degree mirrors the ones that prompted the democratic law-state.

A set of autonomous European bodies makes European-wide law devoted to the Union itself. This is underscored by extended use of qualified majority vote – after the Amsterdam Treaty entered into force – which in most cases, however, goes hand in hand with co-decision with the European Parliament. Co-decision and qualified majority vote are now the standard decision-making procedures. Co-decision, which requires the consent of the majorities in the Council (qualified majority) and the European Parliament (absolute majority), rules out national vetoes. Both developments weaken the position of member states as masters of European integration. Thus one cannot understand the EU's institutional structure merely as a dependent variable; as a product of member states bargaining at IGCs. Institutions are logically prior to institutional choice. They determine the translation of policy objectives into outcomes (Tsebelis and Garrett 2001: 386–7). Instead of the narrow focus of intergorvernmentalism on treaty negotiations, one should, according to Tsebelis (2002), look at interactions among the European Unions's four primary institutions and their role as *collective veto-players*. In addition to the Commission, and the (big) member states which have the upper hand – through the Council – in many legislative issues and which through IGCs control Treaty changes, the role of the ECJ and the increasing power of the EP must be adjusted for when accounting for who has the agenda-setting power. But how to account for the establishment of European post-national, supranational institutions in the first place?

Reflexive Integration

In Europe, the nation-states have voluntarily circumscribed their sovereignty and reduced their autonomy. In many areas, the nation-states have surrendered their veto powers. As noted by the European Court of Justice (ECJ):

> By creating a community of unlimited duration, … having its own institutions, the Member States have limited their sovereign rights and have thus created a body of law which binds both their nationals and themselves.
>
> *(Case 6/64,* Costa v Enel*)*

How is this possible when the European Union is a polity that does not itself have direct control of a given territory; when it lacks a collective identity; truly hierarchical principles of law, and powerful enforcement means? Without a collective identity symbolized by a people, there can be no authority conferred upon a government to rule in the name of all. Such makes up the so-called *non-majoritarian sources of legitimacy* that make collective decision-making possible. Majority rule rests upon allegiance and civic solidarity that is only conceivable in terms of the symbolic establishment of a demos – a people – founded on a sense of unity and allegiance. A solidaristic substrate is required for the formation of a collective identity strong enough to ensure that the compatriots not only see themselves as members of a society based on liberty but also of one based on equality and solidarity (Offe1998; Grimm 2004).

Both positive political science and political theory are struggling to comprehend the genesis and nature of this creature. Whilst positive political science searches for new ways of conceptualizing a political order 'above' intergovernmentalism and 'below' statism, normative theory is struggling with the yardsticks of democracy when assessing a polity which is more than an international regime but less than a state. The *pragmatist approach* is interesting because it is not confined to the nation-state template and its presuppositions of sovereignty, demos, territory, and identity. A collective identity is held to be missing and civic solidarity has often been in short supply in Europe, but this has not prevented the EU from growing in size and competence over time. In Europe, one must therefore look for another basis than pre-political agreement on substantial values, we-feeling, and common interests to explain the integration process. The pragmatist perspective, which turns on the regularized use of knowledge for solving common problems – *experimental inquiry combined with free and full discussion* – offers an interesting perspective on transnational and supranational decision-making systems, which to a large degree lack forceful compliance mechanisms as well as identitarian personification. The argument is that experimental inquiry and political deliberation – free opinion and will-formation processes – can ensure justification and learning and sway actors to adopt a common position without a pre-existing value consensus. In Dewey's concept of democratic experimentalism actors faced with problematical situations only deals with them cogently as far as they make full use of the available knowledge through 'intelligent experimentation, reflection, and discussion' (1991: 2276; see also Eriksen 2005).

In this perspective, polity building is seen to stem from simple forms of cooperation on resolving problematic situations through the collective inquiry of the citizens. Notions of the common good and of justice are not a function of values and convictions that exist prior to processes, but something that is created through these processes. Deliberation is problem-solving discussion. It is an error-detecting and truth-finding as well as justificatory device (Eriksen 2009:170). Deliberation is a cognitive process for the assessment of reasons in a practical situation in order to reach fair and binding decisions. There is no postulation of a collective identity or common interest at the outset, but these are established during the process of attending to and solving the problems facing the actors: 'Recognition of evil consequences brought about a common interest which required for its maintenance certain measures and rules, together with the selection of certain persons as their guardians, interpreters, and, if need be, their executors' (Dewey 1927:17). When consequences are recognized and deliberated upon indirect and wide-ranging interaction lead to the formation of public spheres. Subsequently, a polity becomes organized and establishes regulative schemes of action.

This perspective is relevant for the EU, as European cooperation started out as piecemeal collaboration on coal and steel, which increasingly caught on and had polity consequences. In causal terms, we may conceive of integration beyond the nation-state as a process where states and non-state actors cooperate in joint problem-solving sites across national borders in Europe in solving problematic situations, thereby creating a *transnational society*. As the activities increase, common standards, rules, and dispute-resolution mechanisms – regulation and coordinating mechanisms – are needed, which, in turn, trigger reflexive and self-reflexive processes conducive to the establishment of authoritative institutions that can control and command obedience in the name of all.

Integration through Deliberation

In the EU, voting and threat-based bargaining are difficult to make use of, as the non-majoritarian resources of democracy – the common values – are weak, and bargaining chips are few. Generally, transaction costs are low, information and ideas are abundant and widely distributed among states (Moravscik 1998: 479ff). Because formal instruments of power are weak, ensuring agreement is an essential part of the nature of EU decision-making. This system is set up as, and functions as, a *consent-based system*, where unanimous voting procedures go together with more complex processes and procedures for deliberation and sounding out. Very substantial resources are expended to foster and ensure consensus. Non-agreement is difficult for such joint-decision systems, as it leads to loss of control and reduces the 'independent capabilities of action over their member governments' (Scharpf 1988: 258). It leads to loss in efficiency, as well as in legitimacy. The requirement of consensus is apparent in the institutional structure, and in the relations among the institutions. For instance, 'resort to explicit majority voting is often viewed as something of a political failure … '. The undertakings and procedures employed prior to decision-making indicate that the EU practises a kind of *extreme consensus democracy* (Lord 1998: 47–8). Although unanimity decreases efficiency and sometimes also rationality in decision-making, it may heighten legitimacy, and is seen as a necessary price to be paid.

Until recently, developments have expanded the size of – and the scope for – problem-solving through deliberation within the institutional nexus of the EU. Students of European governance underscore the salience of experimental inquiry and expert-based deliberation within the EU and its conduciveness to trust, learning, and collective decision-making (Gerstenberg 2002; Zeitlin and Trubek 2003). Transnational networks have increased the ability to coordinate rule-development and implementation through argumentation and learning. Comitology committees have managed to combine market integration with social measures, such as the protection of health and safety; have raised the standards of environmental protection; and have fostered consent and integration. It is a setting for *learning* and long-term socialization into common European norms. Here, solutions have been found that are more than the politics of the lowest common denominator. Committee deliberation has made for the pooling of competences and knowledge to the degree that there is no basis for collective decisions other than an outcome that leaves all better or at least as well off as before (Joerges and Neyer 1997; Joerges and Vos 1999; Marks *et al.* 1996; Neyer 2003). Hence the possibility for Pareto improvements. Science figures prominently as the basis on which agreements can be reached. In knowledge-based systems there is an incentive to exploit asymmetrical information to identify positive-sum solutions (Haas 1998). Transgovernmental actors who have no formal authority to 'initiate, pass or strike down legislation' work through informal mechanisms to 'shape agendas, mediate disputes and mobilise support'. These actors possess a *wealth of first-hand experience* that is of interest to policy-making bodies, and may use this to 'frame issues to overcome objections to proposals' (Newman 2008: 120, 121). The cooperative use of competencies and expertise in identifying and solving problems under conversational constraints fosters trust. Informal and entrusted modes of social coordination are needed to solve numerous collective action problems, and hence prepare a move beyond intergovernmentalism.

However, only under certain conditions will deliberation compel decision-makers to explain and justify their preferences to the citizens; and revise them when criticized. Under conditions where criteria of *freedom and equality* apply, double standards and cognitive dissonance will be problematic. The EU's institutional nexus includes mechanisms that compel reason-giving and the handling of claims to justification. Critical scrutiny, judicial review, an ombudsman arrangement, transparency and openness clauses have been put in place, so as to ensure inclusion and the hearing of different interests and their grievances. Moreover, the existence of a 'higher-ranking' European law and authorized decision-making bodies induces a deliberative logic on the proceedings. The justification of power as well as of particular standpoints must be conducted with reference to law. Actors depend on reaching agreements under unanimity rules or being able to establish a viable coalition under QMV, and must therefore be able to explain and justify their preferences with regard to material and procedural norms. Legal orders force the actors to abstain from simply issuing threats and warnings. The language of law, so to say, replaces the language of power (Kratochwil 1989). Law is a reflexive mechanism for solving conflicts in modern societies.

The Dynamics of Integration

In Europe, what began as piecemeal problem-solving for the member states – underpinned by the peace motive – has ended up in a supranational order subjecting the constituent parts to collectively binding decisions. The unbridled sovereigns authorized by the Westphalian order are now brought under the rule of a supra-national polity which disposes of an authoritative dispute resolution mechanism. World Wars I and II profoundly affected the states and citizens all over Europe, and all depended on each other for a peaceful restoration of post-war Europe. Cooperation was initially problem-solving for the members caused by their intense *interdependence*. The solving of common problems led to learning and more cooperation, the building of trust relationships, and to the discovery of new problems of common concern. Increasingly, supranational polity formation took place with conflict resolution and goal attainment institutions of its own, which, however, spurred new questions about the legitimacy basis of such a polity.

> In the beginning, [the European Union] was more of an economic and technical collaboration. … At long last, Europe is on its way to becoming one big family, without bloodshed, a real transformation clearly calling for a different approach from fifty years ago, when six countries first took the lead.
>
> *(European Council 2001)*

The pragmatist approach depicts cooperation as a response to social problems, and institution formation as a response to the indirect consequences of such, which increasingly catches on and has polity consequences. Polity-building is thus seen as the result of deepened integration driven by intelligent problem-solving, but problem-solving leads to juridification; to the imposition of a legal scheme upon subjects who can not change its terms.

More legal regulation triggers claims to democracy or to *reflexive juridification*. Hence the integration process is not a linear mono-causal process driven by unintended consequences as analytical functionalism suggests, nor by 'the hidden hand' of Jean Monnet who foresaw a federation as the necessary outcome of closer cooperation (Monnet 1978: 392ff). The integration process is to a large degree driven by *contestation and opposition* as it came to be seen as a technocratic, elite-driven project conducted in isolation from the people. The inclusion of affected parties is biased, the transnational communicative infrastructure is deficient, and criticism thrives.

The obvious response from the power holders was democratic reforms, which, however, implied more integration and supranationalism. The response is also obvious because in democratic states there is a presumed link between the normative validity of a political order and the social acceptance of this order. One can expect that when integration has reached a point where the supranational institutions wield influence over the citizens and the states – when the EU is not merely an international organization – there is a requirement of democracy because this is the only justifiable standard of political legitimation available in Europe (cf. Rittberger 2005: 5).

The Maastricht popular referenda which marked the *end of the permissive consensus* are important. Then people (in particular, but far from only, the Danes and the French) removed their 'tacit consent to integration' (Abromeit 1998), with the effect that the Union's power-holders were increasingly subjected to profound criticisms of the EU as a technocratic and elite-driven juggernaut (Siedentop 2000). The cry for more openness and democracy became ever-present as during the 1990s *democracy struck back* (Smith and Wright 1999). In the words of one key analyst: 'It is the public reaction, frequently and deliciously hostile, and the public debate which followed which almost sunk Maastricht which count in my book as the most important constitutional 'moment' in the history of the European construct' (Weiler 1999: 4). Public opinion came to acknowledge and embrace the notion that the Union harbours a democratic deficit. Politization and contestation took off (Hooghe and Marks 2009). The leaders recognized that the strong opposition and the many vociferous criticisms of this state of affairs were threatening the viability and stability of the integration process and therefore that remedial action was required.

The post-Maastricht politicization of the integration process has, if anything, been driven by resistance to Brussels-driven 'homogenization', a fear that draws some of its impetus from the experience with national nation-building processes. Europe's recognition of diversity is reflected in a subtle shift in the Union's credo: from the 'ever closer union' of the Rome and Maastricht Treaties to Laeken's *unitas in diversitas* – 'united in diversity'. But this raises the question of how societies can hang together 'in diversitas'. What is the cement of Europe? There is an unsettled issue, even in a pragmatist perspective, with regard to the social or cultural substrate required for integration. A minimum level of trust and confidence is needed to square contestation with the need for consensus: a *modicum of non-egoistic commitment* is necessary for cooperative goal attainment and conflict resolution to come about – for fair play and promise-keeping. Absence of trust paralyzes collective action (Offe 1999).

A Cosmopolitan Subset

Trust functions to absorb the risk of social disintegration that may arise when political orders are reproduced only through the mechanisms of law and deliberation. Under modern conditions, the proclivity to let oneself be bound by reasons 'rests on specific kinds of trust that are supposedly rationally motivated' (Habermas 1984: 302). The sources of trust must rest on solid grounds as it vegetates on the possibility of being tested in a rational discourse (Luhmann 1979: 55–6). Trust is thus both the pre-requisite for cooperation or deliberation and the result of cooperation. The research problem has to do with squaring the following circle. How much trust is needed for cooperation to come about, how much cooperation is required before common commitments become obligatory commitments?

What could a rationally motivated trust consist in at the European level if not in the conviction that the inclusive procedures constituted by the rights of the citizens to participate and hold to account can bear the burden of legitimation? This refers to the bare bones of the democratic law state's cognitive rational principles – rule of law, democracy, and citizenship – in contrast to the pre-political we-feeling and allegiance making up the *existential common ground* of nationhood, of love of country. As the Union is not existentially grounded, it can only justify itself through drawing on the principles of human rights, popular sovereignty, and law – even when dealing with international affairs – underscoring the cosmopolitan law of the people. There is no intrinsic reason why reflexivity should be confined to the hermeneutical clarification of the primordial self-understanding of a particular 'European community of fate' because common constitutional traditions that span territories are in place. What is more, eventual disagreement over the meaning of principles does not mean that they cannot constitute the core reference point of a common identity. The discourse on procedures, on citizenship and participation, and not on substantive values, could provide the requisite normative frame for identification.

It is a rather thin normative basis for this type of allegiance, as it must be based only on what human beings have in common, viz., their right to freedom, equality, dignity, democracy, and the like. But how does this square with the fact that to have things in common requires that other things are excluded? Collective identity stems from membership in a community of compatriots. Such is rather weak in an all-inclusive society. The world's citizens do not have much in common apart from the shared 'humanity' (Maus 2006; Habermas 2001: 108). However, there is no reason why the universality of an ideal cannot also be rooted in a life-world and be the ideal for a specific community. Moreover, the question of Europeanization of identities is not about creating a 'new supra-identity' but rather should be seen 'as a growing reflexivity within existing identities' (Delanty 2005: 140). Hence there is a plea for a European cosmopolitan identity.

Even though cosmopolitanism 'is not part of the self-identity of the EU' (Rumford 2005: 5), scholars nevertheless recognize the EU as a post-national political community and part of, and as a vanguard for, an emerging democratic world order (Archibugi 1998; Beck and Grande 2007; Eriksen 2009, 2011). It is seen to connect to the changed parameters of power politics through which sovereignty has turned conditional upon respecting democracy and human rights. The EU can be posited as one of several emerging entities that intermediate between the nation-state and the UN, and which become recognized as a legitimate independent source of law. The EU can be seen as a *regional subset* of an emerging larger cosmopolitan order, and one which provide the 'international community' with some agency. In such a perspective the borders of the EU could be drawn both with regard to what is required for the Union itself in order to be a self-sustainable and well-functioning democratic entity and with regard to the support and further development of similar regional associations in the rest of the world.

This notion implies that the Union would be a political order whose internal standards are projected onto its external affairs; and further, that it would be a polity that subjects its actions to higher-ranking principles – to 'the cosmopolitan law of the people' in the advent of a reformed and democratisized UN. The law-enforcement capacity, as well as the democratic mandate, is weak although the moral salience of such an order is high. In other words, such a regional subset of the cosmopolitan order may be strong in terms of legitimacy as it can draw on a far-reaching consensus on moral individualism and human rights protection. Such an entity would be an answer to the claim that one should *not replicate the state model* at the European level as the 'system of states' is what makes necessary international organizations in the first place. Nations create problems for each other as well as for the universal protection of human rights, and to upload the state model to the European level would only replicate the problems at the global level.

Conclusion

Hostility and harsh competition has been replaced by peaceful cooperation in Europe. For the first time in human history, we witness the development of a supranational political order that recognizes the difference of its constituent parties. The EU is not brought about by brute force nor is it based on a culturally homogenized people. However, democratic sustainability requires a criterion according to which Europeans are equals. Boundary-construction, the dual processes of inclusion and exclusion, aims at establishing a particular balance between contextualized identities, democratic practice, and global justice. This balance has not been established in the multi-level constellation that makes up the EU. Nevertheless, the EU testifies to a *large-scale experiment* searching for binding constitutional principles and institutional arrangements beyond the mode of rule entrenched in the nation-state. It testifies to the fact that learning processes have taken place and have been institutionalized.

References

Abromeit, H. (1998) *Democracy in Europe Legitimising Politics in Non-state Polity*, New York: Berghahn Books.

Archibugi, D. (1998) 'Principles of Cosmopolitan Democracy', in D. Archibugi, D. Held, and M. Köhler (eds) *Re-imagining Political Community*, Cambridge: Polity Press.

Beck, U. and E. Grande (2007) *Cosmopolitan Europe*, Cambridge: Polity Press

Bohman, J. (2005) 'Reflexive Constitution-making and Transnational Governance', in E. O. Eriksen (ed.) *Making the European Polity: Reflexive Integration in the EU*, London: Routledge.

——(2007) *Democracy across Borders: From Dêmos to Dêmoi*, Cambridge, MA: MIT Press.

Cohen, J. and C. F. Sabel (1997) 'Directly-deliberative Polyarchy', *European Law Journal*, 3 (4): 313–42.

Delanty, G. (2005) 'The Quest for European Identity', in E. O. Eriksen (ed.) *Making the European Polity: Reflexive Integration in the EU*, London: Routledge.

Dewey, J. (1927) *The Public and its Problems*, Chicago, IL: Gateways Books.

Eriksen, E. O. (2005) 'Reflexive Integration in Europe', in E. O. Eriksen (ed.) *Making the European Polity: Reflexive Integration in the EU*, London: Routledge.

——(2009) *The Unfinished Democratization of Europe*, Oxford: Oxford University Press.

Eriksen, E. O. and Fossum, J. E. (2011) "Bringing European Democracy back in. Or how to read the German Constitutional Court's Lisbon Treaty ruling", *European Law Journal* 17.

European Council (2001) Council Regulation (EC) 381/2001 of 26 February 2001 creating a rapid-reaction mechanism, OJ L57 of 27 February 2001.

Frankenberg, G. (2000) 'The Return of the Contract: Problems and Pitfalls of European Constitutionalism', *European Law Journal*, 6 (3): 257–76.

Gerstenberg, O. (2002) 'The New Europe: Part of the Problem – or Part of the Solution to the Problem?', *Oxford Journal of Legal Studies*, 22 (3): 563–71.

Grimm, D. (2004) 'Treaty or Constitution? The Legal Basis of the European Union after Maastricht', in E. O. Eriksen, J. E. Fossum, and A. J. Menéndez (eds) *Developing a Constitution for Europe*, London: Routledge.

Haas, E. B. (1968) *The Uniting of Europe: Political, Social, and Economic Forces 1950–57*, Stanford, CA: Stanford University Press.

——(1998) 'Compliance with EU Directives: Insights From International Relations and Comparative Politics', *Journal of European Public Policy*, 5 (1): 17–37.

Habermas, J. (1984 [1981]) *The Theory of Communicative Action*, Vol. 1, Boston, MA: Beacon Press.

——(2001) *The Postnational Constellation: Political Essays*, Cambridge: Polity Press.

Hooghe, L. and G. Marks (2009) 'A Postfunctional Theory of European Integration: From Permissive Consensus to Contraining Dissensus', *British Journal of Political Science*, 39 (1): 1–23.

Joerges, C. and J. Neyer (1997 'From Intergovernmental Bargaining to Deliberative Political Processes: The Constitutionalisation of Comitology', *European Law Journal*, 3 (3): 273–99.

Joerges, C. and E. Vos (eds) (1999) *EU Committees: Social Regulation, Law and Politics*, Oxford: Hart Publishing.

Kratochwil, Fr V. (1989) *Rules, Norms and Decisions*, Cambridge: Cambridge University Press.

Lord, Chr. (1998) *Democracy in the European Union*, Sheffield: Sheffield University Press.

Luhmann, N. (1979) *Trust and Power*, New York: John Wiley & Sons.

Majone, G. (1996) *Regulating Europe*, London: Routledge.

Marks, G., L. Hooghe, and K. Blank (1996) 'European Integration from the 1980s: State-centric v. Multi-level Governance', *Journal of Common Market Studies*, 34 (3): 341–78.

Maus, I. (2006) 'From Nation-state to Global State, or the Decline of Democracy', *Constellations*, 13 (4): 465–84.

Monnet, J. (1978) *Memoirs*, New York, NY: Doubleday.

Moravcsik, A. (1998) *The Choice for Europe: Social Purpose and State Power from Messina to Maastricht*, London: UCL Press

Newman, A. L. (2008) 'Building Transnational Civil Liberties: Transgovernmental Entrepreneurs and the European Data Privacy Directive', *International Organization*, 62 (1): 103–30.

Neyer, J. (2003) 'Discourse and Order in the EU', *Journal of Common Market Studies*, 41 (4): 687–706.

Offe, C. (1998) ' "Homogeneity" and Constitutional Democracy: Coping with Identity Conflicts through Group Rights', *Journal of Political Philosophy*, 5 (2): 163–82.

——1999 'How Can We Trust Our Fellow Citizens?', in M. E. Warren (ed.) *Democracy and Trust*, Cambridge: Cambridge University Press

Offe, C. and U. K. Preuss (2007) 'The Problem of Legitimacy in the European Polity: Is Democratization the Answer?', in C. Crouch, and W. Streek (eds) *The Diversity of Democracy: Corporatism, Social Order and Political Conflict*, Cheltenham: Edward Elgar.

Putnam, H. (1991) 'A Reconsideration of Deweyan Democracy', in M. Brint and W. Weaver (eds) *Pragmatism in Law and Society*, Boulder, CO: Westview Press.

Rittberger, B. (2005) *Building Europe's Parliament*, Oxford: Oxford University Press.

Rumford, C. (2005) 'Cosmopolitanism and Europe: Towards a New EU Studies Agenda?', *Innovation*, 18 (1): 1–9.

Scharpf, F. W. (1988) 'The Joint-decision Trap: Lessons from German Federalism and European Integration', *Public Administration*, 66 (3): 239–78.

——(1999) *Governing in Europe: Effective and Democratic*, Oxford: Oxford University Press.

Schmalz-Bruns, R. (1999) 'Deliberative Supranationalism: Demokratisches Regieren jenseits des Nationalstaates', *Zeitschrift für Internationale Beziehungen*, 6 (2): 185–244.

Schmitter, P. C. (1969) 'Three Neo-functional Hypotheses about International Organization', *International Organization*, 23 (Winter): 562–4.

Siedentop, L. (2000) *Democracy in Europe*, London: Penguin.

Smith, D and S. Wright (1999) (eds) *Whose Europe? The Turn Towards Democracy*, Oxford: Blackwell.

Tsebelis, G. (2002) *Veto-players: How Political Institutions Work*, Princeton, NJ: Princeton University Press.

Tsebelis, G. and G. Garrett (2001) 'The Institutional Foundations of Intergovernmentalism and Supranationalism in the European Union', *International Organization*, 55 (2): 357–90.

Weiler, J. H. H. (1999) *The Constitution of Europe: 'Do the New Clothes Have an Emperor?' and Other Essays*, Cambridge: Cambridge University Press.

——(2003): 'In Defence of the Status Quo: Europe's Constitutional Sonderweg', in J. H. H. Weiler, and M. Wind (eds) *European Constitutionalism Beyond the State*, Cambridge: Cambridge University Press, 7–28.

Zeitlin, J. and D. M. Trubek (eds) (2003) *Governing Work and Welfare in a New Economy*, Oxford: Oxford University Press.

Transnational Activisms and the Global Justice Movement

Donatella della Porta and Raffaele Marchetti

Transnational activism can be defined as the mobilization around collective claims that are: a) related to transnational/global issues; b) formulated by actors located in more than one country; and c) addressing more than one national government and/or international governmental organization or another international actor. While forms of transnational activism have existed since a distant past, economic and political globalization have increased their frequency, as well as attention to them. Within the wider process of global transformations, the global justice movement (sometimes called anti-globalization movements), represents a key, though not unique, instance of transnational activism.

In the last ten years, the intensification of transnational protests has been followed with attention in various fields of the social sciences, and beyond. Not only political science and sociology, but also anthropology and geography have had a specific focus on transnational social movements, which has produced a substantial body of empirical research and theoretical reflections. At the same time, social and political theory has been an integral part of this renewed interest for transnational protest. In particular, concepts developed in normative theories – such as (global) civil society, cosmopolitanism and deliberative democracy – have been used to investigate the innovations these forms of activism brought about. By clarifying the contextual variations at stake, these studies created a bridge between empirical and normative analysis (on the rapprochement between empirical political sciences and normative political theory, see Bauböck, 2008).

Forms of Transnational Activisms

Transnational activism entails transnational actors. Global civil society, international non-governmental organizations, transnational social movement organizations, the global justice movements are concepts developed to name these actors. In social theory, *global civil society* (GCSOs) is a much used, and much debated term to indicate civil society organizations that represent themselves as a global actor, networking across national borders and challenging international institutions. Similarly, empirical research in international relations has addressed the birth of *international non-governmental organizations* (INGOs), pointing at the recent increase in their number, membership, and availability of material resources, as well as their influence on policy choices. The related concept of *transnational social movement organizations* (TSMOs) was introduced to define the INGOs active within networks of social movements. While non-governmental organizations and social movements developed in parallel to national politics, the formation of INGOS and TSMOs has been seen as a response to the growing politicization of international politics. Research on the *global justice movement* (GJM) have thus understood it as the loose network of organizations and individuals, engaged in collective action of various kinds, on the basis of the shared goal of advancing the cause of justice (economic, social, political, and environmental) among and between peoples across the globe (Della Porta 2007).

Focusing on the interactions between these actors and international governmental organizations (IGOs) (initially especially the United Nations, later on the European Union and other organizations), the first studies emphasized in particular their capacity to adapt to the IGOs' rules of the game, preferring a diplomatic search for agreement over democratic accountability, discretion over transparency, and persuasion over mobilization in the street. Some of these actors have been highlighted as having not only increased in number, but also strengthened their influence in various stages of international policy-making (Della Porta, Kriesi, and Rucht 2009). Their assets include an increasing credibility in public opinion and consequent availability of private funding, as well as specific knowledge, rootedness at the local level, and independence from governments. They are usually considered as actors who enhance pluralism within international institutions by representing groups that would otherwise be excluded and, by turning the attention on transnational processes, making the governance process more transparent. Some of these claims have been challenged, however. Research indicated that, in contrast to business organizations and other economic actors, the actors of global civil society are usually loosely organized and poorly staffed, consisting mainly of transnational alliances of various national groups. Their inclusion in international politics has also been selective: only those organizations that adapt to the 'rules of the game' obtain some access, though usually of an informal nature, to some IGOs. Finally, rootedness at the local level and independence from governments remain variable.

Studies on INGOs and TSMOs highlighted that many of them had nevertheless become increasingly institutionalized, both in terms of acquired professionalism and in the forms of action they employ, devoting more time to lobbying or informing the public than to marching in the street. In this regard, networks constitute a key organizational form (Marchetti and Pianta 2011). A *transnational network* can be defined as a permanent co-ordination among different organizations (and sometimes individuals, such as experts), located in several countries, based on a shared frame for one specific global issue, developing both protest and proposal in the form of joint campaigns and social mobilizations against common targets at national or supranational level. Transnational networking is characterized by voluntary and horizontal patterns of co-ordination, which are trust-centred, reciprocal, and asymmetrical. Networks are in fact eminently non-static organizations: flexibility and fluidity are two major features which allow for adapting effectively to changing social conditions and to keep porous the organizational boundaries (Anheier and Katz 2005; Diani 2003). Transnational networks play a major role in terms of aggregation of social forces and development of common identities.

These actors have also innovated the repertoire of contention. The main activities by transnational networks include spreading information, influencing mass media, and raising awareness, but also lobbying, protest, and supplying of services to constituency. At a more general level, transnational networks are usually characterized by their advocacy function towards the promotion of normative change in politics (Keck and Sikkink 1998; Risse-Kappen 1995) that they pursue through the use of transnational campaigns. In more recent time, innovative forms of transnational protests have been invented and spread. Among them, a new form of transnational protest is the *counter-summit*, defined as the encounter of transnational activists in parallel to official summits of international institutions. Together with countersummits, *global days of action* represent a second new form of protest that brought activists to march, on the same day, in many countries. Finally, since 2001, transnational activism intensified in the *World Social Forum*, as well as its many macro-regional and national version (Della Porta 2009a, 2009b; Smith *et al.* 2007; Della Porta, Kriesi, and Rucht 2009; Pianta and Marchetti 2007; Smith 2007; Tarrow 2005b). Within these events and campaigns, new frames of action developed, symbolically constructing a global self, but also producing structural effects in the form of new movement networks. Not only have supranational events increased in frequency, they have also constituted founding moments for a new cycle of protest that has developed at the national and subnational levels on the issue of global justice. Even though transnational protests (in the forms of global days of action, counter-summits, or social forums) remained a rare occurrence, they emerged as particularly 'eventful' in their capacity to produce relational, cognitive, and affective effects on social movement activists and social movement organizations.

Global Claims: a Global Civil Society?

The global justice movement has contributed to redefine a number of political issues around global justice, and to initiate a process of norm change at the international/global level. While the symbolical reference to the globe is considered by some scholars as nothing really new – referencing the traditional internationalism of the workers' movement or the transnational campaigns against slavery – others have instead stressed the centrality of the global dimension today. Transnational communication helped not only a definition of problems as global, but also the cognitive linkages between different themes in broad transnational campaigns. Whereas in the 1980s social movements had undergone a process of specialization on single issues with 'new social movements' developing specific knowledge and competences on particular sub-issues, the global justice movement has linked together a multiplicity of themes related with class, gender, generation, environment, race, and religion. In fact, different concerns of different movements were bridged in a lengthy, although not always immediately visible, process of mobilization (Della Porta 2007). Accordingly, the global justice movement developed from protest campaigns around 'broker issues' that tied together concerns of different movements and organizations. These processes resonate with some theoretical reflections about the emergence and functioning of a global civil society, characterized by norms of autonomy, respect for differences, and solidarity.

In transnational protest campaigns, fragments of diverse cultures – secular and religious, radical and reformist, younger and older generations – have been linked to a broader discourse with the theme of social (and global) injustice as a common glue, while still leaving broad margins for separate developments. In many reflections on contemporary societies, civil society is referred to as an actor being able to address the tensions between particularism and universalism, plurality and connectedness, diversity and solidarity (Della Porta and Diani 2010). It is, in this sense, referred to as 'a solidarity sphere in which certain kind of universalizing community comes gradually to be defined and to some degrees enforced' (Alexander, 1998: 7). Research on civil society has stressed civility as respect for the others, politeness, and the acceptance of strangers as key values (Keane 2003) as well as autonomy from both the state and the market.

The global justice movement has been said to contribute to and reflect on the spread of composite and tolerant identities. The most innovative feature of this relational, cognitive, and affective process of transnational activism is precisely the capacity to combine the emphasizing of pluralism and diversity with a common definition of the self around a global dimension. At the transnational level, local and global concerns were linked around values such as equality, justice, human rights, and environmental protection. Transnational movements also confirm the growing importance of a conception of autonomy, as emancipation from state power and the market, that has always been central to the definition of civil society. Particularly inspired by new social movements and the movement for democracy in Eastern Europe (Misztal 2001), concerns about personal autonomy, self organization, and private space, independently from both the market and the state, became central (Kaldor 2003: 4). In particular at the global level, the enemy is singled out in neoliberal globalization, which activists perceive as characterizing not only the policies of the international financial organizations (the World Bank, International Monetary Found, and World Trade Organizations), but also the free-market and deregulation policies by national governments. These policies are considered as responsible for growing social injustice, with especially negative effects on women, the environment, the South, and other marginalized groups. Responses to such threat are different and vary from a reflexive continuation of the welfare policies, against both risks of colonization by state power but also of re-economization of society (Jean Cohen and Arato 1992), to the reform or re-foundation of international and would-be global institutions (Patomäki and Teivainen 2004). Rooted global visions, autonomy, respect for diversity, and solidarity are in fact paramount political principles around which the global justice movement coalesced (Marchetti 2009).

Within a global vision, *place-basedness* plays a central role as in opposition to mainstream interpretation of globalization. Contrary to the universalizing perspective that regards the local as provincial and regressive, this principle maintains the importance of localism as an unavoidable and critical resource for social and political life. Rather than accepting mainstream images of dangerous nationalism and bigoted regionalism, the place-based paradigm re-affirms the local and the present as the essential elements for a real political emancipation, though always keeping open and lively the dialogue with the external for cross-fertilization. In this sense, culture plays a relevant role in that it is only through a process of cultural development and self-awareness that collective subjectivity can flourish. Without falling back in a self-enclosed localism, rooted micro-politics, from indigenous movements in Amazon forest to neighbourhood associations in Florence, is thus seen not as a loophole to escape, but as key process for the reorganization of the space from below (Dirlik and Prazniak 2001; Osterweil 2005).

Autonomy is also crucial for distinguishing this perspective from its alternative paradigms. In opposition both to anonymous processes of globalization, and to naïve romanticism and local power positions, the autonomy principle asserts the legitimacy of communal authority. Highlighting pleasures, productivity, and rights of communities, local sovereignty remains grounded on a deep conception of democracy that rejects distant authority. Self-determination is claimed to be able to offer sound solutions to social requirements through a revolution of everyday life where social aims are focused on taking advantage of cultural heritage and traditions rather than seizing power. In many instances, autonomy is interpreted as part of a long process of decolonization which entails struggle against any form of domination, be it intimate, practical, or ideological. The principle of autonomy is mainly twofold for it entails both political independence and economic independence. Concerning the latter, it defends the strengthening of local economies as representing more democratic, sustainable, and economically effective way of production. Food-sovereignty – reoriented towards community needs rather than global market imperatives – forms part of the ideal hereby implied. This indigenous, autonomist, anarchist, and environmentalist perspective aims thus at what has been called global de-linking (Hines 2000; Starr and Adams 2003).

Diversity constitutes a further crucial component. Here the contention confutes the supposedly homogenizing process of globalization that would create a single societal model in which individuals would be deprived of their cultural specificity and reduced to anonymous consumers. In opposition to the single capitalist interpretation of space, time, and values, pluralism is here pursued through a double process. While local cultural are reaffirmed from below, universalizing globalism is critically de-constructed without falling into the equally hegemonic perspective according to which any partial or plural alternative remains incomplete and deficient of something. A different political epistemology is advocated for, one that is not in need of a centralized and unified point of reference. The image envisaged here is thus not a single project, but rather a plurality of cultural projects, a movement of movements, 'a world in which many worlds fit', as the Zapatistas would say. Such complex pluralism is an inevitable result once the point of departure is from below and without central planning, but such diversity is rather considered as a source of mutual learning than as an obstacle. Once this myriad of identities is networked, a new kind of globalism is revealed in the form of a subaltern cosmopolitanism (de Sousa Santos and Rodríguez-Garavito 2005; Tarrow 2005a).

Solidarity represents a final key principle that stresses the importance of transnational collaboration in overcoming local political difficulties. A key factor underpinning the possibility of solidarity is the development of a new interpretation of socio-political problems requiring collective action. The recognition of world interdependence constitutes the turning point for nurturing a process of problem generalization in which local issues circumscribed to the vernacular be no longer. Following from the acknowledgement of the inter-linking of global and local, the principle of solidarity aims to generate a sense of group collective identity, thus of shared fate, which would enhance inter-local coalition to promote global change. In opposition to the neo-liberal logic of individual atomization, local groups would consequently feel they are not alone in their effort and, if acting together, they are able to impact on their lives (Brecher, Costello, and Smith 2000; Smith, Chatfield, and Pagnucco 1997).

Global Movements and Deliberative Democracy

Following from the previous political reflections is the profound reinterpretation of the central theme of democracy as developed by transnational activists. In this respect, it is especially important to note the conception of participatory and deliberative democracy which is elaborated and prefigured in the global justice movements and related transnational networks.

In normative theory and beyond, several studies have indicated that the crisis of representative democracy is accompanied by the (re)emergence of other conceptions and practices of democracy. Empirical research on political participation has stressed that, while some more conventional forms of participation (such as voting or party-linked activities) are declining, protest forms are increasingly used. Citizens vote less, but they are not less interested in or knowledgeable about politics. While some traditional types of associations are decreasing in popularity, others (social movement organizations and/or civil society organizations) are growing in resources, legitimacy, and members.

The global justice movement builds upon some visions of democracy that have long been present in the social sciences' normative and empirical analysis of democracy. These visions however have been (or risk being) removed or marginalized in the 'minimalistic' conceptions of democracy that became dominant in the political as well as the scientific discourse. Social movements do not limit themselves to presenting demands to decision makers; they also more or less explicitly express a fundamental critique of conventional politics, thus shifting their endeavours from politics itself to meta-politics (Offe 1985). Their ideas resonate with 'an ancient element of democratic theory that calls for an organisation of collective decision making referred to in varying ways as classical, populist, communitarian, strong, grass-roots, or direct democracy against a democratic practice in contemporary democracies labelled as realist, liberal, elite, republican, or representative democracy' (Kitschelt 1993: 15). Their critique has traditionally addressed the representative element of democracy, with calls for citizen participation.

While participatory aspects have long been present in theorizing about democracy and social movements, recent developments in transnational activism can be usefully discussed in light of the growing literature on deliberative democracy, with its focus on communication (Della Porta 2005a, 2005b). Several of the scholars who participated in this debate located democratic deliberation in voluntary groups (Joshua Cohen 1989), social movements (Dryzek 2000), protest arenas (Young 2003: 119), or, more in general, enclaves free from institutional power (Mansbridge 1996). Deliberative participatory democracy refers to decisional processes in which, under conditions of equality, inclusiveness, and transparency, a communicative process based on reason (the strength of a good argument) may transform individual preferences, leading to decisions oriented to the public good (Della Porta 2005a, 2005b). In particular, deliberative democracy 'requires some forms of apparent equality among citizens' (Joshua Cohen 1989: 18); as it takes place among free and equal citizens, as 'free deliberation among equals' (Joshua Cohen 1989: 20). Deliberation must exclude power deriving from coercion but also an unequal weighting of the participants as representatives of organizations of different sizes or as more influential individuals. Additionally, deliberative arenas are inclusive: all citizens with a stake in the decisions to be taken must be included in the process and able to express their views. This means that the deliberative process takes place under conditions of plurality of values, including people with different perspectives but facing common problems. Moreover, transparency resonates with direct, participatory democracy: assemblies are typically open, public spheres. In Joshua Cohen's definition, a deliberative democracy is 'an association whose affairs are governed by the *public* deliberation of its members' (Joshua Cohen 1989: 17, emphasis added).

While not always coherently practised, these norms are more and more present in the discourse of contemporary social movements. If norms of equality, inclusiveness, and transparency were already present in social movements, attempts to develop alternative, deliberative, visions and practices of democracy constitute a novelty. Deliberative democracy differs from conceptions of democracy as the aggregation of (exogenously generated) preferences. A deliberative setting facilitates the search for a common end or good (Elster 1998). In this model of democracy, 'the political debate is organized around alternative conceptions of the public good', and, above all, it 'draws identities and citizens' interests in ways that contribute to public building of public good' (Joshua Cohen 1989: 18–19). In particular, deliberative democracy stresses reason, argumentation, and dialogue: people are convinced by the force of the best argument. Deliberation is based on horizontal flows of communication, multiple producers of content, wide opportunities for interactivity, confrontation based on rational argumentation, and attitude to reciprocal listening (Habermas 1981, 1996 [1992]). Decisions rely upon arguments that participants recognize as reasonable (Joshua Cohen and Sabel 1997).

What seems especially new in the conception of deliberative democracy, as developed within transnational networks, is the emphasis on preference (trans)formation with an orientation to the definition of the public good. In this sense, the global justice movement and related networks seem to agree that 'deliberative democracy requires the transformation of preferences in interaction' (Dryzek 2000: 79). They also see their own action as 'a process through which initial preferences are transformed in order to take into account the points of view of the others' (Miller 1993: 75). In the global justice movement these norms entailed a renewed attention to practices of consensus, with decisions approvable by all participants – in contrast with majority rule, where decisions are legitimated by vote.

When applied to the realm of political struggle, these innovative conceptions of democracy have generated a critical attitude towards national and transnational politics. Experimenting in their organizational praxis, transnational activists have elaborated demands for radical changes not only in policies but also in politics. If the social movements of the 1980s and the 1990s were described as more pragmatic and single-issue oriented, research on the global justice movement testifies to its continuous interest in addressing the meta-issue of democracy, with some continuity and innovations vis-à-vis past experiences (Della Porta 2007, 2009a, 2009b). Transnational networks emerged as political actors, mobilizing in various forms in order to produce institutional changes, but also trying to practise those novelties in their internal lives. The prefigurative role of internal democratic practices acquires a particularly important role for the global justice movement organizations, which stress a necessary coherence between what is advocated in the external environment and what is practised inside.

Social movements are also more and more cited as important participants in democratic processes. As Pierre Rosanvallon recently observed, 'the history of real democracies cannot be dissociated from a permanent tension and contestation' (Rosanvallon 2006: 11). In his vision, democracy needs not only legal legitimation, but also what he calls 'counter-democracy'. Citizens' attentive vigilance upon power holders is defined as a specific, political modality of action, a 'particular form of political intervention', different from decision making, but still a fundamental aspect of the democratic process (Rosanvallon 2006: 40). Actors such as independent authorities and judges, but also mass media, experts, and social movements, have traditionally exercised this function of surveillance. The latter, in particular, are considered as most relevant for the development of an 'expressive democracy' that corresponds to 'the *prise de parole* of the society, the manifestation of a collective sentiment, the formulation of a judgment about the governors and their action, or again the production of claims' (Rosanvallon 2006: 26). Surveillance from below is all the more important given the crisis of representative, electoral democracy.

Social movement organizations take the democratic function of control seriously, mobilizing to put pressure on decision makers, as well as developing counter-knowledge and open public spaces. In fact, research indicates that the global justice movements organizations interact with public institutions, at various territorial levels (Della Porta 2009a). In many cases, especially but not only at the local level, they collaborate with public institutions, both on specific problems and in broader campaigns. They contract out specific services, but they are also often supported in recognition of their function in building 'counter' democratic spaces (Rosanvallon and Goldhammer 2009). In particular, these organizations perceive themselves as controllers of public institutions, promoting alternative policies but also, more broadly, calling for more (and different) democracy. While stressing the need for more public and less private, more state and less market, they also define themselves especially as autonomous from institutions and as performing democratic control of the governors. By creating public spaces, they contribute to the development of ideas and practices (Della Porta 2009b). If electoral accountability has long been privileged over the power of surveillance in the historical evolution of procedural democracy, social movement organizations contribute to bringing attention back to the 'counter democracy' of surveillance. Democratic surveillance acquires a special meaning given the perceived challenge of adapting democratic conceptions and practices to the increasing shift of competence towards the transnational level. In this transition, transnational networks contribute to the debate on global democracy, not only by criticizing the lack of democratic accountability and even transparency of many existing IGOs and of the wider globalization process, but also by asking for a globalization of democracy and actually constructing a global public sphere (Smith 2007).

Participation as non-hierarchical and horizontal public engagement constitutes in fact a major element of the political visions constructed by the global justice movement (Marchetti 2008).

Here the critical target consists of all those indirect forms of political representation accused of eroding the political trust between the elected and the electors, or, in the most radical interpretation, of hiding the deception of a the ruling class. Contrary to this supposed elitist view, a model of democratic participation is reasserted in which active engagement of the entire citizenry is expected at all levels and genuinely collective decision-making process thus implemented. In more technical terms, the principle of participation is often associated, as said, with the deliberative turn in political thinking. This input-oriented process is supposed to generate better information, higher solidarity, greater engagement and democratic skills, and enhanced trust in public institutions. In this conception of politics, public institutions are then seen more as facilitators of self-organized open spaces from below, rather than as traditional economic and political leadership from above. Different to previous left ideologies, political parties are for the most part mistrusted while self-organized civil society is called to join politics in first person. Also innovative is an interpretation of politics, according to which self-organization is directed towards changing society rather than taking power and control the state (Fung and Wright 2003; Polletta 2002).

Subaltern, Thick, and Rooted Cosmopolitanism

The global justice movement has not only inspired a new conceptualization of deliberative democracy, but also a peculiar version of the long-standing tradition of cosmopolitanism. In recent years, a sophisticated body of work, mainly (but not exclusively) coming from sociologists and social movement theorists, has provided a robust restatement of cosmopolitan thinking in terms of social cosmopolitanism which is very much indebted to political activism. This third wave of cosmopolitan thinking was generated as a reaction to the first two phases: in opposition to the first ethical phase, which is accused of being too abstract and thin (being linked only to the idea of common humanity), and in opposition to the second institutional phase, which it accused of being too close to a western, dominating agenda and too far from grassroots experience (i.e. resembling the global governance model). In response to these limits, this later version suggests new ways of conceptualizing the socio-political nexus that remains more inclusive and locally rooted. Rather than starting from a normative question of justice (ethical cosmopolitanism's question: *What does global justice imply?*) or a formal question of institutional design (institutional cosmopolitanism's question: *Which institutions best serve global justice?*), here the starting questions are about the agency: *Who needs cosmopolitanism? Who is the genuine actor of cosmopolitanism?* The answer is: the marginalized and excluded people of the world. This marks from the beginning a stark divergence from previous cosmopolitan thinking towards a more socially considerate reflection. What emerges is a third cosmopolitan understanding that combines the aspiration to achieve transnational and global justice with attentiveness to local struggles and realities as they actually exist (Marchetti 2008: ch. 4).

It is highly significant that social cosmopolitanism emerged from an antagonism towards previous cosmopolitan theory. A number of oppositional claims on specific key problems with cosmopolitanism are of particular concern to social cosmopolitanism. They are the following: a) the domination problem, according to which cosmopolitanism is considered too close to neoliberal capitalism; b) the cultural problem, according to which cosmopolitanism is understood to rely on too minimal a set of abstract prescriptions that are far from popular experience; c) the motivational problem, according to which cosmopolitanism fails to connect norms to practices; and d) the political problem, according to which cosmopolitanism fails to champion the claims of local groups, remaining too attached to élites. In response to this critical focus, this new version of cosmopolitanism presents itself as subaltern, thick, embedded, and rooted. It claims to be subaltern because it focuses on those voices that come from minorities, often from the south of the world, and not from the western centres of global governance (de Sousa Santos 2002). It is thick because it is imbued with solidaristic principles of social justice, and is not minimalist in terms of liberal non-harm (Delanty 2006). It is embedded because it is inserted within a social context characterized by intense mutual obligations and feelings of attachment to a comprehensive political experience, rather than referring to loose institutional relationships (Appiah 2006). Finally, it is rooted in that it emerges from local practices and remains tightly connected with political struggles from below, in opposition to élitist management (Tarrow 2005b).

In contrast to the supposedly constitutive *flâneurisme* of cosmopolitanism, social cosmopolitans highlight the inevitability of relying on local factors for building up a viable political community. Social cohesion and solidaristic ties are needed for any political project. Any political struggle needs, in fact, to be embedded within local factors, within local struggles, to be effective and able to mobilize people. Social and political bonds are key elements for generating local and particularistic mutual obligations, which in turn are the true bases for eventual political solidarity, be it local, national, or transnational. The traditional side of communities is important, but this does not mean falling back on a blind acceptance of customs. Previous cosmopolitan thinking developed a problematic denigration of traditions, customs, and all that is related to local con-servatism, including ethnicity and religion. Social cosmopolitanism conversely triggers a new understanding of the social. Pre-given traditions are a fundamental social bond, although they are not the only binding elements. Political visions remain the key component for reforming actual societies towards more democratic systems, but they can only work if they are embedded and engage critically with local traditions. Accordingly, the democratization process cannot be imposed from above (and a fortiori cannot be coercively imported), but it has to grow out of the *Lebenswelt* (lifeworld) – it has to empower individuals within traditions, not against them. A cosmopolitan framework built from below would serve as a facilitator of egalitarian and reciprocal encounters. It would provide the necessary overall framework for a potential reci-procal enrichment rather than for a homogenizing process. Only by beginning from the local can transnational solidarity be built through the formation of transnational and overlapping communities. Unity within locally rooted diversity: this is the model of (transnational) democracy that the social cosmopolitanism defends.

References

Alexander, J. C. (1998). 'Introduction. Civil Society I, II, III: Constructing and Empirical Concept from Normative Controversies and Historical Transformations'. In J. C. Alexander (ed.), *Real Civil Society: Dilemma of Institutionalization*. London: Sage.

Anheier, H. and Katz, H. (2005). 'Network Approach to Global Civil Society'. In H. Anheier, M. Glasius, and M. Kaldor (eds), *Global Civil Society Yearbook 2004/5*. London: Sage.

Appiah, K. A. (2006). *Cosmopolitanism: Ethics in a World of Strangers*. New York: W. W. Norton.

Bauböck, R. (2008). 'Normative Empirical Theory and Empirical Research'. In D. Della Porta and M. Keating (eds), *Approaches and Methodologies in the Social Sciences: A Pluralist Perspective*. Cambridge: Cambridge University Press.

Brecher, J., Costello, T., and Smith, B. (2000). *Globalization from Below: The Power of Solidarity*. Cambridge: South End Press.

Cohen, J. (1989). 'Deliberation and Democratic Legitimacy'. In A. Harmilin and P. Pettit (eds), *The Good Polity*. Oxford: Blackwell.

Cohen, J. and Arato, A. (1992). *Civil Society and Political Theory*. Cambridge, MA: MIT Press.

Cohen, J. and Sabel, C. F. (1997). 'Directly-Deliberative Polyarchy'. *European Law Journal*, 3(4): 313–42.

Delanty, G. (2006). 'The Cosmopolitan Imagination: Critical Cosmopolitanism and Social Theory'. *British Journal of Sociology*, 57(1): 25–47.

Della Porta, D. (2005a). 'Deliberation in Movement: Why and How to Study Deliberative Democracy and Social Movements'. *Acta Politica*, 40(3): 336–50.

——(2005b). 'Making the Polis: Social Forum and Democracy in the Global Justice Movement'. *Mobilization*, 10(1): 73–94.

——(ed.). (2007). *The Global Justice Movement: A Cross-national and Transnational Perspective*. Boulder, CO: Paradigm.

——(2009a). *Another Europe: Conceptions and Practices of Democracy in the European Social Forums*. London: Routledge.

——(2009b). *Democracy in Movement: Conceptions and Practices of Democracy in Contemporary Social Movements*. London: Palgrave.

Della Porta, D. and Diani, M. (2010). 'Social Movements and Civil Society'. In B. Edward (ed.), *Handbook of Civil Society*. Oxford: Oxford University Press.

Della Porta, D., Kriesi, H., and Rucht, D. (eds). (2009). *Social Movements in a Globalizing World*. London: Macmillan, expanded paperback edition

Diani, M. (2003). 'Networks and Social Movements: A Research Programme'. In M. Diani and D. McAdam (eds), *Social Movements and Networks: Relational Approaches to Collective Action*. Oxford: Oxford University Press.

Dirlik, A., and Prazniak, R. (eds). (2001). *Places and Politics in an Age of Globalization*. Lanham, MD: Rowan & Littlefield.

Dryzek, J. S. (2000). *Deliberative Democracy and Beyond*. Oxford: Oxford University Press.

Elster, J. (1998). 'Deliberation and Constitution Making'. In J. Elster (ed.), *Deliberative Democracy*. Cambridge: Cambridge University Press.

Fung, A. and Wright, E. O. (2003). *Deepening Democracy: Institutional Innovations in Empowered Participative Governance*. London: Verso.

Habermas, J. (1981). *Theorie des kommunikativen Handelns*. Frankfurt am Main: Suhrkamp.

——(1996 [1992]). *Between Facts and Norms: Contributions to a Discursive Theory of Law and Democracy*. Cambridge: Polity.

Hines, C. (2000). *Localization: A Global Manifesto*. London: Earthscan.

Kaldor, M. (2003). *Global Civil Society. An Answer to War*. Cambridge: Polity Press.

Keane, J. (2003). *Global Civil Society?* Cambridge: Cambridge University Press.

Keck, M. and Sikkink, K. (1998). *Activists Beyond Borders: Advocacy Networks in International Politics*. Ithaca, NY: Cornell University Press.

Kitschelt, H. (1993). 'Social Movements, Political Parties, and Democratic Theory'. *The Annals of the American Academy of Political and Social Science*, 528: 13–29.

Mansbridge, J. (1996). ' 'Using Power/Fighting Power: The Polity'. In S. Benhabib (ed.), *Democracy and Difference: Contesting the Boundaries of the Political*. Princeton, NJ: Princeton University Press.

Marchetti, R. (2008). *Global Democracy: For and Against. Ethical Theory, Institutional Design, and Social Struggles*. London and New York: Routledge.

——(2009). 'Mapping Alternative Models of Global Politics'. *International Studies Review*, 11(1): 133–56.

Marchetti, R. and Pianta, M. (2011). 'Global Networks of Civil Society and the Politics of Change'. In D. Barrier, M. Pianta and P. Utting (eds), *Social Mobilization, Global Justice and Policy Reform in Europe: Understanding When Change Happens*. London: Routledge.

Miller, D. (1993). 'Deliberative Democracy and Social Choice'. In D. Held (ed.), *Prospects for Democracy*. Cambridge: Polity.

Misztal, B. (2001). 'Civil Society: A Signifier of Plurality and Sense of Wholeness'. In J. R. Blau (ed.), *The Blackwell Companion of Sociology*. Oxford: Blackwell.

Offe, C. (1985). 'New Social Movements: Changing Boundaries of the Political'. *Social Research*, 52: 817–68.

Osterweil, M. (2005). 'Place-based Globalism: Theorizing the Global Justice Movement'. *Development*, 48 (2): 23–8.

Patomäki, H. and Teivainen, T. (2004). *A Possible World: Democratic Transformation of Global Institutions*. London: Zed.

Pianta, M. and Marchetti, R. (2007). 'The Global Justice Movements: The Transnational Dimension'. In D. della Porta (ed.), *The Global Justice Movement: A Cross-National and Transnational Perspective*. Boulder, CO: Paradigm.

Polletta, F. (2002). *Freedom Is an Endless Meeting: Democracy in American Social Movements*. Chicago, IL: Chicago University Press.

Risse-Kappen, T. (ed.). (1995). *Bringing Transnational Relations Back In: Non-State Actors, Domestic Structure and International Institutions*. Ithaca, NY: Cornell University Press.

Rosanvallon, P. (2006). *Democracy Past and Future*. New York: Columbia University Press.

Rosanvallon, P. and Goldhammer, A. (2009). *Counter-Democracy: Politics in the Age of Distrust*. Cambridge: Cambridge University Press.

Smith, J. (2007). *Social Movements for Global Democracy*. Baltimore, MD: John Hopkins University Press.

Smith, J. *et al.* (2007)., *Global Democracy and the World Social Forum*, Boulder CO, Paradigm.

Smith, J., Chatfield, C., and Pagnucco, R. (eds). (1997). *Transnational Social Movements and Global Politics. Solidarity Beyond the State*. Syracuse, NY: Syracuse University Press.

de Sousa Santos, B. (2002). *Toward a New Legal Common Sense: Law, Globalization and Emancipation*. London: Butterworths LexisNexis.

de Sousa Santos, B. and Rodríguez-Garavito, C. A. (eds). (2005). *Law and Globalization Below: Toward a Cosmopolitan Legality*. Cambridge: Cambridge University Press.

Starr, A. and Adams, J. (2003). 'Anti-globalization: The Global Fight for Local Autonomy'. *New Political Science*, 25(1): 19–42.

Tarrow, S. (2005a). 'Cosmopoliti radicati e attivisti transnazionali'. *Rassegna italiana di sociologia*, 46(2): 221–47.

——(2005b). *The New Transnational Activism*. Cambridge: Cambridge University Press.

Young, I. M. (2003). 'Activist Challenges to Deliberative Democracy'. In J. Fishkin and P. Laslett (eds), *Debating Deliberative Democracy*. Malden, MA: Blackwell.

The Transnational Social Question

Thomas Faist

The world's greatest inequalities seem to be defined by national borders in addition to and overlapping with well-known markers such as race, class, or gender. At the beginning of the twenty-first century manifold inequalities characterize relations between social groups: The most widespread measure, inequality among countries' per capita incomes, accounts internationally for two-thirds of overall income inequality. Average incomes in the richest countries far exceed those in the poorest countries, with estimates of incomes that are 40 to 50 times greater in the former (Bourguignon and Morrisson 2002). Equally or more important, access to food, nutrition, formal education, and medical care is vastly unequal. Resulting effects such as malnutrition, ill health, and low life expectancy, and inadequate social protection to protect against risks, threaten the lives of many. This situation is reminiscent of the living conditions of a majority of the population that obtained in a large part of nineteenth-century Europe. At that time and in that particular world region, the 'social question' was the central subject of extremely volatile political conflicts between the ruling classes and working-class movements. Nowadays, the protests of globalization critics, for instance at the World Social Forum, can certainly not be overlooked. There is also an abundance of political groupings and NGOs rallying across national borders in support of numerous campaigns such as environmental, human rights and women's issues, Christian, Hindu or Islamic fundamentalism, or food sovereignty (Evans 2006).

Then and now the social question has several distinct elements: first, the perception of large-scale inequalities between social groups; second, political contention around inequalities; and third, institutionalized efforts at dealing with inequalities, such as – historically in large parts of Europe – social rights within nationally bounded welfare states or, more recently, social standards meant to apply worldwide. Given this context, the starting question is as follows. Do we observe the perhaps gradual emergence of sanctionable global social norms by way of transnational social rights beyond national state borders? In other words, is there a discernible development of global social policy in the twenty-first century, implying a move from national to post-national solidarity and the corresponding rights and duties as well as policies? At the same time, the focus on the transnational aspect of the social question does not mean the occlusion of inequalities, contentions, and rights within and across national states. Quite to the contrary, one of the central issues is how solidarities on one scale may contribute to or exclude solidarities on another through institutionalized mechanisms of social closure such as immigration controls.

439

National welfare states in Europe, for example, can be cast as enabling the social protection of large parts of the population at the expense of those who are not admitted or covered – for example, by way of immigration control.

Historically, one of the solutions to stark social inequalities and pressing issues of the old social question in Europe, North America, and Australia has been the national welfare state and thus the institutionalization of social rights. For political thinking and debate on social inequality, two postulates were of crucial significance: equality of conditions and democracy. These postulates were already the subject of political discourse more than 150 years ago when they were analysed by Alexis de Tocqueville (1986 [1835 and 1840]) in the light of the development of democracy in the United States. In the past, social rights have been tied to (national) citizenship status. Citizenship can be understood as a continuous series of transactions between rulers and subjects. In the tradition of T. H. Marshall (1964 [1950]), citizenship captures the tensions between democracy and capitalism. The central focus is the inherent tension between the idea of democracy, which is based on the notion of equal citizenship, and the social inequalities brought about by capitalism. Marshall argues that the expansion of citizenship rights, and especially the growth of social rights in the course of the twentieth century, enabled a historic compromise between social classes. In his view, social rights and social policies stabilize welfare capitalism as a legitimate system of social inequality on the national level. The possibility of this happening today on a global scale is more a normative utopian idea. There is no feasible concept of citizenship with the postulate of equal political freedom, or of equal political rights, in any kind of global polity, although there is a tendency toward an establishment of social standards in loose association with human rights. The main difference between rights and standards is that the latter are not enforceable by persons through the legal system. Unlike social rights which can, in principle, be claimed in court, social standards are an instance of 'soft law' which implies self-binding of the agents concerned. Nonetheless, without setting the experience of national welfare states as a path for global developments, the question is how the transnational social question is dealt with.

The new transnational social question has not made obsolete the issues dealt with in the old social question, which has found expression in national welfare states in the OECD world. Rather, it has added yet another layer, namely cross-border interdependence and a global horizon. Debates around social inequalities and protection often occur on various scales simultaneously – local, national, and global; hence the phrase the transnational (and not necessarily the global) social question.

The Perception of Growing Interdependence

A cross-border horizon relates to the increasing perception of cross-border interdependencies, such as international migration, military threats, environmental degradation, and climate change. There are empirically identifiable global trends in meta-principles such as the postulates of equality and democracy that show a shift in public awareness concerning transnational exchange and interdependence (Furia 2005). More information, and possibly even greater knowledge of transnational social inequality, are available now than was the case in the past to scholars and publics alike (Inglehart 2003).

The anticipation of mass migration from Eastern to Western Europe in the early 1990s may serve as an example here. The question arose as to whether social rights could also be conferred on persons abroad, for instance in the form of a basic minimum income (De Swaan 1992). Not unlike the emergence of national social welfare in the nineteenth century, such a development, so the argument runs, could be conceivable on a transnational scale. In the nineteenth and early twentieth centuries, de Swaan argued, the (national) ruling classes felt threatened by the 'vagabond poor' to such a degree that some states introduced welfare measures to offset this menace. The perceived threat of mass migration from Eastern Europe and the Third World, so the argument continues, had meanwhile become so great that northern states could see benefits in contributing toward a welfare state at the supranational level. It is in the meantime clear that in the light of effective controls at the borders of European immigration countries there is no forceful argument for implementing this measure to prevent migration. An argument similar to migration could be made relating to environmental destruction, the most visible form of which is today discussed under the label climate change. Yet, again, social destitution and escape from deteriorating conditions by millions of people are not likely to impinge directly upon the welfare of the OECD countries. As is the case with forced migration movements, most persons will probably end up in the same or neighbouring countries.

The consequences of interlinkages are highly politicized, as the mobility of highly-skilled professionals suggests. Their expertise is sought after by technologically and economically advanced centres. For the category of the highly-skilled the limitation of one place of residence determining their life chances is incorrect – indeed, there are divergent interpretations. One side, in the past mostly developing countries, has connected this mobility with 'brain drain', a loss of skilled human power, of the educated and skilled, by marginalized countries. The other side, most often industrialized countries, speaks of 'brain gain' or 'brain circulation' and depicts the situation as beneficial for emigration regions, immigration regions, and the mobile persons alike. While the first emphasizes transnational inequalities, the second speaks of favourable impacts on political and economic development.

Public policies impacting on social protection in the local, national, and international realms have undergone significant changes over the past decades. This is visible in how international, national, and transnational institutions have framed socio-economic or human development. Crucially, social policy and development thinking have moved from a focus on the national state to more emphasis on local government and international institutions (Mkandawire 2004) and terms such as 'global social policy' (Deacon 1997) have flourished. Correspondingly, social rights as human rights have been points of departure. Social rights in international conventions – usually not enforceable in courts – constitute the shared vocabulary from which political debates start. After the Second World War, United Nations organizations began to consider social rights in conjunction with basic rights, along with political and civil rights. Meanwhile, some international organizations no longer discuss social protection and concomitant social rights merely as a factor contributing to economic development, but as intrinsic rights. Explicit reference to the General Declaration of Human Rights (1948), the International Covenant on Economic, Social and Cultural Rights (1966), and even the rights of citizens to a social contract on the national state level is widespread (e.g. UNDP 2005), and so is an emphasis on the universality of human rights and citizens' rights (Brysk and Shafir 2004). They are universal in the sense that, for instance, all member states of the UN are signatories of the International Covenant on Social and Economic Rights. The essential social rights laid down in Articles 22–27 of the Universal Declaration of Human Rights (1948) are a fundamental right to school education, the right to work and to join or form a trade union, the right to a basic or minimum income, food, clothing, housing, medical care, and social security.

Social standards have been legitimated as referring to social rights. The transnational regulation of employment and social standards comprises international institutions and regimes such as the International Labour Organization (ILO), social clauses in trade agreements, public codes of conduct, and the UN Global Compact; but also includes more private transnational regulatory forms such as codes of conduct for specific businesses, international framework agreements, or social labels. The governance of social and labour standards is characterized by a wide diversity of work regulations involving the conventional agents, viz. the state, the trade unions, and employers associations, but also new actors such as social movements and NGOs. It is striking that the justifications for, say, labour and social standards, insofar as they are represented by international organizations like the ILO have in recent decades increasingly merged with the human rights discourse. Another salient point is that sanctionable rights and obligations have to an increasing degree been substituted by employers' voluntary self-regulation, especially in the case of transnational businesses. Such standards are therefore frequently private, voluntary transnational arrangements, or soft law, and their regulation relies on cooperation, rather than sanctions. The major issue for the future is therefore whether in transnational political multilevel systems such norms can be legally claimed at all.

The development of social rights and social standards must be seen within the context of a world that is highly fragmented with respect to the vast range of opportunities that citizens' social rights provide in different countries. Not surprisingly, the citizens of those states that are marginalized and are not integrated to a significant degree through trade and investment in the world economy have hardly anything to do with, for instance, labour and social standards as defined by international conventions. To a greater degree than in the OECD world, in marginalized and so-called developing countries the formal, and implicitly also the informal, means of providing social protection are determined by transnational factors. Such factors are institutional, such as the World Bank, the IMF, and the World Trade Organization (WTO), which determine parameters through rules and the provision of finance; commercial, such as transnational capital and investments of foreign investors; civil societal through transnational non-governmental organizations (NGOs) and the significant role they play in development aid or cooperation; and kinship systems through migrants and their remittances back home. The heavy-handed dominance of OECD countries in the architecture of international organizations also accounts for the resistance of states not only in marginalized countries, but also in newly industrializing and transformation countries, to common social standards through mechanisms such as the WTO. There has been, at least on the part of international organizations, a move from structural adjustment policies vis-à-vis countries in Africa, Latin America, and Southeast Asia to polices that favour a combination of a liberal market approach with market-based insurance and targeted policies for the poor/needy, and a heavy focus on social capital and local community, characterized by keywords such as empowerment and capacity-building.

Various factors discourage one from expecting the establishment of sanctionable global social norms in the form of transnational social rights and social citizenship, but such a conclusion could be altered as a result of the mobilizing force of a politics of rights and obligations. Most important, the framing of the transnational social question as one of social rights or, more broadly, democracy and equality, brings to the fore the crucial issue in political debates and conflicts – the legitimacy of orders of inequality. Given the obvious absence of a Marshallian world on a global scale in which capitalism and democracy are linked by a world welfare state, many persons around the globe readily associate globalization (a convenient shorthand for seminal processes of social transformation; cf. Polanyi 2001 [1944]) with unfair social outcomes and oppose it precisely for this reason; the anti-globalization movement builds on the feeling that prevailing patterns of trading relations and income distribution are unjust and morally reprehensible. If it is true that opposition to globalization and opposition to inequality are closely linked, tolerance of inequality becomes a key factor in the political calculus. The perception of transnational inequality could therefore make a difference. Thus, concerned persons must have some normative notion of what a proper, justifiable, and fair distribution of income should be – a kind of everyday normative political theory. People's beliefs about inequality are relevant because their views and above all practices feed into the political process. Considering people's attitudes, social inequalities are transnational in the sense that those who care about intra-state inequality are also very likely to speak out against the global gap between rich and poor regions (Lübker 2004). There is thus a direct link, at least on the attitudinal level, between perceptions of inequality within demarcated welfare states on the one hand and global concerns on the other. While beliefs about inequality and solidarity are first indicators about the transnational horizon of the social question, the issue of politics looms large. Reviving older notions of class mobilizations but going beyond the well-known channel of working-class politics, Hardt and Negri (2000), for example, put their faith in a 'multitude' of those exploited, which has the potential of becoming a 'class for itself'. Nevertheless, the question which follows is how even organized movements can, aside from performing protests, provide effective levers for action.

Theories: Normative and Political Sociological Approaches to Social Rights

The relatively autonomous world political system, with national states as its main constituents, is central to the inequalities in the distribution of social rights. Place of birth and residence is one of the main determinants of one's position in a transnational hierarchy of inequality (Shachar 2009). Social rights are institutionalized within national states and distinct from objective rights, which protect individuals from violence or restraint. The latter thus include, for instance, freedom of association, freedom of opinion, and religious freedom. Social rights are also defined as positive rights as opposed to negative rights (Höffe 2002), which are rights to liberty, i.e. political and civil rights. Positive rights require the active intervention of the state. The relationship between negative and positive rights is not dichotomous, however. Political rights are necessary, at least in democracies, in order to create social rights. Conversely, the major theorists of citizenship – Aristotle, Cicero, Niccolò Macchiavelli, Edmund Burke, Alexis de Tocqueville, John Stuart Mill, Hannah Arendt – have all argued that, in order to participate fully in public life and to achieve recognized social membership, one needed to be in a certain socioeconomic position. Furthermore, others have pointed out that the formal equality of rights is by no means sufficient for them to be effective. They must be accompanied by substantial liberties and by institutions enforcing them (Marshall 1964 [1950]).

For the conceptualization of emergent transnational social rights and social standards, there are two types of approaches, one stemming from normative political philosophy, and the other from political sociology. In normative political theory, in turn, two branches can be distinguished: a world citizenship – or cosmopolitan – perspective, and a nationality perspective. In a cosmopolitan citizenship perspective, social rights are part of a desirable world citizenship. An optimistic perspective may refer to Max Weber's social and economic history (Weber 1980 [1922]) and argue that citizenship was first conceived and practised at the municipal level in ancient Greece and medieval Europe before it moved up one level and became *de jure* and *de facto* congruous with membership of a territorial national state. Citizenship rights beyond the national state would therefore be an evolutionary leap forward (Heater 2004). Ultimately, this would, however, require a global political community with socio-cultural resources such as reciprocity and solidarity to be drawn on as required. This would be a broad extension of Immanuel Kant's idea of a cosmopolitan right to hospitality (Linklater 1999) by means of a rational development of identities beyond the national level. Such a global political identity is today only conceivable as a transparent, constructed affiliation (Habermas 1998). This perspective would certainly be attractive in terms of the allocation of life chances according to legal citizenship. World citizenship would not acknowledge any privileges passed on by descent or birth within a certain territory, the most prominent of which is indeed citizenship. We would all formally have the same status as members of an all-encompassing global polity. Such a community would, however, be greatly endangered by a 'tyranny of the majority' (de Tocqueville 1986) because of the unavailability of exit options. Equally important, positive rights would require a willingness to redistribute goods. This notion is even less probable and less conceivable on a global scale than it is in regions like Europe (cf. Faist 2001). While these qualities can be observed when disaster strikes or in development policies, they have no legal status and certainly no regulative components on the order of, say, EU social policy.

This critique of the concept of world citizenship highlights the central elements of a republican version of national cosmopolitanism. The republican version conceives of social rights primarily as a close form of solidarity on a national scale. As a consequence, the following conditions can be fulfilled only in a national state: First, citizens of the respective legal citizenship, that is nationality, are counted as valid members of a framed political community viz. polity and in this way reproduce the socio-cultural basis for citizenship, namely reciprocity and solidarity. Second, a common allegiance has a bonding effect on the citizens and enables them to agree on substantive rights and obligations that form the basis for their membership. Third, citizenship confers participatory rights and political representation. Ultimately, world citizenship from this perspective appears to be little more than a vague cosmopolitan idea in a world lacking a fundamental moral consensus. A further criticism is that at best world citizenship would weaken the bonds that hold citizens of a national state together. And only these national bonds ensure that citizens maintain their ties to the rest of humanity (Walzer 1996). This critique of the concept of world citizenship could be disputed, however, based on empirical findings that suggest that world and national citizenship are not necessarily zero-sum notions and that the claim has to be qualified (Furia 2005). Also, it neglects the fact that national citizenship is in itself a mechanism that perpetuates transnational social inequality.

The debate over cosmopolitan vs. national perspectives can also be found in theories of justice. There has been a vivid debate on the moral significance of state boundaries and thus the appropriate frame to which norms and rights should refer which could address transnational inequalities. In *A Theory of Justice* (1971) John Rawls proposed a clear principle of distributive justice: In a nutshell, this 'difference principle' says that economic inequalities within a national society are unjust unless they benefit everyone, including the least advantaged. He argued that distributive justice between different states ('peoples') is not possible because there is nothing to distribute. In his view the society of states is not a scheme of cooperation for mutual advantage and so there is no social product whose distribution is a proper matter for redistribution. Rawls's critics hold otherwise. First, under conditions of interdependence, national societies are not sufficiently separate to justify their being treated as self-contained entities (Beitz 1979). This argument concludes that the world has to be seen, in certain respects, as a single society, and therefore the 'difference principle' applied, so as to benefit the least advantaged. Yet one of the questions that arises is whether such a world society is a scheme of mutual advantage, as Rawls held about national societies; think of the world economic order which systematically disadvantages peoples in the periphery. Second, there is a widespread argument that rich countries are responsible for the poverty of poor countries and that therefore they should acknowledge obligations to the latter. While theories of imperialism and dependency (e.g. Frank 1971; Wallerstein 1983) no longer enjoy widespread intellectual and political currency outside the South, this argument has recently been taken up once again in political theory. For example, according to such a claim, environmental degradation, mass poverty, malnutrition, and starvation are the price paid by the poor to support the lifestyle of all the inhabitants of the advanced industrial world. Thus, global redistribution, such as a tax on the use of natural resources, would be a requirement of global social justice (Pogge 2002). Critics of this position, mostly liberally minded economists, argue that free trade, i.e. an end to industrial and agricultural protection in the advanced industrial world, would do more to help the poor than this kind of world welfarism (Bhagwati 2004). In sum, since Rawls did not apply the difference principle to the international realm, his strongest critics contend, this absence allows for extreme global inequalities (Barry 1991). In this view the application of a principle of justice would require a global difference principle, not just an international one.

Responding to some of this criticism, Rawls later specified that a global difference principle would be untenable because liberal states would then improperly impose social-liberal doctrine on (potentially) non-liberal states. It constituted a kind of intolerance because it would refuse the right of other peoples to live by principles of their own (Rawls 1999). Rawls thus argues in favour of a pluralist idea of principles and an acknowledgement of history in setting norms. This comes out clearly in his answer to a vexing question. What is the extent of obligations of richer toward poorer countries? Most theorists would agree that we have different and more extensive obligations toward those closer to us – family, friends, and fellow citizens – than we have toward distant strangers (see, however, Singer 1972): the key question is how different and how much more extensive. Rawls argues that our obligations extend only to helping societies that are not capable of sustaining internal schemes of social justice to reach the point at which they would be so capable, and he argues against the transfer of actual resources. For example, help could be extended to support the right kind of civil society and state administration which could serve as incubators of social rights.

An even stronger consideration of communal allegiances and pluralism can be found in the work of Amartya Sen. In realizing human capabilities he gives primacy to the idea of freedom (Sen 1999). This basic premise makes room for a world in which people value very different allegiances. Extending Sen's idea, communal allegiance is not only to be considered regarding poor countries. National welfare states, like the Scandinavian ones, are built upon moderate nationalism and strong immigration controls. This model is also increasingly under threat. This aspect is important because – according to national cosmopolitans who see a close link between moderate nationalism and social solidarity – schemes of international cooperation and redistribution depend on the willingness of discrete national states to engage in solidary behaviour (cf. Miller 1995).

These normative considerations must be supplemented by socio-political reflections that can be empirically validated, in order to shift the focus from desirable situations to actually emerging legal constructs and especially their institutional context. In particular, world polity theory, a neo-institutionalist approach (Meyer *et al.* 1997), has been a fertile ground for testing theoretical assumptions. It examines whether there are institutional forms, such as educational systems and social insurance systems, that are common to all states. The underlying idea is that institutional isomorphism, i.e. cases in which national states adopt similar forms of, for example, organizing schooling, can be traced to a Weberian notion of rationalization. This implies that institutions strive to appear 'modern' in adapting dominant ways of organizing social, economic, and political life. Role models can be found in, among others, international organizations such as UNESCO for the educational field, or the EU's 'Bologna Process' for university education. Yet while this kind of neo-institutionalist theory greatly enhances our understanding of the spread of some forms of formal institutions (almost) globally, it has not yet examined how such institutions are structured to contribute to the diffusion of social rights. There is clear evidence, for instance, that in many countries in sub-Saharan Africa and in southern Asia the expansion of the education system, structured into primary, secondary, and tertiary schooling, contributes to even greater social inequality because it is exploited by local elites to secure privileges for their own offspring (Bevans 2004). Similar observations could be made in OECD states such as Germany, where educational inequalities along social class and disability have persisted over the past decades and those along ethnicity are staggering. Another question that has not yet been explored by advocates of the world polity approach is whether or not certain functions are fulfilled by altogether different systems, for instance informal systems of social security. Such systems cannot simply be categorized as 'traditional', as they are primarily the consequence of unfulfilled promises made by postcolonial states and international organizations. Consequently, and this insight goes beyond the discussion of this particular approach, social rights and other, more informal, commitments must not only be sought in state–citizen relations, but also in other arrangements such as family, kinship, and communal systems, or clientelistic political practices.

On a more abstract level, system-oriented world society theory (Luhmann 1997) holds that societal spheres are organized in subsystems, such as the political, legal, economic, or educational systems which fulfil certain societal functions. There is a long-term evolution from segmented systems, in which societies are based on territorial entities, on to stratified systems, of which the national state and class differentiation are expressions, up to functional differentiation. Systems-based world society theory thus assumes that the master mechanism of functional differentiation makes concepts such as class and stratified assumptions about social inequality obsolete. Binary concepts such as inclusion into or exclusion from societal systems replace earlier notions. Two considerations are important. First, the majority of the poor in so-called developing countries are excluded from functional systems such as education and the economy, and therefore ultimately cannot be mobilized on this issue (Luhmann 1997 vol. 2: 632–3). This argument overlooks the fact that social movements and NGOs demand social rights directly as advocates of the poor, or that the poor make claims on their own. Second, and nonetheless, one may argue that solidarity provides the criterion for making distinctions, akin to codes in other subsystems, e.g. power/non-power in the political system or money/no-money in the economic system.

World polity theory and, even more so, world society theory steer our attention to the processes of drawing the boundaries that constitute the objects of inquiry, such as states, markets, or systems more generally. They thus raise questions of the 'state' beyond the nation-state and draw attention to the emergence of a world public sphere. Thus, an open approach to boundaries may be a first step toward capturing the transnational social question. In his 'Basic Sociological Terms' Max Weber did not define society (*Gesellschaft*) or community (*Gemeinschaft*). Instead he discussed the associative and communal relationships (*Vergesellschaftung* and *Vergemeinschaftung*) (Weber 1980 [1922]: 21–3). Drawing explicitly on Ferdinand Tönnies, Weber argued that associations and communities are based on different patterns of interaction and solidarity. This approach serves as an inspiration to pursue the question about the appropriate epistemological stance in dealing with the transnational social question. Instead of starting with the national state and the system of nation-states or with a borderless world, it may be more fruitful to use concepts such as social space to delineate the social formations relevant for the subject areas of social inequality and social protection (Faist 2009).

In sum, a strong concept of world citizenship certainly sheds no further light on the emergence of transnational social rights, and a notion of a linear progression of citizenship from the municipality to the state and then to the global level would be misleading. Then again, normative theories of world citizenship allude to a world society as a horizon of meaning and expectation that already embraces meta-norms such as equality (of opportunity), democracy, and global justice. Political–sociological approaches, on the other hand, such as the world polity approach, not only refer to global horizons of expectation, as the world citizenship approach does, but also to institutional types of multilevel political systems and multi-agency constellations – such as international regimes at state level, or networks of state and non-state organizations. World polity theory may help to shed light on the diffusion of policy models which may not be national models (e.g. emulation of OECD type welfare states), but might include elements of models, such as the combination of liberal market approaches with private insurance, supported by civil society, community, and kinship arrangements. It would be premature, however, to speak of world social regime or policy models akin to welfare state regimes found in the OECD world (cf. Esping-Andersen 1990).

Outlook: Toward Critical Cosmopolitanism

While it is useful to start with the European historical trajectory, we need – in the end – to go beyond this particular experience of the link between of social rights and (political) citizenship. A starting point may be the inclusion of contributions from the different regions of the world to discourses on the transnational social question and social rights. Amartya Sen, for example, approached the question of inequalities not from an institutional vantage point but from the perspective of individual resources. Based on liberal political theory, he has proposed the concepts of entitlement and capability. In his work on famines he does not argue for a 'right to food'. He places the law (social rights) in 'between food availability and food entitlement' (Sen 1981: 165–6). For Sen, entitlements are not (moral) rights but a term for a person's actual ownership and exchange capabilities. Nonetheless, his argument, namely that hunger needs to be tackled at the level of entitlements, and that market mechanisms alone will not achieve this end, does point in the direction of policies that alter legal and socio-political structures. In his later work, Sen defended the idea of a 'metaright' to public policies that would help make the right to food realizable. And he expanded his key concept to 'capabilities', resources to achieve certain functional capacities, such as health or literacy (Sen 1999).

With the help of approaches such as 'critical cosmopolitanism', which goes beyond exclusively European universalistic principles (Delanty and He 2008), the conceptual premises, analytical approaches, methodologies, and methods of contributions to the transnational social question should be scrutinized. One way of doing this is to unearth the different meanings and interpretation of (social) rights and citizenship in various world regions (e.g. Mamdami (1996) on Africa and Taylor (2004) on Latin America). Another venue is to question the facile thinking of a model of ever-growing social solidarity which is underlying concepts such as global social policy. This thinking is not wrong, but by itself it is inadequate. Taking seriously the whole of humanity regarding social protection need not preclude taking seriously the various particular relationships in which humans are constituted and connected to each other. Analysis also needs to pay greater attention to both social solidarities *and* social exclusion. Such an approach necessitates seriously considering markers of heterogeneity, such as social class, race, ethnicity, age, gender, and religion. Eventually, it is important to think of transnationally relevant solidarities and exclusions in the plural, avoiding the illusion that plagued much earlier thought on ethnicity and nationalism – that there was some one basic identity common to all members of a group, be it a clan, a nation, or humanity.

References

Barry, B. (1991) *Theories of Justice: A Treatise on Social Justice*. Vol. 1, Berkeley, CA: University of California Press.

Beitz, C.R. (1979) *Political Theory and International Relations*, Princeton, NJ: Princeton University Press.

Bevans, Philippa (2004) 'The Dynamics of Africa's In/security Regimes', in Ian Gough *et al.* (eds) *Insecurity and Welfare Regimes in Asia, Africa and Latin America*, Cambridge: Cambridge University Press.

Bhagwati, J. (2004) *In Defense of Globalization*, Oxford: Oxford University Press.

Bourguignon, F. and C. Morrisson (2002) 'Inequality among World Citizens: 1820–1992', *American Economic Review* 92(4), 727–44.

Brysk, A. and G. Shafir (eds) (2004) *People out of Place: Globalization, Human Rights, and the Citizenship Gap*, New York: Routledge.

Deacon, B. (1997) *Global Social Policy: International Organizations and the Future of Welfare*, London: Sage.

Delanty, G. and B. He (2008) 'Cosmopolitan Perspectives on European and Asian Transnationalism', *International Sociology* 23(3), 323–44.

Esping-Andersen, G. (1995) *The Three Worlds of Welfare Capitalism*, Cambridge: Polity Press.

Evans, P. (2006) 'Counterhegemonic Globalization: Transnational Social Movements in the Contemporary Global Political Economy', in J. Timmon Roberts and Amy Bellone Hite (eds) *The Globalization and Development Reader: Perspectives on Development and Global Change*, Oxford: Blackwell.

Faist, T. (2001) 'Social Citizenship in the European Union: Nested Membership', *Journal of Common Market Studies* 39(1), 39–60.

——(2009) 'Making and Remaking the Transnational: Of Boundaries, Social Spaces and Social Mechanisms', *Spectrum: Journal of Global Studies* 1(2), 66–88.

Frank, A.G. (1971) *Capitalism and Underdevelopment in Latin America*, Harmondsworth, UK: Penguin.

Furia, P. (2005) 'Global Citizenship, Anyone? Cosmopolitanism, Privilege and Public Opinion', *Global Society* 19(4), 331–59.

Habermas, J. (1998) *Die postnationale Konstellation*, Frankfurt a.m: Suhrkamp.

Hardt, M. and A. Negri (2000) *Empire*, Cambridge, MA: Harvard University Press.

Heater, D. (2004) *World Citizenship*, London: Continuum International Publishing Group.

Höffe, O. (2002) *Demokratie im Zeitalter der Globalisierung*, München: C.H. Beck.

Inglehart, R. (ed.) (2003) *Human Values and Social Change: Findings from the Values Survey*, Leiden: Brill Academic Publishers.

Linklater, A. (1999) 'Cosmopolitan Citizenship', in K. Hutchings and R. Dannreuther (eds) *Cosmopolitan Citizenship*, London: Routledge.

Lübker, M. (2004) 'Globalization and Perceptions of Social Inequality', *International Labour Review* 143(4), 91–128.

Luhmann, N. (1997) *Die Gesellschaft der Gesellschaft*, 2 vols, Frankfurt a.m: Suhrkamp.

Mamdani, M. (1996) *Citizen and Subject: Contemporary Africa and the Legacy of Late Colonialism*, Princeton, NJ: Princeton University Press.

Marshall, T.H. (ed.) (1964 [1950]) *Citizenship and Social Class*, Cambridge: Cambridge University Press.

Meyer, J.W., J. Boli, G.M. Thomas and F.O. Ramirez (1997) 'World Society and the Nation State', *American Journal of Sociology* 103(1), 144–81.

Miller, D. (1995) *On Nationality*, Oxford: Oxford University Press.

Mkandawire, T. (ed.) (2004) *Social Policy in a Development Context*, Basingstoke, UK: Palgrave Macmillan.

Pogge, T. (2002) *World Poverty and Human Rights*, Cambridge: Polity Press.

Polanyi, K. (2001 [1944]) *The Great Transformation: The Political and Economic Origins of Our Time*, 2nd edn, Boston, MA: Beacon Press.

Rawls, J. (1971) *A Theory of Justice*, Cambridge, MA: Belknap Press.

——(1999) *The Law of Peoples*, Cambridge, MA: Harvard University Press.

Sen, A. (1981) *Poverty and Famines: An Essay on Entitlement and Deprivation*, Oxford: Oxford University Press.

——(1999) *Development as Freedom*, New York: Anchor Books.

Shachar, A. (2009) *The Birthright Lottery: Citizenship and Global Inequality*, Cambridge, MA: Harvard University Press.

Singer, P. (1972), 'Famine, Affluence, and Morality', *Philosophy and Public Affairs* 1(1), 229–43.

de Swaan, A. (1992) 'Perspektiven einer transnationalen Sozialpolitik', *Journal für Sozialforschung* 32(1), 3–17.

Taylor, L. (2004) 'Client-ship and Citizenship in Latin America', *Bulletin of Latin American Research* 23(2), 213–27.

Tocqueville, A. de (1986 [1835 and 1840]) *De la démocratie en Amérique*, 2 vols, Paris: Gallimard.

United Nations Development Programme (UNDP) (2005) *Report on the World Social Situation 2005: The Inequality Predicament*, New York: United Nations.

Wallerstein, I. (1983) *Historical Capitalism*, London: Verso.

Walzer, M. (1996) *Thick and Thin: Moral Argument at Home and Abroad*, Notre Dame, IN: University of Notre Dame Press.

Weber, M. (1980 [1922]) *Wirtschaft und Gesellschaft*, 5th edn, Tübingen: J.C.B. Mohr.

Hospitality, Rights, and Migrancy

Meyda Yeğenoğlu

Recent years have witnessed growing enthusiasm about the concept of hospitality in an attempt to understand the relation between immigrants, exiles, foreigners, refugees, and other displaced populations who are in transit and/or without a home and their hosts or the "new" socio-cultural and political "homes" they are situated in. The portrayal of these groups as guests entails discussing the meaning of a series of other concepts and issues such as the host, what does to welcome and receive mean, subjectivity, *ipseity*, and interruption of the self, conditional and unconditional hospitality, hostility, home, ownership, and expropriation (or dispossession). But most important of all, these debates have highlighted the problematic and convoluted nature of the relation between the ethics and politics of hospitality. Three names stand out in any discussion of hospitality: Immanuel Kant, Emmanuel Levinas, and Jacques Derrida. In discussing their ideas, I will particularly focus on the importance of Derrida's recasting of our understanding of the nature of the relation between the ethics and politics of hospitality and the paradox, hiatus, or *aporia* this relation entails.

It is in *Toward Perpetual Peace: A Philosophical Sketch* (1983) that Kant develops his ideas on the issue of hospitality. Perhaps it is important to mention at the outset that it is the Kantian understanding that has constituted the background of the moral and legal codes of hospitality in Western civilization. Moreover, as Derrida notes, all the three monotheisms share the same, what he calls, the Abrahamic understanding of hospitality.

As the philosopher of Enlightenment par excellence, Kant develops his ideas on hospitality in his attempt to disentangle hospitality from its religious and moral bind, and come up with ideas that can possibly mitigate potential hostilities between the nation-states in a modern and global world. So, Kant's notion of hospitality does not have a religious or other spiritual undercurrent that has shaped the understanding of hospitality before him. The territorial expansion and the consequent dissemination of people he witnessed in his age compelled him to ask, while not giving up on the question of national sovereignty, the question of the foreigner in a particular way. How can a stranger who is in our land be responded to respectfully and handled in a peaceful way? One of the key issues that were at stake in cases where a foreigner was to be encountered for Kant was the maintenance of nationhood or national integrity and not to lose peace at the same time. The goal of responding to a stranger not with hostility but hospitality is first of all to maintain peace among the nations. Indeed, Kant's question, as the title of his essay indicates, is to preserve peace. Kant's concern with peace suggests that his starting point is the primacy of a state of war:

> The state of peace among men living in close proximity is not the natural state (*status naturalis*); instead, the natural state is one of war, which does not just consist in open hostilities, but also in the constant and enduring threat of them. The state of peace must therefore be *established*, for the suspension of hostilities does not provide the security of peace, and unless this security is pledged by one neighbor to another (which can happen only in a state of *lawfulness*), the latter from whom such security has been requested, can treat the former as an enemy.
>
> *(Kant 1983: 111)*

So, Kant's question concerns the peaceful regulation of the relation between the nations that is engendered through the mobility of citizens into each other's territory without sacrificing peace or reverting to war. Neither the nations should preclude the movement of people nor the visitors should infringe upon the sovereignty of the host society. The respectful visitation of a stranger therefore is something that needs to be regulated by a common law. The rationale for such a common measure is to regulate the relation of strangers when they visit each other's territory for lawlessness would result in hostility. In "The Third Definitive Article for Perpetual Peace," Kant suggests, "cosmopolitan right shall be limited to conditions of universal hospitality." Hence for Kant, hospitality is not an issue of philanthropy but an issue of right as it "means the right of an alien not to be treated as an enemy upon his arrival in another's country. If it can be done without destroying him, he can be turned away; but as long as he behaves peaceably he cannot be treated as an enemy" (118). Therefore, for Kant, visiting another nation's territory should be regulated by and grounded in maxims that have universal applicability and not left to the benevolence of the host society in question. By removing hospitality from the field of moral or religious responsibility or benevolence, and placing it in the field of rights, Kant recommends situating the issue of hospitality under the command of legal and juridical regulation. Hospitality, for Kant, should be seen first and foremost as a right of visit.

Kant's reduction of the reception of the foreigner to an impersonal, formal, abstract, and indifferent form of relation has implications: it results in the reception of the foreigner, the guest in "our" land and this reception does not result in any form of relation between the host and the guest. The stranger, turned into an object of abstract and impersonal law, is only offered a right. The hospitality offered is a conditional one, for it welcomes the other on the condition that he/she adjust to the *chez soi*, respects the order and rules of the home, nation, and culture, learns and speaks the language, and so on. Here the master remains the master, host remains the owner of the home, and the guest is an invited guest, that is, one who is expected not to alter the rule and order of home but obey them.

As Tracy McNulty (2007) notes, the form of encounter Kant envisions between the host and the guest does not result in an immanent or accidental encounter that is neither foreseen nor legislated and, as such, eliminates "relationality" (65) and thereby privileges "ontology over ethics, identity over relation" (66). She suggests that in Kant's understanding, hospitality does not designate a welcoming of the stranger but refers to a right of visit as Kant does not use the term German *Gastlichkeit* (derived from the root word *Gast*) but uses the word *Besuchrecht*, designating a right of visit (55). She further notes that this usage does not designate welcoming or receiving. This is a very important observation and I will discuss the implications of this usage when I am discussing the notion of hospitality as ethics in Levinas's and Derrida's frameworks and its difference from the Kantian understanding.

Let me briefly discuss how hospitality is circumscribed in Kant's framework. Hospitality does not indicate any openness towards or preparedness for a relation with the other. As part of an impersonal rule and juridical regulation it indicates, an abstract right of the guest. Such an abstract and impersonal law and rule enables the one who is visiting to be treated according to the legal and juridical rules that are signed among the sovereign nation-states. As such, a relation of hospitality is transformed into an abstract, legal, and juridical contract rather than being treated as an "immanent, accidental encounter which can be neither foreseen nor legislated" (McNulty 2007: 65).

Kant's idea on cosmopolitan right of citizens to visit each other's territory without being treated as an enemy is modeled on the givenness of the nation-state and its sovereignty. Hence what is of primary importance in the Kantian treatment of hospitality is the protection of the sovereignty of the nation-state whose sovereignty is not endangered to be dispossessed by the visiting guests. Therefore, in Kant's understanding of hospitality, the sovereignty, possessions, and borders of the nation-states remain inviolable because the guest, upon entering another sovereign nation's territory, is ascribed only a right of visit, implying that this is a right that is granted on the basis of certain conditions. The fundamental condition here is that the borders and sovereignty of the nation have to be respected while one is visiting the other's territory either for commercial or touristic purposes. And the host nation's hospitable response to this temporary visit is something to be transmitted as a legislatable universal right through laws such as laws of citizenship, laws of commerce, and laws of exchange. The laws that regulate the nature and condition of the guest's visit to the sovereign nation-state's territory are based not only on the premise and inviolability of borders but also on the presumption that the guests who are visiting are citizens of another sovereign national entity. Hence the first conditionality to grant a right to visit is introduced by Kant: the visitor must be a citizen of another country. This implies that those who are classified as nomads, asylum seekers, or people who are displaced for a variety of reasons cannot be granted hospitality or a right to visit for they remain a potential menace to the integrity and sovereignty of the nation-state. Hence the conditionality of the right of hospitality is premised on the sacredness of the national borders. McNulty suggests that by situating hospitality within the field of rights and under the sign of a rule or regulated mode of visitation, Kant's understanding removes hospitality from the status of an obligation: "Kant's imperative involves the displacement or even the elimination of hospitality as such, in favor of what he calls an 'unsocial sociability,' an impersonal relation that dispenses with the immediate – and therefore potentially uncomfortable or menacing – penetration of the stranger into the intimacy of the home" (McNulty 2007: xlvi–xlvii).

The Kantian framework is not only based on an understanding that makes the nation's sovereignty fundamental and inviolable, but also the individual host's sovereign identity remains intact while the act of hospitality is offered to the stranger. The conditionality introduced by Kant is based on the premise that the sovereignty of the subjectivity of the host remains intact and that the host as subject should not be dispossessed or interrupted by opening itself to otherness. Here the conditional welcoming of the guest enables that the self-identity of the host does not become vulnerable through being exposed to a relation with the stranger. For this reason, Kant's conceptualization of hospitality can be read as laying the conditions of conditionality while at the same time maintaining the means where the host does not relinquish its sovereignty. As Derrida notes, to welcome the other is to appropriate a place for oneself and then welcome the other, indeed appropriate a place to be able to welcome the other (Derrida 1997: 15–16). McNulty (2007) regards this Kantian privileging of ontology over ethics, identity over relation leading to the elimination of relationality and the unforeseen encounter with a stranger altogether (66). It is with Levinas's view of hospitality and Derrida's particular reading of it that the issue of hospitality is freed from the constricting field of rights but transposed into the field of ethics.

Derrida's reading of Levinas underscores that the Levinasian understanding of hospitality opens it up to the field of ethics and constitutes a challenge to the Kantian account of hospitality and its encapsulation into a matter of juridical legislation of the other nation's citizens right of temporary sojourn and opens it up to the field of ethics. One of the key concerns that motivate Derrida's reading of Levinas is the nature of the relation between the ethics and politics of hospitality. I will address this toward the end of the essay.

While Kant starts with the condition of natural or originary hostility or war, and regards peace as something to be restored through the cosmopolitical rules and laws that arrange the relations between citizens and sovereign nation-states, Levinas, "starts out from a nonnatural yet originary – or, better, preoriginary – peace rather than from a natural state of war, as Kant does" (de Vries 2001: 182). In Levinas, peace is not something that is instituted as a result of legal regulation or prevention of war. According to Derrida's reading, Levinas's ideas on hospitality revolve around what it means to welcome or receive the other. This exploration necessarily leads us to the domain of ethics of hospitality, for hospitality as ethics sets in motion a relation with the other. In *Adieu to Emmanuel Levinas* (1997), Derrida suggests that the question of hospitality in Levinas needs to be understood as "the whole and principle of ethics" (Derrida 1997: 50) or *ethics as such* or *"ethicity itself"* (50). Therefore hospitality is neither a region of ethics, nor a question of political or juridical regulation. When we are in the domain laid out by Levinas, we are dealing with the issue of hospitality that is not simply empirical or thematizable either. This is so because with Levinas, the issue of hospitality is carried onto the field of responsibility. However this is not to say that what Levinas suggests about hospitality does not have pertinence for understanding and engaging with one of the most burning issues of our times: that is, with displaced populations, exiles, refugees, and immigrants. As Derrida notes,

> … Levinas oriented our gaze toward what is happening today, not only in Israel but in Europe and in France, in Africa, America, and Asia, since at least the time of the First World War and since what Hannah Arendt called *The Decline of the Nation State*: everywhere that refugees of every kind, immigrants with or without citizenship, exiled or forced from their homes, whether with or without papers … call for a change in the socio- and geo-political space – a juridico-political mutation, though before this, assuming that this limit still has any pertinence, an ethical conversion … It is intensified, one might say, by the crimes against hospitality endured by the guests (*hotes*) and hostages of our time, incarcerated or deported day after day, from concentration camp to detention camp, from border to border, close to us or far away.
>
> *(Derrida 1997: 70–1)*

If the issue of hospitality has great relevance for understanding issues that are triggered by processes of globalization, then it is important that we engage in the discussion of the nature of the relation that can be established between the *ethics of hospitality* and a *politics of hospitality*. Another way of engaging with this issue is to address the nature of the relation between conditional and unconditional hospitality and whether unconditional hospitality can be adopted as an official policy by the nation-states and open their borders to unconditionally welcome strangers without turning the issue of hospitality into a matter of legal and juridical regulation of the right of visit of strangers. Can we attribute unconditional hospitality the status of a regulative idea?

Derrida's interpretation of Levinas's ideas particularly attends to this question. If the horizon opened up by Levinas compels us to rethink of hospitality different from the conditionality introduced by the Kantian understanding of hospitality as an issue of rights, obligations and duties, then what are the key components involved in rethinking ethics as hospitality? For Derrida, as an ethics, hospitality is infinite and unconditional. But if hospitality as ethics implies unconditionality and irreducibility to politics or legal regulation, how would it operate in a practical politics? Could an ethics of hospitality bring on and lay down the foundations of a particular politics or a law? If Derrida suggests that the burning issues of our times call for a transformation of the socio-geo-political space and therefore an *ethical transformation* (as the above quotation illustrates) in dealing with the problems involved in immigration and all sorts of issues that stem from the transit and mobility of people, then how do we think of the relation between this ethical transformation and politics? Another way of asking this question is whether unconditional hospitality can be treated as a decree and command to formulate a political program.

Derrida's answer is that it is not possible to deduce a politics from the ethics of hospitality. Rather, he thinks the relation between the two with the aid of a number of concepts such as *aporia, hiatus, lacuna, gap* (Derrida 1997: 20), or *constitutive impossibility*. The series of concepts are all devised to warn us to be wary of translating absolute hospitality into a determinate politics or deducing from it an immediately political and juridical regulation and thereby turning hospitality into an issue of granting rights. Rather, by insisting on the hiatus or lacuna between the ethics and a determinate politics of hospitality, Derrida wants to underline the irreducible heterogeneity between the two (Raffoul 1998: 280):

> Let us assume, *concesso non dato*, that there is no assured passage, following the order of a foundation, according to a hierarchy of founding and founded, of principal originarity and derivation, between an ethics or a first philosophy of hospitality, on the one hand, and a law or politics of hospitality on the other. Let us assume that one cannot *deduce* from Levinas's ethical discourse on hospitality a law and politics, some particular law or politics in some determined situation today, whether close to us or far away.
>
> *(Derrida 1997: 20)*

However, this does not mean that there is no relation between the two. Hospitality as ethics demands or calls for a politics of a certain kind. But this relation is not one of the ethical laying the conditions or pinning down the nature of politics. Derrida insists on the non-deducibility of the latter from the former to underline the necessity of a *non-foundational* relation between the two. In suggesting that there is a hiatus or the *aporetic* relation between the two, he does not mean their non-relationality but insists on the necessity of leaving their relation to one of non-determination and thus leaving the interval open so as to situate political decision to be determined. The lacuna between the two does not indicate absolute absence of rules.

> How, then are we to interpret this impossibility of founding, of deducing or deriving? Does this impossibility signal a failing? Perhaps we should say the contrary. Perhaps we would, in truth, be put to another kind of test by the apparent negativity of this lacuna, by this hiatus between ethics … on the one hand, and, on the other, law or politics. If there is no lack here, would not such a hiatus in effect require us to think law and politics other-wise? Would it not in fact open – like a hiatus – both the mouth and the possibility of another speech, of a decision and a responsibility, as we say, *taken*, without the assurance of

an ontological foundation? … Beyond this appearance or convenience, a return to the conditions of responsibility and of the decision would impose itself, between ethics, law and politics.

(Derrida 1997: 20–1)

The hiatus or aporia neither indicates a non-relation between the two nor lack of rules. It is precisely when a hiatus remains between the ethical and the political, or when the relation between the two is left undetermined that political action and decision can take place and responsibility can be exercised. The hiatus, gap, or lacuna thus indicates the irreducible heterogeneity between the two (Raffoul 1998: 280). As Derrida notes "without the hiatus, which is not the absence of rules, but the necessity of a leap at the moment of ethical, political, or juridical decision, we could simply unfold knowledge into a program or course of action. Nothing could make us more irresponsible; nothing could be more totalitarian" (Derrrida 1997: 117). Derrida's intervention is to invite us to think ethics and politics otherwise than the one implied in the Kantian tradition of hospitality where legal and juridical regulation of rights and the universality of law are equated with issues of morality and justice.

For hospitality to be hospitable and capable of welcoming the other, it needs to be extended without the imposition of any condition to a guest who is unexpected or unanticipated. It is precisely by not envisaging the nature of the guest – that is, without asking any question, including his/her name, identity, language, where he/she is coming from etc. – that a welcome can be offered to the one who visits. According to Derrida, for hospitality to be a hospitable welcome, it should be a hospitality of *visitation* not of *invitation*. In that sense, hospitality needs to be extended without being conditioned. For this reason it needs to be extended to anybody and everybody without even asking the name of the visitor. However, on the other hand hospitality needs to be a singular act as well. As Naas (2003) suggests, "hospitality requires that the guest be welcomed as a somebody, not as a serialized nobody" (159).

There are a number of other issues and stakes that are closely connected with the unconditional welcoming or hospitality as *ethicity as such*. One such issue pertains to home, ownership, and proprietorship and the other concerns subjectivity, *ipseity*, and sovereignty. No doubt they are interrelated. Taking Levinas's ideas on responsibility and welcoming as his guide, Derrida offers a radical reconsideration of these issues. A brief sketch of these themes will also reveal the radical difference between the Kantian understanding of conditional hospitality and the ethical hospitality suggested in the writings of Derrida. In the last section, I will discuss the implications of these two approaches on hospitality in terms of the relation between citizens and foreigners, strangers, or immigrants.

In Derrida's understanding, absolute or unconditional hospitality can exist only as unconstrained and hence entails a restructuring of the relationship between the host or the master of the house and the guest, the *hostis* or the foreigner. Such a restructuring implies a deconstruction of the at-homeness of the host, because an unconditional welcoming opens the home to a sharing with the new visitor and freely shares it. This requires that the ownership and control of the house be relinquished and that the home becomes hospitable to its owner. In Derrida's understanding this would turn the host (owner) a host received in his "own" home, a guest who is also welcomed or a a owner turned into a tenant. This would imply that the home is not owned or is owned only in a very particular form. Derrida puts it as follows: " … at least it is owned, in a very singular sense of this word, only in so far as it is already hospitable to its owner. The head of the household, the master of the house, is already a *received hôte*, already a guest in his own home" (Derrida 1997: 42–3). Utilizing the ambiguity of the French term *hôte*, which designates both the host and guest, Derrida wants to refer to the fact that, when there is unconditional hospitable welcoming, then there is no at-homeness from which the subject is able to receive, whereas with conditional hospitality, the guest is welcomed but still the ownership of the home is retained. Opposing to this kind of understanding of hospitality, Derrida warns us against the risk or danger of a usurpation of a position of power by the conditional welcoming of the other: "to dare to say welcome is perhaps to insinuate that one is at home here, that one knows what it means to be at home, and that at home one received, invites, or offers hospitality, thus appropriating for oneself a place to *welcome* (*acceuellir*) the other, or worse, *welcoming* the other in order to appropriate for oneself a place and then speak the language of hospitality" (Drrida 1997: 15–16).

Emphasizing the importance of the Levinasian conception of hospitality and its difference from the conditional one, Derrida underlines how the structure of unconditional or absolute hospitality not only involves a peculiar reversal of the meaning of the host (becoming a guest in his home and being welcomed by whom he welcomes), but it also implies a radical transformation of the ownership and possession of the home. For this reason, absolute hospitality cannot be dissociated from issues of propriety and possession. On the basis of this peculiar reversal, Derrida identifies what he calls the "implacable law of hospitality". "[T]he *hôte* who received (the host), the one who welcomes the invited or received *hôte* (the guest), the welcoming *hôte* who considers himself the owner of the place, is in truth a *hôte* recived in his own home. He receives the hospitality that he offers *in* his own home; he receives it *from* his own home – which, in the end, does not belong to him. The *hôte* as host is a guest" (Derrida 1997: 41).

When the distinction between host and guest breaks down, the position of master of the house is dismantled and through this unconditionality the issue of possession of the home becomes limited only to a legal ownership, but making hospitality more open, absolute, or generous. The inhabitant dwelling in this way, inhabits the land "as a refuge or of an exile, a guest and not a proprietor" (Derrida 1997: 37). For this reason, absolute hospitality precedes property (Derrida 1997: 45)

Given that absolute hospitality implies a radical dispossession of the home, it also implies loss of sovereignty. The loss of sovereignty pertains not only to the land that one inhabits but also concerns the very concept of subjectivity. Defining the subject as that very welcome or as openness to the other, Derrida's reading of Levinas has radical implications for a reconsideration of the concept of subject that is not understood as self-identity or *ipseity*. The welcome offered to the other entails the subordination or putting the sovereignty of the subject into question. The intentional attention to the other involves an interruption of the self as other. The responsibility to the other, the subject's being a host, is about putting the subject's being in question. In Derrida's reading of Levinasian hospitality, ethics precedes ontology, relationality precedes being and identity. For this reason, for Derrida (1997), the host is a hostage when its being is put into question. As he puts it, the subject "not the being of the questioner or of the questioned, but the being-in-question, where, so to speak, it finds itself under accusation [*mis en cause*], where it passively finds itself and finds itself contested interpellated, implicated, persecuted, under accusation" (56). It is this "other way of inhabiting, of welcoming or of being welcomed" that puts the subjectivity of the host into question: "the host [*hôte*] is a hostage insofar as he is a subject put into question, obsessed (and thus besieged), persecuted in the very place where he takes place, where as emigrant, exile, stranger, a guest [*hôte*] from the very beginning, he finds himself elected to or taken up by a residence [*élu á domicile*] before himself electing or taking one up [*élire domicile*]" (56). Thus, unconditional hospitality not only involves the interruption of a full possession of a place called home and reversal of the owner becoming a tenant in his/her "own" place, but also entails the freedom of the self from auto-affirmation. This means that the subject is no longer sovereign. Instead, it is placed as guest and host at the same time, because its being is welcomed as guest. So, the subject, in being responsible for the other, is "heteronomous – subject to another – rather than autonomous" (Bankovsky 2005: 161). The welcoming that is offered to the quest entails that the self is interrupted as *ipseity*, authority, mastery, and indissoluble sovereignty contradict with absolute hospitality. In relinquishing sovereignty, the host gives up possession of his subjectivity and is no longer in possession of himself. Therefore, in offering absolute hospitality, "the host who welcomes the other and offers hospitality does so also as a subject displaced from his/her own subjectivity, a subject other than and no longer in possession of her/himself" (Carroll 2006: 825). As I noted above, the radical dispossession that the implacable law of hospitality implies is not only pertinent for the dispossession of the ownership of home, but also has bearing on the way in which subjectivity is defined. As Raffoul notes, defining the subject as welcome of the other

> does not mean that the subject would have, among other attributes, the ability to welcome the other. More importantly, this means that the subject, as such, is a welcome and hospitality of the other, before any self-posited identity. … The welcome of the other defines the subject. As such the subject is that very welcome, that very openness to the other. Its identity is thus fractured and opened by the irruption or invasion of the other. The first revolution brought about by the thought of hospitality, then, concerns the concept of subjectivity. The subject is no longer a self-identity, an ego, a consciousness, even an intentional consciousness. The subject is an openness to the other.
>
> *(Raffoul 1998: 277)*

This interruption of the subject cannot be brought out by a decree or law, but is produced in the intentional attention to the other. This implies the subordination or subjection of the *subjectum* and hence enables the birth of a subject with freedom: the subject being put into question by the responsibility offered to the other.

Conclusion

If the Kantian conceptualization of hospitality, by limiting it with an issue of rights and legal regulations, does not involve any interruption of sovereignty, entails no risk, no accidental encounter, or unforeseen relation to Otherness, then it means that the other's *alterity* is not welcomed. When hospitality is turned into a regulated reception, then home, nation-state, or the sovereign subject is not opened to otherness because the relation with the other occurs only as a result of an invitation not of visitation.

However, following Derrida, to insist on the irreducibility of unconditional hospitality into a determined political program or juridical and legal regulation, does not mean that the concept of hospitality and the questions of ethics are not inextricably linked. On the contrary, it has great ramifications for thinking the socio-political manifestations of otherness and hence issues that are related to immigrants, asylum seekers, strangers, and other displaced people and invites us to bring and translate issues of hospitality to these concerns. Without this translation, as Hent de Vries (2001) suggests, the issue of hospitality would remain "an empty dream" (184). But this does not mean that hospitality can be reduced to its concrete and particular instances or issues of laws and juridical regulations. The Levinasian/Derridean understanding of hospitality invites us to question our given ideas and politics on issues of immigration, nation-state, citizenship, and rights. Being hospitable to the idea of unconditional or absolute hospitality invites us to be more hospitable to the interruptions of our given ideas on sovereignity and open ourselves to different understandings of politics that is beyond the familial nation-state's juridical regulative models and the confines a decree or a political program.

Derrida notes that the relation between conditional and unconditional hospitality is heterogeneous. Even though one cannot deduce a political program from uncoditional hospitality and even though unconditional hospitality cannot be reduced to a legal formulation that the conditional hospitality implies, the two are nevertheless indissociable. That is, one cannot deduce from unconditionality that nations, cultures, or governments open their houses unconditionally to strangers and aspire to make unconditional hospitality their official policy. This is because, like justice, unconditional hospitality is *impossible*. But this impossibility does *not* mean that a *politics of hospitality is impossible*. Like the relation between law and justice, where justice enables one to deconstruct law, unconditional hospitality enables one to deconstruct conditional hospitality. Certainly the improvement of laws of immigration and other legal regulations is necessary but it is insufficient to assure unconditional hospitality: it is futile to expect these regulations to guarantee unconditional hospitality, because unconditional hospitality is not the name of a political program correcting global injustices and/or an injuction that can lead to a better management of the nature of the relation with immigrants and strangers. Despite this impossibility, for Derrida, one has to constantly aspire for unconditionality as it is through this aspiration that the condition of possibility of the prefection and improvement of conditional hospitality is possible. Yet, the realm of action and practical regulation always remains heterogeneous to theory. To quote Derrida:

> It's impossible as a rule, I cannot regularly organise unconditional hospitality, and that's why, as a rule, I have a bad conscience, I cannot have a good conscience because I know that I lock my door, and that a number of people who would like to share my house, my apartment, my nation, my money, my land and so on so forth. I say as I rule, but it may happen, pure forgiveness may happen, just as an act of forgiveness, some forgiveness may happen, pure forgiveness may happen. I cannot make a determinate, a determining judgment and say: 'this is pure forgiveness,' or 'this is pure hospitality,' as an act of knowledge, there is no adequate act of determining judgment. That's why the realm of action, of practical reason, is absolutely heterogeneous to theory and theoretical judgments here, but it may happen without even my knowing it, my being conscious of it, or my having rules for its establishment. Unconditional hospitality can't be an establishment, but it may happen as a miracle. … in an instant, not lasting more than an instant, it may happen. This is the. … possible happening of something impossible which makes us think what hospitality, or forgiveness, or gift might be.

> *(Derrida 2001: 15–16)*

If unconditional hospitality is distinct from this or that specific right and something that cannot be guaranteed by law, it needs to be thought of in conjunction with Derrida's idea about democracy. For Derrida, democracy is the possible happening of something impossible, and needs to be thought as something to come (*a venir*). Speaking of democracy, Derrida (1991) states that "it is not something that is certain to happen tomorrow. Not the democracy (national, international, state or trans-state) of the *future*, but a democracy that must have the structure of a promise – *and thus the memory of that which carries the future, the to-come, here and now*" (78). The "happening as a miracle" and "lasting more than an instant" implies the necessity that the politics of hospitality has to be immanent to the present and require the transformation of present conditions of conditional hospitality, yet it will never be capable of exhausting all the possibilities of unconditional hospitality.

References

Bankovsky, Miriam (2005). "Derrida Brings Levinas to Kant: The Welcome, Ethics, and Cosmopolitan Law", *Philosophy Today*, Summer, 49 (2): 156–70.

Carroll, David (2006). "Remains of Algeria: Justice, Hospitality, Politics", *MLN*, 121: 808–27.

Derrida, J. (1991). *The Other Heading: Reflections on Today's Europe*, trans. P.-A. Brault and M. B. Naas, Bloomington and Indianapolis, IN: Indiana University Press.

——(1997). *Adieu To Emmanuel Levinas*, trans. P.-A. Brault and M. B. Naas, Stanford, CA: Stanford University Press.

——(2001). "A Discussion with Derrida", <http://muse.jhu.edu/journals/theory_and-event?v005/5.1 derrida.html> (5 January)

Kant, I. (1983). "To Perpetual Peace: A Philosophical Sketch (1795)", in *Perpetual Peace and Other Essays*, trans. T. Humphrey, Indianapolis, IN: Hackett Publishing, pp. 107–43.

McNulty, T. (2007). *The Hostess: Hospitality, Femininity, and the Expropriation of Identity*, Minnesota, MN: University of Minnesota Press.

Naas, M. (2003). *Taking on the Tradition: Jacques Derrida and Legacies of Deconstruction*, Stanford, CA, Stanford University Press.

Raffoul, F. (1998). "On Hospitality, Between Ethics and Politics", *Research in Phenomenology*, Fall: 274–83.

de Vries, H. (2001). "Derrida and Ethics: Hospitable Thought", in T. Cohen (ed.) *Jacques Derrida and the Humanities: A Critical Reader*, Cambrdige: Cambridge University Press, pp. 172–92.

Social Suffering and the New Politics of Sentimentality

Iain Wilkinson

In recent years, the concept of 'social suffering' has been widely adopted in social science as a means to refer us to lived experiences of pain, damage, injury, deprivation, and loss. Here it is generally understood that human afflictions are encountered in multiple forms and that their deleterious effects are manifold; but a particular emphasis is brought to bear upon the extent to which social processes and cultural conditions both constitute and moderate the ways in which suffering is experienced and expressed. With reference to 'social suffering' researchers aim to attend to the ways in which subjective components of distress are rooted in social situations and conditioned by cultural circumstance. It is held that social worlds comprise the embodied experience of pain and that there are often occasions where individual suffering is a manifestation of social structural oppression.

'Social Suffering' also serves as a label for an interdisciplinary field of inquiry that combines the social sciences, humanities, and medical science in an attempt to understand how suffering is made part of people's experience, and how in turn they are liable to respond to this (Kleinman *et al.* 1997). In the sociology of health and medical anthropology this is associated with efforts to broaden the biomedical conceptualization of pain so that recognition is brought to the ways in which both the experience of pain and a person's responsiveness to its 'treatment' are moderated by cultural conditions and social contexts (Bendelow 2006; Delvecchio Good *et al.* 1992). It is also featured as part of a critical engagement with conventions of health care practice that aims to make these more attuned to the social distresses borne by people under the experience of mental and physical suffering (Kleinman 1988, 2006). Under these terms, a broader conception of 'health' tends to be incorporated within critical debates relating to the quality of people's working environments and living conditions. Particularly in the contexts of French sociology and psychology, the focus on 'social suffering' is used to highlight the cumulative miseries of ordinary life that are perennially marginalized within arenas of political debate; or rather, are 'explained away' as unfortunate and unavoidable 'side-effects' of social life in capitalist societies (Dejours 1998; Bourdieu *et al.* 1999; Renault 2008). The concern to 'bear witness' to the experience of 'marginality', and especially the plight of the poorest sections of society, has also drawn many to place problems of 'social suffering' at the centre of the attempt to draw public attention to the experience of people living in developing societies. Here the documentation of experiences of people suffering from diseases of poverty is taken up as a means to engage in public debate over the structural conditions that systematically reproduce the material and social deprivation of the so-called 'Third World' (Farmer 1997, 1999, 2005). Indeed, the advocacy of human rights and humanitarian social reform is made explicit in many instances where 'social suffering' is deployed as a descriptive tool and/or analytical device for conveying the human consequences of the physical violence, emotional distress, and social deprivation experienced in contexts of war, civil conflict, and totalitarian abuse (Das 1995, 2007; Scheper-Hughes 1992, 1997, 1998).

It is often the case that in this work critical attention is brought to the symbolic forms of culture by which people's suffering is represented in public life (Sontag 2003; Chouliaraki 2006). Much debate surrounds the potential for texts and visual imagery to be carefully crafted to effect a 'moral education'. It is argued that it is possible to cultivate an 'ethics of emotions' that gives rise to political solidarities in the pursuit of human rights (Barreto 2006; Farmer 2006). In this context, researchers also seek to understand the ways in which victims of suffering might find the cultural and moral resources to recover from their experience via the 'healing' initiated through the social recognition that is brought to their plight (Das et al. 2001). Moral sentiments of 'pity', 'sympathy', and 'compassion' are analysed both in terms of the power relations they set up between the victims and witnesses of suffering and in relation to the contribution they make to bonds of civil society (Nussbaum 1996, 2001; Halpern 2002; Spelman 1998).

The new 'visibility' of human suffering that is made possible via modern communication media has given rise to a great deal of analytical controversy and moral concern. John Thompson contends that via television and the Internet, we are regularly brought into contact with extreme forms of death and destruction that would be unknown to previous generations (Thompson 1995: 225–7). Similarly, when highlighting the peculiarity of the cultural and moral landscapes we occupy, Michael Ignatieff observes that such technologies have made us routine 'voyeurs of the suffering of others, tourists amid their landscapes of anguish' (Ignatieff 1999: 11). Accordingly, it is important to recognize that, when working to understand the social production of moral sentiment, researchers are challenged to make sense of cultural processes of reproduction and exchange that are without precedent and for which they struggle to produce an adequate framework of analysis.

We have scarcely begun to chart the moral contradictions that arise for people in connection with the experience of being positioned as remote witnesses of the suffering of other people. Whilst some venture to articulate a moral point of view on the *possible* social consequences of these cultural conditions, very little is known about how these are *actually* working to transform popular outlooks and political dispositions. On a negative account, Luc Boltanski (1999) holds that the widely shared experience of being a 'detached observer' of human affliction intensifies a shared sense of political powerlessness and moral inadequacy; for he contends that people routinely find that they have no adequate means to respond to the imperative of action that the brute facts of suffering impresses upon their sensibilities. A further, and perhaps more despairing, perspective suggests that even where moral responsibilities and possible courses of action are made imminently clear to people, they all too easily deny the call to take care of others (Cohen 2001; Moeller 1999). On a more positive note, a number of writers argue that the public priority and popular support given to global humanitarian social movements in countries such as the United Kingdom speak of a growing level of responsiveness towards the moral appeal made through suffering (Sznaider 2001; Tester 2001). Accordingly, whilst recognizing that people's experiences of suffering may be 'culturally appropriated' for competing political, moral, and commercial ends, and that there are also many conflicts of interpretation with regard to their overall impacts on society, some argue that it remains possible for mass media to be used as a positive force within the education of compassion (Hoijer 2004; Ignatieff 1999; Nash 2008).

In summary, 'social suffering' calls for a new project of social science. It involves researchers in the attempt to understand how social and cultural conditions moderate the experience of suffering. It also brings a critical focus to the ways in which such experience serves to expose the moral character and structural force of society within people's lives. Whilst attending to the particular ways in which individuals struggle to make 'the problem of suffering' productive for thought and action, it also works to understand how, through to the level of collective experience, this contributes to wider dynamics of social change.

Historical Antecedents

It is only since the 1990s that 'social suffering' has been taken up as a pivotal matter for socio-logical and anthropological research; however, it has a much longer history as a term for describing components of human affliction. From the late eighteenth century onwards it is possible to find writers making occasional references to experiences and events of 'social suffering' (Wordsworth 1952: 9 [1793]; Frothingham et al. 1862: 26; Blaickie 1865: 30; Schilder 1938; van Sickle 1946). For most of this time, the concept was used either as a means to label state policies as the primary cause of people's miseries or to comment in general terms upon the social hardships that result from physical disability or mental illness. In this respect, it can be taken to mark the arrival of a cultural and political outlook that holds that there are many occasions where an inordinate amount of suffering takes place as a result of social circumstance and that the meaning and causes of this experience should be sought through a process of social inquiry. It also signals the development of a commitment to gathering the resources to oppose the deleterious effects of suffering via programmes of social reform. The mobilization of the concept of 'social suffering' in commentary on public affairs points to a new understanding of the moral meaning of human suffering and of 'the social' as a governing force over people's lives.

In order to grasp the magnitude of sociological issues at stake here, it is important to attend to the late-eighteenth-century origins of the concept of 'social suffering' and the cultural circumstances under which this was forged. It is now widely understood that the second half of the eighteenth century witnessed a revolution in social attitudes towards human suffering; and that this in turn was heavily implicated within nascent conceptions of the 'the social' as a domain constituted by bonds of 'fellow-feeling' (Barker-Benfield 1992; Denby 1994; Ellis 1996; Vincent-Buffault 1996). On many accounts, the public reactions to events such as the Lisbon earthquake of 1755 represent a dramatic shift in the interpretation of the causes and consequences of human affliction that involved both the rejection of Providential thought and the consolidation of a cultural disposition that relates to suffering as an experience for which there is no sufficient moral meaning or purpose (Besterman 1962). Whilst already provided with some intellectual currency via Pierre Bayle's *Historical and Critical Dictionary* (1965 [1695–7]), such convictions are voiced in a more popular vein in works such as Voltaire's *Candide* (1947 [1759]) and in many of the 'sentimental' novels of the period. They are also understood to have provided a vital spur to early movements of humanitarian social reform. In campaigns to abolish the slave trade, movements in opposition to the use of torture in criminal proceedings, and more generally under the attempt to mobilize discourse on human rights, considerable efforts are made to profile excessive experiences of human suffering as a means to set agendas for moral and social debate (Hunt 2007). In this context, both the social realm and the possibility of this becoming a part of a person's political imagination are held to be animated by the force of moral sentiment (Smith [1976 [1759]).

The politics of sensibility have always courted controversy. At its origins many were inclined to question the authenticity of expressions of fellow feeling and were worried by the possibility that this could be enjoyed as an end in itself or be used as a force of ideological manipulation (Ellis 1996: 190–221). This inevitably involved dispute over the character and force of human society as well as the grounds of human sociality; for these were understood to be established and sustained by the sentiments with which we relate to one another. In questioning the meaning and virtue of moral feeling the reality of the social realm was made a matter for debate and became conceivable as an object for reform. In this respect the acquisition of a sociological imagination is wedded to 'the navigation of feeling'; and the subsequent development of sociology as a 'science' or as 'social literature' may be assessed in terms of the relative importance accorded to this matter (Lepenies 1992; Reddy 2002).

With regard to the main task at hand, it is important to note there are many instances where the character and parameters of contemporary debates addressed to problems of 'social suffering' mark a *return* of interest to issues and questions that were aired in the late eighteenth and early nineteenth centuries. Being conversant with the fates that befell earlier movements is a necessary part of the attempt to take stock of the present. Certainly there is much here to draw sociology into debate with the traditions of theory and research that have shaped its disciplinary formations to date; and here researchers may well be brought to question whether the effort to recover nascent concepts of 'the social' might serve as the means to inspire better conceptions to fit our times.

Key Influences

The new gathering of interest around the phenomenon of 'social suffering' is not easy to explain. There is no single event that stands out as a decisive factor in making this a matter for debate; rather, a considerable range of social developments, intellectual interests, and ethical concerns is involved here. In part, the labelling of social problems in terms of 'social suffering' can be attributed to the influence of Pierre Bourdieu and Arthur Kleinman over their respective fields of inquiry. It is often with a mind to contribute to debates featured in the works of Kleinman and Bourdieu that scholars account for their analytical practices and research priorities.

For Bourdieu, the attempt to bring public attention to the force and parameters of 'social suffering' comprises a broader programme of critical inquiry into the moral character of contemporary 'neo-liberal' capitalism, and the increasingly authoritarian forms of technocracy through which the government of populations takes place. In *La Misère du Monde* (1993) (translated in 1999 into English with the title *The Weight of the World*), he draws attention to the *painfully* dull compulsion of everyday life that leaves people with an overriding sense of alienation and engrained attitudes of despairing ennui. Here 'social suffering' is held to be an experience takes place within 'the most intimate dramas' of everyday life; and as such, is largely unformulated as a matter of public discourse and remains beyond the purview of official surveys and opinion polls. (Bourdieu and Wacquant 1992: 102). It is apprehended through the stumbling language, awkward silences, and humiliated look of individuals living in poor housing conditions and working for low wages in the most demeaning circumstances. Whilst it is often the case that 'social suffering' takes place in contexts of social and material deprivation, on this account, it more directly concerns the damage done to a person's sense of dignity and worth when the field of possibilities before them is heavily circumscribed by structural conditions that offer no means of respite or escape.

Here the evidence of social suffering is taken as a moral register of political processes and economic conditions that create social conditions in which people experience themselves and others as alienated, superfluous, and without hope. It is also featured as a moral rebuke to neo-liberal state policies that abandon welfarist principles so as to promote the market as a disciplinary force of regulation in matters pertaining to the maintenance of public housing and the quality of people's working environments. In this context, Bourdieu is widely understood to have fashioned his sociological writing as a form of political engagement (Boyne 2002; Charlesworth 2005; McRobbie 2002; Renault 2008; Vittelone 2002).

In Arthur Kleinman's publications the term 'social suffering' has a wider sphere of reference. It is applied to any situation in which experiences of pain, trauma, and disorder take place as a result of 'what political, economic and institutional power does to people and, reciprocally, from how these forms of power themselves influence responses to social problems' (Kleinman et al. 1997: ix). Accordingly, whilst it is used to document the 'corrosion of character' that takes place in situations of material deprivation and social breakdown, it is also identified as a component of the harms done to and pains borne by people in contexts of ill health, interpersonal violence, large-scale social conflict, and cultural collapse. The suffering experienced in contexts of 'advanced' industrial capitalism is set alongside ethnographically detailed accounts of the pains and hardships borne in 'developing' and 'under-developing' sectors of the globe. Here efforts are made to have us recognize the global multiplicity of human conditions and the extent to which experiences of and responses to suffering are comprised by the many contingencies of social life in process.

For Kleinman, a focus on 'social suffering' serves as a means to highlight the moral challenges faced by individuals set in, and moving through, particular socio-political spaces. His interest lies in the extent to which 'social suffering' always takes place within morally charged environments where individuals experience life in terms of 'what really matters' (Kleinman 2006). 'Social suffering' casts the existential plight of individuals in stark relief; but always with attention being drawn to the moderating force of prevailing social structures and established cultural practices on people's moral sensibilities and cognitive dispositions. In this regard, Kleinman presents his work as a contribution to a new 'anthropology of subjectivity' that aims to expose the shifting social grounds of moral experience and its bearing upon the myriad ways in which individuals struggle to make sense of their lives whilst beset with the task of forging and maintaining relationships with others (Kleinman and Fitz-Henry 2007).

In a more critical vein, Kleinman seeks to alert us to a series of radical transformations that are taking place across the dynamic fields of local experience as forces of 'rationalization', 'media-tization', and 'commodification' acquire a heightened technological and institutional capacity to intrude upon, and routinely discipline, the ways we relate to ourselves and other people (Kleinman 1999). A substantial component of his research focuses upon the experience of social suffering in the context of health care. In this respect it is the ever-intensifying forces of ratio-nalization experienced during the 'medicalization' of people's health problems that occupy his critical attention; particularly in contexts where the possibility of attending to a person's illness experience is sacrificed to a drive for technical efficiency and the dictates of bureaucratic process (Kleinman 1988, 1995a). Kleinman highlights the socio-political and technological processes in which abstruse forms of measurement and analytical practice are used to gloss over the moral obstinacy and interpersonal turmoil of human experience. On the understanding that many social procedures and cultural conventions are being disciplined to operate 'without regard for persons', he stands with Max Weber in decrying the dehumanizing force of rationalization.

Kleinman also raises troubling ethical questions in relation to the cumulative impacts of media representations of the suffering of distant others on the 'moral-emotional processes' by which we acquire a capacity for empathy and compassion (Kleinman 1995b; Kleinman and Kleinman 1997). He argues that such experience is now making it all too easy for us to dissociate ourselves from the call to respond to the suffering of others with social care and political action. On this account, the mass dissemination of the imagery of suffering via commercial forms of cultural reproduction and exchange is effecting a major transformation in the experience of social subjectivity; for this 'normalizes' a vivid awareness of others' suffering in contexts that foreclose possibilities for participation in public debate and withhold the option of a compassionate engagement with human needs.

Kleinman calls upon social scientists to bring a renewed focus to 'the particularity of experience' so as to 'affirm that our subjectivities and the moral processes within them are forever in flux – not static, abstract, biologically fixed, or divorced from political, social and econonomic processes, but fluid, contingent and open to transformation' (Kleinman and Fitz-Henry 2007: 55). He maintains that it is in the context of 'ordinary lives' that we stand to apprehend the moral dilemmas and political possibilities afforded under present conditions of modernity; and that this is where we must start to engage with the task of building better social worlds. Here a priority is placed on documenting human experience in social context and importance is placed on the effort to attend to the varieties of social practice that create our world. Kleinman advocates a critical anthropology that works from experience 'on the ground' to question how local practices might gather the force to change social structure and cultural process.

Politics and Ethics

In both French and American contexts, research and writing on 'social suffering' takes place at 'the intersection of social science, politics and civic ethics' (Bourdieu and Wacquant 1992: 200). For those working in these fields, it is readily acknowledged that the task of understanding social life involves us in open expressions of moral worth and political longing; and further, that it is via a thoroughgoing examination of such commitments that we move to understand how 'the social' is experienced and made in people's lives. This is also taken as the grounds on which to inquire into the social practices that enable people to live through and beyond their experience of suffering and how these might contribute to progressive movements for social change.

A 'critical humanism' tends to feature within most of the work that takes place here (Plummer 2001). This is manifested in the commitment to documenting a great variety of human conditions and possibilities; and, more directly, in a careful attendance to the moral tensions and political frustrations borne by individuals in conditions of extreme hardship and adversity. It is also displayed in the effort to understand how the witness of suffering serves to establish social bonds of empathy and the political imperative to care for others (Tronto 1993). In this context, a privileged position is given to the task of understanding how the cultural capacity to 'feel for' the suffering of others can be nurtured to establish principles of human rights (Turner 1993; 2006); and, more importantly, it seeks to understand how this can be used to inspire the social actions that make for their practical realization in people's lives (Farmer 2006).

It is important to note that whilst the larger part of debates on the politics of pity and compassion is concerned with matters of abstract principle, in the context of 'social suffering' a privileged role is given to *lived experience* as a guide to moral values and political commitments. In this regard, those engaged with the study of 'social suffering' tend to draw inspiration from traditions of pragmatism; though it would be a mistake to identify this as aligned to the standpoint of figures such as Richard Rorty. Where Rorty's critique of 'human rights foundationalism' leads him to conclude that 'sad stories' do more to advance the recognition of human rights than arguments that appeal to abstract philosophical principle, whether such stories are drawn from experience or not, does not appear to matter too much to him (Rorty 1998). By contrast, this matters a great deal to those with a commitment to studying problems of 'social suffering'.

Here researchers tend to be acutely alert to the 'sentimentalist fallacy' outlined by William James as a situation where individuals 'shed tears over abstract justice and generosity and beauty, etc., and never know these qualities when (they) meet them in the street, because circumstances make them vulgar' (James 1907: 153). On these grounds Richard Rorty may be portrayed as 'insufficiently pragmatic', for he is too narrowly focused on problems of language and not sufficiently engaged with the task of understanding the harms that are done to people *in experience* and how such *experience* might be made to change (Kloppenberg 1996).

It is possible to characterize a great deal of research and writing on 'social suffering' as a form of critical praxis that seeks to establish the right of people to have rights (Arendt 1973). Some are inclined to label what takes place here as a 'politics of recognition'. Axel Honneth argues that it is often the case that contexts of social suffering are discussed as part of a 'disclosing critique' that aims to make known the 'pathologies of the social' in which 'the other of justice' is denied moral recognition and respect for their rights (Honneth 1995). For example, Paul Farmer contends that 'a failure of imagination is one of the greatest failures in contemplating the fate of the world's poorest', and aims to use ethnographic texts and photography as a means to shock his readers into questioning the human values and responsibilities that bind them to the victims of suffering (Farmer 2006: 145). He uses whatever 'rhetorical tools' are available to him to convey the experience of individuals dying from AIDS and seeks to offend readers' sensibilities with images of the physical torment suffered by people living in circumstances of extreme material deprivation. Farmer uses such methods to advocate an expanded notion of human rights that gives as much importance to the right to 'freedom from want' as to civil and political rights.

Similarly, Veena Das explains her work as an attempt to devise 'languages of pain' by which social sciences might be crafted as a textual body on which 'pain is written' (Das 1997a: 67). Her ethnographic practice is designed to fashion a re-entry to 'scenes of devastation' and worlds 'made strange though the desolating experience of violence and loss (ibid.). Here the efforts made to convey the standpoint of women who have been subjected to brutal acts of violence in the internecine conflicts of India's civil wars are intended as a means to 'convert' such experience into a script that can be used to establish ties of empathy and communal self-understanding. Das presents this as part of a 'work of healing' that creates a social space for the recognition of human rights and possibilities for a retrieval of human dignity (Das 1994, 1995, 2007; Das *et al.* 2001).

Whilst engaging with such struggles for recognition, writers such as Farmer and Das tend to present this as merely a point of beginning. Here the foregrounding of people's experiences of social suffering is intended not only as a plea for recognition but also as a means to initiate a wider set of inquiries into the institutional foundations of civil society and the grounds upon which it may be possible to realize people's social and economic rights. For example, Farmer writes:

> [R]ecognition is not enough … We need another modern movement, a globalized movement that will use whatever stories and images it can to promote respect for human rights, especially the rights of the poor. For such a movement to come about, we need to rehabilitate a series of sentiments long out of fashion in academic and policy circles: indignation on behalf not of oneself but of the less fortunate; solidarity; empathy; and even pity, compassion, mercy, and remorse … Stories and images need to be linked to the historically deeper and geographically wider analyses that can allow the listener or the observer to understand the ways in which AIDS, a new disease, is rooted in the historically defined conditions that promote its spread and deny its treatment; the ways in which

genocide, like slavery before it, is a fundamentally 'transnational' event; the reasons why breast cancer is inevitably fatal for the most affected women in who live in poverty; the meaning of rights in an interconnected world riven by poverty and inequality. In short, serious social ills require in-depth analyses.

(Farmer 2006: 185)

In this context, Das seeks to reposition problems of 'theodicy' as a key matter for analysis and holds that there is much to be gained through the recovery of classical traditions of sociological inquiry into the ways in which populations are liable to come under a compulsive struggle to make the experience of suffering productive for thought and action (Das 1997b). Accordingly, Max Weber's studies of the impact of repeated attempts to solve problems of theodicy on wider processes of rationalization may be set alongside Emile Durkheim's account of the social origins of moral individualism and Karl Marx's focus on the ways power is exercised through the toil of work, as indispensable components of a movement to expose how social forces condition the experience of suffering and set limits on the ways this is acknowledged and responded to in the political realm (Wilkinson 2005). Das calls for the development of 'secular theodicies' that bring a sociological frame of analysis to bear upon the ways in which harms are caused and distributed; and holds that these should also work to account for the many different ways in which experiences of suffering might be 'culturally appropriated' for competing moral and political ends (Das 1997b: 570).

Whilst theodicies traditionally worked to establish a 'higher' divine purpose for suffering that was not immediately apparent to believers, a secular 'sociodicy' proceeds in a more pragmatic vein that holds that it may always be the case that a substantial part of suffering will appear to be utterly 'useless' and without meaning (Levinas 1988). In this respect, the experience of 'useless suffering' may well be identified as the means by which 'bare life' is brought into relief and we encounter the moral demand to be responsible for others (Agemben 1998); though, of course, this is a demand that is all too often denied (Cohen 2001). In this context, the relevance of research and writing on social suffering for human rights might well lie in the extent to which the former can be used to open up avenues of inquiry into the ways in which the latter now serves as a primary means to address problems of 'sociodicy' (Morgan and Wilkinson 2001).

Ongoing Issues and Work in Progress

Social suffering is a troubled field of inquiry; it calls upon researchers to place the harms that are done to people and that we do to one another at the heart of the attempt to make sense of society and our social condition. It challenges social science to attend to the particular ways in which individuals and societies experience suffering as well as the historical and cultural conditions under which this is ascribed with moral meaning. The experience of suffering, particularly in its most acute forms, is identified as a decisive element within the formation of individual personalities and within the overall character of societies. The social practices by which individuals struggle to live through this experience, and the institutional arrangements that are set in place under the effort to minimize its deleterious effects on human life, are held to exert a major influence over the formation of political cultures and the dynamics of social change.

On many accounts, social suffering unsettles the conventions of social science. Here it is almost always the case that researchers are made to question the adequacy of their frames of social representation and analysis. In this context, they are made to broker with many destabilizing tensions; to many it appears impossible to surmount the difficulty of providing a morally sufficient account of what suffering does to people. On many of the points raised in the above, it may not yet be possible to provide a clearsighted view on how these can be made productive for further thinking and action.

In the historical record of human suffering, we repeatedly come across the extreme paradox that through experiences that entail the most terrible uprooting of life, people are brought under the compulsion to reach out for what really matters in their lives. This appears to be engrained in the character of the work that takes place here. With a focus on problems of social suffering, social science is continually set to confront its limits; but almost always with a commitment to making these more suited to grasp what is existentially at stake in the human social condition. On these grounds, it may be possible to both revise the ways we relate to the history of modern times as well as the ways we live towards the future.

References

Agamben, G. (1998) *Homo Sacer: Sovereign Power and Bare Life*, Stanford, CA: Stanford University Press.

Amato, J. A. (1990) *Victims and Values: A History and a Theory of Suffering*, New York: Greenwood Press.

——(1994) 'Politics of Suffering', *International Social Science Review*, 69(1–2): 23–30.

Arendt, H. (1963) *On Revolution*, Harmondsworth: Penguin.

——(1973) *The Origins of Totalitarianism*, New York: Harcourt Brace Janovich.

Barker-Benfield, G. J. (1992) *The Culture of Sensibility: Sex and Society in Eighteenth Century Britain*, Chicago, IL: University of Chicago Press.

Barreto, J. M. (2006) 'Ethics of Emotion as Ethics of Human Rights: A Jurisprudence of Sympathy in Adorno, Horkheimer and Rorty', *Law & Critique*, 17(1): 73–106.

Bayle, P. (1965 [1695–7]) *Historical and Critical Dictionary*, Indianapolis, In: Bobbs-Merrill.

Bendelow, G. (2006) 'Pain, Suffering and Risk', *Health, Risk & Society*, 8(1): 59–70.

Besterman, T. (1962) 'Voltaire and the Lisbon Earthquake or, The Death of Optimism', in T. Besterman (ed) *Voltaire: Essays*, Oxford: Oxford University Press.

Blaickie, W. G. (1865) *Heads and Hands in the World of Labour*, Alexander Strathern: London.

Boltanski, L. (1999) *Distant Suffering: Morality, Media and Politics*, Cambridge: Cambridge University Press.

Bourdieu. P. et al. (1999) *The Weight of the World: Social Suffering in Contemporary Life*, Cambridge: Cambridge Polity Press.

Bourdieu, P. and Wacquant, L. (1992) *An Invitation to Reflexive Sociology*, Chicago, IL: Chicago University Press.

Boyne, R. (2002) 'Bourdieu, Social Suffering and Bourdieu: From Class to Culture, *In Memorian* Pierre Bourdieu 1930–2002', *Theory, Culture & Society*, 19(3): 117–28.

Charlesworth, S. (2000) 'Bourdieu Social Suffering and Working-Class Life', in B. Fowler (ed.) *Reading Bourdieu on Society and Culture*, Oxford: Blackwell.

Chouliarki, L. (2006) *The Spectatorship of Suffering*, London: Sage Publications.

Cohen, S. (2001) *States of Denial: Knowing About Atrocities and Suffering*, Cambridge: Polity Press.

Das, V. (1994) 'Moral Orientations to Suffering: Legitimation, Power and Healing', in L. C. Chen, A. Kleinman, and N. C. Ware (eds) *Health and Social Change in International Perspective*, Boston, MA: Harvard School of Public Health.

——(1995) *Critical Events: An Anthropological Perspective on Contemporary* India, Delhi: Oxford University Press.

——(1997a) 'Language and Body: Transactions in the Construction of Pain', in A. Kleinman, V. Das, and M. Lock, *Social Suffering*, Berkeley, CA: University of California Press.

——(1997b) 'Sufferings, Theodicies, Disciplinary Practices, Appropriations', *International Journal of Social Science*, 49: 563–57.

——(2007) *Life and Worlds: Violence and the Descent into the Ordinary*, Berkeley, CA: University of California Press

Das, V., Kleinman, A., Ramphele, M., Lock, M., and Reynolds, P. (eds) (2001) *Remaking a World: Violence, Social Suffering and Recovery*, Berkeley, CA: University of California Press

Dejours, C. (1998) *Souffrances en France: La banalization de l'injustice sociale*, Paris: Seuil.

Delvecchio Good, M.-J., Brodwin, P. E., Good, B. J., and Kleinman, A. (eds) (1992) *Pain as Human Experience: An Anthropological Perspective*, Berkeley, CA: University of California Press.

Denby, D. (1994) *Sentimental Narrative and the Social Order in France, 1760–1820*, Cambridge: Cambridge University Press.

Ellis, M. (1996) *The Politics of Sensibility: Race, Gender and Commerce in the Sentimental Novel*, Cambridge: Cambridge University Press.

Farmer, P. (1997) 'On Suffering and Structural Violence: A View from Below', in A. Kleinman, V. Das, and M. Lock(eds) *Social Suffering*, Berkeley, CA: University of California Press.

——(1999) *Infections and Inequalities: The Modern Plagues*, Berkeley, CA: University of California Press.

——(2005) *Pathologies of Power: Health, Human Rights and the New War on the Poor*, Berkeley, CA: University of California Press

——(2006) 'Never Again? Reflections on Human Values and Human Rights', in G. B. Peterson (ed) *The Tanner Lectures on Human Values*, Salt Lake City, UT: University of Utah Press

Frothingham, N. L. *et al.* (1862) *Society for the Relief of Aged and Destitute Clergymen: Extracts from Records Relating to its History and Objects*, Boston, MA: John Wilson & Son.

Halpern, C. (2002) *Suffering, Politics and Power: A Genealogy in Modern Political Theory*, Albany, NY: State University of New York Press.

Henderson, L. (1987*)* 'Legality and Empathy', *Michigan Law Review*, 85(6): 1574–1653

Hoijer, B. (2004) 'The Discourse of Global Compassion: The Audience and Media Reporting of Human Suffering', *Media Culture & Society*, 26(4): 513–31.

Honneth, A. (1995) *The Struggle For Recognition: The Moral Grammar of Social Conflicts*, Cambridge: Polity Press.

Hunt, L. (2007) *Inventing Human Rights: A History*, New York: W. W Norton & Co.

Ignatieff, M. (1999) *The Warrior's Honour: Ethnic War and the Modern Conscience*, London: Vintage.

James, W. (1907) 'Pragmatism's Conception of Truth', *Journal of Philosophy and Scientific Methods*, 6(4): 141–55.

Kleinman, A. (1988) *The Illness Narratives: Suffering, Healing and the Human Condition*, New York: Basic Books.

——(1995a) *Writing at the Margin: Discourse Between Anthropology and Medicine*, Berkeley, CA: University of California Press.

——(1995b) 'Pitch, Picture, Power: The Globalization of Local Suffering and the Transformation of Social Experience', *Ethnos*, 60(3–4): 181–91.

——(1999) 'Experience and Its Moral Modes: Culture, Human Conditions and Disorder', in G. B. Peterson (ed) *The Tanner Lectures on Human Values*, Salt Lake City, UT: University of Utah Press.

——(2006) *What Really Matters: Living a Moral Life Amidst Uncertainty and Danger*, Oxford: Oxford University Press.

Kleinman, A. and Fitz-Henry, E. (2007) 'The Experiential Basis of Subjectivity: How Individuals Change in the Context of Societal Transformation', in J. Biehl, B. Good, and A. Kleinman (eds) *Rethinking Subjectivity: Ethnographic Investigations*, Berkeley, CA: University of California Press.

Kleinman, A. and Kleinman, J. (1997) 'The Appeal of Experience; The Dismay of Images: Cultural Appropriations of Suffering in Our Times', in A. Kleinman, V. Das, and M. Lock (eds) *Social Suffering*, Berkeley, CA: University of California Press.

Kleinman, A. Das, V., and Lock, M. (eds) (1997) *Social Suffering*, Berkeley, CA: University of California Press.

Kloppenberg, J. T. (1996) 'Pragmatism: An Old Name for Some New Ways of Thinking?', *Journal of American History*, 83(1): 100–13.

Lepenies, W. (1988) *Between Literature and Science: The Rise of Sociology*, Cambridge: Cambridge University Press.

Levinas, E. (1988) 'Useless Suffering', in R. Bernasconi and D. Wood (eds) *The Provocation of Levinas: Rethinking the Other*, London: Routledge.

McRobbie, A. (2002) 'A Mixed Bag of Misfortunes? Bourdieu's Weight of the World', *Theory, Culture & Society*, 19(3): 129–38.

Moeller, S. (1999) *Compassion Fatigue: How the Media Sell Disease, Famine, War and Death*, London: Routledge.

Morgan, D. G. and Wilkinson, I. (2001) 'The Problem of Suffering and the Sociological Task of Theodicy', *European Journal of Social Theory*, 4(2): 199–214.

Nash, K. (2008) 'Global Citizenship as Show Business: The Cultural Politics of Make Poverty History', *Media, Culture & Society*, 30(2): 167–81.

Nussbaum, M. C. (1996) 'Compassion: The Basic Social Emotion', *Social Philosophy and Policy*, 13(1): 27–58.

——(2001) *Upheavals of Thought*, Cambridge: Cambridge University Press.

Plummer, K. (2001) *Documents of Life 2: An Invitation to Critical Humanism*, London: Sage.

Reddy, W. M. (2001) *The Navigation of Feeling: A Framework for the History of Emotions*, Cambridge: Cambridge University Press.

Renault, E. (2008) *Souffrances Sociales: Philosophie, Psychologie et Politique*, Paris: Editions La Découverte.

Rorty, R. (1998) 'Human Rights, Rationality and Sentimentality', in *Truth and Progress: Philosophical Papers*, Volume 3, Cambridge: Cambridge University Press.

Scheper-Hughes, N. (1992) *Death Without Weeping: The Violence of Everyday Life in Brazil*, Berkeley, CA: University of California Press.

——(1997) 'Peace Time Crimes', *Social Identities*, 3: 471–97.

——(1998) 'Undoing: Social Suffering and the Politics of Remorse in the New South Africa', *Social Justice*, 25(4): 114–42.

Schilder P. (1938) 'The Social Neurosis', *Psychoanalytic Review*, 25: 1–19.

van Sickle J. V. (1946) 'Regional Aspects of the Problem of Full Employment at Low Wages', *Southern Economic Journal*, 13(1): 36–45.

Skultans, V. (1998) *The Testimony of Lives: Narrative and Memory in Post-Soviet Latvia*, London: Routledge.

Sontag, S. (2003) *Regarding the Pain of Others*, London: Hamish Hamilton.

Smith, A. (1976 [1759]) *The Theory of Moral Sentiments*, Oxford: Clarendon Press.

Spelman, E. V. (1998) *Fruits of Sorrow: Framing Our Attention to Suffering*, Boston, MA: Beacon.

Sznaider, N. (2001) *The Compassionate Temperament: Care and Cruelty in Modern Society*, Lanham, MD: Rowman & Littlefield.

Tester, K. (2001) *Compassion, Morality and the Media*, Buckingham: Open University Press.

Thompson, J. B. (1995) *The Media and Modernity: A Social Theory of the Media*, Cambridge: Polity.

Tronto, J. C. (1993) *Moral Boundaries: A Political Argument for an Ethic of Care*, New York: Routledge.

Turner, B. S. (1993) 'Outline of a Theory of Human Rights', *Sociology*, 27(3): 489-512.

——(2006) *Vulnerability and Human Rights*, Pennsylvania, PA: Pennsylvania State University Press.

Vincent-Buffault, A. (1986) *The History of Tears: Sensibility and Sentimentality in France*, Basingstoke: Macmillan.

Vitellone, N. (2004) 'Habitus and Social Suffering: Culture Addiction and the Syringe', in L. Adkins and B. Skeggs (eds) *Feminism After Bourdieu*, Oxford: Blackwell Publishing/Sociological Review.

Voltaire (1947 [1759]) *Candide or Optimism*, Harmondsworth: Penguin.

Wilkinson, I. (2005) *Suffering: A Sociological Introduction*, Cambridge: Polity Press.

Woodward, K. (2002) 'Calculating Compassion', *Indiana Law Journal*, 77(2): 223–46.

Wordsworth, W. [1952–9 [1793]] 'Descriptive Sketches', in E. de Selincourt (ed.) *The Poetical Works of William Wordsworth*, Oxford: Clarendon Press.

New Forms of Value Production

Adam Arvidsson

> As soon as labor in the direct form has ceased to be the great well-spring of wealth, labor time ceases and must cease to be its measure and hence exchange value [must cease to be] the measure of use value.
>
> Karl Marx, *Grundrisse* (1973 [1939]: 705)

'Value' is one of the most difficult and contested subjects in the social sciences (Graeber 2001). After the long, mainly Marxist debates of the 1970s (Bellofiore 1997) the concept has faded from the agenda of the social sciences, to reappear in recent years (De Angelis 2006; Stark 2009). This new interest in 'value' has been triggered by three developments: the growing size and importance of financial markets (McKenzie 2008, Zaloom 2006), the perception that an important structural change is underway within the very 'spirit' of the capitalist economy (Boltanski and Chiapello 1999), and, finally, the development of a number of alternative forms of value creation that do not operate according to the established logic of corporate capitalism: what many now refer to as 'social production' (Benkler 2006; Carson 2008; Coleman 2005; O'Neil 2009). This chapter will argue that these trends are interconnected. It will suggest that contemporary corporate capitalism is marked by a persistent value crisis, where, as the opening quote claims, exchange value no longer adequately reflects use value, or, to put it in less cryptic terms, there is a general sensation that a lot of the real values that circulate in our economy cannot be adequately represented. It will go on to suggest that this value crisis is caused by the emergence and growing centrality of 'social production' as a source of value. Consequently a lot of the value that circulates in our economy is produced in ways that established systems of value representation and management have difficulties in capturing (Vormbusch 2008). Our existing systems of value-representation and capture have emerged, along with the modern industrial corporation, with the managerial revolution that began in the 1880s. That development was largely triggered by the need to capture new forms of value production that derived from the extended, more complex chains of industrial production that were made possible by means of novelties like electricity, the assembly line, and the telegraph (Chandler 1977; Burchell *et al.* 1985). In the last decades new networked information and communication technologies have empowered a further extension of productive cooperation to reach beyond the organizational boundaries of the corporation and involve a number of external actors, such as subcontractors, participants to open or user-driven innovation projects, or even co-producing consumers. This has socialized the production process to the extent that a large part of the value actually produced evades capture by established systems of representation. Of course, this does not mean that there are no attempts to capture, measure, and represent the value that is produced in such new forms of social production. On the contrary, we can understand the host of new managerial attempts known as 'post-bureaucracy' as driven by the attempt to include and subsume such new, socialized value producing practices (Du Gay 2007; Kunda 2006; Maravelias 2003). Finally, this chapter will argue that social production is difficult to subsume under the institutionalized corporate logic, not because it has no value as many Web 2.0 prophets have suggested (Tapscott and Williams 2006), but rather because it moves according to a different value logic. In brief, I will suggest that value in social production is not primarily linked to the deployment of labor time or other scarce means of production, but to the ability to install the kinds of virtuous social relations that give coherence, purpose, and direction to highly complex and mobile productive systems. In other words, social production operates according to an ethical logic of value. The existence of such a different, but distinct value logic points at a possible direction for the development of a new principle for value representation and distribution, a new 'law of value', so to say. This possibility will be briefly explored in the last section.

The Flight of Value

The inability of the corporate economy to adequately represent the value that derives from social production is clearly visible in the valuation of corporate assets. One of the most important economic developments in the post-war years had been the rising importance of intangibles. The term *intangibles* generally refers to things such as brand value, intellectual capital, or reputation (a number of different terms are tossed around) that are reflected in the market valuations of companies, and that have a notable impact on business performance, but that are only partially reflected in established accounting practice. (For example, since 2001, the US Financial Accounting Standards Board enables companies to take up purchased brands and other forms of 'goodwill', but investments in brand building and in R&D are treated as expenditure, rather than investment.) Even when these resources are taken up in official accounting they are valued in different ways in different contexts. In contrast to the well-established standards for valuing 'material' assets, official accounting rules differ widely in valuing intangibles. As Nir Kossovski, executive secretary of the Intangible Assets Society, an advocacy group that is working to develop new standards and practices for monetizing intangible assets, laconically concludes: 'there is not the rigor and uniformity that governs the valuation of tangibles' (Caruso 2007). The same thing goes for the valuation of intangibles outside of official accounting rules. A study of the valuation of intangible assets on the part of credit rating agencies such as Moody's or Standard & Poor, show that these have little in terms of systematic rules for the valuation of such assets, but generally rely on 'the analysts experience and intuition' (Del Bello 2007: 187).

This means that a *growing number of companies increasingly rely on assets that they cannot measure and account for in any rational way*. Or to put it in the more sober, academic terms of an accounting scholar: 'There is indeed a vast agreement in the scholarly and professional community that the value of firm performance is not adequately portrayed by the traditional financial measurement tools, which appear to many as incapable of representing the multi-dimensional nature of that performance' (Cordazzo 2007: 67). This is quite serious since intangible assets, although per definition impossible to precisely measure, do amount to a significant economic reality: intangibles are estimated to account for some 7 per cent of US investments in

2000–3, or a bit more than US$1 trillion. Similarly, data on the 100 most traded companies on the London Stock Exchange estimate the share of market price attributable to intangibles to have increased from about 20 per cent in 1950 to about 70 per cent in 2000; data on Fortune 500 companies show similar results (Mandel *et al.* 2006; Nakamura 2001; Lev 2001; Hulten and Hao 2008). So a significant and growing share of the US economy (about 7 per cent of investments) and of other advanced knowledge economies (estimates from, for example, Finland show very similar results, cf. Hussi 2003) is *beyond measure*, so to say (cf. Negri 1999). It cannot be adequately represented within established systems of measurement, accounting, and governance. This becomes even more serious if we consider that such intangibles are generally considered the strategically most important resources in the information society (cf. Higson *et al.* 2007).

Why are intangibles so difficult to measure? It is not because they are immaterial or made of air, after all a lot of immaterial things, such as cleaning or taxi rides, find very precise values within the capitalist economy. Rather it is simply because they are produced in processes that are not reflected by the value logic within which the capitalist economy operates. Intangibles are difficult to measure because, to a large extent, they are produced 'outside' the sorts of pro-cesses that existing accounting systems have been designed to measure (Vormbusch 2008). Intangible assets are to a large extent produced in processes that unfold beyond the control of companies, deploying resources that are generally not owned by anyone. Let us take a look at the nature of today's most important kinds of intangibles: knowledge, brand, and flexibility. Knowledge stands both for the codified and for the tacit knowledge at a firm's disposal. This can be a matter of codified patents, or other IPRs: often it is a matter of the implicit know-how and tacit knowledge embodied in social processes. Brand stands for the affectively significant relations that a company is able to install with its stakeholders, consumers, employees, sub-contractors, and the public at large. This would include reputation, goodwill, and perceptions of social responsibility. Finally 'flexibility' stands for the ability of a company to respond quickly to market changes, to 'breath with market' (Marazzi 2008). The production of these three kinds of intangible assets has a common trait. It is increasingly a matter of putting to work commonly available, socialized competences, 'collective intelligence', or what Marx called General Intellect (see below). While some Intellectual Property might result from the salaried labor of engineers and scientists in corporate R&D departments, the trend is for R&D to be ever more dependent on socialized and diffuse forms of knowledge production, through user-led innovation schemes (like Procter & Gamble's famous 'connect & develop' program, Huston and Sakkab 2006) or through clever utilization of transversal communities of practice (as in the case of Linux or other open source products now receiving substantial corporate support, cf. Rometti 2006). Even when this is not the case, corporate R&D has always depended heavily on public investments in research and education. We are approaching a situation where, as Peter Drucker (1993:176) put it, no company or industry has any natural advantage in the knowledge economy, rather com-petitive advantage tends to depend more and more on the ability to organize and capitalize on *universally available knowledge*. Flexibility builds on the ability of employees to quickly construct and re-construct adequate relations of production and to build functioning and complex net-works of cooperation all along a value chain (producers, logistics, distribution, customer rela-tions, call-centres, and so on). These are processes that put to work the common affective, linguistic, and social skills that employees possess, as members of society. Increasingly such value chains come to involve consumers and other members of the public as well (Zwick *et al.* 2008). Indeed, the third category – the brand – builds on a putting to work of the social and affective potentials of public communication (cf. Arvidsson 2006).

This points to a general movement of value creation from the 'core' to the 'edge'(Hagel and Brown 2005): from the resources that a company can directly control – like its machines or what its employees can be commanded to do – to resources that it cannot control, like public opinion or the 'creativity' or sociality of its employees that cannot be directly commanded. Across the advanced sectors of the economy, the boundaries of organizations become more fluid and the production processes comes to rely on a number of resources that are located in the environment of the firm, either internally, as in the social capacity of employees or their affective attachments to the company or to each other, or externally, as in the communication processes that unfold between consumers, or the knowledge sharing that takes place among suppliers. This means that the company increasingly 'swims' in a sea of productive externalities that it tries to translate into measurable value. This allows us to suggest that the growing importance of intangibles in the information economy is a reflection of a growing importance of external resources in the production process. Since present accounting systems are organized to adequately represent value creation that derives from proprietary resources they have great difficulty in dealing with such external resources. So the value crisis is essentially a crisis of representation.

Ethical Economy?

In recent years the increasing socialization of wealth creation has acquired a lot of attention. Within the business world, a series of publications such as *Wikinomics* (Tapscott and Williams 2006), *Revolutionary Wealth* (Toffler and Toffler 2006), and *The Wisdom of Crowds* (Surowiecki 2004), together with the present focus on user-led innovation or open business (von Hippel 2005), have directed the attention of managers towards the potential gains that can derive from involving consumers, suppliers, and other external stakeholders directly within the value chain. Similarly, the impact of Yochlai Benkler's (2006) *The Wealth of Networks*, and a host of related works, has established such new productive forms on the agenda of the social sciences. These approaches share a common perspective: the business literature as well as most academic analyses view these new forms of social production as a free resource: either as a 'free lunch for business' available for appropriation (to use Toffler's and Toffler's expression), or as a new set of commons that make possible radically new productive relations that move beyond the commodity form (Dyer Withford 2006; Negri, 1999). The processes of social production on which business relies in the accumulation of intangibles are indeed 'free' in the sense that they generally do not move according to the established corporate value logic. However, it is important to understand that these productive processes *do* follow a distinct value logic, albeit one that is markedly different from the value logic that governs the corporate economy. In order to understand what that value logic looks like we need to once again examine the nature of intangible assets like knowledge, brand and flexibility.

We have argued that these intangibles are produced in part by processes that unfold outside of the direct control of companies. Consequently contemporary brand and knowledge management is concerned with the organization of mechanisms by means of which value can be abstracted from these common competences by the ability to give them a distinct organizational form. Knowledge, innovation and intellectual capital management is about constructing an environment that is particularly conducive to creativity or where tacit knowledge connects and comes out in the open as 'collective intelligence'. In some cases this environment can become more important than the actual knowledge produced. Many successful high-tech companies (like the Italian Arduino, Thompson 2008) now decide to provide open access to their designs and other knowledge capital. What they lose in rendering their product easy to copy is more than compensated for by the innovation and knowledge sharing community that they are able to construct. This gives them easy access to user-based product developments and positions them at the centre of a knowledge economy where services around the product are becoming a more important source of revenue than the product itself. Similarly, agility and flexibility are max-imized by empowering employees to self-organize their productive processes and, importantly, to develop flexible yet robust forms of logistics and supply-chain management (the real advantage of companies such as Zara or IKEA). Brand management can similarly be seen as a sort of logistics of meaning and affect, the ability to organize and give direction to largely autonomous flows of public opinion and sentiment. In all of these areas value is primarily produced by the ability to construct affectively significant ties: ties that bind a brand or a company to its con-sumers, employees, or other stake-holders in ways that go beyond contractual obligations. You cannot order an employee to be creative or a consumer to share his or her ideas about product improvements. Such offers need to be voluntary; they need to be motivated by some form of affective affiliation. Such relations are not free, they require time and energy to build. If corporate social responsibility used to be seen as a peripheral matter of philanthrophy or doing good, this practice is now increasingly integrated within the strategically important business of brand building. Seen this way, CSR is mainly about cultivating the kinds of virtuous relations to stakeholders that can create value for the company by, for example, facilitating the recruitment and retention of 'talented' personnel, motivating suppliers to take part in a collective innovation process, or creating durable ties between consumers and the brand (Vogel 2006).

We can make similar observations about the host of productive practices that have developed outside of the capitalist economy. Within the FLOSS world the radical nature of GNU/Linux, the fact that such a complex thing as an operating system could be created through socialized 'open' forms of production (something nobody thought possible before) depends not on the abundance of programming-labor at the community's disposal, or on the unusual skill of its programmers *per se*, but on the organizational form of the GNU/Linux brand-community that has been able to attract vast quantities of 'free labor' from the public and channel those diffuse energies into the completion of such a complex task (Weber 2004; O'Neil 2009). Most big cities possess an abundance of 'talent' in the form of people with an artistic bent, but only those cities that provide an ambience where this talent can organize itself with ease (essentially, many occasions for face-to-face encounters) are able to capitalize on this resource. And even there, most of what is produced is accomplished by a small number of entrepreneurs that distinguish themselves by the size of their networks and the respect and social capital that they can com-mand (Florida 2002; Currid 2007; Lloyd 2006). In all of these instances what creates value is not measured inputs of scarce productive time (labor or machine time), but the ability to build social relations that organize and motivate essentially abundant resources: 'free labor' and col-lective intelligence. *The production of value in networks of socialized production is the same thing as the construction of ethically binding social relations*, that is relations that are able to motivate and organize cooperation in absence of external sanctions.

Indeed, the scarcity of this ability to give coherence and organization to productive processes is set to rise with the growing socialization and complexity of such productive networks. Tra-ditionally the solution to this problem has consisted in including such forms of productive cooperation within bureaucratic organizations. But, as David Stark (2009) has argued, along with many other economic and organizational sociologists, bureaucracy is ill suited to handle productive systems that are marked by a wide diversity of value horizons and strong pressures towards temporal and spatial flexibility (cf. Boltanski and Chiapello 2009). Many organizational scholars have pointed at the emergence of new forms of post-bureaucratic organizations as a solution to this problem (Maravelias 2003; Du Gay 2007; Kunda 2006). Going back to the fashion for values-based management in the early 1980s, post-bureaucracy essentially entails attempts to manage through the installation of an *ethos*, an affective climate that can give sense and direction to productive development in ways that need not be explicitly stated or spelled out. This way post-bureaucracy amounts to a managerial recognition that it is the ability to install such an *ethos* – the brand that ties consumers together into an imaginary and fragile community, the sentiment that motivates members of the project team to maximize their efforts – that constitutes the most important source of value in practices of social production. Similar points have been made in a number of recent studies. Most famously perhaps Maurizio Lazzarato describes contemporary knowledge work as 'immaterial labor', where the main source of value consists in the ability to put affective and communicative competences to work in producing the very relations of production that can give direction and coherence to extended processes of cooperation. Indeed, Lazzarato goes so far as to suggest that in immaterial labor 'the production of value tends to coincide with the production of ethicity (*eticità*)' (1997: 13; cf. Virno 2004). Gabriela Coleman makes a similar point in her analysis of the free software project, Debian. In her description it is the ability to create social relations, what she calls 'ethical labor', rather than programming labor, that is the most important source of value in the Debian community. Programming is abundant; in contrast to Microsoft, Debian does not need to pay people to program, on the contrary the community needs to devise complicated entry rituals to keep potential programmers out. What is scarce is the ability to build and maintain the complicated web of relations that keeps Debian functioning as a productive community and that maintains the ability of the Debian brand to keep attracting vast supplies of free programming labor. Conversely, along with technical brilliance, it is the hard 'ethical labor' of building the community that ultimately confers on participants the charisma and reputation in which their relative value is manifested. This picture is not too different from the ways in which management scholars have described work in networked, knowledge intensive 'post-bureaucratic' organizations (Maravelias 2003). Indeed, a wide and quite disparate literature on free/open software (Coleman 2005; O'Neil 2009), social, open, or user-led innovation (von Hipple 2006), web 2.0 (Benkler 2007), brand management and viral marketing (Arvidsson 2006), knowledge work, and creativity (Du Gay 2007; Arvidsson 2007), suggests similar things. Indeed, inspired by Durkheim's notion of 'organic solidarity', Adler and Hecksher (2006: 22; cf. Adler *et al.* 2008) suggest that while 'capitalist development does indeed corrode traditional community ... the demand for complex, knowledge-based and solutions-oriented production in the modern capitalist economy has stimulated significant progress towards a new form of community'; what they call 'collaborative community' where the main source of value relies precisely in what they call 'interdependent self-construals' – 'rather than orienting to a single source of morality and authority, the personality must reconcile multiple conflicting identities and construct a sense of wholeness from competing attachments and interactions' (Adler *et al.* 2008: 17). In his analysis of what he calls heterarchical organization David Stark (2009) makes a similar point, albeit at a different level of abstraction. In a situation in which established modernist classificatory schemes have exploded into a variety of different value standards, what creates value is the ability to create a common definition of the situation in which such diverse perspective can be reconciled. So what really creates value in an economy of commons, is the ability to create a common, to put communicative and affective capacities to work in the construction of an however temporary *ethos* that can determine, in relation to a particular situation, what the values are, and in what direction to proceed. The creation of economic value becomes a matter of *ethical practice*.

Ethics, Finance, and General Intellect

The term 'ethical economy' would imply something quite radical: that ethics is not to be conceived as an extrinsic limitation to economic pursuits but, on the contrary, as an intrinsic source of economic value. This requires a different understanding of ethics. To most of the tradition of business ethics, as well as to modern (post-Kantian, or even post-Augustinian) discussions of ethics more generally, ethics has been taken to mean something like 'the elaboration of general rules for moral action'. More recently such formalistic theories of ethics have been challenged by more 'post-modernist' approaches, such as those of Alain Badiou, Imanuel Levinas, Judith Butler, and, long before postmodernism, Michail Bahktin (cf. Bauman 1993). Common to these authors is a rejection of universal ethical rules in favor of an approach to ethics as the practice of creating values and norms of action (a *nomos*) that is particular to the specific situation at hand. To put it in the words of Gabriela Coleman, 'the hard labor of ethics, its demanding phenomenology, is an outgrowth of taking risks, putting in the effort to engage with others and choosing to confront the situation at hand in its specificity' (Coleman 2005: 60). In this version, ethics is less about the elaboration of universal moral laws (such as the Kantian imperative) and more about creating the values and norms that keep a particular web of social relations together: ethics is about producing a *koinonia* or 'common' in however transitory form. Curiously, such 'postmodern' definitions of ethics come very close to what Aristotle had in mind. For him, ethics – conceived, importantly, as a craft, rather than as a science – was about the construction of community through the mutual balancing of affects and passions (*ethoi*). In their free interaction as ethical beings, the citizens construct the kinds of social relations that make the good life (*eudaimonia*) attainable within the *polis*. Ethics in this sense of the balancing of affect and the construction of relations is the very foundation of the political project of constructing a thing in common. Above I have argued that we can see the emergence of precisely this Aristotelian version of ethics as the fundamental value-creating practice in a number of central contemporary business developments.

Why is this the case? Social production in its various corporate and non-corporate manifestations deploys as its most important productive resource skills and competences that are commonly available and highly socialized – what Marx, in a famous and much quoted passage in the *Grundrisse*, called General Intellect (Marx 1973 [1939]: 705–9). Marx said two important things about General Intellect. First, that this is a common resource, freely available to workers by means of their membership in a productive context; their status as social individuals. Second, that to the extent that the capitalist production process becomes more complex-as it has with the processes of globalization and hyper-networking that mark the information economy, the importance of such General Intellect would dwarf that of labor time as a source of value.[1] But since General Intellect is common, and hence abundant, it cannot, by definition, constitute the basis of value. Hence Marx concludes that the massive importance of General Intellect as a source of wealth will ultimately explode the 'law of value' on which the capitalist economy builds, and propel us directly into communism, where the most important productive resource would remain 'beyond value' (Negri 1999). What Marx did not foresee was that the very expansion and complexity of the productive process that has promoted this new importance of General Intellect also creates the conditions for a new standard of value. When production is hyper-complex and networked and builds on commonly available resources, the scarce element becomes the ability to coordinate such complex and mobile processes in real time in ways that ensure the successful appropriation and utilization of General Intellect. Economic value becomes contingent on the ability to build however transient social values and norms that are able to coordinate particular and situated productive processes, to construct the temporary, particular, and situated *nomos* that allows a flexible and complex productive process to go on. In other words, value becomes contingent on ethical practice.

The value of such ethical practice resides in its ability to construct however temporary forms of order in complex productive networks, in particular in situations where abundant recourse to common resources and 'free labor' (or forms of labor that are difficult to command, like the 'creativity' of employees) renders the two classic forms of capitalist coordination, identified already by Coase (1937), market and contract, insufficient. This takes two important forms. First, 'the right kind of ethics' confers order and direction on productive cooperation, it creates the kind of trust and social capital to facilitate cooperation in complex networks. Second, 'the right kind of ethics' is able to attract externalities that are difficult both to command or remunerate (like customer input to open innovation systems, or programmer labor in free software). The emergence of such an ethical economy, and the concomitant confluence of ethics and economics, would then seem to be the result of the growing socialization and increasing complexity of production processes that have resulted from the ongoing expansion and globalization of capitalism in the post-war years.

If the institutions of the modern corporate economy emerged as a response to the new challenges posed by more complex and extended industrial value chains (Chandler 1977) then that institutional framework is now being undermined by a second wave of socialization of the production process, greatly empowered by networked information and communication technologies. Is it already possible to now discern the beginnings of a corporate response to this challenge, a 'second managerial revolution' that attempts to include social production within a new societal law of value? Boltanski and Chiapello (1999) along with many others have pointed at how new 'post-bureaucratic' forms of management are driven by the goal to include and command things like creativity and 'social capital' that are difficult to subsume under a traditional, bureaucratic job description. Others have focused on how the turn to 'biopolitical' power within management, and society more generally, amounts to a putting to work of subjectivity by means of which the whole life process, and not just labor time, is 'put to work' for capital (Berardi 2009; de Angelis 2006). While the shift of focus, from labor time to 'life time' is clearly part of such a new managerial response, these approaches do not address how the value of such non-salaried activities is determined, nor how the surplus thus accumulated is distributed.

The massive increase in the turn-over of financial markets *vis-à-vis* commodity markets makes it reasonable to suggest that whatever new regime of value that emerges out of this period of transition will rely on financial markets as its main medium of redistribution. This has already happened within the corporate world, where the shift to shareholder-oriented governance and the massive shift over to financial rent as a main source of profits has inscribed the maximization of (often short-term) value of shares over the longer term stability of Chandlerian memory as the main parameter of corporate governance (Harvey 2007).

At the level of everyday life processes this tendency manifests itself in the decreasing centrality of the wage relation as a mechanism for the redistribution of social wealth. Instead household income tends to derive from a multitude of diverse sources: regular salaried employment, short term work, children's work, unpaid forms of social production that can be monetized in different ways, entrepreneurship, engagements with the growing informal economy, and, for the middle and upper classes, real-estate speculation and other forms of financial rent (Warren 2007). Conversely, the financialization of everyday life, particularly through the expansion of mortgage and credit card debt, provides a way of capturing value from a multitude of activities that lie outside the wage relation proper: In the Fordist model the labor contract guaranteed the worker a secure long-term access to the means for the reproduction of life, and the capitalist a secure long-term and predictable stream of surplus labor (in the form of the productivity of the working day that exceeded the cost of labor). In the post-Fordist model the financial system anticipates necessities for the reproduction of life (a house, health insurance, etc.) and receives in turn a long-term and (relatively, or at least calculably) secure value stream in the form of interest payments. The interest payments become a direct extraction of surplus from the whole-life practice, and not just from the working day. This way we can argue that the financial expansion that has marked the last decades has not just been a reaction to a declining rate of profit, but also, at least in part, a rational response to a situation where the production of value tends to occur beyond the command of the wage relation.

But how are such financial values set? A combination of recurrent financial boom-and-bust cycles, together with a growing empirical interest in the actual operations of financial markets, has undermined the rational expectations hypothesis that guided the discipline of financial economics since its inception (Fox 2009). A growing interest in 'behavioral finance' among economists combined with a growing interest in financial markets among sociologists have opened up the hypothesis that financial values are largely 'social' (Stark 2009) or 'linguistic' (Marazzi 2008) constructs. To put it in simpler terms, the financial values of corporate assets are largely determined by the ability to construct a convention that guides investors in a particular way. Such a convention can be constructed in two ways. This can be done politically, by some form of agreement among the some 10–15 large actors among investment banks and central banks that control financial markets that now, for example, is the time to invest in dot.com shares. Alternatively, and on a more everyday level, this can be done by cultivating the kind of reputation that, in the form of brand equity, can motivate a market valuation of 2–3 times above book value (a normal figure for Fortune 500 companies today, and there is an emerging consensus in the managerial literature that the reputational value deriving from CSR activities has a discernable effect on market valuation). In other words, it seems possible to suggest that financial markets are part of an ever more important reputation economy. This reputation economy manifests itself in many other key areas of the contemporary information economy: consumers value brands according to their reputation, the value of knowledge workers' skills and labor is largely set by their networks and reputation (Forlano 2008; Wittel 2001), the reputational capital of celebrities is becoming an ever more central asset to the media industry (Hearn 2008), and, finally, the growth of social networking sites enables reputation and networks to be objectified in novel and interesting ways (Illouz 2007). Could a combination of financial distribution and reputational valuation become the cornerstones of a new law of value? This would require that the determination of reputation be democratized, that is, that reputation formation would no longer be controlled by the actors who control media access and attention. It would also require that the link between ethical use value, a person's real ability to 'matter' in new productive processes, and reputational exchange value be made transparent. Present developments in social media carry some promise in that respect.

Note

1 This does not mean that labor disappears, but that its value becomes related to its ability to exploit General Intellect. Rather than the disappearance of labor, this situation presupposes an enormous expansion of the global labor force and hence of the availability of an enormous mass of productive skill that can be networked into General Intellect.

References

Adler, P. and Heckscher, C. (2006) 'Towards Collaborative Community', in Heckscher, C., and Adler, P. (eds) The Firm as Collaborative Community, Oxford: Oxford University Press, pp. 11–105.

Adler, P., Seok-Woo, K., and Heckscher, C. (2008) 'Professional Work, the Emergence of Collaborative Community', Organization Science, 19 (2).

Anderson, C. (2009) Free: The Future of a Radical Price, New York: Random House.

Adam Arvidsson

Arvidsson, A. (2006) *Brands: Meaning and Value in Media Culture*, London: Routledge.

——(2007) 'Creative Class or Administrative Class: On Advertising and "The underground"', *Ephemera*, 7 (1): 8–23.

Bauman, Z. (1993) *Postmodern Ethics*, Oxford: Blackwell.

Bellofiore, R. (1997) *Marxian Economics: A Reappraisal*, London: St Martin's Press.

Benkler, Y. (2006) *The Wealth of Networks*, New Haven, CT: Yale University Press.

Berardi, F. B. (2009) *Soul at Work*, New York: Semiotext(e).

Boltanski, L. and Chiapello, E. (1999) *Le nouvel ésprit du capitalisme*, Paris: Gallimard.

Burchell, S., Clubb, C., and Hopwood, A. (1985) 'Accounting in its Social Context: Towards a History of Value-added in the United Kingdom', *Accounting, Organizations and Society*, 10: 381–413.

Carson, C. (2008) *Nowtopia: How Pirate Programmers, Outlaw Bicyclists, and Vacant-lot Gardeners are Inventing the Future Today!*, San Francisco, CA: AK Distribution.

Caruso, D. (2007) 'When Balance Sheets Collide with the New Economy', *New York Times*, 9/9.

Chandler, A. 1977, *The Visible Hand: The Managerial Revolution in American Business*, Cambridge, MA: Harvard University Press.

Coase, R. (1937) 'The Nature of the Firm', *Economica*, 4 (16): 386–405.

Coleman, G. (2005) *Three Ethical Moments in Debian*, available at: <http://anthropology.usf.edu/cma/ssrn-id805287.pdf>.

Cordazzo, M. (2007) 'IC Statement vs. Environmental and Social Reports: An Empirical Analysis of Their Convergences in the Italian Context', in S. Zambon and G. Marzo, eds, *Visualizing Intangibles: Measuring and Reporting in the Knowledge Economy*, Aldershot: Ashgate, pp. 67–96.

Currid, E. (2007) *The Warhol Economy: How Fashion, Art and Music Drive New York City*, Princeton, NJ; Princeton University Press.

De Angelis, M. (2006) *The Beginnings of History. Value Struggles and Global Capital*, London: Pluto Press.

Del Bello, A. (2007) 'Credit Rating and Intangible Assets: A Preliminary Inquiry into Current Practices', in S. Zambon and G. Marzo, eds, *Visualizing Intangibles: Measuring and Reporting in the Knowledge Economy*, Aldershot: Ashgate, pp. 165–92.

Drucker, P. (1993) *Post-capitalist Society*, New York: Harper Collins.

Du Gay, P. (2007) *Organizing Identity*, London: Sage.

Dyer-Withford, N. (2006) 'The Circulation of the Common', Paper presented at the 'Immaterial Labour Conference', Cambridge (UK), April 2006, available at: http://ning.p2pfoundation.net/Circulation_of_the_Common>, accessed 1 November 2010.

Florida, R. (2002) *The Rise of the Creative Class*, New York: Basic Books.

Forlano, L. (2008) 'When Code Meets Place: Collaboration and Innovation at Wifi Hotspots', Ph.D Dissertation, Columbia University, New York.

Fox, J. (2009) *The Myth of the Rational Market*, New York: Harper Business.

Graeber, D. (2001) *Towards an Anthropological Theory of Value*, London: Palgrave.

Hagel, J. and Brown, J. (2005) *The Only Sustainable Edge: Why Business Strategy Depends on Productive Friction and Dynamic Specialization*, Boston, MA: Harvard Business School Press.

Harvey, D. (2007) *A Brief History of Neoliberalism*, Oxford: Oxford University Press.

Hearn, A. (2008) 'Meat, Mask, Burden: Probing the Contours of the Branded "Self"', *Journal of Consumer Culture*, 8(2); 163–183.

Higson, C., Rivers, O. and Deboo, M., (2007) *Creative Business: Crafting the Value Narrative*, London: London Business School.

von Hippel, E. (2006) *Democratizing Innovation*, Cambridge, MA: MIT Press.

Hulten, C. and Hao, J. (2008) 'Intangible Capital and the "Market to Book Value" Puzzle', The Conference Board.

Hussi, T. (2003), 'Reconfiguring Knowledge Management. Combining Intellectual Capital, Intangible Assets and Knowledge Creation' Discussion Papers 849, Helsinki: Research Institute of the Finnish Economy.

Huston, L. and Sakkab, N. (2006) 'Connect and Develop: Inside Procter & Gamble's New Model for Innovation', *Harvard Business Review*, March: 58–66.

Illouz, E. (2007) *Cold Intimacies: The Making of Emotional Capitalism*, Cambridge: Polity.

Kunda, G. (2006) *Engineering Culture: Control and Commitment in a High-tech Corporation*, Philadelphia, PA: Temple University Press.

Lazzarato, M. (1997) *Lavoro immateriale*, Verona: Ombre Corte.

Lev, B. (2001) *Intangibles: Management, Measurement and Reporting*, Washington, DC: Brookings Institute.

480

Lloyd, R, (2006) *Neo-Bohemia: Art and Commerce in the Post-industrial City*, New York: Routledge

McKenzie, D. (2008) *An Engine, Not a Camera: How Financial Models shape Markets*, Boston, MA: MIT Press.

Mandel, M., Hamm, S., and Farrell, C. (2006) 'Why the Economy is a Lot Stronger than You Think' *BusinessWeek*, 13/2, available at: <http://www.businessweek.com/magazine/content/06_07/b3971001. htm>, accessed 15 October 2010.

Maravelias, C. (2003) 'Post-bureaucracy: Control through Professional Freedom', *Journal of Organizational Change Management*, 16(5): 547–66.

Marazzi, C. (2008) *Capital and Language*, London: Pluto Press.

Marx, K. (1973 [1939]), *Grundrisse*, London: Penguin.

Nakamura, L. (2001) 'Investing in Intangibles. Is a Trillion Dollars Missing from GDP?', *Business Review*, 04: 27–37,available at <http://www.philadelphiafed.org/files/br/brq401ln.pdf>, accessed 15 October 2010.

Negri, A. (1999) 'Value and Affect', *Boundary 2*, 26 (2): 77–88.

O'Neil, M. (2009) *Cyber Chiefs: Autonomy and Authority in Online Tribes*, London: Pluto Press.

Rometti, G. (2006) *Expanding the Innovation Horizon: The Global CEO Survey*, IBM Enterprise Stark, D. (2009) *The Sense of Dissonance: Accounts of Worth in Economic Life*, Princeton, NJ: Princeton University Press.

Surowiecki, J. (2004) *The Wisdom of Crowds*, New York: Brown.

Tapscott, D. and Williams, A. (2006) *Wikinomics: How Mass Collaboration Changes Everything*, New York: Portfolio.

Thompson, C. (2008) 'Build It, Share It, Profit! Can Open Hardware Work?', *Wired*, 20 October, available at <http://www.wired.com/techbiz/startups/magazine/16–11/ff_openmanufacturing?currentPage=all>, accessed 15 October 2010.

Toffler, A. and Toffler, H. (2006) *Revolutionary Wealth*, New York: Kopf.

Virno, P.(2004) *A Grammar of the Multitude*, London: Pluto Press.

Vogel, D. (2006) *The Market for Virtue: The Potential and Limits of Corporate Social Responsibility*, Washington, DC: Brookings Institute Press.

Vormbusch, U. (2008) 'Talking Numbers: Governing Immaterial Labour', *Economic Sociology Newsletter*, 10, 1, November: 8–11.

Warren, E. (2007) 'The Vanishing Middle Class' in J. Edwards, M Crain, and A. Kallenberg, eds, *Ending Poverty in America: How to Restore the American Dream*, New York: New Press.

Weber, S. (2004) *The Success of Open Source*, Cambridge, MA: MIT Press.

Wittel, A. (2001) 'Towards a Network Sociality', *Theory, Culture and Society*, 18(6): 51–76.

Zaloom, C. (2006) 'Trading on Numbers', in M. Fisher and G. Downey, eds, *Frontiers of Capital: Ethnographic Reflections on the New Economy*, Durham, NC: Duke University Press, pp. 58–85.

Zwick, D., Bonsu, S., and Darmondy, A.(2008) 'Putting Consumers to Work: Co-creation and New Marketing Govermentality', *Journal of Consumer Culture*, 8, 2: 163–96.

Memory Practices and Theory
in a Global Age

Daniel Levy

Collective memory has become an ubiquitous term dominating the public and scholarly imagination since the late 1980s. True to its multidisciplinary character there has been little agreement on a concise definition (Olick and Robbins 1998). Nevertheless, much of the literature draws on the works of Maurice Halbwachs, for whom memories are not simply mediated but structured by social arrangements and constituted in social frameworks. 'It is in society that people normally acquire their memories. It is also in society that they recall, recognize, and localize their memories' (Halbwachs 1992: 38). Studying and theorizing memory is thus not a matter of exploring the subjective mind or its neurological functions but of identifying shifting social frames within which memories are embedded. The forms memories take thus vary according to social organization, and the groups to which individuals belongs.

Differences notwithstanding there is a minimal consensus that collective memories will be sustained by the social frameworks within which they are produced (Halbwachs 1992), have an intersubjective (Misztal 2003), and intertextual (Olick 2007) dimension. Leaving aside the more individualistic psychoanalytical and neurological orientations, cultural memory is commonly characterized by intentional, organized, and ritualized mnemonic manifestations. Producing memory types that transcend particular experiences and sustain trans-generational long-time memories thus requires institutionalized repositories.They rely on external media and institutions onto which experiences, memories, and knowledge are inscribed (e.g. archives, museums, libraries).

The decision to refrain from offering a specific definition of collective memory is driven by the central claim that memory and the theoretical concepts underwriting its study should not be reduced to a static concept but need to be addressed in their respective historical contexts. They provide the epistemological underpinnings circumscribing the essential features of memory techniques and attendant social, cultural, and political practices. As Patrick Hutton has pointed out: 'The expressive, collective memory, of oral tradition gives way to the introspective, personal memory of literary culture. Memory, first conceived as a repetition, is eventually reconceived as a recollection. Over the long run, the appreciation of memory as a habit is displaced by one of memory as representation' (Hutton 1993: 16). Here changing modes of communication are co-extensive with different apprehensions of memory: 'orality with the reiteration of living memory; manuscript literacy with the recovery of lost wisdom; print literacy with the reconstruction of a distinct past; and media literacy with the deconstruction of the forms with which past images are composed' (Hutton 1993: 16). During this last stage of media literacy then, memory has become a self-conscious device which, I argue here, is a crucial development for how memory is linked to political, social, and cultural theory (PSCT).

What we are studying when we apply collective memory as an analytic lens to society are changing temporal conceptions of the past–present–future triad. George Orwell's observation, by now a cliché, that 'whoever controls the present controls the past' has long been a central theme in the memory literature. Most conceptual statements and empirical undertakings seem to revolve around this kind of instrumentalist approach. According to this perspective present political concerns and dominant (nation-state) interests are projected onto the past instrumentalizing memory for the political needs of the present (Hobsbawm and Ranger 1983). This research tradition is in line with Orwell's perception of a controlling hegemonic party. Challenging this state-centric view, another popular research strand draws on Michel Foucault's notion of counter-memory, paying attention to sub-national units of analysis such as ethnic minorities, gender, and other subaltern groups with counter-memorial agendas (Foucault 1975). Despite their different vantage points, both orientations essentially consider political expediencies about the generation of power and socio-cultural orientations revolving around identity in the present as leading to the invention or construction of the past.

Far less (theoretical) attention has been paid to the future and its relation to the temporal modes of present and past, beyond Orwell's other instrumentalist insight that 'whoever controls the past controls the future'. On a polemical level this omission has frequently been associated with the critique that memory supposedly is merely backward looking, and that contemporary preoccupations with the past come at the expense of a progressive future agenda (Maier 1993). This view is echoed in John Torpey's critique of the proliferation of memory tropes associated with transitional justice mechanisms. 'The global spread of reparations demands and the preoccupation with the past to which it bears witness reflect an unmistakable decline of a more explicitly future-oriented politics' (Torpey 2006: 5). My point here is not so much to dispute this charge (the neglect of either temporal dimension, after all, is by itself an important finding) but to underscore that collective memory involves all temporal registers, generating meanings for the future as well. Paradoxically, the critics of the memory boom who lament the alleged absence of a future vision reproduce this limitation by dismissing memory tout court rather than engaging with its significance for the social articulation of futures.

As Alasdair MacIntyre puts it: 'An adequate sense of tradition manifests itself in a grasp of those future possibilities which the past has made available to the present. Living traditions, just because they continue a not-yet-completed narrative, confront a future whose determinate and determinable character, so as it possesses any, derives form the past' (1984: 223). Here memory and its association with a particular past are not an impediment for the future but a prerequisite to enunciate a narrative (bridge) over the present. A shared sense of the past becomes a meaning-making repository which helps define aspirations for the future. In his historical analysis of times and temporalities Reinhart Koselleck points out that the present is situated between past experiences, which is 'present past, whose events have been incorporated and can be remembered', and a horizon of expectations, which refers to 'the future made present, it points to the not-yet, to that which has not been experienced, to that which can only be discovered' (Koselleck 1985: 272). What matters for our discussion is that the preoccupation with the past and the (secularized) command to remember have become sources of political legitimacy and cultural affirmation. As such they are perceived as central mechanisms for the transmission of values to future generations. On this view, memory is not only an intricate parcel of meaning-making activities but can also become an empowering resource for a wide variety of groups, as the popularity of the aforementioned notion of counter-memory attests to.

Despite the prominence of memory in public discourse and the proliferation of memory studies, the topic remains a marginal theme in political, social, and cultural theory. It is instructive to briefly consider why memory is addressed as epiphenomenal rather than as an integral and constitutive part of theory. This omission needs to be understood with reference to the genealogy and epistemological conditions under which PSCT originated and evolved. Much of modernity (and along with it the social sciences) was a forward-looking intellectual enterprise, establishing rather a-historical dichotomies between the past and the present (e.g. *Gesellschaft* and *Gemeinschaft*). Time and memory were frequently subjected to linearity and rationality. The emphasis on change and progress instead of tradition (which was closely associated with memory and conceptions of pre-modernity) left little theoretical space for the incorporation of memory. Paradoxically, it was precisely the perception that progress destroyed the past which triggered the nineteenth-century preoccupation and (re)invention of memory, to paraphrase the famous observation by Eric Hobsbawm and Terence Ranger (1983). The invention of traditions was largely a response to provide a sense of continuity (and foundation) for the new nation-state eager to establish a connection to the past (Smith 1986) and an imagined community (Anderson 1983). Early twentieth-century references to the past resembled many of the transitions and transformative anxieties associated with modernity that have given rise to the contemporary memory boom. The establishment of museums as a means to preserve the past was perhaps the most emblematic feature of a wave of public commemorations (Lowenthal 1985). Another sign of growing attention to memory at the beginning of the twentieth century was the shift from its association with tradition and ritual to a more scientific realm, embodied in the works of Sigmund Freud and others (Hacking 1995).

Memory as Heuristic Device in the 'Commemorative Era'

Yet this plethora of memory phenomena, both in the realm of study and as a political–cultural marker of modernity, has done little to alleviate the theoretical paucity alluded to. The conceptual lacuna, that is the missing link of memory in PSCT, is especially surprising considering that memory is a necessary condition for our cognition and values. It is essential for the development of attachments, and various forms of belonging. 'It is closely connected with emotions because emotions are in part about the past and because memory evokes emotions' (Misztal 2003: 1). Memory is indispensable for our ability to make sense of the present as it 'functions in every act of perception, in every act of intellection, in every act of language' (Terdiman 1993: 9). From a phenomenological perspective every social act is permeated with memory. Edward Casey notes that

> in the case of memory, we are always already in the thick of things. ... Not only because remembering is at all times presupposed, but also because it is always at work: it is continually going on, often on several levels and in several ways at once. ... Indeed, every fiber of our bodies, every cell of our brains, holds memories – as does everything physical outside bodies and brains, even those inanimate objects that bear the marks of their past histories upon them in mute profusion.
>
> *(Casey 2000: xix)*

The identity dimension of memory is not confined to this phenomenological perspective but extends to the very core of how we exist in and through history. As Philip Abrams put it:

> Doing justice to the reality of history is not a matter of noting the way in which the past provides background to the present; it is a matter of treating what people do in the present as a struggle to create a future out of the past, of seeing that the past is not just the womb of the present but the only raw material out of which the present can be constructed.
>
> *(Abrams 1982: 8)*

Memory – relating past and present – is thus a central faculty of being in time, through which we define individual and collective selves. In short, the stuff around which PSCT revolves.

Memory is situated in *social* frameworks (e.g. family, national, and personal experiences anchored by symbolic markings), externalized in *cultural* markers (e.g. archival repositories such as memorials and museums), and shaped by *political* circumstances (e.g. wars, catastrophes, and debates generating lasting meanings of these events). Social frameworks and historical circumstances change over time and with them the aforementioned alignments of temporalities (e.g. the discourse of progress in modernity). Studying (and theorizing) memory allows us to shift our focus from time to temporalities, and thus to understand what categories people, groups, and cultures employ to make sense of their lives, their attachments, and the concomitant ideals that are validated – that is, the political, cultural, and social theories which command normative attention.

Following Hans-Georg Gadamer, I suggest that the theoretical surplus of memory consists of its heuristic value:

> Hermeneutics must start from the position that a person seeking to understand something has a relation to the object that comes into language in the transmitted text and has, or aquires, a connection out of which the text speaks. ... The place between strangeness and familiarity that a transmitted text has for us is that intermediate place between being a historically intended separate object and being part of a tradition. The true home of hermeneutics is in that intermediate area.
>
> *(Gadamer 1975: 262–3)*

And it is memory that occupies this intermediate realm as it provides the necessary temporal distance and thus the clarifying conditions in which understanding takes place.

The current theoretical value of memory, I argue, is primarily derived (though not limited) from the specific context of the aforementioned memory boom, which is challenging existing conceptual categories and their attendant theories. A short look at the origins of the memory boom and some of its political, cultural, and social expressions is instructive for situating memory as an integral part of PSCT. What follows should not be mistaken as an exhaustive explanation of the memory boom let alone a genealogy of memory. Rather it is an attempt to specify the epistemological conditions for the centrality of memory in PSCT.

Recent public and scholarly attention to memory works and the work of memory originated during the 1980s and has shown no signs of slowing down. According to Pierre Nora (2002) two interrelated phenomena explain the current upsurge in memory. One is the 'acceleration of memory' which suggests 'that the most continuous or permanent feature of the modern world is no longer continuity or permanence but change. And increasingly rapid change, an accelerated precipitation of all things into an ever more swiftly retreating past' (Nora 2002: 1). On this view, memory 'has shattered the unity of historical time, that fine, straightforward linearity which traditionally bound the present and the future to the past. In effect, it was the way in which a society, nation, group or family envisaged its future that traditionally determined what it needed to remember of the past to prepare that future; and this in turn gave meaning to the present, which was merely a link between the two' (ibid: 1). Andreas Huyssen (1995) has addressed the digital age as an instantiation of this acceleration and the cultural responses evidenced in the preoccupation with memory (e.g. the surge of auto-biographies, memoirs, and the popular interest in genealogy). History writing itself has been affected as earlier delineations between memory and history have given way to a blurring of the two (Klein 2000). Together, these developments 'have introduced an element of relativism into historiography. ... Accordingly the problem of memory comes to the fore. History becomes a politics of what we in the present want posterity to remember' (Hutton 1994: 100).

This move from history to memory (a division which is merely analytic and has itself become the subject of historiographic attention) is echoed in the proliferation of heritage sites. 'In the movement from history to heritage there is an evaluation of the past in order for the present to judge what legacy it should derive from history' (Delanty 2008: 36). The current heritage movement, whose origins can be dated to the 1970s, represents a self-conscious effort to integrate memory as a meaning making activity. 'An important aspect of heritage is a memory conceived of as a mode of interpretation. The memories that are encapsulated in a heritage allow a society to interpret history and the relation of the present to history. To speak of heritage in such terms is to see it as a cultural model of interpretation' (ibid: 38). This heuristic device is closely related to the acceleration of memory, which has resulted in the paradox that the less we are embedded in actual 'milieux de mémoire' the more we cultivate 'lieux de mémoire' (Nora 1989). The loss of memory corresponds to an obsession with memory. The 'age of commemoration' is marked by the cultivation and preservation of heritage sites on a global scale. The so-called 'heritage industry' has entwined political (conservativism), cultural (growth of museums and private collections), social (identity forming), and economic (commodification of the past) functions (Lowenthal 1985). A correlate to the heritage industry is the resurgence of nostalgia. Both are cultural preoccupations that characterize epochal transitions. Nostalgia was also part of the *fin de siècle* memory boom during which the political, cultural and social foundations of modernity were theorized in the context of a paradox in which time threatened memory and memory sought to restrain time.

The second reason for the memory boom speaks to the emergence of identity politics. The nexus of memory and identity is sustained by the basic premise that group identities require a sense of permanence. 'Identities and memories are not things we think *about*, but things we think *with*. As such, they have no existence beyond our politics, our social relations, and our histories' (Gillis 1994: 5). What characterizes the memory boom is that 'the common feature underpinning most contemporary manifestations of the memorycraze seems to be an insecurity about identity. We might postulate a rule: when identity becomes uncertain, memory rises in value' (Megill 2000: 43). Nora speaks about the 'democratization' of history. He ascribes the popularity of this emancipatory discourse to three types of decolonization:

> *international* decolonization, which has allowed societies previously stagnating in the ethnological inertia of colonial oppression access to historical consciousness and the rehabilitation (or fabrication) of memories; *domestic* decolonization, within traditional western societies, of sexual, social, religious and provincial minorities now being integrated with the mainstream and for whom reaffirming their 'memory' in actual fact, their history – is a way of having their 'particularism' recognized by a community that had previously refused them that right, while at the same time cultivating their difference and their attachment to an identity threatened with disintegration.
>
> *(Nora 2002: 5)*

Previously marginalized groups seek to reaffirm their identities through the discovery and rehabilitation of their (counter)-memories.

The third type of decolonization is *ideological*. It refers to the re-emergence of long suppressed memories unleashed by the end of the Cold War and linked to the collapse of totalitarian and authoritarian regimes in Eastern and Central Europe, Africa, and Latin America. This trend is associated with the growing attention to human rights discourses and the appearance of transitional justice studies (Levy and Sznaider 2010). Truth and justice are linked with traumatic memories imposing challenges for societies to remember their collective wrongs and pursue different forms of reconciliation through a host of mechanisms including: symbolic acknowledgment of past injustices through rituals of forgiveness (e.g. apologies) and related commemorative activities (e.g. post-heroic memorials); the recognition of victims and the responsibility of perpetrators (e.g. truth commissions); material compensation through a variety of restitutive measures; and legal procedures (e.g. human rights or war crime trials). Transitology is by now a vast field and its details are beyond the scope of this essay. What matters for our theoretical purposes is that the prominence of memories of past injustices is reflective of and contributes to emerging forms of cultural identifications, collective self-understandings, and political legitimacy. Political legitimation has always depended on collective memory (myth, etc.). What distinguishes today's version is that it is driven by a critical introspection of one's negative pasts, what Jeffrey Olick (2007) has termed the 'politics of regret.' On this view, the central questions 'for a sociohistorical theory of regret concern the ways regret is modern and the way modernity is regretful' (Olick 2007: 130).

The popularity of the memory boom among memory enterpeneurs is matched by conceptual developments on the observer level. On the analytical side, these international, domestic, and ideological transformations tie in with the consolidation of memory studies as a field which includes scientific institutes, multi-disciplinary scholarship, curatorial work, oral history projects, and an ongoing stream of publications mirroring and accentuating the commemorative vigor of contemporary societies:

> Where baby-boomers worry about the living death of Alzheimer's disease, neuro-scientists search for its biological basis. Where trauma victims seek to overcome their on-going suffering from post-traumatic stress, psychologists develop frameworks for treatment. Where past oppression has seemingly become the coin of identity, cultural theorists inquire into the origins of the politics of victimhood. And where societies confront the legacies of their misdeeds, social and political scientists analyze the conditions for successful transition and salutary commemoration. All of these, and more, are constituents of what has come to be referred to as the new 'memory studies', which has acquired its own journals, been elaborated in countless edited volumes, has established research centers, received grants, and been the subject of university courses.
>
> *(Olick, Vinitzky-Seroussi, and Levy 2010: 2)*

Mnemo-history and Theory

The theoretical value of memory is best assessed with a mnemo-historical approach. According to Jan Assmann (1997) mnemo-history is not about the exploration of the past per se but rather is concerned with how a particular past is remembered. How histories are remembered (and by extension distorted over time) emerges as the main focus of our analytic pursuits. Jan Assmann reminds us that what matters is not so much the factuality of these memories but their actuality. By historicizing memory as a contingent phenomenon we can simultaneously elucidate the reasons for distinctive memory cultures and capture the specificities of memory. This process oriented approach suggests that 'memory is not only storage of past "facts" but the ongoing work of reconstructive imagination. In other words, the past cannot be stored but always has to be "processed" and mediated. This mediation depends on the semantic frames and needs of a given individual or society within a given present' (Assmann 1997: 14). However, there are two conceptual reflections a mnemo-historical approach needs to take into consideration.

The first concerns the specific characteristics of the mnemonic reference group:

> Every group – be it religious, political or economic, family, friends, or acquaintances, even a transient gathering in a salon, auditorium, or street-immobilizes time in its own way and imposes on its members the illusion that, in a given duration of a constantly changing world, certain zones have acquired a relative stability and balance in which nothing essential is altered.
>
> *(Halbwachs 1980: 126)*

An obvious, but sometimes neglected point here is that memory practices are mediated by idiosyncratic group features of temporal experiences and distinctive cultural dispositions towards specific pasts and pastness in general. Attentiveness to the kind of cultural validations specific groups attribute to temporal phenomenon such as progress, change, innovation and memory itself is therefore indispensable.

A second characteristic of great concern for a mnemohistorical approach attuned to how different cultures may apprehend temporality relates to questions of noncontemporaneity. There is a tendency in the academic literature to privilege a mostly Western conception of memory. Therefore, the need to 'de-provincialize' the notion of memory arises, since it is frequently situated in an ideal(ized) sequence of modernity that is characterized, among other things, by its alleged anachronistic relationship to the past and traditions. Not to mention the kind of linear assumptions which have long informed social and political modernization theories. Much of the literature addressing the memory boom operates with a conception of modernity stipulating a certain universalism that loses track of the particular conditions that shape memory cultures. They share a 'modernist' bias, which leaves little empirical let alone conceptual space for the existence of noncontemporaneities. Instead of reproducing a view of memory that presupposes a particular sequence of temporalities, we need to be attentive to the different figurations the temporal triad of past, present and future can manifest itself. 'What engenders noncontemporaneity is the advance of modernity itself, and the more rapidly the modern replaces the pre-modern, or the late modern replaces the early modern, the more sizable amounts of noncontemporaneity get produced' (Gross 2000: 142). The entwinement of differential historical experiences and distinctive group orientations circumscribes the kind and scope of memory. David Gross (2000: 142ff) delineates three types of temporal realignment: *Absolute noncontemporaneity* refers to a past that has been obliterated. It is a lost past for which we have mere fragments that are preserved in museums and subject to archeological speculations, but have no bearing on present-day experience. Then there is *relative noncontemporaneity* which is a past that has passed too but has left behind some traces that can still be evoked (e.g. residual forms of behavior dating back to but also severed from earlier times such as certain codes of honor, outmoded manners). Lastly, there is *enduring noncontemporaneity*, addressing unmitigated thoughts and conducts from the past that are clearly incongruous with current behavioral practices. A mneno-historical approach seeks to resolve the aforementioned tension between the synchronic imperatives globalization imposes and diachronic dimensions suggesting a theoretical perspective in which the objects and subjects of our inquiries are historically constituted.

Pledging close attention to the a-synchronic features of noncontemporeaneity then is not a matter of cultural relativism but of analytic pragmatism.

Conclusion: Epochal Memories and Their Epistemological Foundations

If we accept the mnemo-historical premise that memory practices and their heuristic value need to be understood in specific cultural and historical contexts, we must explore the distinguishing political, cultural, social, and technological features shaping and transforming the character of memory cultures. Mnemo-history is concerned with the epochal features of memory, being situated between local conditions and global currents. Which mnemonic practices prevail and characterize a particular epoch and/or culture? During the late nineteenth and for the first three quarters of the twentieth century memory was identified with the hegemonic aspirations of the nation-state seeking to forge a united and unifying narrative of the past. While nation-state memories were a self-conscious top-down and territorialized effort, the late twentieth and early twenty-first century signal a self-reflexive turning point attributing legitimacy to nation transforming forms of memory.

The literature on memory, however, remains widely wedded to a nation-state model. Ironically, the territorial conception of national culture – the idea of culture as 'rooted' – was itself a reaction to the enormous changes that were going on as the nineteenth century turned into the twentieth. It was a conscious attempt to provide a solution to the 'uprooting' of local cultures that the formation of nation states necessarily involved. Sociology understood the new symbols and common values, transmitted primarily through the consolidation of cultural memories by establishing links to foundational pasts, as means of integration into a new unity. The triumph of this perspective can be seen in the way the nation-state ceased to appear as a project and construct, and instead was perceived as something natural. Accordingly, the nation-state reflects a

> spatial understanding of the possibility of political community, an understanding that necessarily gives priority to the fixing of processes of historical change in space. Not only does the principle of state sovereignty reflect a historically specific resolution of questions about the universality and particularity of political community, but it also fixes that resolution within categories that have absorbed a metaphysical claim to timelessness. … Time and change are perceived as dangers to be contained.
>
> *(Walker 1990: 172–3)*

Since about 1990 we have witnessed a cultural (and by extension temporal) turn in the social sciences and humanities. At the beginning of the twenty-first century, globalization is posing a challenge to the idea that binding history and borders tightly together is the only possible means of social and symbolic integration.

This crisis of territoriality has significant theoretical implications as the spatially rooted understanding of culture is being challenged by the uncoupling of nation and state in the context of a cosmopolitanization of memories (Levy and Sznaider 2002). This cosmopolitanization of memories consists of a process that shifts attention away from the territorialized nation-state framework that is commonly associated with the notion of memory. Rather than presuppose the congruity of nation, territory, and polity, cosmopolitan memories are based on and contribute to nation-transforming idioms, spanning territorial and linguistic borders. The formation of cosmopolitan memories does not eliminate the national perspective, but renders nationhood into one of several options of collective identification. The cosmopolitan turn suggests that particular orientations toward the past need to be reevaluated against the background of global memory scapes (Levy and Sznaider 2005). This is not to say that memory is no longer articulated within the nation-state, but that we witness a pluralization of memory – both in formal terms and pertaining to its normative validation – which has given way to a fragmentation of memory, no longer beholden exclusively to the idea of the nation-state. The key interpretive issue here is the transition from heroic nation-states to a form of statehood that establishes internal and external legitimacy through its support for skeptical narratives challenging foundational quasi-mythical pasts, which previously served as generation transcending fixed points. Empirically those post-heroic symptoms of statehood are predicated on a critical engagement with past injustices, manifested, among other things, in the proliferation of historical commissions and the salience human rights norms occupy in public debates about usable pasts.

This transformation of memories involves to the fragmentation of memories and their related privatization, reflecting a reconfigured relationship of memory and history. During the last two decades we can observe the appearance of 'memory history' (Diner 2003). The difference to conventional historical narratives is instructive. History is a particularized idea of temporal sequences articulating some form of (national) development. Memory, on the other hand, represents a co-existence of simultaneous pasts. (National) history corresponds to the telos of modernity (as a kind of civic religion). Memory dissolves this sequence, which is a constitutive part of history. 'Memory history' implies the simultaneity of phenomenon and a multitude of pasts. 'Memory history' is a particular form of memory which moves away from a state-supported (and state-supporting) national history. The previous (attempted) monopoly by the state to shape collective pasts has given way to a fragmentation of memories carried by private, individual, scientific, ethnic, and religious agents. To be sure, the state continues to exercise an important role in how we remember its history, but it is now sharing the field of meaning production with a host of other players. This brief sketch elucidates a shift from assumptions of homogeneous time and hegemonic memories to non-contemporaneous and fragmented memories.

The theoretical thrust of memory is closely tied to the self-reflexive political, cultural, and social engagements with changing conceptions of temporal links. As Barbara Misztal points out: 'Since memory practices are increasingly seen as the central characteristic of contemporary cultural formations, studies of social memory are becoming an important part of an examination of contemporary society's main problems and tensions. Thus, it is concluded that studies of collective memory can provide important insights for a general theory of modernity' (Misztal 2003: 8). Moreover, the memory boom along with the rise of memory studies contributes to the co-existence of analytic and actor perspectives. Following Anthony Giddens (1987), this supports the status of memory as a double hermeneutic fermenting its relevant status for PSCT. 'The concepts of the social sciences are not produced about an independently constituted subject-matter, which continues regardless of what these concepts are. The "findings" of the social sciences very often enter constitutively into the world they describe' (Giddens 1987: 20). Like class, gender, and ethnicity, memory is now being self-consciously deployed for analysis and in mnemonic practices. In other words, memory assumes a reflexive character. This is not to be mistaken as another version of instrumentalism, but rather an attribute of a period during which memory is articulated as 'the essential aspect of reflexivity and the multiple time frames that enter into the construction of an object to the extent that it is envisaged as a production situated in time and space. ... it is not so much the temporal dimension in itself as the incidence of a plurality of temporalities involved in the identification and construction of the objects that is in question' (Werner and Zimmermann 2006: 45). Memory encourages us to explore questions 'concerning scale, categories of analysis, the relationship between diachrony and synchrony, and regimes of historicity and reflexivity' (ibid: 32). The conversation on memory has been moving from one about a struggle over the meaning of the past to encompassing theoretical debates over the political, cultural and social meanings of memory itself, that is the extent to which it is theoretically generative.

References

Abrams, P. (1982) *Historical Sociology*, Ithaca, NY: Cornell University Press.

Anderson, B. (1983) *Imagined Communities*, London: Verso.

Assmann, J. (1997) *Moses the Egyptian: The Memory of Egypt in Western Monotheism*, Cambridge, MA: Harvard University Press.

Casey, E. (2000) *Remembering: A Phenomenological Study*, Bloomington, IN: Indiana University Press,

Delanty, G. (2008) 'The European Heritage: History, Memory and Time', in C. Rumford (ed.) *Handbook of European Studies*, London: Sage, 36–51.

Diner, D. (2003) *Gedächtniszeiten: Über Jüdische und andere Geschichten*, München: C.H. Beck

Foucault, M. (1975) 'Film and Popular Memory: An Interview with Michel Foucault', *Radical Philosophy*, 11: 24–9.

Gadamer, H.G. (1975) *Truth and Method*, London: Sheed & Ward.

Giddens, A. (1987) *Social Theory and Modern Sociology*, Cambridge: Polity Press.

Gillis, J. (1994) 'Memory and Identity: The History of a Relationship', in J.R. Gillis (ed.) *Commemorations: The Politics of National Identity*, Princeton, NJ: Princeton University Press, 3–27.

Gross, D. (2000) *Lost Time: On Remembering and Forgetting in Late Modern Culture*, Amherst, MA: University of Massachusetts Press.

Hacking, I. (1995) 'Memory Sciences, Memory Politics', in P. Antze and M. Lambek (eds) *Tense Past: Cultural Essays in Trauma and Memory*, Routledge: London, 67–88.

Halbwachs, M. (1980 [1950]) *The Collective Memory*, ed. M. Douglas and trans. Francis J. Ditter Jr and Vida Yazdi Ditter, New York: Harper Colophon.

——(1992) *On Collective Memory*, Chicago, IL: Chicago University Press.

Hobsbawm, E. and T. Ranger (eds) (1983) *The Invention of Tradition*, Cambridge: Cambridge University Press.

Hutton, P. (1993) *History as an Art of Memory*, London: University Press of New England.

——(1994) 'Review Essay: History and Memory', *History and Theory*, 33 (1): 95–107.

Huyssen, A. (1995) *Twilight Memories*, London: Routledge.

Klein, K.L. (2000) 'On the Emergence of Memory in Historical Discourse', *Representations*, 69: 127–50.

Koselleck, R. (1985) *Futures Past: On the Semantics of Historical Times*, Cambridge: MIT Press.

Levy, D. and N. Sznaider (2002) 'Memory Unbound: The Holocaust and the Formation of Cosmopolitan Memory', *European Journal of Social Theory*, 5 (1): 87–106.

Levy, D. and N. Sznaider (2005) *Holocaust and Memory in the Global Age*, trans. A. Oksilof, Philadelphia, PN: Temple University Press.

——(2010) *Memory and Human Rights*, Philadelphia, PA: Penn State University Press.

Lowenthal, D. (1985) *The Past is a Foreign Country*, Cambridge: Cambridge University Press.

MacIntyre, A. (1984) *After Virtue: A Study in Moral Theory*, Notre Dame, IN: University of Notre Dame Press.

Maier, C.S. (1993) 'A Surfeit of Memory? Reflections on History, Melancholy and Denial', *History and Memory*, 5(2): 136–52.

Megill, A. (2007) 'History, Memory, Identity', in Megill, A. *et al* (eds) *Historical Knowledge, Historical Error: A Contemporary Guide to Practice*, Chicago, IL: University of Chicago Press pp. 41–62.

Megill, A., Shepard, S., and Honenberger, P. (2007) 'History, Memory, Identity', in *Historical Knowledge, Historical Error: A Contemporary Guide to Practice*, Chicago, IL: University of Chicago Press.

Misztal, B. (2003) *Theories of Social Remembering*, Maidenhead: Open University Press.

Nora, P. (1989) 'Between Memory and History: Les Lieux de Memoire', *Representations*, 26: 7–25.

——(2002) 'The Reasons for the Current Upsurge in Memory', *Transit*, 22: 1–6.

Olick, J.K. (2007) *The Politics of Regret, On Collective Memory and Historical Responsibility*: London: Routledge.

Olick, J.K. and Robbins, J. (1998) 'Social Memory Studies: From "Collective Memory" to the Historical Sociology of Mnemonic Practices', *Annual Review of Sociology*, 24: 105–40.

Olick, J.K., Vinitzky-Seroussi, V, and Levy, D. (2010) *The Collective Memory Reader*, New York: Oxford University Press.

Smith, A.D. (1986) *The Ethnic Origins of Nation*, Oxford: Blackwell.

Terdiman, R. (1993) *Present Past: Modernity and the Memory Crisis*, Ithaca, NY: Cornell University Press.

Torpey, J. (2006) *Making Whole What Has Been Smashed*, Cambridge, MA: Harvard University Press.

Walker, R.B.J. (1990) 'Sovereignty, Identity, Community: Reflections on the Horizons of Contemporary Political Practice', in R.B.J. Walker and S. H. Meendlovitz (eds) *Contending Sovereignties: Redefining Political Community*, Boulder, CO: Lynne Rienner.

Werner, M. and Zimmermann B. (2006) 'Beyond Comparison. Histoire Croisée and the Challenge of Reflexivity', *History and Theory*, 45: 30–50.

Post-secular Society

Austin Harrington

If it can be said that theoretical controversies in the social sciences in the 1980s and 1990s revolved first predominantly around debates about modernity and "postmodernism" and then moved to an overriding focus on concepts and experiences of "globalization", a strong case can be made for religious, ethical, and axiological inquiries as a third paradigmatic key of investigation since the turn of the millennium.

Unquestionably spectacular events on the global stage have brought matters of religion to the forefront of public and academic attention in recent years. Noisy disputes in the mass media about Islam and the West, about religious education and the wearing of religious clothing in schools, about diversity politics, citizenship, and free speech, and fears of global terrorism have all placed religion inescapably in the limelight. Arguably, however, the roots of the new sensibility reach deep into structural social and attitudinal transformations of the later twentieth century and elude comprehension simply in terms of ephemeral shifts of media fashion and hyperbole.

Jürgen Habermas (2001) has described these transformations in terms of an emerging consciousness of the "post-secular society" – a phrase which may seem to suggest some kind of end of secularism and the onset of a new era of religiosity in contemporary social and political self-understanding. A more illuminating reading of the term, however, as Habermas and others have stressed, would be to see it as marking a certain importantly new dimension of reflexivity in the ongoing secularist self-understandings of contemporary democratic pluralist societies. Ideas of a "return of religion" in this frame may then be said to name less any substantive *increase* in religious attachments than rather a new-found awareness of, and sensitivity toward, *continuities* of religious values and legacies in contemporary political life. The term may thus be read as raising one central question for contemporary social theory. What is religion's place in processes of modernization? In particular, must religion always be seen as in some way an obstacle to these processes or can religion also be seen as acting as a vehicle or medium of forms of modernity?

The following survey addresses these questions in relation to four main clusters of recent work on religion in social theory. A first cluster comprises challenges to "classical secularization theory"; a second covers debates about the place of religion in contemporary liberal democratic public spheres; a third domain concerns work on religion in comparative historical studies of world civilizations; and a fourth field encompasses engagements with religion from the side of left-wing traditions of social and political theory.

Classical Secularization Theory

Although some scholars continue to mount robust defences of secularization as an overarching explanatory frame for conditions of modernity, an ever growing body of work in recent years has come to see classical social-scientific concepts of secularity and secularization as in need of serious revision (Bruce 2002; Berger 1999; Martin 2005; Joas and Wiegandt 2007; Joas 2008; Pollack and Olson 2008). This work has argued that undeniably real developments in Western societies over the last four decades suggest that classical sociological equations of conditions of modernity with processes of secularization can no longer be plausibly sustained. Doubts about secularization theory in this perspective extend not only to the nineteenth century's Eurocentric, teleological, and evolutionistic philosophies of history – all of them variously positing religion as an inferior stage in the cognitive maturation of humanity. The doubts also extend in this perspective to more sophisticated varieties of evolutionary social theorizing arising from Marxian historical materialism and Marxian varieties of ideology-critique, as well as from liberal reformist traditions of social thought represented by Durkheimian and post-Kantian ideas of the progressive transla- tion of religious images of the sacred into civic humanist moral norms. Even Max Weber's highly nuanced analyses of processes of rationalization in terms of experiences of the "disen- chantment of the world" have been seen as implying in some respects a rather questionable coupling of modernity with the retreat of religion to a space of purely private life, irrelevant to wider social and political dramas.

In particular, greatest critical attention has been directed in recent years toward an assumption that processes of differentiation between religious and political fields of institutional authority in modern societies necessarily entail decline in the overall impact of religious organization on public life as a whole (Casanova 1994; Martin 2005). This, it has been stressed, was the assumption that underpinned structural–functionalist conceptions in the 1950s that saw modern social forms as evolving along more or less uniform lines toward a configuration of structures marked by the relegation of claims to faith-based normative sanction to a space of purely private personal conduct of life. One landmark work critical of this assumption is José Casanova's *Public Religions in the Modern World* (1994), which pinpoints ways in which modern church– state separation processes in Christian countries do not automatically result in general cognitive and cultural decline of religious life in civil society and public spheres. Clearly the situation of the United States, where levels of religious mobilization have always remained comparatively high, and have done so in many ways not in spite of but rather precisely because of the Constitution's "wall of separation" between politics and faith, stands as one major counter- example to any generalization from specifically Western European experiences of religion's gradually declining cultural significance, either with respect to the West in particular or in relation to the world as a whole. In a truly global perspective, it has been stressed, Western European experiences of secularization must be considered more an exception than the norm (Davie 2000, 2006).

Much of this assessment finds particular support from the experience of post-communist and post-dictatorship countries at the end of the twentieth century. In post-communist Eastern Europe, it has been argued, religion's return to open public life occurred not only as a con- sequence of the lifting of state repression but at least in part also as an actor in its own right in the democratic transition process – notably, for example, in Catholic Poland, but also to a certain extent in a comparatively more secular country such as the former GDR (Pollack 1994). In Latin America in the 1980s church representatives played a significant role in the social–agrarian emancipation movements of post-dictatorship states. In India and in regions of the Middle East, Hinduism and Islam have played a part in the shaping of at least relatively pluralistic political public spheres and institutions since the end of colonialism – fundamentalist and ethnic-nationalist tendencies notwithstanding. In Turkey, similarly, the electoral popularity of the AK Party since the turn of the millennium has shown how a religiously shaped democratic political mass movement can emerge from a state founded on staunchly secular–national political norms and win a position of transformative hegemony within this state oriented to ongoing processes of institutional and juridical reform.

As scholars have underscored, these and other cases tend to suggest that while some process of differentiation between political and religious institutional authority remains one indispensable precondition for general modern societal structures, this process can take many different forms and need not always lead to religion's wholesale disappearance from politically relevant channels of public contention and deliberation. Where the historic existence and subsequent abolition or functional disabling of state churches seems to have been responsible for comparatively high levels of religious indifference in European countries, the historic absence of state churches in other major countries of the world such as the United States seems to have helped make possible the growth of often quite diverse spiritual "market-places", populated by confession-based voluntary associations whose activities and energetic modes of organization have significantly influenced public communication about religious matters and general civic values in public spheres (Stark and Bainbridge 1987).

Measurements of levels of religious belief and involvement vary greatly with the precise framing of statistical indicators, but general data suggest consistently that while overall rates of belief remain in steady decline in Europe and North America alike, the pace and extent of the drop is not as great as was once commonly assumed. Levels of engagement turn out to be noticeably higher where the emphasis of interrogation falls on matters of personal belief and on relatively open-ended reference to higher powers and spiritual feelings, as distinct from subscription to more formal articles of faith and formal participation in established institutions. "Believing without belonging" or "vicarious religion" (Davie 1994, 2006) or "invisible religion" (Luckmann 1967) have been influential catchwords for this pattern. "Vicarious religion" describes a state of majority passive acceptance of the ministrations of a religious minority, to whose services the majority turn occasionally for special ritual purposes such as for marriages and funerals, and mirrors a preponderance of growth in sect-based or evangelical "low-" rather than "high-church" forms, such as Pentecostalism, particularly among congregations of African descent (Martin 2002). In addition, in Europe since the Second World War, immigrant communities from former colonial territories have brought with them the religious traditions of their native lands and generally have sustained these traditions over the generations, possibly also in part from a search for psychological self-reassurance in a sometimes unwelcoming environment. The result has been a dramatic transformation of the cultural landscape of European countries that no previous general secularization theory of modernity could have possibly anticipated.

One conclusion to be drawn from this would seem to be that secularization cannot be held to provide any decisive *explanation* of modernizing processes, however well it might describe certain *consequences* of these processes. Connections between modernization and secularization may be less intrinsic than once thought, and religion may merit recognition as an independent rather than merely dependent variable in explanatory analysis in this regard. Differentiation between political and religious sites of authority may engender increasing general levels of indifference to religion through history, but not necessarily. As the next section of this chapter considers, any such inference seems to be particularly belied by the dramatic profile of religious or religion-related controversies in Western public spheres in recent years.

Religion in the Public Sphere

Religious life and association in Western societies seems to have become not "privatized" but rather increasingly "de-privatized" in character over the last thirty years (Casanova 1994). One explanation for this would seem to need to point to a way in which conditions of citizenship in Western democratic nation-states can no longer be described reliably and neutrally by reference to purely or unreflexively secularist definitions of public rights and responsibilities today. An awareness has grown in many states in recent years that freedom of religious expression has in practice remained a comparatively inadequately realized constituent of the principles of value pluralism on which these states claim to found themselves. Transformations in the social constitution of Western democracies in the wake of immigration flows and general global erosion of nation-state boundaries have exposed a way in which formal principles of equality regarding liberty of conscience have not been implemented in ways adequate to social facts on the ground (Davie 2000). Just as formal legislation against racial and sex discrimination has often in practice fallen short of alleviating substantive realities of inequality between the sexes and between majority and minority ethnic groups, so formal principles of equality of rights for Christians, non-Christians, and non-believers seem not to have addressed real differences of life chances for particular social groups.

As demonstrated perhaps most clearly by the case of France, formal norms of secular citizenship qua *laïcité* no longer appear to respond adequately to real differences of opportunity for religious communities in French society, most notably for Muslims, whose entitlement to behave freely in public in ways that do not infringe the freedom of others to behave freely in the same space seems to have been in at least one way significantly proscribed – namely in relation to the freedom of Muslim women and girls to wear the *hijab* in schools (Asad 2003; Göle 2005). Far from guaranteeing equality of rights to all citizens of the French state, *laïcité* in this case seems only to have infringed these rights. Far from treating all citizens inclusively and impartially, *laïcité* seems to have been implemented juridically in ways that have been experienced as exclusionary and divisive.

Other similar cases in Britain, Germany, the Netherlands, Denmark, and elsewhere suggest equivalent conclusions. With the dissolution of the once relatively culturally homogeneous white-majority social democracies of the post-war period has come a need for an ever more rigorous redrawing of the substantive meaning of equality, solidarity, and liberty of citizens. Democratic states in Europe and the West continue to be much more problematically influenced by Christian cultural history than their elected representatives have often been willing to acknowledge. Recent controversies have seen different kinds of acts of mobilization by non-Christians, non-believers and not least, by practising Christians themselves, against varieties of perceived curtailment of entitlements to free expression in civic spaces. A continuing predominance of Christian-based public holidays and of Christian-based moral education in schools has not gone without contestation from non-Christian as well as non-believing sections of populations. Yet moral education curricula in schools that avoid religious reference, likewise may not necessarily represent a fair and inclusive response to problems of cultural value pluralism. Instead, they may, from at least one perspective, seem typically to disavow ways in which civic humanist values are themselves cognitive products of religious intellectual and semantic history.

Values of tolerance in these situations, it has been emphasized, would seem to require something more than mechanical acts of appeal to existing constitutional democratic legislation. In some instances tolerance may be invoked in ways that mask real underlying currents of oppressive intolerance toward minority groups. Arguably, one case of this includes the anti-Muslim cartoons published in the Danish newspaper *Jyllands-Posten* in 2006, which some sections of Danish public opinion at the time came to defend in rather disingenuous terms by appeal to worldview-neutral rights to free speech. Tolerance, it has been argued, requires an energetically self-critical willingness on the part of conflicting parties in civil society to take up positions on value-questions, to defend these positions with criticizable reasons, and at the same time to accept the possible limits of sovereignty of such positions from within the worldview-specific premises of these positions themselves (Forst 2003). Just as a democratic state's worldview-neutrality cannot be tied down to any substantively unchanging legislative precept, so tolerance in relation to religious and anti-religious advocacy movements seems best intelligible in terms of an ongoing argumentative achievement of communicative struggles in public spheres, always open to qualitative reinterpretation.

Ideals of "civil religion" in democratic states, it has been argued, consequently signify something importantly different today from the kind of neo-Roman classical republican expression of these ideals dramatized by Jean-Jacques Rousseau two centuries ago in *The Social Contract*. As Robert Bellah first showed in the late 1960s, references to "God" in Western constitutional documents and oaths of office (most famously in the American Declaration of Independence) essentially stand as place-holders for an unnamed instance of transcendent authority above state sovereignty – and therefore *a fortiori* above restriction to any definite confessional or definite non-confessional tradition (Bellah 1991).

Religion in Comparative Historical Sociology

A sense of the inescapability of normative inter-faith and inter-worldview contention in civil societies in recent years has nurtured a welter of historical–sociological studies aimed at establishing the variety of religious and civilizationally distinct pathways of evolutionary development followed by societies of the modern world. Renewed appreciation has grown in recent academic work for various pre- and supra-national religiously inflected roots of contemporary political and legal orders, stretching deep into the past and across the once taken-for-granted civilizational boundaries of the historically predominantly Judaeo-Christian West (Eisenstadt 1986, 2000; Joas and Wiegandt 2007).

A widespread understanding now exists in public discussion generally that ideas of "human rights" do not spring from any kind of civilizationally indifferent historical vacuum. The philosophers of the eighteenth-century Western European radical Enlightenment, whose ideas fed into the French and American Revolutions, it has been stressed, were not absolute originators of ideas of the rights of man. Rather, as the German-Jewish jurist Georg Jellinek (1979) first showed in a seminal study of 1895, ideas of the rights of man first developed in effect not in revolutionary France but rather, at an earlier stage, among Puritan settlers in the New World – notably in Rhode Island, under the leadership of the Baptist minister Roger Williams – seeking freedom of religious conscience and coming gradually to recognize similar strivings among peoples of other faiths and denominations as a universal concern of humanity. Human rights, Jellinek argued, therefore had to be seen as at least in part religious in origin and motivation, and not only as secular.

At the beginning of the century, Ernst Troeltsch (1931) in Germany and other scholars began to extend this general thesis to a wider genealogical survey of the roots of modern natural-law doctrines in a sequence of fusions between Greco-Roman Stoic philosophy and early Christian theological understandings of the sanctity and solitude of individual souls before God. Max Weber (2003 [1915–20]) then adapted this project to a comparative historical sociological study of "the economic ethics of the world religions", ranging from ancient Confucian and Buddhist China and India to ancient Israel and early Islam.

Weber's non-evolutionistic synopsis of multiple contingently unfolding zones of religious–civilizational change would remain largely unexplored by scholars for several decades. However, in 1949, in his book *The Origin and Goal of History*, synthesizing Weber's sociology with existentialist philosophy, Karl Jaspers inaugurated a line of inquiry that has since become of particular interest to recent scholarly work. Within an ancient time-frame that Jaspers called the "Axial Age", marked approximately by the years 800–200 BCE, Jaspers argued that at least five or six different civilizations witnessed the genesis of a set of multiple understandings of ideas of "transcendence" or rupture between intra-mundane customary life and extra-mundane instances of higher spiritual authority. These different spiritual understandings, Jaspers argued, essentially set the decisive developmental paths traced subsequently by the course of world history. Thus in Jaspers's picture, not *one* "axis of world history" existed, as Hegel had described the birth of Jesus Christ in *The Philosophy of History* (Hegel 1956: 319). Rather, Jaspers argued, multiple such axes existed, from ancient China to ancient India, Iran, Israel–Palestine, and Greece, each with their own intrinsic founding capacities for sustaining long-enduring structural societal transformations constitutive of the modern world.

In the 1980s, the Israeli historical sociologist Shmuel Eisenstadt adapted Jaspers's philosophical vision to a wide-ranging empirical programme of inter-civilizational comparative historical–sociological research. In the year 2000, in collaboration with other researchers, Eisenstadt also went on to propound a conception of "multiple modernities", identifying different pathways of societal and institutional modernization, each inflected by different religiously significant founding "transcendental visions" – from Japan to China to the Middle East to the Atlantic West (Eisenstadt 1986, 2000). Reconceptualizing Talcott Parsons's originally functionalist evolutionary analysis of various globally dispersed societal "universals", Eisenstadt and Robert Bellah (both of whom had been pupils of Parsons in the 1950s) have sought to pinpoint a range of variant trajectories of modern societal, cognitive, and religious evolution, each starting from different autochthonous global centres (Bellah 2005). World history on this understanding offers examples of a variety of processes of societal differentiation between political and religious institutional and intellectual forms, all of them divergent in important ways from the specifically occidental phenomenon of secularization experienced by Judaeo-Christian Western Europe and North America.

It can be said that the central insight of this work is that processes of modernization can unfold historically not necessarily against the resistance of religious normative inheritances but more often precisely by *means* of or by *virtue* of such inheritances. To this extent, eighteenth-century Western Europe's radical anti-clerical Enlightenment cannot be considered any exclusive paradigm of enlightenment experiences in general. Historical investigation offers every reason not to speak of wholly antagonistic relations to the church as preconditions for intellectual modernity – such as in the manner emblematized, say, by the satires of Voltaire. Rather, different manifold scenes of negotiation can be descried between rational scientific culture on the one hand and faith, revelation, and sacred tradition on the other. These may range from the forms of Anglo-American Puritan–utilitarian modernity at the forefront of Max Weber's concerns in *The Protestant Ethic and the Spirit of Capitalism* to more philosophically introverted forms of cultural modernity prevalent in Lutheran northern Europe in the eighteenth and nineteenth centuries, or to Jewish enlightenment rationalism in the same period, or to legal–institutional reform experiences of the Ottoman empire and the Arabian Middle East and Iran in the nineteenth and twentieth centuries, or finally to the diverse institutional modernization programmes of twentieth-century post-colonial Africa and Far Asia. All of these cases, it has been stressed, are misunderstood if religious factors are viewed simply as hindrances to the legitimization of institutional and intellectual pluralism in these regions.

Many compelling reasons thus exist to support a view that faith-based religious orientations need not be seen in principle as in conflict with social and political ideals of collective liberty, autonomy, and social justice and cognitive ideals of enlightenment in global settings.

Yet might it not still be the case that religiously mobilized social traditions do frequently present obstacles to the pursuit of these ideals in contemporary reality? Can post-secularist redefinitions of contemporary normative political discourse and historical self-understanding genuinely withstand worries about elements of persistent ideology, irrationalism, and oppressive social conservatism in religious life and organization today? These concerns are taken up in the last section of this essay.

Religion and the Left

Clearly, fundamentalist and dogmatist religious forms, in which large masses of the dispossessed, estranged, or undereducated can tend to be galvanized by small bands of clerical elites into affirming morally simplistic, truncated, and retributive pictures of the world, need not be the only way in which religious language can respond to felt injustice and suffering in the world. It can be appreciated that an involvement of a particular tradition of religious norms in oppression of women, persecution of non-majority groups, war-mongering, and other expressions of violence and aggression can meet just as often with reproof from these norms as sanction from them. Contemporary secular humanism looks upon religiously sanctioned acts of killing and violence as an offence to humanity precisely because the universalizing religious traditions to which this same humanism owes its ultimate inception – in its embrace of unconditional values of love, peace, forgiveness, and human dignity – *also* experience such acts as an offence to humanity (cf. Kippenberg 2008).

Yet still, important questions inevitably have to be asked at this point about the susceptibility of religious creeds, particularly in countries of the developing world, to feed upon the poor, the weak, and the materially and psychologically insecure, and generally to aggravate rather than to ameliorate conditions of life for such groups.

Studies of the World Values Survey compiled by Ronald Inglehart (1997; Norris and Inglehart 2004) and other researchers have highlighted some clear correlations between patterns of religious affiliation and high rates of poverty, reduced life expectancy, and high birth rates in the developing world (www.worldvaluessurvey.org). From at least one angle, these correlations would seem to underwrite traditional Marxian materialist arguments about religion as transcendental compensation for material privation on this earth (Marx 1974 [1844]). Where persistent rates of belief in more affluent countries of the world seem to be explicable in Inglehart's analysis in terms of a reorientation toward "post-material values" – building in a kind of supplementary fashion on already achieved conditions of comfort and security – religious mobilization in the developing world seems to be inextricably causally connected to generally negative consequences of processes of economic globalization in recent decades. It seems no coincidence that religious activism and conflict most often appear to flare up in those parts of Africa and the Middle East most linked to geopolitically strategic global export markets for raw materials – in the first instance for oil – where one-sided economies led by super-rich dynastic elites tend to leave behind a mass of the disenfranchised. Where reconstruction in the post-colonial world fifty years ago tended to found itself on predominantly secular–national and socialist programmes of industrial modernization, the end of the Cold War and the rise of Atlantic-centred global neoliberal economic governance regimes appears to have helped bring about a noticeable shift in the cultural and political self-understanding of large sections of populations in the developing world toward emphatic religious and ethnic identity movements. The question then arises as to how far such movements genuinely articulate these populations' interests in an autonomously realized project of collective social life.

Yet in the developed world too, religious mobilizations in contemporary public spheres appear to have proceeded in tandem in at least one relevant way with shifts toward the curtailment of state welfare and social security spending and wealth-redistribution policies in favour of ever greater reliance on voluntary-sector actors, such as charitable foundations, churches, and other religious organizations. Where the profile of such voluntary services has long been a factor behind the resilience of religious life in American public discussion, the rise to prominence of church-based public actors appears to be a new feature of the political landscape of many European countries over the last twenty years, particularly – but not only – in post-communist Eastern Europe.

Perhaps more fundamentally, general societal processes of socio-economically mediated *individualization* appear to have lent extra impetus to more specific processes of religious individualization – with a net effect of possibly intensifying recourse to faith-based personal value-orientations in contemporary Western social mores. As almost all commentators agree, if any one master trend exists in modern religious history, it is a trend toward the "subjectiviza-tion" or transformation of contents of religious belief and practice into objects of individual choice, deliberation, selection, and recombination – into items of "consumption", on the analogy of shopping (Berger 1967; Stark and Bainbridge 1987; Davie 2006). It might seem at this point that it is particularly at a time of heightened pressures of socio-economic individua-lization, brought about by the closing down of public agencies of collective social solidarity, that this peculiarly subjectivized character of contemporary religiosity is given added weight. In a world of more and more precarious and flexibilized individual employment practices, faith-based value-attachments may seem to provide a special kind of unconditional emotional reassurance and resource of moral motivation and dedication for individuals (Bell 1996).

Yet it must be stressed that not all such processes of religious individualization can be explained exclusively in socio-economic terms. Though some significant connection may well exist between the rise of democratic pluralism and the multicultural society on the one hand and capitalistic market liberalization processes on the other, a view of increases in forms of subjectivized personal religiosity as purely a reflection of the force of individualistic entrepre-neurialist norms in competitive labor markets may be too simple. A more subtle account, along lines suggested by theorists such as Ulrich Beck (2008) and Niklas Luhmann, might point rather to personal religious value-attachments as signifiers of experiences of the bisection of societal normativity by a space of the inviolably and incommunicably interior (Pollack 1988). In this way, rises in a religious sense of the "God-within-me" might be explicable not as expressions of growth in some kind of type of narcissistic competitive subjectivity but rather as the cipher of increasingly widely felt insight into the limits of purely societally constituted orders of moral law.

This last remark should be the occasion for a few general concluding caveats about the limits of predominantly materialist determinations of the scope of religious self-understanding in contemporary cultures and societies.

A longstanding preponderance of secularist attitudes among broadly left-liberal audiences in Western intellectual circles since the Second World War no longer appears as self-evident as it once did. Indeed today it seems more often belied than boosted by the rather knee-jerk reactive and positivistically reductive diatribes against religion published in recent years by popular atheist authors such as Richard Dawkins (2006) in the UK. In public and academic discussion generally, a recognition seems to have grown in recent years that criticism of the rationality-claims of religious thought and practice need by no means preclude appreciation of the cognitive transformative and transfigurative potentialities of religious imaginaries. As recent interventions by such prominent and diverse thinkers as Habermas (2001, 2002, 2008), Charles Taylor (2007), Jacques Derrida (2002), Hans Küng (1998), or Slavoj Zizek (Zizek and Milbank 2009) suggest, a great many different kinds of positions can be taken up on ways in which religious experience might be said to gesture toward a productive "space for faith" beyond the all too often restrictive and prescriptive "limits and boundaries" of reason and rationalistic culture. For Habermas these potentialities have revolved around a task of reclaiming the "semantic contents" of religious language for projects of normatively generalizable discursive communication in civil society. For Derrida, Zizek, Badiou, Agamben, and others, the actuality of the religious has turned on a revisiting of the messianic utopian moment in modern religious social thought after figures such as Benjamin, Bloch, and Scholem and their Biblical and historic antecedents – from Moses and Isaiah to St. Paul, Thomas Münzer, or Lenin (cf. Milbank 1990; De Vries 1999). For others, taking a lead from thinkers from Carl Schmitt to Leo Strauss, Eric Voegelin, Reinhold Niebuhr, Georges Bataille, Roger Caillois, Claude Lefort, Jacob Taubes, Karl Löwith, Hans Blumenberg, and others, contemporary social and political philosophy has shown itself to be inextricably entangled in engagement with the question of the spiritual legitimacy of the modern age in relation to theologico-religious antiquity.

All of the four clusters of recent work reviewed in this chapter point generally to a conclusion about the amenability rather than sheer resistance of religious heritage to modern projects of collective self-determination and reflective self-understanding. Ideas of the post-secular society can be understood in this frame as expressing fundamentally the continuation rather than simple abrogation of modernity's "unfinished project of enlightenment". Contemporary religious movements on the global stage can and should be seen as capable of reactivating resources of reflective self-renewal over against more dogmatized and rigidified expressions of their own traditions. Recent interest in religion in contemporary Western public spheres seems unlikely to be a temporary phenomenon of adjustment to a post-Cold War and/or post-modernist social world; and it seems unlikely to disappear with processes of ongoing assimilation of populations to capitalist-consumerist ways of life around the world (*pace* e.g. Anderson 2009). In sum, every reason exists to consider religious life today simply as one more manifestation of modernity's ever-shifting repertoire of dimensions of reflexive self-articulation.

References

Anderson, Perry (2009) *The New Old World*, London and New York: Verso.

Asad, Talal (2003) *Formations of the Secular: Christianity, Islam, Modernity*, Stanford, CA: Stanford University Press.

Beck, Ulrich (2008) *Der eigene Gott: von der Friedensfähigkeit und dem Gewaltpotential der Religionen*, Frankfurt am Main: Suhrkamp.

Bell, Daniel (1996) [1976] *The Cultural Contradictions of Capitalism*, New York: Basic Books.

Bellah, Robert (1991 [1967]) "Civil Religion in America", in id., *Beyond Belief: Essays on Religion in a Post-traditionalist World*, Berkeley, CA: University of California Press.

——(2005) "What is Axial about the Axial Age?", *Archives européenes de sociologie / European Journal of Sociology*, 46: 69–89.

Berger, Peter L. (1967) *The Sacred Canopy: Elements of a Sociological Theory of Religion*, Garden City, NY: Doubleday.

——(ed.) (1999) *The Desecularization of the World: Resurgent Religion and World Politics*, Washington, DC: Ethics and Public Policy Center.

Bruce, Steve (2002) *God is Dead: Secularization in the West*, Malden, MA: Blackwell.

Casanova, José, (1994) *Public Religions in the Modern World*, Chicago, IL: University of Chicago Press.

Davie, Grace (1994) *Religion in Britain since 1945: Believing without Belonging*, Oxford: Blackwell.

——(2000) *Religion in Modern Europe: A Memory Mutates*, Oxford: Oxford University Press.

——(2006) "Religion in Europe in the 21st Century: The Factors to Take into Account", *Archives Européenes de Sociologie*, 47 (2): 271–96.

Dawkins, Richard (2006) *The God Delusion*, Boston, MA: Houghton Mifflin.

De Vries, Hent (1999) *Philosophy and the Turn to Religion*, Baltimore, MD: Johns Hopkins University Press.

Derrida, Jacques (2002) *Acts of Religion*, ed. G. Anidjar, London: Routledge.

Eisenstadt, Shmuel (ed.) (1986) *The Origins and Diversity of the Axial Age Civilizations*, New York: SUNY Press.

——(ed.) (2000) "Multiple Modernities", *Daedalus*, 129 (1): 1–29

Forst, Rainer (2003) *Toleranz im Konflikt: Geschichte, Gehalt und Gegenwart eines umstrittenen Begriffs*, Frankfurt am Main: Suhrkamp.

Göle, Nilüfer (2005) *Interpenetrations: L'islam et l'Europe*, Paris: Galaade.

Habermas, Jürgen (2001) *Glauben und Wissen*, Frankfurt am Main: Suhrkamp.

——(2002) *Religion and Rationality: Essays on Reason, God, and Modernity*, ed. E. Mendietta, Cambridge, MA: MIT Press.

——(2008) *Between Naturalism and Religion: Philosophical Essays*, trans. C. Cronin, Malden, MA: Polity Press.

Hegel, G.W.F. (1956 [1831]), *The Philosophy of History*, trans. J. Sibree, New York: Dover.

Inglehart, Ronald (1997) *Modernization and Postmodernization: Cultural, Economic, and Political Change in 43 Societies*, Princeton, NJ: Princeton University Press.

Jaspers, Karl, (1953 [1949]) *The Origin and Goal of History*, trans. M. Bullock, London: Routledge.

Jellinek, Georg (1979 [1895]) *The Declaration of the Rights of Man and of Citizens*, trans. M. Farrand, Westport, CN: Hyperion Press.

Joas, Hans (2008) *Do We Need Religion? On the Experience of Self-transcendence*, trans. A. Skinner, Boulder, CO: Paradigm Publishers.

Joas, Hans and Klaus Wiegandt (eds) (2007), *Sakularisierung und die Weltreligionen*, Frankfurt am Main: Fischer.

Kippenberg, Hans (2008) *Gewalt als Gottesdienst: Religionskriege im Zeitalter der Globalisierung*, Munich: C.H. Beck.

Küng, Hans (1998) *A Global Ethic for Global Politics and Economics*, New York: Oxford University Press.

Luckmann, Thomas (1967) *The Invisible Religion: The Problem of Religion in Modern Society*, New York: Macmillan.

Martin, David (2002) *Pentecostalism: The World Their Parish*, Malden, MA: Blackwell Publishers.

——(2005) *On Secularization: Towards A Revised General Theory*, London: Ashgate.

Marx, Karl (1974 [1844]) "A Contribution to the Critique of Hegel's Philosophy of Right", in *Karl Marx: Early Writings*, trans. R. Livingstone and G. Benton, London: Penguin.

Milbank, John (1990) *Theology and Social Theory*, Oxford: Blackwell.

Norris, Pippa and Inglehart, Ronald (2004) *Sacred and Secular: Religion and Politics Worldwide*, New York: Cambridge University Press.

Pollack, Detlev (1988) *Religiöse Chiffrierung und soziologische Aufklärung : die Religionstheorie Niklas Luhmanns im Rahmen ihrer systemtheoretischen Voraussetzungen*, Frankfurt am Main: P. Lang.

——(1994) *Kirche in der Organisationsgesellschaft: Zum Wandel der gesellschaftlichen Lage der evangelischen Kirchen in der DDR*, Stuttgart: Kohlhammer.

Pollack, Detlev and Olson, Daniel V.A. (eds) (2008) *The Role of Religion in Modern Societies*, New York: Routledge.

Stark, Rodney and Bainbridge, William Sims (1987) *A Theory of Religion*, New York: P. Lang.

Taylor, Charles (2007), *A Secular Age*, Cambridge, MA: Harvard University Press.

Troeltsch, Ernst (1931 [1912]) *The Social Teaching of the Christian Churches*, 2 vols, trans. O. Wyon, London: Allen & Unwin.

Weber, Max (2003 [1915–20]), *The Essential Weber*, ed. S. Whimster, London: Routledge.

Zizek, Slavoj and Milbank, John (2009) *The Monstrosity of Christ: Paradox or Dialectic?* Cambridge, MA: MIT Press.

Index